THE saddam HUSSEIN READER

THE saddam HUSSEIN READER

Edited by
Turi Munthe

Thunder's Mouth Press
New York

THE SADDAM HUSSEIN READER

Published by Thunder's Mouth Press
An Imprint of Avalon Publishing Group Incorporated
161 William St., 16th Floor
New York, NY 10038

Library of Congress Cataloging-in-Publication Data

The Saddam Hussein reader / edited by Turi Munthe.
p. cm.
Collection of articles previously published.
Includes bibliographical references.
ISBN 1-56025-428-9
1. Iraq—Politics and government—1979-1991 2. Iraq—Politics and government—1991- 3. Hussein, Saddam, 1937- I. Munthe, Turi.

DS79.7 .S196 2002
956.7044—dc21

2002075273

9 8 7 6 5 4 3 2 1

Book design by Sue Canavan
Printed in the United States of America
Distributed by Publishers Group West

With great anticipation and love, this book is dedicated to Annibale, the bump.

Acknowledgments

I would like to thank my editor at Thunder's Mouth Press, Dan O'Connor, for all his suggestions and help, Noga Arikha, Iradj Bagherzade, Efrat Cohen, Angus Cook, Carmit Gai, Noa Gimelli, Kanan Makiya, Tobias Munthe, Jamal Nusseibeh, Jonathan Tepper, Daniel Swift, and most of all Muzia, great with child, beautiful and here.

Publisher's Note

No convention governs the transliteration of Arabic names into English and we have not imposed uniformity upon the many variant spellings found herein. All names appear as translated in their source publications.

Contents

Part II

Part III

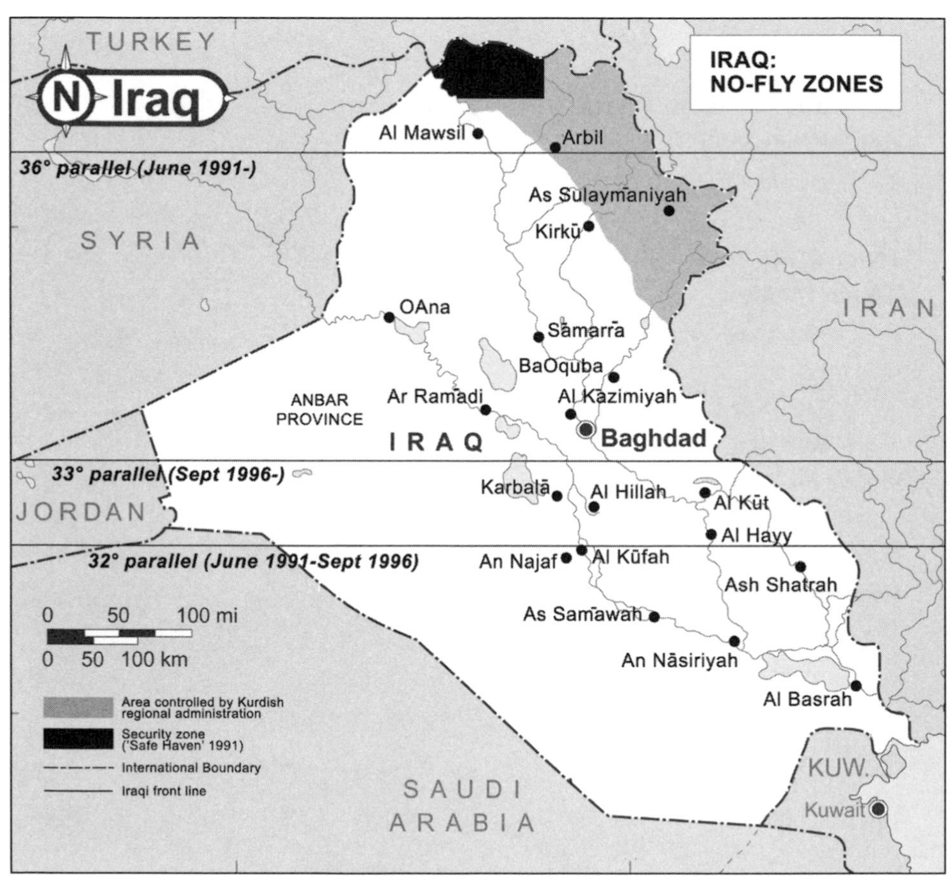
IRAQ:
NO-FLY ZONES
Iraq
N
TURKEY
SYRIA
IRAN
JORDAN
KUW.
SAUDI ARABIA
36° parallel (June 1991-)
33° parallel (Sept 1996-)
32° parallel (June 1991-Sept 1996)
Al Mawsil
Arbil
As Sulaymaniyah
Kirkū
OAna
Sāmarrā
BaOquba
Al Kāzimiyah
Baghdad
ANBAR PROVINCE
Ar Ramadi
IRAQ
Karbalā
Al Hillah
Al Kūt
Al Hayy
An Najaf
Al Kūfah
Ash Shatrah
As Samawah
An Nāsiriyah
Al Basrah
Kuwait
0 50 100 mi
0 50 100 km
Area controlled by Kurdish regional administration
Security zone ('Safe Haven' 1991)
International Boundary
Iraqi front line

Timeline and Glossary

Saddam Hussein was born on 28 April 1937 near Tikrit, on the Tigris River in northwest Iraq, into a poor but influential Sunni family.

1947 Hussein is sent to live with his uncle in Baghdad, the capital of Iraq, where he becomes involved in the Arab nationalist movement, joining the Baath Party in 1957. In 1958, while a secondary student, he is involved in the assassination of a prominent communist in Tikrit. He is arrested and imprisoned for six months.

1958 The Iraqi monarchy is overthrown in a coup on 14 July and a republic is declared, although instability continues to reign as communists led by the Iraqi Communist Party struggle with the Baath Party and other nationalist groups for dominance.

1959 Hussein is recruited by Baath Party leader general Ahmed Hassan al Bakr for an attempt to assassinate brigadier Abd al-Karim Qassem, the communist-sympathising head of the Iraqi government. The attempt occurs in October. Qassem is injured but not killed. Hussein is wounded in the leg and flees to Syria then Egypt, where he completes his secondary school studies. Others in the Baath Party are arrested and tried for treason. Hussein is sentenced to death in absentia on 25 February 1960.

1962 He studies at the Cairo Law School.

1963 The Baath briefly attains power when Qassem's government is overthrown on 8 February but is in turn ousted by a coup in November. Hussein, who has returned to Iraq to study at the Baghdad Law College, is arrested on 14 October 1964 and sent to prison. While in prison he is elected to the Baath leadership. Baath resurfaces as a force in 1965, with Bakr as secretary general. Hussein is made Bakr's deputy in September 1966.

1967 Hussein escapes from prison.

1968 On 17 July, the Baath returns to power in a bloodless coup that Hussein helps organise, leading the storm of the presidential palace. A group of Sunni Iraqis from Tikrit, the birthplace of Hussein, take the top posts in the new Baath government. Bakr is made president. Hussein is appointed as acting deputy chairman of the Revolutionary Command Council (RCC - the government's most powerful decision-making body) in July.

On 30 July he takes personal charge of a purge to rid the new government of old-guard figures. Two months later, following an unsuccessful coup attempt against it, the Baath government cracks down again. Hussein and Bakr direct a further series of purges designed to eliminate opposition to the government. A new constitution is introduced on 22 September.

1969 Already a central figure in the Baath Party, Hussein becomes the dominant force. He is confirmed as deputy chairman of the RCC and placed in charge of internal security on 9 November and personally directs attempts to accommodate the Kurd's wish for self-government.

1970 The constitution is modified on 16 July 1970 and again in 1973 to entrench Baath power. The party forms a covert surveillance network headed by Hussein and establishes its own militia. Power within the party gravitates to three members of the Talfah family from Tikrit-Bakr, Hussein and general Adnan Khayr Allah Talfah, Hussein's brother-in-law. A permanent settlement with the Kurds appears near when they accept a peace agreement offering them limited autonomy.

1971 Hussein obtains a degree in law from the University of Baghdad. He is ranked as a lieutenant general in the Iraqi military from 1973 to 1976, when he is promoted to general. On 1 February 1976 he is awarded a master of arts honours degree in military science together with a staff degree.

1972 In June, Hussein directs the nationalisation of Iraq's oil industry.

1974 Hussein extends autonomy negotiations with the Kurds but following an attempt by the Baath to assassinate the Kurdish leadership in March full-scale fighting breaks out. The Kurd dissidents receive support from Iran, Syria, Israel, and the United States and are able to inflict heavy losses on the Iraqi forces.

1975 In an effort to weaken the Kurds, Hussein signs an agreement with the shah of Iran under which Iraq drops claims on territory on the northern border with Iran in return for the ending of Iranian assistance to Kurdish separatists. A long-running dispute with Iran over the border at the Shatt al Arab (the confluence of the Tigris and Euphrates rivers) is resolved with an agreement to set the midpoint as the boundary. With their support base compromised, Kurds are forcibly relocating from their heartland in the north and all Kurdish villages along a 1300 kilometre stretch of the border with Iran are razed.

1976 Hussein turns his attention to the domestic economy, introducing a successful state-sponsored industrial modernisation program based on Baath socialist principles. The program increases social wealth, improves education and health care, and promotes the equitable redistribution of land. With the home front secure, Hussein focuses on regional politics, advocating Arab unity against foreign intervention. His November 1978 denouncement of Egyptian president Anwar Sadat's signing of the Camp David Accords on peace between Egypt and Israel brings Hussein regional and international prominence.

1977 With Bakr ailing, Hussein assumes full control of the government.

1979 The shah of Iran is overthrown in an Islamic revolution in February. The new Islamic Republic of Iran is headed by the Shi'ite cleric Ayatollah Sayyid Ruhollah Musavi Khomeini, who Hussein had expelled from Iraq in 1978. When Bakr resigns on 16 July, Hussein is formally appointed as president. He also becomes secretary general of the Baath Party Regional Command (the party's executive), chairman of the RCC, and commander-in-chief of the armed forces. Days after becoming president Hussein orders a purge of the party, government, and military.

1980 Iraqi Shi'ites, inspired by the revolution in Iran, organise into a religiously based opposition and during the spring attempt to assassinate members of the Iraqi cabinet. Hussein responds by ordering the deportation to Iran of thousands of Shi'ites of Iranian origin and the arrest and execution of the Shi'ite opposition leader.

Conflict over the sovereignty of the Shatt al Arab resurfaces when Hussein cancels the agreement of 1975 and claims the entire waterway as Iraqi territory. Iraqi troops march across the Shatt al Arab into southwestern Iran on 23 September, beginning the eight-year Iran-Iraq war.

The war initially goes well for Iraq, but by May 1982 the Iraqis are on the defensive. Hussein orders the withdrawal of troops from Iranian territory in June 1982 and attempts to negotiate a cease-fire but the Iranians continue to advance, crossing the Shatt al Arab in the south and capturing mountain passes in the north, where they are aided by Kurds. The Iraqis are able to contain and reverse the Iranians but cannot remove them entirely from their territory. Kurd resistance is quelled by the reported use of chemical weapons and forced deportation to Iran.

The war bogs down to a stalemate. With neither side able to press a decisive initiative both resort to the use of chemical weapons. It is reported that Iraq is summarily executing thousands of Iranian prisoners of war and Kurdish civilians.

1984 The University of Baghdad awards Hussein an honorary doctorate in law. Diplomatic relations with the US are restored during the year, allowing the US to provide Iraq with aid to end the war.

1988 A cease-fire is declared on 20 August. The war has claimed approximately 75,000 Iraqis killed and about 250,000 wounded. More than 50,000 are being held as prisoners of war in Iran. Property damage is estimated in the tens of billions of dollars, with the destruction especially severe in the southern part of Iraq.

In the north, the Iraqi government moves against the Kurd dissidents who had aided the Iranians during the war. It is reported that thousands of Kurds are killed when villages are attacked with poison gas. An estimated 4000 villages and towns are razed. Hundreds of thousands of Kurds are "cleansed" from the region by forced deportation. Many Kurds flee across the borders with Turkey and Iran. Over 100,000 Kurdish civilians are reported as "disappeared." By the end of 1989 the Kurdish resistance has been crushed. Relations between the US and Iraq sour.

1990 Hussein accuses neighbouring Kuwait of overproducing oil to force the price down and further damage the war-crippled Iraqi economy, claiming that the action amounts to a declaration of war. Iraqi troops invade Kuwait on 2 August, quickly overrunning the country. On 6 August the United Nations imposes trade sanctions on Iraq, including an embargo on sales of Iraqi oil.

1991 On 16 January, after Hussein ignores a UN security council demand for Iraq's unconditional withdrawal, a coalition of 33 world nations led by the US counterattacks, starting the six-week Gulf War, also known as "Operation Desert Storm." The Iraqis are forced out of Kuwait and chased as they retreat. Tens of thousands die and much of Iraq's infrastructure is destroyed.

The war ends on 27 February. Hussein accepts the UN terms for a permanent cease-fire in April and moves to quell rebellions by the Kurds in the north and Shi'ites in the south. Iraq places an economic blockade on its Kurdish regions and public servants are ordered to return to secure Iraqi territory. The internal blockade is exacerbated by the international trade sanctions against Iraq. About two million Kurds flee across the borders with Turkey and Iran. The international community imposes "no fly zones" over the north of Iraq to prevent attacks on the Kurds by the Iraqi airforce.

In the south, the Iraqi government launches a campaign against the Shi'ite marsh Arabs, with much of the area being drained. It is reported that villages are being razed, their occupants deported, and that thousands of civilians are being summarily executed. No fly zones are also imposed on Iraq's southern regions.

1992 Following the Gulf War Iraq comes under intense and continuing international pressure to dismantle weapons of mass destruction and to allow verification by a UN weapons inspection team. Weapons inspectors are allowed in but are given only limited access to some sites. Trade sanctions and the oil embargo remain in force.

1994 Hussein is appointed as prime minister of Iraq. In an effort to break the trade sanctions Hussein masses Iraqi troops near the Kuwait border but is forced to back down. The sanctions remain in place.

1995 Following a national referendum in October, Hussein is given another seven-year term as president.

1996 An "oil for food" deal is agreed at the UN in May. It allows Iraq to sell a limited amount of oil in exchange for food and humanitarian supplies. The dispute over weapons inspections remains. Hussein attempts to ban US nationals from the inspection teams and refuses unlimited access to presidential palaces. By February 1998 it appears that the dispute may be resolved and in March access to the presidential sites is granted. The sanctions remain in place.

1997 The Iraqi government orders the forced expulsion of Kurds and other minorities from the Kirkuk region 260 kilometres north of Baghdad. The region is resettled with ethnic Arabs.

1998 The weapons inspections dispute flares again in August when Hussein demands that US influence on the program be reduced. Iraq withdraws cooperation in October. The weapons inspectors leave Iraq in December, just before the US and Britain launch punitive air strikes against suspected weapons facilities.

Reports in January 1999 that some weapons inspectors have been supplying information to the US do not stop the attacks, which continue into March 1999. In December 1999 the UN agency responsible for the weapons inspections is replaced by a new body, although its authority is immediately rejected by Hussein.

1999 A senior Iraqi Shi'ite cleric, Ayatollah al Sayyid Mohammad Sadiq al Sadr is murdered on 19 February, fanning renewed unrest in the south of Iraq. In August the UN Children's Fund (UNICEF) reports that child mortality in the centre and south of Iraq, where the Iraqi government administers the "oil for food" program, has more than doubled during the sanctions, and warns of an impending humanitarian emergency. UNICEF estimates that 500,000 Iraqi children have died because of the privations caused by the sanctions.

UNICEF also reports that in the north, where the UN administers the program, child mortality has fallen below pre-Gulf War levels.

In December the "oil-for-food" deal is expanded.

2000 The International Committee of the Red Cross reports on the catastrophic breakdown of the health system, hygiene, and water supply in Iraq. UN secretary-general, Kofi Annan expresses grave concern over the humanitarian crisis. It is reported that Hussein is using the funds generated by the "oil for food" program for personal enrichment and to shore up the support of the Iraqi elite. Hussein is alleged to have spent over US$2 billion on presidential palaces.

2001 Ten years after the end of the Gulf War the sanctions and air strikes against Iraq continue, although in February the US announces the sanctions will be eased. The weapons inspections carried out since the end of the Gulf War have found no evidence of biological or nuclear weapons but have discovered chemical agents.

2002 Following the 11 September 2001 terrorist attacks on the World

Trade Center and the Pentagon, US president George W. Bush nominates Iraq as one of the members of an "axis of evil" that also includes Iran and North Korea. The US begins to agitate for a resumption of the armed conflict with Iraq in order to overthrow Hussein. However, the suggestion is rebuffed by the Arab states.

A meeting of the Arab League in March officially rejects "the threat of an aggression on some Arab countries, particularly Iraq, and assert(s) the categorical rejection of attacking Iraq or threatening the security and safety of any Arab state, and consider(s) it a threat to the national security of all Arab states." In return Iraq agrees to recognise Kuwait as an independent state and to not invade it again. Iraq also agrees to work with the UN in implementing post-Gulf War ceasefire provisions and to join an initiative to settle the conflict between the Arab states and Israel.

Meanwhile, it is reported that since late 2000 Hussein has provided aid of more than US$10 million to Palestinians fighting the Israeli government. The families of more than 800 Palestinians killed in clashes with the Israeli military had each received "martyr" payments of US$10,000. Palestinian fighters with serious injuries were given US$1,000. Those with light injuries received US$500. In March the amount handed to the families of the killed is increased to US$25,000.

On 14 May, the UN security council approves a revision of the sanctions against Iraq, introducing a goods review list (GRL) to streamline the vetting of imports under the "oil for food" program. Under the US-crafted resolution only imports that include items on the 302-page list will be subject to scrutiny. The revision is designed to reinforce military sanctions while eliminating most of the restrictions on trade in civilian goods. Humanitarian goods will be allowed in virtually automatically. Goods that have both military and civilian applications will be excluded. The new system is scheduled to come into effect on 1 June.

On 17 June it is reported that US president Bush has ordered the Central Intelligence Agency (CIA) to undertake a covert operation to topple Hussein. The order directs the CIA to use all available tools, including increased support to Iraqi opposition groups, expanded intelligence gathering, and the possible use of special forces teams authorised to capture Hussein and kill him if they are acting in self defence.

The same day it is reported that Hussein has adopted a three-pronged strategy to repel the US—Iraq's defences are being bolstered and reorganised to allow local commanders to act autonomously if attacked; strained relations with the rest of the Arab world are being repaired; and aid is being provided to potential foreign allies. It is reported that Hussein's younger son and heir-apparent, Qusay Hussein, has been instrumental in rebuilding the ties with the Arab world.

Qusay Hussein controls the Special Security Organisation, Iraq's secret police, and plays a leading role in foreign affairs.

On 20 June coalition planes bomb a military command facility in southern Iraq in retaliation for increasing attacks on British and US aircraft patrolling the no-fly zones in the country's north and south. A US fighter also bombs an antiaircraft artillery site in northern Iraq. The attacks continue the following day. On 26 June US planes bomb an air defence site in northern Iraq after coming under fire from anti-aircraft guns.

p.6 **Gamal Abd al-Nasser,** the most charismatic political figure in the Arab world at his time, was president of Egypt between 1956 and 1970.

p.8 **Omar, Othman and Ali** are respectively the 2nd, 3rd and 4th caliphs of the Islamic world. Along with **Abu Bakr,** the first caliph of Islam who succeeded Muhammad as head of the Muslim community at his death in 632AD, they are considered to be the Rashidun, or "Rightly-guided" caliphs.

p.10 **Nebuchadnezzar** was one of Babylon's most famous kings, lived between 630 and 563BCE. He built the hanging gardens, and under his rule, Babylon was the largest city in the world.

p.10 **Salaheddin** was the first Ayyubid sultan. Born in Tikrit (where Saddam Hussein was also born) in 1138, he was famous for recapturing Jerusalem from the Crusaders.

p.10 **Mouawiya** was the first ruler of the Umayyad dynasty, which made its capital Damascus. He became Caliph in 661AD.

p.10 From 711AD to 1492AD, Arab kingdoms covered large parts of Spain, particularly in the south. The Arabic name for the region was **Al-Andalus,** from which we get the word Andalucia.

P. 12 **Khalid ibn al-Walid** was an early convert to Islam, and became the chief Muslim general in the conquest of Syria, Egypt, Iraq, and Persia, taking Damascus in 635AD. Muhammad gave him the title "The Sword of God."

p.43 **General Ahmed Hasan al-Bakr** was president of Iraq from 1968 until his forced resignation in 1979 in favour of Saddam Hussein.

p.44 The **Camp David Accords** were signed on 17 September, 1978 between Egyptian President Anwar al-Sadat and Israeli Prime Minister Menachem Begin. In them, Egypt recognised Israel as a state, bringing peace between the two countries but creating an uproar across the Arab world.

p.49 **Ahmed Chalabi** runs the Iraqi National Congress (INC), Saddam Hussein's main opposition group, based in London.

p.54 **Abdel Khaliq Samarai** (Wafic al-Samarrai) was former chief of Iraqi Military Intelligence, since defected to the West.

p.76 **Mu'ammar Qaddafi** has ruled Libya since 1969.

p.83 **Shi'i** is a branch of Islam which places great importance on the 4th caliph, Ali and his children Hassan and Hussein. They represent the second largest group in Islam, with under 100 million adherents, predominantly in Iran. The vast majority of Muslims are Sunnis.

p.83 **Sunni** is a branch of Islam, which places great importance on the revelations of Muhammad and acknowledges the first four caliphs as the rightful successors of Muhammad. About 90 percent of all Muslims are Sunni.

p.120 **Sargon** was the founder of the city of Babylon, and **Hammurabi** was its greatest king.

p. 133 **Iran-Contra Affair,** 1983-1988, was perhaps the most significant scandal to touch Reagan's presidency. It was finally proved that the US had sold arms to Iran during their war with Iraq, and had used part of the proceeds to fund the activities of the rebel Nicaraguan Contra movement.

p.180 **Brigadier General Abd al-Karim Qassem** overthrew the Hashemite monarchy of Iraq in 1958, and ruled the country until his own assassination in 1963.

p. 185 **General Hussein Kamel Hassan** was Saddam Hussein's son-in-law and ran Iraq's weapons program until his defection in August 1995. He returned to Iraq where he was assassinated—most probably on the orders of Uday Hussein, Saddam's eldest son.

p.246 Jad al-Haqq is the former **Sheikh al-Azhar.** He later went on to become the rector of Al-Azhar University in Cairo, the world's oldest university and Sunni Islam's foremost seat of learning.

Introduction

Turi Munthe

Saddam Hussein is a tyrant, at the head of a regime that has turned violence into an instrument of state, leading a broken people and a shattered country along what many believe to be a sure road to destruction. He is also, by any standards, a heroic leader: a fatherless boy from a poor clan in Tikrit, he rose to become President of one of the most powerful countries in the Middle East. As deputy chairman of the Revolutionary Command Council in the 1970s, Saddam Hussein turned Iraq into a near-model Arab nation. He had hoisted half the country's population into the middle class, and Arabs the world over (from the Gulf, to Palestine, Jordan and the Maghreb) came to study at Iraqi universities. Erudite, efficient, and hugely energetic, he seemed to many in the Arab world, but also in the West, to be an ideal leader for Iraq's complex polity, and a model for his neighbours.

He has played out these contradictions on a global scale. The wary West's darling in the Iran-Iraq war, he is now its arch-pariah, and across the Arab world, he has been seen as the new Saladdin—the only Arab leader capable of standing up to the West—as well as the biggest threat to regional stability.

Today, he is America's greatest embarrassment, but an embarrassment they must perpetuate. In the current climate, Saddam Hussein's image must remain that of the world's most ruthless tyrant, with a history of psychopathy and anti-Americanism that stretches back to his first days in power. If, in the demonization process, the American public is reminded of their government's consistent support of him throughout that period, that is a price the present administration has to pay.

In the Arab world, Saddam Hussein exposes a similarly tragic paradox. What he has done to his own people is unnameable, but on the streets of Arab towns from Fez to Ramallah, he symbolises courage and defiance to an enormous demographic group that has the opportunity for neither. The tragedy is that defiance (a meaningless pose), regardless of the context or consequences, has become an ideal in itself. It is as morally empty and shocking as it is understandable—sprung from a despairing pride that has nothing to anchor it.

The West, more particularly America—to whom, as this book will make clear, Saddam Hussein owes his immediate power most directly—is once again ambivalent about him. Pulled between two extremes—attack or ignore—the US has seen the most unlikely alliances form.

The traditional hawkish Right—dominated by the Defense Department under Donald Rumsfeld and Paul Wolfowitz—has seen its ranks swelled by the vast majority of Iraq's exiled opposition, as well as by large sections of the Left, outraged at Saddam Hussein's hideous human rights record. That competing alliance of economic, political, and humanitarian interests claims the mantle of enlightened imperial liberalism. In qualifying their demand for Saddam Hussein's demise with vocal support for democracy in Iraq, they promise the end of the dictator and the end of America's most consistent policy in foreign affairs: across the world, and since World War II, the US has unashamedly supported autocrats they knew, rather than risk the threat of an unknown elected leader. They have done so with Saddam Hussein for decades.

The Doves are just as ill-assorted. Headed by the unlikely Colin Powell, they include old-fashioned isolationists, the majority of the mainstream Republican State Department, as well as the most Left-leaning anti-globalisation protesters of Seattle and Genoa. Cynical political and military caution with regards to both the US and Israel (within striking distance of Iraq's Western desert), has teamed up with the intellectually fashionable artillery of anti-imperialism in righteous self-interest. They herald their disengagement as the intelligent humility of true power.

Saddam Hussein—curse or hope, tyrant or saviour—has been near-universally presented as a phenomenon in his own right. His own self-image contributes to this, but he can and should also be seen within the wider context of Middle East politics in the period.

One of Saddam Hussein's favourite epithets is "The Struggler" and his four turbulent decades' long hold on power in one of the most volatile states in the Middle East is testament to its appropriateness. To maintain that power, he has had to bend with the prevailing winds of political sentiment. His political persona and discourse represent a model of the changes in mainstream Arab politics across the Middle East.

As a young man, he joined the Baath Party, a socialist pan-Arab organisation with proto-mystical undertones linking political freedom with spiritual growth. Pan-Arabism, at the time, was in fashion. With immense political idealism it dreamt of homogenising the Middle East, and establishing a single Arab Nation based on shared culture, shared interests, and shared political values—values which had much to do with reasserting the global power of the Arab Umma (or community) against Western hegemony. That single Arab Nation remains a political Narnia, but in the 1950s, following the Suez Crisis of 1956, and the creation of the short-lived United Arab Republic incorporating Egypt and Syria in 1958, it was an idea to be taken very seriously. Saddam Hussein was one of many would-be Middle Eastern leaders following in the footsteps of his generation's hero, Gamal 'Abd al-Nasser.

Saddam Hussein risked his life for that common ideal, and, as proof, walks with a limp, the same charismatic flaw as Tamurlane and Byron. In 1959, aged twenty-three, on Rashid Street in Baghdad, he took a bullet in the leg while fleeing the scene of a failed assassination attempt. His target had been 'Abd al-Karim Qassem, the prime minister and leader of the coup that had toppled the Hashimite monarchy in 1958. Brigadier Qassem's Iraqism had pushed the Baathists from centre stage, and threatened pan-Arabism across the Middle East.

Pan-Arabism suffered terribly in the years that followed, and most forcefully after the June 1967 war against Israel. The wholesale humiliation of the united strength of the Arab world forced a retrenchment: the greater vision had failed, and Arab leaders across the Middle East turned to their backyards. When Saddam took the presidency in 1979, he did so against a pan-Arab move by his predecessor Ahmed Hassan al-Bakr to yoke Syria and Iraq. Again Saddam

Hussein's politics were not unique. Hafiz al-Asad, Syria's Baathist president at the time, welcomed the chance to focus inwards and consolidate his Alawite constituency's hold on power. The climax of that process occurred in 1983, when upwards of 30,000 people were buried under the ancient city of Hama, following an uprising by the Muslim Brotherhood there. Arab Nationalism had taken over. In 1979, Egypt, the cultural and political figurehead of the Arab World, would make peace with Israel. The pan-Arab ship had sunk and Saddam Hussein was watching from dry land.

The late 1970s saw the spread of an entirely new phenomenon in the region—political Islamism. The Shi'ite Islamic Revolution that placed Ayatollah Khomeini at the head of the Iranian polity in 1979 sent shockwaves through the Muslim world. Islam, both Shi'ite and Sunni, both cultural and political, had regained a firm hold on the Middle East. Saddam Hussein's politics shifted. As many others, like President Mubarak of Egypt, he cracked down heavily on Islamist activity but bent his discourse to their terms. He portrayed his 8-year long war against Iran as a second Qadissiya—the battle in which, in 636, Saad bin Abi Waqqas defeated the Sassanian army and brought Islam to Persia and beyond. Iraq, in his speeches, was Mesopotamia—the oldest civilization in history—but Iraq was also the last stronghold of resistance to the infidel imperialist foe and its Zionist acolyte. In a Baghdad library, commissioned in 1997 on the occasion of his sixtieth birthday, stands a Qur'an that is written entirely in Saddam Hussein's own blood.

Saddam Hussein's immense flexibility and his hypersensitivity to the currents of political change are the marks of an extraordinary political survivor. The importance of these reinventions, however, lies not in the changes themselves but in the phenomenon they represent: where power had been vision's handmaiden, Saddam inversed the roles. As a political revolutionary in his early twenties, he was as idealistic as anyone of his generation—the Middle East was unharnessing itself from the colonial yoke and was on the threshold of a new era. Even as the young vice-president of the Revolutionary Command Council of the Baath Party in the 1970s, he was hailed as its most faithful son, and became the favourite protégé of the Party's charismatic theoretical founder and luminary, Michel 'Aflak. With power, steeped in blood within days of his assumption of the presidency, Saddam Hussein's political idealism metamorphosed into self-idealisation. He became Iraq's vision, Iraq's future, Iraq's ideal.

Iraq is shrouded in his image. A likeness of him stands on every boulevard and high street in every town and village of the country—as soldier, business man, sportsman, father, in every uniform, in every pose. Saddam Hussein would make himself normative. Saddam's degradation from the visionary he might have been to the tyrant he has become is etched into the Iraqi state. There, consensus is grounded not on success, nor on idealism, but in violence and the fear it breeds amongst the Iraqi people.

The historical and political circumstances that formed Saddam Hussein bred, almost uniformly across the Middle East, an entire generation of brutal rulers. They share many of the same challenges—populations divided by faith, tribe and ethnicity; no firmly established basis for consensus or legitimacy; immense separation between rich and poor; deep-seated historical grievances; arbitrary borders. . . . Governing the Middle East has not been easy, but it has been done disastrously—to the immense cost of the people governed. If Saddam Hussein is unique, it is in scale—an unfortunately human one.

Saddam Hussein, as I hope the pages that follow show, is the creature of deeply flawed and narrowly self-interested Western policy in the region, and of the tragic failure of the Middle East to hoist itself to greatness once again. He is also the most cancerous form of that tragedy; he embodies it and perpetuates it. Whatever happens in Iraq in the foreseeable future, one thing is certain—that the suffering of its people will continue, and the death toll, already in the hundreds of thousands, will rise.

The story of Saddam Hussein has no single possible narrative. He has meant and means too much, and too politically, to too many people. Unlike a standard biography, a Reader need not plug a particular line—there is its advantage.

There are truths expressed by his most virulent enemies, just as there are truths to come from his apologists. The essays and articles in this volume are collected with the broadest scope in mind, to offer the general reader an insight into the immensely complex question mark that hangs over Saddam Hussein's Iraq today. Included is the work of the major commentators and observers, and the best historians and analysts of the region. An incalculable amount of material exists concerning Saddam Hussein and the country that he has been ruling since the 1970s. I have chosen historians for their concision and reliability, and commentators for the scope or influence of their opinions and the extent to which their views were representative of wider currents of thinking in the political community.

Part I covers the years up to 1990—from Saddam Hussein's rise to power, through the Iran-Iraq War. Part II deals in depth with the Gulf War, a war which lasted a hundred hours, caused untold destruction to Iraq, and ultimately failed when George Bush Sr. refused to back the uprising in southern Iraq that would have swept Saddam from power. Part III looks at the years since—long years for the Iraqi people, living with the effects of exposure to the hundreds of tons of depleted uranium used by US forces during the Gulf War, in a country that has been crippled by more than a decade of sanctions, under a regime that has taken political and social repression to new heights.

The pieces should be read with their authorship very much in mind. There is no shortage of axes to grind on the subjects of Iraq and Saddam Hussein—it is almost impossible to write about them outside a politicised framework. Within that context, I have tried to bring to light the issues that have formed the policy of and on Saddam Hussein over the last four decades, and have made Iraq and its president what they are today.

London, September 2002

THE saddam HUSSEIN READER

Part I

The Young President: An Interview with Saddam Hussein in 1980

Fuad Matar

from *Saddam Hussein*

The following interview with President Saddam Hussein was conducted over several meetings that lasted for seventeen hours. The first session was held a few weeks after the President took over full responsibility for the Party and the State on 17 July 1979.

Fuad Matar: How did you become a Baathist? One would have expected your childhood and youth, filled with social hardship, to lead you towards Marxism. If you had read about Marxism before discovering the Baath ideas and principles, would you not have chosen Marxism?

President Saddam Hussein: Traditionally Marxism attracts the oppressed. This, however is not the case in the Arab nation. I had a meeting with President Julius Nyerere of Tanzania only yesterday, during which we discussed world problems including economic ones. These are problems which had already been raised during the Non-Aligned Summit in Havana. I repeated my point of view on the matter. I told President Nyerere that we cannot solve the problems of Tanzania or those of the Third World, and yet we would like to awaken the world's conscience and change its thinking about the relationship between the oppressed and the oppressors. The Tanzanian President remarked that it was unique to find such an opinion coming from a people which was not poor, and to find a country that wanted only to help not to exploit. I replied that, though this might seem strange, if we went back in Arab history, we would find that most of the calls for socialism were made by people who did not come from the oppressed classes. The socialist programmes in Arab history did not always come from the poor, but from men who had known no oppression and became the leaders of the poor. The Arab nation has never been as class-conscious as other nations. It is true that social differences exist, but today class differences exist mostly between Arabs and non-Arabs. This was not so obvious amongst the Arabs of pre-Islamic times.

I used to have a Communist friend at school. He's dead now, God rest his soul. He spent most of his time reading communiques and declarations to us, his schoolmates. All we did was make fun of him. We never felt that what he was reading had anything to do with us. The main reason for our indifference was that we knew his theories came from abroad; they had been introduced by a foreigner, not an Arab. Our problems were not simple ones: they were problems of partition, of a struggle against Zionism and against class differences. At the time, the peasants in the northern and southern parts of Iraq felt the oppression of the existing feudal system. In the central parts of Iraq where I come from, the situation was not the same, and we had no feudal class. That is why I never felt at a social disadvantage, even I, a peasant's son. The greatest feudalist amongst us was the cousin of President Ahmad Hassan Bakr, an uncle of mine. If he got angry he beat his relatives, but they gave back as good as they got. As a matter of fact, they hit him much more often than he did them. He certainly was not the feudalistic figure that would make a human being feel oppressed. The feudal authority that invaded so many parts never reached my region, which is why we never lived a life of humiliation. Our heads remained high and we never lost our self-respect.

Besides this, my maternal uncle was a nationalist, an officer in the Iraqi Army. He spent five years in prison after the revolution of Rashid Ali Kaylani. 'He's in prison,' was my mother's constant reply whenever I inquired about my uncle. He always inspired us with a great nationalistic feeling, which is why I never isolated the socialist programme from my national outlook. The nation's problems were part of my conscience and the Party was a part of me before I became a member.

Fuad Matar: As a revolutionary, you are against Marxism. Why? Do you have doubts about the nationalist feelings of Arab Marxists?

President Saddam Hussein: I believe that all human civilisation from the beginning of history is interwoven. This also applies to the revolutionary theories which have emerged in the world: they are connected to, and influenced by, human trial and error over the ages. They cannot possibly cross the current of events without being influenced by some of them. In order for a revolutionary theory, any revolutionary theory, to be human, it must be responsive to fresh ideas. Lenin is one of the world's great thinkers whose books I have most enjoyed because he deals with life in a lively manner. I have also read Mao Tse Tung. I am not against Marxism. I am for responding to human thought, but with spirit and character; the theorist should be willing to give and take, not just to look at a country in terms of what it can offer. Our nation is capable of making Marxism aware that it is no longer equipped to deal with all of the new notions of life today. In addition to my faith and trust in the nation and its capabilities, I am always against the mechanical transfer of theories, just as I am against isolationism and rigidity.

I respect the original programme of Marxism and I respect Marxists. But I have no respect for those Communists who use their association with Marxist theories to drum up followers, in whatever nation of the world. In both my thinking and my programme, I differentiate between the Soviet Union and America and never give both an equal status. The Party has spelt out the reasons for this on more than one occasion. When it comes to adherence, however, I make no distinction between he who follows America and he who follows the Soviet Union. In this I am adamant, using neither courtesy nor diplomacy. It is our Party policy. I believe that people who use their Marxist connections to draw up a programme that means political adherence to any country outside the Arab nation are in the wrong. That is why I differentiate between Arab, African and Asian Communists, for example. I neither blame nor criticise Africans who have adopted Marxism, and I am ready to discuss with any African the true manner of adhering to Marxism. And since neither Africans nor Asians have the traditions or the history of the Arab nation, why should they not adopt Marxism? Marxism is a revolutionary solution and the way to change life. What does an African in Rhodesia have to lose when he adopts Marxism, since he does not have the historical depth or the intellectual heritage of the Arab nation, a heritage which offers all the theories necessary for a life of change and progress? The Arab nation is the source of all prophets and the cradle of civilisation. And there is no doubt that the oldest civilisation in the world is that of Mesopotamia. It is not an Iraqi civilisation in isolation from the Arab nation. It is a civilisation which developed thanks to the strength and ability of the Iraqi people, coupled with the efforts and heritage of the nation.

Fuad Matar: Do you not find that the three slogans of the Baath (Unity, Freedom, Socialism) have been placed in an order that is based more on hope than on practical possibilities, and that the order in which **Abdel-Nasser** placed them (Freedom, Socialism, Unity) is more realistic? What has the Baath learned from Abdel-Nasser's experience and vice versa?

President Saddam Hussein: The arrangement 'Unity, Freedom, Socialism' was intentional. The Arabs must struggle for a national truth; they cannot achieve true liberty without nationalism and the struggle towards Arab unity. This does not mean that the Party believes that Arabs cannot achieve freedom without Arab unity; it means that the Party's programme is based on the fact that an Arab must be a nationalist to achieve true liberty. This must ultimately lead to unity, and from there to socialism. Let us stop here awhile and talk about Iraq. Is Iraq's freedom today the same as it would be if it became part of a greater Arab nation?

In today's world of blocs and superpowers, where sharks roam the sea around us, it is difficult to say that Iraq's freedom in international politics is what it would enjoy as part of a united Arab nation. At the same time, life cannot consist of pure theory; it is a slow and inevitable process towards revolutionary achievement. Arab unity is like all the other goals of national struggle: difficult to achieve through nothing but theories. Had we all been one Arab nation today, the freedom an Iraqi citizen would have enjoyed would be different, because his liberty today is linked with his relationships and dealings with the outside world. Liberty is linked automatically with the way things stand today. A human being who is capable and self-confident, who is at peace with himself, will grant freedom more easily than a coward. That is why I believe that the order in which our three slogans are placed as goals to be achieved by the Party is correct and needs no change.

We have profited greatly from the experience of Abdel-Nasser. The Party had three historical experiences to refer to when it began to build the nation after the July 1968 Revolution: failure in Syria, failure in Iraq and the experience of Abdel-Nasser. Following Abdel-Nasser's death, and once Egypt had recovered, we could see his efforts as they really were; we used this reality to deal with the problems of our own society, economic, political and social, without forgetting the causes of Abdel-Nasser's failures. The study of the latter is what made Egypt's recovery easier and more complete.

As for the advantages that Abdel-Nasser may or may not have derived from the Baath Party, I am unable to answer this question accurately or at length, since I was not one of the Party leaders at the time of the union between Egypt and Syria. I do wish to say, however, that the programme Abdel-Nasser—God rest his soul—initially set out to accomplish was not the one that he seems to have adopted in the end. Thus one can say that there was some interaction between Abdel-Nasser and the Baath. Abdel-Nasser profited from his experience in that he rose before the Arab nation from a national horizon and not from Egypt alone. This is one of the most important points in the 23 July Revolution in Egypt led by Abdel-Nasser, especially during and after the 1956 Suez war.

Fuad Matar: Can you tell us about the special relationship that exists between you and President Ahmad Hassan Bakr, as well as your relationship with Michel Aflaq? The reasons for the question are as follows. First, it is probably unique for a Vice-President to exercise all the power and authority invested in the president of a republic for ten years without ever deciding to take over the presidency. Secondly, you continue to respect Michel Aflaq, although circumstances have changed since you became President of the Republic. This is also unusual.

President Saddam Hussein: I do not consider respect a sign of weakness; it is more a proof of a strong personality. When someone is said to be polite, this does not mean he is a weakling; it is a proof of strength because he is courteous and diplomatic in his political relationships. This is true strength of character. President Bakr was Secretary of the Regional Command. In our Party we were always brought up to respect our elders. Besides, a relationship is not a one-way street. A Baathist may be a brilliant thinker; does that mean this is the only image I would want for a Baathist? No. A Baathist is a human being who lives the cause of the people, believes in principles and behaves accordingly in his everyday life, even if his political and intellectual abilities are limited.

Let us go back to our history because it is constantly before my eyes, especially its most glorious and enlightening moments. Let us go back to the relationship between **Imam Ali, Omar ibn al-Khattab** and **Abu Bakr al-Seddiq.** What was that relationship like? Was Abu Bakr al-Seddiq stronger than Omar ibn al-Khattab and Ali bin Abi Taleb? When Omar ibn al-Khattab asked for advice from Imam Ali, did that mean Imam Ali had less strength and ability than Omar ibn al-Khattab? And what of the relationship between Imam Ali and **Othman,** who was by far the weakest? Principles were the basis of the respect between the Rashidi Caliphs. When one of these great men was asked his point of view, he was always accorded total respect and given all the necessary support for leadership and action.

My relationship with President Bakr is one of comradeship; it is also brotherly and paternal. The latter is not meant in the traditional way, but in the civilised sense which involves respect, freedom of thought and opinion, and the full exercise of one's role. It might have seemed that, in an emergency, I conducted myself with the authority of a head of state; this may also have happened in private, but I never turned this 'emergency status' into one that was permanent. When the emergency was over, I became once more the Vice-President of the Revolution Command Council. Constitutionally, I would respectfully return to my place.

Some find it strange that, when President Bakr used to telephone me and ask me to step into his office, I refused to do so until his aide-de-camp went in and announced me. I truly believe in this code of behaviour and it certainly does not make me a weak character or personality; it is a source of strength. As a matter of fact, the Arab nation has deserted its old traditions only to become decadent and weak, especially in moral terms. At this point, what is most wanted of Arab comrades is to stir the Arab nation's conscience by upholding ideal relationships, whatever the sacrifice, since this is nothing compared to the final result, a renaissance in Arab morality.

It is certain that matters would have been accomplished faster had I become the Republic's President five years earlier. This was also President Bakr's conviction. But I used to contradict him because I did not want him to leave his post as President. If I had not behaved in this moral way, what would I have told the people? What would I have had to say about my unique experience? Nothing. My situation would have been exactly like any other revolutionary situation in the world or in the Arab nation, with no clear-cut moral difference. If the one who is better takes over his friend's place and seeks only the reward, then we would be exactly like so many other revolutionary movements, whereas this is far from the truth.

Thus it is Michel Aflaq who created the Party and not I. How can I forget this? How can I forget what Michel Aflaq has done for me? Had it not been for him, I would not be in this position. It is true that Michel Aflaq did not carry out the Revolution and that I achieved my present position because of my own qualities. Yet the spirit in which I carried out the Revolution, the spirit in which the Baathists united, struggled and made sacrifices, and the principles to which I was loyal, were those of the Baath. Baathists carried out the Revolution, struggled and made sacrifices, and the Baath was founded by Michel Aflaq. That is why I must respect him, despite my official position and despite my past and my abilities. It is a unique situation, that is true, but the Party is a unique institution. The Party's principles, morality and goals are unprecedented in the current age.

Fuad Matar: You have often spoken of 'direct strategic moments' that may be used against one by imperialism, of moments when expertise has failed to produce the right result, of errors committed in recruitment. What do you mean by this?

President Saddam Hussein: The expressions 'strategic', 'technical', and 'expertise' belong to an encyclopaedia that is part of a revolutionary and military way of thinking. Let us for instance take the existence of Zionism. Zionism exists and so do the Arabs. Imperialism uses Zionism as a strategic arm against Arab unity, progress and development. This is a well-known fact. How can the Arabs deal with this? They are the ones giving imperialism the chance to use this strategy against the Arabs. It is the enemy that benefits strategically so long as the Arabs are divided. As an example, let us take the Palestinians. They differ as to the kind of democracy they want for their state, a state that they do not yet have. This can be used by the enemy, since it has been given a golden opportunity to turn the Palestinians against each other, making them forget the main issue. The enemy has used both strategy and expertise, turning the Palestinians' mistakes to its own advantage. The Palestinians have the right to disagree at times but now is certainly not the time for them to be divided. Only when they have reached their goal can they differ. But since the goal is still far away, even in the eyes of those referred to as the 'moderates', all the division, discussion and disagreement can only produce a golden opportunity for imperialism and Zionism.

Another point to be made is that different tribes and minorities exist in our society and in the Arab world and cannot be ignored. However, how is one to deal with them without giving imperialism the opportunity to use them against our goals? If one deals with them on the battlefield, in a way that is primitive and narrow-minded, one merely turns confessions into confessionalism, tribes into tribalism and minorities into fanatic opponents of Arab nationalism. That is why we always warn the revolutionary to behave wisely and not to commit tactical errors. It is not the enemy's ability, but these errors—errors due mainly to the stupidity of the revolutionary—that benefit the enemy and contribute to his success.

Fuad Matar: What do the following names mean to you: **Nebuchadnezzar; Salaheddin al-Ayoubi;** Ghandi; Lenin; Gamal Abdel-Nasser; de Gaulle; Che Guevara; Mao Tse Tung; Ho Chi Minh; Tito; Nehru; Castro; Ali bin Abi Taleb; Omar ibn al-Khattab; **Mouawiya; Al-Andalus;** Jerusalem; Egypt?

President Saddam Hussein: Nebuchadnezzar stirs in me everything relating to pre-Islamic ancient history. I am reminded that any human being with broad horizons, faith and feeling can act wisely but practically, attain his goals and become a great man who makes his country into a great state. And what is most important to me about Nebuchadnezzar is the link between the Arabs' abilities and the liberation of Palestine. Nebuchadnezzar was, after all, an Arab from Iraq, albeit ancient Iraq. Nebuchadnezzar was the one who brought the bound Jewish slaves from Palestine. That is why whenever I remember Nebuchadnezzar I like to remind the Arabs, Iraqis in particular, of their historical responsibilities. It is a burden that should not stop them from action, but rather spur them into action because of their history. So many have liberated Palestine throughout history, before and after the advent of Islam.

As for Salaheddin al-Ayoubi, he was of the same calibre but with the spirit of Islam in him. He was a Muslim Iraqi. This is why, at a Farmers' Congress held in Baghdad in November 1979, I said, 'Do not be surprised if a Palestinian dies a martyr in Palestine without having been born there, or if the martyr is an Iraqi, a Lebanese, a Syrian or any other Arab.' Besides this, I consider Salaheddin al-Ayoubi a great leader because he was able to make use of the nation's spirit; he breathed life into it, united it, and gave it one aim and purpose, and thus won a brilliant victory over the Crusaders.

The greatness of Ghandi lies in that he held power in his hands without the use of arms, an unconquerable power which Ghandi knew was the essence of the personality of the people of India. Ghandi's movement would have failed in a country like Iraq or Syria. Ghandi inspired resistance against the colonialists under the emblem of passive resistance.

Che Guevara's courage and romanticism are attractive, but they are not enough to make a leader out of a man.

Mao Tse Tung's greatness lies in that he was able to liberate China, build up socialism and choose a special road within Marxism, taking into consideration China's particular circumstances, an outlook which certainly differs from that of Lenin.

Ho Chi Minh was a great revolutionary leader. I never met him and I have not read enough about him. Yet I can sense the simplicity of the man and admire him for this and for his relationship with his revolutionary comrades.

As for Tito, he was a great revolutionary leader who, in the face of great difficulties and with the least possible violence, was able to bring different populations together and turn them into one happy, united people. This is what makes him different from all other Communist regimes.

Nehru's name evokes that of Ghandi, the teacher with great respect for the student who became a political leader and a great thinker.

Castro, whom I know well, is characterised by directness and courage. Most revolutionary leaders are daring but Castro is endowed with particular courage.

Ali bin Abi Taleb was a man of principle. What I admire in Omar ibn al-Khattab is his sense of justice and in **Khalid bin al-Walid** his sense of chivalry. As for Mouawiya, I have no special opinion to give. All I can say is that I have not benefited directly from his history. From what I have read, it seems to me that Mouawiya worked more for this world than for the next, and such people are of no interest to me.

Jerusalem represents the glory of the Arabs throughout their great history and is one of their sacred shrines. The history of Palestine has important links with the history of the Arabs in Andalusia, a fact which has never been given enough credit. The Arab nation is different from other nations: when the latter conquered, they also colonised, whereas the former established constructive relationships based on a deep understanding of nationalist feelings and religions. This is clear in their conquest of Andalusia and their liberation of Palestine. Besides, the Arabs left Spain with a great heritage which the country still uses to attract tourism.

Egypt in the time of Abdel-Nasser was the fulcrum of the Arab nation, a fact of which we must be proud, whatever we may think of Abdel-Nasser's experiment. He was the only leader at the time to express the opinion of the whole Arab nation before the world, no matter how that opinion may have been expressed. And this period in Egypt's history should be the one present in our minds today.

There remains de Gaulle, the knight whose chivalry I most admire. I always remember a conversation between de Gaulle and Churchill, when the former was offered aid. He replied, 'Let it be put on record that France refuses to take unrecorded aid.' This is a great attitude.

Fuad Matar: Is revolution an endless process, or is it an introduction to a flexible situation, as in the case of China? The reason behind the question is your constant warning against the transformation of the revolutionary into a flexible liberal who enjoys the situation and little by little drowns in it, in order to make up for time lost during the revolution. Is not revolution like war, and the revolutionary its soldier? A soldier wages war and, if victorious, automatically takes the spoils. Does this not also apply to the revolutionary when he has taken power?

President Saddam Hussein: Revolution is a process that does not end with the application of its principles. It varies and changes shape according to the changing circumstances of life. That is why one's opinion of a revolution will develop as the revolution does and keep in step with the changes in the revolutionary leader and the revolutionary member of society. It is in the light of society's understanding of rights and duties that one can fully and correctly comprehend a revolution. That is why we find that the definition of democracy and liberty will change in shape and form as the revolution passes from one stage to another, depending on its success. The same applies to the revolution's stand against its enemies. Throughout its progress, a revolution must always remain in the service of the people for whom it essentially takes place. It is true that I always warn the revolutionary against the threats of 'flexible liberalism' and a new settled life that may make him a prey to illegal desires, making him forget his nationalist duties and obligations. However, this does not mean that I forget that the revolutionary is a human being entitled to his rights like any other ordinary human being, as long as these rights and needs are legal.

A Baathist must remember that his duty is not only to safeguard the Party within Iraq; he also has an obligation towards the whole Arab nation. Had we been revolutionaries for Iraq alone, we would not have issued so many warnings. That is why the Iraqi revolutionary must be a light that shines throughout the Arab nation and that is why so much is required of him. If we turn to our ancestors' history, we will see that this matter was always given a very important place in Islam. Omar ibn al-Khattab kept most of his followers within the Arabian peninsula in order to avoid any unwanted external influence. A simple, ascetic life meant that his men were always ready to pick up their swords, mount their horses and go into battle, to emerge victorious. That is why Omar ibn al-Khattab did not distribute the land of Iraq amongst his Muslim followers after its conquest from the Persians.

That is why we warn our people in the revolution against flexible liberalism. We are part of a big nation and would like to be a shining example to it. That is why a revolution has no beginning and no end; it is not like war and its soldiers must not profit from its spoils. It is something continuous, it is a message to life, and the human being is only the bearer of the message.

Fuad Matar: Now that you have achieved revolutionary power, which is the more difficult: working to achieve it, or working to retain it?

President Saddam Hussein: The hardest part is not reaching a position of power; it is rather how to turn this power into a constant means to serve the people. This is the most difficult task, even more difficult than the hardships of the underground life endured by the Party. But I do not draw a distinction between the spirit during the days of struggle and the expression of principles through the means of power. Only true comrades are true revolutionaries and only they can turn power into a means to serve the people.

Fuad Matar: Can you explain your understanding of the difference between a revolution and a *coup d'état?*

President Saddam Hussein: The revolution and the *coup d'état* are technically similar, in that they both change power through the use of force. Yet there is a difference in depth and involvement, as well as in the programme adopted and its outcome. Those who overthrow a regime may be revolutionary human beings who reject what the people have also rejected. Yet if they have come to power without either preparation or understanding of the life that surrounds them, they are simply responsible for a *coup d'état.* Those who carry out a *coup d'état* are to be respected if they overthrow and change a bad leader. Yet if they have no pre-arranged programme in hand, they have achieved nothing but a limited *coup d'état.* That is the difference.

Fuad Matar: What is the role of the Army in Iraq? Is it technical or political?

President Saddam Hussein: Had the Army's role been only technical, the July 1968 Revolution would have been nothing but a *coup d'état.* The Army's role is primarily political. Soldiers in the Army are members of the July Revolution, and primarily Baathists, who make use of their technical abilities for the good of the revolutionary Baath programme. This is the main role of the Army.

Fuad Matar: When can one consider that national independence is a reality? What is your opinion of the Arabs' wealth and how this can be used for the good of the nation?

President Saddam Hussein: National independence can be achieved in stages. One of the most important steps in today's world is to possess a national economy that cannot be influenced by external circumstances. Another is to have a strong army, capable of defending one's sovereignty and beliefs. One must be endowed with power based on a political, economic, social and military structure, built up as a result of one's position within the nation and one's relationship with Arab and foreign countries. This enables one, for instance, to receive arms shipments without pre-conditions or attempts to influence one's programme, one's independence or one's sovereignty; that is, if one is unable to manufacture arms oneself. This is the way for a truly independent and nationalist human being.

We in Iraq have used our resources in order to strengthen our national independence. Had our wealth been less than it is today, our independence would have also differed, since principles and resolutions are not enough for real independence in today's world. Wealth can lead either to enslavement or to sovereignty. We have used ours as a means of strengthening our sovereignty, our independence and our happiness.

Fuad Matar: What made you give the Kurds their autonomy since you feel strongly about unity. Is the Kurdish problem over? What is the relationship between the Iraqi Arab and the Kurd? What would have happened to the Kurds had there been unity between Iraq and Syria?

President Saddam Hussein: There are two main causes for the decision for self-rule: the principles of our Party, and its respect of the desires of the people. It is a fact that our Kurdish people wanted self-rule. Part of the people were incited to act against the Revolution under the guise of seeking self-rule. Yet the latter would never have been established had it not been at the request of the people of Kurdistan. The Kurds wanted self-rule; had we not granted it to them this would only have led to bloodshed, and division among the people. On the contrary, granting self-rule to the Kurds has brought us together. Self-rule for the Kurds does not stand in the way of Arab unity, and was one of the points that we planned to introduce on the agenda of the union constitution discussed with the Syrian regime. This would always be an essential condition in the event of a union between Iraq and any Arab country since we know that if the Kurds ever feel threatened in their autonomy by Arab unity they will rise up against the Arabs which is certainly not to our benefit. Nor is Kurdish self-rule a threat to our principal aim, Arab unity.

Fuad Matar: It is often said that the Arab nation cannot be a strong and able one without 'a powerful Iraq'. Can you please explain this saying? Does this mean that if Iraq remains strong, the Arab nation will be powerful although many individual states are not?

President Saddam Hussein: First and foremost, I would like to point out that what I mean by a 'powerful Iraq' is an Iraq based on the Arab Socialist Baath Party. It is my right to feel that the road to save the Arab nation is through these principles. Yet this outlook on life does not ignore the actual relationship with the Arab nation. Whatever the nationalist movement, if it exists we must co-operate with it. That is why I believe that Iraq today, with its principles, is an extraordinary power within the nation. Yet its power is not sufficient if it is only surrounded by weak regions. It can most certainly help in the development of the nation, through the power invested in it by the principles of the Party. Iraq can assist in the strengthening of other regions in the Arab nation, both directly and indirectly.

Fuad Matar: I have some questions about socialism and its application:

First, I notice that socialism is not applied absolutely; at the same time, the 'open door' is not fully open. If I may say so, there is a half-socialism and a half-open policy, and the two together have led to a new form of socialism. Is this form an established one and is it the solution?

Second, do you not think that certain gaps in the application of socialism have been exploited by Marxism on the one hand and Islamic ideology on the other; is this why it was important for you to find a new form of socialism?

Third, Abdel-Nasser saved the Baath from committing certain errors in the application of socialism, since he was the first to apply it. Has the Baath benefited from these errors, in that they were not repeated in Iraq?

Fourth, the Baath has succeeded in setting up effective cadres for unity on the political level, yet it has not been able to do the same on the socialist level. Do you not think that these cadres should exist in the socialist sector as well? I say this because I tend to believe that the principal aim of national struggle in the Baath seems to be Arab unity rather than socialism.

Fifth, are the benefits that have been achieved by socialism for the good of the citizen in Iraq, and in the rest of the Arab countries, equal to the sacrifices he has made?

Sixth, is it not strange that, after twenty years of socialism and its application, it is still rejected by the majority in many Arab countries? Is it because socialism is closer to Marxism than to Islam, or is it simply because of an incorrect application of socialism?

President Saddam Hussein: Our socialist programme has never consisted of collecting elements from elsewhere and stringing these ideas and thoughts together into a common denominator for the use of Iraq. We are open to influence. We do not overlook the experiences and theories of others, but we always have the Baath in mind; we do not go to others with empty minds but always with our own principles and ideas in mind. We believe human thought should interact all over the globe; this is the correct attitude. We do not go to Marxism to take whatever small element pleases us in its laws. Marxism is a revolutionary theory, but it is not the only one, nor is it the oldest.

The theory of the Prophet Muhammad applied divine laws on earth, through Islam. The theories of our Muslim Arab leaders and rulers are much older than Marxism, since they are 1,400 years old. Therefore when we study Marxism, we do so in the hope that we may benefit from it in accordance with the Baath system and not in accordance with Marxism. That is why we have no intention of collecting the theories and experiences of others for our own benefit. Even when we study Abdel-Nasser's experience we do so not to copy it, rather to learn from it, to know when to beware of traps and dangers, since Nasser's experience is not far from that of the Baath.

When I talk about the application of socialism, I talk of the Baath and the application of its theories in Iraq. Socialism in other Arab countries is another matter. I do not think that we have fallen into any trap such as is the case in other countries, whereby mistakes in the application of socialism were committed in a manner that repelled people. Some people may have a wrong concept of what socialism means and therefore become rightist as a reaction. A most significant example is Egypt itself. One of the most important weapons used by those who are against socialism is to tell people that the ideology allows for no private activity, or does so only minimally. Saying that the private sector is non-existent in socialism is as incorrect as to say that there is 'free' competition between the socialist and the private sectors without any interference from the State.

This does not mean that we have not made mistakes. Yet there is a difference between natural, human error and falling into a trap. Our mistakes can be treated and resolved. We are capable of correcting them, thanks to the understanding of our people and the Party, our financial resources, and our cadres.

Our dream is not only one of Arab nationalist struggle for Arab unity, it is also the construction of one united Arab socialist democratic nation. And yet, as I mentioned earlier, the Party wanted to place unity before all else, before liberty and socialism.

There is no lack of understanding of socialism among our cadres, although they lack numbers. However, national philosophy has, since the beginning of this century, always stressed the importance of national struggle, giving it preference over the means of using socialism. There should be a dialectic of interaction between national struggle and social struggle. Those Arab countries which attempted to unite, while at the same time building a socialist society, found that the Party, as well as all other nationalist movements, lacked the cadres to which I referred. I can state with certainty that our Party has the cadres capable of understanding and applying Baathist socialism, and yet we can do more by continuing to develop the cultural and intellectual programme among our cadres.

Fuad Matar: You have always stressed the issue of the Arab woman's liberation. Yet it is acknowledged that it is easier to wage a revolution against petroleum monopolies and foreign interests than to go against the traditions that chain the Arab woman. The Revolution hesitates to adopt any forceful measures that go against the inherited customs and the traditions which stand in the way of liberation, which means postponement of the issue.

You have stated on one occasion, 'If the Revolution does not deal with the rights of women on an equal basis, taking into consideration their role in history, then the Revolution will certainly lose a part of its people.' What would happen if this part were indeed lost, although this could be prevented by educating people gently and ending forever the unfair and unjust traditions? If the women are lost, the loss will be permanent, but traditions go on spreading. Can you also tell us about the nature of women's lack of freedom, and what would have happened had you acted with force?

President Saddam Hussein: Whenever I warned against forceful action to liberate women and give them equal status, I always differentiated between this kind of action and that used against foreign companies. We do not lack daring—yet the issue of women is directly linked to the traditions of our society, whereas driving out monopolies is in line with the will of our people, since the companies are foreign parties exploiting our wealth. In using force to deal with the monopolies and in nationalising oil, I placed all the people on the same front, facing the foreign economic occupier. That is why I warn against applying this method in dealing with the social problems of our people. I mention this in connection with a comment made by one of our woman comrades at a women's congress I attended. She said that the leadership which had successfully nationalised oil should also fight against reactionary thoughts and liberate women just as quickly. I answered that there was a difference between the two. Postponing the issue for three years, for instance, was better than losing people from our ranks. Nevertheless, only a year after this comment a law was passed concerning the role of women and the achievement of equality between the sexes.

In this, as in other issues, we do not use the same methods as those adopted by the opposition (even ours) when we were not in power: they thought that solving the problem was merely a matter of issuing a set of laws and applying them. A revolution that does not translate its thoughts into laws remains a verbal revolution. The revolution must become both the law and the tradition if we are to build a new society. Yet we do not look at the woman's situation within the context of law and the study of law. Her situation is different, in that she is a part of the social movement. For instance, we believe that by educating women and making it easy for them to find jobs in both the economic and the social fields, we have partly helped them on the road to liberation. We have also set up children's nurseries to enable mothers to go to work without their husbands objecting and insisting that a woman's duty begins at home.

This is certainly not enough. What is needed is to change society's state of mind. This does not take place in a year, or two, or three, or four . . . It is when one applies a twelve-year plan in one year that one loses part of the people. We do not wish to do this unless we have to. Some socialist revolutions lost followers by the millions in order to apply socialism. We do not want to fall into this trap. This is why we must learn the lesson of others; it also explains why our losses are few. Our programme continues, and the road towards the liberation of women takes its natural course. We do not wish to make only socialist changes, but social changes as well.

Fuad Matar: The West is in the throes of a great crisis, and one of the reasons is that men and women are both forced to work. This has created a sense of emptiness in both sexes, and is resulting in the breakdown of society. So when we talk of women's liberation in the Arab world, do we mean that we want them to be equal to Western women? Does the President not feel that a deeper study should be made, and new theories developed, so that liberation will not create new burdens for women?

President Saddam Hussein: Our Party is aware of this fact. It certainly does not claim that women can work in all fields and under all circumstances. This would only be harmful. Moreover, they themselves do not wish to be treated in this manner. I mentioned at an open session of the Federation of Iraqi Women that legal, practical and theoretical equality between men and women is a weapon against women. We cannot possibly ask women to undergo those hardships endured by men in order to attain equality. In the capitalist West, the end justifies the means. That is why Western women are forced to work in order to help financially and to strengthen family relations. However, the burden and the responsibilities involved lead these women to realise that the spirit of the family has been lost. There is a great difference between a woman working in order to co-operate and one doing so under duress.

In our case, the situation is different because the understanding differs. Salaries are in line with the needs of the individual. Just as we provide jobs for women, we also have laws that strengthen family relationships. As an example, a pregnant working woman is granted leave long before she has given birth and resumes her duties only after she is satisfied with her health and that of the newborn baby. Such a long period of leave is detrimental to our economy, and yet it is granted because the economy should first and foremost serve our socialist society. This is not the only law that we have decreed in order to preserve the family and for women's liberation. Other steps will be taken and become law as soon as they are fully discussed. All these laws will give priority to family relationships.

Fuad Matar: After the developments in Iran, it seems to me that there is a contradiction between Arab revolution and Islamic revolution. Do you not believe there should be a way to make one support the other? Iraq has confronted both regimes, the Shah's and the present one; which Iran did Iraq prefer as a neighbour? What is your analysis of the Iranian situation in general?

President Saddam Hussein: We rejoice at any revolution that takes place with the spirit and goals of Islam, even if it is outside the Arab nation. We see it as a bridge between the Arab nationalist movement, which is working towards a new society, and the non-Arab Islamic nations. Any revolution within an Islamic society which does not abide by the spirit of Islam goes against the Arab revolution. Any revolution that hides behind Islam in order to attain its goals and then confronts the Arab revolution is detrimental to the Arabs, as well as to the cause of Islam, because it is not based on co-operation and understanding.

It is natural for me to welcome any revolution inspired by Islam after 1,400 years, since it can only create a bridge of understanding between the revolutionaries and ourselves: we would then share the same traditions and beliefs, as well as the same feelings towards injustice and oppression. This is why all Arabs rejoiced at the fall of the Shah, not only because he was a tyrannical ruler but because his regime was corrupt; the fall of any such ruler is a proof of the victory of right over wrong, good over evil. The Shah fell in an Islamic society, a society which stands on the borders of the Arab nation. That is why all Arabs rejoiced in the hope that the new circumstances would be a bridge between the Iranian and the Arab revolutions; the Arab revolution is not simply a system of laws on earth, but derives its spirit from heaven.

Yet the Iranians, particularly those in responsible positions, behaved as though they naturally assumed that there were contradictions between their revolution and ours. They were chauvinistic and isolationist in their outlook towards the Arabs, whether historically or as regards their present interests. Moreover, in the case of a confessional movement, conflict is inevitable, since the Arab revolution is by no means a confessional one.

The Iranian revolution is dreaming if it intends to liberate the Arabs. It can help by freeing certain Arab societies from their corrupt regimes, but it certainly cannot be of any assistance through fanaticism and narrow-mindedness in religion. There is absolutely no contradiction between the Arab revolution and one which takes its inspiration from true Islam. We do not wish to force people to accept pre-established ideas or ready recipes. This is why we see the spirit of the Baath in all young people, Baathist or non-Baathist, who work in the spirit of Islam against corrupt regimes, Arab or non-Arab. Any Muslim who stands up to corruption is a revolutionary, wherever he is. There is no difference between people fighting against corrupt regimes, confessionalism and reactionary powers. Yet I would ask them to realise that 1,400 years have passed since the coming of Islam, that people have changed and society has progressed and developed, and all of this must be taken into consideration. It remains to be seen how successful these revolutionaries will be in building a new society.

It is not our business to give advice. Yet we reserve the right to think that the rulers of a society like Iran, composed as it is of five ethnic groups, must face this reality for the ultimate happiness of the people and to safeguard against interference by foreign powers. The Iranians claim that their revolution is based on the concepts of Islam; therefore they must understand that there is no contradiction between the values of Islam and the Persian and four non-Persian groups in their society—the Arabs, the people of Baluchistan, the Kurds and the people of Azerbaijan. As for Arab existence within the state of Iran, that is a fact. The Arab minority does not number thousands there; it numbers millions. It is up to them, and to them alone, to decide their own future.

If it based itself on the principles and truths I have already mentioned, Iran could be a good neighbour to Iraq.

Fuad Matar: How did you become involved with Palestine and when did your view of Palestine change from a romantic to a more realistic one? What do you think you could have accomplished for Palestine if you had been in power at an earlier date? Now that you are in power, what are the barriers that prevent you from achieving these things? What contribution has Iraq made to the Palestinian cause from 1948 to 1979? And for which Palestine are you fighting?

President Saddam Hussein: No movement can create a new society without a revolutionary vision, although it should not base itself on this alone. Through this vision, the revolutionary sees life as he wishes it to be, although he realises its present state. He sees clearly the life for which he fights and struggles, and nothing can separate him from his vision. This is a legitimate dream. Revolutionary romanticism in this sense still exists within me, and I find more pleasure in it than ever. I feel the need for it more than before, in order to be able to face the tasks of practical everyday life. Having said this, it is only natural that I have not yet been able to achieve all my ambitions.

What have we contributed to the Palestinian cause? We would have wished to offer more. We will never be content with our contribution, although we have certainly given more than any other Arab country without exception, apart from the special circumstances of those countries whose territory was occupied. There has been no war in which Iraq has not taken part. We have constantly called for the support of Palestinian revolutionaries. We are in the forefront of this support and will remain so. As for the Palestine that we want, it is a Palestine devoid of the presence of the Zionist usurpers. This is not a call for the existence of a Palestine without Jews. Arabs have never in their history been either religious or racial fanatics. However, the long road to our ultimate goal requires patient planning and optimism.

Fuad Matar: Within this context I would like to ask you, as a revolutionary comrade, the following questions. How can the Palestinian revolution become more effective? Was Iraq's encouragement of a greater number of resistance operations, especially of the kind planned by the late Dr Wadi Haddad, helpful to the cause?

President Saddam Hussein: The Palestinian revolution would be more successful if it rid itself of certain negative currents within the Arab nation and extricated itself from the game of international politics. The Arab nation is its source of inspiration and strength, yet some of its negative aspects may impede the Palestinian revolution. On the other hand, the Arabism of the revolution is also the basis of its strength, its optimism and its success. Although Arabism is sometimes a burden, the Palestinian revolution will never reach its goals without it. Arabism has made the revolution a part of Arab politics and this has laid it open to interference and intervention by Arab rulers, good and bad. The Palestinian revolution could have avoided the negative aspects of Arabism, but it failed to do so. The Palestinian revolutionaries' reasons may have been geographic as well as political, since the revolution had no other base of its own. One can imagine the importance of interaction between the Arab revolution as a whole and the Arab Palestinian revolution. They both have the same goal: the liberation of Palestine.

As for our support of operations, we do so in view of the circumstances. We are in favour of any operations, even suicidal ones, that may serve the Palestinian cause, either within the occupied land or outside it. We will not change this stand—even if we now hold a different opinion as to methods, which may make it appear that we have changed. We are in favour of any method used to express the Palestinian and Arab conscience, as long as this does not set world public opinion completely against it. This is our Party's line.

Fuad Matar: Some of Iraq's heroes have done great deeds for Palestine—I am thinking of Nebuchadnezzar and Salaheddin, for example. May I presume that you too dream of a similar role? Is this possible in your view, or are the circumstances of three thousand years ago different from those of today?

President Saddam Hussein: By God, I do indeed dream and wish for this. It is an honour for any human being to dream of such a role. But like all the revolutionaries of today, Baathists or Arabs, I also realise that the world of today is unlike the world of Nebuchadnezzar and Salaheddin. Today we know that in order to liberate Palestine we must first awaken the nation, liberate it from its chains, and give it confidence. This is understood by all Arab comrades. The genius of any leader should be a reflection of that of his nation. By this I do not mean to belittle any leader, nor do I wish to make comparisons. On the contrary, we must all work together as one nation. There is no more time to be lost by the Arab nation; there are many challenges to be faced and there is too much international involvement in the Arab world. This has certainly limited the advent of great leaders like Nebuchadnezzar and Salaheddin who were in the image of their nation. And yet anyone has the right to dream and try to achieve what these leaders achieved. We may hope to do what they did for Palestine, without ever forgetting that the great powers are trying to threaten Iraq. Iraq will continue to look to its history as an example, and will look forward to the constant advancement of humanity. In any game, even a simple one in the countryside, a would-be winner is always surrounded and stifled so as to prevent him succeeding. I feel that the great powers are behaving exactly in this manner towards Iraq. Despite all this, and despite the limitations, I feel nothing but optimism. I know that one day the nation's spirit will shine, no matter what the trials and despite the moves that will be made against it.

Fuad Matar: I have the following questions to ask you about Arab unity and understanding:

First, when shall we reach the stage when each Arab state will feel the need for unity with other Arab states?

Second, what are the barriers that stand between us and this unity? Is it because of a lack of conviction, or is it a fear of losing our identity?

Third, do you not think that it is impossible for the Arab nation to unite as long as there are problems of minorities? Could there possibly be another intermediate step before complete unity?

Fourth, do you feel optimistic about Arab unity? When, and under what circumstances, can it take place? Since you believe in flexibility, is there not a way other than unity in order to reach understanding?

Fifth, how do you explain the fact that traditional regimes get along better with one another than the revolutionary ones do?

President Saddam Hussein: Reactionary and rightist Arabs have one plan and one political line, although they may differ in the application of their principles; this explains their stable relationships. They share the same interests, the same capitalist and feudal outlook, whereas progressive regimes are still on the way to building a dual existence: one based partly on tradition and partly on new laws and a new way of life which have to be accepted by the people. The ambitions of reactionary regimes are more realistic than those of progressive regimes. Many progressive regimes find that the greatest challenge to their existence comes from other so-called 'progressive' regimes. Thus we find that differences become open conflict, rather than remaining differences. There are many reasons for this, mainly the lack of maturity and depth in the general outlook and behaviour, as well as a lack of self-confidence. One can also add to this the effect of international currents, which are now affecting progressive regimes as well as reactionary regimes. We would work better and more effectively if only we could all realise that there is enough space within our region for several different progressive movements (as long as they are not influenced by foreign powers), with no danger of one encroaching upon the other. Had there been enough understanding of joint Arab action, we could have found a vast field for Arab action, and for co-operation between all the national and progressive regimes and organisations.

Now we come to the subject of unity: twenty years ago we believed that unity could be achieved through a common constitution, and that it was a political act, as in the case of the unity between Egypt and Syria in 1958. Today we who fight and struggle for unity see it differently. We consider it an honourable goal, and we strive for a constitutional and political union between two or more Arab regions, in order to reach the ultimate goal: complete unity. This can only be achieved through a common constitution and policy. We also try other methods that would bring us closer to unity. For instance, we believe that economic ties may serve to promote unity, but are not in themselves unity. The problem is that people either have their gaze fixed on the future and neglect to do anything for the present, or they work only for the present and reach a form of Arab co-ordination which they see as unity.

We must not belittle the importance of any links between the Arabs; they may all contribute to unity on a constitutional and political basis. Yet we must not think that these steps will necessarily lead to unity, since sometimes they do not have unity as their aim. After the year 1958, co-operation between one Arab region and another was often incorrectly referred to as unity or union. I can give several examples of this: 'unity' between Syria, Egypt and Libya; unity between Egypt and Libya; unity between Egypt and North Yemen at the time of the late Gamal Abdel-Nasser; talk of unity between Syria and Jordan. It is only when the Arabs are convinced of the importance of uniting that they will do so. It is only when they realise that they must unite in order to be truly effective in society that they will do so. It is the Arab belief and faith in unity that will make them reach the ultimate goal, always bearing in mind that they must rely on themselves.

Fuad Matar: During the days leading up to a revolution, democracy comes first and foremost on the agenda, and it is believed that democracy will spread once the comrade comes to power. But then the concept of democracy changes so that it is no longer an issue. Do you believe that the concept of democracy is unsuited to the Arab world or do you have a practical definition of it? As a leader who has fought for twenty years, half in the Revolution itself and the other half in power, can you not install a democracy that would be peculiar to the Baath?

President Saddam Hussein: I do believe that we can establish a form of democracy in Iraq that can be imitated in the Arab nation. If we are not able to do so, then what is the use of my believing in the Baath and why does our Party struggle in the entire Arab nation? But if you ask me whether Western democracy is suitable for the Arab nation, my answer is no. Let us go back in history to the time of the early Arab Muslims. Their democracy never followed a Western pattern, and they relied on consultation rather than a parliament. That is why our own understanding of democracy should be based on the particular characteristics of our nation, as well as of our Party. Democracy has to develop and change with the times, while taking into account the political and legal rights of the citizen and his role in building the nation, together with his relationship with the Party. We cannot automatically apply democracy through imitation; this would only be detrimental to us as well as destructive, whether the source of imitation is Western or Eastern. How can our society, which is less developed than some, adopt the patterns of a very advanced society?

What is the right way of introducing a developed democracy within a traditional society? This is what we have been implementing in stages since 30 July 1968. If you were to ask the Iraqi people today who 'Abu Dolof' is, they would immediately answer, 'He is Karim al-Jassem, the head of the General Federation of the Farmers' Unions.' Karim al-Jassem is a farmer's son and a farmer himself; an Iraqi who can barely read or write, he has become an important social figure in Baath society, a personality who is the leader of millions of farmers. How could he have reached this level of leadership in his relationship with the farmers if there had been no democracy in revolutionary action? This is an active expression of the will of the people, applicable since 30 July 1968, and yet always changing with the times.

We have not yet dealt directly with the exercise of democracy on a constitutional level. Until now the Revolution Command Council has been the only body to adopt higher constitutional resolutions directly. However, the draft laws for the National Assembly and the Legislative Assembly for the Autonomous Region, which the people are now discussing, will ensure that the people's representatives participate in constitutional decisions and in shaping the higher policy of the nation. We do not believe that the liberal democratic experience is suited to our society because it was founded and developed on the basis of a capitalist society. Its context differs from ours, which is mainly based on our Revolution. According to the Western concept, for example, a society must have a free economy, even at the expense of other freedoms; yet one cannot possibly isolate the economy from life itself.

Fuad Matar: You know more than most people about Arab human rights because you faced difficult social circumstances in your childhood, because this stage was followed by one just as difficult, and because you were willing to make sacrifices, to the point of martyrdom, in your stand against a regime which had no use for human rights. In view of this, I would like you to define minimum and maximum Arab human rights. Under what circumstances will the Arab attain his political and social rights? What are the rights the Arab has attained in Iraq? What rights has he not yet attained, and how will he be able to attain them?

President Saddam Hussein: First we must agree that the matter of human rights is dynamic, not static. If we go back to early Arab Islamic history, to which I attach great importance, we find the Arabs' concept of rights was not rigid. It adapted to the times, from the coming of the Prophet and throughout the era of his followers until decadence set in. Rights changed with each new circumstance but were always based on principles. Even at the beginning, divine laws were based on the conditions and circumstances that prevailed at the time. That is why the advent of Judaism, Christianity and Islam came in that order, by the will of God, to be carried out by His prophets and their followers according to the times and circumstances . . .

Was preaching the only means that the Islamic religion used, or did it also make use of knowledge, education and the sword for its conquests? The answer is well known: Muslim Arabs used both, the Quran and the sword. But did they later use the sword as fervently as they did at the beginning of their mission? Did the Prophet Muhammad make as much use of the sword in the eleventh year of Islam as he did in the first years? The answer is no. That is why we say that human rights will depend on the time, the conditions and the circumstances. They will always be in step with the Revolution and its principles. The concept of human rights today is different from what it was four years ago, for instance, because the Revolution has progressed in the last twelve years.

Yet the basic principle of human rights remains the same: man was born to be free but not to be alone in his freedom; he must also take society's rights into consideration, as well as the freedom and rights of others. The interests of man and society are interrelated. Our view of human rights is different from that held by capitalism, which is based on the assumption that the individual's freedom and interests are equal to society's freedom and interests . . . Human rights outside society's rights are based on self-interest alone. So Americans can talk of human rights in the Soviet Union when they themselves are killing human beings in other societies, and we find Communist societies discussing the same subject when they, too, destroy human rights in their own lands and in another people's territory.

We must always remember our history, although I do not wish to do so in order to imitate it. Each Arab must learn the lessons of our heritage and our past. Some of the sons of our nation have a firm belief in our history, its greatness and its depth, and, finding themselves unable to follow in the path of their ancestors, decide to leave history well alone. This is wrong.

Fuad Matar: Yesterday I spent some time with your children to see how they live, and what sort of relationship you have with them. When I talked to your eldest son Uday, I saw he was wearing a military uniform and that he is being trained in the use of weapons despite his youth. It occurred to me to ask him the standard question: what do you want to be when you grow up? His answer reminded me of an important question I had prepared earlier for you. Your son said he wanted to become a nuclear scientist. My question to you was the following: is Iraq planning to procure a nuclear bomb?

President Saddam Hussein: Science must always be based on solid foundations. I do not believe nuclear weapons can be used for peaceful, scientific purposes in an underdeveloped, bedouin society. Money alone does not mean that a state possesses the key to the correct use of nuclear weapons for peaceful purposes. The use of such a weapon has its own conditions, circumstances and demands. It cannot be separated from the rest of life, society, international politics, the state's interests or the people's demands for a better life. However, I think that if you ask any person in the world whether he would like to possess a nuclear bomb, he will tell you that he would. A nuclear bomb is not a child's toy. It is a heavy responsibility, although it may not seem so. And if you asked countries such as Djibouti, India, Dubai, Nepal or Japan—all countries which have entered into special treaties since the Second World War—they would tell you that the nuclear bomb is definitely a burden. However, there is no doubt that within our essential programme we attach great importance to the peaceful uses of nuclear power, both technologically and scientifically.

Fuad Matar: Do you not think it is time to evaluate the Baath's principles now that it has been in existence for thirty-five years, especially as regards its view of Islam? We are living in the midst of an Islamic awakening or, if one may say so, in a state of Islamic 'baath'. The reason behind this may be that the generation of the seventies is suffering from the failure of nationalism. The Baath has always stressed the importance of secularism. You are in the best position to judge this analysis: you are in power, and the Islamic 'baath' stands a good chance of attracting a generation of Arabs, whom the national Baath appears to have failed to attract.

President Saddam Hussein: The Party's outlook on religion is not only based on the inspiration it derives from Islam, nor is it neutral before faith and apostasy; the Party is for faith. When we say that we are not neutral between apostasy and faith, we mean that Baathists are like all other believers, free to worship as they wish. They pray, fast and carry out their religious duties towards God. They have a direct relationship with their religion, whereas those who have a scientific outlook on life may stand on the borderline between faith and apostasy, or may even have a materialistic outlook on life. Yet, although we may be inspired by religion and its laws, we do not deal with life by following a religious path. Today, after 1,400 years, religion has taken many new paths, new meanings, new conduct, new schools of thought. We do not believe in dealing with life through religion because it would not serve the Arab nation. It would only serve to divide the nation into different religions and numerous sects and schools of thought. We discussed this point before the Iranian revolution took place and we find that our predictions have come true: differences have arisen amongst the believers in everyday religious matters. What I wish to point out here is that we have two relationships with religion: an inspiration stemming from the main principles and lessons, and the fact that, like all ordinary citizens, we are believers who worship without any interference from those in power. That is why I do not see the need for an analysis of the Baath's attitude towards religion.

However, we must pause here and analyse the reasons behind the politicised religion of some of the young men who use religion as a weapon in their struggle against corrupt regimes, instead of using the Baath as a way of achieving their goals. We all have the same aims. The Baath is not operating in a limited field; on the contrary, it is spreading, and so are the religious movements of these young men. They deserve our attention, not because we are afraid of them, but because they are in the image of the Baathists in that they are fighting against corruption, injustice, confessionalism and reactionary movements. Whether they will succeed—and they have not yet done so—is another matter.

We believe in religion and it is ever-present in our daily life and in our Party. Therefore we do not find any contradiction between these young men and us, inasmuch as they struggle, often under the seal of secrecy, against injustice and without foreign aid for the unity of the Arab nation. Yet we still believe that the road taken by the Baath is the best one to deal with injustice, in that it has greater experience and is more capable of bringing happiness to Arab society. In our struggle it is just as important to find a way to build a better society within the framework of religion, its principles and traditions, as it is to erase corruption.

We follow the dictates of Islam fully, as we are people who come from a religious society; yet the manner of worship is free of any state interference, since each human being practises in accordance with his religion, his sect and his customs.

We are content, although not completely, with our calculations and our programme. We are content in that the application of our Party's principles has taken the right road in the Iraqi region, and we find Baathists fighting against corruption and injustice and dying for their honourable cause wherever the need arises in the Arab world.

How long is it since the revolution took place in Iran? Eleven months. Has it taken development into consideration, its circumstances and its demands? If it does not do so, then it must explain each development which may lead to the creation of a new school of thought, and even to a new sect. We believe that if the Iranian revolution continues on its present path, it may split from the Shia sect and become a new sect. This is why our Party and its early leaders looked upon Arab life as they did, believing that the Baath was the right way. This is also our view of the matter. We do not deal with life through religion, but at the same time we are linked to religion through worship, which takes into consideration freedom of worship. Had the Arab world been one nationality and one religion it would have been easy to resolve this. However, it is surrounded by new and hostile currents which seek to exploit the weak points in the Arab nation and thus prevent its development. We truly believe that the Baath's road will save the nation from dangers and bring about a new and flourishing civilisation, free from corruption and injustice, where happiness and justice will prevail.

As for the religious awakening you mentioned earlier, I would like to point out that it is not the first time that our young men have rebelled against injustice, taking the principles of Islam as their inspiration (whether they succeed in their call or not is another matter). For example, the Muslim Brothers used their religious beliefs as a weapon to resist the British in Egypt. Religious movements flourished in the Arab nation in the forties and fifties. This was the case, for instance, amongst our own young men in Iraq before the Revolution of July 1958.

The explanation for this recent awakening is that corruption is more widespread in the Arab world today than ever before. Some regimes are the image of corruption itself. The presence of mosques has been a great help towards the creation of such movements, since mosques are sacred places on which assaults and attacks would be strongly discouraged, although some rulers have taken such steps. Mosques, if I may say so, are the ideal headquarters for underground activities in the context of a religious direction of the struggle. We rejoice and feel deeply with any young man who believes in the Islamic call and is ready to die for it in his struggle against corruption. In the past this has only occurred in Egypt and Algeria; today, it is more widespread. However, the Baathists fight for the same causes and are ready to die for them.

Fuad Matar: Do you sometimes wonder why the Arabs were greater in the past and why they have changed so drastically? And why is it that the Arabs are now only good at poetry and imitating others, whereas the whole region was once a shining light for other civilisations? And why were the Arabs an example of chivalry in the past, unlike today? Why are they living through a religious crisis when they were the very source of religion? Why are they facing a crisis of legislation when they were the source of law? They were pioneers in medicine, yet today they send their patients to be treated abroad. They were the masters of philosophy, but have become the followers of Western thought today. They were the source of history and are now given a fleeting reference in history books. Why?

President Saddam Hussein: It is natural for me to wonder about all this, but I still believe that our nation is capable of a renaissance. There is no nation that has given as much to humanity as the Arab nation has. There is no other nation that has risen, fallen and risen once more, without being colonialists or aggressors, and with only human interests in mind. A nation goes through life just as a human being passes through different stages: infancy, childhood, youth, middle age, old age, then death. There are reasons behind this which I do not wish to go into. Decadence sets in when man loses faith and its incentives. There are other reasons which account for the decadence of the Arab nation at certain points of its history.

But let us also ask ourselves the following question: where were the other nations when the Arab nation was at the height of civilisation? They were then at the stage of receiving knowledge. We must point out that the Arab nation is not made up of a single civilisation but of many—civilisations that were unique in their humanity. Non-Arab nations were still living in darkness when the Arab nation's civilisation shone throughout the world.

When the nation starts to weaken and becomes decadent it is the fault of those in power, because they have lost their belief in the principles of life and forgotten the importance of a nation's role, its message and its values. We can state without hesitation that our nation has a message. That is why it can never be an average nation: throughout history our nation has either soared to the heights, or fallen into the abyss through the envy, conspiracy and enmity of others. Any rising nation attracts enemies who have only one wish, to stand in the way of its development.

If one asked whether the Arab nation today is on the ascent or in decline, the answer would have to be that it is on the ascent as compared with the previous ten years; indeed, it is experiencing a renaissance. Do we have the necessary means today for a new renaissance? The answer is no. However, our young people have faith, and believe in taking the necessary steps to save the nation. We are reaching a crucial stage in the struggle for the nation's renaissance. Your questions are natural and meaningful, yet the state in which we find ourselves today as compared to that of our ancestors will not sap my energy, nor can it prevent me from stating that the nation can and will rise again.

There have been many opportunities of which the Party could have made use. However, they did not do so. This does not mean that the Party was incapable of doing so; but rather that the Party would not at that time have been able to emerge as a popular leader over the whole Arab nation rather than over Iraq alone, as is our ambition. It is not only the difficult moments the Party has lived through which are responsible for this, it is also a lack of the right opportunities. There were shortcomings in the use of the Party's capabilities, as well as a certain neglect in the way the Party's beliefs were explained. This could have been done better. The Arab nation would be in a stronger position today if the February Revolution in Iraq and the March Revolution in Syria had both taken our same Baathist path.

Although we recognise our mistakes and try to learn from them, we do not stop to cry over the negative aspects. We must consolidate our struggle and strengthen our purpose to push ever forward. Ours is a great nation, and it will be even greater in time. This is the solemn pledge made by all our comrades.

Baathism

Michel Aflak

from *Choice of Texts from the Ba'th Party Founder's Thought*

Whereas the "Unionists" of fragmentation consider unity something automatic that can be reached by political unification when circumstances and opportunities become propitious and that unity needs only political preparation, to be conducted through negotiations and manoeuvres. As for ideological preparation this is, at best, nothing more than a generalised lip service to unity which is so wide that it includes all sorts of improvisations and incongruities, and whereas unity represents, in the eyes of regionalist parties with their well-known practices, a superficial thing which lacks seriousness and comes last in priorities when compared with regional preoccupations which practically dominate the interest of such parties, unity, as seen by the "Arab Baath", is a fundamental and living idea. It has a theory in the same way as freedom and socialism have theories. Like them it has its principled, organised daily and continuous struggle as well as its stages of application which enhance the power of that struggle and pave the way for the final victory.

"The revolutionary nature of the Arab unity, 2—February, 1953".

Arab unity is an ideal and a standard. It is not the outcome or a consequence of the fight of the Arab people for liberty and socialism, it is a new ideal which should accompany and direct that fight. The potentialities of the Arab nation are not the numerical sum of the potentialities of its parts when they are in the state of separation; they are greater in quantity and different in kind.

"The revolutionary nature of the Arab unity, 2—February, 1953".

The serious danger to unity comes from those who affect it, brag about it, who, when clinging to it, do so in order to fake it, suck out its blood, stifle it, and put on its mouth what it does not want to say, in order to make it a prisoner in their hands. They can then use it as a threat and bargain for it in exchange for base positions and personal leadership.

"On the unity of Egypt and Syria, its direction and obstacles on its way, 2—April 7, 1956".

Unity has been a pursuit of the Arab nation since it has been afflicted with fragmentation. The Baath did not create the demand or the objective of unity, but gave it a new conception that makes it realisable. Unity, in the view of the Baath, is a revolutionary idea and a revolutionary action in contrast to the concept prevalent in the past, whose consequences survive to this day. That concept meant merely putting together and binding the parts of the Arab homeland, whereas the revolutionary understanding of unity means creativeness in thought and struggle which stand opposed both to the state of fragmentation and to what has been bequeathed and fabricated by fragmentation in terms of mentality, emotions, interest and political, economic and social conditions inside every region of the nation.

Thus unity, in its revolutionary conception becomes linked with the two other revolutionary objectives, liberty and socialism, interacts with them, nourishes them and nourished by them. Thus unity enters, for the first time in many generations, into the very fabric of the life of the Arab people and into the innermost points of its struggle for its freedom, independence, political rights, and its daily bread as well as for the economic and social condition conducive to its human dignity and its national mission.

"Questions and Answers >, 1—1957".

We want independence and liberty because they are right and just and because they are the means to the release of our great gifts and creative capacities, so that we can realise on this earth, which is our land, our aim and the aim of every man—complete humanity.

"The age of heroism, 1—1935".

We represent liberty, socialism and unity. This is the interest of the Arab nation, I mean by nation the greater number of the people and not that disfigured and deviating minority which has denied its identity, the minority enslaved by its selfishness and private interests, for it is no longer a part of the nation.

"The Arab Baath is the will of life, 1—April, 1950".

Everything that Islam has achieved in victories and culture was in the germinal stage in the first twenty years of the message. Before they conquered the lands, the Arabs had conquered themselves and penetrated into the innermost of their souls. Before they governed nations, they governed themselves and controlled their passions and were in possession of their wills.

"In memory of the Arab Prophet, 1—April, 1943".

We might not be seen among those who pray and we might not fast with those who fast, but we believe in God because we are in dire need of Him. Our burden is onerous, our road is rough and our aim is high. We have reached this faith, we did not start with it. We arrived at it through sufferings and hardships and did not receive it by inheritance nor was it handed down to us conventionally. For this reason it is invaluable for us, being the fruit of our efforts.

"In memory of the Arab Prophet, 1—April, 1943".

Until now the life of the prophet was regarded from the outside, as an admirable image for our appreciation and consecration. We now have to start looking at it from within, so that we can live it. Every Arab at present can live the life of the Arab prophet even though by comparison he is no more than a stone to the mountain or a drop of water to the sea. Naturally, no man, however great he is, is capable of doing what Mohammed did. It is also natural that any man, however small his capacity, could be a miniature of Mohammed, so long as he belongs to the nation which concentrated all its powers to produce Mohammed. Or rather, so long as this man is one with a nation which Mohammed concentrated all his efforts to produce. Sometime in the past the life of a whole nation was summarised in one man. Today the whole life of this nation in its revival should be the detail of the life of its great man. Mohammed was all the Arabs. Let all the Arabs of today be Mohammed.

"In memory of the Arab Prophet—April, 1943".

But does this mean that Islam has come to be confined to the Arabs? If we say this we shall be far from the truth and so deviate from reality. Every great nation, deeply connected with the eternal meanings of the universe, moves in its very genesis towards the eternal and universal values. Islam is, therefore, for the Arab people in its actuality and for all mankind in its ideal objectives. The message of Islam is to create Arab humanism.

"In memory of the Arab Prophet, 1—April, 1943".

Therefore the meaning which Islam reveals in this historic and important epoch and at this decisive stage in development is that all the efforts should be directed to strengthening the Arab and awakening them and that these efforts should be within the framework of Arab nationalism.

"In memory of the Arab Prophet, 1—April, 1943".

A day will come when the nationalists will find themselves the only defenders of Islam. They will have to give a special meaning to it if they want the Arab nation to have a good reason for survival.

"In memory of the Arab Prophet, 1—April, 1943".

The pure nationalist idea in the West was consistent with itself when it separated nationalism from religion. Religion entered Europe from the outside, therefore it is alien to its character and history. It is a combination of otherwordly faith and morals. It was not revealed to them originally in their languages. It did not express the needs of their environment nor was it fused with their history. Islam, on the other hand, is to the Arabs, not only an otherworldly faith nor is it merely a moral code, but it is also the dearest expression of their universal feeling and their view of life. It is the strongest expression of the unity of their personality in which word, feeling, thought, mediation, action, soul, and destiny, are all integrated and work in harmony together.

"In memory of the Arab Prophet, 1—April, 1943".

The connection of Islam to Arabism is not, therefore, similar to that of any religion to any nationalism. The Arab Christians, when their nationalism is fully awakened and when they restore their genuine character, will recognise that Islam for them is nationalist education in which they have to be absorbed in order to understand and love it to the extent that they become concerned about Islam as about the most precious thing in their Arabism. If the actual reality is still far from this wish, the new generation of Arab Christians has a task which it should perform with daring and detachment, sacrificing for it their pride and benefits, for there is nothing that equals Arabism and the honour of belonging to it.

"In memory of the Arab Prophet—April, 1943".

Islam is nothing but offspring of sufferings, the sufferings of Arabism. These sufferings have come back to the Arab land in a degree of violence and depth unknown to the Arabs of Jahilyah (Pre-Islamic Arabs). How many more such sufferings will be brought by a cleansing revolution equal to the revolution that Islam carried on its banner? Only the new Arab generation can shoulder the responsibility for such a revolution and appreciate its necessity, for the sufferings of the present time have prepared it to do so. Its love of its soil and history has prepared it for knowing its spirit and orientation.

"In memory of the Arab Prophet, 1—April, 1943".

Yes, it is an extraordinary experience, that of the Party in Iraq. It is the experience of the Party which is not going to be surpassed. Not because we have reached all our aims for we are at the beginning of the road. But this genuine beginning is the only one which will take us to the victorious end. Some minutes ago I said to our dear comrade Saddam that the idea of the Party was from the start a rigorous idea that required a rigorous revolutionary standard as you know from the writings in the early life of the Party. I told him that the conditons of Syria where the Party emerged were not of the same degree of difficulty and cruelty. It was natural that Arabic Iraq, with its tragic and cruel conditions, to be the starting point for a serious realisation of this idea.

> "The experiment of the Baath in Iraq is a starting point for the Arab revolution, 7—A speech to the advanced cadres of the Arab Baath Socialist Party in Baghdad—June 24, 1974".

How Saddam Hussein Came to Power

Said K. Aburish

from *Saddam Hussein: The Politics of Revenge*

There is no denying the social and economic achievements of the Ba'ath's first decade in power, 1968–78, under the stewardship of Saddam Hussein. Iraq had become a welfare state which was envied by the other Arabs and admired by the USSR and the West. In fact, only one thing stood between Iraq and being a model state—the human cost. The articles of the provisional constitution which purported to protect the rights of the individual—and each government which followed the monarchy had one—were never observed. But Saddam's regime differed from what had gone before. Both its accomplishments and its dictatorial ways were incomparably greater than those of the previous governments. To most Iraqis, including the Shias and the Kurds, the Ba'ath was behind the improvement in their standard of living. A minority, however, were subjected to a level of suffering that the country had never before experienced. Celebrating or condemning the Ba'athist government became an individual matter and reduced the importance of people's ethnic or religious origins.

Saddam's efficient 1970s dictatorship and its popularity with broad segments of the Iraqi people also impressed others. Outsiders too concentrated on the results and ignored the methods, a case of the ends justifying the means.

The image that Iraq projected to the outside world was similar to the one celebrated by leftist Western intellectuals writing about the Soviet Union and its leaps forward in the 1930s. Like Stalin, Saddam appeared to make sense out of an unwieldy country. The improving standard of living produced stability, which in turn produced ethnic and religious harmony. Saddam was on his way to proving that full bellies would overcome and replace people's desire for a democratic system of government. Everybody agreed with him, and the tables of statistics showing economic growth figures and subsidiary achievements were better known to the rest of the world than the contents of the few reports about his human rights record.

By 1978 everything in Iraq was running smoothly under Saddam's personal control. The Army, which had been totally mechanized and expanded to over four hundred thousand, was under the command of Adrian Khairallah, Saddam's cousin, childhood playmate and brother-in-law and Khairallah Tulfah's son. Although he was married to Bakr's daughter, Adrian's loyalty was to the real leader of the country, his cousin. Saddam's half-brother Barazan had become head of the *mukhabarat* branch of the security service following the Kazzar conspiracy and had claimed some of the functions of the other security departments. (The fortunes of the various branches of the security apparatus rose and fell depending in the importance of their chiefs, and Saddam trusted Barazan and depended on him.) The National Security Office, which oversaw all security functions, was run by his cousin Sa'adoun Shaker who reported directly to Saddam. Half-brother Watban had become governor of the expanded province of Tikrit, renamed Salaheddine in honour of the legendary Muslim warrior 'Saladin'. Sabawi, the last of the half-brothers, had been made deputy chief of police. The Popular Army was still under Izzat Douri, Saddam's deputy in the RCC and his unwavering obedient follower. The Popular Army was expanding even faster than the regular Army and numbered around 150,000. The number of party members, followers and supporters had increased and, though different figures have been cited, became one million strong. The Iraqi command of the Ba'ath (the Regional Command Council in charge of the country), which had been placed under the RCC, had created a structure of loyalists through the formation of seven divisions which reported directly to it: the military office, propaganda office, labour office, peasant office, student office, office of professional organizations and office for relations with the party.

Saddam's Tikriti relations and a handful of unthreatening followers used the party as a front. The Ba'ath existed as a structure, but Saddam and his small group ran its various aspects on all levels. It was a merger between the family and the party, with the former using the latter as a vehicle to control the country. The party reported to the family and justified its rule, but the family acted in the name of the party. Saddam, as head of the family, needed a personality to preside over the family's pre-emption of the party. Using the colossal propaganda machinery of the government, he began to portray himself as the embodiment of every strand of Iraqi history.

Bakr was still there, but without much to do. A former Iraqi Ba'athist, who does not wish to be identified, asserts that Bakr's residence became known as 'the tomb of the well-known soldier'. Aflaq compensated for his own effeteness and inability to participate directly in the running of the country by watching the progress of his protégé with undisguised pleasure. The spiritual leader of the party limited himself to issuing what amounted to songs of praise with little philosophical or ideological content.

The opposition, made up of Kurds, religious Shias and Communists, continued to exist, and they had not changed their policies towards the regime. The Kurds kept up their demands for autonomy in their usually confused way, while the Shias wanted to participate in the running of their country and were incrementally raising their demands. The Communists were calling for 'democratic rule'. But all three groups had been weakened by the emergence of a docile, happy middle class created by Saddam. According to Iraqi historian and sociologist Faleh Abdel Jabbar, the percentage of the population that qualified to be included in this social grouping rose from 28 in 1970 to 58 in 1979.

Furthermore, there was now a lack of the outside support on which all three opposition groups had depended in the past as a necessary ingredient for changing Iraqi governments or forcing change on them. Despite an occasional resort to arms, the West was not ready to back the Kurds as extensively as it had done before, and they missed the charismatic leadership of Mulla Mustapha Al Barzani who had taken refuge in the USA after the 1975 Saddam–Shah Algiers Agreement and was suffering from cancer. Iranian support for the Shias had declined considerably since the 1975 agreement, and the alliance between the anti-Shah Khomeini and the Iraqi Shias made its resurrection unlikely. The 1979 assumption of power of Khomeini was to signal a new phase in this relationship and the intensification of Shia opposition. But before that moment, relations between the Shah and Saddam had become so good that Empress Farah visited the Shia holy places in Iraq, an act which dispirited Saddam's Shia opponents. And the USSR had all but given up on the Iraqi Communist Party's chances of participating in the government of Iraq. The Communist Bloc as a whole showed more concern for saving its overall influence in the country and the Middle East from Western encroachment. This was particularly so after the Soviet invasion of Afghanistan and Saddam's open opposition to it. In 1978, the opposition to Saddam was weaker than at any other time since the Ba'ath had assumed power in 1968.

Another historical source of trouble for the rulers of Iraq, the ability of other Arab countries to influence its internal events, was in suspension. **The Camp David Agreement** had isolated Egypt and reduced its position as a factor in Arab politics. Saudi Arabia and Kuwait had nothing to complain about because 'brother Saddam' had been friendly and not threatened them or made claims against them, to the extent of taking no more than a day to settle several small border incidents with Kuwait. Poor countries within the Arab League, such as Somalia and Sudan, were appreciative of Saddam's financial help and wanted it to continue. Arafat and the PLO had made their peace with the Iraqi regime and were more interested in maintaining it as a backer than in anything else. They repaid Saddam by publicizing his contributions to the cause.

Saddam's inward-looking policies, which since 1973 had emphasized economics over ideology, had succeeded in the Arab arena. Only Syria was still a problem, but a minor one because its supposedly leftist-leaning branch of the Ba'ath party did not have the financial means or the following inside Iraq to threaten Saddam.

It was the Iraq-first policy which guaranteed Western support for Saddam, or at least acquiescence in what he was doing. He pursued his long-term plans quietly, without any agitation that might generate Western disapproval, so the West judged him by day-to-day political happenings and decided that he was not threatening—not even bothering—anyone except his own people. Meanwhile, his crackdown on the Communists in 1977—earned him credit in Western capitals because it was judged in political rather than human rights terms. His expulsion of Khomeini, the man who was threatening the pro-West Shah, was welcomed, even when it was accompanied by the imprisonment of thousands of Iraqi Shias.

The West perceived the Kurds as troublemakers who stood in the way of stability, the word which the West then associated with Saddam. This and the constant divisions in their ranks overshadowed Saddam's attempts to subdue them violently or to change the ethnic character of Kurdistan by resettling over half a million Kurds (the figure is disputed) in the southern part of Iraq, Nassirya, Afaq and Diwaniya. By the late 1970s the increase in this resettlement activity, known as *mujama'at,* resembled the deportation of ethnic groups to Siberia under Stalin, and well over a thousand Kurdish villages were depopulated. To avoid being forcibly resettled, several hundred thousand Kurds escaped to Iran. The Iraqi regime, as it was to do on a larger scale later, encouraged Sunni Arabs to move to the mostly Kurdish cities of Kirkuk, Suleimaniya and others.

Even Saddam's tilt towards a market economy and his ending of collectivization could not but help him in Western circles. The one element which could have disturbed this picture, a perceived threat to Israel, was something which he studiously manipulated. During this period he never went beyond what the most pro-West of Arab countries was saying. Moreover, the hawkish Menachem Begin was now Prime Minister of Israel, and his exaggerations of the Arab threat and messianic zeal made the USA and others dismiss him—not to speak of the Carter administration's antipathy towards the Israeli leader and its desire to include Iraq in an eventual peace agreement with all the Arab countries. This background included the promotion of good relations between Saddam and civilian and military suppliers in the USA and Europe.

In one of those twists of Arab politics which leads the wise investigative writer never to take anything for granted, it was none other than Bakr who finally challenged Saddam and shattered his aura of invincibility. Bakr's move subscribed to an old Iraqi saying, *'Aydain bil qadr ma tutbukh'*, which can be loosely translated as 'Too many cooks spoil the broth'. It also proved that Bakr's *de jure* position as head of state, which he had failed to utilize to control his deputy in the past, still provided him with clout. The reason that Bakr used to try to curb or remove Saddam was a legitimate one acceptable to all believers in Ba'athist ideology, and he knew that he could count on the support of most if not all members of the party. Bakr's belated move took the form of an attempt to unite Syria and Iraq as one country under a single Ba'ath Party. Even Saddam could not object to this aim; it was a perfect cover.

President Sadat of Egypt's Camp David Agreement of 17 September 1978 had provided Bakr with the real or nominal reason to attempt this move. All Arabs, including the leadership of both branches of the Ba'ath party, were agreed that the response to Sadat's peace initiative had to include a strengthening of the Arab eastern front, opposing Israel with, namely Iraq, Syria and Jordan. Jordan's special relationship with the West and vulnerability to Israeli military retaliation precluded its involvement in any unification schemes, but there was nothing to stop the other two countries responding to their peoples' wishes—and their people wanted their leaders to overcome the quarrels which had separated them and to concentrate on facing 'the common Zionist enemy'. To the average Syrian and Iraqi, creating a country big enough and strong enough to face Israel was more important then any commitment to individual leaders. They wanted to compensate for the loss of Egypt from the Arab side. Besides, the similarities between the two countries have always made this prospect more enticing than other Arab unification schemes. Misgivings based on past experience, including that of the short-lived United Arab Republic of Egypt and Syria, were set aside.

On 1 October Iraq announced that it was willing to send troops to reinforce Syria in its confrontation with Israel. This pledge was made by Bakr who, acting on his own and courageously, followed it with an open-ended offer to merge his country with its erstwhile enemy. There was no way that President Hafez Assad of Syria could refuse such an offer. On 26 October he accepted an invitation to visit Baghdad and held a summit conference with Bakr and Saddam. After condemning the policies of Sadat, the three announced a Charter for Joint National Action to coordinate their anti-Israeli efforts. On 7 November they formed a joint Higher Political Committee to supervise their efforts. The leaders described their activities as measures aimed at turning the two countries into 'one state, one party and one people'.

Behind the populist statements a struggle for power had developed which reflected the realities of the situation. To the elderly Bakr, this was a last chance to leave a mark on Arab history. He proposed an immediate union and the creation of one country under his leadership but with Assad as his deputy and successor. Although the challenge to Saddam was clear, Assad doubted Bakr's ability to deliver his part of the bargain. He knew that Saddam controlled all centres of power in Iraq, and was afraid that Iraq's natural wealth and strength would eventually play into his competitor's hands and allow Saddam to edge him out regardless of any succession arrangement reached with Bakr.

Assad refused to contemplate immediate union and declared that the dispatch of Iraqi troops to Syria was unnecessary. He came out in favour of unification but via a more deliberate step-by-step approach that would take several years. Bakr tried to change Assad's mind and to circumvent the developing impasse. He visited Syria in January 1979 and reduced his demands to an immediate merger of the two branches of the Ba'ath Party as a first step. But this too was rejected by the Syrian leader. Assad, to many the most astute Arab diplomat of the century, simply refused to budge. For a while things were held in abeyance.

This state of limbo represented a threat to Saddam's position. Because the Iraqi people and the nominally important Ba'ath's Regional Command Council were in favour of union to the extent of sacrificing Mr Deputy, he had to close the door on the whole business. Acting in character, Saddam decided against leaving anything to chance. As luck would have it, this was the time of the Islamic fundamentalist victory against the Shah in Iran. Khomeini returned to his country on 12 February, and suddenly good relations between Iran and Iraq were a thing of the past. The tepid reply to Bakr's congratulatory cable to Khomeini revealed a deep level of mistrust. Bakr's wishes of regional peace were answered by a terse 'Peace is with those who follow the righteous path.' This excluded the secular Ba'ath.

The Iraqi fear of emerging change in the regional balance of power stood in sharp contrast to the favourable Syrian reaction. Assad, and even the PLO's Arafat, felt that Khomeini's Iran gave the anti-Israeli forces depth. Saddam, however, saw the Islamic regime as a menace because Khomeini placed loyalty to religion ahead of loyalty to the state. He was anti-Ba'athist and committed to helping the Shias of Iraq topple their country's government. Assad's perception of Khomeini as a new ally prompted him to send the Imam a telegram to which, in contrast to his reply to the Iraqis, the latter responded enthusiastically. The developing amity with Iran lessened Assad's need to depend on Iraq. Meanwhile, Khomeini's enmity to the Iraqi Ba'ath took the form of calls for rebellion against the regime. One week after he assumed power in Tehran, he declared that he 'wanted Najjaf' one of the Shia holy cities in Iraq. In response, Saddam recalled the days of the Shah's old threats to Iraq and described the cleric as nothing but 'a Shah in religious garb'. But worse things were on the way.

The Iraqi-Syrian differences over the new Islamic regime in Iran turned the hitherto personal competition for position between Assad and Saddam into an ideological issue which provided Saddam with a more acceptable reason for cancelling the plans to unite the two countries. He responded in his usual methodical way to the unexpected challenge to his paramountcy within Iraq from Bakr's blatant attempt to curb his power, and to the threat posed by Khomeini's control of Iran. First, he took steps to tighten his control on all aspects of life within the country. Although the various branches of the security apparatus, Popular Army and regular armed forces had been totally Ba'athized by 1977, he conducted cleansing operations in the ranks of these organizations and eliminated anyone whose loyalty to him was suspect, or not guaranteed. This attempt to place these organizations totally in Mr Deputy's hand was carried out by Saddam's reliable Tikriti relations, and it was so pervasive it included schoolteachers. Thousands of government and party workers were dismissed and hundreds were imprisoned.

He followed this with a two-pronged attack. Unable to go back on Bakr's unification offer because of its popular appeal, he resorted to making it unacceptable. He capitalized on the Syrian leader's reluctance by presenting Assad with an ultimatum: either immediate union or the termination of all negotiations towards one. Once again, Assad read the situation correctly. He surmised that Saddam would never opt for the total merger of the two countries unless it meant that he was capable of toppling Bakr and assuming the leadership of the new political entity. When Assad did not respond to Saddam's threat, Saddam withdrew Iraqi participation from the various committees that had been set up to oversee the merger. The committees had in any case ceased to function since mid-1978; with the Iran problem they were disbanded. There is little doubt that it was Saddam who brought about the end of the discussions towards union.

The time for demanding Bakr's resignation had come. According to a Ba'athist source, Saddam's first step was to surround the presidential palace with troops loyal to himself. With that and other security measures in place, he went to Jordan in early July 1979 to visit King Hussein and secure support for the physical removal of Bakr. It was Saddam's personal experience in the 1963 coup, his awareness that the CIA and others were capable of influencing events within Iraq, which made him seek guarantees against interference in the ousting of Bakr by outside powers. According to opposition **INC Chairman Ahmed Chalabi,** King Hussein promised Saddam support and followed that by traveling to Saudi Arabia to secure that country's blessing for Saddam's plans. A former colonel in the Jordanian Army corroborates and expands Chalabi's story. He asserts that Jordanian Prime Minister Abdel Hamid Sharraf, King Hussein's cousin and an astute operator, was party to the discussions. Furthermore, during this trip Saddam also had meetings with several unnamed CIA operatives stationed in Amman.

The reason behind the attitude of Jordan, Saudi Arabia and perhaps the CIA is not mysterious: all of them were opposed to Iraqi–Syrian union. The prospect of a large, strong neighbor was a threat to Jordan's independence, or at least to its ability to follow independent policies. Saudi Arabia entertained similar fears and, as always, opposed any Arab unification schemes that might snowball to include it. And the CIA had always opposed any cooperation between Syria and Iraq lest it threaten its client states, Israel, Saudi Arabia and Jordan. Saddam's personal target was Bakr, but this did not interest the others greatly except in terms of Bakr's advocacy of an Iraqi union with Syria. In other words, Saddam offered them a package: he was willing to intercept the plans for Syrian–Iraqi union in return for a promise of non-interference in his removal of Bakr.

What started as a stuggle over who would preside over a united Iraq and Syria after Bakr, ended up being something else. In helping Saddam to remove Bakr, the pro-West Arab countries and the CIA administered a blow to the ideology of the Ba'ath Party. Of course, Jordan, Saudi Arabia and the rest of the Arab countries had viewed Khomeini's rise to power with unease. Though not as directly threatened as Iraq, they had already reached the conclusion that a confrontation with Khomeini was inevitable. Saddam, unlike Bakr, agreed with them. The USA's problems with Khomeini were developing. Although the hostage crisis did not start until November 1979, Washington was already adopting anti-Khomeini policies. Along with traditional opposition to Syrian–Iraqi unity, this guaranteed American support for Saddam.

On 16 July 1979, a weary-looking Bakr appeared on Iraqi television to announce his retirement. He attributed this to personal reasons, ceded power to comrade Saddam Hussein and nominated the colourless and uninspiring Izzat Douri as Saddam's deputy. I have interviewed more than a hundred Iraqis, a knowledgeable collection of people who belong to different political groupings with different agendas, and not a single one accepts the Bakr resignation on face value. All of them insist that what took place in Baghdad in July 1979 was a coup within the Ba'ath party. To them, Saddam simply ordered Bakr to go home—under guard. Because of Saddam's history, authors and journalists accept this conclusion unquestioningly. This is indeed correct, but the activities which preceded Bakr's political demise deserve closer examination.

The fact that Saddam felt he needed outside help or acquiescence in the removal of Bakr proves that his assumption of the presidency of Iraq was opposed within the leadership of the Ba'ath Party, and that he felt insecure. Saddam attributed the 'resignation' to Bakr's loss of his wife, son and son-in-law during the previous two years and to poor health. This and the praise that he heaped on Bakr supports the allegations by Saddam's opponents that he needed to justify his action to limit the opposition to it. But Arab history and belief in individual leadership does not provide examples of presidents ceding power willingly. In fact, more than solid proof that Bakr was forced to resign showed in what followed Saddam's takeover.

Before analyzing the real reasons for Bakr's removal as they manifested themselves after he disappeared in Tikrit, it is worthwhile to note what Aflaq did. As usual, he produced a pamphlet about the subject of his constant adoration and wrote on 'what God had endowed you with to make you the brave leader and inspired struggler to realize the dreams of the party'. This time, Saddam's need to have his move blessed by the founder and spiritual leader of the Ba'ath had sound underlying reasons. To his comrades, Saddam's individualism and lack of ideology disqualified him. His success meant subordinating whatever ideology was left to the person of Saddam. This is analogous to what happened in Stalin's time. But in Iraq, as in the Soviet Union, the party did not cede its prerogatives without a fight.

On 28 July 1979, less than two weeks after replacing Bakr as President of Iraq, Saddam reverted to the methods he had employed during the early days of the regime and announced the discovery of a Syrian plot to overthrow him. This was followed by the trial of the conspirators in a revolutionary court and a Stalinist purge of the leadership of the Ba'ath Party. Although there had been disturbances by Shia elements in southern Iraq, Saddam began by focusing on the government and the party.

One third of the members of the RCC were shot. The party, security, Army, People's Army, trade unions, student unions, professional and other associations and departments were purged of 'all suspect elements'. For several weeks, a reign of unprecedented terror enveloped Iraq. Although it had begun secretly, shortly before 'the resignation' and several weeks before 'the Syrian plot', its sheer scale precluded keeping it secret and forced Saddam into the open.

Saddam started with Muhi' Abdel Hussein Mashhadi, the Secretary General of the RCC. He was relieved of his duties three days before Bakr's dismissal, but the news of his removal was temporarily withheld. In fact, Mashhadi had been arrested, tortured and convinced to turn against his colleagues. This and what followed attest to a power struggle within the party which had been in progress for months. By all accounts, many in the Ba'ath command had anticipated Saddam's dethronement of Bakr through analyzing his cleansing operations of the various government departments, and had appealed to the elderly president to resist Saddam's plans. They not only refused to accept Saddam as president, but asked for time to counter his moves and stop him. Though Bakr had stood up to Saddam regarding the fate of a hundred Shia dissidents sentenced to death, and refused to sign their execution order, he was too tired to contemplate another confrontation.

Bakr's inability to oppose Saddam adds to the importance of Mashhadi's removal. As Secretary General of the RCC he was capable of convening meetings to discuss the resignation and succession. With him out of the way, the party's ability to intercept Saddam was compromised. However, to Saddam's surprise the rest of his Ba'athist opponents refused to be cowed. This forced his hand. Either he believed that their stubbornness originated in a plot against him sponsored by outsiders, or he concocted one to justify their removal and execution. Despite general agreement by writers who have analyzed the plot and agree with Iraqi political exiles that the whole thing was an invention, my first-hand experience leads me to a different conclusion. Although the first phase of my work with Iraq had by then come to an end, I was contacted by some of Saddam's security people and asked to look into the possibility that Dalloul was part of an anti-Saddam plot. It was a nonsensical request to which I never responded.

What happened on 18 July 1979 is recorded on video. Saddam personally ordered the filming of the proceedings of a meeting of the Regional Command

Council and other top party officials of the Ba'ath, four hundred in all, in a conference hall which looked like a cinema that he had had built for international meetings. The film shows Saddam running the meeting by himself. He is on stage, sitting behind a large table with four microphones in front of him and a large cigar in his hand. Occupying the first row are his loyalists: Izzat Douri, his second-in-command in the Iraqi Ba'ath Party and Deputy Secretary General of the RCC; Taha Yassin Ramadan, his Vice President; Foreign Minister Tareq Aziz; and others including his cousin, brother-in-law and Chief of Staff, General Adnan Khairallah.

Saddam stood up and walked slowly, as if with a heavy heart, to a lectern with two microphones on it. He spoke to the gathered leadership in the manner of a relaxed lecturer addressing a group of supplicants. He not only announced the existence of a plot, but gestured with a wide sweep of his arm and told his followers that they would have a chance to determine the veracity of his statement. Mashhadi was summoned from behind the curtain and took Saddam's place at the lectern while the latter went back and sat behind the table, still puffing on his huge cigar.

For two hours, Mashhadi regaled the listeners with details of the conspiracy, dates, places of meetings and names of participants. It was obvious that his presentation was rehearsed. He referred to the so-called conspirators as traitors, and as he mentioned each name plain-clothed security officers were filmed escorting the person mentioned out of the hall. When one of them tried to speak to the gathering, Saddam shouted, *'Itla', itla'*, or 'Get out, get out!' Heads bowed, every single one walked out with his grim-looking escorts, never to be seen again. No one said anything while the camera panned across the faces of Douri, Aziz and Khairallah.

What was happening, one of the most hideous recorded examples of the working of a dictatorship, finally became clear to the rest. Some of them stood up and started to cheer Saddam. He responded with a broad smile, twice thanked people who stood up to praise him and offer their fealty. Encouraged, others stood up to speak of Saddam leading them on a march to liberate Palestine, and the camera showed a happy Saddam content with what he was hearing.

Saddam reserved for himself the right to make the closing statement. Tearfully, he mentioned how the conspirators had tried to drive a wedge between him and Bakr and 'weaken the glorious Ba'ath Arab Socialist party'. When he repeated the names of the accused who had been close to him, Andan Hamdani among others, he appeared to wipe tears from his eyes. The audience followed suit; Douri led the way and suddenly everyone had a handkerchief in his hand and was wiping away tears. Towards the end Saddam was in good spirits and laughed, and the whole audience laughed with him.

The most dramatic situation was that of Hamdani, Saddam's close personal friend, one-time head of his personal office, member of the RCC and partner in the Committee for Strategic Development. The camera closed in on him as he was forcibly taken out by security officers. He had no opportunity to speak up for himself. The same happened to Mohammed Ayish and Ghanim Abd Al Jalil, to Saddam 'brothers who betrayed us'.

A special court was set up under Naim Haddad, a Shia member of the RCC and naturally a Saddam loyalist, who acted quickly on the leader's accusations. The secret trials lasted less than two weeks: twenty-two Ba'ath leaders were executed and well over forty others were imprisoned. Mashhadi was among those executed. Five hundred high-ranking Ba'athists who were not implicated in 'the Syrian plot' were nevertheless detained. Vagueness, inconsistencies and lack of solid proof of the charges against the accused did not matter. Although Saddam took time out during the meeting to offer Bakr fulsome praise, all of the latter's supporters and advocates of unity with Syria were now gone. These moves were repeated throughout the country, and special courts were set up to deal with suspects on all levels of the elaborate party command structure. Copies of the videos of the meeting in which Saddam identified 'the traitors' and supposedly also tapes of some of the trials (I have not been able to obtain copies of the latter) were distributed to all security offices, to be shown to the public as a warning to 'other traitors and conspirators'.

If there was any doubt that Iraq was undergoing a massive purge of all anti-Saddam elements, the gratuitous execution of **Abdel Khaliq Samarai** put an end to it. Although he had been in prison since 1973, he was brought out now to face a firing squad with the rest. His execution by Saddam was an act of revenge by someone who knew that Samarai still commanded respect among many of the party faithful. This was followed by another commitment to revenge, one in which Saddam asked all Iraqis to join him. A special telephone number, supposedly his own, was flashed on television screens to be used by informers wishing to squeal on 'enemies of the revolution'. An unknown number of innocent people fell victim to the pettiness of personal vendettas with no political content.

The way the execution of his opponents among the party leadership was carried out is an original Saddam invention. The victims were taken to the basement of the building where the plot was announced and executed by their comrades, Saddam and his supporters in the RCC and cabinet. Saddam gave every member of the *ad hoc* execution squad a handgun and asked them to participate in carrying out the hideous act. Of course, he led the way. So all of his inner circle were implicated in an act of murder, which guaranteed their loyalty to Saddam. None of them showed any hesitation, perhaps out of the kind of fear that Stalin instilled in others who carried out his crimes. In fact, Iraqi tribalism played into Saddam's hands. Because the relations of the victims would have demanded the blood of the executioners of their kin, implicating his loyalists provided Saddam with an even greater guarantee of their loyalty and subservience than would have been the case in non-Arab countries.

Perhaps what was happening in Iraq is best told through a joke which became current during that period. A twelve-year-old schoolboy stands up in class and asks his teacher whether elephants can fly. The teacher admonishes him for this stupidity and orders him to sit down. Unabashed, the boy repeats the question several times, only to receive more stern admonishments. Finally, when the class ends, he sheepishly approaches the teacher and in a hushed voice says, 'Our leader [Saddam] says elephants can fly.' The teacher looks around him and replies, 'Yes, but not for a long time.'

The executions were followed by extremely odd behaviour on Saddam's part. According to a Lebanese journalist who knows Saddam and has solid connections to the Tikriti regime which continue to this day, the new President locked himself up in his bedroom and would not come out for two days. When he finally emerged, his eyes were so bloodshot and swollen that he could hardly open them, and he had difficulty speaking. He had been crying his black heart out. I am unable to bring this story to any conclusion because, though many within Saddam's new circle knew about what he did, none of them has ever dared ask him about this episode. The reasons for it, like his reprieve of a Jew who had been kind to him when he was a poor boy selling cigarettes on the streets of Baghdad, and his generosity to an unknown Egyptian doorman, remain locked in the dark recesses of his mind.

According to the same Lebanese source—and he is definitely in a position to know—Saddam's strangeness at this time did not stop there. A few days after the executions he paid a personal visit to the widow of Adnan Hamdani, the person closest to him among the victims. He unashamedly paid his condolences, and weeping loudly, told the grieving woman that 'national considerations' took precedence over personal ones. To Saddam, her husband was a man whom he loved like a brother, but he had had no choice but to sacrifice him 'for the cause'. Continuing this incredible statement, which deserves the attention of a professional psychiatrist, Saddam assured Mrs Hamdani that 'she would never need, as long as he was alive'. Some time later he lived up to his promise and ordered the building of a substantial villa along the Tigris for the Hamdani family. My informant, a Saddam supporter, was under the impression that this story demonstrated the president's inherent humanity.

This peculiar second story was confirmed to me by six other people beside the Lebanese journalist and, like my original informant, all of them verified it on non-attribution basis because it touches on the workings of Saddam's mind. Revelations about what moved and motivated him, certainly anything which revealed human weakness, always made him dangerous and set him on the road to revenge—even when the motive of the people who revealed these weaknesses was innocent. And there is more to make this story among the most bizarre that I have ever heard. Why was Hamdani, who was utterly loyal to Saddam, executed? The answer complicates rather than solves the mystery. It is an established fact that Hamdani came from a known, well-to-do family. During their young revolutionary days he had seen to it that Saddam was never short of money. In other words, Hamdani had subsidized him. If the killing of Samarai was an act of revenge against a former senior comrade who towered above Saddam intellectually, then the murder of Hamdani was one against a benefactor.

There was a third execution which supports my belief that Saddam was intolerant of people with superior attributes or lineage to the point of eliminating them. Ghaleb Mawloud Mukhlis, the son of the man behind the Tikritis' original entry into the armed forces, was also executed during this period. Ghaleb was close to Bakr, but most people dismiss this as a reason for the execution. They believe that it was aimed at eliminating the legend of his father, to remove any risk that Saddam's success might be attributed to the older Mukhlis. Saddam had resented Samarai and secretly rejected his dependence on Hamdani, and erasing the image of the Mukhlises as Tikrit's benefactor followed. He did not want the world to know that he owed anyone anything, or that someone else was behind Tikrit's ascendance. Perhaps that was why he felt a need to repay Hamdani through attending to the needs of his widow.

The execution of Hamdani reduced the leadership of the Committee for Strategic Development to Saddam and Adnan Khairallah. That lessened its effectiveness as the supreme body in charge of non-conventional weapons development within the country and as the source of direction for hundreds of people who worked for Saddam outside Iraq. Many of the people on whom Hamdani had depended in the Ministry of Planning were also purged. Even people who emulated Saddam and saw fit to offer their condolences to Hamdani's widow were executed or imprisoned for their crime of manifesting human sympathy towards the family of a traitor. The procurement network did not escape suspicion, either, and Ramzi Dalloul was one of the victims, because Saddam never trusted him again.

Recently a number of writers have published stories about Dalloul, which include allegations that his services were terminated because he and Hamdani were realizing high commissions. This is something I do not accept. Neither man put money before commitment to Iraq. If I may jump ahead of the story once again, in early 1982, during my second phase of cooperating with Saddam's government, I was questioned about Dalloul's connection with Hamdani. The Iraqis obviously believed Dalloul was politically loyal to Hamdani and that he had known about 'the conspiracy'. My reaction was to deny it; again, my knowledge of Dalloul precludes any dishonest or violent behaviour on his part.

The purge of 1979, followed by comparatively minor ones of the Baghdad-based pan-Arab Ba'ath leadership in 1980 and the consequent open abandonment of ideology, are landmarks in Saddam's leadership. Having used the party to control the Army, then merged the party with family and put relations in charge of the merger, and supported this primacy through other aspects of Tikriti, Douri and 'Ani tribalism, all power in the country was vested in Saddam's person as the head of the family and tribe. Douri, Ramadan, Aziz, Haddad and Adnan Khairallah were the new members of the RCC, but had no power except to carry out Saddam's orders. Newly appointed members of the cabinet had even less power. Aflaq, whose loyalty to Saddam made him forget the original ideology of the Ba'ath, became more decorative than ever before. The slogans of 'One Arab nation with an eternal mission' and 'Unity, freedom and socialism' became things of the past. As for Bakr, although he had been a figurehead for some time, and despite a desperate last-minute attempt to reimpose himself as leader of the country, his removal signalled the removal of the last hurdle to Saddam's assumption of absolute power.

Saddam still worked sixteen to seventeen hours a day, but there was a perceptible change in the way he ran the country which showed almost immediately when he became President. Unleashing government propaganda organs as if they had been held in check awaiting this occasion, the Iraqi media began calling him 'knight', 'struggler', 'leader', 'son of the people' and comparing him to Peter the Great. This was a new approach, which, for unknown reasons and until the war with Iran, dispensed with recalling the legacies of the ancient kings of Mesopotamia, famous Muslims and others.

But the change in Saddam went beyond his use of titles and comparing himself to historical figures. Instead of his former meticulous planning and precision in implementing government programmes, Saddam began issuing 'directives', 'orders' and 'national guidelines'. Because he was on television daily, pompously carrying on about everything under the sun, the functional aspect of his thinking was surrendered to others, reducing the effectiveness of what he had in mind. On television, his mellow voice and slow, unemotive delivery, aimed to reassure people that their future was secure, failed to disguise the menace of his imposing physical presence. The legendary *gada'* of the Ba'ath's early days became the God Father of a ruling family, with everything that goes with this description. He was a benevolent father figure taking care of his immediate and extended Iraqi family, a poor boy with a remarkable record of achievements. But everybody whispered about how the achievements were built on the bones of the hundreds of people who dared to oppose him.

Not for the first time Saddam was reinventing himself. On the surface, his exercise of power as Bakr's Mr Deputy had been unhindered and open. But the new persona which emerged after the purge revealed that he had suffered a surprising level of frustration on most levels. The first aspect of the new Saddam concerned his personal behaviour. The suddenness with which he proceeded to indulge himself and the grandiose way in which it was expressed leaves no doubt that the presence of the fatherly Bakr and the existence of a party structure had acted as checks on his Tikriti instincts.

Soon after Saddam became President, his security people started using sticks and electric rods to administer shocks on people who wanted to approach him during his walkabouts. Furthermore, he seemed to walk stiffly and in an excessively formal way, which, if intended to imbue him with an air of dignity, was self-defeating. According to others who corroborate the story about the use of sticks, this was not a security measure but a gratuitous exercise of power. So in yet another manifestation of contradictory behaviour, Saddam was maintaining the legend of the benevolent leader who wanted direct contact with the people while feeling that he was above being touched.

During the same period, it became evident that Saddam had a bottomless wardrobe. Those who watched him on television in his elegant clothes began to speak of his dandyism, something that the tough Iraqis do not admire. His former Ba'athist colleague Dr Tahseen Mua'la claims that Saddam possessed over four hundred belts. In fact, Saddam had a personal tailor by the name of Haddad (also known as Sarkis Sarkis) and the rest of his clothes were tailor-made in Geneva. Soon he had a private Indian doctor, a resident soothsayer and no fewer than ten drivers. In keeping with his new image, he began to walk and talk in a more deliberate way.

The oddest Saddam story of the time is the one recalled by Dr Mahmoud Othman, the Kurdish politician who negotiated with him for nearly thirty years and whose observations of the personal and political behaviour of the Iraqi leader would fill an entire book. Following Saddam's declaration, upon becoming President, of a political amnesty for all his opponents, Othman had made an appointment to discuss the Kurdish problem. They were to meet at 7 a.m., and the meticulous Othman was at the palace on time. The previous night, Saddam had worked in his special small office in the palace until the early hours. As was his habit when he did this, he had slept in the office (which very few people had ever seen) instead of returning to the residential wing. When told of Othman's presence by an aide, Saddam told the men to apologize to the Kurdish leader and usher him in without delay, while he was still in his pyjamas.

What Othman saw—and he is probably the one person outside Saddam's personal entourage to have witnessed this—was truly puzzling. Saddam had slept on a small cot, almost military in its simplicity, in the corner of the room and had put on a robe to receive Othman, which he did warmly. But it was other things which baffled the usually unflappable Kurdish leader. Next to the bed were 'over twelve pairs of very expensive shoes. And the rest of the office was nothing but a small library full of books about one man, Stalin. One could say he went to bed with the Russian dictator.' Othman managed to hide his surprise and he and Saddam conducted one of the many meetings which marked the lives of both men, but without making any progress. To this day, Othman is unable to control a change in his voice when telling this story.

There were further signs that Saddam's new persona was spinning out of control, that his image of himself as a figure of historic importance (by the looks of things modelled on Stalin) had over-shadowed the real Saddam. Some time during this period he pompously told his biographer Iskandar that he was not concerned with what the people thought at the time but with 'what people will say about us 500 years hence'. He followed this with a statement to Fuad Matar which suggested that he no longer had anything to fear 'because most Iraqis are Ba'athists'. In his own eyes he had become an immortal person speaking for an Iraqi people who obviously followed his Ba'athist philosophy and in the process surrendered their judgement and entrusted everything to him. According to Saddam, 'Iraq was too young for democracy.'

A country too young for democracy, and obediently following its leader, needed a leader who could give it direction. Saddam decided that his television and radio monologues, often three or four hours long, were not enough. His already prodigious literary output, which eventually reached over two hundred books, articles and essays, gained momentum. He 'wrote' about everything and, like his essay to justify making the birthday of Imam All a national holiday, the rest of his published work was aimed at creating a philosophy for what he was doing.

Surprising to most people as these manifestations of the new Saddam were, there was a small group of Iraqis who had suspected that these traits lurked within him. These people, or their children, had seen similar inherent weaknesses of character in his sons' behaviour. In 1980 Udday and Qussay were sixteen and fourteen respectively and were attending Al Kharkh Al Namouthajiya School (the Kharkh Exemplary). Until he became President, this school had been run by Saddam's wife Sajida, and her presence and the high level of education it ostensibly afforded made it a place for the privileged few. Saddam spoke of it with special pride, but, as with many other model achievements, the facade of modernity and quality hid a darker side.

Ahmad Allawi of the Iraqi National Council was a classmate of Udday, Saddam's oldest son. Tamara Daghastani's children were among the students, and one of them knew Saddam's second son Qussay. Latif Yahya was another of Udday's classmate's, who resembled the leader's son so closely in physical appearance that he was later used as his double. The recollections of these three Iraqis provide irrefutable proof that Saddam's (and indeed his wife's) complexes first showed in the way they brought up their children. Although the habit of the newly rich to spoil their children to compensate for the deprivation of their own youth is well known, what Saddam allowed his children to get away with exceeded anything of which I have ever heard.

Tamara Daghastani distinguished between Saddam's two sons by stating that, according to her children, Udday was loud and vulgar while Qussay was quiet and calculating. 'Both received special treatment and never obeyed any rules or regulations. One shouted about it and the other didn't, but both of them came first in their class, though Udday never did any work. Naturally, nobody dared get near them and even the classrooms were guarded so heavily, it affected the performance of other students. Of course, leaving to go to another school was out of the question because one had to explain why they would want to leave an exclusive school attended by the president's children. It became hell on earth for others.'

Ahmad Allawi's eye witness account goes further. 'They [Udday and Qussay] always violated the dress code. They came to class in dish-dashs and Udday occasionally used a bandanna instead of a belt and had live ammunition in it. One time Udday came to class with a headdress made of bamboo sticks, and naturally the teacher said nothing and we pretended we were seeing nothing. There were so many security people, the classrooms were of a huge size to accommodate them. I was there when Udday demanded extra time to finish his test and the teacher had to obey him and gave us all fifteen minutes more. Then he finished in six minutes and told the teachers to stop the rest from continuing. The whole thing was really sick—Udday had so many cars and generated so much fuss. One time he ordered the driver to drive up about ten stairs because he did not want to walk that number of steps. Allah help anyone who had a good car the like of which Udday did not have—he'd send his guards to confiscate it. Even then their [Udday's and Qussay's] cars had special licence plates which didn't make sense—they had on them "O Salaheddine

[Saladin], O Iraq", all nonsense. The rest of us were there to keep them company, that's all. When Udday broke his leg, the class moved to the lower floor to make it easy for him. Qussay was more intelligent. He did the same things, but he didn't abuse people verbally or show off like his brother.'

Latif Yahya's book confirms what Daghastani and Allawi had to say and reveals that Udday started having girlfriends quite early in life, an oddity in a Muslim society. There is a suggestion here that the girls in question had little choice in the matter. There are also stories of Udday smoking cigars at an early age, and others of him later demanding an office similar to his father's. And, of course, also to be taken into account were his arrogance, an early inclination to resort to violence and the huge sums he spent on clothes and cars.

Why Saddam, the man who for years had refused to enter Bakr's office without being announced, accepted this behaviour by his children and thought it would escape public scrutiny is unknown. To say that he was too busy and Sajida was behind her sons' misbehaviour is to excuse and absolve Saddam who, after all, was an Arab husband obeyed by his wife (in his own family, Saddam never ceased to believe in the tribal primacy of the head of the household). Moreover—and despite the fact that he might not have known about his children's behaviour because people did not dare tell either parent about it—Udday's future criminality and Saddam's acceptance of it rule this out. In reality the boys were no different from the relations of other Middle Eastern dictators, such as the over indulged offspring of the House of Saud or the Kuwaiti royal family. Their lack of proper upbringing is another testimony that even in Ba'athist Iraq, ideology was only skin-deep and family connections have always taken precedence.

When these and other stories about Udday and Qussay eventually became common knowledge, they shattered overnight an image of Saddam that many Iraqis had admired, that of a self-made family man. Together with a long list of stories about the financial manipulations of Uncle Khairallah, who used his position as Governor of the Province of Baghdad to control twenty-five companies, they dealt a lasting blow to the popularity of the new President. However much people opposed him politically, very few had ever suspected him of corruption. Even his later dismissal of Khairallah did not save him from being associated with that image of other Arab leaders.

These revelations, significant though they are in exposing Saddam the tribal dictator, should not stand in the way of detailing the other important activities which followed his assumption of the office of president of Iraq. Some of these activities contained a glimpse of the old Saddam and his commitments to populism, but others were new, forced on him by circumstances as a response to developments inside Iraq, regionally and internationally. If Saddam the populist leader was hindered by his tribal inner mind, then Saddam the international leader was an utter disaster. But, even at the risk of preempting events that speak for themselves, it is well to remember that the West aided and contributed to the many problems that President Saddam Hussein bequeathed to the rest of the world.

Among his first acts as President was a decree prohibiting the use of family names. This simple-sounding measure was anything but—it was an attempt at instilling equality among the Iraqi people. Except for some establishment families with solid lineage, the concept of family names was a relatively recent development in Iraq and most people were named after the town or village from which they came—the Tikritis from Tikrit, 'Anis from 'Ana, and so on down the line. Their place of birth gave them identity, and with it social status, or lack of it which could impede their advancement. For example, the poor Christians from Tel Keif in northern Iraq were janitors and servants. Saddam issued the decree to prevent people suffering because of their social origins.

Simultaneously, he expedited the end of the collective farm scheme. In no time at all the only farms which remained in the hands of the government were ones which individual farmers did not want to own. To replace them, he developed schemes which gave the peasants the right to the land but saw to it that government assistance was made available. And there were other measures which were a continuation of undertakings he had started during his early years in government. All schools were ordered to install central heating, mortuaries were to be refrigerated and grocers' pricing practices were rigorously monitored. Distribution of housing was increased, although Saddam cleverly favoured Ba'ath members and put them ahead of the general public.

Perhaps it was the holding of elections for a National Assembly in 1980 which represented Saddam's most ambitious move. As already mentioned, he dangled a carrot to the people immediately upon becoming President by declaring a general amnesty. The response from the Shias and Kurds was less than enthusiastic; they simply did not trust him. But he followed this by deciding to install a National Assembly. The way he created this body does not subscribe to the Western concept of an acceptable democracy, and most representatives were appointed rather than voted in, but it was a step in the right direction which contained the seeds of possible improvement. The mere mention of every fifty thousand people being represented by someone who spoke on their behalf, and ensuring that no fewer than 40 per cent of the seats were occupied by Shias, amounted to the first serious consideration of democracy since the days of the monarchy.

These populist decrees and their consequences were taking place against a background of internal political developments which were determining foreign policy and external considerations which affected Saddam's behaviour inside his country. The two developments which occupied his mind and rendered inevitable the march towards his first regional war were the emergence in February 1979 of Islamic fundamentalism in Iran and the invasion of Afghanistan by the USSR in December that year. Both had a direct influence on the thinking of the Iraqis and their relations with the West and the USSR. And the influences of both affected the policies of other countries towards Iraq in a way which contributed to Saddam's overestimation of Iraq's capabilities, its role and his own personal importance. Both drew Iraq and the USA into a cynical embrace, the results of which remain to this day.

The appearance of an anti-Ba'ath regime in Iran encouraged Saddam's enemies, who saw it as a much-needed benefactor and backer to reignite their flagging activities against the central government of Iraq. For instance, the Kurdish leader Mulla Mustapha's sons Massoud and Idris cabled their congratulations and support to Khomeini soon after his takeover. Despite their different purposes, the contacts between Iran and the Kurds continued for years, and a while later Mulla Mustapha himself cabled Khomeini assuring him of Kurdish support against the Ba'ath. However, important as this was, the rebelliousness of the Kurds was something to which Saddam had grown accustomed and it was the Iranian revolution's influence on the Shias which threatened him more seriously.

Khomeini's exhortations to the Iraqis to overthrow the Ba'ath exceeded in both intent and intensity the usual meddling of Middle Eastern leaders in the affairs of neighbouring states. His calls to the Shias of Iraq to rid themselves of the 'non-Muslim Ba'ath' were reinforced by Iraqi Shia leader Sadr's response that 'other tyrants [beside the Shah] have yet to see their day of reckoning'. Riots followed each of Khomeini's calls to religious rebellion, not only in Iraq but in the rest of the Gulf countries which had Shia populations—Saudi Arabia, Bahrain and Kuwait. Khomeini, exaggerating his own powers and underestimating his opponents' ability to respond to his appeals, was pushing these countries towards an alliance.

Once again, Saddam resorted to his carrot-and-stick tactics. At first he stepped up the distribution of TV sets, refrigerators and other goods in Shia areas, but the magnitude of the challenge to his authority reduced this to a hollow gesture. When Sadr openly placed religion ahead of loyalty to the state and accepted Khomeini as the overall leader of the Shias, Saddam uncharacteristically tried to avoid a confrontation by asking the latter to rescind his newly declared fealty. But Sadr, made of the same stuff as Saddam, refused to do so and began issuing his own inflammatory statements as Khomeini's deputy in Iraq.

Unfortunately for the Shias of Iraq, Sadr's behaviour during this period reduced their cause to a struggle between two individuals, and his acceptance of Khomeini's leadership played right into Saddam's hands. The chants of the rioting crowds in Najjaf and other Iraqi cities amounted to open rebellion: *'Ash Al Khomeini wil Sadr weddine lazim yantasser'* means 'Long live Khomeini and Sadr, and the faith will prevail.' There was no way for Saddam to overlook this, or the *fatwa* against membership in the Ba'ath declared by Sadr, and survive. Slogans celebrating Khomeini were being coined every day, among them some which touched on the very identity of Iraq such as: *'Kulana lak fada' Khomeini'* or 'We are for you to sacrifice, Khomeini.' This was followed by reports that the Shias, with Iranian help, were undergoing training in the use of small arms.

For reasons which are hard to explain, Saddam's initial response, however severe or even savage, was not directed at the source. Referring to the slogan-chanters as Khomeinites, Saddam arrested hundreds of people and executed ninety-four, including a ninety-one-year-old cleric. But Sadr was not touched. He had been arrested in 1972, 1974, 1977 and for two days in 1979, but each arrest only added to his popularity and standing among his people. However, things were moving toward their inevitable climax. Khomeini had followed the reports of arrests and executions in early 1980 with an open appeal to Sadr not to leave Iraq—probably what Saddam had hoped for by leaving him free. Sadr had responded by assuring Khomeini that he was staying put until their common aim was achieved.

On 1 April 1980, members of Sadr's Dawa Party, which had murdered a score of government officials in 1979, tried to assassinate Deputy Prime Minister and RCC member Tareq Aziz. The attempt took place when Aziz was visiting Mustinsirya University to attend a conference of the National Union of Iraqi Students. Aziz himself was only slightly wounded, but there were an unknown number of dead and injured. Twenty-four hours later, Saddam made an announcement which ended all hope of a peaceful end to the Shia rebellion: 'Yesterday, a miserable agent caused the very dear blood of Mustinsirya students to be shed . . . Our people are ready to fight to protect their honour and sovereignity, as well as maintain peace among the Arab nations.' On 5 April, when a Dawa hit squad attacked the funeral of those who had died in the attempt against Aziz and killed more people, Saddam responded by making Dawa membership a crime punishable with death. Hundreds were executed.

Saddam did not stop there. The following day his special forces entered Najjaf and arrested Sadr and his sister Amina, known to Shias as Bint Al Huda or the daughter of the righteous. Obeying shoot-to-kill orders, they overwhelmed the few who tried to oppose them and brought their prisoners back to Baghdad. There is little doubt that the cleric and his sister were tortured, but nothing short of final settlement of the problem would satisfy Saddam. On 9 April, the two were executed. There is no record of a trial. Riots broke out in southern Iraq, scores of people were shot to death and thousands arrested, many never to be seen again. Along the Iranian–Iraqi border, skirmishes between the two countries' armies became a common occurrence.

Saddam followed the executions with the rigid implementation of the nationality law which he had used against the Shias in the past. The absurd interpretation of lineage was augmented by summary deportations of 'people who had secretly entered Iraq'. Tens of thousands of poor innocents were forced to leave without their possessions. As if to prove his statement to biographer Iskandar that he was not afraid of death, Saddam followed this with a visit to Najjaf to demonstrate his lack of fear and the fact that the Shia stronghold was under central government control. Having told them in 1979 that he was the grandson of Ali, founder of the Shia branch of Islam, this time he recalled his name to justify his harsh measures: 'I am the son of Ali and I kill with his sword.' He went on to make declarations about the Arabism of Iraq and how it took precedence over religion.

In an attempt to gain the support of fellow Arab governments for his growing confrontation with Khomeini, Saddam dispatched personal envoys carrying explanations of what was happening in Iraq. Because Khomeini and other kinds of Islamic fundamentalism were a common threat, his envoys were received with open arms. This was particularly true in Saudi Arabia and Egypt. The former supported him because Saudi Shias in the oil-producing province of Hasa had rioted in February 1980, not for the first time, and the latter because of the growing danger of local fundamentalism. Saddam also sent his version of events to Fidel Castro in his capacity as head of the Non-Aligned Nations Conference and to UN Secretary General Kurt Waldheim. But it was what was happening behind the scenes which mattered most.

The tilt towards the Arab countries and the cynical amity with America both of which began to reveal themselves in the aftermath of Sadr's execution had in fact begun some time earlier. On 8 February 1980 Saddam announced an Eight-Point Arab National Charter, essentially a guideline for behaviour among the Arab governments. While there was nothing new in its calls for placing Arab brotherhood ahead of all else and rejecting the influence of outside powers, the charter was to become more important with the passage of time.

Saddam's rejection of the USSR had started in July 1978, while he was Vice President. In an interview with the *International Herald Tribune* he had declared that, '[The Soviet Union] will not be satisfied until the whole world is Communist.' This criticism, born as it was out of his problems with the Iraqi Communist party, was followed by further condemnation after the Soviet invasion of Afghanistan. The Arab National Charter not only confirmed his rejection of the USSR's invasion of Afghanistan, it signalled an attempt by Saddam to endear himself to the moderate Arab countries. Furthermore, the charter contained an explicit commitment to settling all inter-Arab issues in an amicable way, which he himself was to violate by invading Kuwait.

While it is impossible to prove, many believe that the charter was part of Saddam's design to attack Iran and that it was aimed at pleasing the West as much as the Arab countries. The late Hani Fkaiki, the former Ba'athist turned opposition leader, told me that, with the blessing of Saddam, the CIA had opened a Baghdad office in late 1979. To make the same point, others underscore Saddam's criticism of Soviet actions in Afghanistan, South Yemen and Ethiopia and his growing friendship with Jordan's King Hussein. Of course, the frequency of visits to Saudi Arabia by members of Saddam's government contributed to the theory that an Iraqi-Jordanian-Saudi-American conspiracy against Iran was in the making.

It is impossible to verify whether this 'conspiracy' was detailed or amounted to nothing more than discussions on issues of mutual interest. Kenneth Timmermann claims that what started as a mutuality of interest culminated in a July 1980 meeting between Saddam and Carter's national security adviser, Zbigniew Brzezinski in Amman. Brzezinski himself denies that this meeting, first reported by the *New York Times*, ever took place. In the end, the mystery of this meeting is superseded by two proven facts. In April 1980, while Saddam was executing dozens of Shias and deporting thousands, Brzezinski declared, 'We see no fundamental incompatibility of interests between the United States and Iraq.' And Saddam himself cleverly ignored certain developments of the kind which in times past had prompted him to denounce the United States and other Western countries and accuse it of complicity with Israel. In April 1979, Mossad agents blew up a ship carrying atomic reactor cores to Iraq before it left the French port of Toulon. Some time later, on 14 June 1980, an assassination with implications for the future shape of Middle East politics took place in Paris. This time Mossad killed Yahya Al Mashed, the Egyptian atomic scientist working for Saddam. The issue of Saddam's non-conventional weapons was beginning to surface.

The results of my own investigation support the conspiracy theory but do not implicate the former national security adviser. According to a member of King Hussein's cabinet, a former general in his Army and Iraqi leader Ahmad Chalabi, the meeting which took place in Amman was between Saddam and three CIA operatives, Rance Haig, Tom Twitten and psychological warfare specialist Tom Alan. Saddam's presence in the Jordanian capital when the CIA men were there is an established fact. But the specifics of the actual meeting remain elusive. What is undoubtedly true is that both sides met with King Hussein, and both sides and the Jordanian monarch were preoccupied with the problem of Iran. Even if a meeting between the parties did not take place, an indirect meeting of minds through King Hussein definitely did. Among the many services which the King is supposed to have provided Saddam was a meeting with Iranian opposition leaders, who assured the Iraqi leader that Khomeini's popularity was waning and that the time to attack Iran had come.

There were several other developments which confirmed that a pattern of cooperation between the United States and Iraq was emerging. Ahmad Chalabi and members of the Jordanian government at the time confirm that the USA had 'told' Hussein to stop providing assistance to the Kurds." (That the Jordanian King was helping the Kurds while entertaining Saddam falls within the scope of political machinations as they occur in the Middle East.) Iraq signalled its readiness to expand commercial relations with the United States by making a request to buy five Boeing-747s, which was eventually approved by the Reagan administration in 1981. Using as evidence the news of the General Electric engines for Italian boats and the request to purchase Boeings, American business magazines began to promote business opportunities in Iraq. Above all, the improving relations between the leader of the Gulf countries, Saudi Arabia, and Iraq could not have taken place without Saudi determination that America had no objection to this happening.

Against the background of an orchestrated Iraqi media campaign condemning the 'Persian' enemy (recalling centuries-old rivalries and enmities), which had been in progress for several months, Saddam arrived in Saudi Arabia on 5 August 1980 after making a quick stopover in Jordan. He wore his military uniform, carried a gun and looked grim. His meetings with Fahd, then the country's crown prince and strong man, lasted more than ten hours. According to Saudi Arabia's Ambassador to the UK, Ghazi Al Gosaibi, Saddam told Prince Fahd of his plans to attack Iran. A former Saddam aide, Sa'ad Bazzaz, supports this by making the unequivocal statement: 'We told them we're going to attack Iran.'

Although both chroniclers stop there, others claim that Fahd promised Saddam billions of dollars in aid and free use of the Saudi port of Jeddah to compensate for not being able to use Basra after the start of hostilities. Even if this is only partly true, there is little doubt that Saudi Arabia encouraged Saddam and that it must bear some of the responsibility for the start of the war. Upon his return to Baghdad, the media campaign which was emphasizing Iraq's Arabness reached an unusual level of shrillness. Little doubt existed that war was on the way, and Saddam promised 'to turn Iraq into a bloodbath if the imperialists invade it'. Border incidents between Iraq and Iran were taking place on a daily basis. After making several visits to Iraqi Army units along the Iranian border, on 17 September Saddam abrogated the Algiers Agreement which had ceded to Iran control of half of the Shat Al Arab waterway at the head of the Gulf. The Iraqi Army invaded Iran on 22 September 1980. The US media, though it lamented the war in the way people should, expressed its support for Saddam Hussein.

Saddam's Word

Ofra Bengio

from *Saddam's Word: Political Discourse in Iraq*

In an article marking the first anniversary of the Gulf War, *al-Qadisiyya* wrote: "We have Saddam Husayn and they have their democracy." It attacked the United States for acting according to the "law of the jungle" and for expecting "others" to do the same, as if they had no history of their own, no tradition of government, and no leaders capable of sacrifice for the honor of their country. Iraq was telling the United States, the article went on, that "we have rejected, are rejecting, and shall always reject" such values. "Let them enjoy their democracy . . . but we are content to have an Arab leader, a Muslim seeker of justice ['adil], Saddam Husayn, may God preserve him." In other words: other places might have democracy as their form of government, but in Iraq, Husayn was a "form of government" in himself—he *was* the regime. The two systems were utterly opposed to each other; in preferring Husayn's one man rule, Iraq was following the old Muslim tradition of a single honest, just ruler—the embodiment of good government.

To reinforce his one-man rule, Husayn drew on the models of Mesopotamian and Arab rulers of the distant past to whom he likened himself. True, he used the modern party apparatus (unparalleled in older Arab history) as a principal vehicle for his rule, but within the party he was autocratic. Indeed, the Arabic *"hizb,"* though commonly translated as "party," is not fully synonymous with the latter. In classical Arabic, it was used in a neutral or a positive sense to denote a group, association, or circle of people, or negatively to describe divisiveness. Only when political parties were formed in Arab countries around the turn of the twentieth century was the term applied consistently to them. In Iraq, too, parties sprang up in the twentieth century, but they differed from the Western model in two respects: first, in their weakness compared with the armed forces (in the last account, the army shaped political events); second, in their inability to compete with each other except by using force. Under the Ba'th, even such vestiges of pluralism disappeared altogether. After the communist and the Kurdish parties had gone underground in the 1970s, Iraq turned into a single-party state. The cadres of this single party, the Ba'th, were at the sole disposal of the ruler.

The methods of state and party propagandists, even though they used all modern information techniques, were surprisingly similar to those of ancient times. As in the past, poets, writers, men of religion, and professional propagandists now combined their efforts to glorify Husayn and to mock and vilify his adversaries. However exaggerated and magnified this personality cult became, there is no denying that it contained an element of historical authenticity and continuity. In Iraq, it may have evoked a note familiar from the past and may therefore have been easier to obey.

The Indispensable Leader

In early 1978, a historical novel entitled *The Long Days* was published in Iraq. Its author, 'Abd al-Amir Mu'alla, explained that his intention had been to describe the emergence of a leader *(qa'id)* "who has reached his position by virtue of his qualities, a leader who has struggled and opposed, has been expelled from his land and has suffered, but has not renounced his revolutionary principles." He called his hero Muhammad bin Husayn al-Saqr (the Falcon) and described how he had taken part in the unsuccessful attempt on Qasim's life on 7 October 1959 and had subsequently been forced to flee to Egypt. Even though the attempt had failed, al-Saqr had already shown his heroic qualities and his great love of Iraq; when he fled abroad, "half his heart" remained behind in Baghdad. The practiced Iraqi reader would have had no trouble equating al-Saqr with Husayn. However, at the time (about a year and a half before Husayn's final takeover), the author preferred to present a fictional figure, albeit one to which he attributed all the qualities and all the biographical details of the real man. He may have wanted to deepen the mystery surrounding Husayn, or he may have wished to prepare the ground for Husayn's emergence as the sole leader, or he may have feared to play up Husayn under his real name at a time when Ahmad Hasan al-Bakr was still president. Bakr might have exploited such a publication to block Husayn's way.

A few months after the novel was published, another writer, ʻAbd al-Jabbar Muhsin, discussed the qualities needed in a leader in an article in *al-Thawra.* "The leader is a requirement of history [*ibn al-darura al-ta'rikhiyya],"* Muhsin wrote; "he sets historical events into motion." (Muhsin may have been influenced by debates among European historians about the role of the individual in history and about the concept of "historical inevitability.") The leadership that took over in July 1968, he goes on, received "the people's love even before it began to rule"—an allusion to Husayn taking second place until 1979. He then quoted the following verse from the Qur'an: "As for the scum, it vanishes as jetsam, and what profits men abides in the earth." Whether he wanted this to be applied to Bakr on his way out and to Husayn on the way up is a moot point.

Saddam Husayn took an active part in preparing for the personality cult that he developed fully after his takeover. His relations with his "court writers" form an instructive chapter in the study of social mobility in Ba'thi Iraq, as well as in understanding how certain political phrases were turned into household words. Husayn started the debate on the issue of leadership back in 1975, well before his assumption of the presidency. He wrote that "the leader must, at one and the same time, be the son of society and its father." But being the "father of society" did not mean that he was a "backward tribal father" who acted as the "guardian" of his tribe. Rather, "his fatherhood is in the framework of democratic-revolutionary relations." In another essay written about a year later, Husayn distinguished between "leader" (*qa'id*) and "ruler"(*hakim*). In order to lead, he stated, "you must give those you lead the feeling that you are just, even if circumstances require you to act with a heavy hand." If a person is not just, he may be a ruler but cannot be a leader. A ruler could achieve power in many ways; a leader only through the people and by virtue of their "extraordinary affinity [with him] and their constant loyalty." If these conditions were fulfilled, then the advent of the leader was "a historic birth" (emphasis added) and not merely an "artificial" event.

The purpose of such theorizing was to project an ideal image of a single leader, as opposed to "collective leadership" (*al-qiyada al-jama'iyya*). The latter had originally been adopted by the Ba'th as a basic point of its doctrine, and ostensibly the party remained committed to it. Here, however, we encounter a remarkable ambiguity. During the decade from the Ba'th takeover until the beginning of Husayn's presidency, the principle of collective leadership was extolled in public, at times by Husayn himself; yet at the same time, the ideal of the single leader was fostered vigorously, with Husayn's unmistakable encouragement. This was plainly a matter of pure political pragmatism: as long as Bakr was president, Husayn and his associates were interested in upholding collective leadership in order to circumscribe Bakr's powers and enhance their own. At the same time, talk of a single leader was to ready people's minds for the moment when Husayn would set up his one-man rule. Until then, caution was indicated. Husayn therefore joined others in calling Bakr by the title of *qa'id*, and at times "father-leader"(*al-ab al-qa'id*).

While preparing to replace Bakr, Husayn made ready to appropriate his titles, too. He preferred that of *qa'id* over its possible alternative. Qasim had borne the title of *za'im,* and so had Bakr during the first period of Ba'th rule. But any word associated with Qasim was best avoided. Moreover, in classical Arabic *za'im* could be used to denote a commander or leader but also a usurper. *Hakim,* though always used in a positive sense, with associations including wisdom, medical science, and justice, was disliked by Husayn, as was *hukuma* (government). He explained that he preferred terms such as "leadership" or "command council." Indeed, the word *hukuma* disappeared almost entirely from public parlance during his tenure, being replaced by *majlis al-wuzara'* (council of ministers).

Husayn apparently understood *hakim* to denote a rather narrow, technical function of leadership, while to him *qa'id* connoted innate qualities and a superior, almost metaphysical, station. This led him to call political rivals, most particularly Hafiz al-Asad, by the name of *hakim.* He called Asad a dictator and said that his only objective was to stay in power. Another "Arab *hakim*" was **Qadhdhafi.** A journalist, using the always fashionable rhyming technique, wrote: "*Al-Qadhdhafi—wahl fi-l-ard wa-shawk fi-l-fayafi*" (Qadhdhafi—dirt on the earth and a thorn in the desert). Such people, one of the "court writers" declared later, did not act with honesty and justice. That was why their people punished them, just as the Iraqis had punished their earlier leaders.

The title *qa'id* suited Husayn's taste particularly well because it meant both a military commander and a civilian leader. In the Middle Ages, the term had been used specifically to refer to the supreme commander of the armed forces. This was important to Husayn not only because, taking both meanings together, the title indicated integrated total rule but also because it made his command over the armed forces seem legitimate. He had never served in the army, and the need to project the image of a genuine military leader turned into an obsession with him—in a trait no doubt connected with his violent and expansionist aspirations. Indeed, the use of the title *qa'id* began in 1975, about the time that he "promoted" himself to the rank of general *(fariq awwal).* (Later, when he became sole ruler, he took the rank of field-marshal [*mubib*].) This seems to have caused some dissatisfaction among senior officers who had risen to their present ranks through the laborious procedure of graded promotion. He answered them indirectly by saying that "according to our tradition, each of us, regardless of his status or rank in the armed forces, is a *qa'id* and serves the people in his particular capacity."

Husayn's ideas were taken up dutifully by the writers at his disposal, who elaborated on them and gave them general currency, a labor often resulting in great benefits to themselves. After Husayn's final takeover, for instance, Mu'alla became director-general of the General Authority for the Cinema and the Theater. Using his new position, he had his novel made into a film as well as into a television series and, apart from their distribution in Iraq, had them marketed in other Arab countries. Needless to say, in the film version, the fictional name of the hero was abandoned and he was called Saddam Husayn. The role of the hero was played by Saddam's cousin and son-in-law, Saddam Kamil. Later,

Mu'alla published two more parts of his novel. *Al Jumhuriyya* noted that they were received enthusiastically by readers who were eager to learn more details of the life "of the historic leader [*al-qa'id al-ta'rikhi*], the hero Saddam Husayn . . . who realized the dreams of the Iraqis and the Arabs of what a real leader should be." In 1980, Mu'alla was elected to the national assembly. 'Abd al-Jabbar Muhsin, by then also a member of the house, became director of the research center attached to the Revolutionary Command Council. In 1981, he was appointed deputy minister of culture and information. Later, he became the chief military spokesman and director of the department for political indoctrination in the Ministry of Defense.

Muhsin's conception of "the leader" seems to have made its way directly into the political report of the 1982 party congress. As a matter of fact, the language in the report makes it likely that he himself worded the relevant section. The congress was held in an atmosphere of crisis: Iraq had just been forced out of Iranian territory; Khomeini had challenged the Ba'th by making the end of hostilities conditional on the removal of Husayn from power; and the party itself had apparently become restive. One way to meet these challenges was to reinforce the myth of the indispensable leader. The report therefore devoted a very long chapter to the image and the tasks of Husayn. Nothing similar had been included in the report of the preceding congress, held in 1974 when Bakr was still president. The 1982 report spoke of Husayn as the man who had sustained and consolidated the party after its overthrow late in 1963; who had led it back to power in 1968; who, within the space of a few years, had given Iraq stability and prosperity; and who had commanded the army in a brilliant campaign against Iran—the most successful war ever fought by the Arabs. The campaign had been so extraordinary because there had been "full coordination between the political and the military leadership . . . both headed by the same leader."

The report coined a new expression that later turned into a household phrase: *al-qa'id al-darura* (approximately, the leader by necessity). This combination had originally been used by Muhsin and became current despite its strange, grammatically incorrect form. How, then, was it to be understood? The report explained that "in bitter, hard circumstances there appeared *al-qa'id al-darura*. . . . Saddam Husayn's leadership of the party and of the revolution had been a historical necessity right from the start and it was incumbent on every party struggler with a sense of honor to maintain it." Over time, his leadership became "a national necessity" *(darura wataniyya)*.

Darura can be understood in its customary sense, indicating historical inevitability—a sense suited to a determinist worldview. But there *is* a more meaningful way to interpret it, and it is that meaning that may have underlain the choice of the word. That meaning is connected with its use to denote the sources or roots of Islamic religious law. There had originally been four such roots: the Qur'an, the *sunna* (tradition), *al-giyas* (analogy), and *ijma'* (consensus). But some later jurists recognized additional categories as applicable for rulings on points of religious law, among them *darura* and *haja* (compulsion, force of circumstances). Later still, the idea of *darura* was extended from legal to political use. The famous eleventh-century theologian Abu Hamid al-Ghazali, for instance, justified citizens subjecting themselves to tyranny on the principle of *darura*. Religious law recognizes *al-daruriyyat al-khams*, the "five necessities" that must be upheld under all circumstances: religion, the soul, the intellect, the honor of the family, and the right to property. It may be assumed that the author or authors of the political report had these verbal associations in mind when they chose the term. Overall, the word carried a clear message to Iraqis that perhaps also implied a refutation of Khomeini's demand to rid themselves of Husayn. Saddam Husayn, the message read, was leader by force of necessity, and his leadership was no more to be questioned than a good Muslim would question an authoritative ruling on a point of religious law.

It may be significant that one of the first newspapers to introduce the term *al-qa'id al-darura* was the organ of the armed forces, *al-Yarmuk*, which was apparently already under Mushin's control. From then onward, the expression was used almost as a synonym of Saddam Husayn. There were, however, other attributes by which he became known: *qa'id al-nasr* (the victorious leader), *qa'id al-salam* (the leader of peace), and eventually, after the invasion of Kuwait, *qa'id al-umma* (leader of the nation, implying all-Arab leadership). He was described as the *sani'* (shaper) of history; the founder of modern Iraq; and "the man of the long days" *(al-ayyam al-tawila)*—the days of Arab glory. In the pre-Islamic heroic poetry, *ayyam* meant the days of battle and tribal glory.

Another writer close to Husayn, Zuhayr Sadiq Rida al-Khalidi, asked rhetorically: What other leader could have "created a new Arab man," and who could have produced an invincible Iraq? Husayn was an "eternal" *(khalid)* leader whose influence would be felt long after his disappearance as an actual "historical leader." Even the new national anthem contained an implicit reference to Husayn in a line calling on the leader "to make the horizon the limit of the revolution." Children, too, were mobilized for the personality cult. The poet Faruq al-Sallum wrote an operetta for the use of kindergartens entitled, "The Leader and the Future."

The Myth of Saddam Husayn

"Myth has an impressive quality: it is expected to work immediately. . . . Its influence is much stronger than the rational explanations which are likely to invalidate it later on." Clearly, myths, appealing to emotions and instincts as they do, overcome or lull the intellect. From the start, the men in charge of shaping Husayn's image were keenly aware of this, and they strove to make him a living legend. Mu'alla's novel *The Long Days* was only one link in a long chain. Layer by layer, his image was created in poetry, prose, and the arts, all of which were made subservient to this aim. The more distressing realities were, the more the myths abounded. The shapers of Husayn's myths combined the ancient and the modern in remarkable ways. The images and the symbols were taken from the past, most often from the distant past, but the means employed to market them were the most modern available to the mass media. The press became a subcontractor of sorts for the propagandists; at times, half the space in the papers was filled with pictures and sayings of Husayn and with descriptions of his activities. Commercial advertising hardly exists in the Iraqi newspapers, but when it appears, it takes the form of a picture of Husayn, accompanied by greetings or congratulations on the part of the advertiser. Altogether, Iraqi propaganda methods recall modern marketing techniques, always thinking up new gimmicks to sell the product.

Husayn himself directed these campaigns, whether directly or indirectly. In 1988, *The Political Dictionary of Saddam Husayn* was published. It contained 500 entries of his political expressions, collected and interpreted by the poet Muhammad Salih 'Abd al-Rida. *The Complete Writings of Saddam Husayn* was published in eighteen volumes. Another method—one with the advantage of brevity—was to collect his witticisms and bons mots *(ida'at)* and place them at the top of newspaper pages. One such saying was "Democracy is the source of strength of the individual and of society." Politicians and journalists acquired the custom of weaving such sayings into their speeches and articles. Their endless repetition eventually gave them currency among the public at large.

One method used consistently was to equate Husayn with Iraq, with the Iraqis, and with Arabs everywhere. This led to an interesting and novel use of political language meant to underline the bond between the man and his country: *'Iraq Saddam Husayn* (the Iraq of Saddam Husayn), a use or misuse of the Arabic genitive case to indicate an inseparable link. Similar expressions were *Saddam al-'Arab* (Saddam of the Arabs) and *Saddam al-Fath* (the Saddam of conquest). The poet Ghazay Dir' al-Ta'i took this method a step further; in a song for children, he wrote:

> We are Iraq and its name is Saddam;
> We are love and its name is Saddam;
> We are a people and its name is Saddam;
> We are the Ba'th and its name is Saddam.

Another approach to the same goal used terms taken from family life: *Abu-l-'Iraq al-jadid* (the father of the new Iraq) or *Baba Saddam* (Daddy Saddam, perhaps recalling the name of Ataturk, father of the Turks). At other times, he was spoken of as the son or the elder brother of the Iraqi people. The theme of fatherhood was first employed by Husayn himself. In a speech in January 1981, he told his listeners that over the last few months he had received thousands of letters from children and old people, and all had called him "our father and begetter" *(waliduna)*. At times, he was addressed as *Saddamuna* (our

Saddam). "Saddamism" as a term for a historical phenomenon was used as an overall reference to all that was good in the Arab character.

While such images were meant to evoke feelings of closeness, others were used to place Husayn far from the common people, in a realm of the superhuman, not to say the supernatural. He was likened to light and rain, to the sun and the moon, to the sea and to a river, to a flower and to a tree in paradise. He was like a lion or an eagle, like gold, or like a fortress. All these metaphorical images are found in the descriptions of medieval Islamic rulers, and the writers working for Husayn used them just as the court poets of earlier times had. Of particular interest are images taken from the earliest Arab-Muslim cultural environment: *khayma* (tent), *kufiyya* (the traditional desert headdress), *sayf* (sword) and *faris* (knight). The last two terms are in special favor with Husayn. He is called *sayf al-Islam al-battar* (Islam's sharp sword) and *faris al-'arab* or *faris al-umma al-'arabiyya* (knight of the Arabs or Knight of the Arab nation).

Husayn gave instructions to research the historical significance of these terms, and the army organ *al-Qadisiyya* wrote an article explaining that, in ancient times, the word "sword" had been the synonym of strength, might, and honor. Arabs would keep their swords by their sides day and night, and compose poems about them. Muhammad had said: "He who girds his sword for the sake of Allah, Allah will gird him with a belt of honor"; his grandson, the Imam 'Ali, had spoken of the sword as a "blessing"; and—the article goes on to say, as if it were a perfectly natural transition—Saddam had said: "The sword is the weapon of the strugglers who defend the land, [their] principles, and sovereignty." The sayings here attributed to Muhammad and 'Ali are not found in any of the accepted *hadith* collections I have been able to consult. This is significant in two ways. It attests to the need to rely on old authorities, and it shows that the production of new *hadith* items goes on today as it did at so many earlier stages of Muslim history. Husayn ordered a "sword of *Qadisiyya*" made, produced from parts of the weapons of soldiers who had fallen in combat against Iran and from jewelry donated by Iraqi women for the war effort. It was awarded to war heroes.

The army newspaper *al-Qadisiyya* also examined the historical concept of *faris* (knight) and found that it was used to denote all that was good in the Arab character: manliness, tolerance, knowledge, talents superior to all other mortals, and the capacity for revenge. Such a man, the article proclaimed, was Husayn. "After the Arab nation had become detached from its past and ancient glory, God sent it one of its sons [Husayn]," who possessed all the qualities of knighthood and who remade Iraqi history. Through his genius, he linked the present with the past.

Husayn's Role Models

In August 1990, a few days after the invasion of Kuwait, Husayn sent a message to Egyptian president Muhammad Husni Mubarak, attacking him for making common cause with the United States and Saudi Arabia against Iraq. He reinforced his political argument by referring to Mubarak's lowly origin from a peasant family not connected with the families of Egypt's former rulers. He contrasted this with his own origin from a most illustrious family that traced its origins back to the Qurayshis, the tribe of Muhammad; he claimed descent from the prophet's grandson Husayn, the son of 'Ali bin Abi Talib and Fatima. This was not his only reference to his genealogy, whether actual or imaginary. On the contrary, it was part and parcel of the buildup of his image among Iraqis and among Arabs everywhere. This pride in ancestry *(al-mufakhara bi-l-hasab wa-l-nasab)* goes back to the most ancient period of desert culture. It remained a vital element in Islamic political culture because descent from the tribe of Quraysh (and even more so from its Hashim subtribe, to which Muhammad's family belonged) was one of the means of establishing the legitimacy of a Muslim ruler. Descent from 'Ali, the prophet's cousin, son-in-law, and closest associate, would of course lend a leader a potent claim to legitimate leadership. Moreover, Shi'is would consider any leader not descended from 'Ali a usurper (even if the leader came from Quraysh).

The claim to such lineage was only one aspect of Saddam Husayn's endeavors to liken himself to the great leaders of the Arab and Muslim past. There was probably an element of compensation in such effort, for in fact Husayn was born into a simple farmer's family in the village of 'Awja near the town of Tikrit. But an aura of greatness derived from an affinity with great figures of the past was more likely to arouse the imagination of Iraqis and engage their loyalty than being a Tikriti. The historical figures Husayn wished to liken himself to varied with changing circumstances. His small army of poets, writers, and journalists made the changes required by the course of events and by Husayn's varying preferences.

Among the first model figures Husayn wished to equate himself with was of course 'Ali bin Abi Talib. The timing of Husayn's first use of 'Ali as a personal model was not coincidental. It came some time after Khomeini's Islamic Revolution in Iran (February 1979) and Husayn's own final takeover (July 1979) and was intended to achieve three goals: to ingratiate himself with the **Shi'i** population of Iraq; to counter the contagion likely to spread to them from Iran through Khomeinist propaganda; and to give Husayn the image of an "authentic" Shi'i in contrast with Khomeini's non-Arab, hence "false," Shi'ism. In a speech in August 1979, Husayn praised 'Ali as representing "the spirit and the meaning of the Islamic message." The present Iraqi leadership was likewise seeking such "godly values." He went on to establish his own link with 'Ali by saying: "We are the grandchildren of the Imam Husayn [bin 'Ali]." But since everybody knew he was a **Sunni,** this seemed not enough. After a while, he published an "official" genealogy to "prove" his descent from 'Ali. One of his establishment writers, Amir Ahmad Iskandar, took the matter a step further, explaining that, precisely as in the manner approved by tradition, Husayn's family tree established his descent "link by link" *(jidhr ba'd jidhr).* Iskandar went on to say that Husayn had not mentioned this point previously because he did not wish to dwell on his own historical and religious roots in front of those who had none.

The employment of professional "image-builders" and writers to acquaint the widest possible public with Husayn's genealogy exemplifies the technique of taking up a remark of his—originally perhaps a quite inconsequential one—making it common knowledge, and eventually turning it into a "fact." Did the publication of the family tree give Husayn's claim greater credence among Iraqis? Perhaps, as had often been the case with tribal genealogies, the ambitious pretension behind it was accounted more important than the facts; legend counted for more than reality. One way or another, Husayn was a past master of building up such myths layer by layer until they became an established part of the Iraqi political discourse. Since no one publicly questioned the official genealogy, it was perfectly easy to go on reinforcing it and even to export it beyond the borders of Iraq. 'Izzat Ibrahim al-Duri, a senior Ba'th functionary and Husayn's right-hand man, declared with a ring of inner conviction that "the values of the Imam 'Ali are being renewed in the leader of our revival." As we have seen, Husayn did not hesitate to cite the point in his note to Mubarak as if it was beyond question.

At a later stage, Husayn placed the caliph al-Mansur at the center of his historical image-building effort. The purpose here was to create an impression of political and military greatness rather than of moral rectitude. Al-Mansur was the second Abbasid caliph, reigning from 754 to 775. His name is linked with the suppression of Shi'i opposition to his dynasty and with the elimination of the remaining supporters of the Umayyads (who had preceded the Abbasids). He expanded Abbasid territory to the north and the east; he built Baghdad and made it the splendid, even legendary, imperial capital as which it is remembered. He was thus a fine role model to use in wartime.

In 1985, while the war against Iran was at one of its peaks, an establishment writer wrote (in a piece that was half poem/half article): "Saddam Husayn al-Mansur will continue to be [our] moon and Iraq will be the flag of victory." "Al-Mansur" is used here with a twofold meaning: the literal meaning of "victorious by the grace of Allah," and the added connotation of the caliph so named. A year or so later, the first meaning was made more explicit by calling Husayn *al-mansur b-i-llah* ("by the grace of God"), but here again we find an echo of the names of past rulers, such as al-Mustansir b-i-llah, al-Mustansid b-i-llah, and al-Muntasir b-i-llah. In order to underline the continuity between Mansur I (the caliph) and Mansur II (Husayn), *al Jumhuriyya* used the expression *Baghdad al-Mansurayn* (the Baghdad of the two Mansurs), "the one bearing witness to Mansur's wondrous foundation, the other bearing witness to Mansur Saddam Husayn's wondrous rebuilding of it." The paper thought it significant that the date of the foundation of Baghdad, the anniversary of the formation of the Ba'th, and Husayn's birthday all fell in the month of April. For one of his birthdays, the inhabitants of Baghdad gave Husayn a model of the caliph's city made of pure gold. The use of *al-mansur* was not discontinued at the time of Iraq's severe defeats at the hands of the Iranians. A journalist spoke of the Iraqi soldiers in the field as "millions of al-Mansur Saddam Husayn."

Another suitable role model was Saladin who, although a Kurd, was a native of Tikrit. Quite apart from his historical achievements against the European crusaders, he could therefore be a useful symbol for Arab-Kurdish unity—a symbol much needed in the modern era of prolonged warfare between the two peoples in Iraq. His successful reunification of the Muslims in consequence of his victories over the crusaders was taken as a signal to the Arabs that they, too, could unite, provided a new Saladin stood at their head. It is not clear when Husayn first began to model his own image after that of Saladin. The uncertainties of Husayn's birth may have had something to do with his choice; the accepted version held that he was born in 'Awja near Tikrit, but others believed that he was born in Tikrit itself. Furthermore, the population register of the ministry of the interior records the year of his birth as 1939, while his official biographies give the year as 1937. There have been several attempts to explain the difference. The most plausible is that he wished to appear as having been born precisely 800 years after Saladin (1137/1937). In fact, Husayn did have a point in common with Saladin: both had a vast propaganda machine working for them. Just as, according to some historians, Saladin was driven to fight the battle at Hattin by his own propaganda claims, so Husayn's own propaganda methods dragged him into the Gulf War.

Primary targets of Ba'th propaganda were children. From a tender age, they were exposed to official indoctrination and taught to admire Iraq's leader. In this particular context, comparing Husayn with the great figures of Arab history was a useful device. In 1987, a Baghdad publisher of children's books printed a booklet entitled, *The Hero Saladin.* Its cover picture showed a portrait of Husayn, with sword-wielding horsemen in the background. The first, shorter, section was a presentation of Saladin's life, with the accent on his reconquest of

Jerusalem and of "Arab Palestine." The second and longer part was devoted to the "new leader," whom it called "the noble and heroic Arab fighter Saladin II Saddam Husayn." Throughout the booklet, Husayn was referred to as "Saladin II," and his life story was told in a manner meant to establish the similarity between the two. To do so, Husayn's "heroism" in the war against Iran was given particular salience. It was Husayn, the booklet said (addressing itself to its "young friends"), who "personally coordinated most of the battles, so as to demonstrate to the Arab and the international world that a leader must be at the head [of his forces]." So also Saladin had done. Again, like Saladin, Husayn was spoken of as the leader of the Arab nation in its entirety. The booklet concluded with greetings and blessings from the children to "Saladin II."

Sometime later, *al-Qadisiyya* published a long article written at the insistence of Husayn and entitled, "Saladin, the Liberator of Egypt, Syria [*al-Sham]* and Palestine." There was no specific reference to Husayn's affinity with Saladin, but the article began by speaking of the "real" hero who was " a glowing star . . . [that] melts the snows of despair." In July 1987, a colloquium on Saladin was held at Tikrit under the title, "The Battle of Liberation—from Saladin to Saddam Husayn." Latif Nusayyif al-Jasim, the minister of culture and information, dwelt on the "wonderful coincidence" that Saladin and Husayn were born in the same district, "two sons of Iraq and of the Arab nation with its glorious history." A newspaper spoke of the line linking the original battle of Qadisiyya to Hattin and again to the modern Qadisiyya (the war against Iran).

The mythology equating Husayn with Saladin continued after the war against Iran and may have served (whether intentionally or not) as a sort of preparation of public opinion for the "liberation of Jerusalem" and, in consequence, the encounter with the world of the infidels (i.e., the Gulf War, in terms used in Iraq). Characteristic of this trend is an article in *al-Qadisiyya* under the heading, "Our Saddam Is the Saladin of the Arabs and the Kurds." It said that just as history had caused the rise of "our grandfather" Saladin, so it would witness the rise of Husayn, "the best of sons to the best of fathers." The following day it elaborated on the theme, saying that "Palestine is embracing Baghdad" because the latter was the spring of hope for the Arabs and hope would erupt from it despite its enemies, who were trying "to stop the light shining [from there] on the Arab lands." Or, as another newspaper put it: "For the first time since Saladin" Arab hearts were beating with hope—the hope given them by Husayn.

Little wonder, then, that in some people's minds the Gulf War took on eschatological dimensions. At the height of the war, a newspaper wrote: "We smell the smell of Hattin and of the battle for the innermost sanctum." The "campaign of oppression" against Iraq had really started back in 1987, recalling that Hattin had been fought in 1187. Just as Saladin had foiled an attack by the crusaders in 1191, so his modern embodiment would defeat the "new crusaders" in 1991.

Unlike with Saladin, no direct affinity with the prophet Muhammad could possibly be established without being interpreted as blasphemous. Only indirect and cautious hints were at all admissible, and only veiled, evocative expressions could be used. We have seen that the fictitious hero of *The Long Days*—Husayn's "double," as it were—was called Muhammad. After the invasion of Kuwait, Husayn took the additional name of 'Abdallah, possibly an allusion to the name of Muhammad's father, possibly to be understood in its literal meaning of "servant of God," possibly both. Somewhat more tangible was the use of the word *rasul* (messenger) in connection with Husayn: he was at times called *rasul al-shams* (messenger of the sun) or *rasul al-'Arab* (messenger of the Arabs). Even though *rasul* was often enough used for "messenger" in the day-to-day sense, such titles could hardly fail to evoke an association with Muhammad's appellation of *rasul Allah*. Moreover, it had become customary to describe Muhammad as *al-rasul al-qa'id* (the messenger and the leader). This was an anachronistic use, since the word *qa'id* in the sense of "leader" did not exist in the seventh century, but it established an affinity between the prophet and Husayn, the leader. Calling Husayn's annual birthday celebrations *mawlid al-qa'id* also had some similarity with the prophet's birthday, called *'id al-mawlid al-nabawi al-sharif.* Another hint lies in the stress on Husayn having been born an orphan on his father's side and having grown up in his paternal uncle's house, just as Muhammad had grown up in the house of his paternal uncle Abu Talib.

A long time passed between Muhammad's death and the appearance of the first written account of his life (called *sira,* or more specifically *al-sira al-nabawiyya).* Husayn, for his part, had a biography of himself written in his lifetime and called it *sira.* Late in 1990, the national assembly passed a law establishing a special committee to oversee the writing of what might be called Husayn's official biography. The assembly rejected a proposal to call the biography *sifr* (book, large volume), preferring *sira*, notably because of its association with the prophet. It explained its choice by saying that the biography was intended to keep Husayn's memory alive "for hundreds of years." To call his biography *sira* was one way of establishing a link with the prophet; another was calling his personal aircraft *al-Buraq,* the name given to the legendary animal that bore Muhammad from Mecca to Jerusalem and back in a single night (the "night's journey" that became a Muslim holiday). *Al-Jumhuriyya* spoke of Husayn's "special relationship" with his plane, adding: "Who said that an aircraft is a [mere] thing bereft of understanding?"

Breaking the otherwise cautiously observed taboo on direct comparisons, between Husayn and Muhammad, a scholar named Ahmad Sawsa wrote that Husayn was following in the prophet's footsteps and turning his teachings into realities. That was so, he explained, because "the purpose behind the appearance of the prophet in his time was to accomplish the unity and rebirth of the nation." There had, he went on, never been an Arab leader like Husayn; even Saladin had only begun the work of unification but had not completed it. Even more daring was a poet, Ghazay Dir' al-Ta'i, who wrote:

> O our lord Saddam
> You have brought the light of God
> To the Arab tribes
> And broken their idols
> In times long past.

In a similar vein, the poetess Shafiqa al-Daghistani wrote that the Arab chosen from on high to carry the torch of the mission of mankind was the very man (Husayn) who was now standing guard on Iraq's eastern frontiers. "Just as the paths of Mecca . . . knew him, so the borders of the homeland know him today, as he stands firm against the gods of evil." *Al-'Iraq* compared Husayn's war against the "apostates and the ignorant" of Iran with Muhammad's wars for the true faith. Amin Jiyad wrote that the man now living among us "has become a prophet."

Muhammad's name is never mentioned without adding the blessing *salla Allah 'alayhi wa-sallam* (God's prayers and peace upon him). If Husayn resembled him, it was natural to link his name with a blessing of his own. And indeed, the words *hafizahu Allah* (may God preserve him) became almost a part of Husayn's name. Some, wishing to enlarge upon the theme, began saying, *Hafizahu Allah wa-ra'ahu* (May God preserve and protect him). The first to use this blessing was 'Abd al-Ghani 'Abd al-Ghaffur, director-general of the ministry for youth affairs, in 1981. He wrote of Husayn that he resembled the caliph 'Umar in his search for justice and 'Ali in the firmness of his principles; he then added, "*hafizahu Allah.*" Three years later, having served in the meantime as minister of religion and of religious endowments and having become a member of the top party leadership, he published an "open letter to the President, the leader Saddam Husayn, may God preserve him." From then on, members of the armed forces, party men, writers, and journalists, as well as people from the public at large who understood which way the wind was blowing, added the blessing to each and every mention of Husayn. This was particularly noticeable in times of crisis or when Saddam Husayn seemed to be in danger, or else when the user of the phrase felt threatened. One such time was the Gulf War and its immediate aftermath. Even scholars followed suit: the historian Hasani wrote of "the beloved leader Saddam Husayn, may Allah preserve him."

Do these things have a significance beyond being indications of the prevalent personality cult? They became current under the pressure of circumstances, but they teach us something about how political language is shaped through the interrelationship between the ruler and the ruled, with the latter learning to sharpen their senses to pick up the new usages as quickly as possible. Do they do so as a protective screen as a defense mechanism? Or is there an element of inner persuasion? These questions must remain moot.

In Praise of Saddam Hussein

Amir of Bahrain

translated from *al-Khalij al-'Arabi (The Arab Gulf)*

HH Sheikh Issa bin Salman Al Khalifa, Emir of the State of Bahrain, praised the national stances taken by Iraq, reasserting that these positions are a source of pride for all Arabs, and above all for the Arab people of Bahrain. His Highness's comments came during his reception of a delegation from *Alef Ba'* magazine, in the presence of Mr Tarek Abd El Rahman Al Moayyad, the Bahraini Minister of Information.

HH referred to the ancient ties that bind Iraq to Bahrain, and said: "We take pride in Iraq and in the people of Iraq, because we are one people and one state . . ." adding: "[i]f the Arab nation unites, she will become a great and unrivalled power, able to face every danger and truly become a force to be reckoned with." HH then said: "I am positive that Iraq, under the leadership of Saddam Hussein, will be the hope and bastion of the Arab nation, and that he will achieve for our brethren the Arab people of Iraq what we ourselves aspire to."

US-UK Realpolitik in the Gulf Up to 1980

Avi Shlaim

from *War and Peace in the Middle East: A Critique of American Policy*

Realpolitik in the Gulf

The Cold War outlook that dictated America's policy toward the Arab-Israeli conflict from the Eisenhower administration on also guided its approach to the Persian Gulf. A Gulf policy was simpler to formulate, however, because Israel's security was not directly involved. In the Gulf, America had only two major interests: to bolster the independence, security, and stability of the oil-producing states, thus ensuring access to their vast oil resources, and to contain the spread of Soviet military power and influence. These mutually reinforcing objectives pointed to the preservation of the political status quo. The problem of reconciling America's commitment to Israel with other U.S. interests did not arise in the Gulf. Hence the persistent American attempt to treat the Arab-Israeli problems and those of the Persian Gulf as separate and unrelated.

Superficially, American policy, particularly policy on Soviet containment, may look like an extension of Britain's approach throughout the nineteenth century, but the stakes were different. Britain's involvement in the Gulf started for strategic reasons and gradually encompassed politics and economics; America's involvement started for economic reasons and later encompassed politics and security. Britain paid close attention to local and regional threats to the status quo, whereas America focused on the Soviet threat. The British conception of Gulf security was intimately linked to regional politics and the internal conditions of individual states; the American conception was more closely linked to military alliances, balance of power, and arms supplies.

Before Britain's withdrawal from east of Suez, President Nixon exaggerated the power vacuum such a move would create. By doing so, he hoped to overcome congressional opposition to funding the Indian Ocean military facility closest to the Saudi oil fields. The more critical area, however, was in and around Iran, the center of much of the world's oil production. Britain was no longer willing to defend the area, and America, mired in the costly and unpopular Vietnam War, was unable. But Mohammad Reza Pahlavi, shah of Iran since 1941, was eager to become the Gulf's policeman, a role President Nixon and Henry Kissinger encouraged him to play.

America's disillusion with its part in the Vietnam War led to the 1969 Nixon Doctrine: America would overcome the political and economic constraints on its power by relying on friendly local powers as regional policemen. In the Middle East, two candidates nominated themselves for this role: Israel and Iran. Iran became the key pillar of support for American interests in the Gulf, a bastion of regional stability and a protector of the status quo. The United States selected Saudi Arabia as the other pillar in what became known as the "two-pillar" strategy.

The two-pillar policy implied equal reliance on Iran and Saudi Arabia, the largest and wealthiest pro-Western monarchies. But given Saudi Arabia's limited military capability, the United States acknowledged that Iran would have to be the main source of strength. Another difficulty was the quarrelsome relationship between the two pillars. The Saudi royal family was jealous of the Iranian dynasty and expressed it in petty and petulant ways, like calling the Persian Gulf the Arabian Gulf. Moreover, Saudi Arabia was not just a Gulf power; it was also a member of the Arab League and an enemy of Israel. Iran, Islamic but not Arab, enjoyed covert cooperation with Israel. Iran supplied Israel with oil, while Israel supplied Iran with arms and related services. Iran did not participate in the 1973 oil boycott of countries supporting Israel. Israel in turn supported Iran in the Iran-Iraq War, which lasted from 1980 to 1988. Regarding oil, however, Americans were closer to the moderate Saudis than to the shah, who pressed for higher prices and a higher share of the revenues. The two-pillar policy was thus more problematic than its name suggests. It was subjected to two severe tests, in 1973–74 and in 1978–79.

Under the two-pillar strategy, America extended a security commitment as well as arms and technical assistance to both Iran and Saudi Arabia. The quality and quantity of arms supplied to the shah, whose policy was to buy the best equipment in the largest possible quantities, increased at a staggering pace. American policy was to indulge rather than curb the shah's desire for arms. Fear of Soviet advances, particularly in Iraq, outweighed restraint. During a May 1972 visit to Tehran, Nixon and Kissinger agreed to let the shah purchase anything he wanted short of nuclear weapons. By mid-1970s Iran accounted for half of American arms sales abroad, and arms sales became the central component in U.S.-Iranian relations. The sales increased as American companies scrambled for lucrative contracts, contributing to Iranian domestic problems. The overspending on arms led to inflation and corruption as some American company officials offered "commissions" in return for government contracts. The increased exposure to Western ideas also disturbed Islamic fundamentalists. All these factors progressively alienated the Iranian people from their ruler.

Nixon and Kissinger tolerated the shah's repression of human rights such as freedom of speech because he was the only card they had to play against the Soviet Union in Central Asia. They used him to weaken the Soviet Union and its allies, especially Iraq, where secular Arab militants—the Ba'athists—had gained power in 1968. The United States pointed to Soviet arms supplies to Iraq to justify its own policy toward Iran. Although the Soviets made various arms-control proposals, Nixon and Kissinger refused to give them any say in Gulf affairs. They, not the Soviets, were therefore primarily responsible for the unbridled superpower rivalry and for the dangerous escalation of the arms race that accompanied it.

Nixon and Kissinger also aided the shah in his campaign to destabilize the Ba'ath regime in Baghdad. In 1972 they agreed to covert American-Israeli-Iranian action in support of the Kurdish rebels in northern Iraq. A report four years later by the House Select Committee on Intelligence Activities revealed the calculations behind this policy:

> Documents in the committee's possession clearly show that the president, Dr. Kissinger, and the foreign head of state [the shah] hoped that our clients [the Kurds] would not prevail. They preferred

> instead that the insurgents simply continue a level of hostilities sufficient to sap the resources of our ally's neighboring country [Iraq]. This policy was not imparted to our clients, who were encouraged to continue fighting.

The White House policy treated the Kurds as pawns in a geopolitical game, supporting them only as long as they were useful. America tilted now toward Iran; it would tilt in favor of Iraq when circumstances changed and when it deemed such a tilt advantageous. In the long run this strategy built suspicion and resentment of America on all sides. But its architects were oblivious to the long-term consequences.

In 1973, just as the United States deemed the Nixon Doctrine a success, the Yom Kippur War broke out between Israel and Egypt allied with Syria. The Arab Gulf states made a dramatic and unexpectedly effective contribution to the Egyptian-Syrian war effort by restricting the production and export of oil to America and other supporters of Israel. The action caused panic and disarray in the Western camp; the American policy of separating the Arab-Israeli conflict from relations with the Gulf states lay in ruins, as did the separation of business from politics. By the end of 1974, the Organization of Petroleum Exporting Countries (OPEC), supported by Iran and Saudi Arabia, had raised the price of oil fourfold. The balance of power between the Arabs and the West was about to tilt in favor of the Arabs.

One consequence of the 1973–74 oil shock was a massive transfer of resources from the industrialized countries to the oil producers. The Arab states used their mounting revenues to buy arms, goods, and services from the West and to invest in its financial markets. This created a new kind of linkage between the Western and Gulf economies. Western governments became eager to boost their exports. Consumer demand, led by the shah, and the push of Western arms manufacturers propelled arms transfers in particular. Iran and Saudi Arabia alone ordered $30 billion of American arms between 1973 and 1980. The Gulf became heavily militarized without any perceptible gain in either regional security or internal stability. America committed a serious error in flooding the Gulf with the most advanced weapons, and the local rulers committed an even more serious one by squandering their wealth on military hardware.

Countless disputes over land, water, and oil persisted among the Gulf states following the British withdrawal. The most persistent and dangerous of these pitted Iran against Iraq for control of the strategically vital Shatt al-Arab waterway, which lies along the borders between the two countries. Britain had done well by Iraq in persuading Iran to sign a 1937 agreement that set the border on Shatt al-Arab's eastern shore. In 1969, after Saddam Hussein's Ba'ath Party assumed power, Iran renounced the 1937 treaty and began to challenge Iraqi control of Shatt al-Arab. In 1975 Saddam, the Iraqi vice president and strongman of the regime, concluded an agreement with the shah of Iran that set the border along the median line of the waterway. In return the shah and his American backers agreed to end their support of the Kurdish insurgency in northern Iraq, thus exposing the Kurds to the tender mercies of the Ba'ath regime. It was not the first time America betrayed the Kurds, nor was it to be the last.

Nixon defined security in military terms. Jimmy Carter's presidency emphasized morality. Two important Carter policies resulting from that emphasis—human rights and restrictions on arms sales—threatened the cozy relationship with the shah. Yet U.S.-Iranian relations maintained a remarkable continuity despite the transition from Republican to Democratic rule. One reason for this was the permanent bureaucracy that sustained American defense commitments and regional strategy. Another was that Jimmy Carter appreciated Iran's importance to Western oil supplies, both as a major exporter and as a regional power. There was no obvious alternative to close relations with the shah. What Carter did bring about was a subtle shift in the two-pillar policy relying more heavily on Saudi Arabia than on Iran.

Carter and his aides thought that a new regional stability had begun. But they misunderstood the process of internal change that led to the 1979 overthrow of the Pahlavi dynasty. No sooner had Carter pronounced Iran an "island of stability" than a revolution forced the shah out of the country. Carter and his advisers were surprised to discover that a large army, police force, and security apparatus could not save the Peacock Throne. They failed to grasp until too late that although the shah had built up his armed forces to assert Iran's independence, most Iranians believed his policy served only his regime and perpetuated their country's dependence on America. Confusion in Washington and conflicting signals during this critical period may also have emboldened the opposition forces and contributed to the shah's downfall.

Carter's ambivalent policy toward the shah explains why both globalists and regionalists have blamed him for the "loss" of Iran. Globalists on the right blamed his human-rights policy and his failure to stand by the shah against Iran's domestic opponents. Regionalists dismissed Carter's human-rights policy as more bark than bite. They blamed him for not persuading the shah to liberalize his regime and for pandering to the shah's whims with unlimited arms supplies. Both globalists and regionalists exaggerate America's influence. The shah's fall was due more to his own domestic and foreign policies than to American policy. As Iran expert R. K. Ramazani has argued, it was not America that lost Iran but the shah who "wooed, won, but also lost America."

With the collapse of the shah's regime, a decade of efforts to develop a viable Gulf strategy ended in spectacular failure. The main prop of the Nixon Doctrine in the region had been demolished. America lost not only prestige, credibility, and a close ally but also its links with the Iranian military, its monitoring stations near the Soviet frontier, and one of its most lucrative export markets. Even more serious, the oil-price increase from $13 to $34 a barrel had profound consequences for the world economy.

At first Carter made an effort to come to terms with the new regime of the elderly and inflexible Ayatollah Ruholla Khomeini. Khomeini had been an outspoken critic of the shah's subservience to America and of his alliance with Israel, regarding both as inimical to Islam. He promptly severed contacts with Israel, and when Iranian students took American diplomats hostage at the Tehran embassy, he severed relations with America as well. An abortive U.S. military mission to free the hostages further embittered relations and dealt another blow to American prestige.

The Islamic revolution reversed Iran's traditional foreign policy, turning

America and other former allies into enemies. Iran's new leaders were ideologically opposed to the status quo both at home and in the international system. They believed their revolution would not be secure until Saudi Arabia and Iran's other neighbors threw off American protection. A fundamental tenet of the revolution was that Iran had a God-given mission to export the Islamic system of government to the corrupt pro-Western and anti-Islamic countries of the Persian Gulf. While denouncing America as "the Great Satan," however, the new leaders did not embrace the Soviet Union. On the contrary, they regarded the superpowers as equally guilty of imperialism and sought to free the region from the stranglehold of both. Ayatollah Khomeini's "neither East nor West" was not a mere slogan but a central principle in revolutionary Iran's foreign policy. It implied the creation of an Islamic bloc powerful enough to stand up to both superpowers. This is why the Soviet Union did not welcome the revolution. But to the Americans the new regime was threatening because it challenged the status quo and legitimacy of America's conservative allies in the Gulf.

The Soviet invasion of Afghanistan in December 1979 heightened American unease. For the first time since World War II, large numbers of Soviet troops were committed outside the communist bloc. The effect was to eliminate a buffer state and bring the Red Army closer to the Indian Ocean and the oil fields of the Persian Gulf. Washington feared that the invasion was a prelude to Soviet expansion in the Gulf.

President Carter articulated this concern in his January 1980 State of the Union address: "Let our position be absolutely clear. An attempt by any outside force to gain control of the Persian Gulf will be regarded as an assault on the vital interests of the United States of America, and such an assault will be repelled by any means necessary, including military force." This declaration, which quickly became known as the Carter Doctrine, clarified what American presidents had been saying since 1947. It also bore a striking resemblance to the Lansdowne Declaration of 1903, in which the British foreign secretary of the day warned rival great powers to keep out of the Persian Gulf.

Influenced by events in the "Arc of Crisis," which stretched from

Afghanistan to Iran, South Yemen, and Ethiopia, President Carter's foreign policy shifted from regionalism to globalism. Having begun his presidency emphasizing the need to resolve regional disputes and cooperate with the Soviet Union, Carter ended it by focusing on the threat of Soviet expansionism. At the time Carter issued his portentous statement, the American capacity for projecting military power into the Gulf was limited; there had been no military draft for several years, and the United States had no bases in the Gulf. Although Carter emphasized the build-up of the Rapid Deployment Force, a well-trained force able to go anywhere on short notice, it had hardly progressed by the end of his presidency.

On September 22, 1980, shortly before Carter left office, Iraq launched a massive attack on Iran. The animosity between America and the Khomeini regime gave rise to a conspiracy theory that implicated the Carter Administration as an accomplice. Iranians of all factions believed that Great Satan encouraged the attack. Some liberal critics of America also believed this theory. Christopher Hitchens, Washington editor of *Harper's Magazine*, for example, charged that America knew Iraq was planning an assault on a neighboring country and, at the very least, took no steps to prevent it.

Upon close inspection, however, the circumstantial evidence pointing to an independent Iraqi decision outweighs the conjectural. Saddam Hussein, by now president of Iraq, had the motives, the military capability, and the opportunity to attack Iran. The motives were to settle old scores with an ancient foe, assert control over the disputed Shatt al-Arab waterway, and establish primacy in the Gulf. The provocative behavior of the new Iranian regime, especially its call to Iraqi Shiites to overthrow Saddam and establish an Islamic state like Iran's, supplied another Iraqi motive for war. The rupture between revolutionary Iran and its principal source of arms and spare parts enhanced Iraq's military advantage. And the chaotic state of affairs within Iran after the revolution led Saddam Hussein to believe, erroneously as it turned out, that he could achieve swift victory. Saddam thus needed no encouragement from America or anyone else to launch his war on Iran.

America's Persian Gulf policy oscillated during the 1970s from the globalism of the Nixon administration to the regionalism of the early days of the Carter administration and back toward globalism at the end of Carter's term. Numerous events challenged America's position during this decade: the Yom Kippur War, the oil shocks, the full-scale Iranian revolution, and the 1980 Iran-Iraq War. All these threats to oil supplies and regional stability sprang from within. None could be blamed on the Soviet Union. There was thus some inconsistency in Carter's adoption of the Soviet-instigation argument as the basis of American planning for defense of the Gulf. It was left to his Republican successor, however, to use this argument as the basis for America's entire global strategy in what came to be known as the Second Cold War.

The Iran–Iraq War and the Iraqi State

Charles Tripp

from *Iraq: Power and Society*

The capacity of Iraq to survive nearly eight years of war with Iran raises a number of questions regarding the nature, the causes and the effects of this success. It also raises the question of what exactly is meant by 'Iraq' in such a context. In outward form, it would seem that the state of Iraq proved, through the test of war, to have had a greater degree of definition and to have possessed stronger foundations as a territorial organization of power than had been suspected prior to the war. Led by Saddam Hussein, the government which started the war remained more or less intact, as did the administrative structure of the state. In spite of massive casualties, the armed forces expanded during the years of war and, if anything, improved in quality during that time. Apart from the rebellion in some areas of Kurdistan and isolated acts of violence by the Shi'a based al-Dawa organization, there was no evidence of significant popular disaffection with the government, despite the increasingly onerous nature of its demands. On the contrary, the government was able to organize the population on an unprecedented scale in order to counter the Iranian military threat. In general, this was successful and the territorial integrity of the Iraqi state was maintained.

The question which arises, therefore, is whether the Iraqi state itself was similarly strengthened, not simply as an organization of power, but, crucially, as an authoritative institutional expression of collective interests. There are two features to note in this connection. The first is that while one could see the fact of resistance to Iran and of mass obedience to the government's directives, the motives of the Iraqis themselves cannot be easily ascertained. There was no voice in Iraq independent of the control of the government. That which is now in the common domain was a product of a government strategy to safeguard its own power, as well as to maintain the war effort against Iran. Consequently, it is impossible to disentangle real motive from projected myth. However, the way in which the myth was presented is in itself of significance. This is because it underlined and was used to support the second feature of Iraqi politics during the war: the strengthening of the autocracy of Saddam Hussein.

Whilst Saddam Hussein utilized all the images appropriate to the collective organization of power, he made certain that both in symbolic terms and in reality such an organization, indeed the definition of such a collectivity, should only find expression in his person, not in the impersonal office which he occupied. The reinforcement of so exclusive a claim to personal power would seem to suggest that it is perhaps not the foundations of the state which were strengthened during the war, but the rule of one man, Saddam Hussein. The fact that he was so apparently successful in using both the structures and myths of state power should not disguise the solitary nature of the endeavour.

Nevertheless, it raises the question of the degree to which the organization of power, whatever its public rationale, corresponds to a system of greater indigenous material and moral significance than the forms of the European state which appear to characterize the dispensation of power in Iraq. Where the implications of the latter do not seriously impede or contradict the former, they can prove to be valuable amplifiers of the power of the autocrat. Equally, in using these instruments, particularly under the stress of war, it is possible that processes will have been set in motion, appropriate to the rationale and the transformations associated with the structure of the state, which may ultimately undermine so individual a claim to rule.

Patrimonialism and Its Implications

Quite apart from the ubiquitous and unforeseeable workings of chance, success in politics generally results from the capacity to pursue a course which is regarded as both fitting and practical by those whom it affects. This consideration embraces not simply those who are required to obey the policies in question, but also those whose task it is to carry them out. Success of this kind had been a very obvious part of Saddam Hussein's eleven-year rise to absolute power in Iraq, culminating in his assumption of the presidency in 1979. As important as the notorious *tarhib wa-targhib* [terror and enticement, or stick and carrot] formula, was his knowledge not only of the proper recipients, but also of the channels through which punishment and reward should be doled out. In this respect, Saddam Hussein's relative advantage was that he placed no reliance whatsoever on either institutions or ideologies as sufficient guarantors of men's loyalties and political behaviour. Whilst others might have seen institutions as having an autonomous existence, defined by certain rules which, in turn, determined the relations between those who staffed them, Saddam Hussein seemed to have little faith in the intangible and abstract compulsions of formal procedures. He might—and often did—use the organizations in question and their respective rationales as a way of justifying and extending his own power. Equally, he was content to use such devices insofar as they became the focus of others' beliefs and activities. Quite apart from anything else, this placed a certain restraint on their imagination and action. However, Saddam Hussein himself had no intention of becoming beholden to such insubstantial entities.[1] Instead, he relied increasingly on the informal mechanisms of socially accepted patronage to reinforce and indeed to justify his growing power.

The fact that Saddam Hussein was so successful in erecting a system of power largely based on this patrimonial principle, indicates its continued efficacy in the society and politics of Iraq. Given the various histories of the peoples who inhabit the country, as well as the record of the development of the formal institutions of the Iraqi state, this is perhaps scarcely surprising. However, where Saddam Hussein—and indeed others before him—was markedly successful, was in combining the social efficacy of the networks of patronage denoted by the term *al-intisab*, with the administrative organization of power inherent in the formal structure of the state.

From this perspective, the offices of state have come to be regarded as so many prizes to be captured on one's own behalf, and on that of the network of clients who depend upon all prominent individuals. The normative expectations associated with the idea of *al-intisab* [lit. 'membership' or 'affiliation', but also signifying kinship and linkage, as well as suitability or appropriateness] sustain such networks. Under this heading, the more generally understood logic of patron-client relations comes into play, with the weak serving the strong in exchange for protection and reward. The relationship benefits both parties, since the greater the entourage of the patron, the greater his prestige and the wider the circle of his power and influence. This, in turn, amplifies the capacity of the weaker client and enhances his own standing. In order to be taken on as a client, an element of personal trust is necessary. In the first place, this might be founded on kinship, clan and tribal ties. Here the expectations vested in the patron would be that much greater, as would the augmentation of his authority for being seen to help so generously those whom it was felt 'natural' or fitting that he should help. However, beyond these family circles, reassurance of the kind necessary for trust and expectations to develop might also be afforded by common provincial, sectarian or ethnic origin.[2]

From this perspective, the power and resources available through control of the administrative machinery of the state, are not regarded as being for the common good of the unknown and possibly mistrusted other inhabitants of the state as a whole. Rather, they are deemed to be primarily for the benefit of these informal, but highly resilient and efficacious client groupings. Their very cohesion depends upon the manifest ability of the patron to acquire and to share the fruits of office with his followers. Failure to do so means social disgrace and political oblivion, as clients defect to someone who can more successfully protect and advance the interests of those who pledge their service to him. Saddam Hussein was able to prevent this from happening, not simply through the physical elimination of potential rivals, but also through the placating and cultivation of those whose support made the exercise of absolute power both worthwhile and possible.

The implications of the sustained operation of such a system are various. Most importantly, in this context, has been the vicious circle which it established in regard to the operation of the formal institutions of the state. Clearly, the resilience of such a social mechanism as that associated with *al-intisab* is both cause and effect of the lack of faith among much of the Iraqi population, including the political leadership, in the authority or efficacy of the impersonal institution of the Iraqi state. If people already believe that the power to reward and to punish lies in the hands of networks based on family trust, or common provincial and/or sectarian origins, they will seek to operate the logic of such a system to their own advantage. In doing so, they further strengthen the very principles of efficacy and authority which sustain these networks, and consequently assist in the degradation of the normative framework of the institutions of the state. By this means, one can see how the foundations of such patrimonially based systems of power tend to reproduce themselves, despite the elaboration of formal institutional structures and despite the apparent contradiction with the public justification for the exercise of power.

Further important political outcomes of such a system of power have been the reinforcement of a sense of communal privilege and the tendency towards autocracy. The sense of communal privilege may not be explicit, but it has been implicit in the whole system of trust and mutual favour denoted by *al-intisab*, and the way in which this has taken over the machinery of the state. To admit that other principles might govern the allocation of power in the state would be to acquiesce in the dismantling of the networks which guarantee the advancement of those already entrenched. Given the history of the foundation of the Iraqi state and its subsequent development, those best placed to benefit from such a dispensation of power have come disproportionately from the clans and families of the Sunni Arabs. To suggest another principle for the organization of power—such as democracy, nationalism or constitutionalism—might be to suggest the theoretical equality of all inhabitants of the Iraqi state. This would leave the twenty per cent who were Sunni Arab in a position where they might be ruled by someone from the remaining eighty per cent. He could be, therefore, in theory at least, a Shi'i, a Kurd, a Christian, a Jew, a Turkoman, a Sabean or a Yazidi. Quite apart from the specific prejudices which colour one group's views of the others, such a development would turn the political world upside down. It would automatically exclude most Sunni Arabs from the networks of kinship and communal trust emanating from the new holders of power.

Saddam Hussein used this system to good effect. He observed its conventions and played upon the fears and hopes which it encourages. He may have propagated the myth of Iraqi nationalism and national identity, but he did not let it determine the pattern of his appointments to positions of real power in the state. Whilst he frequently appointed people who were not Sunni Arabs to positions of relative prominence in the public hierarchy of the state, the inner circle of those with substantial delegated power remained almost exclusively Sunni Arabs, largely drawn from the clans of Saddam Hussein's tribe, the Al Bu Nasir.[3] Parallel to the formal, institutional structures and hierarchies of the state, there existed another structure, governed by the rules of patronage, in which the power and rank of each was determined by their position in relation to Saddam Hussein himself. Naturally, the overlap is close, not least because Saddam Hussein, after all, heads most of the formal organs of the state itself. However, it is the informal, clan-based hierarchy which is the true repository of power and authority. Unsung in the public propaganda of the regime, but implicit in its very organization, this is the order which Saddam Hussein could only have disrupted at his peril, even had he wanted to.

Conversely, as long as he maintained the proprieties, he was assured of a large measure of support from the wider circles of the Sunni Arabs. In addition, all those who benefitted from his patronage, or believed themselves in a position where their social connections would allow them to do so, whatever their sectarian or ethnic origins, have helped to maintain a system with which they are familiar. This generalized fear of being forced to deal with the unfamiliar, unknown personnel of an alternative dispensation was a significant reinforcement for autocracy under Saddam Hussein, but also under his predecessors. The powerful Sunni Arab leader who could dispense favours and who stood at the apex of a pyramid of patronage, might be resented for any number of reasons, but could be relied upon not to overturn the whole system. As long as such a leader existed, there was always a chance of advancement. Above all, however, there was little chance that another community could monopolize the power and resources which were regarded as rightfully belonging to the Sunni Arab inheritors of the Ottoman Empire's successor states.[4]

Iraqi Autocracy and War with Iran

A feature of autocratic rule is the desire for authority, control and order through the manipulation of the beliefs of the population concerning the rightness, uniqueness and indispensability of the ruler, without relying for this on any form of institutional solidity that might eventually challenge that authority or call the leader to account. To invest an institution with authority and to give it the licence to act upon that authority, is to create a potential base of opposition. Autocracy is, therefore, in many respects the antithesis of the institutional and, above all, impersonal order suggested by the Western idea of the state. Yet, at the same time, it is clear that the autocrat, no less than any other ruler, has need of organizations that will amplify his power, extending surveillance and control throughout the population he intends to govern, maintaining thereby an order that does not threaten his hold on power. These were the considerations which apparently underpinned Saddam Hussein's progressive domination of both the Party and the administrative structure of the state in Iraq.

This domination was facilitated by his ability to assemble around himself an inner core of men whose loyalty was to him personally, either because they were members of his family, of his provincial community or because they had proved their personal loyalty during the long years of association with him in the conspiracies of the Baath. They owed their position neither to their official rank in the institutions of the state, nor to their position within the ideological vehicle of the Party. They did not, therefore, represent any principle of impersonal authority. On the contrary, they were placed in positions of seniority in both organizations precisely because of their pre-existing relationship with the person of Saddam Hussein. It was this which they had chiefly in common and, therefore, it allowed Saddam Hussein to control in a particularly effective way their activities, even if he was perforce obliged to delegate some of his own powers to them.[5]

The cohesion of this inner core allowed Saddam Hussein progressively to dominate the Party and, through the insertion of Party cadres, to dominate the apparatus of the state. The provincial governorates, the principal ministries, the intelligence and security services, the judiciary and the armed forces were either in the hands of men whose main allegiance was to Saddam Hussein, or were dominated by Party bureaux which were themselves the creation of Saddam Hussein. When, in July 1979, he finally persuaded his uncle the President to stand aside, he himself became President of the Republic, Chairman of the RCC, Secretary General of the Baath and Commander-in-Chief of the armed forces. In addition, he presided over the Cabinet, the Office of Financial Supervision, the Planning Council, the Intelligence Directorate and, whenever necessary, the Revolutionary Tribunal. He was, therefore, in a strong position to purge all organs of the state and Party of the few remaining figures of authority who had shown themselves to be lukewarm to the prospect of Saddam Hussein's personal ascendancy. The spate of executions of senior officials in both party and state administrations which accompanied his assumption of absolute power demonstrated not only his absolute ruthlessness, but also his inability as an autocrat to compromise with those who might adhere to principles of rule and of order other than those dictated by Saddam Hussein himself.

At the same time, a personality cult of truly impressive proportions was in the making, in which Saddam Hussein was portrayed as the only figure who could unite the various communal identities existing within the Iraqi population. On a symbolic level, this meant appealing to the various communities by presenting himself as one of them and, therefore, as uniquely qualified to apprehend their true interests. Saddam Hussein was variously portrayed masquerading as a Kurd, as a Shi'i tribesman from the lower Euphrates, a Bedouin sheikh and, even more ambitiously, as a descendant of the Caliph Ali ibn Abi Talib. This campaign appears to have been due less to some desire for an abstract national unity—to the principles of which Saddam Hussein himself might have been held accountable. Rather, it seems to have been designed to persuade people of all the other communities of Iraq—however they defined their communal identity—that Saddam Hussein was their rightful leader. Whatever their identities, he had their true interests at heart, he was the source of all benefits and, therefore, it was to him that they should give their unquestioning obedience. Not only did he intend thereby to derive from these people the kind of support he had enjoyed among the clans of the Sunni Arab northwest, but he was also determined to displace their own communal leaders in the affections of their people. He had to establish that it was not only prudent to obey him, but fitting to do so as well. There was, in addition, a second reason why, in 1980, Saddam Hussein should have sought to stress the unity of the Iraqi people under his command, and to project himself as their sole authoritative leader.

The rapid deterioration of relations with Iran since the revolution of 1979 had left the Iraqi state potentially vulnerable in two respects: firstly, the Kurds might have thought once more of exploiting Iraqi-Iranian enmity in order to carve out a degree of autonomy from the control of central government in Baghdad; secondly, there was considerable fear in Iraq that significant numbers of Iraq's Shi'i majority might take inspiration and encouragement from the Islamic Republic in Iran and rise against the Iraqi government. Potentially, therefore, there existed two disaffected communities within the territory of the Iraqi state which, if mobilized to seek political power appropriate to their particular communities, would mean the dismemberment of that state, or, at the very least, a radical reshaping of the political order. In a speech in February 1980, Saddam Hussein, unusually, gave voice to this fear, declaring that unless the inhabitants of Iraq demonstrated their loyalty to a specifically Iraqi state, the country would be divided into three 'mini-states': one Arab-Sunni, one Arab-Shi'i and one Kurdish.[6] It was in this regard that increasing stress was to be placed on the common history and common interests of those who occupied the territory of Iraq.

Saddam Hussein had long been associated with those in the Baath who believed that if the Iraqi government were to dedicate the resources at their disposal to the creation of a pan-Arab state, and thus neglect the non-Arab inhabitants of Iraq, this might destroy both the Party and the state. This had been evident in his attempts to resolve the problem of Kurdish separatism in the early 1970s. However, it was clearly a delicate task, if conducted from within a Party whose raison d'être was apparently the creation of an Arab state coterminous with the territory inhabited by the Arab nation. It was also dangerous for a Sunni Arab ruler, whose chief constituency lay among the Sunni Arabs who saw him as their champion, if necessary against the other communities inhabiting Iraq. As his influence grew during the 1970s, however, it was noticeable that the government gave increasing encouragement to the idea that all Iraqis were the cultural heirs to the great civilizations of Mesopotamia. Sumerian, Babylonian and Assyrian themes were stressed in much of the government sponsored art and architecture of those years. Amongst many of the Arab nationalists of the Baath there was evidently some unease, but the rise of Saddam Hussein to a position of political dominance allowed him to be bolder in his assertion of a specifically Iraqi collective identity. As he was to declare in 1979:

> As long as we place Iraq at the core of the Arab nation, we are not afraid that strengthening Iraqi identification would occur at the expense of the Arab nation, much as we talk, with great pride, of Iraq's present, past and future.[7]

The coincidence of his assumption of the Presidency and the growing threat of the Iranian revolution to Iraq's social cohesion and territorial integrity led to an increasingly explicit attempt to inculcate a belief in the moral value of Iraq's territory amongst its inhabitants. Thus, in his effort to transfrom the Baath into a party of mass mobilization, open to general membership, Saddam Hussein stated that 'The new organizational structure of the Party includes all Iraqis who believe in Iraqi soil'.[8] In May 1980, during the mass expulsions of thousands of Iraqi Shi'is who had even the most tenuous family links with Iran, or who simply bore a name of Persian origin, Saddam Hussein declared: 'Those who do not love Iraq and are not ready to shed blood in the defence of Iraqi territory and dignity, must leave Iraq'.[9]

As relations with Iran deteriorated to a point where open conflict seemed highly probable, these themes were repeated with much emphasis by Saddam Hussein. It is true that, at the same time, he was careful to allude to the Arab identity of Iraq, as well. Clearly, in a struggle with the Iranians, where the crucial question was the loyalty of the Iranians' Arab Shi'i co-sectarians in Iraq, this was as important as the stress on a specifically Iraqi identity. Two other factors appear also to have played a part. Saddam Hussein was simultaneously, making irredentist noises about the need to 'liberate' the Arab-speaking inhabitants of the Iranian province of Khuzestan. He was also seeking pan-Arab approval for his defiance of Iran, hoping thereby to extend Iraq's, and thus his own influence throughout the anxious Arab states of the Gulf, as well as in the Arab world generally.

Saddam Hussein's attempt to establish himself as undisputed master of the Iraqi state had led in the first instance to his successful domination of the apparatus of the state. It had also led him to stress the identity of all Iraqis, their supposed common history and purpose, and his own unique qualifications to represent and to further that purpose. At the same time, as a means of giving definition to the Iraqi community that was held to underpin this sense of identity and to legitimate its submission to a unitary state apparatus, the territoriality of the Iraqi state was emphasized. In September 1980, all three elements led Saddam Hussein to order the Iraqi armed forces to invade Iran. War had come to seem not only an appropriate activity, but also perhaps the only possible activity that, if successfully conducted, would finally legitimate Saddam Hussein's exclusive claim to rule Iraq.

The rapid and decisive humbling of Iran seemed to have been intended to achieve three objectives pertinent to the cohesion of Iraqi society under the domination of Saddam Hussein. Firstly, it would inhibit the crystallization of communal disaffection among either the Shi'i or the Kurds, by demonstrating that it would be useless to look to Iran for aid. Secondly, it would enhance the authority of Saddam Hussein in the Arab world, thereby satisfying not only a Sunni Arab and Baathist constituency in Iraq, but also greatly promoting the influence of Iraq and of Saddam Hussein in the region. Thirdly, and equally importantly, it was intended to wring territorial concessions from Iran.

The latter point is of considerable significance, since it relates both to the territorial definition of the Iraqi state and to the obligations which Saddam Hussein appeared to have assumed in claiming the right to rule the state. In 1975 he had been the principal architect of the Algiers Agreement which, in the face of Iran's overwhelming military might and its persistent aid to the Kurdish rebellion, surrendered Iraq's claim to territorial sovereignty over the whole of the Shatt al-Arab waterway which runs between Iraq and Iran at the head of the Gulf. Since this made no difference to the actual use by Iraqi vessels of the waterway, but did stipulate that, thenceforth, they would have to fly the Iranian flag if they crossed the median line that constituted the new frontier between the two states, the shame of this surrender was largely symbolic. It was no less keenly felt, for all that. Saddam Hussein's determination to use war as a means of reasserting Iraq's territorial sovereignty seems to have been due to the belief that failure to do so would seriously weaken his own authority, since it would weaken his claim to be the sole competent defender of the territorial integrity of Iraq. Consequently, his ability to restore the 'lost honour of Great Iraq', by forcing the Iranian government to acknowledge Iraqi territorial sovereignty, was to be the measure of his success as guardian and ruler of the Iraqi state.

The interesting feature of this aspect of the conflict was that it represented a synthesis, or apparent hybridization, of two different principles of state power, originating in two different state traditions. On the one hand, there was the 'state of Iraq' organized by Saddam Hussein as his own personal following—the obedience of all Iraqis in a patrimonial system of power constituted the moral foundation of the state, the pattern of beliefs which allowed his reach and command to extend to the four corners of his domain. This was *al-sulta* ['power', but also, interestingly and significantly, 'authority' and 'sovereignty'] which ensured that his will would be obeyed. It had been constructed on the basis of all the many networks of reward and punishment which had bound people to him precisely because he was so obviously in a position to promote or harm their interests, as well as those of their own followings. Regional powers made their appearance as rivals for the loyalties and support of the circles which Saddam Hussein had assembled. Their prestige could only be won at the expense of Saddam Hussein. Conversely, as their power was seen to wane, so the reach of Saddam Hussein could be extended.[10] The competition was, therefore, seen as a contest between rival leaders to extend their respective followings.

Interestingly, in 1980, the abstract question of territorial sovereignty over a waterway (and over some small areas of land), and not over people or populations, became the token and symbol of this competition. Precisely because of the relative insignificance of the material value of the physical areas in dispute, it was the moral or normative aspects of the territorial state which appeared thereby to be emphasized. That is, Saddam Hussein had decided to make this issue a test of his own authority within Iraq—as President of the territorial state of Iraq—and in relation to the rulers in Tehran. It is unlikely that many in Iraq knew or cared where Iraqi sovereignty began and Iranian sovereignty ended in the waters of the Shatt al-Arab.

However, once Saddam Hussein had decided to make the extensions of formal Iraqi territorial sovereignty a test of his own power relative to that of the government in Iran, few in Iraq could be in much doubt about what was at stake in the conflict. At this stage, before the full gravity of the situation had become apparent, this was clearly a struggle for relative regional prestige and influence between Saddam Hussein and Khomeini. Were Saddam Hussein to fail in his bid to compel the Iranian ruler to acknowledge Iraq's, and thus his own ascendancy, the population of Iraq might not transfer their allegiance to Khomeini. However, significant numbers of them might well transfer their allegiance away from Saddam Hussein and towards a domestic rival who could protect their standing, as well as their material interests more effectively. In this respect, it was not the Shi'a whom Saddam Hussein had most to fear, but the

Sunni Arab clans who had hitherto benefited from his patronage and basked in the glow of his ascendancy.

War and the State in Iraq

War is an activity which to some extent both defines and tests the state. The latter idea has given rise to a rather suspect school of thought which claims to see in the fact of successful prosecution of war proof of the moral superiority of the victorious community, defined as the state and the nation which is believed to find its proper expression in the state. Nevertheless, leaving aside the sinister overtones of such speculation, there is a sense in which a state at war is being tested on the three levels that constitute its definition: as an organization of power, capable of exercising its power through the use of violence; as an 'ethical community' whose members have a sense of their own identity and who actively participate in the violent protection or extension of certain commonly defined interests; as a territorial unit capable both of being maintained in the face of attack and the definition of which has entered into the imagination of its inhabitants in the belief that this territory is worth defending with their lives.

In examining the relationship of war to the state, therefore, one will be examining the ways in which the strategies required for the conduct of successful war may have consequences for the three areas central to the definition of the state. The consequences of these policies may be the reinforcement of the foundations of the state in the moral perspective of its inhabitants, as well as its strengthening as a political unit able to withstand external attack. Nevertheless, success of this kind may be a hollow one for the architects of victory, since their very strategies may set in motion processes among their subjects which would throw into doubt their right to continue in the exercise of power. The endeavour by Saddam Hussein in Iraq to ensure that his strategies for strengthening the outward forms of the state in its war with Iran should not erode his own autocratic power forms the subject of the following pages. That is, the degree to which the conduct of a prolonged war forced him to attend to the definition and foundation of the Iraqi state, whilst at the same time his own preoccupation with the exercise of highly personalized power led him to seek to avoid becoming beholden to the obligations of impersonal, collective authority that underly such a conception of the state.

The Instruments of Violence

In Iraq, under the pressure of the war, considerable transformations had necessarily to take place within the organization of the armed forces. Not only were they expanded to nearly one million men (four times their peacetime strength), but the earlier methods of ensuring their complete obedience to the leadership no longer seemed so advisable. The ubiquity of Baathist commissars in all units, the appointment of officers whose chief qualification was loyalty to Saddam Hussein, rather than military competence, the rapid rotation of officers to ensure that they formed no bonds of solidarity either with each other or with the men under their command, the confusion of lines of command and the denial of any independent initiative to local commanders—these had been the techniques whereby loyalty, or at least absence of effective conspiracy had been assured.

The lacklustre performance of the armed forces in the early years of the war and the realization after 1982 that the Iraqi government would have to organize an effective defence if it was to hold back the Iranian onslaught, necessitated considerable changes. A crucial component of that defence was to be the increasing professionalization of the military. This entailed the encouragement and promotion of competent officers, the establishment of clear lines of command, the effective delegation of authority based on rank, the reduction in the role of the Baathist political officers and the enhancement of unit solidarity. In short, attention was paid to the establishment of an institutional order within the armed forces, unparalleled in any of the other organs of the Iraqi state.

The structual, institutional solidity, as well as the moral element, the *esprit de corps*, which Saddam Hussein found himself compelled to encourage in the armed forces, were dictated by the urgent need to defeat the forces of Iran on the battlefield. Whilst there was little doubt that this was the common aim of Saddam Hussein and of much of the Sunni Arab dominated—but by no means exclusively either Sunni or Arab—officer corps, there clearly existed a suspicion that this did not necessarily imply the total, uncritical commitment to Saddam Hussein that he demanded of all the organizations of power in Iraq. At times of stress, the perennial fear surfaced that relative institutional independence might encourage army officers to see in their immediate superiors, or amongst their colleagues, individuals more fitted than Saddam Hussein to supervize the war effort. This was particularly in evidence when Saddam Hussein's strategic judgement and personal intervention interfered with the conduct of operations and threatened to bring about disaster on the battlefield. The military set-backs of 1982 and of the first half of 1986 witnessed precisely such a development, probably with good reason.[11]

Consequently, whilst obliged to grant the armed forces a measure of independent initiative and to routinize their internal organization, Saddam Hussein sought to ensure his personal control in a manner similar to that in which he attempted to retain control over all the principal organs of the state. The prowess of the armed forces was regularly extolled as evidence of Saddam Hussein's military genius and unparalleled strategic vision; in victory, they were called the 'Army of Saddam Hussein'; the idea was maintained that there was something exceptional in carrying out the commands of Saddam Hussein, since only in this way were the armed forces truly serving the people of Iraq.[12]

At the same time, Saddam Hussein was careful to ensure that key positions of command were held only by those who owed him personal loyalty, preferably as kinsmen. His first cousin and brother-in-law, the late General Adnan Khairallah Tulfah, was the Minister of Defence, deputy Commander-in-Chief and overall commander of the Southern Region. Another first cousin, Ali Hasan al-Majid, headed the Military Bureau of the Baath and was placed in overall command of the Northern Region in order to supervize the campaign against the Kurdish insurgents during 1988. The most prominent of the serving generals, Mahir Abd al-Rashid, was allied to Saddam Hussein by marriage and commanded the Army Corps fighting on the crucial Basra/Fau front. The commanding officer of the Air Force, Hamid Shaban al-Takriti, was a member of Saddam Hussein's provincial community and of his tribal clan. The same applied to Hussein Kamil al-Majid al-Takriti, who commanded the divisions of the Presidential Guard and of the Baghdad garrison, and who cemented his alliance with Saddam Hussein by marrying one of the latter's daughters. In this way, it was clearly hoped by Saddam Hussein that the links of blood and clan loyalty would counteract any tendency within the armed forces to make use of the relative autonomy they had been granted during the war to question the capacity and the right of the 'imperative leader' to command absolute, unconditional obedience.

The Question of Community and Differentiation

The problems that may arise with particular piquancy in regard to the armed forces, may also apply to some degree to the inhabitants of the state as a whole. It is in the interest of those who rule the state and who conduct the war, to insist upon the particularity and community of those who inhabit the territory of the state. Underlying all the rationales for sacrifice in war lies the idea that in risking personal extinction, the individual is helping to protect a collective reality that has prior claim on his loyalty, since it incorporates a set of values that give meaning to his collective existence.[13] This is all the more important in an age when the successful organization of force depends upon the ability to transform, through mass mobilization, large numbers of individual subjects into an army. Visible in all these efforts is the attempt to convince those who are mobilized that they share a history as an identifiable community, that they share values which mark them off from others and that they share with those who are commanding them to fight, a common concern for a benign order, guaranteed by the territorial integrity of the state, but now threatened by the activities of the enemy.

These themes were much in evidence in Iraq during the war. At the 9th Baath Party Regional Congress in July 1982, it was decided that

> For the first time in many centuries, Iraqi nationalism [sic] becomes the prime bond for all the children of this people, and a symbol of which the Iraqis are so proud that they are ready even for martyrdom. Equally, this deep, strong and creative Iraqi nationalism

> has for the first time been linked to the Arab nationalist bond, constituting a living and abundant tributary of it and a steel base guarding it against the evil of enemies and covetous forces'.[14]

Precisely in order to communicate the fact that Iraq's geographical territory was coterminous with a moral community, Saddam Hussein was to state in 1987 that 'others must remember that Iraq is not simply a geographical entity, but is now also a will. This state of affairs exists and the matter is now at an end. There is no force capable of reversing it'.[15]

The war years are full of exhortations by Saddam Hussein, his associates and the Iraqi media which all convey the message that Iraq as a whole was worth defending. That is, the territorial state was represented as having a moral value, in the sense that its physical existence and the integrity of its borders were portrayed as being necessary conditions for the security of all. This was clearly intended to mean not simply the physical security of its inhabitants, but also the values which made life worthwhile. An example of the genre should suffice to give the flavour, but more importantly also to illustrate the kinds of themes which the leadership seemed determined to communicate. In a speech by Saddam Hussein to the 1st Army Corps on 28 May 1987, he declared:

> How do you give expression to your life? Defending it is defending what? Defending your blood . . . your free will . . . defending the present and the future, your home and the laws, whether your home is in Jisan or in Baghdad. The enemy, if he were to reach Jisan and find no man there capable of confronting him, would then reach al-Kut. And if all the men were only to be found in Baghdad, he would attack Baghdad as well . . . Because defence of the homeland in its remotest parts, is the defence of it all, of every home, of every compatriot, of the present and the future.[16]

It is, of course, impossible to measure the effects on the Iraqis of Saddam Hussein's campaign to elaborate a myth of Iraqi nationalism. The organization of the successful defence of Iraq during the years following the disasters of 1982 may have been influenced by the government's relentless attempt to persuade the Iraqis of the essential otherness of the Iranian enemy and of their common plight as victims of Iran's historical enmity. In doing so, it was noticeable, however; that the Iraqi authorities were not content simply to stress the uniqueness and continuity of the Iraqis as a distinct people, although this was certainly the most prominent of the arguments used. Often simultaneously, other images and themes were deployed which appeared to be aimed at the various communities inhabiting Iraq.

Thus, in exhorting his troops to fight in 1987, Saddam Hussein was to appeal not simply to Iraqi patriotism, but also to the sense of Arab national duty:

> Do not believe that your sacrifices in the difficult march of your revolution, particularly your sacrifices in the Qadisiya battle are only a defence of Iraqi territory, although this deserves sacrifices and martyrdom. These sacrifices are more than this: they are for the future of the Arab nation, as well as for the future of Iraq.[17]

This was an important theme to stress, in view of the suspicion with which many Iraqi Sunni Arabs have regarded the idea of Iraqi nationalism. Precisely because the widespread acceptance of the idea of an Iraqi nation would, at best, make them no more than the equals of their non-Sunni and non-Arab compatriots, adherence by the government to such a principle would indicate a radical shift of power within Iraq. Ostensible adherence to Arab nationalism, however, ensures Sunni dominance.

In encouraging popular commitment to a war against a professedly Islamic republic, the Islamic aspects of the community of Iraqis were also stressed. For the first time, therefore, the Baath Congress devoted itself to lengthy discussion of Islam. Taking as its cue Saddam Hussein's statement that 'We are not neutral between belief and unbelief. We are believers', the Congress stated that:

> The Party does not call for the creation of a religious state, but

> for a state based on patriotic links within the framework of one country, and based on pan-Arab links throughout the great Arab homeland. Such a state should be inspired by Islam as a mission and a revolution.[18]

The chief purpose appears to have been to convince the Iraqi Muslims, especially the Shi'i, that the Iranian leaders' claim to speak authoritatively in the name of Islam itself was a sham. Consequently, the speeches of the war years are full of passages denouncing Khomeini and his supporters as bogus Muslims. They are accused of being 'Magians' [Zoroastrians], working hand in hand with the Jews, in an attempt to further the imperialist designs of Persia. Given the history of Islam, especially in Mesopotamia, the twin themes of Arabism and Islam could be felicitously combined with the accusation that the Iranian forces were no more than 'Shu'ubists'.[19] Saddam Hussein now denounced the Iranian regime for using the cover of religion to assert their fundamental hostility to the Arab nation:

> The Arabs are a religious nation, charged with the task of conveying to the peoples of the world the religion's message . . . especially that of Islam . . . It is the Arab man who correctly understands religion more than any other non-Arab pretender . . . The Shu'ubi movement's anti-Arab activity through religion will surface when the Arabs abandon their bright leading role and also when the Arabs play their bright leading role. In the first case, the Shu'ubis will fill the vacuum and in the second they will move to resist the tide and the leading role of the Arabs.[20]

Taking their cue from the President, books appeared such as Dr Faruq Umar's *Mabahith fi al-haraka al-Shu'ubiya* [Studies in the Shu'ubi Movement]. Ostensibly a historical study of the Shu'ubiya under the Abbasids, this had a clear contemporary purpose, as the author explicitly stated in the Conclusion:

> A common feature of all the various religio-political movements that emerged in Persia was their hostility to the Arabs and to the latter's Arab, Islamic Caliphate. In all these movements, the Shuʻubiya played its part . . . It is clear that the roots of the Khomeinism which Iran is presently experiencing lie in this. The research has demonstrated that it is influenced by Magian-Batini-Shuʻubi trends in its values, strategies and goals.[21]

Whatever the images of the community used to stiffen the morale of the Iraqis in the war, they shared two common features. The first was that of the essentially foreign nature of the Iranians, whether as non-Iraqis, non-Arabs, non-Arab Muslims, or even as non-Muslims. Only the first of these corresponded to a specific attempt to inculcate loyalty to a territorial Iraqi state. In a war against Iran, where the victory of the latter could be portrayed as a potential disaster for the values associated with these other communities, images such as these might have been thought equally effective, however tenuous a hold the notion of loyalty to an Iraqi nation-state might be. The second common feature was, of course, the centrality of the person of Saddam Hussein, as an Iraqi, an Arab and a Muslim, the symbol and true guarantor of the values associated with these identities, as well as of the Baathi revolution. Combining in his person the qualities and interests associated with all the various peoples of Iraq, it was Saddam Hussein who most truly represented them and to whom they were tied by a personal bond of loyalty and service.[22]

As Saddam Hussein is reported to have said to his Cabinet in late 1980:

> We know of no other place on earth where people, old and young, the very families of martyrs, face Saddam Hussein and tell him that those they lost were a 'sacrifice to you'. They do not utter such words merely because the person they address is actually Saddam Hussein. No. What they want to express to him, and to the Revolution through him, is that what they say and feel represents the essence of the prevailing new spirit of the Iraqis.

He proceeded to spoil the relatively selfless tone of the above by adding, somewhat disingenuously:

> Now we may wonder what makes an old father, or a widow of a martyr, say to us: 'What is important is (not the person we lost but) that you should be alive and well and keep yourself in good health?'[23]

The Legitimation of Rule

Saddam Hussein's prime consideration was that he should not find himself under an obligation as ruler to those who, in obeying his commands, so greatly extended his reach and power. This concern had underpinned the structure whereby he had sought to delegate a measure of non-threatening power to the armed forces. It had also been evident in his handling and presentation of the myths of Iraqi national identity. For instance, in the elaboration of these myths of Sumerian, Assyrian or Babylonian antecedents for Iraq as a whole, it often seemed that the parts played by the absolute rulers, such as **Hammurabi, Sargon** or Nebuchadnezzar, were being stressed as much as, if not more than the other achievements of these civilizations.

Similarly, whilst talking of democracy, openness and participation, it was evident that Saddam Hussein had two principal objects in mind. The first was that not he, but those to whom he delegated a measure of power should be accountable for their activities. His idea of accountability was that they should answer to him, but with the forms of popular backing granted by such organizations as the National Assembly. The second intention was to make it clear that participation should mean participating in common obedience to him as:

> the Leader-Necessity . . . the man who at a certain stage represents the aspirations and basic interests of the Party and the people. Therefore it is in the interest of the Party and the people to preserve this (Necessity) and adhere to it in a sincere and genuine manner and within the context of democratic practice, collective

> leadership and sound and genuine Party-related and national relations. . . Rejecting such a (Necessity) or leaving its strategic line is not an individual stance or special interpretation. Rather, it is an act aimed at inflicting direct and deliberate damage on the basic aspirations and interests of the Party and the people.[24]

There was evidently not much space here for the people themselves to participate in the definition of their own interests, except by giving unqualified support to Saddam Hussein.

When Saddam Hussein felt compelled to talk about the virtues of law and legality, it was clear from his description of the process which he seemed to believe was open and democratic, that his was to be the final word. The function of everyone else—legal experts, ministers, members of the RCC—was simply to give him their advice, in the manner of the absolute monarch. He would then make his decision, on the basis of this counsel and of what he considered to be correct.[25] By this means, as he stated in an earlier interview, he would ensure that the rule of law would not be equated with unthinking respect for existing legislation. He went on to say that the person who had the capacity [*al-iqtidar*] to do so, must use it to legislate and enforce conformity with the law. His guiding principle should be the ideals of the revolution because they correspond with the fundamental interests of the people. Saddam Hussein was thereby carving out for himself a crucial position as law giver and legal arbiter. He himself should be the sole legal innovator and the people would participate simply through their devotion to him, since he embodied and was aware of their true interests.[26]

The very confidence with which he set out the qualities of his own supreme leadership and the relationship between that and the dispensation of power in Iraq, indicate the degree to which he conceived of the state itself as an emanation of his own person. It may also have been possible that, in doing so, he felt that he was basing his claims on a more indigenous conception of the state which was both more comprehensible and more readily accepted among those on whose obedience he ultimately depended. Although constant reference was made to 'the people' and to their true interests, it was clear that these were only to find their proper definition in the person of Saddam Hussein himself. His was to be the will which animated the organs of the state and supervized their performance; the community of all Iraqis was to find expression in common devotion to Saddam Hussein himself, who was the symbol and epitome of the historical myth which linked them to the glorious past of 'Great Iraq'. It was he, after all, who saw himself as the leader produced by historical necessity to liberate, unify and defend a single people, for too long unaware of their common interests. War and the nature of his revelatory leadership, he proclaimed, had changed this:

> The people have bestowed their trust in the regime and in the leadership of the regime step by step. The people have discovered that the leadership is in their interest and they have given their allegiance to it. This is the allegiance they have demonstrated by spilling their blood in the battle of Qadisiya.[27]

Conclusion

In many respects, the nature of the autocracy which Saddam Hussein established in Iraq seems to be the very antithesis of the principle of power and authority embodied in the formal structure and rationale of the Iraqi state. The definition of power is individual, not collective. The claim to the right to rule is personal, not institutional. It is maintained, in the last analysis, by personal and private networks of trust, not by organized, public alliances or coalitions. Yet at the same time, it is evident that Saddam Hussein found the European model of the state, as structure of power and as collective myth, of some utility in the reinforcement and amplification of his own control. This appears to have served him well in the war with Iran. It also served the interests of most of the inhabitants of Iraq, if those interests could be taken to include a desire not to be subject to the rulings of the Iranian government, however perceived. Whether such a coincidence of interests exists on any other level, remains to be seen. In some respects, it would be considerably to the advantage of Saddam Hussein if such a definition of collective identity and of common interest had failed to crystallize around anything more positive than simply resistance to the armed forces of Iran.

In view of the nature of the Iranian threat, very few sections of the Iraqi population had any reason to welcome an Iranian victory. On the contrary, whilst it would have meant the end of Saddam Hussein's rule in Baghdad, it would also have meant domination by people who are regarded as foreigners by whatever definitions of community exist amongst the peoples of Iraq. Such a victory also raised the spectre of the intercommunal conflict that has frequently been associated with the collapse of effective power at the centre. These social cataclysms were apparently deemed too high a price to pay. The effect of this process was to extend the circle of those who implicitly obeyed the commands of the 'imperative and indispensable' leader, greatly contributing to the war effort by their obedience, but also enhancing thereby the retinue and reach of the autocrat. Although the principles would seem to be wholly different, there does not appear to have been any serious conflict between the European *forms* of state organization and the more locally derived perceptions of how power can and should be organized. Personal service of the leader, whether through a desire to preserve communal or even family advantage, or through an acknowledgment that he and his clan's protection are necessary to stave off a worse evil, has less to do with the legitimacy of the state than with the perceived efficacy of a given dispensation of power. The nature of the war with Iran tended to reinforce such perceptions in Iraq.

These developments have given an appearance of solidity to the state, but it may be merely the product of expediency caused by the unusual circumstances of the war. Had the state been strengthened as an impersonal organization of power, founded on collectively accepted principles of authority and maintained by the rule of law, it would have set a limit on the degree to which Saddam Hussein could maintain so self-centred and personal a style of rule after the ending of the war. Consequently, it appears to have been the intention of Saddam Hussein that no such crystallization of impersonal, institutionalized authority should take place. The organization of power had been useful to him in a multitude of ways. However, the possibility that these organizations should in some sense become autonomous was seen as the real danger. After the ending of the war, it was noticeable, therefore, that Saddam Hussein did his utmost to disrupt the 'institutional memory' which might have formed the basis of self-sustaining, and thus self-willed, institutions. This was particularly visible in the armed forces. As far as his own immediate survival was concerned, it may also have been particularly necessary in that sphere of the state's organization of power.

The impressive edifice of power which Saddam Hussein constructed in Iraq depends ultimately upon his own capacity to service it and to keep it subject to his will. As developments during the years following the end of the war with Iran showed, this is an undertaking fraught with risks, hazardous not only for those inside Iraq, but also for those who find themselves drawn into the strategies by which Saddam Hussein seeks to maintain this edifice. It also suggests that it will only be as long-lived as he himself. This does not mean that the state as an administration or as a territorial entity will vanish, unless his passing is accompanied by a series of regional developments that would mobilize sufficient force and ambition to encompass the territorial partition of Iraq. More probable, is the emergence of another leader and another clan well placed—possibly because of the position they already occupy within it—to take over the state administration and use it in the service of their power. A sense of community is at work, but it is of a community that does not appear to correspond to a political community of Iraqis. Despite the images projected by the Iraqi government during the war and despite the mobilization of much of the Iraqi people in a common war effort, there is as yet little evidence that such a conception has emerged, let alone that it acts as an organizing principle of power or as the impersonal collectivity that justifies the tenure of office. In its absence, the question of the moral foundations of the Iraqi state must remain in doubt.

Notes:

[1] A vivid example of this can be seen in his address to party officials: 'Since the earliest days of the revolution, various writers used the epithet "strong man" when writing about me. I did not want my colleagues to read those articles, because I

was worried about the effect it might have on them especially since—officially—I was only No. 2. However, thank God, those circumstances have now passed'. *Al-Thawra* 23 August 1986 (5).

[2] N.T. Al-Hasso, *Administrative politics in the Middle East: the case of monarchical Iraq 1920–1958* (PhD Thesis, University of Texas at Austin, 1976) pp. 60–65.

[3] See A. Baram, 'The ruling élite in Ba'thi Iraq 1968–86; the changing features of a collective profile', *International Journal of Middle East Studies* 21 (1989) pp. 476–493; *The Economist* 29 September 1990.

[4] H. Batatu, *The old social classes and the revolutionary movements of Iraq* (Princeton University Press, 1978), pp. 13–16.

[5] 'Document: La Nomenklatura Irakienne', *Les Cahiers de l'Orient*, 8/9, 1987/88.

[6] BBC/SWB/ME 12 February 1980 (A/2-3).

[7] A. Baram, 'Culture in the service of wataniyya', *Asian and African Studies, 17 (1983), p. 266.*

[8] A. Baram, 'The June 1980 elections to the National Assembly in Iraq', *Orient*, September 1981, p. 393.

[9] BBC/SWB/ME 5 May 1980 (A/9).

[10] Saddam Hussein on 20 July 1980: 'An Iraqi ruler who bows to Khomeini or to anyone else will be trampled upon by the Iraqis . . . we are not the kind of people to bow to Khomeini. He has wagered to bend us and we have wagered to bend him. We will see who will bend the other' BBC/SWB/ME 24 July 1980 (A/12).

[11] See S. Chubin and C. Tripp, *Iran and Iraq at war* (London, 1988), pp. 89–90, 118–9.

[12] See, for instance, the special number of *al-Thawra* 6 January 1987, published to coincide with Army Day, its headline reading 'The army of Saddam Hussein is the army of great victory'.

[13] See Ben Anderson on the importance of timelessness/historical continuity in defining the bonds which constitute a feeling of national community, B. Anderson, *Imagined communities* (London, 1986), pp. 28–40. Saddam Hussein seemed to echo these concerns in his speech of 22 April 1987 to air force officers, when he said: 'This generation, to which we belong, will pass and a new generation will come after us, pursuing the same course, because this course . . .

was not intended to be for only ten, twenty or thirty years . . . all must remember that Iraq holds fast to this spirit and will continue to do so for hundreds of years to come', Saddam Hussein, *Al-muallafat al-kamila*, Part 15, 1986–87 (Baghdad, 1987–90), pp. 295–6.

[14]. The Arab Baath Socialist Party, Iraq *The central report of the ninth regional congress June 1982* tr. SARTEC, Lausanne, C.H. (Baghdad, January 1983), p. 40.

[15] Saddam Hussein, *op. cit.*, Part 15, 1986–87, p. 295.

[16] Saddam Hussein, *op. cit.*, Part 15, 1986–87, p. 359.

[17] BBC/SWB/ME 7 May 1987 (A/9). The war had come to be called 'Saddam's Qadisiya'. Qadisiya was the name of the battle in 636 A.D. when the Arab Islamic armies had defeated the armies of the Sassanian Empire, thus opening up Persia to conversion to Islam.

[18] O. Bengio, 'Iraq', in C. Legum, H. Shaked and D. Dishon, eds., *Middle East contemporary survey 1982–1983* (London, 1985), p. 624; Arab Baath Socialist Party, *The central report of the ninth regional congress*, pp. 245–283.

[19] The Shu'ubiya was a movement under the Abbasid Empire which was centred largely among that Empire's Persian-speaking subjects. It was mainly a literary and cultural movement which challenged the Arabs' claim to primacy within the Islamic dispensation and championed the cause of non-Arab, especially Persian, cultures.

[20] Saddam Hussein, *Religious political movements and those disguised with religion* [in English] (Baghdad, *1987), pp. 8, 14.*

[21] Faruq Umar, *Mabahith fi al-haraka al-Shu'ubiya (Baghdad, 1986), p. 161.*

[22] It was significant that the 'referenda' and demonstrations of support, organized particularly in 1982, were generally referred to as being evidence of the Iraqi people giving to Saddam Hussein the *baya*—the traditional Arab-Islamic oath of homage to the person of the ruler.

[23] *President Saddam Hussein addresses the cabinet on conflict with Iran*, tr. N.A. Mudhaffer (Baghdad, 1981), pp. 27, 28.

[24] Arab Baath Socialist Party, *The central report of the ninth regional congress*, pp. 39–40.

[25] See Saddam Hussein's speech at a conference to discuss legislation and the drafting of laws on 14 December 1987, Saddam Hussein, *Al-muallafat*, Part 16, 1987–88, pp. 299–301.

[26] *Al-Thawra* 23 August 1986 (5).

[27] *Al-Thawra* 23 August 1986 (4).

Iraq's Strategic Culture

Anthony H. Cordesman

from *Iraq and the War of Sanctions: Conventional Threats and Weapons of Mass Destruction*

There is a danger in generalizing about Iraq's "strategic culture." It is all too easy to confuse Saddam Hussein's ambitions and the ambitions of those around him with the views and ambitions of the Iraqi people. It is equally easy to forget that Saddam Hussein and his supporters are drawn from a relatively small mix of tribal and clan elites centered around Tikrit, and that they do not even represent the mainstream of Iraqi Sunni history and culture. At least 75–80% of the total population of Iraq is also Shi'ite and/or Kurdish, and Iraq is now a highly urbanized, educated nation.[1] As the fall of other dictatorships has shown, leaders are not peoples, and "strategic cultures" can change rapidly with the regime.

Nevertheless, Saddam Hussein and those around him currently are the Iraqi state, and Saddam's views currently are Iraq's "strategic culture." Saddam has few checks on his power. Although he supposedly was confirmed "president" for seven years by a stage-managed referendum on October 15, 1995, he is a self-appointed authoritarian leader with almost total personal control over the state. He is not only president, but prime minister, minister of defense, minister of finance, commander-in-chief, Secretary General of the Ba'ath Party, and Chairman of the Revolutionary Command Council. He controls the Ba'ath

Party Military Bureau, the Defense Council, and the National Security Council.

Saddam and his immediate supporters can exercise direct rule over every aspect of the Iraqi government and the Ba'ath Party. Saddam can rule by decree and exercise his power over every position in the Iraqi civil government, military forces, and security services. He personally approves every promotion in the Iraqi military forces of any field grade rank, and appoints every official down to the level of under-secretary. He can overrule any decision of the National Assembly, and the Revolutionary Command Council of the Ba'ath Party is totally under his control. He can bypass any aspect of Iraq's institutions by formally decreeing martial law or by taking private action in any way he chooses. He secures this rule through a web of overlapping intelligence and internal security services, many of which he controls directly through his youngest son, Qusay, and the Office of the Presidential Palace.

There is little point, therefore, in trying to assess Iraq's military intentions by looking at its public strategic doctrine, or the ideology of the Ba'ath Party. At least for today, Iraq's strategic doctrine is Saddam Hussein, as are its intentions. Iraq is bound only by the limits to Saddam Hussein's personal rule, and to his ability to use Iraq's military forces to further his ambitions.

The Impact of History

There is nothing historically inevitable about Iraq's present regime or its militarism. At the same time, much of its current "strategic culture" does not seem to be regime-specific, and the goals and character of its regime may not change radically with the departure of Saddam Hussein. Iraqis are a proud and often warlike people, and Iraq has been highly nationalistic ever since it emerged as a modern state. Iraqi politicians and officers charged that Iraq had been exploited and "cheated" out of just territorial claims long before Saddam came to power. They made claims to the territory of neighboring states, and exhibited desire to be the Arab leader of the Gulf. Several showed a desire for regional hegemony, and fear or resentment of Iran, Turkey, and the West.

Iraq's history has shaped the perceptions of its past leaders, and it is likely to affect the attitudes of its ruling elites long after Saddam is gone. Like other Arab nationalists, Iraq's Arab military and political figures felt that Britain and France betrayed the "Arab nation" following World War I. Iraq, however, had a more troubled genesis than that of many other Arab states. Britain's occupation of Turkish Mesopotamia in 1918 was followed by growing tension between Britain and the native Arab population, the killing of British officers, and a full-scale tribal revolt in June, 1920. This revolt lasted until 1921 and cost Britain 450 dead and over 1,500 wounded.[2]

The creation of Iraq as an independent state did little to ease these tensions. Britain acquired a mandate over Iraq in 1920, and the formal deposal of the Ottoman Sultan in November, 1922 did not create borders that suited the ambitions of either Iraqi nationalists or surrounding states. The resulting border settlements left Arab territories like Kuwait under British control, failed to deal with Iraqi and Arab concerns regarding Iraq's border with Iran and Turkey, limited Iraq's access to the Gulf, and failed to create the desired border with the area that became modern Saudi Arabia and Jordan.

Iraq did not begin to achieve true independence until Britain and Iraq signed a treaty ending the British mandate in 1929, and Iraq was not admitted to the League of Nations until 1932. The Hashemite monarchy that ruled between 1932 and 1958 was seen by some Iraqis as an alien elite of British origin, and came into conflict with the Iraqi military on a number of occasions. This led to five military coups d'etat, beginning in 1936, and a split between nationalists and pro-British Iraqis, which reached the crisis point in 1939. Britain invaded Iraq following a nationalist coup in 1941 and occupied the country until 1945.

Britain effectively dominated Iraqi politics until 1958, often causing the removal of hostile or nationalist Iraqi officials and military officers and exploiting Iraq's oil interests to serve British interests. During this period, Britain made sure that Iraq did not act on any of its major claims and grievances regarding its neighbors, and it pressured Iraq into joining the Baghdad Pact (which included Turkey, Pakistan, and Iran) in 1955. This led to significant clashes and anti-British riots in 1948, 1952, and 1956—all of which had a broader anti-Western character and all of which were suppressed by force.

The coup that overthrew and slaughtered Iraq's Hashemite rulers on July 14, 1958, placed a series of highly nationalist and authoritarian Iraqi leaders in power. The first was a military junta led by Abd al-Karim Qasim, which lasted from 1958 to 1963. The new Iraqi regime almost inevitably turned to Russia and China. It began a series of arms imports from Russia in 1959 that helped institutionalize a continuing arms race between Iraq and Iran. It supported radical political movements that threatened the ruling regimes of virtually all of its neighbors, and made new claims to Kuwait and part of Iran's border area. In fact, Qasim's failure to make good on his attempt to claim Kuwait in 1961 and Britain's successful deterrence of an Iraqi invasion was one of the major reasons for his eventual fall.

The Rise of the Ba'ath and Saddam Hussein

The Ba'ath Party coup that deposed Qasim on February 8, 1963, was an alliance of even more nationalist and pan-Arab officers and politicians. While the leaders of the coup were soon replaced in a new junta under Abd al-Salam Arif, which came to power in November, 1963, the end result was still a regime that was ideologically opposed to the West, a British-dominated Southern Gulf, and a pro-Western Iran, Turkey, and Saudi Arabia. The new regime also sustained the arms race between Iraq and Iran, and Iraq's support of anti-regime movements in neighboring states.

A new Ba'ath coup succeeded on July 17, 1968, that brought General Ahmad Hasan al-Bakr and a small Ba'ath elite to power. This elite ruled through a Revolutionary Command Council (RCC) of which Saddam Hussein became vice chairman. It also adopted policies toward the control of Iraq's oil resources, which led to a steady rise in oil revenues that allowed Iraq to exploit massive rises in oil prices that took place during 1973–1974.

Iraq stepped up its arms imports and military ties to the Soviet Union at precisely the time the United States made Iran the major "pillar" of its policy in the Gulf, and the Shah of Iran began to demonstrate his vaulting ambitions for regional hegemony. Reinforced by the rivalries of the Cold War, this led to a massive acceleration in the Iraqi-Iranian arms race. Further, during the early

1970s, the Shah responded by exploiting an uprising of Iraqi Kurds with the covert support of the CIA. This led to a proxy border war between Iran and Iraq that forced Iraq to concede to Iran partial control of the Shatt al-Arab, its main shipping channel to the Gulf. Iraq also had to make a number of other territorial concessions in its border area with Iran.

Saddam Hussein was the main negotiator of the Algiers Accord that ratified these agreements in 1975. He saw both the extent of the CIA support of the Kurds before the accord, and the way in which the CIA suddenly abandoned them at the Shah's direction within days of its signing. While Saddam's character and ambitions are unique, they must be kept in a broader context. The man who formally shoved General Ahmad Hasan al-Bakr aside on July 16, 1979—and then launched the Iran-Iraq War in September, 1980—came to power as part of an Iraqi ruling elite that has fears and ambitions which are not the product of one man or one party, and which are likely to shape the attitudes of many Iraqi political and military figures long after Saddam and his immediate coterie are gone.

The Iran-Iraq War

Saddam Hussein tacitly supported the Iranian revolution and attempted to reach a modus vivendi with Khomeini, once Khomeini returned to Iran and became the leader of the revolution. Khomeini rejected Saddam's overtures, however, and called for the overthrow of the secular regime in Iraq. He also sent religious "messengers" to the Shi'ites of Iraq, who attempted to provoke an Islamic revolution. During 1980, Iran and Iraq engaged in a steadily escalating series of border clashes and military incidents.

Saddam may have felt threatened by Khomeini and the Iranian revolution, but he also attempted to exploit Iran's apparent military weakness. Iran's military forces underwent a series of purges and upheavals. The new revolutionary government began a series of civil struggles with opposition movements like the People's Mujahideen and hostile ethnic groups like the Kurds. The US embassy hostage crisis cut Iran off from Western arms and military support, and further tensions emerged between the regular Iranian military and new revolutionary militias.

Saddam began by rejecting the Algiers Accord, and then invaded Iran on September 22, 1980. He sent his forces into the oil-rich areas of southwestern Iran, and claimed that this was in support of an Arab uprising. During the time Iraqi forces advanced into Iran, Saddam attempted to claim that much of Iran's richest oil reserves were part of an "Arabastan" that should either be a separate country or part of Iraq.

Saddam's "victory," however, was only the prelude to eight years of war. Iraq could not sustain its advance into Iran, no meaningful popular Iranian support existed for Iraq, and there was no Iranian Arab uprising in what had become a largely ethnic Persian region. Iraq's forces had little capability for urban warfare, failed to seize key strategic objectives like Dezful when they were vulnerable, and then encountered growing popular Iranian resistance. Within a few months, Iraq's slow-moving and road-bound forces were being defeated piecemeal by a steadily growing mass of Iranian Revolutionary Guards, while Iran's regular army deployed and often defeated Iraqi forces.

Between 1981 and 1982, Iran drove Iraq out of virtually all of Iran's territory and began to advance into Iraq. Iraq was forced to use virtually all of its capital reserves to pay for the war and the massive arms imports it needed to compensate for its military incompetence. By 1982, Iranian forces had advanced within 70 kilometers of Basra, and had begun to actively threaten Iraq's control over its Shi'ite south. Iran also had largely defeated its own Kurds, and was supported by key factions of the Iraqi Kurds in their revolt against Saddam. Iran started another front in Iraq's northern border area, and built up its forces in areas that could threaten Baghdad.

Iran retained the military initiative from 1982 to early 1988. However, a war of attrition developed in which Iran relied on revolutionary fervor and human wave attacks, and Iraq relied on a massive superiority in firepower and armored mobility. Iran often scored major initial gains and breakthroughs against Iraqi forces, but lacked the force cohesion and mobility to exploit them. Iraq then concentrated its defenses and inflicted massive casualties on Iran's advancing forces.

Iraq survived near bankruptcy and the loss of most of its oil-export capabilities because of massive aid and loans from Kuwait and Saudi Arabia, and large transfers of modern arms from Europe and the Soviet Union. Iraq made up for its often lackluster military performance with money and weapons, while Iran attempted to improve its methods of attack, exploit surprise, infiltration, night warfare, and attacks through mountain and marsh areas where Iraq could not bring its superiority in arms to bear.

By late 1987, Iran appeared to be winning. It had managed to seize the Faw (Fao) Peninsula in spite of massive Iraqi counter-attacks. It threatened Basra, and Iranian forces had begun to make steady advances in Iraq's northern border areas. Iran was still advancing into Iraq as late as March 15, 1988, when it fought the battle of Halabjah, triggering Iraq's first massive use of poison gas against Iraqi civilians.

Iraq experienced growing difficulties in getting further aid and loans from Kuwait and Saudi Arabia during 1987, and in getting support from other Arab states. **The Iran-Contra** scandal had cast great uncertainty on the reliability of the support it was getting from the United States, and Iraq had steadily increasing problems in getting French and Russian financing for more arms orders, although deliveries from past orders continued to pour in.

Iran, however, also faced major problems. It had never really succeeded in exploiting its potential advantage in manpower and had begun to experience major recruiting problems. Iranian morale and fervor had faded as Iranian casualties increased. The divisions between Iran's regular and revolutionary forces further undercut Iran's military effectiveness, and Iran had major problems obtaining any resupply for its Western arms and was forced to rely on relatively low-grade Chinese and North Korean weapons.

Several factors decisively tipped the balance during the spring of 1988. Iraq's military capabilities improved more quickly than those of Iran's, partly because Iran's forces were affected by the political divisions within Iran and partly because Saddam Hussein was forced to give his best commanders greater independence and initiative in order to survive. Iraq had built up an advantage in air and long-range missile power that allowed it to strike at Iran's cities and to further undercut morale.

Beginning in 1984, Iraq had slowly developed the capability to conduct massive chemical warfare attacks. By 1987, its growing stockpile of weapons, its wide variety of delivery systems, and improved planning of how to make joint use of its chemical forces and conventional operations resulted in large-scale chemical attacks that were highly effective by regional standards. While these attacks did not produce massive numbers of death, they reached a scale by 1987 where they inflicted many casualties, paralyzed Iranian offensive action, disrupted Iranian rear areas, and steadily undercut Iranian morale. Iraq had decisively "out-proliferated" Iran.

Iraq had slowly developed the capability to effectively attack Iran's oil export facilities in the Gulf and tankers moving to key Iranian loading facilities, such as Kharg Island. Iran had responded by threatening all tanker traffic through the Gulf, especially shipments from Kuwait. It sought both to force other nations to put pressure on Iraq to end its attacks on Iran, and to intimidate Kuwait and Saudi Arabia into reducing their support for Iraq. The end result was the "re-flagging" of Kuwaiti tankers with US flags and US escorts of the reflagged tankers. This led to Iranian missile and mine attacks on Kuwaiti and US ships, and a "tanker war" between Iran and the US Navy. The end result was a decisive defeat of the Iranian navy and further reductions in Iran's oil revenues.

Seven years of war had taught the Iraqi army a great deal. It developed a cadre of more competent regular divisions. Iraq's defeats in 1986 led to a rapid expansion of Iraq's elite Republican Guard and forced Saddam to give his corps and divisions commanders far more independence of action. Many of these Iraqi forces regrouped and retrained during late 1987 and early 1988, and Iraq created carefully rehearsed plans to liberate Faw and drive Iran away from Basra.

These Iraqi forces spearheaded a massive Iraqi attack on Iran's positions in southern Iraq in the spring of 1988, and achieved strategic surprise. Iran did not believe Iraq could attack so effectively, and it was unprepared for the scale of chemical warfare that took place. Iran's leaders failed to realize how fragile Iranian morale had become, and they were unprepared for the sudden collapse of their forces.

Iran was decisively defeated during May–July, 1988. Iraq advanced deep into Iran's border area, Iran suffered massive new casualties, and Iran's land forces lost nearly half of their equipment. Khomeini announced the "poison pill" of his acceptance of UN resolutions calling for a cease-fire on July 18, 1988, and " a cease-fire came into effect in August. Saddam had won the Iran-Iraq War to the point that he had forced Iran to accept a cease-fire, although he had no real gains to show for eight years of war, had bankrupted Iraq, and had nearly $70–80 billion worth of debt to his neighbors and the West. He had, however, emerged from the Iran-Iraq War with a large and well-equipped military, one which was the most effective and experienced force in the Gulf region.

Iraq's "Strategic Culture" After the Iran-Iraq War

The end of the Iran-Iraq War did not change Iraqi perceptions of its neighbors and the West. While Arab and outside aid was crucial to Iraq's survival and eventual victory during the period between 1982 and 1988, many Iraqis saw this as an opportunistic exploitation of Iraq. Outside arms sales had to be paid for on terms that scarcely encouraged gratitude, and France was the only supplier that backed its sales with useful tactical advice and support.

Saddam and his coterie saw Kuwait's and Saudi Arabia's refusal to forgive its debts and enhance Iraq's oil revenues as ungrateful and as part of a US-led effort to weaken Iraq. The Ba'ath interpreted the growing ties between the United States and the Southern Gulf states that followed the "Tanker War" as part of an effort to encircle Iraq, and the decline of Soviet power as a further threat to its interests. It was this set of conspiracy theories, as well as greed and ambition, that led to Iraq's invasion of Kuwait in August, 1990.

Many Iraqis had come to feel that the United States was deliberately prolonging the Iran-Iraq War to weaken both countries. The Iran-Contra deal reinforced Iraq's distrust of the United States, while occasional Russian tilts towards Iran scarcely led to a solid Iraqi-Russian friendship. Syria's and Libya's hostility to Iraq caused new sources of distrust, and many Iraqis felt that other Arab states should have provided military forces.

Iraq's "Strategic Culture" Since the Gulf War

The aftermath of the Gulf War has scarcely improved this climate. For nearly a half-decade, the "war of sanctions" has kept Iraq under a mix of sanctions, inspection regimes, and export and import controls that have isolated it politically and crippled its economy. During this time, Iraq has been deprived of overt access to arms imports and the technology it needs to proliferate. Iraq's neighbors, including Iran, have been able to continue their efforts to proliferate and to build up their conventional forces, as well as to develop their economies.

Kuwait remains independent, but Iraq has been forced to transfer key territory near its small coastline on the Gulf to Kuwait. Iraq has also been forced to allow UNSCOM and the International Atomic Energy Agency (IAEA) to supervise the destruction of most of its weapons of mass destruction and its ability to produce them, to allow Coalition forces to enforce military restrictions and "no fly zones," and to allow Coalition forces to create an independent Kurdish enclave in Iraq.

During this period, Saddam Hussein has repeatedly shown that he has three major priorities: his own survival; the rebuilding of his conventional military forces; and the preservation of his capability to manufacture and deploy weapons of mass destruction. From the first days of the cease-fire to the present, he has systematically attempted to violate the terms of the cease-fire. He has fought and won a brutal civil war against his Shi'ite opposition in the south, and has kept up constant pressure on the Kurdish enclave in the north. He had mobilized and deployed his army towards Kuwait. He has constantly challenged UNSCOM's efforts to destroy his weapons of mass destruction.

There has never been a three-month period since the cease-fire in early 1991 in which Saddam Hussein has not provoked a new confrontation with the UN, his neighbors, or the West. He has systematically impoverished his people and mortgaged their hopes for future economic development by concentrating Iraq's scarce resources on rebuilding his military forces. He has refused economic aid and relief from limits on Iraq's capability to export oil in an effort to break out of sanctions. He has made constant efforts to divide the Arab world, and he has courted key nations like France and Russia with oil deals and promises of future economic concessions. To all practical purposes, he has turned his defeat and the cease-fire into an extension of war by other means.

The sanctions crisis that Saddam Hussein provoked since the fall of 1997 is simply another series of steps in what has become a near-ritual aspect of Iraqi policy. Every fall since the Gulf War has seen some new challenge to the UN. At the same time, it is clear that Iraq is intensifying its efforts to exploit "sanctions fatigue" and that it has found that it can use UNSCOM as a tool to divide the Security Council. Iraq is increasingly coupling its efforts to rebuild its military forces with propaganda that exploits the hardships of the Iraqi people, the near-collapse of the Arab-Israeli peace process, and the concern Arab nations feel about Iraq's sovereignty and territorial integrity, and the fear that many Southern Gulf states still have of Iran. The individual battles in the "war of sanctions" have often focused on military and security issues, but the strategic goals behind the war are much broader and have clear links to Iraq's "strategic culture."

This mix of history and current strategic priorities helps explain why Saddam Hussein has continued to commit Iraq to new military confrontations with the US-led Coalition. It explains why Iraq has been willing to forgo nearly $120 billion in oil export revenues, and why Iraq's present leaders will continue to use every possible means to break out of UN-sanctioned import restrictions. At least for the foreseeable future, Iraq's official policy towards the rebuilding of its conventional forces and proliferation will continue to be a mix of denial and lies, with occasional bluster and indirect threats. These lies will be told to Iraq's people, media, intellectuals, and military officers, as well as to other nations.

Iraq will make every effort to conceal its true plans and the full nature of its military efforts, and only Saddam Hussein and a few trusted supporters will have any overview of Iraq's military progress and capabilities. Furthermore,' Iraq's plans and polices will remain opportunistic and unstable. Iraq's leaders will be unable to predict the exact areas where they will be successful in evading or vitiating UN sanctions and controls. As a result, their strategy, military doctrine, and force development efforts can be expected to evolve on a target-of-opportunity basis. The only thing that seems certain is that Iraq will make a continuing effort to obtain advanced conventional arms and to proliferate in every way that Iraq can conceal.

After Saddam

It is far from certain that Iraq's current "strategic culture" is dependent on whether Saddam and his immediate supporters remain in power. There is little democratic and moderate opposition to Saddam Hussein. The most likely alternative to Saddam, following a "one-bullet election," is another narrowly based authoritarian Sunni elite, and if any "moderates" do seem to rise to power in the immediate aftermath of Saddam's fall, they may end as short-lived figureheads than remain real leaders.

A "quieter Saddam" who patiently waits to acquire significant nuclear or highly lethal biological warfare capabilities and then exploits such capabilities in a more cautious and calculating manner might prove to be just as serious a threat as Saddam the instigator. Few Iraqi regimes of any character are likely to ignore the potential threat of proliferation by Iran, Israel, and Syria. Any civil turmoil or conflict following Saddam's departure might also lead to the use of surviving or covert capabilities against the Iraqi population, and might create new forms of extremism. Regimes may then emerge that are openly revanchist in character, and/or face future financial crises that lead them into new forms of military risk taking.

Nevertheless, any change in Iraq's leadership is likely to be for the better, and such a change might create a very different Iraq. Many, if not most, ordinary Iraqis do not share Saddam's ambitions, near-xenophobia, and paranoia. Figures like Kemal Ataturk and Anwar Sadat have shown that brilliant, moderate leaders can suddenly emerge and change the strategic culture of their nations, and an Iraqi leader with vision might well conclude that focusing on rebuilding Iraq's oil wealth, economic development, and the unification of Iraq's diverse ethnic elements would offer a far greater place in history than continuing with expensive military build-ups and the search for regional hegemony.

Little about the Gulf War or the sanctions that have followed seems likely to reduce Iraqi nationalism or prevent the addition of a strong element of revanchism to Iraq's "strategic culture." Iraqis have little reason to admire the West or Iraq's neighbors. They have obvious reason to resent Britain, Kuwait, Saudi Arabia, and the United States, and no reason to trust Syria, Iran, Jordan, and Turkey.

Iraqis must be aware that virtually all of Iraq's present "friends" and "supporters" are opportunists seeking future trade and investment opportunities and have no real sympathy for the regime. Further, no Iraqi can ignore the fact that the average Iraqi per capita income was well under one-tenth of its level at the time the Iran-Iraq War began, and that Iraq faces a massive potential reparations and debt repayment bill once sanctions are lifted. There are striking parallels between the cost of peace to Iraq and the cost to Weimar Germany, and the economic consequences of the peace could easily be very similar.

Yet any Iraqi ruling elite must deal with the region in which it lives. Iraq's geography will always present problems in terms of access to the Gulf and dealing with powerful neighbors. Regardless of how friendly a given regime is today, there will always be uncertainties regarding tomorrow. Iraq must deal with other proliferators like Iran and Israel, which remain very real military threats.

Iraq's internal divisions will also present continuing problems. The issue of Kurdish nationalism is unlikely to disappear, and tensions between the Sunni and Shi'ite are unlikely to end—creating inevitable complications in terms of relations with Iran. There will always be tension with fellow exporters, and with importers, over Iraq's need to maximize its oil export revenues. Even a relatively defensive Iraqi regime is likely to feel compelled to go on acquiring weapons of mass destruction to counterbalance the capabilities of Iran and Israel and to limit American power projection options. Any Iraqi regime that survives over time is likely to be highly centralized, relatively ruthless, and to see its neighbors and the West as a potential threat.

Notes

[1] Estimates differ according to source, and other sources are quoted later in this report. This estimate is taken from the International Institute for Strategic

Studies (IISS), *Military Balance, 1997–1998*, London, Oxford Press, 1997, p. 127.

[2] See David Fromkin, *A Peace to End All Peace,* New York, Henry Holt, 1989, especially pp. 449–462.

Arms Sales to Iraq

Stephen Shalom

Z magazine

The war between Iran and Iraq was one of the great human tragedies of recent Middle Eastern history. Perhaps as many as a million people died,[1] many more were wounded, and millions were made refugees. The resources wasted on the war exceeded what the entire Third World spent on public health in a decade.

The war began on September 22, 1980, when Iraqi troops launched a full-scale invasion of Iran. Prior to this date there had been subversion by each country inside the other and also major border clashes. Iraq hoped for a lightning victory against an internationally isolated neighbor in the throes of revolutionary upheaval. But despite Iraq's initial successes, the Iranians rallied and, using their much larger population, were able by mid-1982 to push the invaders out. In June 1982, the Iranians went over to the offensive, but Iraq, with a significant advantage in heavy weaponry, was able to prevent a decisive Iranian breakthrough. The guns finally fell silent on August 20, 1988.

Primary responsibility for the eight long years of bloodletting must rest with the governments of the two countries—the ruthless military regime of Saddam Hussein in Iraq and the ruthless clerical regime of the Ayatollah Khomeini in Iran. Khomeini was said by some to have a "martyr complex," though, as U.S. Secretary of State Cyrus Vance wryly observed, people with martyr complexes rarely live to be as old as Khomeini. Whatever his complexes, Khomeini had no qualms about sending his followers, including young boys, off to their deaths for his greater glory. This callous disregard for human life was no less characteristic of Saddam Hussein. And, for that matter, it was also no less characteristic of much of the world community, which not only couldn't be bothered by a few hundred thousand Third World corpses, but tried to profit from the conflict.

France became the major source of Iraq's high-tech weaponry, in no small part to protect its financial stake in that country.[2] The Soviet Union was Iraq's largest weapon's supplier, while jockeying for influence in both capitals. Israel provided arms to Iran, hoping to bleed the combatants by prolonging the war. And at least ten nations sold arms to both of the warring sides.[3]

The list of countries engaging in despicable behavior, however, would be incomplete without the United States. The U.S. objective was not profits from the arms trade, but the much more significant aim of controlling to the greatest extent possible the region's oil resources. Before turning to U.S. policy during the Iran-Iraq war, it will be useful to recall some of the history of the U.S. and oil.

Some Crude History

Much of the world's proven oil reserves are located in the limited area of the Persian Gulf (called by Arab nations the "Arabian Gulf," and by those who try to keep their gazetteers politically neutral, simply "the Gulf").

Less than four percent of U.S. oil consumption comes from the Gulf, but, according to the official argument, Western Europe and Japan are extremely dependent on Gulf oil and hence if the region fell into the hands of a hostile power, U.S. allies could be brought to their knees, and U.S. security would be fundamentally and irreparably compromised. If one examines the history of U.S. policy in the Gulf, however, protecting the oil interests of Western Europe and Japan never seemed to be one of Washington's foremost goals.

As far back as the 1920s, the State Department sought to force Great Britain to give U.S. companies a share of the lucrative Middle Eastern oil concessions. The U.S. Ambassador in London—who happened to be Andrew Mellon, the head of the Gulf Oil Corporation (named for the Mexican, not the Persian/ Arabian, Gulf)—was instructed to press the British to give Gulf Oil a stake in the Middle East.[4] At the end of World War II, when the immense petroleum deposits in Saudi Arabia became known, Secretary of the Navy James Forrestal told Secretary of State Byrnes, "I don't care which American company or companies develop the Arabian reserves, but I think most emphatically that it should be *American*."[5] And it wasn't the Russians that Forrestal was worried about. The main competition was between the United States and Britain for control of the area's oil.[6]

In 1928, Standard Oil of New Jersey and Mobil had joined British and French oil interests in signing the "Red Line Agreement," under which each pledged not to develop Middle Eastern oil without the participation of the others. Nevertheless, after World War II these two U.S. firms (together with Texaco and Standard Oil of California) grabbed the Saudi concessions for themselves, freezing out the British and French. When the latter sued on the grounds that the Red Line Agreement had been violated, Mobil and Jersey told the court that the agreement was null and void because it was monopolistic.[7]

In the early 1950s, oil was used as a political weapon for the first time—*by* the United States and Britain and *against* Iran. Iran had nationalized its British-owned oil company which had refused to share its astronomical profits with the host government. In response, Washington and London organized a boycott of Iranian oil which brought Iran's economy to the brink of collapse. The CIA then instigated a coup, entrenching the Shah in power and effectively un-nationalizing the oil company, with U.S. firms getting 40 percent of the formerly 100 percent British-owned company. This was, in the view of the *New York Times*, an "object lesson in the heavy cost that must be paid" when an oil-rich Third World nation "goes berserk with fanatical nationalism."[8]

In 1956 the oil weapon was used again, this time by the United States against Britain and France. After the latter two nations along with Israel invaded Egypt, Washington made clear that U.S. oil would not be sent to Western Europe until Britain and France agreed to a rapid withdrawal schedule.[9] The U.S. was not adverse to overthrowing Nasser—"Had they done it quickly, we would have accepted it," Eisenhower said later[10]—but the clumsy Anglo-French military operation threatened U.S. interests in the region.

In October 1969 the Shah of Iran asked the U.S. to purchase more Iranian oil as a way to boost his revenues. But the Shah's request was rejected because, as an assistant to then President Nixon explained, "a substantial portion of the profits from these purchases would go to non-American companies if Iranian oil were sought," while if Saudi oil were purchased, the U.S. share would be larger.[11]

By the end of the sixties the international oil market was far different from what it had been two decades earlier. Oil supplies were tight, the number of oil firms had grown, and the producing countries, joined together in the Organization of Petroleum Exporting Countries, were seeking to improve their financial position.

Crucial talks on oil prices began in 1970 between U.S. companies and the government of Libya. Significantly, Washington did not weigh in on the side of the companies, and in fact, the companies themselves did not put up much resistance to the price increases. For the oil companies, higher prices would be beneficial, making profitable their growing investments in the developed nations (for example, in Alaska and the North Sea).[12] Any higher prices could be passed on to consumers—and, indeed, in 1972-73 the companies raised their prices to a greater extent than crude costs alone warranted.[13]

In 1972, the Nixon administration was advocating higher oil prices.[14] According to a study by V. H. Oppenheim, based on interviews with U.S. officials, "The weight of the evidence suggests that the principal consideration behind the indulgent U.S. government attitude toward higher oil prices was the belief that higher prices would produce economic benefits for the United States vis-a-vis its industrial competitors, Western Europe and Japan, and the key Middle Eastern states, Saudi Arabia and Iran."[15] And Henry Kissinger has confirmed that this was U.S. Government thinking: "The rise in the price of energy would affect primarily Europe and Japan and probably improve America's competitive position."[16]

Amid growing warnings about a possible oil embargo, the industrialized Western countries held meetings to decide their response. Showing its concern for its allies, the United States proposed that resources be shared, but on the basis of each country's sea-borne imports, rather than on the basis of total energy requirements. Since the U.S. was much less dependent on imports than other countries, this formula meant that in the event of an embargo U.S. energy supplies would be cut far less than those of its "allies."[17]

After the October 1973 Middle East war broke out, but before the Arab embargo, U.S. oil company officials wrote to Nixon, warning that the "whole position of the United States in the Middle East is on the way to being seriously impaired, with Japanese, European, and perhaps Russian interests largely supplanting United States presence in the area, to the detriment of both our economy and our security."[18] Note that the Russian threat was considered only a possibility, the allied threat a certainty.

In late 1973 and on into 1974, the Arab oil producers cut their production and imposed an embargo against the United States and the Netherlands for their pro-Israeli position. The public has memories of long lines at the gas pump, rationing, and a crisis atmosphere. In fact, however, in Kissinger's words, "the Arab embargo was a symbolic gesture of limited practical impact."[19] The international oil companies, which totally monopolized petroleum distribution and marketing, pooled their oil, so the shortfall of Saudi supplies to the U.S. was made up from other sources. Overall, the oil companies spread out the production cutbacks so as to minimize suffering, and the country most supportive of Israel—the U.S.—suffered among the least. From January 1974 to March, oil consumption in the U.S. was only off by 5 percent, compared to 15 percent in France and West Germany.[20]

Even these figures, however, overstate the hardship, because in fact, *there was at no time a real shortage of petroleum on the European market.* Consumption simply responded to the increase in prices. . . . Between October, 1973, and April, 1974, the reserves of oil products in the countries of the European Community never descended below the 80-day equivalent of consumption; and in Italy the reserves in fact increased by 23 percent."[21] In Japan, there were about two million barrels of oil more than the government admitted, as the bureaucracy, the oil industry, and industrial oil users sought to exploit the crisis for their own advantage.[22]

In the aftermath of the embargo, U.S. allies tried to negotiate their own bilateral petroleum purchase deals with the producing nations without going through the major international oil companies. Washington opposed these efforts.[23] In short, the well-being of U.S. allies has never been the key consideration for U.S. policymakers.

Nor for that matter has the crucial concern been the well-being of the average American. One former Defense Department official has estimated that it cost U.S. taxpayers about $47 billion in 1985 alone for military expenditures related to the Gulf;[24] former Secretary of the Navy John Lehman put the annual figure at $40 billion.[25] What could be worth these staggering sums?

These expenditures have *not* been necessary for the survival of the West. In extremis, according to former CIA analyst Maj. Gen. Edward B. Atkeson, if all Gulf oil were cut off, the elimination of recreational driving (which in the U.S. accounts for 10% of total oil consumption) would reduce Western petroleum needs to a level easily replaceable from non-Gulf sources. Even in wartime, Atkeson concluded, Gulf oil is not essential to Western needs.[26] And in a protracted global conflict, one can be sure that oil fields would not last very long in the face of missile attacks.

The billions of dollars, however, are a good investment for the oil companies, given that they are not the ones who pay the tab. To be sure, the multinationals no longer directly own the vast majority of Gulf crude production. But they have special buy-back deals with the producers, whereby they purchase at bargain prices oil from the fields they formerly owned. For example, according to former Senator Frank Church, U.S. firms "have a 'sweetheart' arrangement with Saudi Arabia, notwithstanding the nominal nationalization of their properties. . . ."[27] Radical regimes want to sell oil as much as conservative ones do, but a change of government in any Gulf state might eliminate the privileged position of the oil companies.

The internal security of regimes like Saudi Arabia depends heavily on outside, particularly U.S., support. Many Saudis believe that in return their country has been overproducing oil to please the United States, to the detriment of their nation's long-term interests. Selling oil beyond the point at which the proceeds can be productively invested is economically irrational, particularly given the fact that oil in the ground appreciates in value.[28] More democratic or nationalistic governments in the Gulf may not be so willing to sacrifice their own interests. And such governments will also be less willing to accommodate a U.S. military presence or to serve as U.S. proxies for maintaining the regional status quo.

And thus for more than forty years, through many changed circumstances, there has been one constant of U.S. policy in the Gulf: support for the most conservative available local forces in order to keep radical and popular movements from coming to power, no matter what the human cost, no matter how great the necessary manipulation or intervention. The U.S. has not been invariably successful in achieving its objective: in 1979, it lost one of its major props with the overthrow of the Shah of Iran, who had policed the Gulf on Washington's behalf. But the basic pattern of U.S. policy has not changed, as is well illustrated by its policy toward the war between Iran and Iraq.

The Gulf War

The United States did not have diplomatic relations with either belligerent in 1980 and announced its neutrality in the conflict. One typically humanitarian State Department official explained in 1983: "we don't give a damn as long as the Iran-Iraq carnage does not affect our allies in the region or alter the balance of power."[29] In fact, however, the United States was not indifferent to the war, but saw a number of positive opportunities opened up by its prolongation.

The need for arms and money would make Baghdad more dependent on the conservative Gulf states and Egypt, thereby moderating Iraq's policies and helping to repair ties between Cairo and the other Arab states. The war would make Iran—whose weapons had all been U.S.-supplied in the past—desperate to obtain U.S. equipment and spare parts. The exigencies of war might make both nations more willing to restore their relations with Washington. Alternatively, the dislocations of war might give the U.S. greater ability to carry out covert operations in Iran or Iraq. And turmoil in the Gulf might make other states in the area more susceptible to U.S. pressure for military cooperation.

When the war first broke out, the Soviet Union turned back its arms ships en route to Iraq, and for the next year and a half, while Iraq was on the offensive, Moscow did not provide weapons to Baghdad.[30] In March 1981, the Iraqi Communist Party, repressed by Saddam Hussein, beamed broadcasts from the Soviet Union calling for an end to the war and the withdrawal of Iraqi troops.[31] That same month U.S. Secretary of State Alexander Haig told the Senate Foreign Relations Committee that he saw the possibility of improved ties with Baghdad and approvingly noted that Iraq was concerned by "the behavior of Soviet imperialism in the Middle Eastern area." The U.S. then approved the sale to Iraq of five Boeing jetliners, and sent a deputy assistant secretary of state to Baghdad for talks.[32] The U.S. removed Iraq from its notoriously selective list of nations supporting international terrorism[33] (despite the fact that terrorist Abu Nidal was based in the country)[34] and Washington extended a $400 million credit guarantee for U.S. exports to Iraq.[35] In November 1984, the U.S. and Iraq restored diplomatic relations, which had been ruptured in 1967.[36]

The Soviet Threat and the Rapid Deployment Force

At the same time that the war was furthering the U.S. position in Iraq, it was also extending U.S. military relations with the other Arab Gulf states.

Washington typically justified its desire for military ties in the Gulf and the development of forces for use there by warning of the Soviet threat. In January 1980, President Carter proclaimed the "Carter Doctrine," declaring that the U.S. was willing to use military force if necessary to prevent "an outside power" from conquering the Gulf. As Michael Klare has noted, however, the real U.S. concern was revealed five days later when Secretary of Defense Harold Brown released his military posture statement. Brown indicated that the greatest threat was not Soviet expansionism but uncontrolled turbulence in the third world. "In a world of disputes and violence, we cannot afford to go abroad unarmed," he warned. "The particular manner in which our economy has expanded means that we have come to depend to no small degree on imports, exports and the earnings from overseas investments for our material well-being." Specifically, Brown identified the "protection of the oil flow from the Middle East" as "clearly part of our vital interest," in defense of which "we'll take any action that's appropriate, including the use of military force."[37]

Brown did not explicitly state that the United States would intervene militarily in response to internal threats, like revolution, but after he left office he explained what could be said openly and what could not: "One sensitive issue is whether the United States should plan to protect the oil fields against internal or regional threats. Any explicit commitment of this sort is more likely to upset and anger the oil suppliers than to reassure them."[38]

Gulf touchiness on explicit U.S. commitments to "defend" the oil fields had two sources. First, the sheikdoms do not like to be seen as dependent on U.S. force against their own populations. And, second, the Gulf states were made nervous by the frequent talk in the United States about taking over the oil fields in the event of another embargo.[39] There was even a Congressional study of the feasibility of seizing the oil fields; and though the study concluded that such an operation would be unlikely to succeed militarily, the mere fact that this was considered a fit subject for analysis did not instill confidence in Gulf capitals.[40]

Given this sensitivity, Brown advised that the United States should prepare plans and capabilities for intervention—against coups and other threats—but should avoid an explicitly declared policy to this effect.[41]

The Carter administration began the formation of a Rapid Deployment Force (RDF) to project U.S. military power into the Gulf region. Originally proposed in 1977, the planning did not make much progress until after the Soviet invasion of Afghanistan. The fundamental purpose of the RDF was always, in the words of Carter's National Security Adviser, "helping a friendly government under a subversive attack";[42] nevertheless, to justify the RDF the Soviet threat had to be magnified. Accordingly, Carter spoke in apocalyptic terms about the strategic significance of the invasion of Afghanistan, even though U.S. military experts were aware that a "thrust through Afghanistan would be of marginal advantage to any Soviet movement through Iran or the Gulf."[43]

In 1980, the Army conducted a gaming exercise called "Gallant Knight" which assumed an all-out Soviet invasion of Iran. The Army concluded that they would need 325,000 troops to hold back the Soviet colossus. According to a former military affairs aide to Senator Sam Nunn, the Army deliberately chose this scenario to guarantee that immense forces would be required.[44] And though an RDF of this size might seem unnecessarily large for combating Third World troublemakers, the Pentagon noted that in the mid-1980s Third World armies were no longer "barbarians with knives." The U.S. could no longer expect to "stabilize an area just by showing the flag."[45]

When Reagan became president, he added what became known as the "Reagan Codicil" to the "Carter Doctrine," declaring at a press conference that "we will not permit" Saudi Arabia "to be an Iran."[46] The codicil did not represent new policy, but merely made explicit what had always been policy.

Under Reagan, the CIA secretly concluded that the possibility of a Soviet invasion of Iran was "remote"[47]—not surprisingly, given that the Red Army was hardly having an easy time with the Afghanis, who had half the population and were much less well equipped.[48] The remoteness of the Soviet threat, however, did not slow down the build up of the RDF.

In 1982 the Pentagon's secret *Defense Guidance* document stated that the Soviet Union might extend its forces into the Gulf area "by means other than outright invasion." It continued: "Whatever the circumstances, we should be prepared to introduce American forces directly into the region should it appear that the security of access to Persian Gulf oil is threatened. . . ."[49] In the Senate, many argued that there was too much emphasis on countering the USSR, whereas the focus should be on "deterring and, if necessary, fighting regional wars or leftist or nationalist insurgencies that threatened U.S. and allied access to the region's oil supplies."[50]

The official line was that the RDF would be deployed when a government invited it in to repel a Soviet attack. But, as a Library of Congress study noted, this view was belied by "guidance documents which say that the forces must be capable of coercive entry without waiting for an invitation."[51] Senators Tower and Cohen stated that they favored greater emphasis on marines who could shoot their way ashore against military opposition. The administration pointed out that RDF plans all along had included a "forcible entry" option, relying on Marines. "We must be able to open our own doors," the Marine Commandant testified in March 1982.[52] In short, these folks are not just "barbarians with knives."

To support the RDF, the Pentagon needed a network of bases, and not just in the Middle East, but worldwide. "To all intents and purposes," a former senior Defense Department official observed, "Gulf waters' now extend from the Straits of Malacca to the South Atlantic."[53] Nevertheless, bases nearer the Gulf had a special importance, and Pentagon planners urged "as substantial a land presence in the [54] as can be managed."[55] The Gulf states were reluctant to have too overt a relationship with the United States, but the Iran-Iraq war served to overcome some of this reluctance. In 1985, as Iranian advances seemed ominous, the *New York Times* reported that Oman "has become a base for Western intelligence operations, military maneuvers and logistical preparations for any defense of the oil-producing Persian Gulf."[56] A few months later, a secret U.S. report was leaked indicating that Saudi Arabia had agreed to allow the United States to use bases in its territory in a crisis.[57] The doors to U.S. influence were opening wider.

Two Tracks to Teheran

U.S. policy with respect to Iran was more complicated, because it followed two tracks at once. On the one hand, U.S. officials saw "a great potential" for a covert program to undermine the government in Teheran;[58] on the other hand, Washington tried to build ties to that same government.

U.S. actions in pursuit of the first track showed quite clearly that Washington's opposition to the Khomeini regime had nothing to do with its lack of democracy, for the groups that the U.S. backed against Khomeini were often supporters of the previous dictator, the Shah.

Starting in 1982 the CIA provided $100,000 a month to a group in Paris called the Front for the Liberation of Iran, headed by Ali Amini, who had presided over the reversion of Iranian oil to foreign control after the CIA-backed coup in 1953.[59] The U.S. also provided support to two Iranian paramilitary groups based in Turkey, one of them headed by General Bahram

Aryana, the Shah's army chief, who had close ties to Shahpur Bakhtiar, the Shah's last prime minister.[60]

In 1980, under the Carter administration, the United States began clandestine radio broadcasts into Iran from Egypt, at a cost of some $20-30,000 per month. The broadcasts called for Khomeini's overthrow and urged support for Bakhtiar.[61] Other broadcasts contained anti-Soviet material.[62] In 1986, the CIA pirated Iran's national television network frequency to transmit an eleven minute address by the Shah's son over Iranian TV. "I will return," Reza Pahlavi vowed.[63]

Simultaneous with these activities, the U.S. pursued its second track: trying to establish ties with the Iranian mullahs based on the interest they shared with Washington in combating the left. The U.S. purpose, Reagan announced in November 1986, after the Iran-Contra scandal blew open, was "to find an avenue to get Iran back where it once was and that is in the family of democratic nations"—a good trick, as Mansour Farhang has commented, since pre-1979 Iran was hardly democratic.[64]

According to the Tower Commission, "In 1983, the United States helped bring to the attention of Teheran the threat inherent in the extensive infiltration of the government by the communist Tudeh Party and Soviet or pro-Soviet cadres in the country. Using this information, the Khomeini government took measures, including mass executions, that virtually eliminated the pro-Soviet infrastructure in Iran."[65] These massacres elicited the expected level of concern from U.S. officials. "The leftists there seem to be getting their heads cut off," remarked an undersecretary of state from the Carter administration.[66] The U.S. also passed to the Iranians "real and deceptive intelligence" about the Soviet threat on Iran's borders.[67]

Reagan administration officials claimed that their efforts in Iran were designed to build ties to moderates. In fact, however, they were aware that they were dealing with the clerical fanatics. Oliver North told Robert McFarlane and John Poindexter in December 1985 that the anti-tank weapons the U.S. was secretly providing to Iran would probably go to the Revolutionary Guards, the shock troops of the mullahs.[68] In August 1986, the special assistant to the

Israeli prime minister briefed George "Out-of-the-Loop" Bush, telling him, "we are dealing with the most radical elements. . . . This is good because we've learned that they can deliver and the moderates can't."[69]

The idea of building a strategic connection to Iran had wide support in the U.S. government, though the policy of using arms transfers to achieve it did not. The Tower Commission, for example, stated that while it disagrees with the arms transfers, "a strategic opening to Iran may have been in the national interest."[70] And it should be made clear that a strategic opening does not simply mean beginning a dialogue with or acting civilly toward a former adversary; rather, it was part of a policy to prevent any comparable access for the Soviet Union. Thus, a CIA position paper in 1985 noted that whichever superpower got to Iran first would be "in a strong position to work towards the exclusion of the other."[71] Another CIA official wanted to achieve "a securing of Iran" so that it would again "have a relationship with the U.S." and be "denied to the Soviets."[72] And McFarlane cabled to Poindexter after a secret meeting in Teheran in May 1986: "we are on the way to something that can become a truly strategic gain for us at the expense of the Soviets."[73]

Arms to the Ayatollah

The main tool by which U.S. policy makers sought to secure their position in Iran in 1985 and 1986 was secretly providing arms and intelligence information. As a proclaimed neutral in the Iran-Iraq war, the United States was not supposed to supply weapons to either side. Nevertheless, U.S. allies kept the combatants well-stocked.[74] Israel transferred vast quantities of U.S.-origin weapons to Iran;[75] to what extent U.S. permission for these shipments was obtained (as required by U.S. law) is not known, but surely the U.S. had enough leverage to prevent the transfers if it had wanted to.

In 1984, because of Iranian battlefield victories and the growing U.S.-Iraqi ties, Washington launched "Operation Staunch," an effort to dry up Iran's sources of arms by pressuring U.S. allies to stop supplying Teheran.[76] U.S. secret arms sales to Iran in 1985 and 1986 thus not only violated U.S. neutrality, but undercut as well what the U.S. was trying to get everyone else to do.

The cynical would note that Operation Staunch made the U.S. arms transfers to Iran that much more valuable.

When this arms dealing became known, the Reagan administration was faced with a major scandal on several counts. Proceeds from the arms sales had been diverted to the Nicaraguan contras in violation of the Boland Amendment. And though the administration's professed uncompromising stand on terrorism was always hypocritical, given its sponsorship of terrorism in Nicaragua and elsewhere, being caught trading "arms-for-hostages" was particularly embarrassing.

Now, in fact, this would not have been the first time the U.S. offered Teheran arms for hostages. In October 1980 the Carter administration had declared that spare parts for U.S. military equipment could be sold to Iran if the U.S. embassy hostages were released promptly.[77] There was even talk among U.S. officials about pre-positioning some spare parts in Germany, Pakistan, and Algeria so that the Iranians could get the equipment as soon as possible.[78] Republicans charged that Carter was trying to buy the hostages out in time for the election; there is some evidence that the Republicans in the meantime were engaged in an election maneuver of their own: negotiating with Iran to keep the hostages until after the election to ensure a Reagan victory.[79]

In any event, political influence not hostages was the Reagan administration's objective. Regardless of what was in the President's mind (as it were), the National Security Council was clear that the political agenda was key.[80]

Whatever the arguments for purchasing the freedom of hostages, trading weapons to obtain their release is another matter entirely, since one is exchanging for the lives of some hostages the lives of those who will be fired on by the weapons. And trading weapons for "a strategic opening" is more reprehensible still, particularly so when the weapons are going to the country whose army is on the offensive. Reagan claimed that the weapons were all defensive in nature,[81] but this is nonsense. Anti-tank missiles in the hands of an advancing army are offensive. And U.S. officials knew exactly what Iran wanted the weapons for: for example, as the Tower Commission noted, North and CIA officials discussed with their Iranian contacts "Iran's urgent need" for "both intelligence and weapons to be used in offensive operations against Iraq."[82]

The intelligence that the United States passed to the Iranians was a mixture of factual and bogus information. The CIA claimed that the false information was meant to discourage Iran's final offensive, by for example exaggerating Soviet troop movements on the northern border.[83] But if the U.S. simply wanted to discourage an Iranian attack, it could have done this more easily by telling Iran of Washington's contingency plans to use U.S. air power in the event of an Iranian breakthrough against Iraq.[84] The misinformation about the Soviet Union, however, had the added advantage of inciting Iranian hostility to Moscow and to the local communists.

U.S. intelligence did not deal only with the Soviet Union, but covered the Iraqi front as well. CIA deputy director John McMahon claimed that he warned Poindexter that such intelligence would give the Iranians "a definite edge," with potentially "cataclysmic results," and that he was able to persuade North to provide Iran with only a segment of the intelligence.[85] North, however, apparently gave critical data to Iran just before its crucial victory in the Fao Peninsula in February 1986.[86] It is unclear to what extent North was acting on his own here, but it is significant that despite McMahon's warnings, neither Poindexter nor CIA Director Casey reversed the plans to provide the Iranians with the full intelligence information.[87]

At the same time that the U.S. was giving Teheran weapons that one CIA analyst believed could affect the military balance[88] and passing on intelligence that the Tower Commission deemed of "potentially major significance,"[89] it was also providing Iraq with intelligence information, some misleading or incomplete.[90] In 1986, the CIA established a direct Washington-to-Baghdad link to provide the Iraqis with faster intelligence from U.S. satellites.[91] Simultaneously, Casey was urging Iraqi officials to carry out more attacks on Iran, especially on economic targets.[92] Asked what the logic was of aiding both sides in a bloody war, a former official replied, "You had to have been there."[93]

Washington's effort to enhance its position with both sides came apart at the end of 1986 when one faction in the Iranian government leaked the story of the

U.S. arms dealing. Now the Reagan administration was in the unenviable position of having alienated the Iranians and panicked all the Arabs who concluded that the U.S. valued Iran's friendship over theirs. To salvage the U.S. position with at least one side, Washington now had to tilt—and tilt heavily—toward Iraq.

The American Armada

The opportunity to demonstrate the tilt came soon. Kuwait had watched with growing nervousness Iran's battlefield successes, perhaps made possible by U.S. arms sales and intelligence information. Iran was now also attacking ships calling at Kuwaiti ports, and to protect itself Kuwait decided to try to draw in the United States. In September 1986 (before the scandal broke), it approached both Washington and Moscow and asked if they would be interested in reflagging some Kuwaiti vessels, that is, flying their own flags on Kuwaiti ships and then protecting these new additions to their merchant marine. The initial U.S. reaction was lackadaisical. But when the U.S. learned in March 1987 that the Soviet Union offered to reflag eleven tankers, it promptly offered to reflag the same eleven ships—which would both keep Soviet influence out of the Gulf and give the United States the opportunity to demonstrate its support for Iraq.[94]

The Kuwaitis accepted the U.S. offer, declining Moscow's, though chartering three Soviet vessels as a way to provide some balance between the U.S. and the USSR,[95] the Kuwaitis being less afraid of Soviet contamination than their American saviors were. Undersecretary of Political Affairs Michael H. Armacost explained in June 1987 that if the USSR were permitted a larger role in protecting Gulf oil, the Gulf states would be under great pressure to make additional facilities available to Moscow.[96] The U.S. view was that only one superpower was allowed to have facilities in the region, and that was the United States. Thus, when in December 1980 the Soviet Union proposed the neutralization of the Gulf, with no alliances, no bases, no intervention in the region, and no obstacles to free trade and the sea lanes,[97] Washington showed no interest. By August 1987, the U.S. had an aircraft carrier, a battleship, six cruisers, three destroyers, seven frigates, and numerous supporting naval vessels in or near the Gulf,[98] in what a Congressional study termed "the largest single naval armada deployed since the height of the Vietnam war."[99]

The Reagan administration claimed that the reflagging was merely intended to protect the flow of oil. It warned that "any significant disruption in gulf oil supply would cause world oil prices for all to skyrocket," grimly recalling how events in 1973-74 and 1978-79 demonstrated that "a small disruption—of less than 5%—can trigger a sharp escalation in oil prices."[100]

In fact, however, oil—and oil prices for that matter—were never threatened. There has been a worldwide oil glut since the early 1980s, with much underused production capacity in non-Gulf nations. Despite the horrendous human costs of the Iran-Iraq war, oil prices had actually fallen by 50 percent during the course of the conflict.[101] By the end of 1987, two thirds of all the oil produced in the Gulf was carried by pipeline. The Congressional study noted that even in the unlikely event of an actual shutdown of the Gulf, the impact on oil supplies and prices would be minimal.[102] In no sense then could the Strait of Hormuz be viewed as the "jugular" of the Western economies.[103]

Fewer than two percent of the ships that did transit the Strait came under attack, and even this figure is misleading because many of the attacks inflicted relatively minor damage.[104] Only one Iranian attack in ten caused serious damage.[105]

Significantly, Iran became more aggressive in attacking shipping *because* of the U.S. naval presence.[106] Between 1981 and April 1987, when the U.S. reflagging was announced, Iran struck 90 ships; in the little over a year thereafter, Iran struck 126 ships.[107] As the Congressional study noted, "shipping in the Gulf now appears less safe than before the U.S. naval build-up began."[108]

If the U.S. were concerned with free navigation, it might have given some consideration to a Soviet proposal that the U.S. Navy and all national navies withdraw from the Gulf, to be replaced by a United Nations force.[109] But Washington wasn't interested. Indeed, some, like the *New York Times*, noted that it was the United States that could close the Gulf—to Iranian exports—though the *Times* added that "such action would of course be unthinkable unless requested by the Arab states of the region."[110] So much for freedom of navigation.

It was Iraq that started the tanker war in the Gulf proper in 1981, and that continued these attacks into 1984 without a parallel Iranian response at sea. Two months after Iraq stepped up the pace and scope of its attacks in March 1984, Iran finally began responding.[111] Iraqi attacks, however, outnumbered those by Iran until after the United States announced its reflagging.[112] The U.S. Navy protected the reflagged vessels, and in April 1988 extended its protection to any neutral vessels coming under Iranian attack.[113] In practice, this meant that Iraq could strike at Iranian vessels with impunity, with the U.S. Navy preventing retaliation by Teheran.

Washington justified its policy by noting that Iraq only attacked Iranian ships, while Iran targeted the ships of neutrals: Kuwait, in particular. This was a dubious legal argument on two counts. First, Kuwait was a neutral engaged in rather unneutral behavior. Among other things, it opened its ports to deliveries of war material that were then transported over land to Iraq.[114] Second, Iraq too hit neutral ships, even Saudi Arabian ships—when they called on Iran.[115] Iraq declared certain Iranian waters a "war exclusion zone," but as an international law expert has noted, Iraq's "method of enforcement has closely resembled German methods" in World War II, and "under any analysis the Iraqi exclusion zone cannot be justified." The "attacks on neutral merchant vessels by both sides must be condemned as violations of international law." [116] There was thus no legal justification for the U.S. to take Iraq's side in the tanker war.

Still less was there any sense in which the U.S. Navy could be referred to as a "peacekeeping" force. Gary Sick, a former National Security Council officer in charge of Iran, asserted that American naval units "have been deployed aggressively and provocatively in the hottest parts of the Persian Gulf." "Our aggressive patrolling strategy," he observed, "tends to start fights, not to end them. We behave at times as if our objective was to goad Iran into a war with us."[117] According to a Congressional report, officials in every Gulf country were critical of "the highly provocative way in which U.S. forces are being deployed."[118] When in April 1988 the U.S. turned a mining attack on a U.S. ship into the biggest U.S. Navy sea battle since World War II,[119] *Al Ittihad*, a newspaper often reflective of government thinking in the United

Arab Emirates, criticized the U.S. attacks, noting that they added "fuel to the gulf tension."[120]

The aggressive U.S. posture was in marked contrast to the posture of the Soviet Union. The Soviet Union too was escorting ships in the Gulf, particularly vessels carrying weapons to Kuwait for Iraq. On May 6, 1987, Iranian gunboats attacked a Soviet merchant vessel,[121] and two weeks later one of the Soviet ships chartered by Kuwait was the first victim of a mine attack since 1984.[122] These facts are not widely known, because the Soviet response was extremely mild.

Soviet policy in the Gulf was the subject of a study commissioned by the U.S. Army and written by reputed intellectual heavyweight Francis Fukuyama of the Rand Corporation. Fukuyama concluded that Gorbachev's "new thinking" in foreign policy was only rhetoric as far as the Persian Gulf was concerned because Moscow continued to pursue "zero-sum" (that is, totally competitive) policies vis-a-vis the United States. But the facts presented in the study suggest a rather different conclusion. Fukuyama notes that the "Soviets, it is true, were facing a U.S. administration that was itself playing very much a zero-sum game in the Gulf.... What the Soviets would have done if faced with a more collaborative United States is untestable and consequently unknowable." Nevertheless, for Fukuyama the USSR is to blame since Gorbachev had been accommodative in other areas of policy in the face of U.S. intransigence and thus might have been so in the Gulf as well.[123]

Fukuyama acknowledges that the Soviet Union refrained from following other, more aggressive policies in the Gulf, such as trying to outbid Washington for influence with Kuwait. He observes that Soviet naval units in the Gulf were not offensively deployed, in contradistinction to those of the United States. (Indeed, Fukuyama points out that since the early 1970s Moscow had slowed the development of its power projection capability, unlike the United States.) The USSR sought to use economic and political instruments of policy in the Gulf, rather than predominantly military ones as the U.S. did. And when Moscow did seek its own advantage in relations with Iran, it did so in response to the secret dealings in Teheran by the White House.[124] In short, if Soviet policy in the Gulf can be criticized for insufficient "new thinking," by comparison U.S. policy reflected a Stone Age approach.

The provocative U.S. naval deployments in the Gulf took a heavy toll on innocent civilians. In November 1987, a U.S. ship fired its machine guns at night at a boat believed to be an Iranian speedboat with hostile intent; it was in fact a fishing boat from the United Arab Emirates. One person was killed and three were wounded.[125] The most serious incident was the shooting down by the U.S. cruiser *Vicennes* of an Iranian civil airliner, killing all 290 people aboard. The commander of another U.S. ship in the Gulf noted that while "the conduct of Iranian military forces in the month preceding the incident was pointedly non-threatening," the actions of the *Vicennes* "appeared to be consistently aggressive," leading some Navy hands to refer to the ship as "Robo Cruiser."[126]

These tensions in the Gulf continued to promote one important U.S. goal: they encouraged the Gulf states to enhance their military cooperation with the United States. As noted above, the United States had used the Iran-Iraq war as a lever for obtaining additional basing rights in the Gulf region. The reflagging operation further enhanced the U.S. position. According to an Associated Press report, the U.S. general in charge of the RDF claimed that the "United States gained unprecedented credibility with Arab leaders as a result of its large-scale naval commitment in the Persian Gulf." This commitment, he said, enabled the U.S. to establish better diplomatic and military ties with Gulf states.[127]

Indifference and Diplomacy

Aggressive U.S. naval deployments in the Gulf elicited no dissent from the *New York Times.* The editors acknowledged that Washington's "profession of neutrality is the thinnest of diplomatic fig leaves," that in reality "America tilts toward Iraq." But the tilt was "for good reason," for it was a strategy designed to achieve peace.[128] The administration had been confused, the *Times* admitted, but now Washington had developed "a coherent policy to contain Iran. It has thereby earned the right to take risks in the gulf."[129] And when the risks resulted in the destruction of the Iranian airliner, the editors declared that the blame might lie with the Iranian pilot, but if not, then it was certainly Teheran's fault for refusing to end the war.[130]

This is the common view of the war, widely promoted by Washington—that Iran was the sole obstacle to peace. A review of the diplomacy of the war, however, shows that while Khomeini certainly bears tremendous blame for the bloodshed, the blame does not stop with him.

When Iraq attacked Iran on September 22, 1980, the United Nations Security Council waited four days before holding a meeting. On September 28, it passed Resolution 479 calling for an end to the fighting. Significantly, however, the resolution did not condemn (nor even mention) the Iraqi aggression and did not call for a return to internationally recognized boundaries. As Ralph King, who has studied the UN response in detail, concluded, "the Council more or less deliberately ignored Iraq's actions in September 1980." It did so because the Council as a whole had a negative view of Iran and was not concerned enough about Iran's predicament to come to its aid. The U.S. delegate noted that Iran, which had itself violated Security Council resolutions on the U.S. embassy hostages, could hardly complain about the Council's lackluster response.

Iran rejected Resolution 479 as one-sided—which it was. When Norway called for an internationally supervised withdrawal of forces, Iraq replied—accurately—that this violated 479. Iran refused to engage in any discussions as long as Iraqi forces remained on its soil.[131] In the meantime, State Department officials proposed "a joint U.S.-Soviet effort to promote a settlement," but Brzezinski argued that this "would legitimate the Soviet position in the Gulf and thus objectively undercut our vital interests."[132] No U.S. initiative was forthcoming. A few more unfruitful Security Council meetings were held into October, and then there were no further formal meetings on the subject of the war, despite the immense carnage, until July 1982.[133]

There were a number of third party mediation efforts. The first was undertaken by Olof Palme, representing the UN Secretary General. Palme proposed that as an initial step the two sides agree to have the disputed Shatt al-Arab waterway cleared. Iraq, however, would only agree if it could pay the full costs (thus legitimating its claim to the entire river), and no agreement could be reached.[134] Then, the Nonaligned Ministerial Committee proposed a cease-fire simultaneous with withdrawal, with demilitarized zones on both sides. Iran accepted and, for a while, Iraq did as well. But Baghdad soon changed its mind, hoping to win on the battlefield. In neither of these instances was any significant outside pressure put on Iraq to settle.[135]

In early 1982 another mediation effort was begun by the government of Algeria, which had helped Iran and Iraq reach a border agreement in 1975 and had also served as a go-between for the release of the U.S. embassy hostages. On May 3, 1982, however, an aircraft carrying the Algerian foreign minister and his team of experts was shot down in Iranian airspace by an *Iraqi* fighter plane. Five years later a captured Iraqi pilot was said to have admitted that the attack was intentional, with the objective of having Iran be blamed for the action.[136] Whether this is true or not, the shootdown eliminated from the scene the most experienced mediators.

By the end of May, 1982, Iran had recaptured nearly all its territory and Iraq was looking for a way out of the war. The Islamic Conference Organization and the Gulf Cooperation Council tried to mediate a settlement. On June 3, three men led by an Iraqi intelligence officer attempted to assassinate the Israeli ambassador to Britain, according to one report with the hope of provoking an Israeli invasion of Lebanon that would create the conditions for the Gulf combatants to end their fighting so they might face their common enemy, Israel.[137] Israel needed no encouragement to march into Lebanon; it knew the provocation had nothing to do with the PLO or Lebanon, but invaded anyway. But the Lebanon war did not dissuade Iran from continuing the Gulf war, and may even have derailed the mediation efforts.[138]

Iraq offered to withdraw its remaining forces from Iran and to cease fire. In Teheran a vigorous debate ensued as to whether to accept the offer or to continue on. The militant mullahs had seen their power grow during the war; though the Shah had originally been ousted by a wide range of political forces, the crusade against Iraq had enabled the right-wing clerics to mobilize the population and to prevail over their domestic opponents. In addition, just as Iraq had erroneously assumed that Iran was on the verge of collapse in September 1980, so now it looked to Iran as though Saddam Hussein was about to fall. Khomeini decided to go on with the war, declaring that Iran would not stop fighting until Saddam Hussein was overthrown, Iraqi war-guilt assigned, and reparations paid.

The government of Iran thus bears major responsibility for the death and destruction that followed. But, significantly, no industrial country gave strong support to a peace settlement at this time.[139] Within the United States government, Secretary of State Alexander Haig proposed some sort of international peace conference (though without U.S. participation, and of course with no Soviet participation). The proposal, Haig recalls, "failed to win the attention of the White House." Haig notes that the "war was then at a critical stage, an Iranian offensive having recovered nearly all of Iran's lost territory, and it is possible that a properly designed initiative could have succeeded in ending the hostilities."[140]

On July 12, 1982, the Security Council met on the issue of the war for the first time since 1980 and called for a withdrawal to the pre-war boundaries. Iran considered this further proof of the bias of the United Nations, since the call for withdrawal came at the first moment in the war when Iranian forces held any Iraqi territory.[141]

Iraq responded to Iranian victories on the ground by making use of its advantage in technology: it escalated the tanker war, employed chemical weapons, and launched attacks on civilian targets. Iran retaliated by striking Gulf shipping starting in 1984 and launching its own attacks on civilians, though on a lesser scale than Iraq. Iran charged that the Security Council's handling of each of these issues reflected animus against Iran.

In 1984 the Security Council passed a resolution on the tanker war that was directed primarily against Iran's actions and made no reference to Iraqi conduct except to call for all states to respect the right of free navigation.[142]

On chemical weapons, the Security Council passed no resolution. The United States condemned the use of chemical weapons, but declined to support any Council action against Iraq.[143] The Council did issue a much less significant "statement" in 1985 condemning the use of chemical weapons, but without mentioning Iraq by name; then, in March 1986, for the first time a Council statement explicitly denounced Iraq. This, however, was two years after Iraq's use of chemical warfare had been confirmed by a UN team.[144]

In 1983 a UN team found that both sides had attacked civilian areas, but that Iran had suffered more extensive damage than Iraq. Teheran wanted the Security Council to pass a resolution that indicated Iraq's greater responsibility, but the Council refused to do so, and no statement was issued.[145] In June 1984 the Secretary General was able to get the two sides to agree to cease their attacks on civilians. Both sides soon charged violations, but UN inspection teams found that while Iraq was indeed in violation, Iran was not. By March 1985, the moratorium was over.[146]

At this time, jockeying for position with Moscow was still a crucial consideration for the United States. In a section of a draft National Security document that elicited no dissent, U.S. long term goals were said to include "an early end to the Iran-Iraq war without Soviet mediation. . . ."[147]

Iran remained committed to its maximum war aims, a commitment not lessened by the fact that Oliver North, apparently without authorization, told Iranian officials that Reagan wanted the war ended on terms favorable to Iran, and that Saddam Hussein had to go.[148] But it was not just North's unauthorized conversation that encouraged Iranian intransigence; the authorized clandestine dealings between Washington and Teheran no doubt had the same effect.

In late 1986 the Iran-Contra scandal broke, forcing the U.S. to go all-out in its support for Iraq in order to preserve some influence among the Arab states jolted by the evidence of Washington's double-dealing. In May 1987, U.S. Assistant Secretary of State Richard Murphy met with Saddam Hussein and promised him that the U.S. would lead an effort at the UN for a mandatory arms embargo of Iran; a resolution would be drawn up calling on both sides to cease fire and withdraw, and imposing an embargo on whoever didn't comply, presumably Iran. The U.S. drafted such a resolution, but the non-permanent members of the Security Council altered it to include the formation of an impartial commission to investigate the origins of the war, as Iran had been insisting, and to eliminate the mandatory sanctions. On July 20, 1987 the revised document was passed unanimously as Security Council Resolution 598.[149]

Iraq promptly accepted 598, while Iran said it would accept the cease-fire and withdrawal of forces if the impartial commission were set up first. The U.S. and Iraq both rejected Iran's position, asserting that Iran had no right to select one provision out of many in the resolution and impose that as a first step.[150]

The Secretary General then travelled to Teheran and Baghdad to try to work out a compromise and he made some progress. According to the leaked text of his private report to the Security Council, Iran agreed to accept an "undeclared cessation of hostilities" while an independent commission was investigating the responsibility for the conflict; the cessation would become a formal cease-fire on the date that the commission issued its findings. This was not an acceptance of 598, but an informal cease-fire might have meant an end to the killing as surely as a formal one. Iraq, however, insisted that "under no circumstances" would it accept an undeclared cease-fire.[151] Instead of seizing the Iranian position as a first step toward a compromise, the United States, in the words of Gary Sick, "pressed single-mindedly for an embargo on Iran, while resisting efforts by Secretary General Javier Perez de Cuellar to fashion a compromise cease-fire."[152]

"Could the war have been ended by a compromise in early 1988?" Sick has asked. "The answer will never be known, primarily because the United States was unwilling to explore Iran's offer. The U.S. position—and sensitivities about even the perception of any sympathy toward Iran—were a direct legacy of the Iran-contra fiasco. They may have contributed to prolonging the war for six unnecessary months."[153]

Finally, in July 1988, with Iranian anti-war sentiment growing widespread, Ayatollah Khomeini decided to end the fighting. On July 18, Iran declared its full acceptance of Resolution 598. But by this time Iraq had turned the tide of the land battle, having regained virtually all of its own territory, and Saddam Hussein refused to accept the cease-fire. Baghdad continued offensive operations, using chemical weapons both against Iran and its own Kurdish population.

It was not until August 6 that international pressure got Iraq to agree to a cease-fire, and it went into effect two weeks later.[154] Both regimes continued to kill their own citizens—Kurds in Iraq and dissidents, especially leftists, in Iran—but the Gulf war was over.

The Iran-Iraq war was not a conflict between good and evil. But though both regimes were repugnant, it was the people of the two countries who served as the cannon fodder, and thus ending the war as soon as possible was a humane imperative. Instead of lending its good offices to mediation efforts and diplomacy, however, Washington maneuvered for advantage, trying to gain vis-a-vis the Soviet Union and to undercut the left. The United States provided intelligence information, bogus and real, to both sides, provided arms to one side, funded paramilitary exile groups, sought military bases, and sent in the U.S. Navy—and all the while Iranians and Iraqis died.

Three months after the end of the war, U.S. Deputy Undersecretary of the Navy Seth Cropsy expressed his hope that the outcome of U.S. operations in the Gulf would dispel the "national reluctance to interpose American military forces in third world conflicts when important issues are at stake."[155] Those opposed to U.S. interventionism will not share this hope. Not that there weren't important issues at stake; there were. But they were not the danger of Soviet invasion or the threat that the Western economies might be deprived of oil. For Washington the important issue was whether it would be able to maintain the status quo in a region of great strategic value to the Pentagon and economic value to the oil companies. But for those outside the corridors of power, the real issues have been, and will continue to be, how to promote peace, justice, and self-determination in the Gulf and elsewhere—and these issues do not lend themselves to gunboat diplomacy.

Notes

[1] Casualty figures are uncertain: see Anthony H. Cordesman, *The Iran-Iraq War and Western Security, 1984-87*, London: Jane's Publishing Co., 1987, p. 9; *New York Times*, 10 Aug. 1988, p. A8; in 1982 the U.S. State Dept. estimated that the war had created 2 million refugees: Anthony H. Cordesman, *The Gulf and the Search*

for Strategic Stability, Boulder: Westview, 1984, p. 671; health spending from Ruth Leger Sivard, *World Military and Social Expenditures, 1987-88*, Washington, DC: World Priorities, 1988, table II.

[2] Diana Johnstone, "Little Satan' Stuck in the Arms Export Trap," *MERIP Reports*, no. 148, Sept.-Oct. 1987, pp. 8-9.

[3] Mansour Farhang, "The Iran-Iraq War: The Feud, the Tragedy, the Spoils," *World Policy journal*, vol. 2, Fall 1985, p. 668; see also Cordesman, *Iran-Iraq War . . .*, pp. 23-36; Nita M. Renfrew, "Who Started the War?" *Foreign Policy*, no. 66, Spring 1987, pp. 104-06.

[4] Joe Stork, *Middle East Oil and the Energy Crisis*, New York: Monthly Review Press, 1975, p. 26.

[5] Quoted in William B. Quandt, *Saudi Arabia in the 1980s: Foreign Policy, Security, and Oil*, Washington, DC: Brookings, 1981, p. 48.

[6] See Michael J. Cohen, *Palestine: Retreat from the Mandate*, New York: Holmes & Meier, 1978, pp. 154-55; Stork, *Middle East Oil . . .*, pp. 34-35.

[7] George W. Stocking, *Middle East Oil: A Study in Political and Economic Controversy*, Nashville: Vanderbilt U.P., 1970, pp. 103-06.

[8] Quoted in Stork, *Middle East Oil . . .*, p. 74.

[9] Kennett Love, *Suez: the Twice-Fought War*, New York: McGraw Hill, 1969, p. 651.

[10] Love, *Suez . . .*, p. 387.

[11] Henry Kissinger, *Years of Upheaval*, Boston: Little Brown, 1982, p. 858.

[12] Michael Renner, "Restructuring the World Energy Industry," *MERIP Reports*, no. 120, Jan. 1984, p. 13.

[13] Edith Penrose, "The Development of Crisis," in *The Oil Crisis*, ed. Raymond Vernon, New York: Norton, 1976, p. 49.

[14] V. H. Oppenheim, "Why Oil Prices Go Up; The Past: We Pushed Them," *Foreign Policy*, no. 25, Winter 1976-77, pp. 30, 32-33.

[15] Oppenheim, "Why Oil Prices . . .," pp. 24-25.

[16] Kissinger, *Years of Upheaval*, p. 863.

[17] Robert B. Stobaugh, "The Oil Companies in the Crisis," in *The Oil Crisis*, ed. Raymond Vernon, New York: Norton, 1976, p. 185.

[18] Quoted in Mira Wilkins, "The Oil Companies in Perspective," in *The Oil Crisis*, ed. Raymond Vernon, New York: Norton, 1976, p. 173.

[19] Kissinger, *Years of Upheaval*, p. 873.

[20] Stobaugh, "Oil Companies . . .," p. 193, table 3.

[21] Romano Prodi and Alberto Clo[?missing accent?], "Europe," in *The Oil Crisis*, ed. Raymond Vernon, New York: Norton, 1976, p. 101.

[22] Yoshi Tsurumi, "Japan," in *The Oil Crisis*, ed. Raymond Vernon, New York: Norton, 1976, p. 123.

[23] Horst Menderhausen, *Coping with the Oil Crisis*, Baltimore: Johns Hopkins University Press, 1976, pp. 60-61.

[24] Hearings, *Offshore Oil and Gas Oversight*, Subcommittee on Panama Canal/Outer Continental Shelf, House Merchant Marine and Fisheries Committee, 1984, pp. 469-74.

[25] Richard Halloran, "What Price U.S. Patrols in the Gulf," *New York Times*, 21 Feb. 1988, p. 2E.

[26] Maj. Gen. Edward B. Atkeson, "The Persian Gulf: Still A Vital Interest?" *Armed Forces Journal International*, vol. 124, no. 9, April 1987, p. 54.

[27] Frank Church, "The Impotence of Oil Companies," *Foreign Policy*, no. 27, Summer 1977, p. 49.

[28] Cordesman, *The Gulf*. . . ,p. 264.

[29] *Time*, 25 July 1983, p. 28, quoted in Mansour Farhang, "The Iran-Israel Connection," in *Consistency of U.S. Foreign Policy: The Gulf War and the Iran-Contra Affair*, ed. Abbas Alnasrawi and Cheryl Rubenberg, Belmont, MA: AAUG, 1989, p. 96.

[30] John W. Amos II, "The Iraq-Iran War: Conflict, Linkage, and Spillover in the Middle East," in *Gulf Security into the 1980s: Perceptual and Strategic Dimensions*, ed. Robert G. Darius, John W. Amos II, Ralph H. Magnus, Stanford: Hoover Institution Press, 1984, p. 65.

[31] Cordesman, *The Gulf*. . ., p. 717; Robert O. Freedman, "Soviet Policy Toward the Persian Gulf from the Outbreak of the Iran-Iraq War to the Death of Konstantin Chernenko," in *U.S. Strategic Interests in the Gulf Region*, ed. Wm. J. Olson, Boulder: Westview, 1987, p. 55.

[32] Freedman, "Soviet Policy . . .," p. 55.

[33] Joe Stork and Martha Wenger, "U.S. Ready to Intervene in the Gulf War," *MERIP Reports*, nos. 125/126, July-Sept. 1984, p. 45.

[34] Freedman, "Soviet Policy . . .," p. 63; *New York Times*, 10 Nov. 1982, p. 5.

[35] Stork & Wenger, "U.S. Ready to Intervene . . .," p. 45.

[36] *War in the Persian Gulf: The U.S. Takes Sides*, staff report to the Committee on Foreign Relations, U.S. Senate, Nov. 1987, Committee Print S. Prt. 100-60, pp. 21-22. Hereafter cited as S. Prt. 100-60.

[37] Michael T. Klare, "The RDF: Newest 'Fire Brigade' for U.S. Intervention in the Third World," in *U.S. Strategy in the Gulf: Intervention Against Liberation*, ed. Leila Meo, Belmont, MA: AAUG, 1981, pp. 99-100, 104.

[38] Harold Brown, *Thinking About National Security*, Boulder: Westview, 1983, p. 157.

[39] For examples for policymakers and the press, see Maya Chadda, *Paradox of Power: the United States in Southwest Asia, 1973-1984*, Santa Barbara: ABC-Clio, 1986, pp. 111-12.; and for a particularly gross example, *Business Week*, 19 Nov. 1979, p. 190, quoted in James F. Petras and Roberto Korzeniewicz, "U.S. Policy Towards the Middle East," in *U.S. Strategy in the Gulf: Intervention Against Liberation*, ed. Leila Meo, Belmont, MA: AAUG, 1981, p. 84.

[40] A point made by Chadda, *Paradox of Power*, p. 112.

[41] Brown, *Thinking About National Security*, p. 157.

[42] Zbigniew Brzezinski, *Power and Principle,* New York: Farrar, Straus, Giroux, 1987, p. 450.

[43] *Cordesman,* The Gulf . . ., p. 847.

[44] Deborah Shapley "The Army's New Fighting Doctrine," *New York Times Magazine*, 28 Nov. 1982, p. 47.

[45] Klare, " . . . Fire Brigade," p. 107.

[46] *Public Papers of the Presidents, Ronald Reagan, 1981*, pp. 870-71.

[47] Stephen Engelberg, "Iran and Iraq Got Doctored Data, U.S. Officials Say," *New York Times*, 12 Jan. 1987, p. Al, A6.

[48] Brown, *Thinking About National Security*, makes this point, p. 149.

[49] *New York Times,* 25 Sept. 1982, quoted in Christopher Paine, *"On the Beach: The*

Rapid Deployment Force and the Nuclear Arms Race," MERIP Reports, no. 111, Jan. 1983, p. 11.

[50] Congressional Quarterly Inc., *U.S. Defense Policy*, 3rd ed., Washington. DC: 1983, p. 193. The quote is Congressional Quarterly's summary.

[51] James P. Wooten, *Rapid Deployment Force*, CRS Issue Brief No. IB80027, updated 16 July 1984, p. 4, quoted in Martha Wenger, "The Central Command: Getting to the War on Time," *MERIP Reports*, no. 128, Nov.-Dec. 1984, p. 20; see also Richard Halloran, "Pentagon Draws Up First Strategy for Fighting A Long Nuclear War," *New York Times*, 20 May 1982, pp. 1, 12.

[52] Quoted in Congressional Quarterly, *U.S. Defense Policy*, pp. 195-96.

[53] Cordesman, *The Gulf*. . ., p. 62.

[54] Middle East.

[55] Wenger "Central Command," p. 22, citing Wooten.

[56] Judith Miller and Jeff Gerth, "U.S. Is Said to Develop Oman as Its major Ally in the Gulf," *New York Times*, 25 Mar. 1985, pp. Al, A8.

[57] Bernard Gwertzman, "Saudis To Let U.S. Use Bases in Crisis," *New York Times*, 5 Sept. 1985, pp. Al, A10.

[58] *President's Special Review Board* (*The Tower Commission Report*), New York: Bantam Books/Times Books, 1987, pp. 294-95. Hereafter cited as Tower Commission.

[59] Farhang, "Iran-Israel Connection," p. 95; Bob Woodward, *Veil: The Secret Wars of the CIA, 1981-1987*, New York: Simon & Schuster, 1987, p. 480.

[60] Leslie H. Gelb, "U.S. Said to Aid Iranian Exiles in Combat and Political Units," *New York Times*, 7 Mar. 1982, pp. Al, A12.

[61] David Binder, "U.S. Concedes It Is Behind Anti-Khomeini Broadcasts," *New York Times*, 29 June 1980, p. 3; Woodward, *Veil*, p. 480.

[62] Leslie H. Gelb, "U.S. Said to Aid Iranian Exiles in Combat and Political Units," *New York Times*, 7 Mar. 1982, pp. A1, Alt.

[63] Tower Commission, p. 398; Farhang, "Iran-Israel Connection," p. 95.

[64] Farhang, "Iran-Israel Connection," p. 92.

[65] Tower Commission, pp. 103-04.

[66] Quoted in Jonathan Marshall, Peter Dale Scott, and Jane Hunter, *The Iran-Contra Connection*, Boston: South End Press, 1987, pp. 160-61.

[67] Tower Commission, p. 271.

[68] Tower Commission, p. 194.

[69] Tower Commission, p. 388.

[70] Tower Commission, p. 65.

[71] Tower Commission, p. 113.

[72] Tower Commission, p. 261.

[73] Tower Commission, p. 299.

[74] Cordesman, *Iran-Iraq War . . .*, pp. 23-36.

[75] Leslie H. Gelb, "Iran Said to Get Large-Scale Arms From Israel, Soviet and Europeans," *New York Times*, 8 Mar. 1982, pp. Al, A10; Cordesman, *Iran-Iraq War . . .*, p. 31.

[76] S.Prt. 100-60,p. 21.

[77] Murray Gordon ed., *Conflict in the Persian Gulf*, New York: Facts on File, 1981, p. 163.

[78] Brzezinski, *Power and Principle*, p. 504.

[79] Christopher Hitchens, *Nation*, 20 June 1987 and 4 July 1987.

[80] Tower Commission, p. 27.

[81] *Public Papers of the President, Reagan, 1986*, p. 1546.

[82] Tower Commission, p. 48; see also p. 398.

[83] Tower Commission, p. 427.

[84] Stork & Wenger, "U.S. Ready to Intervene . . .," pp. 47-48, citing *Newsday*, 20 May 1984.

[85] Tower Commission, pp. 239-40.

[86] Cordesman, *Iran-Iraq War. . .*, p. 38.

[87] Tower Commission, pp. 239-40.

[88] Tower Commission, p. 279.

[89] Tower Commission, p. 73; see also Cordesman, *Iran-Iraq War. . .*, p. 38.

[90] Stephen Engelberg, "Iran and Iraq Got 'Doctored Data, U.S. Officials Say," *New York Times*, 12 Jan. 1987, pp. A1, A6.

[91] Woodward, *Veil*, p. 480.

[92] Woodward, *Veil*, p. 480.

[93] Stephen Engelberg, "Iran and Iraq Got 'Doctored Data, U.S. Officials Say," *New York Times*,12 Jan. 1987, pp. Al, A6.

[94] S.Prt. 100-60, p. 37.

[95] S.Prt. 100-60, p. 37.

[96] U.S. Dept. of State, *U.S. Policy in the Persian Gulf*, Special Report No. 166, Washington, DC: July 1987, p. 11.

[97] Freedman, "Soviet Policy . . .," p. 52; Michael Lenker, "The Effect of the Iran-Iraq War on Soviet Strategy in the Persian Gulf," in *Gulf Security and the Iran-Iraq War*, ed. Thomas Naff, Washington, DC: National Defense University Press, 1985, p. 95.

[98] *Washington Post*, 16 Aug. 1987, p. A23.

[99] S.Prt. 100-60, p. ix.

[100] Dept. of State, *U.S. Policy in the Persian Gulf*, pp. 1-2.

[101] S.Prt. 100-60, p. 2.

[102] S.Prt. 100-60, p. 4.

[103] S.Prt. 100-60, p. vii.

[104] Ronald O'Rourke, "The Tanker War," *Proceedings*, U.S. Naval Institute, May 1988, p. 34.

[105] Ronald O'Rourke, "Gulf Ops" *Proceedings*, U.S. Naval Institute, May 1989, pp. 42-43.

[106] S.Prt. 100-60, p. 3.

[107] Rourke, "Tanker War," p. 32; Rourke, "Gulf Ops," p.43

[108] S.Prt. 100-60, p. ix.

[109] Fox Butterfield, "Soviets in UN Council Ask for U.S. Pullout From Gulf," *New York Times*, 16 July 1988, p. 2.

[110] "What If Iran Attacks Again?" *New York Times*, 20 Oct. 1987, p. A34.

[111] Rourke, "Tanker War," p. 30.

[112] Rourke, "Tanker War," p. 32; Rourke, Gulf Ops," p. 43.

[113] Rourke, "Gulf Ops," p. 47.

[114] S.Prt. 100-60, p. 37.

[115] Robert L. Bambarger and Clyde R. Mark, *Escalation of the Conflict in the Persian Gulf*, CRS, May 30, 1984, printed in Hearings, *Offshore Oil . . .*, p. 593.

[116] Ross Leckow, "The Iran-Iraq Conflict in the Gulf: The Law of War Zones," *International and Comparative Law Quarterly*, vol. 37, July 1988, pp. 636-38, 644.

[117] Gary Sick, "Failure and Danger in the Gulf," *New York Times*, 6 July 1988, p. A23.

[118] S.Prt. 100-60, p. 29.

[119] Rourke, "Gulf Ops," p. 44.

[120] Steve Lohr, *New York Times*, 20 Ap. 1988, p. A16.

[121] U.S. Policy in the PG, p. 5.

[122] Rourke, "Tanker War," p. 30.

[123] Francis Fukuyama, *Gorbachev and the New Soviet Agenda in the Third World*, R-3634-A, Santa Monica, CA: Rand Corporation, June 1989, pp. viii, 43.

[124] Fukuyama, *Gorbachev* . . ., pp. 60, 47, 28-29, 53, 45.

[125] Rourke, "Tanker War," p. 33.

[126] Commander David R. Carlson, "The *Vicennes* Incident," letter, *Proceedings*, U.S. Naval Institute, Sept. 1989, pp. 87-88.

[127] AP, "U.S. Wins Arab Respect with Gulf Ship Escorts," *Newark Star Ledger*, 19 Oct. 1988, p. 4; see also Richard Halloran, *New York Times*, 4 Dec. 1988, p. 32.

[128] "Why the U.S. Navy is in the Gulf," *New York Times*, 6 July 1988, p. A22.

[129] "What If Iran Attacks Again?" *New York Times*, 20 Oct. 1987, p. A34.

[130] "In Captain Rogers's Shoes" *New York Times*, 5 July 1988, p. A16.

[131] R. P. H. King, "The United Nations and the Iran-Iraq War, 1980-1986," in Brian Urquhart and Gary Sick eds., *The United Nations and the Iran-Iraq War*, New York: Ford Foundation, August 1987, pp. 10, 14-16, 23.

[132] Brzezinski, *Power and Principle*, p. 453.

[133] King, "The United Nations . . .," p. 10.

[134] Farhang, "Iran-Iraq War . . .," p. 673; King, "The United Nations . . .," p. 18.

[135] Farhang, "Iran-Iraq War. . .,"pp.673-75

[136] Gary Sick, "Trial By Error: Reflections on the Iran-Iraq War," *Middle East journal*, vol. 43, no. 2, Spring 1989, p. 236.

[137] Dilip Hiro, *Iran Under the Ayatollahs*, London: Routledge & Kegan Paul, 1985, p. 211; Noam Chomsky, *The Fateful Triangle*, Boston: South End Press, 1983, 197n.

[138] Hiro, *Iran Under the Ayatollahs*, p. 211.

[139] Farhang, "Iran-Iraq War . . .," pp. 675-76.

140 Alexander M. Haig, Jr., *Caveat*, New York: Macmillan, 1984, p. 334n.

141 King, "The United Nations. . .," p. 17.

142 Leckow, "The Iran-Iraq Conflict. . .," p. 640.

143 Elaine Sciolino, "How the U.S. Cast Off Neutrality in Gulf War," *New York Times*, 24 Ap. 1988, p. 2E.

144 King, "The United Nations. . .," pp. 19-20.

145 King, "The United Nations. . .," p. 18.

146 King, "The United Nations. . .," p. 19.

147 Tower Commission, pp. 117-118.

148 Tower Commission, pp. 49-50.

149 Sick, "Trial By Error," p. 240.

150 Hearings, *Developments in the Middle East, September 1987*, Subcommittee on Europe and the Middle East, Committee on Foreign Relations, Senate, Sept. 1987, p. 19; Sick, "Trial By Error," p. 241.

151 Kuwait KUNA, 19 Sept. 1987, *Foreign Broadcast Information Service*, FBIS-NES-87-183, 22 Sept 1987, pp. 45-47.

152 Gary Sick, "Failure and Danger in the Gulf," *New York Times*, 6 July 1988, p. A23.

153 Sick, "Trial By Error," p. 241.

154 Sick, "Trial By Error," pp. 242-43.

155 Bernard E. Trainor, "Navy Sees Gulf Activity as Portent of New Era," *New York Times*, 25 Nov. 1988, p. B10. The words are Trainor's.

The Institutions of Repression

Human Rights Watch

from *Human Rights in Iraq*

The army was the mainstay of the repressive regimes that ruled Iraq from 1958, when the Hashemite monarchy was overthrown, until 1968, when the Baath party seized power for the second time. It played a major role in internal security and in stamping out dissent. It engineered three successful coups. And it intervened repeatedly in affairs of state.

Though a military coup returned the Baath to power in 1968, and though a Baath military officer, General Hassan al-Bakr, headed the regime for over a decade, the Baath party, under al-Bakr and Saddam Hussein, moved carefully and methodically to subordinate the army to its own authority. It did this through a series of purges and by saturating the army with the equivalent of political commissars—officers whose job it was to give indoctrination lectures and to check loyalty. Senior command positions were filled by party members, and party cadres were assigned to units down to the battalion level. Soldiers were prohibited, on penalty of death, from membership in or activity on behalf of any party other than the Baath. Officers known or suspected to harbor sympathies for other parties—the Iraqi Communist Party, non-Baathist Arab nationalist parties, or Shia and Kurdish opposition movements—were in some cases retired or reassigned, in other cases jailed or executed. In a bizarre twist, the Iraqi army found itself transformed from instrument to object of repression.

While harnessing the military, Baath party leaders also set about subduing the rest of Iraqi society, using many of the same methods. Today, observers of the Iraqi scene speak of the "Baathization" of Iraq as a process long completed. The party is the pillar supporting the regime and the institution most directly responsible for enforcing political and social conformity. But in the years since Saddam Hussein became head of state, the cult of the leader has assumed vast proportions and, in turn, has been employed as a test of loyalty and a means of enforcing conformity. Both the rule of the party and the cult of the leader are enforced by various secret-police agencies, which instill the fear required to sustain the regime's authority.

The Baath Party

The Arab Baath (or Resurrection) Socialist Party was founded in the early 1940s by three French-educated Syrian intellectuals: Michel Aflaq, a Christian; Salah al-Din Bitar, a Sunni Muslim, and Zaki al-Arsuzi, an Alawite. It is a self-professed revolutionary party with a doctrine that combines in vague, romantic, and mystical language a virulent pan-Arab nationalism with a dedication to socialism. In its pristine form, Baath ideology calls for the creation of a simple secular Arab state with equal participation by members of all religious and ethnic groups. "One Arab nation with an eternal message," is one of the party's early slogans. But despite its pretension to embrace the entire Arab world, the Baath party developed a serious following in only Syria and Iraq. Syria has been ruled by one faction or another of the Baath party since 1963. After the Baath seized power in Iraq in 1968, repeated efforts were made to implement the party's pan-Arab program by merging Syria and Iraq. All failed, supposedly owing to disagreement over points of ideology, but perhaps mainly because of personal rivalries and animosities between the leaders of the two states. Today Iraq and Syria, both still ruled by Baath parties, are at drawn daggers, and on opposite sides of almost every regional issue.

In recent years, all the main tenets of Iraqi Baathism have undergone substantial erosion. The idea that the Arab states could be merged into a single unit is now recognized to be impractical in any foreseeable future. The commitment to socialism is gradually giving way to an embrace of capitalism; although heavy industry is still under state management, the agricultural sector has largely reverted to private hands, and private management and capital are officially encouraged in services and light industry. And the Baath itself has become primarily a means to enforce political conformity and to mobilize the population for the benefit of the leadership.

In 1963, after it seized power for the first time in Iraq, the Baath party claimed a following of just under 16,000, only a few hundred of whom were full members. The party's thin membership base was deemed to be one of the reasons for its failure to survive in power through the end of the year. After the second Baath coup in 1968, the party, under impetus from Saddam Hussein, then its second leading figure, undertook an ambitious recruitment drive, with the aim of putting down secure roots throughout the country. By 1980, through a combination of inducements, intimidation, and coercion, the Baath party had mushroomed into a mass organization with a following estimated at 1.5 million, over 10 percent of the Iraqi population at the time and perhaps 30 percent of the active adult population. Relentless pressure to join the Baath party was put on army officers, government officials, professionals, teachers, and students. People who refused recruitment into the party were reportedly threatened, banned from teaching and entry into the university, and even arrested for short periods.

Intensified pressure in 1978 and 1979 led a number of Iraqis to flee the country. One Iraqi émigré interviewed by Middle East Watch described what happened to him in these terms:

> I was only sixteen at the time and in high school but they kept coming around to me and insisting that I join the party. They tried to sign everybody up, and those who did join were then forced to become informers. I told them I wasn't interested in politics, I just wanted to concentrate on my studies, but they wouldn't take no for an answer. Finally we got scared and my mother and I left; my father followed the next year.

The party's various categories of members and followers are believed still today to number about 1.5 million. The core group of "active" or full members, however, has always been small; estimates of its size range from 25,000 to 50,000.

In organization, structure, and method, the Baath party closely resembles a traditional Marxist-Leninist party. Hierarchy, discipline, and secrecy are its dominant characteristics. At the base is the individual cell, the neighborhood unit; followed in the hierarchy by the "division," which may cover a small city; the district "section"; and the provincial "branch," of which there are twenty-one (one for each of the eighteen provinces and three for Baghdad). At the top of the pyramid is the Regional Command, from which, in theory at least, the Regional Command Council, the highest executive and legislative body of the state, is elected.

Like Marxist-Leninist parties, the Baath party is really a state within the state. It has its own training facilities, or "preparatory schools," where cadres and members study ideology, economy, and politics. The party maintains "bureaus" parallel to those of government departments which monitor and sometimes duplicate their work and assure conformity and loyalty. These and other bureaus are charged with organizing and indoctrinating key groups, such as the military, laborers, farmers, and professionals. Along with the army, the teaching profession has been a major target for Baath party recruitment and monitoring because the party is anxious to assure the indoctrination of youth. In 1979, according to a variety of sources, all teachers were required to join the party, and those who refused or were deemed ineligible were fired.

The party also has its own secret police, the Mukhabarat, or General Intelligence Department, and even its own army, the People's Militia. The militia was evidently conceived as a counterpart to the regular army, to discourage the plotting of coups, and is almost as large. In 1980, on the eve of the war with Iran, the People's Militia reportedly numbered about 175,000. During the war it expanded to some 750,000 and is believed to have stayed at about that level despite the cease-fire of August 1988.

Through its pyramidal structure and vast bureaucracy, generally believed to include tens of thousands of cadres, the Baath party has penetrated all walks of life. Membership in the party is a prerequisite to political influence and an important asset for advancement in government, the military, or business. Apologists for the party claim that membership gives only a marginal advantage: "An incompetent Ba'thi is unlikely to be promoted, but all factors being equal, a Ba'thi has a greater advantage than a non-Ba'thi," is the way it has been put. This assertion is disputed by some Iraqis interviewed by Middle East Watch who say that nonparty members need to excel far beyond party members—in addition to being clear of suspicion of disloyalty—to be promoted ahead of party members. Stories abound of junior or incompetent persons being promoted over those more experienced solely on the basis of being members of the Baath party. Party membership is not required for entry into the university, but students who want to study abroad are told they must join.

The party's enormous membership and elaborate structure enable its leaders to mobilize and keep watch on all segments of the population. Civilian informers play a key role in surveillance. According to almost unanimous testimony, Iraq under the Baath party has become a nation of informers. Party members are said to be required to inform on family, friends, and acquaintances, including other party members. Teachers reportedly ask pupils about their parents' views, with the result that parents feel obliged to disguise their thoughts in front of their children. *Index on Censorship* offered the following account of how the duty to inform can be enforced:

> One reliable report concerns a member of the ruling Baath party related to a former senior official, arrested in Baghdad in August [1987] after government informers reported that he had been present at a gathering where jokes were made about President Saddam Hussein. [The party member] was arrested for not informing the authorities, as were the male members of his family: three sons and a son-in-law. During interrogation they were subjected to torture. . . . [A]ll five were subsequently executed and the family's home was bulldozed.

Almost every foreigner who visits Iraq has a story to tell about the oppressive atmosphere in a country where informing is a way of life. A U.S. student of Arab origin, interviewed by Middle East Watch, visited Iraq in the early 1980s and was first followed and then expelled after he went to the University of Baghdad to look for documents for a thesis, even though the research concerned a much earlier period of Iraqi history and a topic of no political sensitivity. A *New York Times* correspondent who visited Iraq in the spring of 1984 reported:

> The hotel lobbies are occupied day and night with idle men filling most available seats, playing with worry beads and keeping an eye on the guests, particularly when the guests meet what in most cases are their Iraqi business contacts. This enhances the claustrophobic feeling to which most foreign residents confess. . . . Whatever the degree of surveillance of aliens, it is far surpassed by the controls that the regime imposes on its own people, according to diplomats and other foreigners working here. "There is a feeling that at least three million Iraqis are watching the eleven million others," a European diplomat said.

The Baath party assures its exclusive hold on power and the loyalty of its members through an extraordinary series of death-penalty laws. In a decree issued in July 1978, the Revolutionary Command Council made the death penalty mandatory for "retired military and police men or volunteers who are released from the service, or whose service has been terminated for any reason whatsoever after July 17, 1968, if their relation or work for, or in the interest of, any party or political group other than the Ba'th party, is proven. Since military service is obligatory in Iraq, this law in effect bars the entire able-bodied male population from membership in or activity on behalf of any political party other than the Baath.

A series of death-penalty decrees promulgated between 1974 and 1978 assures lifetime fidelity by those who join the party. Since 1974, it has been a capital offense for a Baath party member to keep secret his previous party and political membership and links or to have links with, or work for or in the interest of, any other party or political grouping. Even by leaving the Baath party one cannot regain the freedom to join or work for another party, for in 1976 a law was promulgated that establishes the death penalty for former members, "if it can be proven that [they have] a connection with any other party or political grouping or [work] for it or in its interest. Yet another decree, promulgated in 1978, calls for the death penalty for anyone who "recruits to any party or political grouping a person who has, or had, organizational relations with the Arab Baath Party."

The Leader and the Cult of Personality

The Baath party's formidable apparatus was shaped largely by one man, Saddam Hussein, and today it serves to put absolute power in his hands. The list of his titles alone tells much of the story. He is chairman of the Revolutionary Command Council, secretary of the Regional Command, deputy secretary general of the National Command, president of the Republic, prime minister, and commander in chief of the Armed Forces.

A Sunni Muslim, Saddam Hussein was borm in the town of Takrit, northwest of Baghdad, in 1937. He joined the Baath party in his late teens, reportedly first as a hit man. In that capacity he came to notoriety in 1959 as a member of the Baath party squad assigned to assassinate **Qassim.** Baath propaganda has glamorized his role in that particular incident to the point of legend: wounded in the attempt on Qassim's life, the young Saddam Hussein goes into hiding and, without anesthesia, coolly directs a fellow conspirator to dig a bullet out of his leg with a razor; disdainful of the pain of his wound, he makes his way on foot and donkey-drawn cart to his home in Takrit, a journey of several days, in the course of which, through clever ruses of the "Thousand and One Nights" variety, he eludes capture, later to escape across the border into Syria.

By the mid-1960s, Saddam Hussein was an assistant secretary general of the Baath party. According to officially sponsored legend, he masterminded the coup of 1968 that deposed President Abd al-Rahman Arif and returned the Baath to power. Whether or not this was the case, in 1969 he became vice-president of the Revolutionary Command Council, the second highest position in the state. For the next decade Saddam Hussein worked in tandem with President Ahmad Hassan al-Bakr, a distant relative and a native of the town of Takrit, while gradually drawing exclusive power into his own hands. Other relatives (who did not contest his primacy) were put in key positions in the security apparatus, the military, and the government. On July 16, 1979, al-Bakr, then sixty-four and said to have been ailing for several years, went on television to announce his retirement. Saddam Hussein took over.

The takeover may not have been the friendly affair it seemed. Some believe Hussein forced al-Bakr into retirement. In any event, the transfer of power soon became the occasion for a massive purge. Shortly before Saddam Hussein assumed the presidency a large number of arrests took place. On July 28, 1979, the new president announced the discovery of a plot to overthrow the regime. Twenty-two senior officials, among them five members of the ruling Revolutionary Command Council, were sentenced to death and executed after what was described as trial by a special court. Saddam Hussein and other remaining members of the leadership were said to have carried out the executions "in person." These executions were publicly announced. A great many others are believed to have taken place unannounced. One writer puts the number of those executed secretly in the course of Saddam Hussein's takeover at some 500.

Even some Western observers sometimes sympathetic to the regime thought it doubtful that there was really a plot to overthrow Hussein. Historian Phebe Marr put it this way: "Whether or not a fullblown plot existed, Husayn was taking no chances. He decided to inaugurate his presidency by making it clear, once again, that no genuine dissent would be tolerated, not even by his close associates."

The cult of the leader existed in relatively mild form under al-Bakr, and he himself apparently did little to encourage it. Under Saddam Hussein, by the testimony of all who have visited or lived in Iraq in recent years, it has taken on vast proportions, surpassing anything seen elsewhere in the Arab world or, with the possible exception of North Korea, beyond it. Saddam Hussein does enjoy a degree of genuine popularity, in particular among those linked to the regime or who have benefited from it, and many Iraqis regard him as a kind of father figure, albeit a stern one. This notwithstanding, glorification of the Iraqi president has become one of the main enterprises of the country's press, radio, and television, and there is a thriving industry manufacturing posters, pictures, and other likenesses of him. President Hussein's picture appears on the front page of the daily papers regardless of whether there is a story to go with it, and calendars—each with a new picture of the president—are issued frequently throughout the year. Some two hundred songs are said to have been written in adulation of him. The evening television news begins with what Western diplomats in Baghdad call "the Saddam song," presented against a background of victorious soldiers and bursting fireworks by a smiling figure who chants:

> Saddam, our victorious;
> Oh Saddam, our beloved;
> You carry the nation's dawn between your eyes. . . .
> Oh Saddam, everything is good with you. . . .
> Allah, Allah, we are happy;
> Saddam lights our days. . . .

Families name children after him and young men imitate his walk and manner of speech. He has been panegyrized in film and in countless books in Arabic, and at least two extravagantly eulogistic biographies have been published in English. In their early enthusiasm, Iraqi propagandists sought even to carry their campaign to the United States. An advertisement placed by the Iraqi government in *The New York Times* of July 17, 1980, on the first anniversary of Saddam Hussein's takeover, suggested that under his leadership Iraq was on the verge of repeating "her former glories" and compared the Iraqi president to Hammarabi and Asurbanipal of Mesopotamian antiquity and to the two great early Islamic rulers, the Abbasid caliphs-al-Mansur and Harun al-Rashid.

The setbacks experienced by Iraq in its war against Iran, and Iranian demands for Saddam Hussein's ouster, brought an intensification of the cult of the leader. His birthday was declared a national holiday, and in 1982 members of the Iraqi national assembly wrote in their own blood a pledge of loyalty to him. A U.S. visitor to Iraq in 1987 described the scene in these terms:

> Larger than life paintings and cut out posters of Saddam Hussein are omnipresent in Iraqi cities and villages. The paintings,

> some of which are several stories high, depict Saddam in his role as Field Marshal, as a businessman, as a Bedouin Arab in characteristic headdress, as a Kurd, as a comforter of bereaved children, as a devotee in prayer at the holy shrines, as an air force ace, and as a cigar smoking politician. . . . He is venerated on screen and in print. Baghdad's new international airport is named after him; his face adorns calendars, clocks and watches.

Iraqis say that a picture of Saddam Hussein on the living-room wall is a household necessity, if only to ward off suspicion that one is deficient in enthusiasm for the leader and his regime. And as with so many other things in contemporary Iraq, the death penalty has been invoked to reinforce the personality cult. Public insult of the president or of the top institutions of state or party has been made punishable by life imprisonment or death. The decree, issued in 1986 and signed by Saddam Hussein himself, provides:

> Anyone insulting publicly in any way the President of the Republic, or his office, or the Revolutionary Command Council, or the Arab Baath Socialist Party, or the Government, is punishable by life imprisonment and the expropriation of all his property both movable and immovable. The punishment will be execution if the insult or attack is done in a blatant fashion, or is designed to provoke public opinion against the authorities.

The second paragraph of this same decree stipulates a prison sentence of not more than seven years, or prison and a fine, for anyone found to be "publicly insulting in any way, the courts, armed forces or other public authorities and government bodies."

That these provisions are not just on the books but are enforced was suggested by Salaheddin Saeed, editor in chief of the Baghdad daily *Al-Iraq*, during a visit to London in 1987. Asked by a British reporter whether the Iraqi journalists' union would defend members who produced material deemed insulting to President Saddam Hussein, Saeed replied that his organization "does not represent criminals. . . . If you insult the President or the flag, you would be executed."

Evidently, it is left to the courts to determine what constitutes an insult and at what point it becomes flagrant, for the decree in question offers no definition. Even an inadvertent slight can bring trouble. For example, British civil engineer Peter Worth told the London press that he was arrested, beaten, and tortured after he leaned against a wall at a construction project and caused a picture of Saddam Hussein to fall to the ground. According to émigrés interviewed by Middle East Watch, even spilling one's coffee on the picture of Saddam Hussein that appears daily on the front page of the newspaper has been known to lead to arrest and interrogation.

This official personality cult is increasingly used as a means to political control. Observers of the current Iraqi scene have noted that taking part in this cult has become the new benchmark of loyalty, as important as joining the Baath party. For those Iraqis who choose not to become members of the Baath party, it in recent years has come to offer an alternative avenue for gaining access to the many rewards the regime has to offer.

The Secret Police

Observers of the Iraqi scene agree (at least in private discussion) that the secret police are omnipresent, and operate openly with impunity, detaining citizens at will, making arrests without warrant, and routinely torturing and frequently murdering those in custody. Published information on the Iraqi secret police is scarce, but a recent book sheds some light on the subject. It lists three main agencies:

> The Amn, or State Internal Security, said to have had close ties with the Soviet KGB in the early and mid-1970s, before the Iraqi regime's break with the Iraqi Communist party, but believed now to have been somewhat eclipsed.
>
> The Mukhabarat, or General Intelligence Department, the Baath party's security arm, described as "the most powerful and

> feared agency . . . a meta-intelligence organization designed to watch over the other policing networks and control the activities of state and corporate institutions like the army, government departments and mass organizations." The Mukhabarat was headed by Barzan al-Takriti, half brother of Saddam Hussein, from 1978 to 1982 or 1983 (authorities differ on the date).
>
> The Istikhbarat, or military intelligence, which in keeping with the Baath party's policy of subordinating the military to its control, is said to operate only abroad. It performs traditional military intelligence-gathering functions but is also said to have been involved, along with the domestic secret-police agencies, in assassinations and other undercover operations on foreign soil.

Iraqi émigré sources told Middle East Watch that the Mukhabarat in recent years has been substantially reduced in size and authority, and that another organization, the Amn al-Khass, or Special Security, has taken over the role of senior and all-powerful secret-police arm. The Amn al-Khass is described as Saddam Hussein's personal secret police, run out of the president's office. Its rise to preeminence reflects the concentration of power in Saddam Hussein's hands. According to émigrés and an Arab diplomat interviewed by Middle East Watch, the Amn al-Khass is said to be headed by his son-in-law, **Hussein Kamel Hassan,** who is also minister of Military Industry and Military Industrialization.

Just how many people the various security agencies employ is one of the many unknowns of the murky world of Iraq's secret police. The Amn is believed to be part of the Ministry of Interior, which is also responsible for police functions and is said to be the largest governmental department in Iraq. In 1978 it was reported to have 151,301 employees, or nearly 1.5 percent of the estimated population of Iraq at the time. The Presidential Affairs Department, which presumably carries the Amn al-Khass on its payrolls, numbered 57,768 that same year. Today both governmental sectors are believed to have grown still larger, both proportionately and in absolute terms.

The Amn, the Amn al-Khass, and the Mukhabarat operate principally in Iraq itself, but because their activities are shrouded in secrecy, more is known about their operations abroad, where they cannot so easily escape public scrutiny. Even though foreign operations are undoubtedly only a small fraction of those at home, the list of assassinations carried out beyond Iraq's borders that are attributed to its secret-police agencies has grown quite long. Former Iraqi officials, as well as opponents and critics of the regime, have been killed in Arab capitals and in Europe.

In 1971, Hardan al-Takriti, a former member of the Revolutionary Command Council and a rival of Saddam Hussein, was assassinated in exile in Kuwait. In the late 1970s, several dissident Iraqis were murdered in Beirut and Cairo. London became the scene of two successful assassinations and one assassination attempt attributed to Iraqi agents or their surrogates in 1978. In January of that year Said Hamaini, the Palestine Liberation Organization representative in the British capital, was murdered; although the killer escaped, the crime was attributed to the Abu Nidal group, a Palestinian terrorist organization based at that time (and until 1982) in Baghdad.

In February 1978, Dr. Ayad Allawi, a senior Baath party official until his resignation in 1976, was attacked in bed in his home in the early morning hours by a man wielding an ax. Dr. Allawi awoke in time to fight off the assailant, but in the struggle his leg was nearly severed and his wife suffered permanent injury; he himself required a year of hospital treatment to regain use of his leg.

In July 1978, former Iraqi prime minister Abdul Razzaq al-Nayef was shot in London on the steps of the Intercontinental Hotel. This time the members of the assassination team were caught; one was identified as an official of the Iraqi embassy in London, and another acknowledged being a senior Baath party member. They and the gunman reportedly confessed to the killing during police interrogation but later reneged and pleaded not guilty at trial. The assassination moved the British government to expel several members of the Iraqi embassy and to issue a stern warning to Baghdad; U.K.-Iraqi relations remained tense for some time.

In 1979, gunmen operating out of the Iraqi embassy in Aden shot and killed several exiled members of the Iraqi Communist party. When the government of South Yemen took measures against the Iraqi embassy, Baghdad cut off aid and expelled South Yemeni students.

Iraq is said to have been involved in the assassination attempt against Israeli Ambassador Shlomo Argov in London in June 1982, which triggered Israel's invasion of Lebanon. According to one report, the gunmen who shot Argov as he left a London hotel on the evening of June 3 were led by Nawaf Rosan, an Iraqi intelligence colonel who served as deputy to Palestinian terrorist leader Abu Nidal.

Other assassinations are reported by Iraqi émigré groups to have been carried out or attempted by Iraqi services during the 1980s at a variety of locations in Europe, Asia and Africa, including:

> Vienna, in July 1980, where an Iraqi embassy first secretary and attache were expelled for involvement in a bombing in which eight were injured;
>
> West Berlin, in September 1980, where a bomb was placed, but found and defused, at a meeting place for Kurdish rebel factions;
>
> Dubai, in 1981, where Mohammad al-Salman, an Iraqi Shia and a member of the Islamic Opposition movement, was killed;
>
> Sweden, in 1985, where Majid Abdul Karim, reportedly a former Iraqi intelligence officer who had defected, was killed;
>
> Italy, in 1986, where Dr. Mohammad Habush, an Iraqi Shia and a member of the Islamic Opposition movement, was killed.
>
> Pakistan, in March 1987, where Nima Mohammad Mahdi and Sami Mahdi Abid, Iraqi Shias and members of the Islamic Opposition, were killed.
>
> Thailand, in May 1987, where Mohammad Zaki al-Siwaij, an Iraqi Shia clergyman, was wounded while leading prayer services.

In January 1988, in an operation that attracted considerable international attention, Iraqi agents lured Iraqi Shia opposition figure Sayyed Mahdi al-Hakim, an outspoken critic of the Iraqi regime, from the relative safety of his London exile to an Islamic conference in Khartoum and three days after his arrival shot him down in the lobby of the Hilton Hotel. The get-away car used by the gunmen belonged to the Iraqi embassy. When the government of Sudan announced that Iraqi embassy personnel had taken part in the assassination, Iraq closed its embassy in Khartoum.

Ismet Sheriff Vanly, an Iraqi Kurdish scholar and opposition spokesman who holds Swiss citizenship, has given a vivid description of an assassination attempt made against him in 1976 at his home in Lausanne. Vanly recounts, in a book published in 1980, that on October 3, 1976, Iraqi Ambassador Nabil al-Tikriti, a relative of Saddam Hussein, visited him, ostensibly for a discussion about the Kurdish position in Iraq. At the end of the visit, Ambassador al-Tikriti said he had brought Vanly fresh dates from Baghdad but had forgotten them in Geneva. He said he would have them delivered in a day or two. According to Vanly's account:

> On October 7, one of Nabil al-Tikriti's so-called diplomats called at my door. I invited him in and he put the packet of dates on the table in the living room, "with the compliments of Nabil al-Tikriti." I asked him if he would like coffee or an alcoholic drink. The killer, who knew the layout of my house, opted for coffee. I went to the kitchen to make some. I had just turned on the electric cooker when a shot rang out. The "diplomat" had fired at point blank range two 7.65 mm bullets which both smashed into my head, one behind the left ear, the other breaking my lower jaw. The medical report stated that the victim of this assassination attempt "escaped death only by an extraordinary fluke."

Assassinations are only the most visible part of the foreign operations of the Iraqi secret police. Harassment is also common. Iraqi dissidents who have managed to flee have found themselves hounded from one country to the next. In an article published in 1986, an Iraqi writer who took the pseudonym of Raad Mushatat recounted harassment he encountered after he fled his native country in 1979. After escaping across the Syrian border, Mushatat traveled to Italy, where he and a group of other Iraqis started an Arabic magazine. According to Mushatat, "we suffered physical attacks from pro-government Iraqis and some of my friends had to go into hospital." Mushatat fled to the Algerian desert where, in 1984, he again felt compelled to move on.

In the late 1970s, a rash of attacks on Iraqi dissident students in Britain by supposed Iraqi students under government sponsorship prompted the British National Union of Students to withdraw recognition from the Baath student organization, the National Union of Iraqi Students. Nonetheless, throughout the 1980s Iraqi students in Britain who had defected or who were known to be opponents of the Baath regime continued to be harassed by these "students." In December 1988, three supposed Iraqi students were jailed in Swansea for assaulting an Iraqi student at Cardiff University.

Iraq's rapprochement with the West, its desire to gain respectability, and its need for Western credits to rebuild its economy following the war with Iran appear to have brought assassinations in Western capitals largely to a halt in the late 1980s. Lesser acts of violence and intimidation continue, however. In October 1988, Britain, in recent years Iraq's most generous Western creditor, expelled three Iraqi diplomats on charges of "activities incompatible with their status" and asked a fourth not to return. The British press reported that the four were believed to have been spying on and seeking to intimidate the Iraqi opposition in Britain and that they had been found to be walking around London carrying firearms.

Report on al-Anfal

George Black

from *Genocide in Iraq*

Introduction

This report is a narrative account of a campaign of extermination against the Kurds of northern Iraq. It is the product of over a year and a half of research, during which a team of Middle East Watch researchers has analyzed several tons of captured Iraqi government documents and carried out field interviews with more than 350 witnesses, most of them survivors of the 1988 campaign known as Anfal. It concludes that in that year the Iraqi regime committed the crime of genocide.

Anfal—"the Spoils"—is the name of the eighth *sura* of the Koran. It is also the name given by the Iraqis to a series of military actions which lasted from February 23 until September 6, 1988. While it is impossible to understand the Anfal campaign without reference to the final phase of the 1980-1988 Iran-Iraq War, Anfal was not merely a function of that war. Rather, the winding-up of the conflict on Iraq's terms was the immediate historical circumstance that gave Baghdad the opportunity to bring to a climax its longstanding efforts to bring the Kurds to heel. For the Iraqi regime's anti-Kurdish drive dated back some fifteen years or more, well before the outbreak of hostilities between Iran and Iraq.

Anfal was also the most vivid expression of the "special powers" granted to Ali Hassan al-Majid, a cousin of President Saddam Hussein and secretary general of the Northern Bureau of Iraq's Ba'ath Arab Socialist Party. From March 29, 1987 until April 23, 1989, al-Majid was granted power that was equivalent, in Northern Iraq, to that of the President himself, with authority over all agencies of the state. Al-Majid, who is known to this day to Kurds as "Ali Anfal" or "Ali Chemical," was the overlord of the Kurdish genocide. Under his command, the central actors in Anfal were the First and Fifth Corps of the regular Iraqi Army, the General Security Directorate (*Mudiriyat al-Amn al-Ameh*) and Military Intelligence (*Istikhbarat*). The pro-government Kurdish militia known as the National Defense Battalions, or *jahsh*, assisted in important auxiliary tasks.[1] But the integrated resources of the entire military, security and civilian apparatus of the Iraqi state were deployed, in al-Majid's words, "to solve the Kurdish problem and slaughter the saboteurs."[2]

The campaigns of 1987-1989 were characterized by the following gross violations of human rights:

- mass summary executions and mass disappearance of many tens of thousands of non-combatants, including large numbers of women and children, and sometimes the entire population of villages;
- the widespread use of chemical weapons, including mustard gas and the

nerve agent GB, or Sarin, against the town of Halabja as well as dozens of Kurdish villages, killing many thousands of people, mainly women and children;

- the wholesale destruction of some 2,000 villages, which are described in government documents as having been "burned," "destroyed," "demolished" and "purified," as well as at least a dozen larger towns and administrative centers (*nahyas* and *qadhas*);
- the wholesale destruction of civilian objects by Army engineers, including all schools, mosques, wells and other non-residential structures in the targeted villages, and a number of electricity substations;
- looting of civilian property and farm animals on a vast scale by army troops and pro-government militia;
- arbitrary arrest of all villagers captured in designated "prohibited areas' (*manateq al-mahdoureh*), despite the fact that these were their own homes and lands;
- arbitrary jailing and warehousing for months, in conditions of extreme deprivation, of tens of thousands of women, children and elderly people, without judicial order or any cause other than their presumed sympathies for the Kurdish opposition. Many hundreds of them were allowed to die of malnutrition and disease;
- forced displacement of hundreds of thousands of villagers upon the demolition of their homes, their release from jail or return from exile; these civilians were trucked into areas of Kurdistan far from their homes and dumped there by the army with only minimal governmental compensation or none at all for their destroyed property, or any provision for relief, housing, clothing or food, and forbidden to return to their villages of origin on pain of death. In these conditions, many died within a year of their forced displacement;
- destruction of the rural Kurdish economy and infrastructure.

Like Nazi Germany, the Iraqi regime concealed its actions in euphemisms. Where Nazi officials spoke of "executive measures," "special actions" and "resettlement in the east," Ba'athist bureaucrats spoke of "collective measures," "return to the national ranks" and "resettlement in the south." But beneath the euphemisms, Iraq's crimes against the Kurds amount to genocide, the "intent to destroy, in whole or in part, a national, ethnical, racial or religious group, as such."[3]

The campaigns of 1987-1989 are rooted deep in the history of the Iraqi Kurds. Since the earliest days of Iraqi independence, the country's Kurds—who today number more than four million—have fought either for independence or for meaningful autonomy. But they have never achieved the results they desired.

In 1970, the Ba'ath Party, anxious to secure its precarious hold on power, did offer the Kurds a considerable measure of self-rule, far greater than that allowed in neighboring Syria, Iran or Turkey. But the regime defined the Kurdistan Autonomous Region in such a way as deliberately to exclude the vast oil wealth that lies beneath the fringes of the Kurdish lands. The Autonomous Region, rejected by the Kurds and imposed unilaterally by Baghdad in 1974, comprised the three northern governorates of Erbil, Suleimaniyeh and Dohuk. Covering some 14,000 square miles—roughly the combined area of Massachusetts, Connecticut and Rhode Island—this was only half the territory that the Kurds considered rightfully theirs. Even so, the Autonomous Region had real economic significance, since it accounted for fully half the agricultural output of a largely desert country that is sorely deficient in domestic food production.

In the wake of the autonomy decree, the Ba'ath Party embarked on the "Arabization" of the oil-producing areas of Kirkuk and Khanaqin and other parts of the north, evicting Kurdish farmers and replacing them with poor Arab tribesmen from the south. Northern Iraq did not remain at peace for long. In 1974, the long-simmering Kurdish revolt flared up once more under the leadership of the legendary fighter Mullah Mustafa Barzani, who was supported this time by the governments of Iran, Israel, and the United States. But the revolt collapsed precipitately in 1975, when Iraq and Iran concluded a border agreement and the Shah withdrew his support from Barzani's Kurdistan Democratic Party (KDP). After the KDP fled into Iran, tens of thousands of villagers from the Barzani tribe were forcibly removed from their homes and relocated to barren sites in the desert south of Iraq. Here, without any form of assistance, they had to rebuild their lives from scratch.

In the mid and late 1970s, the regime again moved against the Kurds, forcibly evacuating at least a quarter of a million people from Iraq's borders with Iran and Turkey, destroying their villages to create a cordon sanitaire along these sensitive frontiers. Most of the displaced Kurds were relocated into *mujamma'at*, crude new settlements located on the main highways in army-controlled areas of Iraqi Kurdistan. The word literally means "amalgamations" or "collectivities." In their propaganda, the Iraqis commonly refer to them as "modern villages"; in this report, they are generally described as "complexes." Until 1987, villagers relocated to the complexes were generally paid some nominal cash compensation, but were forbidden to move back to their homes.

After 1980, and the beginning of the eight-year Iran-Iraq War, many Iraqi garrisons in Kurdistan were abandoned or reduced in size, and their troops transferred to the front. In the vacuum that was left, the Kurdish *peshmerga*—"those who face death"—once more began to thrive. The KDP, now led by one of Barzani's sons, Mas'oud, had revived its alliance with Teheran, and in 1983 KDP units aided Iranian troops in their capture of the border town of Haj Omran. Retribution was swift: in a lightning operation against the complexes that housed the relocated Barzanis, Iraqi troops abducted between five and eight thousand males aged twelve or over. None of them have ever been seen again, and it is believed that after being held prisoner for several months, they were all killed. In many respects, the 1983 Barzani operation foreshadowed the techniques that would be used on a much larger scale during the Anfal campaign. And the absence of any international outcry over this act of mass murder, despite Kurdish efforts to press the matter with the United Nations and Western governments, must have emboldened Baghdad to believe that it could get away with an even larger operation, without any adverse reaction. In these calculations, the Ba'ath Party was correct.

Even more worrisome to Baghdad was the growing closeness between the Iranians and the KDP's major Kurdish rival, Jalal Talabani's Patriotic Union of Kurdistan (PUK). The Ba'ath regime had conducted more than a year of negotiations with the PUK between 1983-1985, but in the end these talks failed to bear fruit, and full-scale fighting resumed. In late 1986 Talabani's party concluded a formal political and military agreement with Teheran.

By this time the Iraqi regime's authority over the North had dwindled to control of the cities, towns, complexes and main highways. Elsewhere, the *peshmerga* forces could rely on a deep-rooted base of local support. Seeking refuge from the army, thousands of Kurdish draft-dodgers and deserters found new homes in the countryside. Villagers learned to live with a harsh economic blockade and stringent food rationing, punctuated by artillery shelling, aerial bombardment and punitive forays by the Army and the paramilitary *jahsh*. In response, the rural Kurds built air-raid shelters in front of their homes and spent much of their time in hiding in the caves and ravines that honeycomb the northern Iraqi countryside. For all the grimness of this existence, by 1987 the mountainous interior of Iraqi Kurdistan was effectively liberated territory. This the Ba'ath Party regarded as an intolerable situation.

With the granting of emergency powers to al-Majid in March 1987, the intermittent counterinsurgency against the Kurds became a campaign of destruction. As Raul Hilberg observes in his monumental history of the Holocaust:

> A destruction process has an inherent pattern. There is only one way in which a scattered group can effectively be destroyed. Three steps are organic in the operation:

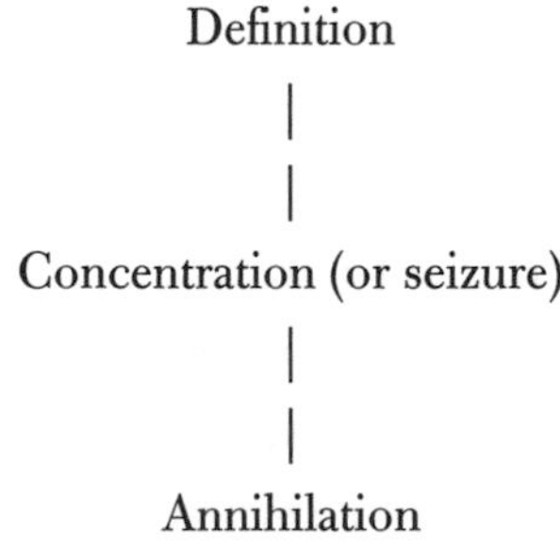

> This is the invariant structure of the basic process, for no group can be killed without a concentration or seizure of the victims, and no victims can be segregated before the perpetrator knows who belongs to the group.[4]

> The Kurdish genocide of 1987-1989, with the Anfal campaign as its centerpiece, fits Hilberg's paradigm to perfection.

In the first three months after assuming his post as secretary general of the Ba'ath Party's Northern Bureau, Ali Hassan al-Majid began the process of definition of the group that would be targeted by Anfal, and vastly expanded the range of repressive activities against all rural Kurds. He decreed that "saboteurs" would lose their property rights, suspended the legal rights of all the residents of prohibited villages, and began ordering the execution of first-degree relatives of "saboteurs" and of wounded civilians whose hostility to the regime had been determined by the intelligence services.

In June 1987, al-Majid issued two successive sets of standing orders that were to govern the conduct of the security forces through the Anfal campaign and beyond. These orders were based on the simple axiom on which the regime now operated: in the "prohibited" rural areas, all resident Kurds were coterminous with the *peshmerga* insurgents, they would be dealt with accordingly.

The first of al-Majid's directives bans all human existence in prohibited areas, to be applied through a shoot-to-kill policy. The second numbered SF/4008, dated June 20, 1987, modifies and expands upon these orders. It constitutes a bald incitement to mass murder, spelled out in the most chilling detail. In clause 4, army commanders are ordered "to carry out random bombardments, using artillery, helicopters and aircraft at all times of the day or night, in order to kill the largest number of persons present in these prohibited zones." In clause 5, al-Majid ordered that, "All persons captured in those villages shall be detained and interrogated by the security services and those between the ages of 15 and 70 shall be executed after any useful information has been obtained from them, of which we should be duly notified."

Even as this legal and bureaucratic structure was being set in place, the Iraqi regime became the first in history to attack its civilian population with chemical weapons. On April 15, 1987, aircraft dropped poison gas on the KDP headquarters at Zewa Shkan close to the Turkish border in Dohuk governorate, and the PUK headquarters in the twin villages of Sergalou and Bergalou, in the governorate of Suleimaniyeh. The following afternoon, they dropped chemicals on the undefended civilian villages of Sheikh Wasan Balisan, killing well over a hundred people, most of them women and children. Scores of other victims of the attack were abducted from hospital beds in the city of Erbil, where they had been taken for treatment of their burns and blindness. They have never been seen again. These incidents were the first of at least forty documented chemical attacks on Kurdish targets over the succeeding eighteen months. They were also the first sign of the regime's new readiness to kill numbers of Kurdish women and children indiscriminately.

Within a week of the mid-April chemical weapons attack Majid's forces were ready to embark upon what he described as a two-stage program of village clearances or collectivization. The first ran April 21 to May 20; the second from May 21 to June 20. More than 700 villages were burned and bulldozed, most of them along the highways in government-controlled areas. The third phase of operation, however, was suspended; with Iraqi forces still committed at the war front, the resources required for such a huge operation were not available. But the goals of the third stage would eventually be accomplished by Anfal.

In terms of defining the target group for destruction, no single administrative step was more important to the Iraqi regime than the national census of October 17, 1987. Now that the springtime village clearances had created a virtual buffer strip between the government and the *peshmerga*-controlled zones, the Ba'ath Party offered the inhabitants of the prohibited areas an ultimatum: either they could "return to the national ranks"—in other words, abandon their homes and livelihoods and accept compulsory relocation in a squalid camp under the eye of the security forces; or they could lose their Iraqi citizenship and be regarded as military deserters. The second option was tantamount to a death sentence, since the census legislation made those who refused to be counted subject to an August 1987 decree of the ruling Revolutionary Command Council, imposing the death penalty on deserters.

In the period leading up to the census, al-Majid refined the target group further. He ordered his intelligence officials to prepare detailed case-by-case dossiers of "saboteurs' " families who were still living in the government-controlled areas. When these dossiers were complete, countless women, children and elderly people were forcibly transferred to the rural areas to share the fate of their *peshmerga* relatives. This case-by-case, family-by-family sifting of the population was to become a characteristic feature of the decisions made during the Anfal period about who should live and who should die.

Last, but not without significance, the census gave those who registered only two alternatives when it came to declaring their nationality. One could either be Arab or Kurdish—a stipulation that was to have the direst consequences for other minority groups, such as the Yezidis, Assyrians and Chaldean Christians who continued to live in the Kurdish areas.[5]

The Anfal campaign began four months after the census, with a massive military assault on the PUK headquarters at Sergalou-Bergalou on the night of February 23, 1988. Anfal would have eight stages in all, seven of them directed at areas under the control of the PUK. The KDP-controlled areas in the northwest of Iraqi Kurdistan, which the regime regarded as a lesser threat, were the target of the Final Anfal operation in late August and early September, 1988.

The Iraqi authorities did nothing to hide the campaign from public view. On the contrary, as each phase of the operation triumphed, its successes were trumpeted with the same propaganda fanfare that attended the victorious battles in the Iran-Iraq War. Even today, Anfal is celebrated in the official Iraqi media. The fifth anniversary in 1993 of the fall of Sergalou and Bergalou on March 19, 1988 was the subject of banner headlines.

Iraqi troops tore through rural Kurdistan with the motion of a gigantic windshield wiper, sweeping first clockwise, then counterclockwise, through one after another of the "prohibited areas." The First Anfal, centered on the siege of the PUK headquarters, took more than three weeks. Subsequent phases of the campaign were generally shorter, with a brief pause between each as army units moved on to the next target. The Second Anfal, in the Qara Dagh region, lasted from March 22 to April 1, 1988; the Third, covering the hilly plain known as Germian, took from April 7 to April 20; the Fourth, in the valley of the Lesser Zab river, was the shortest of all, lasting only from May 3 to May 8.

Only in the Fifth Anfal, which began on May 15 in the mountainous region northeast of Erbil, did the troops have any real difficulty in meeting their objectives. Encountering fierce resistance in difficult terrain from the last of the PUK *peshmerga*, the regime called a temporary halt to the offensive on June 7. On orders from the Office of the Presidency (indicating the personal supervisory role that Saddam Hussein himself played in Anfal), the operation was renewed twice in July and August, with these actions denominated Anfal VI and Anfal VII. Eventually, on August 26, the last PUK-controlled area was declared "cleansed of saboteurs."

By this time, Iran had accepted Iraq's terms for a ceasefire to end the war, freeing up large numbers of Iraqi troops to carry the Anfal operation into the Badinan area of northern Iraqi Kurdistan. The Final Anfal began at first light on August 25, and was over in a matter of days. On September 6, 1988, the Iraqi regime made its de facto declaration of victory by announcing a general amnesty for all Kurds. (Ali Hassan al-Majid later told aides that he had opposed the amnesty, but had gone along with it as a loyal party man.)

Each stage of Anfal followed roughly the same pattern. It characteristically began with chemical attacks from the air on both civilian and *peshmerga* targets, accompanied by a military blitz against PUK or KDP military bases and fortified positions. The deadly cocktail of mustard and nerve gases was much more lethal against civilians than against the *peshmerga*, some of whom had acquired gas masks and other rudimentary defenses. In the village of Sayw Senan (Second Anfal), more than eighty civilians died; in Goktapa (Fourth Anfal), the death toll was more than 150; in Wara (Fifth Anfal) it was thirty-seven. In the largest chemical attack of all, the March 16 bombing of the

Kurdish town of Halabja, between 3,200 and 5,000 residents died. As a city, Halabja was not technically part of Anfal—the raid was carried out in reprisal for its capture by *peshmerga* supported by Iranian Revolutionary Guards—but it was very much part of the Kurdish genocide.

After the initial assault, ground troops and *jahsh* enveloped the target area from all sides, destroying all human habitation in their path, looting household possessions and farm animals and setting fire to homes, before calling in demolition crews to finish the job. As the destruction proceeded, so did Hilberg's phase of the "concentration" or "seizure" of the target group. Convoys of army trucks stood by to transport the villagers to nearby holding centers and transit camps, while the *jahsh* combed the hillsides to track down anyone who had escaped. (Some members of the militia, an asset of dubious reliability to the regime, also saved thousands of lives by spiriting people away to safety or helping them across army lines.) Secret police combed the towns, cities and complexes to hunt down Anfal fugitives, and in several cases lured them out of hiding with false offers of amnesty and a "return to the national ranks"—a promise that now concealed a more sinister meaning.

To this point, Anfal had many of the characteristics of a counterinsurgency campaign, albeit an unusually savage one. And captured Iraqi documents suggest that during the initial combat phase, counterinsurgency goals were uppermost in the minds of the troops and their commanding officers. To be sure, Iraq—like any other sovereign nation—had legitimate interests in combating insurgency. But the fact that Anfal was, by the narrowest definition, a counterinsurgency, does nothing to diminish the fact that it was also an act of genocide. There is nothing mutually exclusive about counterinsurgency and genocide. Indeed, one may be the instrument used to consummate the other. Article I of the Genocide Convention affirms that "genocide, whether committed in time of peace or in time of war, is a crime under international law." Summarily executing noncombatant or captured members of an ethnical-national group as such is not a legitimate wartime or counterinsurgency measure, regardless of the nature of the conflict.

In addition to this argument of principle, many features of Anfal far transcend the realm of counterinsurgency. These include, first of all, the simple facts of what happened after the military goals of the operation had been accomplished:

- the mass murder and disappearance of many tens of thousands of non-combatants—50,000 by the most conservative estimate, and possibly twice that number;
- the use of chemical weapons against non-combatants in dozens of locations, killing thousands and terrifying many more into abandoning their homes;
- the near-total destruction of family and community assets and infrastructure, including the entire agricultural mainstay of the rural Kurdish economy;
- the literal abandonment, in punishing conditions, of thousands of women, children and elderly people, resulting in the deaths of many hundreds. Those who survived did so largely due to the clandestine help of nearby Kurdish townspeople.

Second, there is the matter of how Anfal was organized as a bureaucratic enterprise. Viewed as a counterinsurgency, each episode of Anfal had a distinct beginning and an end, and its conduct was in the hands of the regular army and the *jahsh* militia. But these agencies were quickly phased out of the picture, and the captured civilians were transferred to an entirely separate bureaucracy for processing and final disposal. Separate institutions were involved—such as *Amn, Istikhbarat*, the Popular Army (a type of home guard) and the Ba'ath Party itself. And the infrastructure of prison camps and death convoys was physically remote from the combat theater, lying well outside the Kurdistan Autonomous Region. Tellingly, the killings were not in any sense concurrent with the counterinsurgency: the detainees were murdered several days or even weeks after the armed forces had secured their goals.

Finally, there is the question of intent, which goes to the heart of the notion of genocide. Documentary materials captured from the Iraqi intelligence agencies demonstrate with great clarity that the mass killings, disappearances and forced relocations associated with Anfal and the other anti-Kurdish campaigns of 1987-1989 were planned in coherent fashion. While power over these campaigns was highly centralized, their success depended on the orchestration of the efforts of a large number of agencies and institutions at the local, regional and national level, from the Office of the Presidency of the Republic on down to the lowliest *jahsh* unit.

The official at the center of this great bureaucratic web, of course, was Ali Hassan al-Majid, and in him the question of intent is apparent on a second, extremely important level. A number of audiotapes were made of meetings between al-Majid and his aides from 1987 to 1989. These tapes were examined by four independent experts, to establish their authenticity and to confirm that the principal speaker was al-Majid. Al-Majid was known to have a distinctive, high-pitched voice and the regional accent of his Tikrit district origins; both these features were recognized without hesitation by those Iraqis consulted by Middle East Watch. As a public figure who frequently appears on radio and television in Iraq,[6] his voice is well known to many Iraqis. One Iraqi consulted on this subject pointed out that the principal speaker on the many hours of recordings in Middle East Watch's possession spoke with authority and used obscene language. In contrast, he said: "Others in those meetings were courteous and respectful with fearful tones, especially when they addressed al-Majid himself." Al-Majid, two experts noted, was often referred to by his familiar nickname, "Abu Hassan."

The tapes contain evidence of a bitter racial animus against the Kurds on the part of the man who, above any other, plotted their destruction. "Why should I let them live there like donkeys who don't know anything?" al-Majid asks in one meeting. "What did we ever get from them?" On another occasion, speaking in the same vein: "I said probably we will find some good ones among [the Kurds] . . . but we didn't, never." And elsewhere, "I will smash their heads. These kind of dogs, we will crush their heads." And again, "Take good care of them? No, I will bury them with bulldozers."

Loyalty to the regime offered no protection from al-Majid's campaigns. Nor did membership in the pro-government *jahsh*. Al-Majid even boasted of threatening militia leaders with chemical weapons if they refused to evacuate their villages. Ethnicity and physical location were all that mattered, and these factors became coterminous when the mass killings took place in 1988.

The 1987 village clearances were wholly directed at government-controlled areas, and thus had nothing whatever to do with counterinsurgency. If the former residents of these areas refused to accept government-assigned housing in a *mujamma'a*, and took refuge instead in a *peshmerga*-controlled area—as many did—they too were liable to be killed during Anfal. The same applied to other smaller minorities. In the October 1987 census, many Assyrian and Chaldean Christians—an Aramaic-speaking people of ancient origin—refused the government's demands that they designate themselves either as Arabs or Kurds. Those who declined to be Arabs were automatically treated as Kurds. And, during the Final Anfal in Dohuk governorate, where most Christians were concentrated, they were in fact dealt with by the regime even more severely than their Kurdish neighbors. Those few Turkomans, a Turkic-speaking minority, who fought with the Kurdish *peshmerga* were not spared, because they too were deemed to have become Kurds.

Almost continuously for the previous two decades, the Ba'ath-led government had engaged in a campaign of Arabization of Kurdish regions. The armed resistance this inspired was Kurdish in character and composition. In 1988, the rebels and all those deemed to be sympathizers were therefore treated as Kurds who had to be wiped out, once and for all. Whether they were combatants or not was immaterial; as far as the government was concerned they were all "bad Kurds", who had not come over to the side of the government.

To pursue Hilberg's paradigm a little further, once the concentration and seizure was complete, the annihilation could begin. The target group had already been defined with care. Now came the definition of the second, concentric circle within the group: those who were actually to be killed.

At one level, this was a straightforward matter. Under the terms of al-Majid's June 1987 directives, death was the automatic penalty for any male of an age to bear arms who was found in an Anfal area.[7] At the same time, no one was supposed to go before an Anfal firing squad without first having his or her case individually examined. There is a great deal of documentary evidence to support this view, beginning with a presidential order of October 15, 1987—two days before the census—that "the names of persons who are to be subjected to a general/blanket judgment must not be listed collectively. Rather, refer to them or treat them in your correspondence on an individual basis." The effects of this order are reflected in the lists that the Army and *Amn* compiled of Kurds arrested during Anfal, which note each person's name, sex, age, place of residence and place of capture.

The processing of the detainees took place in a network of camps and prisons. The first temporary holding centers were in operation, under the control of military intelligence as early as March 15, 1988; by about the end of that month, the mass disappearances had begun in earnest, peaking in mid-April and early May. Most of the detainees went to a place called Topzawa, a Popular Army camp on the outskirts of Kirkuk—the city where Ali Hassan al-Majid had his headquarters. Some went to the Popular Army barracks in Tikrit. Women and children were trucked on from Topzawa to a separate camp in the town of Dibs; between 6,000 and 8,000 elderly detainees were taken to the abandoned prison of Nugra Salman in the southern desert, where hundreds of them died of neglect, starvation and disease. Badinan prisoners from the Final Anfal went through a separate but parallel system, with most being detained in the huge army fort at Dohuk and the women and children being transferred later to a prison camp in Salamiyeh on the Tigris River close to Mosul.

The majority of the women, children and elderly people were released from the camps after the September 6 amnesty. But none of the Anfal men were released. Middle East Watch's presumption, based on the testimony of a number of survivors from the Third and bloodiest Anfal, is that they went in large groups before firing squads and were interred secretly outside the Kurdish areas. During the Final Anfal in Badinan, in at least two cases groups of men were executed on the spot after capture by military officers carrying out instructions from their commanders.

The locations of at least three mass gravesites have been pinpointed through the testimony of survivors. One is near the north bank of the Euphrates River, close to the town of Ramadi and adjacent to a complex housing Iranian Kurds forcibly displaced in the early stages of the Iran-Iraq War. Another is in the vicinity of the archaeological site of Al-Hadhar (Hatra), south of Mosul. A third is in the desert outside the town of Samawah. At least two other mass graves are believed to exist on Hamrin Mountain, one between Kirkuk and Tikrit and the other west of Tuz Khurmatu.[8]

While the camp system is evocative of one dimension of the Nazi genocide, the range of execution methods described by Kurdish survivors is uncannily reminiscent of another—the activities of the *Einsatzkommandos*, or mobile killing units, in the Nazi-occupied lands of Eastern Europe. Each of the standard operating techniques used by the *Einsatzkommandos* is documented in the Kurdish case. Some groups of prisoners were lined up, shot from the front and dragged into pre-dug mass graves; others were shoved roughly into trenches and machinegunned where they stood; others were made to lie down in pairs, sardine-style, next to mounds of fresh corpses, before being killed; others were tied together, made to stand on the lip of the pit, and shot in the back so that they would fall forward into it—a method that was presumably more efficient from the point of view of the killers. Bulldozers then pushed earth or sand loosely over the heaps of corpses. Some of the gravesites contained dozens of separate pits, and obviously contained the bodies of thousands of victims. Circumstantial evidence suggests that the executioners were uniformed members of the Ba'ath Party, or perhaps of Iraq's General Security Directorate (*Amn*).

By the most conservative estimates, 50,000 rural Kurds died during Anfal. While males from approximately fourteen to fifty were routinely killed en masse, a number of questions surround the selection criteria that were used to order the murder of younger children and entire families.

Many thousands of women and children perished, but subject to extreme regional variations, with most being residents of two distinct "clusters" that were affected by the Third and Fourth Anfals. Abuses by zealous local field commanders may explain why women and children were rounded up, rather than being allowed to slip away. But they cannot adequately explain the later patterns of disappearance, since the detainees were promptly transferred alive out of army custody, segregated from their husbands and fathers in processing centers elsewhere, and then killed in cold blood after a period in detention. The place of surrender, more than place of residence, seems to have been one consideration in deciding who lived and who died. *Amn* documents indicate that another factor may have been whether the troops encountered armed resistance in a given area—which indeed was the case in most, but not all, of the areas marked by the killing of women and children. A third criterion may have been the perceived "political stance" of detainees, although it is hard to see how this could have been applied to children.

Whatever the precise reasons, it is clear from captured Iraqi documents that the intelligence agencies scrutinized at least some cases individually, and even appealed to the highest authority if they were in doubt about the fate of a particular individual. This suggests that the annihilation process was governed, at least in principle, by rigid bureaucratic norms. But all the evidence suggests that the purpose of these norms was not to rule on a particular person's guilt or innocence of specific charges, but merely to establish whether an individual belonged to the target group that was to be "Anfalized," i.e. Kurds in areas outside government control. At the same time, survivor testimony repeatedly indicates that the rulebook was only adhered to casually in practice. The physical segregation of detainees from Anfal areas by age and sex, as well as the selection of those to be exterminated, was a crude affair, conducted without any meaningful prior process of interrogation or evaluation.

Although Anfal as a military campaign ended with the general amnesty of September 6, 1988, its logic did not. Those who were released from prisons such as Nugra Salman, Dibs and Salamiyeh, as well as those who returned from exile under the amnesty, were relocated to complexes with no compensation and no means of support. Civilians who tried to help them were hunted down by *Amn*. The *mujamma'at* that awaited the survivors of the Final Anfal in Badinan were places of residence in name alone; the *Anfalakan* were merely dumped on the barren earth of the Erbil plain with no infrastructure other than perimeter fence and military guard towers. Here, hundreds perished from disease, exposure, hunger or malnutrition, and the after-effects of exposure to chemical weapons. Several hundreds more—non-Muslim Yezidis, Assyrians and Chaldeans, including many women and children were abducted from the camps and disappeared, collateral victims of the Kurdish genocide. Their particular crime was to have remained in the prohibited majority Kurdish areas after community leaders declined to accept the regime's classification of them as Arabs in the 1987 census.

The regime had no intention of allowing the amnestied Kurds to exercise their full civil rights as Iraqi citizens. They were to be deprived of political rights and employment opportunities until *Amn* certified their loyalty to the regime. They were to sign written pledges that they would remain in the *mujamma'at* to which they had been assigned—on pain of death. They were to understand that the prohibited areas remained off limits and were often sown with landmines to discourage resettlement; directive SF/4008, and in particular clause 5, with its order to kill all adult males, would remain in force and would be carried out to the letter.

Arrests and executions continued, some of the latter even involving prisoners who were alive, in detention, at the time of the amnesty. Middle East Watch has documented three cases of mass executions in late 1988; in one of them, 180 people were put to death. Documents from one local branch of *Amn* list another eighty-seven executions in the first eight months of 1989, one of them a man accused of "teaching the Kurdish language in Latin script."

The few hundred Kurdish villages that had come through Anfal unscathed as a result of their pro-government sympathies had no guarantees of lasting survival, and dozens more were burned and bulldozed in late 1988 and 1989. Army engineers even destroyed the large Kurdish town of Qala Dizeh (population 70,000) and declared its environs a "prohibited area," removing the last significant population center close to the Iranian border.

Killing, torture and scorched-earth policies continued, in other words, to be a matter of daily routine in Iraqi Kurdistan, as they always had been under the rule of the Ba'ath Arab Socialist Party. But the Kurdish problem, in al-Majid's words, had been solved; the "saboteurs" had been slaughtered. Since 1975, some 4,000 Kurdish villages had been destroyed; at least 50,000 rural Kurds had died in

Anfal alone, and very possibly twice that number; half of Iraq's productive farmland had been laid waste. All told, the total number of Kurds killed over the decade since the Barzani men were taken from their homes is well into six figures.

By April 23, 1989, the Ba'ath Party felt that it had accomplished its goals, for on that date it revoked the special powers that had been granted to Ali Hassan al-Majid two years earlier. At a ceremony to greet his successor, the supreme commander of Anfal made it clear that "the exceptional situation is over."

To use the language of the Genocide Convention, the regime's aim had been to *destroy the group* (Iraqi Kurds) *in part*, and it had done so. Intent and act had been combined, resulting in the consummated crime of genocide. And with this, Ali Hassan al-Majid was free to move on to other tasks demanding his special talents—first as governor of occupied Kuwait and, then, in 1993, as Iraq's Minister of Defense.

Notes:

[1] A derisive Kurdish term for the National Defense Battalions, the word *jahsh* means "donkey foals."

[2]"Saboteurs" is the term commonly applied by the Iraqi regime to the Kurdish *peshmerga* guerrillas and their civilian sympathizers.

[3] As defined in the Convention on the Prevention and Punishment of the Crime of Genocide (hereinafter the Genocide Convention), 78 UNTS 277, approved by GA Res. 2670 on December 9, 1948, entered into force January 12, 1951.

[4] Raul Hilberg, *The Destruction of the European Jews* (New York: Holmes and Meier, 1985 student edition), p.267.

[5] While the Yezidis, a syncretic religious sect, are ethnic Kurds, the Assyrians and Chaldeans are a distinct ancient people in their own right.

[6]Al-Majid has served variously over the past five years as Secretary General of the Ba'ath Party's Northern Bureau, Interior Minister, Governor of Iraqi-occupied Kuwait in 1990, and, as Defense Minister.

[7] Rural Kurdish men carry personal weapons as a matter of tradition, regardless of their politics.

[8] Other mass graves have been found elsewhere in Kurdish-controlled territory, containing the remains of *Amn* executions before, during and after the Anfal period.

Part II

Saddam Hussein and the Gulf War

Efraim Karsh and Lawrence Freedman

from *The Gulf Conflict, 1990–1991: Diplomacy and War in the New World Order*

Saddam Hussein was always an unlikely moderate. The use of physical force to promote his political ends had been the hallmark of the Iraqi leader's career from the start: his rise to power in July 1979, for example, was followed by a bloody purge in which hundreds of party officials and military officers, some of whom were close friends and associates, perished. Nevertheless, as far as Iraq's external relations were concerned, Saddam's bark had always been harsher than his bite, as he had preferred to pursue his goals with the lowest risk and greatest economy possible.

During the 1970s, while acting as Vice-President but the *de facto* 'strong man in Baghdad', he effectively pursued an overly pragmatic line which ran counter to his party's outspoken radicalism. In September 1970 he prevented Iraqi troops, then deployed on Jordanian soil, from intervening to stop the bloodshed between the Jordanian Army and the PLO. Similarly, Iraq's military support to the co-ordinated Egyptian-Syrian attack against Israel in October 1973 was extremely limited, and was withdrawn at the first available opportunity. Then, in March 1975, Saddam made a far-reaching concession to the Iranian Shah by concluding the so-called Algiers Agreement which settled the longstanding territorial dispute between the two countries over the Shatt al-Arab waterway on terms favourable to Iran. He observed this agreement throughout the latter part of the 1970s.

Indeed, contrary to the common wisdom, the hazardous move of invading Iran was not motivated by imperial dreams and megalomaniac aspirations. War in the autumn of 1980 could not have been more ill-timed for Saddam Hussein's political career. He assumed the presidency in July 1979, at a time when his country enjoyed unprecedented economic prosperity. Due to the world oil boom Iraqi export revenues had risen to $21 billion in 1979 and $26 billion in

1980, and during the months preceding the invasion these revenues were running at an annual rate of $33 billion, enabling Saddam to carry out ambitious development programmes. War could only put these achievements at risk and, in consequence, render Saddam's domestic standing more tenuous.

Hence, following the overthrow of the Shah in January 1979, Saddam did not attempt to take advantage of the civil strife in Iran to extract territorial or political concessions, but welcomed the revolutionary regime in Tehran, went out of his way to placate it, and emphasized his determination to continue to observe the status quo established by the Algiers Agreement. As late as the spring of 1980 Saddam was publicly airing his fears of Iraq's disintegration into Sunni, Shi'ite and Kurdish statelets.

Only after his gestures of goodwill had been spurned by the Iranians did Saddam change tack. Initially he sought to counter Iranian-inspired Shi'ite restiveness within Iraq, by clamping down on the main Shi'ite underground organization, the *Da'wa* Party ('the Islamic call'), and launching a series of verbal attacks against Ayatollah Khomeini. He also supported Iranian separatist elements, such as the Kurds in northern Iran and the Arabs in the southern Iranian province of Khuzestan, and attempted to orchestrate the Arab Gulf states into a unified front against the Iranian threat.

These countermeasures were significantly upgraded after April 1980, following an abortive Iranian-sponsored attempt on the life of Iraq's Deputy Premier, Tariq Aziz. Deeply shaken by Tehran's ability to hit at the heart of his regime, Saddam resorted to draconian measures against the Shi'ite opposition. Within a fortnight, Iraq's most prominent Shiite religious authority, Ayatollah Muhammad Bakr al-Sadr, who had been under house arrest for several months, was executed, together with his sister, as were hundreds of Shi'ite political prisoners. Saddam effectively sealed the southern part of Iraq, denying foreign, particularly Iranian, worshippers any access to the Shi'i holy shrines. The extent of his anxiety was further illustrated by the expulsion of some 100,000 Iraqi Shi'ites from the country.

As these measures failed Saddam invaded Iran, as a pre-emptive strike to shore up his personal rule. He apparently believed that a limited campaign would suffice to convince the revolutionary regime in Tehran to desist from its attempts to overthrow him, and did not intend to engage in a prolonged drawn-out conflict. If he entertained aspirations beyond the containment of the Iranian danger—as he may have done—they were not the reasons for launching the war but were incidental. As Foreign Minister Aziz put it: 'We want neither to destroy Iran nor to occupy it permanently, because this country is a neighbour with which we will remain linked by geographical and historical bonds and common interests.'

Saddam's limited objectives were also demonstrated by his war strategy. Rather than dealing a mortal blow to the Iranian Army and seeking to topple the revolutionary regime, he sought to confine the war by restricting the Army's goals, means and targets. His territorial aims did not go beyond the Shatt al-Arab and a small portion of Khuzestan. As to means, the invasion was carried out by less than half of the Iraqi Army—five of twelve divisions. Saddam's initial strategy avoided targets of civilian and economic value in favour of attacks almost exclusively on military targets. Only after the Iranians escalated by attacking non-military targets did the Iraqis respond in kind. Most importantly, on 28 September, merely five days after the invasion, Saddam voluntarily halted his troops, while they were still moving forward, and announced his readiness to cease hostilities and to enter into peace negotiations. Hence, when the war turned out to be a far more tortuous experience than he had ever feared, Saddam turned every stone and bent every principle in an attempt to survive this monster of his own making.

The outcome was further moderation in Iraq's regional and global outlook. In March 1979 Saddam had triumphantly hosted in Baghdad an all-Arab conference which expelled Egypt from the Arab League for making peace with Israel; a year later he was desperately pleading with the excommunicated Egyptian President, Anwar Sadat, for military support. During the following years, as Egypt developed into an important military provider, Saddam would toil tirelessly to pave the way for its return to the Arab fold.

Furthermore, whenever his personal survival so required, Saddam had no qualms about accommodating Israel which, for its part, seemed increasingly disillusioned with the prospects of the restoration of a favourable regime in Tehran. In 1985 he sought to buy Israel's acquiescence in the laying of an Iraqi oil pipeline to the Jordanian port town of Aqaba by offering it $700 million over ten years. Covert overtures to Israel were paralleled by growing public indications of readiness to reach a political accommodation with the Jewish state. In 1982 Saddam participated in the Fez Arab summit, which tacitly accepted a two-state solution to the Arab-Israeli conflict. Subsequently, he even voiced public support for peace negotiations between the Arabs and Israel, emphasizing that 'no Arab leader looks forward to the destruction of Israel' and that any solution to the conflict would require 'the existence of a secure state for the Israelis'.

This moderation was sustained into the post-war period. Having survived the deadliest threat to his personal rule, Saddam had no inclination to risk his regime by further foreign entanglements. Even though it was Tehran which eventually pleaded for a cease-fire, the end of the Iran-Iraq War did not imply a lull in Saddam's struggle for political survival. The nature of the threat to his regime had, of course, fundamentally changed as the mullahs in Tehran were no longer calling for his blood. Instead he faced the daunting task of reconstructing Iraq, so as to prove to his subjects that the eight-year war had been won. This, in turn, meant that Saddam's personal interest could be best served by moderation and collaboration rather than antagonism and confrontation, by domestic stability and a relaxed international atmosphere rather than turmoil and heightened tensions.

Hence, the end of the war was followed by unprecedented manifestations of political openness on Saddam's part, such as a public commitment to end the Ba'th's monopoly on power, to establish a democratic multi-party system in Iraq, and to hold direct free elections for the country's presidency. These measures were accompanied by greater liberalization of the Iraqi economy, a process begun in the mid 1970s and accelerated during the war. Price controls on all goods were lifted, and an attempt was made to attract capital from Gulf states and foreign companies. Many state-owned corporations were sold off to the private sector at very attractive prices, and there was much speculation about the eventual privatization of all state enterprises except oil and the military industry.

Equally indicative of Saddam's interest in tranquillity was the continuation of his moderate international policy. He did not revert to his pre-war radical rhetoric but sustained and expanded collaboration with moderate Arabs in an attempt to orchestrate them into a unified bloc that would resist Iranian hegemony, promote the Palestinian cause and pressure Syria. This objective was crowned with success in February 1989 with the formation of the Arab Cooperation Council (ACC) comprising Egypt, North Yemen, Jordan, and Iraq. A month later, during an official visit to Baghdad by King Fahd of Saudi Arabia, a bilateral non-aggression pact was concluded.

Saddam also sustained his positive approach towards a negotiated settlement of the Arab-Israeli conflict, playing an important role, together with President Mubarak of Egypt, in sponsoring the PLO's historic recognition of Israel's right to exist in November and December 1988. Were it not for Iraq's and Egypt's readiness to shield the PLO from Syrian wrath, the Palestinians' political room for manoeuvre would have been severely constrained. Saddam's growing acceptance of Israel was also underlined by the evolution of tacit Iraqi-Israeli collaboration against Syria's interests and its presence in Lebanon. This collaboration was mainly expressed in Israel's abstention from intercepting Iraqi arms shipments to the Christians in Beirut despite its ability to do so. There were also reports that the Israeli port of Haifa was used by Iraq as a transit station for shipping tanks and heavy equipment to General Michel Aoun, the self-styled Maronite President who declared 'war of liberation' to drive the Syrians out of Lebanon.

The West supports Saddam

France had taken the Western lead in courting Saddam. As early as 1963, when the war over Algeria was concluded, France under General de Gaulle had begun to reappraise its Middle Eastern policy, which in the past had been based on deep hostility towards Arab nationalism and close co-operation with Israel (to the point of helping create Israel's nuclear capability). It now went into complete reverse. De Gaulle judged that the future lay with the Arabs and turned against Israel at the time of the 1967 war.

The radical Arab regimes were outside the traditional British sphere of influence in the Middle East, which was still largely based on the monarchies. Taking up the cause of Arab nationalism softened what might otherwise have been stormy relations with France's old North African colonies. It also offered an acceptable alternative for radical regimes which did not wish to be completely dependent on the Soviet Union for arms. However, there were limits to success with this policy. During the 1970s, after the death of Nasser, Egypt under President Sadat gradually moved closer to the Americans. With Syria there were problems because of France's lingering sympathy for the Christian community in Lebanon. Iraq was thus a far more promising avenue and here French policy appeared to pay dividends.

It had been targeted from the moment of the Ba'thi takeover in July 1968. Saddam, for his part, quickly recognized the immense economic, military, and technological potential attending a closer relationship with France. Already in June 1972 he had paid an official visit to Paris, the first ever to a Western capital, where he agreed to sell France nearly a quarter of the oil produced by the Iraq Company for Oil Operations (ICOO). In the autumn of 1974 the French Prime Minister, Jacques Chirac, paid an official visit to Baghdad. The next year it was Saddam's turn in Paris; back came the French Premier, now Raymond Barre, to Baghdad in the summer of 1977. Before long France was Iraq's largest arms supplier after the Soviet Union. In 1976 France agreed to sell Iraq the Osiraq nuclear reactor, which was to be destroyed by the Israeli Air Force in a famous raid in June 1981.

Following the Iranian revolution the French stepped up their support for Saddam. They were fearful of Islamic fundamentalism and saw the Iraqi leader as a bulwark of secularism. This was in addition to his capacity to counter Syrian influence. With the outbreak of the Iran–Iraq War the arms relationship between the two countries grew ever closer—in the first six years of the war France gained some $15–17 billion in military contracts, with an additional $5 billion spent on civilian purchases. A special deal allowed the

Iraqis to use French Étendard aircraft and Exocet missiles, while notionally on loan, to escalate the war with Iran into Gulf shipping.

The British had been somewhat more circumspect. They were aware of Saddam's ruthlessness towards his internal opponents and his brutal treatment of the Kurdish minority. But ruthlessness is a common attribute among successful Middle Eastern dictators, and positive tendencies had been identified in the talk of political reform, an evident tilt towards the West, a generally calm approach towards the Arab–Israeli dispute. In 1989, with the war over, there was hope that Iraq might now turn to domestic reconstruction and some lucrative orders for British companies. A dialogue was set in motion and the results were impressive: by 1990 Britain was Iraq's third largest trading partner. While mindful of the less attractive aspects of Saddam's regime, the Foreign Office was unconvinced of the utility of ostracizing Iraq. As an official briefing paper in September 1988 put it:

> We believe it better to maintain a dialogue with others if we want to influence their actions. Punitive measures such as unilateral sanctions would not be effective in changing Iraq's behaviour over chemical weapons, and would damage British interests to no avail.

In July 1989 London had even considered breaking its previous self-denying ordinance not to sell weapons which could 'materially enhance the danger to each other' to the former disputants in the Iran–Iraq War. Actively encouraged by British Aerospace, as well as by the Ministries of Trade and Industry and of Defence, the Cabinet was asked to consider the sale of about sixty Hawk trainer aircraft to Baghdad. Though dressed up by time limits on both the initial delivery and the associated weapons, had the sale gone through it would have marked a major gesture in Saddam's direction. However, the sale was blocked by John Major, in one of the few decisions taken during his brief sojourn as Foreign Secretary.

Like its allies in London and Paris, the US Administration had gradually come to believe that Saddam could be progressively weaned away from his past militancy and that Iraq could become a source of reason and moderation as well as valuable contracts. For Washington Iraq's most promising feature was that it was Iran's enemy. Since the overthrow of the Shah and the hostage crisis of 1980–81 the regime led by the Ayatollah Khomeini had become something of an obsession for decision-makers in Washington. Hence, if Iraq could keep Iran in check then that in itself was a cause for commendation. So much the better that American friends in the region, such as Saudi Arabia, Jordan and Egypt, also viewed Iraq in the same light.

The first agricultural credits—which were to become the mainstay of the relationship—were agreed in 1982. Some $300 million was made available to buy American produce. At the same time, amid warnings from US intelligence agencies that Iraq was on the verge of defeat, satellite imagery and communications intercepts on Iranian dispositions were passed to Baghdad, and the next year an official blind eye was taken to the seepage of American arms into Iraq from Jordan and Kuwait, who were legitimate clients. As with France, an opportunity was seen to wean Iraq away from its traditional dependence on the Soviet Union, which at this time was unsuccessfully courting Iran as the most strategically significant of the two warring states. By 1884 Iraq had done enough to allow the Reagan Administration to claim that it no longer sponsored acts of international terrorism and so diplomatic relations, severed in 1967 following the Six Day War, were restored. By 1987 Iraq had become one of the main US customers of agricultural and food products, being promised $1 billion credit, the largest loan of its kind to any single country worldwide.

A crisis developed between the two countries following the revelations of the extraordinary Iran–Contra affair, during which high-ranking officials in the Reagan Administration had conspired to get arms to Iran in return for the release of US hostages held by pro-Iranian groups in Lebanon. Embarrassment over this affair perhaps made Washington more willing than might otherwise have been the case to agree to a request from Kuwait (then seen as Iraq's ally) to reflag its ships and provide them with protection against Iranian attacks, which were themselves retaliation for Iraq's attempt to harass Iran's oil trade, and then to accept Saddam's apologies when one of his aircraft mistakenly attacked an American warship, USS *Stark*, in 1987, killing thirty-seven sailors.

Yet while the Reagan and then the Bush Administrations had a consistent policy of cultivating Saddam there was a tension in the relationship, resulting largely from indignation in Congress over Saddam's human rights record, and in particular his repression of the Kurds, including the use of chemical weapons. Saddam had turned on the Kurds with great brutality as the cease-fire with Iran came into effect, and in a number of cases had used chemical weapons. Senate Foreign Relations Committee staff members had been active in publicizing this activity, and it led to Senator Clairborne Pell initiating what was to become a familiar pattern of Congressional attempts to punish Iraq being countered by Administration resistance to sanctions. Pell's bill, starkly named *The Prevention of Genocide Act 1988*, was passed without opposition in the Senate but succumbed to delaying tactics in the House of Representatives and the close of the Congressional session on the eve of the 1988 presidential election. If passed, it would have required the President to impose a trade embargo on Baghdad until it could be certified that Iraq was no longer practising genocide. When the Bush Administration examined policy towards Iraq in its strategic review of 1989 it came to the same conclusion as its predecessor. By 1990 Iraqi loans under the agricultural credits scheme had exceeded $1 billion, while annual trade between Iraq and the United States had grown from around $500 million in the early 1980s to over $3.5 billion.

The message from friendly Arab states, such as Egypt and Saudi Arabia, was that Iraq was well worth some attention and could be turned towards a moderate posture. The Administration's disposition to accept this line was only slightly ruffled by a series of revelations from FBI and Federal Reserve Bank investigators who, after a raid on 4 August, had uncovered the role of the Atlanta branch of the Italian Banca Nazionale del Lavoro (BNL) in financing the build-up of Iraq's military machine by diverting agricultural credits. The bank began in 1984 exploiting the US line of credit for agricultural exports to Iraq. In 1986 it had been caught when Italy decided to ban further credits to Iraq because of a dispute over payment on a major naval contract (eventually settled in 1989 on the basis of a substantial Italian loss). With the war going badly, Iraq was generally considered to be a bad risk at this time. BNL then began to lend money in secret, using its high credit rating to borrow money from other banks which it then lent to Iraq at a higher rate. In 1987 this moved into the funding of military projects. When the scandal broke there were some $4 billion of loans outstanding. News of these revelations generated immediate concern in State and CIA over their impact on US–Iraqi relations.

At a National Security Council meeting the question was posed whether this leopard could change its spots. 'Probably not' said the CIA; 'Perhaps' said the Presidential Advisor Brent Snowcroft; 'It's worth a try' said Bush. National Security Decision Directive 26 (NSDD-26), signed on 2 October, judged that

> Normal relations between the US and Iraq would serve our longer-term interests in both the Gulf and the Middle East. The US government should propose economic and political incentives for Iraq to moderate its behaviour and to increase our influence with Iraq.
>
> As a means of developing access to and influence with the Iraqi defence establishment, the US should consider sales of non-lethal forms of military assistance, eg training courses and medical exchanges, on a case-by-case basis.

The only nod in the direction of anxieties over actual rather than potential Iraqi behaviour was a readiness to consider sanctions and urge allies to do so if Baghdad resumed use of chemical weapons, used biological weapons or tried to develop nuclear weapons. The overall tenor was positive. It was assumed that Saddam would respond to inducements and also, as the intelligence community predicted at the time, that Iraq was so exhausted by its recent war that there was little risk of it turning aggressive toward its neighbours for two to three years.

A few days later, on 6 October, Iraqi Foreign Minister Tariq Aziz visited Secretary of State James Baker in Washington. Aziz accused the Administration of having a 'disturbing' policy towards Iraq, of which he saw evidence in the allegations of bribery and corruption emanating from the BNL scandal. Baker was conciliatory, insisting that no harm to Iraq was intended, that the United States desired good relations and that questions of chemical weapons and nuclear proliferation should be seen as a 'general' problem rather than one specific to Iraq. Aziz set a test. At that time the Agriculture Department was prepared to offer only $400 million new credits. Aziz was concerned that such a cut from the previous year would be seen as a vote of no confidence in Iraqi debt policy. Moreover, he told Baker that this was 'an explosive issue—a government must feed its people'.

Baker set the request for new guarantees worth $1 billion in motion. Those in charge of the BNL investigation were appalled and worked to persuade the Agriculture and State Departments to deny the Iraqi request. The case they produced was devastating. The money which had been made available to Iraq had not always been used to buy agricultural commodities but had been diverted to purchases of military hardware, and even nuclear-sensitive equipment. When agricultural goods were bought bribes were demanded from US businesses if they wished to secure orders. Even then many of the goods received were being bartered with the Soviet Union and other Eastern European states in return for military equipment.

When the issue was addressed at a meeting on 13 October in the Agriculture Department it was minuted that 'although additional research needs to be done, it appears more and more likely that CCC-guaranteed funds and/or commodities may have been diverted from Iraq to third parties in exchange for military hardware'. The same day, a State Department memo observed that the BNL investigation would 'blow the roof' off the Iraq food export programme. 'If smoke indicates fire, we may be facing a four-alarm blaze in the near future.' Even without this scandal, the Federal Reserve Bank's board opposed more credit guarantees for Iraq because of doubts over Iraq's general credit worthiness. It did not seem sensible to allocate one fifth of the credit scheme's fiscal year 1990 budget to a country with such a poor debt-servicing record.

Baker was not prepared to have his Iraq policy blown off course in this manner. His officials decided to assign blame to 'corrupt elements' in Baghdad and put pressure on the Agriculture and Treasury Departments to authorize the new loans. The inclination was to see the BNL scandal as a storm that would blow over if Iraqi sensitivities were not too bruised, rather than as evidence of something rotten at the heart of Iraqi procurement and debt policy. Those who took this latter view received scant attention. Baker himself contacted Agriculture Secretary Clayton Yeutter to drop his objections. On 8 November 'on foreign policy grounds', another $1 billion loan programme was agreed. The only concession to concerns over Iraq's worthiness was that it was to be disbursed in two instalments.

The arguments in London, Paris, Bonn and Washington remained the same: Iraq's war with Iran was over and it was a time for domestic reconstruction and thus good business opportunities. Saddam was undoubtedly ruthless, but at least he was no longer a Soviet client and he had shown a potential for flexibility on the Arab–Israeli dispute. There was no international support for ostracizing the regime—therefore the only logical policy was to cultivate it to advantage, claiming that this could encourage Saddam to stick to a more moderate path. Meanwhile they turned a blind eye to the intensive efforts being made by Iraqis to procure the most sensitive military technologies—especially from Europe.

The relationship deteriorates

Policies based on a hope of Iraqi moderation suffered a severe setback when in the spring of 1990 Saddam made an about-turn in a series of ruthless moves. The most sensational were the execution of the journalist Farzad Bazoft on charges of espionage in March 1990, followed on 2 April by a threat to use chemical weapons against Israel.

A common retrospective explanation of these moves is that they were designed to serve as a smoke-screen to disguise Saddam's aggressive designs against Kuwait, and to prepare the region for its occupation. It has even been argued that Saddam had already conceived of the invasion in the mid-1980s and made the final decision to occupy Kuwait in February 1990. He then engineered an acrimonious encounter with the West to rally the Arabs behind his regime, to secure American and Israeli assurances that he would not be attacked under any circumstances, and to build up the pressure on Kuwait, from which he was trying at the time to extract large sums of money to finance Iraq's economic reconstruction.

This theory, however, fails to take account of Saddam's heavy dependence on the political goodwill and economic support of the West in his effort to revamp the Iraqi economy from the havoc left by the Iran–Iraq War. Rather than a ferocious confrontation with the West and Israel, a low profile and a conciliatory approach would have been more likely to help gain acquiescence in the occupation of Kuwait. The explanation for these events would seem to lie in Saddam's growing desperation during the first half of 1990.

Saddam had a paranoiac obsession with personal and political survival, natural for one operating in one of the region's most hazardous political systems. He had never lost sight of his predecessors' fate. When in July 1958 the pro-Western Hashemite dynasty, which had ruled Iraq since its inception in 1921, was overthrown by a military coup headed by **General Abd al-Karim Qassem,** the mutilated body of the Iraqi regent was dragged by a raging mob in the streets of Baghdad. Five years later, Qassem's bullet-ridden corpse was screened on television to the entire nation. Saddam was determined to use whatever means were required to avoid a similar fate. 'I know that there are scores of people plotting to kill me,' he told a personal guest shortly after assuming the presidency, 'and this is not difficult to understand . . . however, I am far cleverer than they are. I know they are conspiring to kill me long before they actually start planning to do so. This enables me to get them before they have the faintest chance of striking at me.'

That this candid revelation reflected Saddam's mindset could be evidenced by the long trail of victims left during his years in power—both as the *de facto* leader under President Bakr and in the top spot. Pre-empting any dissent through systematic purges and subordinating all domestic and foreign policies to the ultimate goal of political survival, he had transformed the ruling Ba'ath Party into an extension of his will and to cow his subjects into unquestioning submission. Yet the protracted war against Iran had somewhat loosened

Saddam's grip over the officer corps, the main potential threat to his personal rule. In the late war years he confronted what nearly amounted to an open mutiny, when the military leadership questioned his ability to lead Iraq to victory. He survived this challenge because his Generals were not after political power (but rather after the freedom to run the war according to their professional judgement), and because he was sensible enough to give in to their demands—only to purge them at a later stage. But the barrier of fear had been broken, and after the war he apparently confronted several attempts on his life. The first took place in November 1988 and reportedly involved a plan to shoot down his plane on his way from a state visit to Egypt. Another attempt, which reportedly occurred in northern Iraq in late 1988 or early 1989, was ruthlessly suppressed with dozens, if not hundreds of officers executed. The attempt must have been particularly worrying for Saddam since it involved officers from the Republican Guard, his élite bodyguard force. A third coup attempt was aborted in September 1989, and in January 1990 he narrowly escaped an assassination attempt by army officers while he was riding in his car through Baghdad.

There was another major source of frustration. If Iraq did in fact win the war, as its people were urged to believe, the fruits of victory had to be formally sealed, the hatchets officially buried. Then the 65,000 war prisoners could return to their families, alongside hundreds of thousands of demobilized troops. Life would return to normal. Reconstruction would be under way. None of these things happened. The UN-orchestrated peace talks in Geneva quickly ran into a blind alley, as Iran would not negotiate directly with Iraq. In the lack of progress Saddam was forced to look to his guns. The formidable Army remained by and large mobilized, costing the destitute Iraqi treasury a fortune. The social consequences were no less worrying. An entire generation was lost: hundreds of thousands of young conscripts who had been eighteen when the war started were twenty-six by its end and still under arms. They had no private life; they could neither study nor work nor get married. Now that the war had been 'won' they began questioning the necessity of their continued mobilization. Saddam's attempt to defuse the boiling social problem by ordering partial demobilization in 1989 backfired, as it proved beyond the capacity of the shaky Iraqi economy to absorb the huge numbers of young men pouring into the labour market.

There was little else in the foreign policy sphere to provide much comfort. Apart from the formation of the Arab Co-operation Council (ACC), which had boosted his prestige in the Arab world, Saddam's regional policy had little to show for itself. The clash he initiated with Syria in Lebanon brought no results, as his protégé, the maverick General Michel Aoun, made no headway towards his declared goal of 'liberating Lebanon from the Syrian occupation'. Moreover, at the Arab summit in Casablanca in May 1989 he suffered a public humiliation when his proposal for the replacement of the Syrian military presence in Lebanon by a genuine Arab League force was rejected in the face of tough opposition by the Syrian President Asad.

Looking beyond the Middle East, Saddam's anxiety over the stability of his regime was exacerbated by the historic changes in Eastern Europe. The various attempts on his life had been sufficient on their own to ring the strongest alarms in the mind of the ever-vigilant leader. But coming against the backdrop of the collapse of the communist regimes their impact was magnified several-fold. For the West, the events in Europe were a rare moment of spiritual elevation. For Saddam Hussein, like most Arab leaders, it was a development fraught with grave dangers. In his view, the decline of Soviet power and the disintegration of the Eastern Bloc had deprived the Arab world of its traditional allies and left the arena open for a US–Israeli 'diktat'. 'The USSR shifted from the balanced position with the United States in a practical manner, though it has not acknowledged it so far,' he argued at a summit meeting in Amman of the ACC in February 1990. 'It has become clear to everyone that the United States has emerged in a superior position in international politics. This superiority will be demonstrated in the US readiness to play such a role.'

The fall of the Romanian dictator, Nicolae Ceauçescu, was particularly traumatic. Whether or not Saddam actually ordered the heads of his security services to study the videotapes of Ceauçescu's overthrow, as had been widely speculated in the West, this event undoubtedly made him wary. He must have been at least as informed as foreign diplomats in Baghdad that the events in Romania had left a strong impact even within one of the most sensitive centres of power, the officer corps, especially since some officers did not conceal their delight over the fate of the deposed dictator.

A suspicion by Saddam that the Americans, having seen off a succession of dictators in Eastern Europe, would now turn their attention to him may well have been the starting point for the steady decline in Iraq's relationship with the West. Such suspicions were heightened on 15 January 1990, when the Voice of America, in a broadcast celebrating the resurgence of democracy in Eastern Europe and encouraging the overthrow of remaining dictators, described Saddam as a 'tyrant'. Then on 21 February a State Department report was published that discussed human rights abuses in Iraq at length. This was followed by the Foreign Affairs Committee in the House of Representatives condemning Iraq for 'gross violations of human rights'.

Now Saddam was apprehensive, and in a speech to the ACC on 23 February he began to ventilate his anxieties. It was here that he not only spoke of the challenge posed by the Soviet decline but began to revert to an old tune, calling the Americans 'imperialists' and suggesting that their present interest in the Gulf was to support Israel and keep the oil price down. He asked that the residual American maritime force should leave the Gulf, though by now there were only a few ships present compared with the fifty deployed at the height of the war (essentially serving the Iraqi cause).

Israel

Another symptom of the collapse of communism in Europe was the influx of Soviet Jews to Israel which Saddam feared would boost the self-confidence of the Jewish state and would lure it into military adventures beyond its frontiers. Reports in the Western media at the time about secret meetings between Israeli and Syrian representatives in Europe were viewed by the Iraqi President as further indications of 'a dangerous conspiracy' against Iraq. In January 1990 he warned Israel that any attack on Iraq's scientific or military installations 'would be confronted by us with a precise reaction, using the means available to us according to the legitimate right to self-defence'. A month later, during a visit to Baghdad, Ambassador Richard Murphy, former US Assistant Secretary of State for Near Eastern and South Asian Affairs, was told by his hosts that they had reliable information of an imminent Israeli strike against Iraq's non-conventional arms industry, modelled on the 1981 attack on Iraq's Osiraq reactor. A similar message was delivered to the British Chargé d'Affaires in Baghdad in late March, during his meeting with Iraq's Under-Secretary of State for Foreign Affairs, Nizar Hamdoon.

In Saddam's eyes, an Israeli strike against Iraq could be catastrophic. For him, nuclear weapons had always been more than the 'great equalizer', the weapons that could erode Israel's technological edge. They had been a personal obsession. They could be the symbol of Iraq's technological prowess, a prerequisite for regional hegemony, the ultimate guarantee for absolute security. Hence, not only could an Israeli attack on Iraq's nuclear reactor subvert his strategic plans, it would deal his political standing a devastating blow. 'If I am attacked by Israel now,' he told the Saudi Ambassador to Washington, Prince Bandar Ibn Sultan, on 5 April, 'I would not last six hours. When I was attacked the first time [1981], I was in war [with Iran] and could always say I was in war. And now if I am attacked, people will not understand why this happened.'

Bandar had come to Baghdad to help smooth over the consequences of an incautious remark. On 2 April, in an address to the General Command of the Iraqi armed forces, Saddam had threatened Israel with harsh retaliation if it tried to repeat its 1981 attack on Iraq's nuclear installation. 'By God,' he said to the enthusiastic clapping of his audience, 'we will make fire eat half of Israel if it tries to do anything against Iraq.' The statement was immediately deplored by President Bush. Israel, focusing on this threat and ignoring the conciliatory part of the speech, was said to have hinted that an Iraqi chemical attack might be met by a nuclear response.

Though reluctant to lose the newly gained position of inter-Arab prominence, Saddam went out of his way to reassure decision-makers in Jerusalem and Washington that his bellicose statement should not be construed 'in the context of threats or demonstration of power'. Even in his speech he had taken care to underline the purely defensive nature of his threat. 'Everyone must know his limits,' he said within the same breath of issuing his 'burn Israel' threat, 'thanks be to God, we know our limits and we will not attack anyone.' In the following months, this defensive theme was regularly reiterated. 'It should not be assumed,' argued the Iraqi media,

> that if the Arabs have a certain weapon, they will use it while others will not. We talked about using chemical weapons, should Israel threaten us or threaten any Arab nation militarily, including using nuclear weapons that it owns . . . when anyone threatens us with aggression, or tries to raise slogans of aggression, against Iraq or any part of the Arab homeland, then it would be natural for the Arabs to say to him: 'if you try to attack us, we will retaliate against your aggression with the weapons we have.'

These public reassurances were accompanied by covert attempts to convince the Americans and the Israelis of Saddam's 'pure intentions'. In his extraordinary meeting with Prince Bandar, Saddam argued that his words had been misconstrued and that the United States was over-reacting. Vehemently denying any offensive designs, he admitted to his guest that he wished his speech 'had been phrased differently'. 'But you must understand the context in which it had been made,' he continued apologetically,

> it had been delivered to members of his armed forces at a public forum where emotions were running high, with people clapping and screaming. As we both know, it never hurt in the Arab world to threaten Israel, and so I had done it.

Nonetheless, he emphasized that his threat had been made *only* in the context of an Israeli attack against Iraq. He then asked Bandar to assure President Bush and King Fahd that he would not attack Israel, and to request the Americans to secure an Israeli guarantee that it would not attack Iraq either. Having returned to Washington, Bandar conveyed Saddam's message to Bush who, in turn, contacted the Israelis and got their assurance that they were not going to move against Iraq in any way. This was then passed directly back to Saddam.

The Bazoft and 'supergun' affairs

Farzad Bazoft, an Iranian-born journalist working for the London weekly newspaper the *Observer*, had been arrested in September 1989 while probing into a mysterious explosion at a secret military complex near Baghdad. In March he was suddenly put on trial, given a death sentence and summarily executed. Saddam was using Bazoft to send two signals. To potential plotters at home it carried the message that the Iraqi leader was as adamant as ever on exacting the ultimate price from 'traitors'. To the West he was demonstrating the futility of any attempts at coercion.

The exposure of fabricated plots and the punishment of their 'perpetrators' had been one of Saddam's favourite methods of eliminating political dissent and deterring 'treacherous conspiracies' against the regime. However, while his other political victims had been Iraqis, which had enabled him to keep these purges internal affairs, and Bazoft's Iranian origins would not have endeared him to Saddam, he was carrying British travel documents which made his execution an international issue. Whether Saddam might have avoided Bazoft's execution had he foreseen the intensity of Western indignation is difficult to say. His preoccupation with personal survival meant that all aspects of Iraq's domestic and foreign policy were subordinated to this objective. Saddam's meagre understanding of the West may have led him to believe that Bazoft's death might be a useful way of demonstrating his determination to survive without leading to a full confrontation.

This confrontation was particularly galling for Saddam, since it was not confined to expressions of public indignation with the appalling standards of Iraqi justice, but was apparently accompanied by a determined effort on the part of several Western governments to subvert his programme of non-conventional weapons, into which Bazoft had been apparently inquiring. On 22 March 1990 a Canadian ballistics expert, Dr Gerald Bull, was assassinated in Brussels.

Since Bull was involved in developing a 'supergun' for Iraq that would supposedly be capable of launching non-conventional warheads for thousands of miles, the assumption was made by many that he was murdered by a Western security service, or possibly by Israel's Mossad. Soon afterwards, British Customs officials confiscated eight Iraqi-bound large steel tubes, manufactured by a Sheffield company and believed to be destined to form the barrel of Dr Bull's forty-ton 'supergun'. During the next few weeks other parts of the 'supergun' were intercepted in Greece and Turkey. Another blow to Iraq's non-conventional programme was dealt on 28 March, when a joint US–UK Customs operation culminated in the seizure at Heathrow Airport of forty electrical capacitors, devices designed to be used as nuclear triggers.

There was a common theme running through all these conflict points. The enormous resources put into building up Iraq's military power were starting to bear fruit. Determined to reduce his dependence upon overseas suppliers and not to be cowed by Israel's nuclear advantage, Saddam had set about creating an indigenous arms industry capable of producing not only 'conventional' guns and bombs but non-conventional missiles, chemical and nuclear weapons. This had been done by creating an intricate network of agents and companies in the West who had sought out the necessary high-technology equipment and found ways of obtaining finance and getting round export controls. By 1989 the extent of this effort was starting to be recognized and it was transforming international assessments of Iraqi strength. In February the US Government gave its first official warning that Iraq was attempting to become a nuclear power. In April, an Arms Fair took place in Baghdad which displayed weapons manufactured by Iraq at some nineteen identifiable manufacturing plants, most of which had completely escaped the notice of the West. In September there was the devastating explosion at the al-Hillah solid-fuel propellants plant, which had led Bazoft to seek his 'scoop'. In December Saddam boasted of the launch of his first long-range missile; two months later, US intelligence detected construction of five fixed-launch complexes in western Iraq, in range of Israeli cities.

Saddam was aware that the pressures would grow as his additional military strength became recognized—which is why he was becoming increasingly wary of an Israeli strike designed to destroy this strength before it was fully developed. The events which served to thwart the 'supergun' projects and impede his drive for a nuclear capability naturally came to be seen as part of a merging Israeli, American, British conspiracy.

In fact neither the British nor the American Government saw it in this way. They were getting more dubious with regard to Saddam's intentions, but they had not yet diverged from established policy. If anything, all the evidence that Saddam was up to no good convinced them that they must redouble their efforts to strengthen ties. Each Government looked around and was convinced that no other had an interest in a punitive policy. Without collective action such a policy was bound to fail, and the instigating Government would suffer a loss of contracts and influence. Better to persevere along established lines in the hope of steering Saddam back along the path of moderation and domestic reconstruction. Thus these Governments attempted to avoid provocation and insisted that there was no conspiracy and that amicable relations were still sought.

Britain, for example, sent back Ambassador Harold Walker to Baghdad in May after the 'supergun' affair began to blow over. Walker had only been in the post five weeks when the execution of Bazoft had led to him being recalled. In May his instructions were to get back into a dialogue. Saddam must be convinced that there was no UK campaign against Iraq, that the seizure of the capacitors at Heathrow was simply Customs men doing their duty, and that the derogatory comments found in a free press were not Government-inspired. Britain had no desire to rupture relations with yet another Middle Eastern regime. It had broken with Libya and Syria over terrorism and then Iran had broken with it over the Rushdie affair. Walker, therefore, had a developed plan for rebuilding relations, progressing from a scheduled visit by a serious non-Governmental figure, to a substantial showing in the Baghdad trade fair in the autumn, perhaps with a junior trade minister in attendance, and then possibly a visit by the Secretary of State in 1991. He was encouraged in this by the release of Daphne Parish, a nurse who had helped Bazoft and had been sentenced to a long prison term. This was taken as a signal of good will.

There had been a move in the United States to toughen policy on Iraq. To some extent this reflected a growing restlessness over the maltreatment of the Kurds, the use of chemical weapons and the generally repressive nature of the Iraqi state. However these issues were all toned down when on 17 January 1990 George Bush confirmed a policy based on detente and trade. On 12 February 1990 the Under Secretary of State for Near Eastern Affairs, John Kelly, visited Baghdad and met Saddam. He had the first tranche of the new credit but the Agriculture Department was starting to drag its feet on the second. Kelly warned that with relations so fragile such a cut would 'feed Saddam's paranoia'. He told Saddam that he was a 'force for moderation in the region, and the United States wishes to broaden her relations with Iraq'. Saddam's pleasure with this was then somewhat qualified by the Voice of America broadcast which followed three days later and the publication of the report on human rights abuses later in the month. Then came the 'burn Israel' speech of 2 April.

The United States described the threat as 'inflammatory, outrageous and irresponsible'. John Kelly argued against sanctions on Capitol Hill largely on the grounds that they would deny US exporters opportunities and they would not have much effect. Kelly insisted that if sanctions would work in modifying Iraq's behaviour then the Administration would support them, and agreed that Saddam's actions had raised new questions regarding his intentions. The question was how best to 'exercise a restraining influence'. There was a review of policy on 16 April, chaired by Robert Gates, the Deputy Adviser on National Security Affairs. This review has been subject to much speculation, with references to suggestions from both the State and Commerce Departments for an end to favourable treatment on export licences and credits. The policy debate seems to have been half-hearted, with little confidence in the effects of a harder line and uncertainty over how to implement it. The position taken by the presidential National Security Adviser, Brent Scowcroft, was that there was no reason to change policy. As a result of the meeting a paper was prepared by the NSC staff a month later reviewing options. None looked promising. Those in the trade, credits and oil fields were either trivial or more likely to hurt the United States. The political measures could affect the conduct of business.

Even the residual intelligence relationship—on Iran—was deemed valuable because of the access provided to this segment of the Iraqi establishment. All that could be done was not to go forward with the second tranche of the agricultural credits, although even this political signal was moderated by a public rationale unrelated to foreign policy—the illegal 'kickbacks'.

In May it was decided not to proceed with the second half of the $1 billion loan guarantee, largely on the basis of the 'kickback' being received by Iraq from its favoured agricultural suppliers, which included such 'after-sale service' as armoured trucks. There was no desire to be seen to be using the 'food weapon' against Iraq. Even here, an attempt to impose a formal cut in credits was defeated in the Senate.

To the fore in opposing any restraints in relations with Iraq was Senator Robert Dole from Kansas—a major exporter of grain to Iraq. It was Dole who led a group of five Senators, ten days after Saddam's threat to Israel, to meet the Iraqi leader at Mosul. They made it known that they handed over a letter denouncing attempts to get chemical and nuclear weapons. The Iraqis, however, as they did a number of times later to embarrass their past interlocutors, released their own transcript of the meeting. This had Dole reassuring Saddam that President Bush, who had encouraged the trip, did not support a campaign against Iraq, and that the Voice of America man had been sacked (which was not the case). Alan Simpson from Wyoming explained that the problems were with a 'haughty and pampered' press.

The industrial and agricultural lobby were as enthusiastic as ever about a close relationship with Iraq. If sanctions were mentioned they had a well-rehearsed answer: we will be the only losers because nobody else will observe them and they will have no influence on Iraqi behaviour. There was, however, one argument for which they did not have a good answer: Iraq was running out of money.

Saddam's crisis

In the five years from 1984 Saddam had spent $14.2 billion in hard currency in high-technology imports from Britain, France, Germany, Italy and the

United States. At the height of the war with Iran, in 1985, some 60 per cent of Iraq's gross oil revenues were being spent on military equipment and weapons manufacturing technology. In 1989 the BNL scandal was instrumental in bringing out into the open details of Iraqi activities and making other lenders doubly cautious.

Increasingly the most practical issues for Western countries dealing with Iraq concerned lines of credit. Britain's trading position had been achieved in part by extending a line of credit throughout the war. As a result it was being slightly favoured, in that at least some of the debts were being repaid. Yet it was decided in 1990 only to give Iraq further credit to the amount required to turn over existing debts. In May Iraqi repayments fell behind the levels which automatically triggered a halt in new credit coverage from the Export Credits Guarantee Department (ECGD). There were outstanding debts of $100 million.

France had been Iraq's major arms supplier other than the Soviet Union. It had sold Iraq about $5 billion worth of arms, equivalent to about one quarter of the total arsenal. However, reports suggested that Iraq owed France FF28 billion, of which FF15 billion was for military equipment. In September 1989 the two countries had agreed to reschedule the debt so that FF5 billion would be repaid in 1990, but little had been done by Baghdad. An informal arms embargo was imposed and a more formal block on further arms sales was being considered. The French Coface export credit agency stopped covering Iraqi credits, frustrating efforts by Dassault to sell more than fifty Mirage 2000s to Iraq for FF22 billion.

Not even Jean-Pierre Chevènement, a left-winger and founding member in 1984 of the Iraqi–French Friendship Association, could help. He had made full use of his position as Defence Minister to promote the military relationship. In January 1990 he paid an official visit to Baghdad, the first Minister of Defence to do so for ten years, and spoke to Saddam of his intention to 'raise our bilateral relations to a higher level' and how the President enjoyed the respect and esteem of French leaders. Although he obtained some small deals, he was hampered by demands from Paris that all deals had cash up front. An aide to Finance Minister Beregovoy made an observation that was becoming widely shared:

> We note that an enormous share of Iraq's GNP is currently being devoted to military industrialization projects. We do not want to finance regional destabilization. Nor will we issue any more export credit guarantees until the Iraqis make good on the debt rescheduling deal we worked out.

The greatest danger for Saddam in all of this was not simply that the flow of high technology into Iraq would be stemmed but that his creditors would get together to arrange a global rescheduling package which would involve a degree of international surveillance of his economy. This was a far greater danger than economic sanctions. Rescheduling had been mooted in 1988. Saddam dealt then with the challenge on a divide and rule basis. Western Governments were informed that if they resisted this move then they would be rewarded with excellent contracts. The West German Government, with high-technology exports to Iraq booming, was the first to break after Chancellor Kohl had been visited by Tariq Aziz in July 1988. Germany's attitude with regard to the ultimate Iraqi purpose behind the contracts remained relaxed, despite its elaborate domestic legislation aimed at preventing the export of weapons to crisis-ridden areas.

In the first half of 1990, Western finance ministries were coming back to address the problem. Western Ambassadors in Baghdad found credit the abiding topic of conversations with their Iraqi hosts, with each Government being dealt with separately, desperately pitting one against the other to dissuade them from consolidating their interests. Only those prepared to make further loans could expect past loans to be repaid.

All this brought home to Saddam the awful state of his economy. Though Saddam invested huge efforts to depict the end of hostilities with Iran as a shining victory, it increasingly became evident that Iraq had emerged from the war a crippled nation. From a prosperous country with some $35 billion in foreign exchange reserve in 1980, Iraq had been reduced to dire economic straits, with $80 billion in foreign debt and shattered economic infrastructure. Western estimates put the cost of reconstruction at $230 billion.

Even if one adopted the most optimistic (and highly unrealistic) assumption that every dollar of oil revenues would be directed to the reconstruction effort, it would have required nearly two decades to repair the total damage. As things stood a year after the termination of hostilities, Iraq's oil revenues of $13 billion per annum barely covered the military budget. Unless rescheduling could be arranged, half of this would be required to service Iraq's non-Arab debt. With civilian imports approximating $12 billion ($3 billion for foodstuffs), military imports exceeding $5 billion, debt repayments totalling $5 billion, and transfers by foreign workers topping $1 billion, the regime needed an extra $10 billion per annum to balance its current deficit before it could even think about reconstruction. By mid-1990 cash reserves were available for only three months of imports. Yet it was upon this reconstruction that both Saddam's political survival and his long-term ambitions hinged, and it would have to be shelved.

In order to reduce expenditures and to secure jobs for the first demobilized soldiers returning to the labour market, Saddam had begun by squeezing out of Iraq 2 million migrant workers, mainly Egyptians, and slashed the remittances they were allowed to send home. Intensive privatization measures were then introduced but they never stood any chance. With the oil industry, accounting for some 95 per cent of Iraq's income, remaining in the hands of the state, there was no viable basis for the creation of a significant private sector. Moreover, the repressive nature of the regime and its arbitrary convulsions left entrepreneurs wary, investing the barest minimum in future expansion and reaping as much profit as they could in the short term. The high expectations created among the various groups of the society were only matched by soaring inflation, forcing the reintroduction of price controls.

As far as Saddam's personal position was concerned, an immediate economic breakthrough had become critical, for his domestic vulnerability would grow enormously if the state had to be declared bankrupt. On paper, the cure was strikingly simple: a decisive reduction in expenditures and a significant increase in revenues. As Saddam was not one to keep a 'tight ship' when it came to expenditure and the economy was unable to generate extra revenues this created something of a dilemma.

OPEC

At one time Saddam could have hoped to pay for his ambitious modernization plans by means of oil revenues. Not so in the late 1980s. The price of oil was falling. If there was to be any hope of meeting his requirements, Saddam had to find some way of reversing this trend. It was the basic laws of supply and demand which had forced the price down—the industrialized world had responded to artificially high prices as set by the Organization of Petroleum Exporting Countries (OPEC) in the 1970s by exploiting non-OPEC oil reserves and substituting other fuels for oil.

One way to get the price back up was to enforce dramatic cuts in production. Saudi Arabia, with the largest reserves, had been best placed to influence the market in this way, but by the mid-1980s it had become increasingly reluctant to play this role, which meant that it was obliged to accept a disproportionate decline both in production and revenues. To regain market share it decided to take advantage of its relatively cheap production costs by forcing prices even further down, thereby pushing high-cost producers out. At one point the price even went down to below $10 per barrel. In 1986 OPEC agreed to attempt to get the price back to $18 per barrel by sharing out the production cuts. The resulting quota system was complex from the start and honoured as much in the breach as in the observance. The price did not settle.

At issue was as much economic philosophy and circumstances as OPEC discipline. The radical countries such as Iraq not only opposed Western market pressures in principle but, with massive expenditure plans, were desperate for extra revenue. They wanted higher prices but also an extra quota for themselves and less for others. The low-reserve and small production producers were anxious to maximize prices while they could. The Saudis believed that there was no point in pushing the price up too far, but OPEC had given them considerable influence and they were not comfortable with the idea of a wholly unregulated market.

Kuwait, by contrast, was much more inclined to follow market pressures. Only by allowing prices to fall could oil recapture its share of the world energy market. This view was shared by the United Arab Emirates (UAE). These countries did not even pretend to take the idea of quotas very seriously, and refused in June 1989 to hold down production. To the extent that there had to be quotas, they argued, they should be based on reserves and spare capacity and not modernization plans. Also Kuwait had an interest in downstream activities which meant that it had a natural cushion against lower prices.

To the radical states the deliberate flouting of the quota system by Kuwait and UAE was exasperating just as the idea of preserving markets through price moderation was anathema. Yet in practice the economic philosophy of the Kuwaitis was correct and the lower prices of 1986 did revive the demand for OPEC oil, which was surging by the end of the decade. Instead of enjoying the consequent hardening of the price, the major large-reserve producers—mainly to be found in the Gulf—began to position themselves to take a larger share of a growing market by expanding their production capabilities. Inevitably this resulted in an excess of capacity. At the start of 1990, instead of total production by OPEC states sticking at the agreed level of 22 million barrels per day it was approaching 24, with Kuwait and the UAE accounting for 75 per cent of the excess. These two states were pressing for the quota system to be abandoned. Meanwhile the price hawks were becoming alarmed as prices fell once more—from $20.5 a barrel in January to below $18 in March, with the threat of a complete collapse of OPEC discipline.

Saddam's revenue problem was as a result becoming chronic. If he could not get OPEC discipline from these small Gulf states then an alternative was to go to them directly and demand the money with menaces—especially to Kuwait, to which Iraq owed some $10 billion.

Call for Jihad

Saddam Hussein

from *Saddam Speaks on the Gulf Crisis*

Message from President Saddam Husayn to "the Iraqi people, faithful Arabs, and Muslims everywhere" on 5 September 1990 read by announcer. *Baghdad Domestic Service in Arabic 1500 GMT, 5 September 1990.*

In the name of God, the merciful, the compassionate. O great Iraqi people, O faithful Arabs wherever you may be, O Muslims in our Islamic world, wherever you recall your obligations to God as partners in the confrontation of right against falsehood and faith against evil. O sincere Islamists, for whatever path of faith in God and in human rights you have chosen and wherever you perform your duties before God, the great confrontation began on 2 August. Standing at one side of this confrontation are peoples and sincere leaders and rulers, and on the other are those who stole the rights of God and the tyrants who were renounced by God after they renounced all that was right, honorable, decent and solemn and strayed from the path of God until they eventually opposed it when they became obsessed by the devil from head to toe. It is the great confrontation of the age taking place in this part of the world, where the material has overwhelmed the spiritual and all moral and ethical values. Thus, there has been a disruption in the equation that God almighty wanted for humanity, which He conveyed through His books and messengers, whom He asked to convey specific duties to all mankind. Owing to the acts of the evildoers, man has been on the verge of losing even his humanity and being separated from the path of God or the path of God separated from him. It is the confrontation of right against falsehood, the confrontation of faith against infidelity, and a confrontation between the obligations to God almighty against the devil's tendency to appropriate the rights of humanity and misguide the ranks of the feeble.

Almighty God has made His choice, and the gathering of the faithful, militant, and mujahidin who dedicated themselves to principles have responded to His choice. Almighty God has chosen the Arab homeland as the field of confrontation and the Arabs as the leaders of the faithful gathering with the Iraqis as the vanguard force. Thus the message that God has wanted to convey since the first ray of faith emerged is being reaffirmed. This message is that the Arab homeland be the first arena of faith and that the Arabs be impermanent cadre to lead the faithful gathering on the path that pleases almighty God and that leads mankind to real happiness.

It is your turn, O Arabs, to save the entire human race, not only yourselves. Your turn has come to show your values and to highlight the meanings of the message of Islam in which you believe and which you practice. Your turn has come to save humanity from the injustice of the tyrants and usurpers who followed the path of inequity, corruption, dissolution, exploitation, arbitrariness, tyranny, and pride, led along the evil path by the United States of America. Your turn has come as a leading faithful cadre in the human gathering of believers to confront oppression and oppressors, and I do not believe you would relinquish this role to another.

Brothers, when the confrontation began, some thought that it was the outcome of a slogan raised in haste, and that to dissuade the gathering of the faithful from the path and its objectives, it was enough to accumulate a gathering of villains, reprobates, and infidels, and to accumulate the means of destruction on the border of the faithful, patient, and mujahid Iraq, so that the vanguard gathering would be defeated before all the faithful could build upon it. Their thinking and luck has failed them. This is because the kinsfolk of al-Qadisiyya[1] have chosen this path as a result of their deep belief in God and in the nation and its role. And, although they have depended on God in the confrontation, they have taken into consideration the worst that can be launched against them by the arrows of injustice and treachery. When they waged the confrontation, therefore, they did so with faithful hearts that do not know fear or suspicion and that only know the slogan of victory, and only victory, God willing. Ah, verily, the help of God is always near (Koranic verse).

O Arabs, you have proven to the inhabitants of the earth that when God chose you so that your nation would bear witness to the whole of humanity, He was right. Thus, have we made of you an *umma* (nation) justly balanced, that ye might be witness over the nations, and the apostle a witness over yourselves (Koranic verse).

The steadfast stone-throwing people who were assigned by God to perform the duty of showing right against the wrong of the Zionists led your ranks in showing great solidarity for Iraq, and in showing how capable right is, and how weak wrong becomes when it is confronted by right.

The manifestation of solidarity and demonstration of the disparity between right and wrong have followed: from Jordan, Yemen, Tunisia, Algeria, Libya, the Sudan, and Mauritania. The zeal of faith has exceeded the gathering of the faithful to extend to all the sons of the Arab nation and our Muslim world. And, after right was revealed wherever it was revealed correctly, the gathering of supporters extended to the wide expanse of humanity outside the realm of the Arab and Islamic world. Hence, the confrontation has acquired a comprehensive human character.

Brothers, the beginning of any confrontation of this kind always starts with a smaller number that includes only the household ("*Ahl al-Bayt*," meaning the Prophet Muhammad's household). It will then transcend this household to humanity at large. In this confrontation, the household—with due respect to the rights of the Prophet Muhammad's household—is the (Islamic) nation which was chosen by God, so as to possess a leading faith, among the gathering of the faithful. The gathering of the faithful does not presuppose an automatic sequence, but assumes intermingling of an Arab and a non-Arab on the basis of the ruling of the holy verse. Verily, the most honored of you in the sight of God is the most righteous of you.

Considering the circumstances of the confrontation in the time of the Prophet, the most vigorous opponents of the values of the (Islamic) message were among the ranks of the Arabs, led by those who have illegitimate interests, which could never stay where they are or the way they are, except at the expense of the humanity of man.

The evil gathering of those who have taken their side—those whom God has chosen that they not see the right path, having chosen wandering, evil, and corruption, led by those called by the foreigners the rulers of their peoples—are taking a stand against the faithful among the Arabs. But just as God has split the ranks of the infidel, so that people take the guided path from His true religion, He shall disrupt the misguided weak. Indeed, their gathering has been dispersed right from the beginning so that the upper hand will be for the deprived faithful who have known that the road to God is right, through their suffering against the gathering that has lost its path to God, when it degenerated into corruption and corrupted others and sought the help of infidels against faith and the faithful.

As for America's sea and air fleets, its armies and those who slipped with it into the abyss, they will only strengthen in us, the leadership, and the great people of Iraq, our faith in the path that we have chosen in order that God, the people, the nation, and humanity may bless us. The rattling of their weapons and the use of these weapons will only increase our determination to respond to sincere principles, their slogans and their applications, in social justice, in rejecting tyranny, division, and weakness. The motto of the faithful is: There is no going back; the believer will advance. This is our eternal motto which will not be dropped from our hands. Under the banner of faith and jihad, many heads will roll—heads that have never been filled with pride and whose owners never knew the path of faith. Let those who have been promised martyrdom have it.

Muslims everywhere, [King]Fahd, Husni [Mubarak], and their allies from among those who have evil and base records have added to their injustice by repeating the role of Abu-Righal who acted as the guide of the Abyssinian Abraha (who led the attack on Ka'ba before Islam) on the road to pre-Islam Mecca, and was defeated by God with flights of birds and stones of baked clay.[2] Indeed, the part played by Abu-Righal was less vicious than their role when they called in invading armies that have occupied and desecrated the land housing the sacred places of Muslims and Arabs. Thus, we are duty-bound to engage in holy jihad so that we can liberate the two holy mosques from captivity and occupation, after the one who called himself their servant betrayed them.

Your brothers in Iraq will know no peace of mind until the last soldier of occupation departs by choice or is expelled from the land of Arabism in Najd and Hejaz (Saudi Arabia).

We call on all Arabs to do what they can within their means in light of God's laws and the sanctities of jihad and struggle against this infidel and occupying presence to expose, without hesitation and through all means, the actions of traitors and their allies of corruption and oppression.

We appeal to the enduring and afflicted people of Hejaz; the oppressed people of Najd and the eastern province; the people of Mecca, al-Medina, Ha'il, Riyadh, and Jedda; the fraternal people in dear Egypt; and all the sons of our nation wherever they disagree with their rulers due to the differences over dignity, sovereignty, justice, and faith, to revolt against treason and traitors and against the infidel foreign occupation of the land of their shrines. We are with them. And more importantly, God is with them.

O brothers, the children of Iraq will prove, the children of Iraq who are deprived of milk will prove to those greedy invaders and their aides that they are more capable. Those who betrayed their nation, their honor as men, and the meanings and values of humanity will be vanquished before the steadfastness of children. The women of Iraq will prove to them that they are more accurate and skillful in managing things than those who lost the wisdom of management and accurate action. And even before all this, the men of Iraq are beyond comparison, this is because God and His angels are with the good and faithful people at a time when the evil people aligned themselves away from the path of good deeds, dignity, and honor. They went against all noble values. Wretched are their deeds.

Have you known, O brothers, in the history you have studied of someone who tried to starve a nation to death by preventing food from reaching them? Have you seen the acts of Nazism, which the West rants on about, claiming to hoist the banner of confrontation and comparing it to everything loathsome and inhuman . . ., to it, cut off medicine from a whole nation so that the sick will die because there is no medicine? Have you ever seen in the history you have read children dying because of an intentional decision to stop milk from reaching them? If you have not seen or heard about this before, the United States had done all this, urged by Zionism. In doing so, it has been supported by some Western politicians who have been offered a position of rank or have been pushed toward a position of rank by the advertisements of Zionist propaganda and financial institutions; those who have trampled . . . humanitarian principles underfoot, thus adding themselves to the list of those who will be cursed by history.

The Arab and Iraqi nation will not forget their evil deed; they will be backed by the gathering of humanity alongside the gathering of the faithful Muslims, after humanity awakens from its sleep and reveals justice in its true form.

The children of Iraq, before the people of Iraq, do not want us to beg for the milk they need from the infidels and shameless. Their valiant fathers and the glorious daughters of al-Qadisiya will extract life for them relying on God. We will see the portraits of the children who defeated the tyrants and the superpower etched in the hearts of all those who will be liberated and released by this confrontation after the forces of the tyrants retreat and their abortive gathering flees.

History will record immortal pages on those men and women who stand as one against the invaders who desecrated with their soldiers' feet the land of Najd and Hejaz. God will not champion the believers over the infidels unless the believers show that they are well prepared for the confrontation and the sacrifices.

O brothers, your Iraqi brothers have chosen a vanguard position in your group. In light of their long experience, they know that the preparation for sacrifice of those who chose the vanguard position should be in harmony with the position chosen. They know that to God their position in such a choice will be in harmony with the scope of their endurance, patience, and sacrifices. They believe in God and the duty called for by God. They will remain as they have always been—they will make a mockery of the unjust blockade and will not attach any weight other than the weight of evil. They will pray to their mother, the land of Iraq, which will respond with its bounty which it never withheld from its sons. It has always been the supporter of the fighters in every defeat they inflicted on the invaders throughout history. They will be able to defeat the camp of invaders, whether it remains the same or is doubled with the dispatch of other troops.

O Iraqis, and O you brothers everywhere, such a group or a larger group is appropriate for the seriousness with which you have prepared for the confrontation. The believers should not confront a group similar to their own or slightly greater.

Apostle, rouse the believers to the fight. If there are 20 amongst you, patient and persevering, they will vanquish 200; if a hundred, they will vanquish a thousand of the unbelievers, for those are a people without understanding (Koranic verse).

What then will the situation be if we know that the number of Iraqi volunteers who came to sacrifice their lives for principles and the homeland exceeds 5 million Iraqis, not to mention the proud men within the ranks of the armed forces who total more than 1 million combatants? For the invaders to attack this number, they have to mass twice this number. Consequently, the invaders need to mass a minimum of 12 million combatants. O brothers, you know that the air force cannot settle a ground battle, regardless of the sophisticated weaponry. This is the rule governing all conventional and liberation wars. The Vietnamese people were the last to confront this sophisticated capability.

In spite of the fact that the Americans turned what was then South Vietnam into a real base for serving their military operations against what was then North Vietnam and secured there all that would offer their troops comfort and entertainment, these opportunities do not exist—or are not as abundant—on the holy lands of Najd and Hejaz. Their outcome (in Vietnam) is known to you. How would they do then if they were to confront Iraq under completely different circumstances, except for what the people, including the Vietnamese and Iraqi people, have in common: the determination to face the invaders?

Iraq's support at present is all for the honorable leaders and rulers, the Arab nation's people, all the well-meaning and faithful sons of the Islamic nation, the well-intentioned throughout the world led by the oppressed people who are treated unfairly because of the injustice inflicted by the exploiting Americans and others. First and foremost, God is with them.

Those involved will be sorry, and their gathering will be utterly routed if they undertake a military confrontation. Their footprints will be erased from the entire region, and then Jerusalem will be restored, free and Arab, to the lap of faith and the faithful. Palestine will be liberated from the Zionist invaders and the Arab and Islamic nation will see a sun that will never set. They will be in God's protection when they have returned to the Almighty. God is great, God is great, God is great. Accursed be the lowly ones.

(Signed) Saddam Husayn
(Dated) 15 Safar 1411 Hegira, corresponding to 5 September 1990 A.D.

Source: FBIS-NES-90-173, 6 September 1990.

Notes

[1] A site in Iraq famous for the 637 battle in which the Arabs defeated the Persians.

[2] Hijara min sijjil, the Arabic for stones of baked clay, was the name of the long-range missiles which Iraq hurled at Israel during the Gulf War.

Fatwa Against the Iraqi Invasion of Kuwait

Jad al-Haqq, Sheikh al-Azhar

Dar al-Sahwa

The Grand Imam Sheikh Jad Al Haq Ali Jad Al Haq, Sheikh Al Azhar announced in his statement released yesterday to the Arab and Islamic world that the Azhar Al Sharif expresses its grave concern over Iraqi insistence on continuing its aggression against our brother Kuwait. He confirmed that the resort to Arab, Islamic and foreign troops to defend the sacrosanct in Islam was permitted by religion, and that the responsibility of the Islamic armies was to contain the malfeasor so as to prevent his danger from spreading. The statement also called upon President Saddam Hussein and his government to listen to the voice of Islam and of truth, and to desist from the use of force in recognition of their true belonging to the Arab and Islamic nation. The statement reads as follows:

The Azhar Al Sharif has directed an appeal to the peoples of the Arab and Islamic nation and to its leaders, published and broadcast on Friday 19th Muharram 1411 A.H., 10th August 1990 A.D. It coincided with the holding of the Arab summit in Cairo on the same day, at the invitation of President Muhammed Hosni Mubarak, to take cognizance of the nefarious effects on the Arab and Islamic nation resulting from the interference by the leaders of Iraq and their aggression against the State of Kuwait, invading it militarily and occupying its land, and breaching its peoples' rights, as well as all that has been published regarding the pillage of money and the destruction of property. The world has unanimously condemned this grave act, and all international organizations have taken action, such as the Organization of the Islamic Conference, the Conference of Foreign Ministers of Islamic States, the Arab League and the UN Security Council. All this was done on the day the disaster befell, the 2nd August 1990 A.D. Some time has passed since this event that shook the world occurred, and the fleets and armies of different countries, with their arms of terror and destruction, have flocked to our Arab arena where it happened. Yet the leaders of Iraq remain impervious to advice and to the wisdom of Allah in his Book. The Quran calls for aiding the oppressed, and preventing oppression even until the point of fighting it. For this reason, the Azhar Al Sharif today expresses its grave concern for the future of the Arab and Islamic Nation in light of the insistence on this sinful aggression and its excesses. Al Azhar has called on, and repeats its call to President Saddam Hussein and his government to be true to their membership of the Arab and Islamic Nation, and to desist from this action that has aborted the Arab Nation's abilities to progress and to grow, and trapped it in a cycle of killing that will come from whence they know not, as well as reducing its standing among the nations, leaving it bereft of the spirit of empathy, cooperation and friendliness within it. And all this by its own hand, not by the hands of a stranger: one of its leaders erred and left the path of righteousness. He overran a country and people that had lived in comfort and security, performing their duties to their Nation in all domains, and terrorized women, children and the old in their very homes in the dead of night. This is not the deed of a Muslim. The prophet (pbuh) warns of terrorizing Muslims, saying (according to Abu Daoud): "It is not permitted for a Muslim to terrorize another." In another saying related by Al Bazar and others, he said: "Do not terrorize a Muslim, for the terror of a Muslim is a great oppression." In the saying of Abu Huraira, related by Al Tabarani: "Whomsoever looks at a Muslim so as to frighten him without just cause will be frightened by Allah on the Day of Judgment." The prophet (pbuh) also forbade the terrorizing of Muslims by pointing a weapon towards them, saying as related by Al Shaikhan: "Do not point a weapon at your brother for you know not lest Satan pull at your arm and you fall into a pit of fire." In a saying by Muslim of Abu Huraira, "He who points a piece of iron at his brother will be damned by the angels until the end, even if it be his brother to his father or mother." In a saying by Ibn Masoud related by Al Bukhari, "Cursing a Muslim is to stray from the path of righteousness and killing him is to leave the faith." Yet where is all this, regarding what the Iraqi army has done to Kuwait, the destruction, terror, killing, expulsion, plunder and pillage? And what about the Islamic prohibition against terrorizing non-combatants, and killing and torturing them? What happened in terms of the inhumane acts perpetrated by the Iraqi army against Kuwait and its people, as related by the news agencies, is a terrifying and sad thing, refused by Islam and repellent to the conscience of Muslims.

This unenviable situation in which Iraq has placed the Nation, to prepare to face the impending catastrophe that will nigh on annihilate it if the Iraqi leaders continue to the end of their devastating path, requires the Arab and Islamic Nation to respond, and to heed the call to stand against this wrong. Defense of the self and of the Nation requires that armies and forces are sped to surround the ill-doer, so that his harm will not spread; and to contain him as a fire is contained. Allah has permitted fighting the ill-doer: "So fight the malfeasor until it awakens to Allah's commands". And yet the Arab and Islamic forces have heeded the call and come to the aid of the rest of the countries that are exposed to the evil of this catastrophe. They have collaborated in containing the catastrophe in an attempt to stop it, until those in charge of it become aware of the extent of the loss caused by this wicked deed; occupying an Arab Muslim people; breaching the sacrosanct relationship that binds neighbors with a military force vastly superior in numbers and equipment. And let those who are attempting to cause the region to explode, and to destroy it, after they have broken the inviolable sanctity of a country and its people, look what good has come to them of this wickedness? And what has the Nation lost? And are the two equal?

This is great blow that has been dealt to the Nation's dignity and its abilities. Even if the Iraqi army has plundered money and committed sins, this is not a gain but more of the same wickedness. It has been forbidden by Allah; he has warned of the penalties, and ordered that it be combated. The force that overran Kuwait had prepared itself and was more than ready. It entered in the dead of night without prior warning, nay in flagrant breach of treaties and promises made by the leaders of Iraq not to do what they have done, and to sit with their neighbor to discuss and debate their differences. It was a terrible surprise for Kuwait and its people then to be viciously attacked with heavy armor, guns and missiles and all the other implements of modern war. This is not of the courage of Arabs and Muslims, nor of the nature of an Arab to raise his sword except against a foe with a sword; for he would never surprise a foe in safety, nor attack an unarmed opponent. Yet how far this is from what happened. Has this attacking army been bereft of the morals of Arabs and of their nature, and all that runs in the teachings of Islam that forbid the stealth and the use of surprise attacks against a foe that has no arms? If the Arab peoples surrounding Kuwait were afraid and surprised by the actions of the Iraqi army, and called on the armies of the Arab and Islamic states, and of other countries that have the weapons to equal those used by Iraq against Kuwait, there is no wrong in this. Their cry for assistance from these multinational forces is based on the principle of international treaties, and it is their right to defend themselves and to protect their land from this treacherous brother who has heeded no treaty nor promise nor responsibility. Iraq's claim that by doing so, it becomes a *mujahid* is untrue, for *jihad* cannot be in doing wrong, nor in aggression against a fraternal Muslim neighbor. In addition, the claim that the incoming troops have denigrated the land and the sacrosanct is untrue also, for they come with the permission of the owners of that land, and to protect them from aggression. They are Muslim forces or allied to them, and assistance by such troops is permitted in Islam, indeed it is one of the foundations of Islam: one of the rights a Muslim has against another is that he require his help and support to counter oppression, and the same applies to the allied forces also. The claim that the sanctity of the holy land has been breached by allowing foreign troops to set foot in the Kingdom of Saudi Arabia is untrue, for the troops are either Muslim or allied to them, and came to counter aggression and fight oppression. Al Azhar Al Sharif, despite this painful reality and our desire to surmount it, and indeed to uncover the harm that has been done to the Nation, calls on the leaders of Iraq to desist from what they have done, and to withdraw their armies to their own borders; calls for the return of Kuwait's legitimate government to its country and people; and this in order to return to the good and repent from evil, for the return to righteousness is better than continuing in the path of evil, and the best of the sinners are those that repent. "O ye faithful, respond to Allah and to his prophet if he calls you to that which gives you life, and know that Allah is present between Man and his heart, and that to Him you will come."

The Iraqi Invasion of Kuwait

Amatzia Baram

from *Iraq's Road to War*

From the first years of its existence as a nation-state in the wake of World War I, Iraq wanted to gain part or all of Kuwait. But only with Saddam Husayn's decision to invade his neighbor in 1990 did Baghdad make an all-out effort to implement that goal. Saddam's course toward this decision involved Iraq's history and interests as well as his own political environment, ambitions, and thinking.

Iraq's claim for Kuwait has been based chiefly on the argument that it had been a district governed from Basra during the Ottoman Empire. In fact, since 1758, long before the British created the Iraqi state from ex-Ottoman provinces, Kuwait was already an autonomous region under the Sabah family's rule. But Iraq's urge to annex Kuwait was also connected with a need to strengthen its ruling regimes' legitimacy and stability. Iraq's Sunni Arab ruling minority (some 20% of the population) had to keep a Shi'a majority (around 55% of the population) and a Kurdish minority (18 to 20% of the population) under control. A promise to expand Iraq's borders and power was designed to build the masses' enthusiasm and a sense of Iraqi patriotism.[1]

Equally, despite accepting the border with Kuwait in 1923 under British pressure and again in 1932 as a precondition for joining the League of Nations, Baghdad never acquiesced to this situation. Iraq especially objected because the border, following a 1913 Anglo-Ottoman agreement, left it a very short coastline on the Gulf while giving Kuwait two islands, Warba and Bubyan, that controlled the entrance to Umm Qasr, Iraq's only Gulf port.

As early as 1933, official Iraqi government publications began demanding Kuwait's annexation. King Ghazy (1933-1939) broadcast appeals to Kuwaitis to overthrow their rulers and join Iraq. But as long as Britain was both states' patron, Iraq could not go beyond rhetoric.

When Kuwait became independent and the British protectorate ended in

1961, Iraq's anti-British dictator, 'Abd al-Karim Qasim, prepared an invasion that was averted only due to a rapid deployment of British forces.[2] These were soon replaced by Arab League troops. In 1963 Iraq's Ba'thist government accepted the border and recognized Kuwait's sovereignty. But the precise demarcation of the boundary was disputed, and, in 1973 and 1974, Iraqi troops briefly crossed into Kuwait before retreating under U.S.-Iran pressure.

Kuwait consistently refused to cede the two islands. It began asserting sovereignty over them in the early 1970s by establishing border posts and agricultural settlements there; in the late 1980s it planned the town of Sabiya across from Bubyan and connected it by bridge to the barren island. Kuwait's media reiterated more often than before the islands' status as integral parts of Kuwait.[3]

Aside from being deterred by Western protection for Kuwait, Iraq knew that its Soviet patron would not support a confrontation—and possible superpower confrontation—on the issue.[4] In the second half of the 1970s Iraq started to improve its relations with the Gulf Arab states, including Kuwait. Iran's 1978-1979 Islamic evolution and the Iran-Iraq war tightened cooperation among these Arab regimes. During the war Kuwait gave Iraq at least $10 billion in aid and allowed it to receive supplies through Kuwaiti ports. But once the war ended, most of the aid was stopped, and Saddam's attitude toward his Kuwaiti benefactors began to change sharply.

The Iraqi Predicament: Incentives for War

Paradoxically, the post-Iraq-Iran war period was more dangerous for the regime than the war itself. The eight-year-long war sapped the country's resources and made Iraq dependent on financial and strategic support from Kuwait, Saudi Arabia, and other Arab states. Iraqi sources estimated the economic loss from lower oil revenue and higher arms purchases (excluding war-related destruction) at $208 billion. At least 200,000 died, about 400,000 were wounded, and 70,000 were taken prisoner.[5] This was a heavy price for a nation of 17 million people.

Iraqi authorities described the ceasefire as a great victory. Expectations for economic reconstruction, better living standards, and the quick return of prisoners were, however, quickly dispelled as the situation seemed to worsen rather than improve. Iraq's war debt to the Gulf Arab countries was nearly $40 billion which, although creditors did not expect repayment, damaged Iraq's credit rating as long as it was on the books. More pressing was another $40 billion in debts to the non-Arab world, both East and West. Servicing this debt cost nearly $8 billion a year, and—given Iraqi inflexibility—Western banks were averse to make new loans.[7]

Reluctant to use hidden currency reserves, Iraq had to depend on its declining oil income.[8] The severe cash flow problem brought a deep recession that the regime tried to hide through expensive, ostentatious, and economically unproductive reconstruction projects in Basra, Faw, and Mosul.[9] It also tried to distract Iraqis from economic hardship by permitting citizens to go abroad, relaxing some foreign currency regulations, and promising more democracy.[10] But few could afford to travel and no real political changes were made.

Economic stagnation also meant that few soldiers could be demobilized. From August 1988 to August 1990 only 250,000 to 350,000 were released, with over a million still in uniform.[11] The regime preferred to pay soldiers rather than leave them unemployed to create social unrest, especially since the majority of those due to be released were Shi'a whose discontent might trigger a communal revolt. Keeping such a huge standing army, however, required an explanation. Hence Saddam's alarmist speeches beginning in February 1990, blaming two old hate objects—Zionism and Anglo-American imperialism—for preparing to attack Iraq.[12]

Iraq also continued spending huge sums on its military industry.[13] Since 1972 Saddam has been bent on the development of nuclear weapons. Following the June 1981 Israeli raid on his Tammuz reactor, these efforts entered a new, hectic phase that involved also medium-range missiles. Foreign Minister Tariq 'Aziz declared that Iraq needed advanced missiles because it "is still threatened by Iran."[14] Most important, owning these and other nonconventional weapons was a big step toward becoming the Gulf's hegemonic power. These arms could be described as Iraq's contribution to the Arab military effort against Israel, thus turning Iraq into the Arabs' "protector," as its 1981

National Anthem boasts. (For more recent and explicit such promises see below.) By brandishing such weapons Iraq could try to induce the rich Gulf Arabs to offer it much-needed financial aid, indeed, even to impose on them oil quotas and prices that would suit Iraq's interests. This, in turn, promised to make Iraq the most powerful Arab country, economically as well as militarily, and thus to enable Saddam to achieve the Arab hegemony that evaded Gamal 'Abd al-Nasir.[15] But developing these arms put a crushing burden on the crumbling economy.

One of the first casualties of the cash shortage were food subsidies. By the war's end, Iraq's annual imports of foodstuffs cost $2 to 3 billion. Given the regime's reluctance to continue wartime subsidies, food prices rose rapidly. Inflation reached between 25 to 40% annually, but salaries hardly went up.[16] Since Iraq's rulers would not commit more resources to subsidies, living standards deteriorated and, as a safety valve, the press was allowed to publish complaints. For example, a columnist in the party daily complained a few months before the invasion of Kuwait that basic foodstuffs could not be found at government shops at less than twice the official prices, that even these shops were often empty, and that private-market profiteers charged four to five times the official price.[17] The situation created a crisis of expectations.

At the same time, the war's strategic gains seemed to be disappearing as well. The Shatt al-Arab, Iraq's main outlet to the Gulf, remained blocked and Iran refused to allow its reopening. This damaged Iraq's strategic and economic security while undermining Baghdad's claims of victory.

Having never served in the armed forces, Saddam always distrusted the army and its officers' corps. When his party seized power in 1968, Saddam was put in charge of purging the army of disloyal elements. After the Iraq-Iran war ended, he dismissed some of Iraq's most illustrious officers, such as Generals Mahir 'Abd al-Rashid and Hisham Fakhri. Worse still, in January 1989 he arrested and executed scores of army and air force officers for allegedly preparing a coup.[18] Unconfirmed rumors reported another wave of purges and executions in late 1989 and early 1990.

Another development causing the regime great concern were the democratic revolutions in Eastern Europe starting in late 1989: After all, Iraq's system was modeled on these totalitarian regimes.[19] Comments in the Western media equating Arab dictators with Romania's Ceauçescu and predicting Saddam's downfall further alarmed the regime, especially a February 1990 Voice of America (VOA) broadcast which suggested that Middle East dictators, including Saddam, might also be overthrown.[20]

On a strategic level, (some silver lining notwithstanding, see below) the decline of the Soviet Union—the radical Arabs' traditional supporter—was a disaster. To make matters worse, the new regimes in Eastern Europe and the Soviet Union improved relations with Israel, and Moscow allowed a steep rise in Jewish immigration to Israel. Most Arabs saw this as an historic turning point for the worse.[21] Not only had the Arabs lost their main international ally, but it had, in fact, defected to the other camp.

Another Iraqi setback was a failure to evict Syria's army from Lebanon, despite aid to anti-Damascus Christian forces. There are indications that this inspired Iraq to do to Kuwait what Syria had done—with Arab blessing and U.S. acquiescence—to Lebanon. Ten days after invading Kuwait, Iraq urged the problem be dealt with on the same footing as the Lebanese issue.[22] In his January 9, 1991, meeting with Secretary of State James Baker in Geneva, Tariq 'Aziz demanded "an Arab solution" for the Kuwaiti problem similar to the Ta'if agreement that left Syria as hegemonic power in Lebanon.[23] These events all pushed Iraq toward adventurism.

The Territorial Dispute with Kuwait Rediscovered

Between the Iraq-Iran war's end in August 1988 and its invasion of Kuwait two years later, Iraq brought up a series of issues that together created the crisis. These were: the Iraqi-Kuwaiti border dispute; the Israeli-Palestinian issue; the U.S. presence in the Gulf area and the Soviet Union's decline in the Middle East; disputes over oil prices and production quotas; and Iraqi demands for debt forgiveness and financial aid from the Gulf Arabs. The fusing of these questions in Iraqi thinking and propaganda was a step-by-step process. And while there are indications that the Iraqi leadership had been toying with the idea of invading Kuwait at least since 1988, only gradually did Baghdad come to see such an invasion as the solution for all its problems.

In May 1988 Iraq asked Kuwait during the Algiers Arab Summit to let it lease or annex the two Kuwaiti islands astride the Gulf entrance to Umm Qasr.[24] As long as the Faw Peninsula was in Iran's hands, Umm Qasr could not be used anyway, but after Iraq recaptured it in April, the issue reemerged.

Kuwait did not respond to Iraq's overture, apparently fearing Iran's wrath and even more Iraqi demands. In the fall of 1988 an Iraqi brigade occupied Bubyan without publicity, only to leave after a quiet Kuwaiti protest.[25] Iraq's nearby Republican Guard Advanced Command Post, attached during the war to the Seventh Corps Command at Faw, was kept intact after the ceasefire, and Saddam occasionally visited it with great publicity. Another early indication of Iraq's attitude was its request in 1988 for satellite photographs, with military applications, of Kuwait and Saudi Arabia from the French company Spot Image.[26]

In February 1989 Iraq again tried to extricate territorial concessions from Kuwait during the visit of Kuwait's heir apparent and Prime Minister Shaykh Sa'd al-'Abd Allah al-Sabah. Since Iraq's victory over Iran was a service to the whole Arab nation, he was told, it deserved to be rewarded.[27] The impasse was starker given an Iraqi-Saudi nonaggression agreement signed that same month. Saddam later claimed that he offered the same to Kuwait (apparently in return for a satisfactory border deal), but that Kuwait turned it down, "probably under the advice of a foreign power, possibly Britain." Iraq, he asserted, would have never invaded Kuwait had such a bargain been made. "Thank God, Kuwait did not sign that agreement with us!" he exclaimed.[28]

The Kuwaitis, for their part, were frustrated and angry. Just as Iraq felt that it deserved to be compensated by the Gulf Arabs because it saved them from Iran, the Kuwaitis felt that they had supported Iraq strategically and financially, risking Tehran's vengeance.[29]

But both countries retained an outward semblance of normal, even cordial relations. Only an occasional vicious glint in the Iraqi eye revealed that Baghdad was dreaming of revenge.[30]

Turning against the United States and Britain

The next phase in Iraq's increasingly radical turn occurred during the February 1990 meeting of the heads of state of the Arab Cooperation Council. In a speech that took his pro-Western partners, Egypt and Jordan, by complete surprise, Saddam criticized the U.S. Navy's presence in the Gulf, since no Soviet or Iranian threat remained, and came close to demanding its removal. In fact, by then only about 5 of the about 50 ships the U.S. Navy stationed there during the war still remained. This initiative was clearly a bid for unchallenged Iraqi supremacy in the Gulf.

But Iraq's leader went further. Referring to the Soviet Union's decline and the U.S. role as sole superpower, Saddam warned that for the next five years there was a grave danger of U.S. and Zionist machinations and urged Arabs to unite against America. This was the first time since 1980 that Iraqi policy fused together designs for supremacy in the Gulf, vicious anti-Americanism, and vitriolic anti-Israeli propaganda. Saddam also suggested that, with Europe's help, the Arabs could eventually defeat America. While the situation was very dangerous, he implied, the Arabs could reverse matters if they accepted Iraq's leadership.[31] This way Iraq, for the first time, offered itself as a replacement for the Soviet Union in its capacity as the Arabs' protector.

At the time, U.S. officials tended to see this speech as a mere expression of Iraqi anger at the VOA broadcast.[32] Another reason for Saddam's anti-Western mood may have been Turkey's closure of the Euphrates River on January 12, 1990, for 30 days to fill a new dam. This caused hardship to Iraq's farmers in the lower Euphrates basin and produced official protests.[33] The combination of an increasing Iraqi sense of vulnerability and its soaring ambition in the Gulf and Arab world created a very volatile mood in Baghdad. On March 15, Iraq affronted Britain by executing Farzad Bazoft, an Iranian-born, London-based journalist traveling on British papers, on a charge of espionage for Israel.[34] In the past, foreign citizens found guilty of spying were spared in order not to damage Iraq's foreign relations. But now Saddam was willing to risk a $400 million British trade credit promised for 1990. It is quite possible, though, that since the British government had been ignoring its own regulations by selling him dual-purpose machine tools, Saddam felt this was a small danger.[35]

The reason behind the anti-American diatribe and execution seems twofold. Iraq's government wanted to show its citizens that a regime ready to confront great powers would not hesitate to repress its own citizens. Second, by showing America and Britain—Kuwait's protectors—that Iraq was not afraid to antagonize them, Saddam hoped to dissuade them from helping Kuwait when a showdown came and to terrorize Kuwait itself into submission. Relations with Britain and the United States deteriorated further following exposure at the end of March of Iraqi smuggling of such arms' technology as nuclear triggers and a "super-gun" artillery piece.[36]

A few days later Saddam made another quantum jump in his anti-Western rhetoric. On April 19, in a meeting with 'Arafat, Saddam warned that military aggression against him would be met by a counterattack to "sweep away U.S. influence in the region." Saddam even threatened to destroy British and American warships in the Gulf and to use terrorism against U.S. targets.[37]

As a U.S, military attack on Iraq under existing circumstances was unlikely given the Bush administration's great efforts to improve relations, it seems that Saddam was thinking in terms of a very different scenario: an Iraqi assault on a U.S. ally in which he wanted to deter U.S. help for his victim. This possibility is enhanced by a U.S. intelligence report that some Iraqi forces began moving to the Kuwaiti border in the spring of 1990.[38]

The Israeli Angle

The need to divert the public's attention from economic difficulties, the impasse with Iran, events in Eastern Europe, and Iraq's failure to pry Syria out of Lebanon pushed Saddam to make his third important move in 1990. In December 1989 Iraq's leaders began to promise the early liberation of Palestine, something they had not done since 1980. On April 2, 1990, in a speech to military personnel, Saddam disclosed that Iraq had ultra-modern binary chemical weapons "that only the U.S. and the Soviet Union have." Then he warned: "I swear to God that we shall burn half of Israel if it tries to wage anything against Iraq."[39]

That Saddam's speech was designed for a domestic audience is reflected in its language, almost entirely in the Iraqi dialect and full of local images and metaphors, including a variation on the colloquial expression common among Baghdad bullies "I shall burn half your house" *(ukhruk nus beitak)*. It related only secondarily to any Iraqi duty to help other Arab countries defend themselves and was carefully calibrated so as to commit Iraq only to defend its own territory.

The threat against Israel should also be understood in the context that Iraq feared a new Israeli raid against its nuclear industry. Since early 1989 Iraqi spokesmen repeatedly warned Israel against trying to repeat the 1981 raid on Iraq's nuclear reactor by raiding its missile and unconventional arms industry. As disclosed by Iraq's air force commander, at the end of the Iraq-Iran war Iraq's leaders felt that Israel, not Iran, posed the main danger to Iraq's security.[40]

Iraq implied that once it defeated Iran, the West no longer needed its help and thus encouraged Israel to attack. Statements by Israeli politicians and officers that they worried about Iraq's development of an unconventional arsenal, and concern over Iraq's arms industry in the U.S. media, were noted in Baghdad.

Iraq suggested that it could strike anywhere with its missiles (though until April 1990 only conventional warheads were implied) if Israel attacked, while both countries exchanged warnings through covert U.S., Egyptian, and other channels. At least one senior Israeli official met with Foreign Minister 'Aziz, Deputy Prime Minister Sa'dun Hammadi, chief of Iraq's delegation to the United Nations in Geneva (and ex-intelligence chief) Barzan Ibrahim al-Tikriti, Saddam's half brother. The two sides probed each other's positions on a wide range of issues, including the development of unconventional arms, but no binding assurances were made.[41]

In February 1990 Iraq secretly inaugurated its first uranium enrichment site at Tarmiyah. When fully operational, it could produce 33 pounds of weapons-grade, 93%-enriched uranium a year.[42] The proximity in time between this event and the threat on Israel suggests that Iraq worried lest Israel's intelligence had learned what was happening. These fears were heightened when, in March 1990, the United States and Britain exposed an Iraqi plot to smuggle nuclear triggers from the United States via London. Tariq 'Aziz stated that from this time Iraq's leaders feared an Israeli raid due to increased talk in the Western press of an impending war.[43]

In reality, there was no talk of war in the Western press, but there was much criticism of Iraq's unconventional arms industry, which Baghdad may have seen as a campaign to prepare Western public opinion for an Israeli raid. On April 5, Saddam asked Prince Bandar, the Saudi ambassador to Washington, who rushed to Baghdad on Iraq's request, to get him U.S. assurance that Israel was not going to attack. For his part, Saddam promised not to initiate war. According to his own version, in threatening Israel he was motivated partly by his fear of an Israeli raid and partly by the need to distract Iraq's people from daily hardships. Saddam told the prince, "I must whip them into a sort of frenzy or emotional mobilization, so they will be ready for whatever may happen."[44]

Israeli reactions were cautious, designed to deter Iraq while avoiding a military escalation. On one hand, Israeli leaders assured Iraq publicly, and through U.S. channels privately, that Israel had no intention of attacking. On the other, they warned that Israel would retaliate massively against Iraqi aggression, thus implying a readiness to use atomic weapons in response to a chemical attack.

The U.S. and Western European governments made clear their concern while Egyptian officials quietly expressed alarm and promised to "whisper into Iraq's ear: 'cool it.' "[45] It took Iraqi foreign minister Tariq 'Aziz one day to "clarify" that Iraq would use chemical weapons only in retaliation for an Israeli atomic attack on Iraq, a position repeated by Saddam.[46]

Typically, though, the Arab response to Iraq's threats and the international community's alarm was very different from what Egyptians said in private conversations. Part of the Arab world was fascinated and elated; the rest was frightened into submission. King Husayn of Jordan backed his Iraqi patron, saying Western criticism of Iraq "expresses an old enmity towards our Arab nation and a hostile desire to stop it from progressing and building its strength. . . . There are aggressive intentions behind this campaign." 'Arafat's adviser, Basam Abu Sharif, said that criticism of Iraq was part of a "complicated plot to curtail the development of this country as the nucleus [*sic*] of power for the whole Arab nation." Iraq's challenge to the West and Israel, he argued, shifted the power balance in favor of the Arabs and the Palestinian cause.[47]

Even Syria was sympathetic, while even President Mubarak of Egypt, having rushed to Baghdad to tell Saddam to "cool it," declared in a joint press conference with Iraq's ruler that Iraq was acting defensively. Mubarak stressed, "Iraq is not a state that wants war or calls for war."[48] In the Arab world, there was an upsurge of public admiration for Saddam and Iraq. For the first time since Gamal 'Abd al-Nasir, an Arab leader stood up to Israel and fearlessly threatened it with annihilation.[49]

Arab admiration was not lost on Iraq's leader, so desperate to find a way out of his multiple predicaments. This new prestige motivated him to make the next step. On April 22 Saddam's air force commander, Major General Muzahim Sa'b Hasan, announced that Iraq would use "all its might" against Israel in case of an attack on any Arab country, not just against Iraq alone.[50] Such declarations continually escalated. For example, speaking to an Islamic conference in Baghdad in June, Saddam announced: "Yes, we will strike at [Israel] with all the arms in our possession if they attack Iraq or the Arabs. . . . If Iraq remains silent, it will lose the respect of those close to it. . . . Whoever strikes at the Arabs we will strike back from Iraq."[51]

In his April 19 talk with 'Arafat, Saddam also urged the Palestinians to take a hard line and promised to liberate them:

> Brother president ['Arafat], from now on we will not need any concessions or political efforts because you and I know that they are useless. In fact, they increase the enemy's arrogance and indifference to us . . . from now on, we need to strengthen our position and determination . . . no peace, no recognition and no negotiations [with Israel]. . . . We must support the heroism of the brave intifada. You should support it with strong stands and qualitative operations, and we should support it with what we have of qualified air and missile forces to deal a blow to and defeat the enemy, even

> without land fighting or confrontations. . . . We have in no way reduced our military force; we continue to strengthen it."[52]

In Israel, Iraq's warnings were read as relating to Jordan. (On February 19 Iraq and Jordan had announced the establishment of a joint "Pan-Arab" air squadron, and Israel reacted by sending a severe warning to Amman.[53]) But there was a danger that Saddam would be sucked into a war by his own rhetoric. Whatever the case, this was a clear departure from Saddam's long-standing policy of putting Iraq's domestic problems before entanglements in the Pan-Arab arena. Now he reversed priorities: Iraq would solve its own problems by foreign adventurism.

An Overture to Iran

An additional indication that the actual decision to use force against Kuwait (as different from contingency plans that may have existed for a long time) was taken during April 1990 is provided by the Iraqi initiative to improve relations with Iran late that month. It started with a letter that Saddam sent to Iran's 'Ali Akbar Hashemi Rafsanjani suggesting direct talks conducted on the basis of the 1975 Iran-Iraq agreement-which Saddam himself had declared null and void on September 17, 1980. This implied Iraqi concessions on the Shatt al-Arab leading to what Iraqi spokesmen called a "comprehensive and durable peace between Iraq and Iran."[54] Although serious differences between the two countries remained, bilateral meetings between mid-level officials began in June, and more sessions were planned for late August 1990.[55]

Iraq knew that Iran opposed its annexation of the Kuwaiti islands of Warba and Bubyan because any improvement of Iraq's strategic position on the Gulf would seem to be an Iranian loss.[56] According to the Iraqi version of Saddam's July 1990 conversation with Ambassador April Glaspie, Saddam warned—and Glaspie never denied—that if his demands on Kuwait were not met, Iraq would be ready to give up sovereignty over the eastern part of the Shatt al-Arab in exchange for Iran's acquiescence to an Iraqi armed operation against Kuwait.[57] To give his initiative an ideological cutting edge, Saddam also wrote Rafsanjani calling on Iran to create "an Arab-Islamic front against the increasing Zionist dangers."[58]

The Baghdad Arab Summit, May 1990: The Gulf Arabs Under Fire

By late April Iraq's turnabout was nearly complete. Iraq had turned against its wartime allies, the United States and Britain, while trying to befriend its old anti-Western enemy, Iran. And it assumed leadership of the radical Arab camp against Israel, something it had not done since the days of the Camp David Israeli-Egyptian peace agreement. The only missing piece—an aggressive posture vis-à-vis its Arab wartime allies, and Kuwait in particular—was put in place during the Arab summit in Baghdad.

The fact that the Arab summit meeting in Baghdad was neither postponed nor moved was a tremendous victory for Iraq, a de facto endorsement of its aggressive policies and an admission of weakness by moderate Arab states. Iraq and its supporters—chiefly Libya, the Palestine Liberation Organization (PLO), and Jordan—launched an offensive against Israel, Soviet Jewish immigration, the United States, and, by implication, the Arab moderates. The concluding resolutions supported Iraq's "right to take all measures that will guarantee the protection of its national security and . . . the possession of highly developed scientific and technological means" necessary for its defense.[59]

The resolutions added that this must be done in the framework of international law. Yet the "severe denunciation" of "the scientific and technological embargo" imposed on Iraq by the United States and Britain and of the Western media campaign "against [its] sovereignty and national security" meant that the Arabs were collectively denouncing any attempt to stop Saddam's nuclear, chemical, bacteriological, and missile efforts, even defining them as a positive contribution to "pan-Arab security."[60]

Even Mubarak enthusiastically applauded "the right of the Arab peoples to acquire and use modern technology." In context, such a declaration meant support for Iraq obtaining nuclear weapons.[61] Instead of distancing themselves from Iraq's chemical threats against Israel, leaders such as the Arab League's secretary-general praised Iraq as "a pan-Arab defensive shield."[62]

But Iraq did not reciprocate this praise. During the closed sessions, Saddam's real thrust was exposed when he accused some "Arab Brothers" of flooding the world oil market and bringing prices as low as $7 a barrel. Saddam called this an all-out war that gravely damaged Iraq. He added darkly: "We have reached a point when we can no longer withstand pressure."[63]

It seems that this was the moment when Saddam decided to turn the Iraqi masses' frustration from a liability to an asset, blaming their suffering on the rich Arabs and demanding compensation. According to some sources,[64] Saddam also demanded that the Arab summit compel the Gulf Arab states to forgive Iraq its war debt and give it $30 billion in economic aid. He accused Kuwait of stealing oil from an oilfield along the border and demanded that Kuwait give the two islands to Iraq. The summit never discussed the issue, but no one protested and the impression left was that of Arab sympathy for Saddam's demands or, at least, reluctance to confront him. Iraq's leadership interpreted it as further evidence of Iraq's new Arab status, even immunity, and ability to apply brutal pressure on the Gulf Arab states.[65]

Prelude to War: Open Confrontation with Kuwait

Between mid-May and late June Iraq-Kuwait relations showed growing strain. The immediate reason was a decline in oil prices, a blow to Iraq's economy and Saddam's prestige. Saddam told the Saudi oil minister privately after the summit: "I will never agree to let Iraqis starve, and Iraqi women go naked because of need."[66]

But Saddam did not forget the islands, either. Elated by his great success as the summit's host and pacesetter, Saddam asked Kuwait's emir for the use of the islands while driving him back to Baghdad airport. The latter replied, "Even the Emir of Kuwait himself does not have the right to give away a part of his country's lands." Saddam then asked to be allowed to build two pipelines from the Shatt al-Arab to Kuwait City, one for oil, the other for water.[67]

When the emir agreed, Saddam immediately followed up by asking to "build cities, schools and airports along the pipelines." When the emir expressed concern, Saddam suggested that in return Kuwait could use Iraqi territory. "There is no difference between the two countries. Do not worry about the borders," he told the emir.[68] The next quantum leap came in mid-July. Following the summit, the Iraqis scored a limited gain when, on July 10, an Iraqi-Saudi-Kuwaiti-United Arab Emirates (UAE) oil ministers' meeting agreed to abide by the Organization of Petroleum-Exporting Countries (OPEC) quotas. One day later, however, Kuwait announced that in the fall it would review, and possibly revoke, its promise. This way, the Iraqi side felt, Kuwait "killed the agreement."[69]

The Kuwaiti announcement enabled Iraq to present its next move as a defensive one. On July 16, analyzing satellite photographs, the U.S. Defense Intelligence Agency spotted, for the first time, a Republican Guard division, the Hammurabi, being deployed on the Kuwaiti border. The next morning (noon Baghdad time) the whole division was already there and a second one, al-Madina al-Munawwara, was showing up.[70]

In his July 17 Revolution Day speech, Saddam attacked unnamed Gulf Arab countries for plotting against Iraq with "imperialist and Zionist forces." This unholy coalition, he said, used economic means for their evil designs "more dangerous than those produced by the old direct methods." Having delegitimized the Gulf Arabs as the agents of imperialism and Zionism, Saddam then threatened to use force against them if they did not change their policy.[71]

A day later a third Republican Guard Division, *Tawakkalna 'Ala allah,* was monitored moving to the border. That same day Iraq's press published a July 15 letter from Iraq's foreign minister to the Arab League's secretary-general accusing Kuwait of harming Iraq "deliberately and continuously" after the Iran-Iraq war ended. Even during the war Kuwait was said to have exploited Iraq's preoccupation to encroach on its territory. Kuwait was allegedly dumping on world markets oil stolen "from the Iraqi Rumayla oil field" said to be worth $2.4 billion as "part of the imperialist-Zionist plan against Iraq and the Arab nation."[72]

By mid-July, then, Iraq was already past the turning point in its incremental decision to invade Kuwait. It is not clear whether there was anything Kuwait could have done to prevent an invasion at that stage, short of an urgent request to the United States to land troops. But even if the decision to use force could still be reversed provided Kuwait made concessions, as Iraqi spokesmen claimed, only complete surrender could have stopped the Iraqi army in its tracks.

Saddam never embarked on an important adventure without preparing his public. Before attacking Iran in 1980 he laid the groundwork in Iraq's media for five months. This time, preparations were brief and more ambiguous. Even the Revolution Day speech fell short of a sweeping delegitimization of Kuwait's regime, and Iraq's press accused only Kuwait's foreign minister (not the emir) of being "an American agent" plotting against Iraq.[73] The sense of being wronged by ungrateful Gulf Arabs was brought to a crescendo, but there were no claims that Kuwait was an integral part of Iraq. Thus, the occupation of the whole of Kuwait came as a surprise even to senior army—if not Republican Guard—officers.[74] At the end of the war Saddam fired his minister of information, the Shi'a Latif Nusayyif Jasim, for failure to mobilize public opinion behind the war, but this was, clearly, Saddam's own responsibility. Apparently happy that the West did not adhere his warning, he was reluctant to alert it further and thus force it to take preventive action.

Saddam also prepared the home front for war, starting in June 1990, by using Islamic rhetoric, clearly designed to secure mass support. This newly discovered Islam could, indeed, serve as a common platform for an anti-American front with Iran.[75] But Saddam himself undermined this campaign by not introducing Islamic law in Iraq and, trying to distance the Iraqi Shi'a from Iranian-Shi'a influence, by a chauvinistically Arab, anti-Iranian credo emphasizing the Arabs' leading role in Islam.[76]

To safeguard Arab support for an Iraqi invasion without, however, fully alerting them to his designs, Saddam, according to Iraqi sources, tried to convince Mubarak that the Arab wealth should be redistributed and that the "hungry people of Egypt" should be compensated at the expense of the "Kuwaiti Croesus."[77] To give Mubarak a taste of what he could expect after the "Croesuses" were removed, in late July Saddam gave Egypt $25 million "to buy wheat," and promised to deliver $25 million more soon, apparently after the invasion.[78]

But the Kuwaitis did not cave in. Responding to the Arab League's secretary-general, Kuwait expressed "indignation" at the Iraqi "distortion and falsification" of facts. "Iraq has a long record of encroachment on Kuwaiti lands" and always refused to settle the border issue through an impartial Arab arbitration committee. Kuwait never drilled wells in Iraqi territory, rather, Iraq drilled wells that impinged on Kuwait's oilfields.[79] Kuwait also protested to the UN secretary-general, thus internationalizing an Arab conflict, a step Arab countries normally try to avoid.[80] Iraq's foreign minister 'Aziz warned Kuwait "that foreigners will not protect those who conspire against the Arab nation."[81]

The end of July saw a flurry of activity. As reports mounted on July 24, denied by Baghdad, of an Iraqi troop buildup on the border, the Arab League secretary-general and Mubarak arrived in Baghdad. Saddam, Mubarak said, promised him, "There is no intention to attack Kuwait."[82] According to Saddam's own version, he said merely, "I will not use military force until the meeting agreed on is held in Jidda."[83] But Saddam also told Glaspie that he would also await a visit of Kuwait's crown prince to Baghdad "for serious negotiations."[84]

Meanwhile at the OPEC oil ministers' meeting in Geneva, Iraq used its troop buildup on the Kuwaiti border to impose a higher minimum price, contrary to the Gulf Arabs' interests, of $21 per barrel. Iraq's News Agency ascribed the decision by implication to Saddam's threat to use force.[85] Other OPEC ministers were not pleased. "We ought, all of us, to feel ashamed that we live in a world in which a man like Saddam Husayn is accepted by the international community," one minister is quoted as saying. Another noted: "the Saudis will regret this forever." A third delegate said despondently, "I sincerely hope that we can keep OPEC going [in the future] without gunboat quotas."[86]

With this victory, Iraq shifted its main emphasis back to territorial demands.[87] A government newspaper announced Iraq "is claiming its territory that has been infiltrated," the Kuwaiti-held part of the Rumayla oilfield being only part of the land." In short, a few days before the Jidda meeting Iraq already made it clear that it would get its way on all counts or use force.

Probing the U.S. Position

Before invading Kuwait, however, Saddam had to probe the U.S. reaction. After Saddam's Revolution Day Speech President Bush himself expressed concern and his administration spoke of reviewing its policy toward Iraq.[89] On July 18 the State Department announced U.S. determination to ensure the free flow of oil through the straits of Hormuz; defend freedom of navigation; and support "the individual and collective self defense of our friends in the Gulf, with whom we have deep and long-standing ties."[90]

On July 24 Glaspie was instructed to convey again to Iraq the U.S. concern over its threats against Kuwait and the UAE. "The implications of having oil production and pricing policy in the Gulf determined and enforced by Iraqi guns [are] disturbing." She was also to reiterate the State Department formula of commitment to individual and collective self-defense, the free flow of oil, and freedom of navigation in the Gulf. The ambassador delivered this message by phone to Iraq's deputy foreign minister, Nizar Hamdoun.[91] On July 24 the United States also announced joint naval maneuvers with the UAE in response to Iraqi troop concentrations.

Saddam, thus, had to find out what all this meant. In the first place, he decided to try to induce the United States to force Kuwait, Munich style, to make all the concessions Iraq demanded. Failing that, he needed to know whether, in case of an invasion, Washington would rake military action and how this could be deterred by his own threats or proposals.

At 10 a.m. on July 25 Glaspie met Nizar Hamdoun and gave him the same message, this time in person. At noon she was summoned for another meeting at the Foreign Ministry, only to find herself facing Saddam. The transcript of their conversation, published by the Iraqi embassy in Washington in September 1990, was challenged by Glaspie as "a fabrication" and "disinformation." State Department officials acknowledged that it contained omissions but described it as "essentially accurate."[92] Her own report, parts of which were published in American newspapers corroborates much—though not all—of the Iraqi version.[93] Even those parts not in dispute are disturbing. The situation called for an immediate, severe warning to Iraq and an alert in Washington. But due to

Saddam's personal cordiality and because he intentionally blurred his threats somewhat, Glaspie completely misread the situation, sent Washington an all-clear signal, and gave Saddam a mixed message.

According to both versions, Saddam opened by promising the ambassador that Iraq fully sympathized with the U.S. wish for an undisturbed flow of oil but demanded U.S. neutrality in the Iraqi-Kuwaiti dispute. He accused America of using Kuwait to spearhead its anti-Iraqi policy and insisted ominously that Kuwait was threatening Iraq's very livelihood by engaging in "economic warfare," a situation Iraq could not accept.

Instead of responding with equal pressure, Glaspie tried to allay Saddam's fears of U.S. conspiracies against him, insisting that Bush had instructed her to seek better relations with Iraq. The ambassador reported that Saddam then demanded that the thankless rich Kuwaitis keep to their oil quota and "open their purses" to the Iraqis, who spilled for them "rivers of blood."

Saddam told Glaspie that verbal threats and a military buildup was the only way to show Kuwait how much Iraqis were suffering. When Saddam mentioned his promise to Mubarak not to use force if Kuwait met Iraq's demands in the scheduled Iraqi-Kuwaiti meetings, the ambassador regarded this as good news. Saddam also implied skepticism about U.S. resolve to defend its allies, asserting "American society is unable to sustain 10,000 fatalities in one battle," while Iraq did just that during eight years of war.

According to both versions, Saddam also raised the border issue, implying he would like U.S. pressure on Kuwait. The ambassador replied that U.S. policy took no position on such inter-Arab affairs. This assertion was in line with the State Department position. It was designed to avoid diplomatic complications as a result of American involvement in such disputes. But in the context of six Republican Guard armored and mechanized divisions on the Kuwaiti border and two more on the way, this certainly was not a strong warning to Iraq to stick to diplomatic means lest the United States, too, resort to force.

The ambassador never sought any authorization to take a tougher line. This was particularly necessary in view of Saddam's thinly veiled threat that, if

Kuwait did not succumb to his demands, he would make concessions to Iran to bring its acquiescence, then he would attack Kuwait. All the ambassador did was to warn that the United States "cannot forgive" the use of force.

In summing up, the ambassador defined Saddam's attitude during the interview as "cordial, reasonable and even warm." She contended that Saddam was "worried" because he suspected that the joint U.S.-UAE maneuvers meant a U.S. decision "to take sides." Finally, she observed, "His emphasis that he wants peaceful settlement is surely sincere: Iraqis are sick of war. But the terms are difficult to achieve. Saddam seems to want pledges now on oil prices and production to cover the next several months."

It seems that the ambassador forgot altogether about Iraq's territorial demands. But her main purpose was not to warn Iraq but to save, even improve, bilateral relations. Thus, she went out of her way to convince Saddam that the United States was not conspiring against him with Kuwait and others. Her criticisms were expressed in apologetic terms, and she sounded much more convincing when expressing sympathy and promising to work to improve relations. Glaspie not only ignored Saddam's threats but even recommended that public criticism of Iraq would be "eased off" for a while.

The State Department and White House, having concluded that Iraqi troops were not ready for a full-scale invasion, thought Saddam was bluffing[94] and were unwilling to provoke him. Saddam had warned the ambassador that, if offended, he would be compelled to react strongly—even irrationally. The strongest warning they delivered was Bush's verbal message to Saddam sent on July 28 through Glaspie: "We believe that differences are best resolved by peaceful means and not by threats involving military force." The president also put America's friendship with Iraq on the same level as that with "our other friends in the region."[95]

On July 24, 1990, State Department spokeswomen Margaret Tutwiler had asserted, "We do not have any . . . special defense or security commitments to Kuwait." On the day of the Glaspie-Saddam meeting, Ambassador-Designate to Kuwait Edward Gnehm told the Senate Foreign Relations Committee that Iraq was "merely trying to intimidate a small country."[96]

Two days before the invasion, Assistant Secretary of State for Near Eastern and South Asian Affairs John Kelly reaffirmed that the United States had no defense treaty with any Gulf state and considered the Kuwait-Iraq border dispute to be their private affair. After the invasion a senior administration official told the *New York Times* that the government expected an Iraqi invasion to seize a limited border area. "We were reluctant to draw a line in the sand. . . . I can't see the American public supporting the deployment of troops over a dispute over twenty miles of desert territory, and it is not clear that the local countries would have supported that kind of commitment. The basic principle is not to make threats that you can't deliver on." Whatever the truth, the United States behaved as if this was its approach. This caution was enhanced by Mubarak and King Fahd of Saudi Arabia, who assured Washington that Saddam would not invade, arguing that "the best way to resolve an inter-Arab squabble was for the United States to avoid inflammatory words and actions."[97]

U.S. inertia was reflected in a surrealistic meeting between Saddam and U.S. chargé d'affaires Joseph Wilson four days after the invasion. Saddam claimed that because Kuwait "was a state without borders . . . the entry of the Iraqi forces cannot be measured within the framework of the relationship between [normal] states in the Arab world." He later added, "By the way, say hello to President Bush and tell him to consider [Shaykh] Jabir [al-Sabah] finished and history."

Saddam strongly warned the United States "against further meddling in the relations between Iraq and Saudi Arabia" and threatened that if the United States harmed Iraq, Iraq would hurt U.S. interests, again warning America against taking "any bold steps that they can not retreat from." But Saddam also had a proposition: he offered to serve as America's chief ally and—by implication—policeman of the Gulf. In exchange, he promised that there would be a free flow of oil at $25 per barrel.

Wilson merely promised to pass along the message. Not authorized to threaten that unless he withdrew from Kuwait the U.S. would forcefully evict him, Wilson declared: "during these difficult days, it appears to me that it is important that we keep a dialogue between us to avoid making mistakes. This is the only way in which we are going to be able to remove tension and cool emotions."[98]

At the same time it was probing the U.S. position, Iraq also gauged the Soviet stand. According to a Soviet source, some senior Soviet officials promised Iraq that, in case of an attack on Kuwait, the Soviet Union would not support the United States and Britain.[99]

Saddam Goes to War

The Jidda meeting was held on July 31, 1990, and lasted only two hours. If the previous Iraqi demands are any guide, Iraq gave Kuwait an unacceptable ultimatum: to cede or lease to Iraq the two islands and the southern tip of the Rumayla oilfield, to write off Iraq's war debt, and to pay Iraq for claimed financial losses. Iraq was represented at Jidda by a senior delegation led by Revolutionary Command Council (RCC) Vice Chairman 'Izzat Ibrahim al-Duri (whose daughter was married to Saddam's elder son, 'Uday) and including Deputy Prime Minister Sa'dun Hammadi and 'Ali Hasan al-Majid, minister of local government and member of the Ba'th party Regional Leadership (but, most important, Saddam's cousin and one of the chiefs of Iraq's internal security). Sending such a delegation indicated Iraq's seriousness, and Iraq's media warned that Iraq would reject any attempt to "bury Iraqi rights under the rubble of postponements and delays."[100] The fact that the invasion had been fully prepared before the meeting was even convened, however, indicates that Saddam suspected that Kuwait would not accept his demands.

Kuwait's behavior was strange. On the one hand it was ready to stand up to Iraq, refusing to yield territory and offering minimal financial concessions. On the other hand, it put itself at Iraq's mercy, telling foreigners to keep out of this internal Arab affair. "Solving disputes between brothers is not difficult," it argued, and echoed Saddam's view that all Arabs need to cooperate in the post-Cold War world.[101] More dangerously, Kuwait publicly committed itself not to invite foreign troops to defend itself, lulled by U.S., Egyptian, and Saudi promises and, most of all, by their own hope that, if not offended, Saddam would stop short of violence.[102] Very possibly, what the Kuwaitis had in mind was a

Bedouin-style lengthy process of negotiations and bargaining that would end with a compromise: some Kuwaiti and Saudi financial contribution to Saddam's coffers.

There are two versions of the Jidda meeting. According to one, the Iraqi delegation was under orders to obtain Kuwait's full surrender or to walk out.[103] Saddam claimed that his delegation requested a $10 billion "loan." Kuwait agreed to $9 billion and the Saudis offered to contribute the rest, but at the farewell party the Kuwaitis demanded a border agreement as precondition for the loan. Iraq then saw no point in continuing the talks, and they were suspended.[104] The delegations left Jidda and the Iraq-Kuwait border was closed.[105] Early the next day, August 2, 1990, Iraq invaded Kuwait.

Why the Whole of Kuwait? Why Not Saudi Arabia?

In hindsight, Foreign Minister Tariq 'Aziz disclosed that Iraq originally planned to occupy only the islands and the disputed oilfield. He described taking Kuwait City as Saddam's "last-moment" decision just before the invasion. Saddam's argument was that "it would make no difference [to the United States]" how much of Kuwait was conquered.[106] Although, clearly, the Republican Guard was ready for both options, this account sounds credible, if only because it put the blame for the war on Saddam, and thus it placed 'Aziz in jeopardy. ('Aziz never repeated this disclosure.)

The mystery is: What drove Saddam to the strange conclusion that "it would make no difference"? By publishing their version of Saddam's meeting with the American ambassador the Iraqis implied that, due to her vagueness, she at least shared with them the responsibility for their invasion. Saddam's own version was given in an astonishing interview in which he explained his interpretation of Ambassador Glaspie's message:

> "I . . . asked her to persuade [President Bush] to pressure Kuwait if necessary. She replied. . . 'the U.S. does not want to be involved in inter Arab disputes.' I then said: 'we do not want you to be involved either' . . . They said they would not interfere. In so

> saying they washed their hands. What response should I have waited for? We entered Kuwait four days later. Regardless [however], Bush rallied the world . . . and attacked Iraq. What was the problem? They had said that they would not intervene!"[107]

This sounds like feigned naïveté. Judging by the Iraqi transcript, even the overoptimistic Saddam should not have interpreted Glaspie's remark on the border dispute as permission to occupy all Kuwait.[108] Furthermore, by claiming that he did only what he thought the United States allowed him to do Saddam contradicted his own theme, repeated many times between July 17 and August 2, that Kuwaiti behavior was determined by a U.S. plot. Was it logical to expect the United States to plot with Kuwait against Iraq, only to give Iraq green light to invade Kuwait? Alternatively, if, indeed, the Americans were so hostile to Iraq, as Saddam claimed in his pre-invasion speeches, how could he possibly take anything they told him at face value? Why did he not suspect a trap?

Tariq 'Aziz himself explained in his interview with the journalist Milton Viorst that, as he understood it, the reference to U.S. reluctance to get involved did not mean permission, to invade: "Those who say that we regarded what the ambassador said as a green light indicating that the U.S. would not react against Iraq if it launched a military intervention against Kuwait are wrong."[109]

It seems that even those in Baghdad who believed in a U.S. plot against Iraq (and many at least half believed in it) did not think this meant war. Except for Saddam's conversation with Arafat in April, Iraq had only accused the West of economic warfare. Further, the Bush administration's vague commitment to Kuwait's territorial integrity, the ambassador's talk of U.S. reluctance to intervene; and the U.S. government's leniency over Iraq's human rights and other transgressions—along with Arab appeasement—seem to have created a feeling in Baghdad that Washington would take no drastic action over a few miles of Kuwaiti sand and an oilfield.[110]

Why, then, did Saddam not play it safe, staying in Kuwait's northern part? If Iraq's main purpose was to seize a harbor to replace the closed Shatt al-Arab, a far less risky option was to occupy the two islands and develop the Umm Qasr and Mina Bakr ports. But such a mini-invasion, even if including the South Rumayla oilfield, would not have solved Iraq's acute cash-flow problems. In fact, it could worsen them by pushing Kuwait and other Gulf states to overproduce oil again. By taking all Kuwait, however, Saddam could hope to terrorize the Gulf Arabs into total submission, become a hero to most Iraqis and many other Arabs, and, most important in the short run: control Kuwait's huge economic assets. Iraqis estimated Kuwait's assets in the West as $220 billion.[111] But Saddam was also sure that the Kuwaitis, being Bedouins like himself, retained the tradition of keeping a huge stockpile of gold in the vaults of their National Bank. (There is much evidence that he himself did, indeed, retain that tradition.[112])

On the night of the invasion Saddam sent helicopter-borne commando units to three sites: to Kuwait airport, to secure landing facilities for the invading troops; to the emir's palace, in the hope that, in the absence of a legitimate Kuwaiti ruler, Iraq could establish an "interim government" that would siphon Kuwait assets abroad to the Iraqi accounts; and finally he sent a unit, equipped with all the necessary gear, to break into the National Bank. The unit was able to enter the vaults but, to its dismay, found there only relatively small quantities of gold.[113]

All these potential gains were, in Saddam's eyes, big enough to dwarf the risk. But then, Saddam also thought the risk as relatively low, given his conviction that America feared going to war and that the Saudis would not change their historic policy of appeasing radical Arabs to invite U.S. troops.[114] As pointed out above, he thought he had adequately prepared the ground for U.S. and Egyptian inaction. While his understanding of Iraq's internal scene was always superb, Saddam's comprehension of other Arab and Islamic countries was far less impressive.

Saddam thus discounted the likelihood of war, economic sanctions, or a strong Arab front against him resulting from the invasion. He was ready to risk diplomatic confrontation even with the world's sole superpower given the high stakes, but hoped that when faced with a fait accompli, it would make a deal. If

Iraq gained Kuwait's full oil production, together they would pump over 5 million barrels a day, 21% of OPEC's total production, letting them force the West and its Arab allies to accept Iraq's dictates. It will be remembered that, in their post-invasion conversation, Saddam suggested to Joseph Wilson that, in return for a commitment not to invade Saudi Arabia or "harm American interests" elsewhere and to guarantee an undisturbed flow of oil at reasonable prices, the U.S. government would recognize Kuwait's new status and accept him as protector of the Gulf.[115]

Why did Iraq not advance into Saudi territory to seize oilfields as a bargaining card or, later, to attack arriving U.S. forces before they dug in? To claim, as Saddam did, that he was restrained by his 1989 nonaggression pact with Saudi Arabia is unconvincing. More likely, Iraq's leaders were sure the United States would fight to defend Saudi territory. An attack on Saudi Arabia, let alone on the American troops there, would start the war with America that Saddam hoped to avoid.

Aside from his rational thinking, Saddam's decisions are also explained by his entourage's fear of contradicting the leader once his mind was made, and by Saddam's psychology. His self-image was as an invincible warrior and empire-builder, a reincarnation of Gilgamesh, Sargon the Akkadian, Nebuchadnezzar, Salah al-Din, and even the Sumero-Akkadian god Dumuzi-Tammuz.[116] He had invaded Iran only 14 months after becoming president. Saddam became trapped in his own myth. Having emerged as the leading regional power from the Iraq-Iran war, Saddam was eager to win another victory that would provide him with the leaping stone to far greater ambitions. As emerges from his conversation with Joseph Wilson, he intended to become the Gulf's hegemonic power. As he demonstrated in the Baghdad May 1990 Arab summit, as well as in many of his speeches before and after the invasion, he planned to turn himself into the pace-setter for the whole Arab world. Finally, as implied in a few of his speeches following the invasion, using these economic, strategic, and political leverages, his ambition was to become the most influential leader of the Third World. Beyond the immediate rewards of money and an excellent harbor, then, the long-term stakes were global power and glory.

Conclusion: Where Did Saddam Go Wrong?[117]

A number of Saddam's calculations did prove correct. In the first place, he was right in his conviction that his army could easily conquer Kuwait before anybody intervened. Saddam also gained political support from some of the radical Arabs and Jordan. While the Arab regimes supporting him (Libya, Algeria, Yemen, Sudan, and Jordan) did not endorse the annexation of Kuwait, their efforts to prevent war and remove the international embargo objectively helped Baghdad. On the popular level, too, in the Arab world Saddam received mass support in North Africa and Sudan, from Israeli and Palestinian Arabs, and in Jordan. Saddam also managed to launch missile attacks on Israel without provoking an Israeli nonconventional reprisal. Indeed, Israel did not respond at all, but this, if anything, was a disappointment: Saddam planned on a limited Israeli response that would split the Western-Arab coalition against him. Yet, although his missiles failed to split the coalition, he at least won much Arab admiration for being the only Arab leader in half a century to have struck Tel Aviv and to have sent the Israelis fleeing the city.

In the last analysis, however, most of Saddam's calculations were wrong. The Arab radicals gave him little real help. His hope that the masses in countries that opposed him would rise against their rulers proved extremely naive. The main demonstrations occurred in Pakistan, Morocco, and Algeria—all places irrelevant to events in the Gulf—and even there no one was toppled from power. To be sure, revolutions against the pro-Western Arab regimes are still possible, but Saddam needed such revolutions before and during the Gulf War. His wish that Palestinian organizations would sow havoc in Europe and America through terrorism and thus help stop the war proved unrealistic.

Saddam's hope that—in return for cash and a promise of future handouts—Egypt would accept Kuwait's occupation was also wrong. Viewing itself as the Arab world's proper leader, Egypt would not accept Iraqi hegemony. As pointed out earlier, the Saudis, too, disappointed him. Turkey, also, saw Iraq's ambitions as so threatening that it took a strong stand against Saddam.

Saddam was hopeful that Iran would support him against the American "great Satan." To his dismay, he found out that all he could expect from the

Iranians was sympathetic rhetoric and some food supplies at inflated prices. At the war's end Iran helped the Shi'a and Kurdish revolts against him and did not even return the 138 Iraqi warplanes flown by pilots who had taken refuge there.

Saddam also miscalculated the Soviet stance as Moscow cooperated with Washington almost fully. There was some sympathy from Soviet conservatives, especially after the start of the bombing campaign, but the Soviet Union was too weak to make any difference. Saddam's hope, fueled by Paris's highly equivocal policy, that France would extricate him from his predicament also proved a mirage.

More important, Saddam completely misunderstood the U.S. and British positions. For a man who only five months before the invasion had warned Arabs of the American danger to blunder in such a way was, indeed, extraordinary. The U.S. government was ready to tolerate hysterical Iraqi threats against Israel and to some extent threats against the Gulf Arab states; nor would it have fought over a limited border change.

But it had no choice but to go to war over the whole of Kuwait, because acquiescing to an Iraqi occupation would, in effect, mean accepting Iraq's hegemony in the Gulf. Saddam's greatest miscalculation, then, was his failure to predict the U.S. response to an Iraqi occupation of Kuwait. Taking at face value the popular post-Vietnam perception in the Third World of America as a paper tiger, Saddam did not believe that it had the stamina to fight a costly war against him. Whether this perception was right, he was certainly wrong in his assumption that any war against him would be costly for the Americans. Having invaded Kuwait and realized that the Americans might retaliate, Saddam still had the option of withdrawing from most of the country while retaining the two islands and disputed border areas. At first, Iraq did promise an early departure, but the invasion and ensuing annexation had created a new reality. Now that "the branch has returned to the trunk" and "the baby has returned to its mother's lap," as Iraqi spokesmen put it, withdrawing was extremely difficult. This was particularly so in view of Saddam's suspicion that the Americans were bluffing.

Even on January 15 Saddam still could not believe the United States would fight. The ambiguous positions of France and the Soviet Union, antiwar demonstrations in the West, and a pilgrimage of ex-world leaders to Baghdad helped convince him that there was no need to hurry. Surrounded by yes men, Saddam was isolated from the real political atmosphere in Washington and London. No wonder that the war came to him as yet another surprise. Finally, Saddam wrongly believed that, in the ground campaign, his soldiers would still fight to the death and inflict enough casualties on the coalition to deadlock the war. This belief, too, was in error.

Notes

This study was assisted by research grants from the U.S. Institute of Peace; the Bertha Von Suttner Special Project for the Optimization of Conflict Resolution; and Mr. Irving Young of London. I am also grateful to my assistant, Mr. Ronan Zeidel, for his help.

[1] In interviews in London (January 1990) and Haifa (July 1991), Iraqi-born Jews educated in Arab schools in the Shi'a south in the 1940s told the author that teachers promised, to the enthusiastic acclaim of their pupils, "Iraq will conquer [*yahtall*] the Gulf, and make order [*yusawi*] in the Fertile Crescent."

[2] See report by General Khalil Sa'id, commander of the planned operation, *al-Thawra*, August 21, 1992.

[3] On the history of the Ottoman-Kuwaiti and Iraqi-Kuwaiti border issue, see Richard Schofield, *Kuwait and Iraq: Historical Claims and Territorial Disputes* (London, 1991).

[4] See Muhammad Heikal, 'Abd al-Nasir's adviser, in *Illusions of Triumph: An Arab View of the Gulf War* (London, 1992), p. 30, reporting a conversation between 'Abd al-Nasir and Nikita Khrushchev in 1958, following Qasim's coup. Khrushchev urged Nasir to tell Qasim to assure the West that Iraq's oil would continue to flow and all oil agreements would be respected. "If they feel the oil is threatened they will fight," said Khrushchev. Qasim followed the Soviet-Egyptian advice.

[5] Baghdad Radio, July 18, 1990, *Foreign Broadcast Information Service (FBIS)*, July

18, 1990, p. 23. According to Tariq 'Aziz, military hardware cost $102 billion and losses from lower oil sales was $106 billion. The official Iraqi figure for casualties was 100,000 dead. According to *Alif Ba*, 52,948 Iraqis died in Faw alone. The same figure appears on a monument in Faw commemorating the casualties. See *al-Thawra*, April 17, 1992. Casualties in each of the Basra, central, and northern fronts could not have been lower.

[6] *Mahdar mugabalat al-sayyid al-ra'is saddam husayn ma'a al-safira abril klasbi yawm 25.7.90* (Minutes of the Meeting Between President Saddam Hussein and Ambassador April Glaspie on July 25, 1990), p. 4. Iraq's embassy in Washington published the text in September 1990. Western sources vary in their assessment of the debt. According to the *Financial Times* (September 8,1989), by mid-1989 it was somewhere between $65 and 80 billion, half of it to the Arabs and half to countries outside the Middle East.

[7] Interview with a representative in Iraq of a large European bank, London, November 15, 1988.

[8] It later used these reserves to pay for the Kuwait war and domestic expenses after August 2, 1990.

[9] See Iraq's housing minister confirming that rebuilding Basra and Faw was exorbitantly costly, *al-Thawra*, April 13, 1992.

[10] See, for example, Saddam's interview promising a multiparty system, *al-Sharq al-Awsat* (London), March 8, 1989, in *FBIS*, March 14, 1989, pp. 29-30; and the joint meeting of the Revolutionary Command Council and the party's Iraqi Regional Leadership, the country's most important institutions, discussing a multiparty system and other democratizing steps, *al-Yawm al-Sabi'* (Paris), January 22, 29; February 5, 12, 19, 1990.

[11] In June 1989, 150,000 troops from the First Special Army Corps were released (*Iraqi Newt Agency* [*INA*] June 22, 1989, in *FBIS*, June 22, 1989, p. 14).

[12] Baghdad Radio, April 2, 1990, in *FBIS*, April 3, 1990, pp. 33-34.

[13] Iraq spent roughly $5 billion in 1988, or 40% of export earnings on the military. Phebe Marr, "Iraq in the Year 2000", in Charles F. Doran and Stephen W. Buck, *The Gulf, Energy and Global Security*, (Boulder, Colo., 1991), p. 52. In 1989, with the war over and Iran at a clear military disadvantage, Iraq still spent $1.9

billion on arms imports alone (excluding expenditures on its nuclear arms industry). See U.S. Arms Control and Disarmament Agency, *World Military Expenditures and Arms Transfers 1990*, 37.

[14] *INA*, December 13, 1990, in *FBIS*, December 14, 1990, p. 16.

[15] For Saddam comparing himself favorably with Egypt's 'Abd al-Nasir see, for example, his talk with 'Arafat, *al Muharrir* (Paris), May 8, 1990, p. 3 (in *FBIS*, May 9, 1990, pp. 4-5).

[16] Phebe Marr, "Iraq in the '90s," *Middle East Executive Report* (June 1990), p. 13.

[17] *Al-Thawra*, May 13,1990; *Hurras al-Watan*, May 20, 1990.

[18] Consequently, the annual Army Day parade on January 6, 1989, was canceled. Interviews with Western officials in Washington, D.C., February-July 1989, and in London, October-December 1989.

[19] Members of the Shi'a opposition told the author, in London in March 1990, that Saddam ordered that his internal security personnel view videotapes of Ceauçescu's demise to show them the danger.

[20] See Saddam's complaint and U.S. Ambassador April Glaspie's personal apology, her denunciation of the general treatment of Saddam by the American media and her reference to a formal U.S. apology for the Voice of America broadcast, in the Iraqi transcript of her meeting with Saddam on July 25, 1990, *Mahdar al-muqabalat*, p. 4; and partial text in the *New York Times* September 23, 1990, p. 19.

[21] See, for example, *al-Thawra*, October 7 and November 17, 1989; February 6, 1990; *al-Jumhuriyya*, February 6, 1990.

[22] Baghdad Radio, August 12, 1990, in *FBIS*, August 13, 1990, pp. 48-49.

[23] "Minutes of . . . Geneva meeting," *Baghdad Observer*, January 20, 1992.

[24] Iraqi foreign minister Tariq 'Aziz's letter to the secretary-general of the Arab League, Baghdad Radio, July 18, 1990, in *FBIS*, July 18-19, p. 21; INA, July 24, 1990, in *FBIS*, July 24, 1990, p. 24; and interviews with U.S. officials, Washington, D.C., January-August 1989.

[25] Interview with Western official in the United States, January 28, 1992.

[26] See Saddam's visit, *al-Jumhuriyya*, April 18, 1989; For Spot Image, see *Financial Times*, January 11, 1991.

[27] *Al-Thawra* February 8, 1989, cited by *INA*, in *FBIS* February 8, 1989, pp. 21-22. For meetings between Iraq's leaders and Kuwaiti guests see ibid., pp. 19-21.

[28] *Meeting Between President Saddam Hussein and American Chargé d'Affaires Wilson on 6th August 1990*, Iraqi Embassy, Washington, D.C. (September 1990), p. 2.

[29] See, for example, 'Aziz's letter to the Arab League's secretary-general, ibid., p. 23.

[30] See, for example, the Iraqi affront to Kuwait in a Gulf football championship there, the *Economist Intelligence Unit (EIU)-Country Report, Iraq*, no. 2, 1990, p. 11.

[31] "Saddam Hussein Addresses Officials", *INA* in Arabic, February 19, 1990, in *FBIS*, February 20, 1990, pp. 2-3. The Gulf Cooperation Council (GCC) representative at the conference, Sayf Ibn Hayil al-Askari, timidly implied support for the Iraqi demand for an American withdrawal (ibid., p. 2). See also Saddam's speech to the heads of states, *Jordan TV*, February 24, 1990, in *FBIS*, February 27, 1990, pp. 1-3.

[32] Interview with a U.S. official, London, March 8, 1990.

[33] *EIU-Country Report, Iraq*, no. 2, 1990, p. 11.

[34] Tariq 'Aziz to Milton Viorst, *The New Yorker*, June 24, 1991, p. 65.

[35] See report in the *Financial Times* reproduced in *Ha'aretz*, November 13, 1992, of postwar British government encouragement to BSA Tools and Matrix Churchill to export to Iraq machine tools that could be used for arms production. Interview with a senior British official, London, November 16, 1989.

[36] See, for example, *Middle East Economic Digest* (*MEED*), May 18, 1990, p. 16.

[37] *Al-Muharrir* (Paris), May 8, 1990, p. 3.

[38] CIA Chief Robert Gates, reported in *Ha'aretz*, May 10, 1992.

[39] *Iraqi Television* and Baghdad Radio, April 2, 1990, in *FBIS*, April 3, 1990, pp. 32-36.

[40] Lt. General Muzahim Sa'b Hasan, *Hurras al-Watan*, April 22, 1990.

[41] Interview with Major General Avraham Tamir, ex-director general of Israel's Foreign Ministry (Tel Aviv, April 3, 1992). See also *Yediot Ahronot* (Tel Aviv), February 15, 1991. This was not the first such meeting. In 1987 Nizar Hamdun, Iraqi's ambassador to Washington, met two other Israeli generals—Maj. Gen. Avi Yaari and Maj. Gen. Ori Orr (later head of the Knesset Committee on Foreign and Security Affairs)—on study leave at Harvard for an informal discussion at a

private home and later met one of them again. (Both interviewed by the author in 1988.)

42 Report on UN-sponsored International Atomic Energy Agency (IAEA) inspection team in Iraq, UN Security Council, *Note by the Secretary-General*, July 25, 1991, pp. 3-4.

43 *The New Yorker*, June 24, 1991, p. 65.

44 Bob Woodward, *The Commanders* (New York, 1991), pp. 202-203. Saddam received his assurance a few days later.

45 *MEED*, April 13, 1990, p. 18.

46 *Al-Thawra*, April 17, 1990, p. 3.

47 *MEED*, April 13, 1990, p. 18.

48 *Middle East News Agency* (*MENA*) (Cairo), April 8, 1990.

49 Interview with a British official, May 2,1990, and a senior U.S. official, May 7, 1990. On similar Arab responses, see *MEED*, April 13, 1990, p. 22.

50 Radio Monte Carlo, April 22, in *FBIS*, April 23, 1990, p. 13.

51 Baghdad Radio, June 18, 1990, in *FBIS*, June 19,1990, p. 21. Saddam spoke similarly at the Baghdad Arab summit in May. See Baghdad Radio, May 28, 1990, in *FBIS*, May 29, 1990, p. 5, and Saddam's interview in the *Wall Street Journal*, June 28, 1990: "If Israel attacks one [Arab] country and there is no response, then the second country to be attacked surely would be Iraq."

52 *Al-Muharrir*, May 8, 1990, in *FBIS*, May 9, 1990, pp. 4-5.

53 *EIU-Country Report, Iraq*, no. 2, 1990, p. 11.

54 *Al-Siyasa*, May 10-11, 1990, in *FBIS*, May 14, 1990, p. 14. Tariq 'Aziz in Radio Amman, May 15, 1990, *FBIS*, May 15, 1990, p. 8; for Iran's positive response, see Radio Muscat, May 13, 1990, in *FBIS*, May 14, 1990, p. 15.

55 *Al-Siyasa* (Kuwait), June 18, 1990; *Associated Press* from Kuwait, June 18, 1990; and *al-Jazira*, June 19, 1990. In early July it became clear that while Iraq was interested in an early summit meeting, Iran wanted detailed ground work beforehand; while Iraq wanted direct talks, Iran insisted on UN mediation. Finally, while Iraq tried to skirt UN Resolution 598 specifying the order of priority, Iran wanted to follow that resolution. See *al-Sharq al-'Awat* (Riyadh) and *Ha'aretz*, July 8, 1990.

[56] See, for example, Tehran Radio, August 6, 1990, in *FBIS*, August 17, 1990, p. 20.

[57] *Mahdar muqabalat*, p. 14. For Iran's view, see *Le Figaro*, August 13, 1990.

[58] See *al-Thawra, al-'Iraq, Qadisiyya*, June 10, 1990, in *FBIS*, June 14, 1990, pp. 24-25.

[59] *INA*, May 30, 1990.

[60] Ibid.

[61] Mubarak's speech, *MENA* (Cairo), May 28, 1990; the king's speech, *INA*, May 28, 1990.

[62] Shadhli al-Qulaybi to the Arab foreign ministers in Baghdad, *INA*, May 22, 1990, in *FBIS*, May 23, 1990, p. 2.

[63] The May 30, 1990 speech was broadcast only after the Iraqi-Kuwaiti dispute became public. See *FBIS*, July 19, 1990, p. 21.

[64] Interview, September 10, 1990, with a Shi'a opposition leader, and February 5, 1992, with an ex-senior U.S. official; *Komsomolskaya Pravda*, January 5, 1991.

[65] After the Cairo Arab Summit of August 10 denounced Iraq's invasion, Iraq invoked the Baghdad Summit resolutions and demanded that, as they backed Iraq against all "foreign threats," the Arab League should denounce the anti-Iraqi concentration of foreign armies. See Salah al-Mukhtar, *al-Qadisiyya*, February 3, 1992.

[66] 'Aziz in *al-Thawra*, September 9, 1990, in *FBIS*, September 12, 1990, p. 30.

[67] 'Aziz protested to Klibi Kuwait's "procrastination" on Iraq's offer of a water pipeline. See *INA*, July 24, in *FBIS*, July 24, 1990, p. 23. This was strange, bearing in mind that the official Iraqi position had been that it was doing Kuwait a favor.

[68] The emir to the editor of *al-Ahram*, published in *Liwa al-Sadr*, August 18, 1991.

[69] 'Aziz to *The New Yorker*, June 24, 1991, p. 66.

[70] Woodward, *The Commanders*, pp. 205-206.

[71] Baghdad Radio, July 17, 1990, in *FBIS*. July 17, 1990, pp. 22-23.

[72] Baghdad Radio, July 18, 1990, in *FBIS*, July 18, 1990, pp. 21-24.

[73] See, for example, *Yediot Ahronot*, July 24,1990; *al-Thawra, al-Qadisiyya*, July 19,1990; the National Assembly's statement on Kuwait and the UAE, *INA*, July 19, 1990, in *FBIS*, July 20, 1990, pp. 17-18; *Qadisiyya*, July 20, 1990, accuses Kuwait and the UAE of "a large degree of hatred against Iraq's progress."

[74] Interview in Washington, D.C., October 1992, with a U.S. official basing this conclusion on interrogation of senior officers who became prisoners of war.

[75] As suggested by Ofra Bengio, "Iraq," in Ami Ayalon, *Middle East Contemporary Survey* (Tel Aviv University, The Moshe Dayan Center) vol. 14, 1990.

[76] See his "Open Letter" to President Bush, Baghdad Radio, August 16, 1990, in *FBIS*, August 17, 1990, p. 21; Baghdad Radio, September 5, 1990, in *FBIS*, September 6, 1990, pp. 27-29; for "Jesus Christ . . . is the prophet of God and . . . he is an Arab . . . like [all] the [other] prophets from the land of the Arabs," Saddam's Christmas message, *INA*, December 31, 1990, in *FBIS*, January 3, 1991, p. 22.

[77] Baghdad Radio, August 10, 1990, in *FBIS*, August 14, 1990, pp. 32-33.

[78] *October* (Cairo), March 31, 1991, p. 3.

[79] *Middle East Economic Survey*, July 23, 1990, pp. D7-D9.

[80] *Kuwait News Agency* (*KUNA*) July 20, 1990, in *FBIS*, July 23, 1990, p. 15.

[81] *INA*, July 24, 1990, in *FBIS*, July 24, 1990, p. 24. *Al-Thawra*, July 22, 1990, in *FBIS*, July 23, 1990, pp. 29-30.

[82] Cairo Radio, August 811990, in *FBIS*, August 8, 1990, p. 7.

[83] Baghdad Radio, August 10, 1990, in *FBIS*, August 14, 1990, p. 33. While admitting the deadlock in Jidda, Hammadi, Iraq's leading expert on the dispute with Kuwait, apparently unaware of Saddam's intention to invade Kuwait, disclosed that meetings would continue in Baghdad "in accordance with the agreement reached by . . . President Saddam Hussein and President Husni Mubarak . . . and King Fahd" (*INA*, August 1, 1990, in *FBIS*, August 2, 1990, p. 25). This indicates that Mubarak's version was correct. *INA*, July 24, 1990, in *FBIS*, July 25,1990, p. 23. Also *MENA* July 24 ,1990, in *FBIS*, July 24, 1990, pp. 26-27.

[84] Information in author's possession.

[85] *INA*, July 27, 1990, in *FBIS*, July 30, 1990, p. 19.

[86] *The Observer*, July 29, 1990.

[87] Iraqi official spokesman, *INA*, July 27, 1990, in *FBIS*, July 27, 1990, p. 27.

[88] *Al-Jumhuriyya*, July 28, 1990, in *FBIS*, July 30, 1990, pp. 19-20. See also *al-Thawra*, July 28, 29, 1990; *al-Qadisiyya* July 29,1990; *al Jumhuriyya*, July 29, 1990; and *al-Thawra* August 1, 1990, in *FBIS* August 2, 1990, p. 25.

[89] *Ha'aretz*, July 19, 1990; *International Herald Tribune*, July 28-29, 1990.

[90] *New York Times*, March 21, 1991.

[91] *Washington Post*, October 21, 1992.

[92] *New York Times*, March 21, 1991.

[93] See, for example, *New Republic*, August 5, 1990; Washington Post, October 21, 1992.

[94] U.S. analysts were puzzled since Iraq had not carried out exercises, as in the previous war; radio communications were far too low; and logistical preparations seemed inadequate. Woodward, *The Commanders*, pp. 205-12. But these expectations were wrong. Iraq did not need intensive training or large-scale logistics, since the enemy was only Kuwait. Iraq also had already underground logistical centers and telephone lines in the area, kept operational since the Iraq-Iran war.

[95] Leslie Gelb, *New York Times*, April 5,1992; *Washington Post*, October 21, 1992.

[96] Cited by USIA, Norman Holmes, "Freedom of Navigation in Gulf Important to US," Washington, D.C., July 26, 1990, p. 1.

[97] Elaine Sciolino, *New York Times*, September 23, 1990, p. 18; Woodward, *The Commanders*, pp. 213-15.

[98] *Meeting Between President Saddam Husayn and American Chargé d'Affaires Wilson on August 6, 1990,* pp. 1-6. (The Iraqi Embassy, Washington, D.C., *1990).*

[99] *Interview with a Soviet expert, December 13, 1990;* INA, July 28, 1990, in *FBIS*, July 30, 1990, p. 23. There are indications that Iraqi leaders expected the Soviet Union to veto any anti-Iraqi Security Council resolution. Tariq 'Aziz expressed deep frustration that Soviet leaders refused to do so. See *al-Thawra*, February 14, 1992.

[100] *Al-Jumhuriyya*, July 28,1990, in *FBIS*, July 30, 1990, p. 19. Also *al-Thawra*, July 28, 1990, in ibid. p. 20; *al-Jumhuriyya*, July 29, 1990, in ibid., p. 22; *Meeting Between President Saddam Husayn and American Chargé d'Affaires Wilson*, p. 3.

[101] See, for example, *al-Qabas, al-Watan, Kuwait Times, al-Ray al-'Amm*, July 26, 1990, in *FBIS*, July 26, 1990, p. 18.

[102] See, for example, *KUNA*, citing the Iraqi press, July 26, 1990, in *FBIS*, July 26, 1990, p. 18; Woodward, *The Commanders*, pp. 216, 218.

103 Interview with a senior Shi'a opposition figure, September 10, 1990.

104 Saddam's interview to *Hurriyet*, February 10, 1992, in *FBIS*, February 13, 1992, pp. 22-23.

105 Radio Monte Carlo, August 1, 1990, in *FBIS*, August 1, 1990, p. 20.

106 'Aziz to Viorst, *The New Yorker*, pp. 64-67; 'Aziz in *Milliyet*, May 30, 1991, *FBIS*, June 4, 1991, pp. 13-14.

107 Saddam's interview to *Hurriyet*, February 10, 1992, in *FBIS*, February 13, 1992, pp. 22-23.

108 *Mahdar muqabalat*, p. 18.

109 'Aziz to Viorst, *The New Yorker*, pp. 64-67.

110 In 1989 Iraq received $1.1 billion in loans and loan guarantees for buying American foodstuffs, part of which was sold for arms. In 1990 the Bush administration approved half of the $1 billion loan guarantees Iraq requested over the objection of officials investigating the $3-4 billion Banco Nazionale del Lavoro fraud; and of officials at the Export-Import Bank because Iraq defaulted on some repayments. Iraq also received U.S. intelligence at least until May 1990, three months after Saddam criticized the U.S. presence in the Gulf. See *Washington Post*, April 28, 1990; *New York Times*, April 4, 1992; Mark Hosenball, *The New Republic*, June 1, 1992, p. 27. According to the *Statement of Henry B. Gonzalez, Chairman of [the House] Committee on Banking, Finance and Urban Affairs, Before the Senate Committee on Banking and Urban Affairs*, October 27, 1992, "U.S. export licensing policy toward Iraq permitted . . . licenses for conventional military uses. . . . In addition, while many export licenses were denied, the decision to treat Iraq as a close ally of the U.S. made it practically impossible to stem the flow of weapons useful technology to Iraq, despite ample evidence showing that Iraq used . . . U.S. technology for nonconventional weapons purposes" (p. 7).

111 Sa'd Qasim Hammudi, *al-Thawra*, March 16, 1992. In fact, these assets were closer to $100 billion. Immediately after the invasion, Saddam set up a puppet regime. Only on August 8, 1990, when it was clear this regime would be denied access to Kuwait's financial assets abroad, did he announce the annexation.

112 See, for example, his payment in gold that was delivered to Amman for a huge Australian wheat shipment (an interview with a senior Australian diplomat, Haifa,

November 11, 1992). Before the invasion the Iraqi media announced that the new presidential palace would be very richly decorated with gold, which had been accumulated from Iraqi women's (compulsory) contributions during the Iraq-Iran war.

113 Based on an interview with an Israeli intelligence officer after the Gulf War.

114 Woodward, *The Commanders*, pp. 224-32. A well-informed Arab source told Viorst (*The New Yorker*, p. 67) that this was Saddam's view. According to Woodward, *The Commanders*, p. 229, General Norman Schwarzkopf had similar expectations of the Saudis and was surprised when they decided to invite the Americans.

115 *Meeting Between President Saddam Husayn and American Chargé d'Affaires Wilson*, pp. 1-6.

116 For details see Amatzia Baram, *Culture, History and Ideology in the Formation of Ba'thist Iraq 1968-1989* (New York, 1991).

117 For details and sources see Amatzia Baram, "The Kuwait Crisis and the Gulf War August 2, 1990-February 28, 1991: Saddam's Calculations and Miscalculations," in Alex Danchev and Dan Koehane, *International Perspectives on the Gulf Conflict* (London, forthcoming).

Something Evil Has Visited Kuwait City

Robert Fisk

The Independent

What kind of people would do this? That's what we kept asking ourselves in Kuwait City yesterday. Day had been turned into night, so thick was the canopy of smoke, the nation's oil wells burning gold and orange along the black-fringed horizon, Hieronymus Bosch courtesy of the Iraqi army.

They had even used the modern equivalent of a torture wheel. All day, Kuwaiti men, young and old, approached our car with their terrible stories. "They twisted my son on a pole and broke his legs with pieces of wood," a stooped old man said. "They thought he was in the resistance. Now they have taken him away, with all the others, as a human shield."

Then there was Heather Rennison, an English woman married to a Kuwaiti. "A cousin of my mother-in-law was arrested. She was only 19 and they found two-way radios in her bedroom. Three days later they came to her home to ask her parents for clothes and blankets. So her parents thought she would be all right. Then the Iraqis hanged her and dumped her body outside her home. There were burns from electricity on her arms and legs. Of course, the Iraqis kept the clothes and blankets."

Perhaps one needed to walk the pavements of Kuwait City yesterday to understand the extent of what the Iraquis did, that it really does amount to a war crime. "I will show you the mosque where they shot 11 men on Friday," a bearded man shouted to us from his car.

The Abdullah Othman mosque stands in the Palestinian Hawali quarter. The bearded man pointed to a yellow wall. "The Iraqis said that all those at prayer would be taken away—kidnapped—and 11 men stayed in the mosque and refused to go. So they brought them here, blindfolded them, made them stand with their backs to the wall and shot them in the face." The bullets that had hit the worshippers' heads were embedded in the yellow wall. "Don't be surprised," the man said. "I had two neighbours who the Iraqis thought were in the resistance. So they pushed them into drains, closed the grille, poured petrol on them and set them on fire. Their families buried them later—you can't leave bodies in drains."

The figure of 5,000 Kuwaiti men abducted in the last hour before Iraq's retreat seems fantastic until you find—as I did yesterday—that the first three families who offered lifts to various locations in Kuwait City had all lost sons as hostages. The young men had simply been ordered into Iraqi army buses as they walked to work. Three thousand men and women murdered here, the Kuwaitis also tell you. Who could do this?

It is comforting, in trying to come to terms with a reign of terror, to search for some logical reason, historical hatred perhaps, or some aberrant unit of the Iraqi secret police. But this would be fanciful. What is one to think when one walks, as I did yesterday, through the smoking embers of the National Museum, fired by the Iraqis on Tuesday? Or the gutted interior of the parliament? Or the still burning library in the Self Receptor Palace—its magnificent golden clock tower smashed by a tank shell—when I found, lying on a chair, the remains of a book published by the government of India, entitled *The Collected Works of Mahatma Gandhi*? What kind of people burn museums and libraries?

Outside the museum, Kuwait's collection of historic wooden boats had been burned to cinders. The "Islamic house" lay in ruins. The walls of the Emir of Kuwait's Dasman Palace had been torn down with explosions and bulldozers. The Iraqis had used tanks to shoot at the parliament. The great hotels had been systematically fired. The Iraqis had even planted explosives in the bedrooms of the Meridian Hotel. It was like a medieval army which conquered, looted and then burned even on an individual level.

Boat owners found their yachts stolen or deliberately sunk in the marinas. Shopkeepers found their stores burned if they could not be looted, At an abandoned anti-aircraft gun on the coast—where the Iraqis mined the lovely beaches against a non-existent American amphibious landing—I came across piles of brand new women's shoes, made in France, none of them matching, all wrapped inside Iraqi army blankets along with body-building magazines. Why did they do this, these soldiers? Why had they stolen, too, an exhibition display of women's eye shadow? There were cartridge cases across the forecourt of the great museum, bullet-holes in the cracked walls of the building that once contained Kuwait's finest—and long ago looted—national treasures. What was he thinking, this soldier, when he opened fire at a museum?

The seafront restaurants have been torn down, the high, glass-covered landmark water towers machine-gunned. At al-Ahmadi, the Iraqis set off explosives every hour at the two oil farms, each containing 20 tanks. The fine old British "White House" there was burned down along with the control room that operates the oil pipelines.

I suppose one sensed in Kuwait yesterday that something very wicked, at times evil, had visited this city. Not just an occupation army, not even the Iraqi Ba'ath

Party apparatus, but something which intrinsically links dictatorship and corruption. "Down with the dirty [King] Fahd, [Sheikh] Sabah [of Kuwait] and Hosni [Mubarak]," said a blood-red graffito on the wall of one of the burned palaces. "Long live Saddam Hussein." In the little, looted museum of Kuwait peasant art, I found a poster of Saddam stapled to the wall. "Most victorious of all Arabs, the great leader Saddam Hussein—God bless him," the caption said.

Whoever uttered such prayers? Colonel Mustapha Awadi, of the Kuwait resistance movement, offered to show me. In a bleak housing estate in the suburb of Quwain, he took me to a school—the Iraqis used schools as interrogation centers—and in a classroom I found 16 young Iraqi soldiers. They sat on the floor, legs crossed, moustachioed, miserable ordinary men with tired, dirty faces and grimy uniforms. "They were happy to surrender," the colonel said. "See? We even give them food and tea. I promise they will be handed over unharmed to the Kuwaiti Army."

Two of the men had been wounded in the face—their bandages were fresh—and they all smiled when I greeted them and they heard me tell the colonel in Arabic that I would mention their presence to the Red Cross. One could not help but feel sorry for these defeated teenagers with their sad smiles. So what kind of men had raped Kuwait?

Horror, Destruction and Shame Along Saddam's Road to Ruin

Robert Fisk

The Independent

Saddam Hussein's road to ruin stretches for 100 miles up the highway from Kuwait City to the Iraqi border at Safwan. It is a road of horror, destruction and shame: horror because of the hundreds of mutilated corpses lining its route, destruction because of the thousands of Iraqi tanks and armoured vehicles that lie charred or abandoned there, shame because in retreat Saddam soldiery piled their armour with looted carpets, jewellery, video sets, vacuum cleaners, children's toys, even stolen copies of the Koran. No wonder he lost.

The dead are strewn across the road only five miles out of Kuwait City and you see them still as you approach the Iraqi frontier where 52 of the Rumeilah oilfield's earning wells are squirting into the sky. At one point, I saw wild dogs tearing to pieces the remains of Iraqi soldiers.

It is, of course, the horror that strikes you first. Scarcely 15 miles north of Kuwait City, the body of an Iraqi general lies half out of his stolen limousine, his lips apart, his hands suspended above the roadway. You can see his general's insignia on his stained uniform. He had driven into the back of an armoured vehicle in the great rout on Monday night. Farther up the road, corpses lay across the highway beside tanks and army trucks. One Iraqi had collapsed over the carriageway, curled up like a foetus, his arms beside his face, a neat moustache beneath a heavy head, the back of which had been blown away.

Only when ambulance drivers arrived and moved his body did we realize that his left leg had also gone. In a lorry which had received a direct hit from the air, two carbonised soldiers still sat in the cab, their skulls staring forward up the road towards the country they never reached. Kuwaiti civilians stood over the bodies laughing, taking pictures of the Iraqis' last mortal remains.

The wholesale destruction begins 15 miles farther on, beneath a motorway bridge which stands at the bottom of a low hill called Mutla. It was here, trapped by allied bombing of the road at the top of the hill, that the Iraqis perished in their hundreds, probably their thousands. Panic-stricken they must have been, as they jammed themselves in their vehicles, 20 abreast, four miles in length, picked off by the American and British bombers.

There were tanks and stolen police cars, artillery and fire engines and looted limousines, amphibious vehicles, bulldozers and trucks. I lost count of the Iraqi corpses crammed into the smouldering wreckage or slumped face down, in the sand. In scale and humiliation it was, I suppose, a little like Napoleon's retreat from Moscow. There must have been all of two divisions up this road.

Napoleon's army burned Moscow and the Iraqis tried to burn Kuwait but the French did not carry back this much loot. Amid the guns and armour I found heaps of embroidered carpets, string beads, pearl necklaces, a truck load of air conditioners, new men's shirts, women's shoes, perfume, cushions, children's games, a pile of hardbacked Korans on top of five stolen clocks. There were crude rubber gas masks and anti-gas boots—the Iraqis had prepared themselves for chemical warfare—and thousands of rifles, rocket-propelled grenades, shells and bayonets.

Our car bumped over unspent grenades and rifle barrels. I discovered several tanks and armoured vehicles abandoned in such terror that the keys were in the ignition, the engines still running. I found one that had been loaded with suitcases of matches, rugs, food mixers and lipstick. A child's musical box lay in the sand still playing "and a happy new year, and a happy new year . . . ." Iraqi equipment—daggers, belts, berets and helmets—lay everywhere with their owner's name written on the straps.

On top of one armoured vehicle, its engine still idling, I found the helmets of Lieutenant Rabah, Homeida and Private Jamal Abdululah. They had stood no chance, for in front of their vehicle lay another two miles of clogged Iraqi military traffic, at the end of which stood a squad of American soldiers from the US Second Armoured Division, whose motto—Hell on Wheels—appropriately summed up the fate of the thousands in the ghoulish traffic jam below them. No film could do credit to this chaos. It was both surreal and pathetic. Saddam Hussein had called it an "orderly withdrawal".

Around the carnage and dust drove two British Land Rovers of the 26th Field Regiment Royal Artillery, a giant Union Flag floating above both of them. It was Staff Sergeant Bob Halls and Gunner Barry Baxter who showed us the track through the sand to reach the Mutla summit, picking ther way past unexploded cluster bombs and live shells. "You can't really take in what war does till you've seen it," Baxter said. "Why did this happen? Saddam's forces are nothing to be reckoned with, are they? They didn't want to go to war. They just wanted to put their hands up. They are our enemy but they didn't want to be in the war in the first place. They are a sorry sight to see."

They were. The prisoners we saw—remnants of the world's fourth-largest army—were unshaven and exhausted, herded by soldiers of the 16/5th Lancers, trudging through the desert, throwing personal arms on to a pile of weapons 15ft high, guarded by US troops.

All the way to the Iraqi border we found the detritus of the Iraqi retreat, tanks and armour across the road, on their sides in the ditches, scattered over the flat desert on either side. Some were still smouldering. The British and the Americans looked at all this with a mixture of awe and relief.

Lieutenant Andrew Nye and Roy Monk of C Company, 1st Battalion the Staffordshire Regiment, had spent part of the morning burying the dead. They included women and children, Iraqis or perhaps Kuwaiti and Egyptian refugees fleeing the battlefront and caught in the last allied air attacks or by Iraqi artillery.

Lt Nye had lost one of his own men in the fighting. "One of our blokes was killed," he said. "He was hit in the chest by a rocket-propelled grenade after some Iraqis had raised the white flag. It may be that some of the Iraqis didn't know others had surrendered. By then we had grown so used to the prisoners, we had seen so many of them and heard about the huge numbers of PoWs on the radio. You have to feel this to believe it. There are booby-traps here and the Iraqis who died on this road were stripping Kuwait City. But I shudder to think what it would have been like in their position."

As we neared the Iraqi frontier, Egyptian refugees began to straggle down the highway, some weighed down with blankets and begging for water, others pushing their surviving possessions in rusting supermarket trollies, a few asking for cigarettes. Many were too tired to talk, having walked 60 miles from Basra.

"They shoot all Egyptian people in Iraq," one of them said, but would not add to that chilling remark. A group of American soldiers said they had heard the Iraqis were shooting at refugees on the border.

Critique of the Belligerents

Edward Said

The Nation

From the moment that George Bush invented Desert Shield, Desert Storm was all too logical, and Poppy turned himself into Captain Ahab. Saddam Hussein, a dictator of the kind the United States has typically found and supported, was almost invited into Kuwait, then almost immediately demonized and transformed into a worldwide metaphysical threat. Iraq's military capabilities were fantastically exaggerated, the country verbally obliterated except for its by now isolated leader, UN sanctions given a ludicrously short run, and then America began the war.

Since 1973 the United States has wanted a physical presence in the Persian Gulf to control oil supply, to project power and above all, recently, to refurbish and refinance its military. With his crude brutality no match for U.S. and Israeli propaganda, Saddam Hussein became the perfect target, and the best excuse to move in. The United States will not soon leave the Middle East.

The electronic war to destroy Iraq as a lesson in retributive power went rapidly into full swing, the press managing patriotism, entertainment and disinformation without respite. As a topic, civilian "collateral damage" was avoided and unasked about; no one discussed how Baghdad, the old Abbasid capital, might survive the appalling rigors of technological warfare, or how the bombing of its water, fuel and electrical supplies, which sustain four million people, was necessary to this "surgical" war (a larger replay of Israel's destruction of Beirut). Few commentators questioned the disproportion of 200,000-plus air sorties against a country roughly the size of California.

It is curious, but profoundly symptomatic of the Gulf conflict, that the one word that was tediously pronounced and repronounced and yet left unanalyzed was "linkage," an ugly solecism that could have been invented only in late twentieth-century America. "Linkage" means not that there is but that there is no connection. Things that belong together by common association, sense, geography, history, are sundered, left apart for convenience' sake and for the benefit of U.S. imperial strategists. Everyone his own carver, Jonathan Swift said. That the Middle East is linked by all sorts of ties, *that* is irrelevant. That Arabs might see a connection between Saddam Hussein in Kuwait and Israel in Lebanon, that too is futile. That U.S. policy itself is the linkage, this is a forbidden topic to broach.

Never in my experience have nouns designating the Arab world or its components been so bandied about: Saddam Hussein, Kuwait, Islam, fundamentalism. Never have they had so strangely abstract and diminished a meaning, and rarely did any regard or care seem to accompany them, even though the United States was not at war with all the Arabs but very well might have been, except for its pathetic clients such as Mubarak of Egypt and the various Gulf rulers.

In all the mainstream debate in the U.S. since August 2, 1990, much the smallest component in the discussion was Arab. During the Congressional hearings that went on for two weeks in December 1990, no significant Arab-American voice was heard. In Congress and in the press, "linkages" of all kinds went unexamined. Little was done to report oil-company profits, or the fact that the surge in gasoline prices had nothing to do with supply, which remained plentiful. The Iraqi case against Kuwait, or even the nature of Kuwait itself, liberal in some ways, illiberal in others, received next to no hearing; the point would not have been to exculpate Saddam Hussein but to perceive the longstanding complicity and hypocrisy of the Gulf states, the United States and Europe during the Iran-Iraq war. Efforts were made to grapple with Arab popular rallying to Saddam Hussein, despite the unattractive qualities of his rule, but these efforts were not integrated into, or allowed equal time with, the distortions in American Middle East policy. The central media failing has been an unquestioning acceptance of American power: its right to ignore dozens of United Nations resolutions on Palestine (or even to refuse to pay its UN dues), to attack Panama, Grenada, Libya, and also to proclaim the absolute morality of its Gulf position.

From prewar television reports of the crisis I cannot recall a single guest or program that raised the issue of what right "we" had to get Iraq out of Kuwait;

nor any exploration of the enormous human, social and economic costs *to the Arabs* of an American strike. Yet on January 7, I heard a well-known "Middle East expert" say on TV that "war is the easy part; what to do afterward?" as if "we" might, in an afterthought, get around to picking up the pieces and rearranging the area. At the farthest extreme were the unmistakably racist prescriptions of William Safire and A.M. Rosenthal of *The New York Times* as well as Fouad Ajami of CBS, who routinely urged the most unrestrained military attacks against Iraq. The underlying fantasy strongly resembles the Israeli paradigm for dealing with the Arabs: Bomb them, humiliate them, lie about them.

From the beginning, when Arabs appeared on television they were the merest tokens: a journalist or two eager to show Arab failings and weaknesses (which were real and had to be pointed out); the Saudi or Kuwaiti Ambassador, more enthusiastic about war than most Americans; the Iraqi Ambassador, who defended the Husseinian view of the world with cautious amiability; the tiny group of Arab-Americans like myself whose position was neither with Iraq nor with the U.S.-Saudi coalition. Once, in the fifteen seconds I was given, when I began to elucidate an argument about the relationship between Iraqi aggression and American imperialism, I was cut off abruptly: "Yes, yes, we know all that."

Seen from the Arab point of view, the picture of America is just as constricted. There is still hardly any literature in Arabic that portrays Americans; the most interesting exception is Abdel Rahman Munif's massive trilogy *Cities of Salt*, but his books are banned in several countries, and his native Saudi Arabia has stripped him of his citizenship. To my knowledge there is still no institute or major academic department in the Arab world whose main purpose is the study of America, although the United States is by far the largest outside force in the Arab world. It is difficult to explain even to well-educated and experienced fellow Arabs that U.S. foreign policy is not in fact run by the C.I.A., or a conspiracy, or a shadowy network of key "contacts." Many Arabs I know believe the United States plans virtually every event of significance in the Middle East, including, in one mind-boggling suggestion made to me last year, the *intifada*!

This mix of long familiarity, hostility and ignorance pertains to both sides of a complex, variously uneven and quite old cultural encounter now engaging in very unmetaphorical warfare. From early on there was an overriding sense of inevitability, as if George Bush's apparent need to get down there and, in his own sporty argot, "kick ass" *had* to run up against Saddam Hussein's monstrous aggressiveness, now vindicating the Arab need to confront, talk back to, stand unblinkingly before the United States. The public rhetoric, in other words, is simply undeterred, uncomplicated by any considerations of detail, realism or cause and effect.

Perhaps the central unanalyzed link between the United States and the Arabs in this conflict is nationalism. The world can no longer afford so heady a mixture of patriotism, relative solipsism, social authority, unchecked aggressiveness and defensiveness toward others. Today the United States, triumphalist internationally, seems in a febrile way anxious to prove that it is Number One, perhaps to offset the recession; the endemic problems posed by the cities, poverty, health, education, production; and the Euro-Japanese challenge. On the other side, the Middle East is saturated with a sense that Arab nationalism is all-important, but also that it is an aggrieved and unfulfilled nationalism, beset with conspiracies, enemies both internal and external, obstacles to overcome for which no price is too high. This was especially true of the cultural framework in which I grew up. It is still true today, with the important difference that this nationalism has resolved itself into smaller and smaller units. In the colonial period as I was growing up, you could travel overland from Lebanon and Syria through Palestine to Egypt and points west. That is now impossible. Each country places formidable obstacles at its borders. For Palestinians, crossing is a horrible experience, since countries that make the loudest noises in support of Palestine treat Palestinians the worst.

Here, too, linkage comes last in the Arab setting. I do not want to suggest that the past was better; it wasn't. But it was more healthily interlinked, so to speak. People actually lived with each other, rather than denying each other from across fortified frontiers. In schools you could encounter Arabs from everywhere, Muslims and Christians, plus Armenians, Jews, Greeks, Italians, Indians and Iranians all mixed up, all under one or another colonial regime, interacting as if it were natural to do so. Today the state nationalisms have a tendency to fracture. Lebanon and Israel are perfect examples of what has happened. Apartheid of one form or another is present nearly everywhere as a group feeling if not as a practice, and it is subsidized by the state with its bureaucracies and secret police organizations. Rulers are clans, families and closed circles of aging oligarchs, almost mythologically immune to change.

Moreover, the attempt to homogenize and isolate populations has required colossal sacrifices. In most parts of the Arab world, civil society has been swallowed up by political society. One of the great achievements of the early postwar Arab nationalist governments was mass literary; in countries such as Egypt the results were dramatic. Yet the combination of accelerated literacy and tubthumping ideology, which was undoubtedly necessary at some point, has proved far too longstanding. My impression is that there is more effort spent in bolstering the idea that to be Syrian, Iraqi, Egyptian, Saudi, etc. is a quite sufficiently important end, rather than in thinking critically, perhaps even audaciously, about the national program itself. Identity, always identity, over and above knowing about others.

Because of this lopsided state of affairs, militarism assumed too privileged a place in the Arab world's moral economy. Much of it goes back to the sense of being unjustly treated, for which Palestine was not only a metaphor but a reality. But was the only answer military force—huge armies, brassy slogans, bloody promises and, alas, a long series of concrete instances, starting with wars and working down to such things as physical punishment and menacing gestures? I speak superficially and even irresponsibly here, since I cannot have all the facts. But I do not know a single Arab who would disagree with these impressions in private, or who would not readily agree that the monopoly on coercion given the state has almost completely eliminated democracy in the Arab world, introduced immense hostility between rulers and ruled, placed a much higher value on conformity, opportunism, flattery and getting along than on risking new ideas, criticism or dissent.

Taken far enough this produces an exterminism common to the Arabs and the United States, the notion that if something displeases you it is possible simply to blot it out. I do not doubt that this notion is behind Iraq's aggression against Kuwait. What sort of muddled and anachronistic idea of Bismarckian "integration" is this that wipes out an entire country and smashes its society with "Arab unity" as its goal? The most disheartening thing is that so many people, many of them victims of exactly the same brutal logic, appear to have identified with Iraq and not Kuwait. Even if one grants that Kuwaitis were unpopular (does one have to be popular not to be exterminated?) and even if Iraq claims to champion Palestine in standing up to Israel and the United States, surely the very idea that nations should be obliterated along the way is a murderous proposition, unfit for a great civilization like ours.

Then there is oil. While it brought development and prosperity to some, wherever it was associated with an atmosphere of violence, ideological refinement and political defensiveness, it created more rifts than it healed. It may be easy for someone like myself to say these things from a distance, but for anyone who cares about the Arab world, who thinks of it as possessing a plausible sort of internal cohesion, the general air of mediocrity and corruption that hangs over a part of the globe that is limitlessly wealthy, superbly endowed culturally and historically, and loaded with gifted individuals is a great puzzle, and of course a disappointment. We all *do* ask ourselves why we haven't done more of what other peoples have done—liberate ourselves, modernize, make a distinctive positive mark on the world. Where is excellence? How is it rewarded? There are first-rate novelists, poets, essayists, historians, yet all of them are not only unacknowledged legislators, they have been hounded into alienated opposition. For an author today to write is perforce to be careful, not to anger Syria or the Islamic authorities or a Gulf potentate or two.

What seems intellectually required now is the development of a combination discourse, one side of which is concretely critical and addresses the real power situation inside the Arab world, and another side that is mainly about affection, sympathy, association (rather than antagonism, resentment, harsh fundamentalism, vindictiveness). Many of the Arab thinkers of what the historian Albert Hourani calls the liberal age, the late eighteenth to the early twentieth century, were reformers eager to catch up with developments in the West. We've had too much since then of thinkers who want to start from scratch and zealously, not to say furiously, take things back to some pure, sacred origin. This has given all sorts of pathologies time and space enough to take hold in the middle distance, now, with their structures left unscrutinized, while intellectuals go off looking for what *would* have been better, what *would* have been just, and so on. We need to know what it is about the present that we should hold on to, and how. What is just, why is it just, why should we hold on to it? We need odes not to blood and mythology or uprooted, mourned or dead plants but to living creatures and actual situations. As the novelist Elias Khoury says, we need a language that allows one to write neither of a discredited past nor of an immensely distant future.

The supreme irony is that we Arabs are *of* this world, hooked into dependency and consumerism, cultural vassalage and technological secondariness, without much volition on our part. The time has come where we cannot simply accuse the West of Orientalism and racism—I realize that I am particularly vulnerable on this point—and go on doing little about providing an alternative. If our work isn't in the Western media often enough, for example, or isn't known well by Western writers and scholars, a good part of the blame lies with us. Hassanein Heykal, the great Egyptian journalist, has proposed a broadly focused pan-Arab cooperation authority for such things as development, coordinated industry, agriculture and the like. But we should also devote energy to an intellectual coordination effort that opens lines of communication among Arabs internally and externally with the rest of the world. The idea of equal dialogue, and rightful responsibility, needs to be pressed. The provincial and self-pitying posture that argues that a largely fictional and monolithic West disdains us ought to be replaced with the discovery that there are many Wests, some antagonistic, some not, with which to do business, and the choice of whom to talk to and how depends greatly on us. The converse is equally true, that there are many Arabs for Westerners and others to talk to. Only in this way, I think, will imperial America not be our only interlocutor.

If as Arabs we say correctly that we are different from the West, as well as different from its image of the Arabs, we have to be persuasive on this point. That takes a lot of work, and cannot be accomplished by a resort to clichés or myths. George Bush's idea that a new world order has to flow from an American baton is as unacceptable as the big idea that Arabs can muster a big army led by a big tough hero and at last win a few wars. That is dangerous nonsense. Americans, Arabs, Europeans, Africans—everyone—need to reorient education so that central to common awareness is not a paranoid sense of who is top or best but a map of this now tiny planet, its resources and environment nearly worn out, its inhabitants' demands for better lives nearly out of control. The competitive, coercive guidelines that have prevailed are simply no good anymore. To argue and persuade rather than to boast, preach and destroy, *that* is the change to be made.

The war was catastrophic and has only distorted the Arab world further. And there already are enough residual problems to start up another confrontation in the Middle East in a matter of seconds. We should be looking for political mechanisms with the Europeans and the nonaligned that would bring a lasting peace and send everyone—including Palestinians—home. It is good to be reminded of that phrase by Aimé Césaire which C.L.R. James, that great champion of liberation, liked to quote: "No race possesses the monopoly of beauty, of intelligence, of force, and there is a place for all at the rendezvous of victory." This may be utopian idealism, but as a way to think about an alternative to conflicts that go from cultural hostility to full-scale war, it is both more inventive and practical than shooting off missiles.

Islam and the Gulf War

John Esposito

from *The Islamic Threat: Myth or Reality*

If Saddam Hussein had his way, Iraq would have emerged from the Gulf War as the defender of Islam against Western imperialism. However, the war again undermined stereotypical images of monolithic Arab and Muslim worlds gripped by Pan-Arabism or Pan-Islam. The Gulf crisis of 1990–91 divided the Arab and indeed Muslim worlds.[1] Similarly, it witnessed multiple appeals to

Islam by Muslim political and religious leaders to legitimate each side in the conflict and tested the ideology and allegiances of Islamic movements.[2] The greatest incongruity, perhaps, was that Saddam Hussein, the head of a secularist regime who had ruthlessly suppressed Islamic movements at home and abroad, would cloak himself in the mantle of Islam and call for a jihad.

The Gulf crisis simultaneously presented an apparently united Arab response to a rapacious, expansionist Iraq and, at a deeper level, an Arab and indeed a Muslim world divided to an unparalleled extent. The Arab League and the Organization of the Islamic Conference, a Saudi-supported organization of forty-four Muslim states (today fifty-five states), condemned Saddam's invasion of Kuwait. Emphasis on Arab and Muslim government support for the alliance against Saddam Hussein obscured deeper divisions. Only twelve of the Arab League's twenty-one members supported the anti-Saddam forces. Moreover, as the crisis dragged on, Saddam came to enjoy a degree of popular sympathy often not fully appreciated by Westerners, who tended to equate the position of Arab and Muslim governments with their people and tended not to distinguish among the differing perspectives of the Western-led coalition supported by their Arab and Muslim allies and the views of a significant portion of the populace, whose deep-seated grievances were given a new voice and champion in Saddam Hussein.

Stunned by the unexpectedly quick and broadly based international condemnation, Saddam increasingly emphasized the Arab and Islamic rationales for his actions and thus created popular pressure on Arab and Muslim rulers. He stepped into a leadership vacuum in the Arab world. Although not a charismatic leader, he created a popular persona by appealing to Arab nationalism and Islam, shrewdly exploiting long-standing issues: the failures of Arab governments and societies (poverty, corruption, and the maldistribution of wealth), the plight of the Palestinians, and foreign intervention leading to Arab dependency. Like the Ayatollah Khomeini, Saddam appealed to Islam to enhance his image as the champion of the Palestinians, of the poor and oppressed, and the liberator of the holy places, as well as to legitimate his call for a holy war against Western (especially U.S.) occupation of Arab lands and control of Arab oil. In addition, he called for the overthrow of Arab regimes that opposed him. The espousal of populist causes, issues that transcend the individuals who champion them from time to time, enabled Saddam the secular despot to be transformed into a popular hero among many; the messenger was transformed by the message.

The deep divisions within the Muslim world were reflected in competing appeals to Islam and calls for jihad. Leading religious leaders in Saudi Arabia and Egypt legitimated the presence of foreign troops in Saudi Arabia—the home of Islam's holy sites and cities (Mecca and Medina), access to which is forbidden to non-Muslims. At the same time, Saddam Hussein, Iran's Ayatollah Khomeini, and the Jordanian ulama and Muslim Brotherhood called for a jihad against foreign intervention.[3]

Islamic movements, reflecting their societies, were initially pulled in several directions. At first, most condemned Saddam Hussein, the secular persecutor of Islamic movements, and denounced his invasion of Kuwait. But this initial rejection of Saddam gave way (despite the relationship that many had to supporters in Saudi Arabia) to a more populist, Arab nationalist, anti-imperialist support for Saddam and the condemnation of foreign intervention and "occupation" of Islam's homeland as large numbers of foreign troops poured into the Gulf. The key catalyst was the massive Western (especially U.S.) military buildup in the region and the threat of military action and a permanent Western presence.

For many in the Muslim world, the buildup of foreign troops, announced after the American elections in November 1990, transformed the nature of the conflict from a defensive operation to an offensive force. Operation Desert Shield had been transformed into Operation Desert Storm, or what its Muslim critics called "Desert Sword"; the defense of Saudi Arabia and the liberation of Kuwait had become not just a war against Saddam Hussein but an all-out attempt to destroy Iraq politically and militarily. Who was thought to benefit most from the resulting power vacuum? America and its ally Israel.

Domestic politics—pressure not to run counter to popular sentiment more than religious conviction and ideology—influenced support for Saddam and his call for jihad by Islamic activists, as witnessed in Algeria, Tunisia, Morocco, Jordan, Pakistan, and Egypt. Thousands of Muslim activists in Algeria had initially demonstrated against Iraq's invasion of Kuwait; on a subsequent visit to Baghdad, however, Abbasi Madani, the leader of the Islamic Salvation Front, declared that "any aggression against Iraq will be confronted by Muslims everywhere."[4] In Jordan, the Muslim Brotherhood had also initially condemned the Iraqi invasion. However, after the deployment of American forces, it called for a jihad against "the new crusaders in defense of Iraq and the Islamic world." One American Muslim observer noted that "people forgot about Saddam's record and concentrated on America. . . . Saddam Hussein might be wrong, but it is not America who should correct him."[5] In Egypt, the Muslim Brotherhood denounced the Iraqi invasion and supported the government's anti-Saddam position. As the war continued, however, the brotherhood joined with other opposition groups and criticized the massive presence of foreign (Western) forces in Saudi Arabia.

Even in countries that sent forces to support the anti-Saddam "international alliance," popular sentiment often differed from that of the government. A majority in Pakistan had opposed the annexation of Kuwait, but in a poll taken by *The Herald*, a Pakistani magazine, 86.6 percent of those polled responded negatively when asked, "Should U.S. troops be defending the Muslim holy places in Saudi Arabia?"[6]

In Southeast Asia, Malaysian and Indonesian government support for U.N. resolutions was accompanied by general condemnation of Iraqi aggression in Kuwait. However, this did not translate into popular support for foreign troops or the threat of massive military action in the Gulf. Saddam Hussein's aggression and the Bush administration's portrayal of him as a new Hitler were not isolated, in the minds of many, from the turbulent politics of the Middle East or the obvious self-interest of the Western-led coalition and many of its allies. Defending Saudi Arabia and liberating Kuwait was one thing, attacking Iraq quite another. Many in Malaysia and Indonesia (reflecting or in solidarity with populist sentiment throughout much of the Muslim world), although critical of Saddam's annexation of Kuwait, were equally strong in their condemnation of the U.S. "double standard," excoriating Saddam for violating international law and calling for vigorous enforcement of U.N. resolutions while continuing to refuse to take the very same stand with regard to U.N. resolutions condemning Israel's annexation and continued occupation of the West Bank and Gaza.[7] (Similar criticisms were made with regard to the West's failure to come to the defense of Bosnian Muslims.)

An independent Malaysian publication reflected the strong feelings of many in the Muslim world:

> Given the magnitude of the US military buildup in the Gulf and its past records of invasions of and interferences in Third World countries, it is likely that the situation in the Gulf will lead to full scale war. . . . It is indeed hypocritical for the US to come to the aid of Kuwait while it remains silent about Israel's invasion and occupation of the West Bank, Gaza Strip, Golan Heights, Lebanon and its bombing of Tyre, Sidon, and West Beirut, which wounded and killed hundreds of civilians. Instead of economic sanctions, Israel received an increasing amount of US aid. At present, Israel is receiving $4 billion a year from the US. $400 million of US aid goes to help settle Jews from the Soviet Union in Israel's occupied territories therefore legitimating Israel's territorial expansion. In addition, the US had consistently vetoed all attempts by the Security Council to condemn Israel for ignoring United Nations' demands that it withdraw from Lebanon. This double standard was again observed by the US in regard to the Palestinian intafada in which the Israeli military killed over 700 Palestinians including some 160 children. The UN resolution calling for international observers to investigate the situation in the occupied territories was vetoed by the US.[8]

Reluctance by the United States to link (or to acknowledge the linkage of) the two issues—enforcement of U.N. resolutions regarding Iraq's invasion and occupation of Kuwait and Israel's occupation of the West Bank and Gaza—in resolving the Gulf crisis was seen by many in the Muslim world as an attempt to disengage two already interlocked realities.

In Pakistan Qazi Hussein Ahmad, the leader of Pakistan's Jamaat-i-Islami and a member of Pakistan's senate, addressed a large anti-American rally, calling upon Pakistan's government to give up its pro-American foreign policy. Characterizing the American-European alliance as "anti-Islamic forces," he warned that the United States intended to establish its hegemony in the region, not liberate Kuwait. Europe and America had joined hands to "destroy the fighting power of the Islamic world."[9] Thus, he concluded, there would be no place for the Islamic world in the New World Order. Populist support for Saddam Hussein became more strident with pro-Saddam and anti-American rhetoric, demonstrations, protest marches, and, at times, violence across the Muslim world: in Algeria, Tunisia, Morocco, Mauritania, Sudan, Libya, Nigeria, Lebanon, Jordan, the West Bank and Gaza, Yemen, Egypt, India, Pakistan, Bangladesh, Iran, Malaysia, Indonesia, and even among South Africa's Muslim community. Scud missile attacks on Tel Aviv were celebrated by many Arab nationalists and Islamic activists alike. Saddam was seen as the first Arab leader to actually hit the heart of Israel. Those convinced that Israel supplied intelligence information on Iraq, fought its wars with the Arabs on Arab territory, and freely carried out retaliation attacks against Tunis, Baghdad, Beirut, and southern Lebanon, hailed Saddam for bringing the experience and human costs of war home to the Israelis. Algeria, Morocco, Tunisia, Mauritania, and the Sudan witnessed large demonstrations. Saddam's appeals to Arab Nationalism, Islam, and the Palestinian cause resonated with memories of French colonialism and the struggle of many to root their identity more indigenously in an Arab Islamic past. In Rabat on February 3, 1991, 300,000 demonstrators took to the streets demanding the withdrawal of Moroccan troops from the multinational coalition. Lebanon experienced some of the largest demonstrations since the beginning of the Lebanese civil war, along with bombings of Western banks and airline offices. In Iran anti-American demonstrations took place in many major cities. President Rafsanjani, while carefully maintaining

Iran's official position of "neutrality," was equally cautious, aligning himself with populist Muslim sentiment within both Iran and the broader Muslim world: "the leader of imperialism is destroying a Muslim nation and ruining the resources of Muslims."[10] The Indonesian government supported U.N. resolutions on the Gulf, and many Indonesians denounced the annexation of Kuwait. However, Saddam's linkage of his actions with resolution of the Palestinian problem, the presence of U.S. forces in the Gulf, and the subsequent devastation of Iraq produced a growing level of anti-American criticism in the press and among intellectuals, Muslim leaders, and student groups.[11]

Coalition members such as Morocco, Bangladesh, Egypt, Syria, and Pakistan, who had sent troops to the Gulf, were increasingly subjected to domestic pressure to remove their forces. Islamic activists joined with other opposition groups in protesting the war. In Egypt, the Muslim Brotherhood joined with the left and many professional associations. An anti-government weekly carrying the headline "Muslims! Your Brothers Are Being Annihilated. Hurry to Aid Iraq in Its Heroic Steadfastness" sold out within hours.[12] Pakistan saw religious organizations like the Jamaat-i-Islami involved in massive public demonstrations throughout the country as hundreds flocked to centers to volunteer for the jihad.

As in other instances, the Gulf War revealed a diversity of positions within the Muslim world—a multiplicity of voices representing differing perspectives and priorities: differences among Muslim governments, between some governments and their people, among religious leaders and Islamic movements. Although images of the Crusades, imperialism, and a clash of civilizations were raised by Saddam in the name of Islam, they were rejected with equal force by other Muslim countries and religious leaders such as the official ulama of Egypt and Saudi Arabia.

Notes

[1] See John L. Esposito, "Jihad in a World of Shattered Dreams: Islam, Arab Politics, and the Gulf Crisis, *The World and I*, February 1991, pp. 512–27.

[2] Piscatori, ed. *Islamic Fundamentalisms and the Gulf Crisis*; Yvonne Y. Haddad, "Operation Desert Shield/Desert Storm: The Islamist Perspective," in *Beyond*

Desert Storm: The Gulf Crisis Reader, ed. Phyllis Bennis and Michel Moushabeck (New York: Olive Branch Press, 1991), chapter 23.

[3] See *Washington Post*, September 14, 1990; and *Los Angeles Times*, September 22, 1990.

[4] "Islam Divided," *The Economist*, September 22, 1990, p. 47.

[5] Abdurrahman Alamoudi in *The Washington Report on Middle East Affairs*, October 1990, p. 69.

[6] *The Herald*, September 1990, p. 30.

[7] "The Gulf Crisis," *Aliran* 10, no. 8 (1990), p. 32.

[8] "Exposing US Motives: A Third World View," *Aliran* 10, no. 11 (1990), p. 38.

[9] *Dawn*, February 1, 1991.

[10] *Christian Science Monitor*, January 24, 1991.

[11] *Far Eastern Economic Review*, January 24, 1991.

[12] *The Economist*, January 26, 1991.

Charge of War Crimes Against US

Ramsey Clark

from *War Crimes: A Report on United States War Crimes Against Iraq*

Initial Complaint
Charging

George Bush, J. Danforth Quayle, James Baker, Richard Cheney, William Webster, Colin Powell, Norman Schwarzkopf and Others to be named

With

Crimes Against Peace, War Crimes, Crimes Against Humanity and Other Criminal Acts and High Crimes in Violation of the Charter of the United

Nations, International Law, the Constitution of the United States and Laws made in Pursuance Thereof.

Preliminary Statement

These charges have been prepared prior to the first hearing of the Commission of Inquiry by its staff. They are based on direct and circumstantial evidence from public and private documents; official statements and admissions by the persons charged and others; eyewitness accounts; Commission investigations and witness interviews in Iraq, the Middle East and elsewhere during and after the bombing; photographs and video tape; expert analyses; commentary and interviews; media coverage, published reports and accounts gathered between December 1990 and May 1991. Commission of Inquiry hearings will be held in key cities where evidence is available supporting, expanding, adding, contradicting, disproving or explaining these, or similar charges against the accused and others of whatever nationality. When evidence sufficient to sustain convictions of the accused or others is obtained and after demanding the production of documents from the U.S. government, and others, and requesting testimony from the accused, offering them a full opportunity to present any defense personally, or by counsel, the evidence will be presented to an International War Crimes Tribunal. The Tribunal will consider the evidence gathered, seek and examine whatever additional evidence it chooses and render its judgment on the charges, the evidence, and the law.

Background

Since World War I, the United Kingdom, France, and the United States have dominated the Arabian Peninsula and Gulf region and its oil resources. This has been accomplished by military conquest and coercion, economic control and exploitation, and through surrogate governments and their military forces. Thus, from 1953 to 1979 in the post World War Il era, control over the region was exercised primarily through U.S. influence and control over the Gulf sheikdoms of Saudi Arabia and through the Shah of Iran. From 1953 to 1979 the Shah of Iran acted as a Pentagon/CIA surrogate to police the region. After the fall of the Shah and the seizure of U.S. Embassy hostages in Teheran, the U.S. provided military aid and assistance to Iraq, as did the USSR, Saudi Arabia, Kuwait and most of the Emirates, in its war with Iran. U.S. policy during that tragic eight year war, 1980-1988, is probably best summed up by the phrase, "we hope they kill each other."

Throughout the seventy-five year period from Britain's invasion of Iraq early in World War I to the destruction of Iraq in 1991 by U.S. air power, the United States and the United Kingdom demonstrated no concern for democratic values, human rights, social justice, or political and cultural integrity in the region, nor for stopping military aggression there. The U.S. supported the Shah of Iran for 25 years, selling him more than $20 billion of advanced military equipment between 1972 and 1978 alone. Throughout this period the Shah and his brutal secret police called SAVAK had one of the worst human rights records in the world. Then in the 1980s, the U.S. supported Iraq in its wrongful aggression against Iran, ignoring Iraq's own poor human rights record.[1]

When the Iraqi government nationalized the Iraqi Petroleum Company in 1972, the Nixon Administration embarked on a campaign to destabilize the Iraqi government. It was in the 1970s that the U.S. first armed and then abandoned the Kurdish people, costing tens of thousands of Kurdish lives. The U.S. manipulated the Kurds through CIA and other agencies to attack Iraq, intending to harass Iraq while maintaining Iranian supremacy at the cost of Kurdish lives without intending any benefit to the Kurdish people or an autonomous Kurdistan.[2]

The U.S. with close oil and other economic ties to Saudi Arabia and Kuwait has fully supported both governments despite the total absence of democratic institutions, their pervasive human rights violations and the infliction of cruel, inhuman and degrading punishments such as stoning to death for adultery and amputation of a hand for property offenses.

The U.S., sometimes alone among nations, supported Israel when it defied scores of UN resolutions concerning Palestinian rights, when it invaded Lebanon in a war which took tens of thousands of lives, and during its continuing occupation of southern Lebanon, the Golan Heights, the West Bank and Gaza.

The United States itself engaged in recent aggressions in violation of international law by invading Grenada in 1983, bombing Tripoli and Benghazi in Libya in 1986, financing the contra in Nicaragua, UNITA in southern Africa and supporting military dictatorships in Liberia, Chile, El Salvador, Guatemala, the Philippines, and many other places.

The U.S. invasion of Panama in December 1989 involved the same and additional violations of international law that apply to Iraq's invasion of Kuwait. The U.S. invasion took between 1,000 and 4,000 Panamanian lives. The United States government is still covering up the death toll. U.S. aggression caused massive property destruction throughout Panama.[3] According to U.S. and international human rights organization estimates, Kuwait's casualties from Iraq's invasion and the ensuing months of occupation were in the "hundreds"—between 300 and 600.[4] Reports from Kuwait list 628 Palestinians killed by Kuwaiti death squads since the Sabah royal family regained control over Kuwait.

The United States changed its military plans for protecting its control over oil and other interests in the Arabian Peninsula in the late 1980s when it became clear that economic problems in the USSR were debilitating its military capacity and Soviet forces withdrew from Afghanistan. Thereafter, direct military domination within the region became the U.S. strategy. With the decline in U.S. oil production through 1989, experts predicted U.S. oil imports from the Gulf would rise from 10% that year to 25% by the year 2000. Japanese and European dependency is much greater.[5]

The Charges

1. The United States engaged in a pattern of conduct beginning in or before 1989 intended to lead Iraq into provocations justifying U.S. military action against Iraq and permanent U.S. military domination of the Gulf.

In 1989, General Colin Powell, Chairman of the Joint Chiefs of Staff, and General Norman Schwarzkopf, Commander in Chief of the Central Command, completely revised U.S. military operations and plans for the Persian Gulf to prepare to intervene in a regional conflict against Iraq. The CIA assisted and directed Kuwait in its actions. At the time, Kuwait was violating OPEC oil production agreements, extracting excessive amounts of oil from pools shared with Iraq and demanding repayment of loans it made to Iraq during the Iran-Iraq war. Kuwait broke off negotiations with Iraq over these disputes. The U.S. intended to provoke Iraq into actions against Kuwait that would justify U.S. intervention.

In 1989, CIA Director William Webster testified before the Congress about the alarming increase in U.S. importation of Gulf oil, citing U.S. rise in use from 5% in 1973 to 10% in 1989 and predicting 25% of all U.S. oil consumption would come from the region by 2000.[6] In early 1990, General Schwarzkopf informed the Senate Armed Services Committee of the new military strategy in the Gulf designed to protect U.S. access to and control over Gulf oil in the event of regional conflicts.

In July 1990, General Schwarzkopf and his staff ran elaborate, computerized war games pitting about 100,000 U.S. troops against Iraqi armored divisions.

The U.S. showed no opposition to Iraq's increasing threats against Kuwait. U.S. companies sought major contracts in Iraq. The Congress approved agricultural loan subsidies to Iraq of hundreds of millions of dollars to benefit U.S. farmers. However, loans for food deliveries of rice, corn, wheat and other essentials bought almost exclusively from the U.S. were cut off in the spring of 1990 to cause shortages. Arms were sold to Iraq by U.S. manufacturers. When Saddam Hussein requested U.S. Ambassador April Glaspie to explain State Department testimony in Congress about Iraq's threats against Kuwait, she assured him the U.S. considered the dispute a regional concern, and it would not intervene. By these acts, the U.S. intended to lead Iraq into a provocation justifying war.

On August 2, 1990, Iraq occupied Kuwait without significant resistance.

On August 3, 1990, without any evidence of a threat to Saudi Arabia, and King Fahd believed Iraq had no intention of invading his country, President Bush vowed to defend Saudi Arabia. He sent Secretary Cheney, General Powell, and General Schwarzkopf almost immediately to Saudi Arabia where on August 6, General Schwarzkopf told King Fahd the U.S. thought Saddam Hussein could attack Saudi Arabia in as little as 48 hours. The efforts toward an Arab solution of the crisis were destroyed. Iraq never attacked Saudi Arabia and waited over five months while the U.S. slowly built a force of more than 500,000 soldiers and began the systematic destruction by aircraft and missiles of Iraq and its military, both defenseless against U.S. and coalition technology. In October 1990, General Powell referred to the new military plan developed in 1989. After the war, General Schwarzkopf referred to eighteen months of planning for the campaign.

The U.S. retains troops in Iraq as of May 1991 and throughout the region and has announced its intention to maintain a permanent military presence.

This course of conduct constitutes a crime against peace.

2. President Bush from August 2, 1990, intended and acted to prevent any interference with his plan to destroy Iraq economically and militarily.

Without consultation or communication with Congress, President Bush ordered 40,000 U.S. military personnel to advance the U.S. buildup in Saudi Arabia in the first week of August 1990. He exacted a request from Saudi Arabia for U.S. military assistance and on August 8, 1990, assured the world his acts were "wholly defensive." He waited until after the November 1990 elections to announce his earlier order sending more than 200,000 additional military personnel, clearly an assault force, again without advising Congress. As late as January 9, 1991, he insisted he had the constitutional authority to attack Iraq without Congressional approval.

While concealing his intention, President Bush continued the military build up of U.S. forces unabated from August into January 1991, intending to attack and destroy Iraq. He pressed the military to expedite preparation and to commence the assault before military considerations were optimum. When Air Force Chief of Staff General Michael J. Dugan mentioned plans to destroy the Iraqi civilian economy to the press on September 16, 1990, he was removed from office.[7]

President Bush coerced the United Nations Security Council into an unprecedented series of resolutions, finally securing authority for any nation in its absolute discretion by all necessary means to enforce the resolutions. To secure votes the U.S. paid multi-billion dollar bribes, offered arms for regional wars, threatened and carried out economic retaliation, forgave multi-billion dollar loans (including a $7 billion loan to Egypt for arms), offered diplomatic relations despite human rights violations and in other ways corruptly exacted votes, creating the appearance of near universal international approval of U.S. policies toward Iraq. A country which opposed the U.S., as Yemen did, lost millions of dollars in aid, as promised, the costliest vote it ever cast.

President Bush consistently rejected and ridiculed Iraq's efforts to negotiate a peaceful resolution, beginning with Iraq's August 12, 1990, proposal, largely ignored, and ending with its mid-February 1991 peace offer which he called a "cruel hoax." For his part, President Bush consistently insisted there would be no negotiation, no compromise, no face saving, no reward for aggression. Simultaneously, he accused Saddam Hussein of rejecting diplomatic solutions.

President Bush led a sophisticated campaign to demonize Saddam Hussein, calling him a Hitler, repeatedly citing reports—which he knew were false—of the murder of hundreds of incubator babies, accusing Iraq of using chemical weapons on his own people and on the Iranians knowing U.S. intelligence believed the reports untrue.

After subverting every effort for peace, President Bush began the destruction of Iraq answering his own question, "Why not wait? . . . The world could wait no longer."

The course of conduct constitutes a crime against peace.

3.President Bush ordered the destruction of facilities essential to civilian life and economic productivity throughout Iraq.

Systematic aerial and missile bombardment of Iraq was ordered to begin at 6:30 p.m. EST January 16, 1991, eighteen and one-half hours after the deadline set on the insistence of President Bush, in order to be reported on television evening news in the U.S. The bombing continued for forty-two days. It met no resistance from Iraqi aircraft and no effective anti-aircraft or anti-missile ground fire. Iraq was defenseless.

The United States reports it flew 110,000 air sorties against Iraq, dropping 88,000 tons of bombs, nearly seven times the equivalent of the atomic bomb that destroyed Hiroshima. 93% of the bombs were free falling bombs, most dropped from higher than 30,000 feet. Of the remaining 7% of the bombs with electronically guided systems, more than 25% missed their targets, nearly all caused damage primarily beyond any identifiable target. Most of the targets were civilian facilities.

The intention and effort of the bombing of civilian life and facilities was to systematically destroy Iraq's infrastructure leaving it in a preindustrial condition. Iraq's civilian population was dependent on industrial capacities. The U.S. assault left Iraq in a near apocalyptic condition as reported by the first United Nations observers after the war.[8] Among the facilities targeted and destroyed were:

- electric power generation, relay and transmission;
- water treatment, pumping and distribution systems and reservoirs;
- telephone and radio exchanges, relay stations, towers and transmission facilities;
- food processing, storage and distribution facilities and markets, infant milk formula and beverage plants, animal vaccination facilities and irrigation sites;
- railroad transportation facilities, bus depots, bridges, highway overpasses, highways, highway repair stations, trains, buses and other public transportation vehicles, commercial and private vehicles;
- oil wells and pumps, pipelines, refineries, oil storage tanks, gasoline filling stations and fuel delivery tank cars and trucks, and kerosene storage tanks;
- sewage treatment and disposal systems;
- factories engaged in civilian production, e.g., textile and automobile assembly, and
- historical markers and ancient sites.

As a direct, intentional and foreseeable result of this destruction, tens of thousands of people have died from dehydration, dysentery and diseases caused by impure water, inability to obtain effective medical assistance and debilitation from hunger, shock, cold and stress. More will die until potable water, sanitary living conditions, adequate food supplies and other necessities are provided. There is a high risk of epidemics of cholera, typhoid, hepatitis and other diseases as well as starvation and malnutrition through the summer of 1991 and until food supplies are adequate and essential services are restored.

Only the United States could have carried out this destruction of Iraq, and the war was conducted almost exclusively by the United States. This conduct violated the UN Charter, the Hague and Geneva Conventions, the Nuremberg Charter, and the laws of armed conflict.

4. The United States intentionally bombed and destroyed civilian life, commercial and business districts, schools, hospitals, mosques, churches, shelters, residential areas, historical sites, private vehicles and civilian government offices.

The destruction of civilian facilities left the entire civilian population without heat, cooking fuel, refrigeration, potable water, telephones, power for radio or TV reception, public transportation and fuel for private automobiles. It also limited food supplies, closed schools, created massive unemployment, severely limited economic activity and caused hospitals and medical services to shut down. In addition, residential areas of every major city and most towns and villages were targeted and destroyed. Isolated Bedouin camps were attacked by U.S. aircraft. In addition to deaths and injuries, the aerial assault destroyed 10–20,000 homes, apartments and other dwellings. Commercial centers with shops, retail stores, offices, hotels, restaurants and other public accommodations were targeted and thousands were destroyed. Scores of schools, hospitals, mosques and churches were damaged or destroyed. Thousands of civilian vehicles on highways, roads and parked on streets and in garages were targeted and destroyed. These included public buses, private vans and mini-buses, trucks, tractor trailers, lorries, taxi cabs and private cars. The purpose of this bombing was to terrorize the entire country, kill people, destroy property, prevent movement, demoralize the people and force the overthrow of the government.

As a result of the bombing of facilities essential to civilian life, residential and other civilian buildings and areas, at least 125,000 men, women and children were killed. The Red Crescent Society of Jordan estimated 113,000 civilian dead, 60% children, the week before the end of the war.

The conduct violated the UN Charter, the Hague and Geneva Conventions, the Nuremberg Charter, and the laws of armed conflict.

5. The United States intentionally bombed indiscriminately throughout Iraq.

In aerial attacks, including strafing, over cities, towns, the countryside and highways, U.S. aircraft bombed and strafed indiscriminately. In every city and town bombs fell by chance far from any conceivable target, whether a civilian facility, military installation or military target. In the countryside random attacks were made on travelers, villagers, even Bedouins. The purpose of the attacks was to destroy life, property and terrorize the civilian population. On the highways, civilian vehicles including public buses, taxicabs and passenger cars were bombed and strafed at random to frighten civilians from flight, from seeking food or medical care, finding relatives or other uses of highways. The effect was summary execution and corporal punishment indiscriminately of men, women and children, young and old, rich and poor, all nationalities including the large immigrant populations, even Americans, all ethnic groups, including many Kurds and Assyrians, all religions including Shia and Sunni Moslems, Chaldeans and other Christians, and Jews. U.S. deliberate indifference to civilian and military casualties in Iraq, or their nature, is exemplified by General Colin Powell's response to a press inquiry about the number dead from the air and ground campaigns: "It's really not a number I'm terribly interested in."[9]

The conduct violates Protocol I Additional, Article 51.4 to the Geneva Conventions of 1977.

6. The United States intentionally bombed and destroyed Iraqi military

personnel, used excessive force, killed soldiers seeking to surrender and in disorganized individual flight, often unarmed and far from any combat zones and randomly and wantonly killed Iraqi soldiers and destroyed material after the cease fire.

In the first hours of the aerial and missile bombardment, the United States destroyed most military communications and began the systematic killing of soldiers who were incapable of defense or escape and the destruction of military equipment. Over a period of forty-two days, U.S. bombing killed tens of thousands of defenseless soldiers, cut off most of their food, water and other supplies and left them in desperate and helpless disarray. Without significant risk to its own personnel, the U.S. led in the killing of at least 100,000 Iraqi soldiers at a cost of 148 U.S. combat casualties, according to the U.S. government. When it was determined that the civilian economy and the military were sufficiently destroyed, the U.S. ground forces moved into Kuwait and Iraq attacking disoriented, disorganized, fleeing Iraqi forces wherever they could be found, killing thousands more and destroying any equipment found. The slaughter continued after the cease fire. For example, on March 2, 1991, U.S. 24th Division Forces engaged in a four-hour assault against Iraqis just west of Basra. More than 750 vehicles were destroyed, thousands were killed without U.S. casualties. A U.S. commander said, "We really waxed them." It was called a "Turkey Shoot." One Apache helicopter crew member yelled "Say hello to Allah" as he launched a laser-guided Hellfire missile.[10]

The intention was not to remove Iraq's presence from Kuwait. It was to destroy Iraq. In the process there was great destruction of property in Kuwait. The disproportion in death and destruction inflicted on a defenseless enemy exceeded 1,000 to one.

General Thomas Kelly commented on February 23, 1991, that by the time the ground war begins "there won't be many of them left." General Norman Schwarzkopf placed Iraqi military casualties at over 100,000. The intention was to destroy all military facilities and equipment wherever located and to so decimate the military age male population that Iraq could not raise a substantial force for half a generation.

The conduct violated the Charter of the United Nations, the Hague and Geneva Conventions, the Nuremberg Charter, and the laws of armed conflict.

7. The United States used prohibited weapons capable of mass destruction and inflicting indiscriminate death and unnecessary suffering against both military and civilian targets.

Among the known illegal weapons and illegal uses of weapons employed by the United States are the following:

- fuel air explosives capable of widespread incineration and death;
- napalm;
- cluster and anti-personnel fragmentation bombs; and
- "superbombs," 2.5 ton devices, intended for assassination of government leaders.

Fuel air explosives were used against troops-in-place, civilian areas, oil fields and fleeing civilians and soldiers on two stretches of highway between Kuwait and Iraq. Included in fuel air weapons used was the BLU-82, a 15,000-pound device capable of incinerating everything within hundreds of yards.

One seven mile stretch called the "Highway of Death" was littered with hundreds of vehicles and thousands of dead. All were fleeing to Iraq for their lives. Thousands were civilians of all ages, including Kuwaitis, Iraqis, Palestinians, Jordanians and other nationalities. Another 60-mile stretch of road to the east was strewn with the remnants of tanks, armored cars, trucks, ambulances and thousands of bodies following an attack on convoys on the night of February 25, 1991. The press reported that no survivors are known or likely. One flatbed truck contained nine bodies, their hair and clothes were burned off, skin incinerated by heat so intense it melted the windshield onto the dashboard.

Napalm was used against civilians, military personnel and to start fires. Oil well fires in both Iraq and Kuwait were intentionally started by U.S. aircraft dropping napalm and other heat intensive devices.

Cluster and anti-personnel fragmentation bombs were used in Basra and other cities, and towns, against the convoys described above and against military units. The CBU-75 carries 1,800 bomblets called Sadeyes. One type of Sadeyes can explode before hitting the ground, on impact, or be timed to explode at different times after impact. Each bomblet contains 600 razor sharp steel fragments lethal up to 40 feet. The 1,800 bomblets from one CBU-75 can cover an area equal to 157 football fields with deadly shrapnel.

"Superbombs" were dropped on hardened shelters, at least two in the last days of the assault, with the intention of assassinating President Saddam Hussein. One was misdirected. It was not the first time the Pentagon targeted a head of state. In April 1986, the U.S. attempted to assassinate Col. Muammar Qaddafi by laser directed bombs in its attack on Tripoli, Libya.

Illegal weapons killed thousands of civilians and soldiers.

The conduct violated the Hague and Geneva Conventions, the Nuremberg Charter and the laws of armed conflict.

8. The United States intentionally attacked installations in Iraq containing dangerous substances and forces.

Despite the fact that Iraq used no nuclear or chemical weapons and in the face of UN resolutions limiting the authorized means of removing Iraqi forces from Kuwait, the U.S. intentionally bombed alleged nuclear sites, chemical plants, dams and other dangerous forces. The U.S. knew such attacks could cause the release of dangerous forces from such installations and consequent severe losses among the civilian population. While some civilians were killed in such attacks, there are no reported cases of consequent severe losses presumably because lethal nuclear materials and dangerous chemical and biological warfare substances were not present at the sites bombed.

The conduct violates Protocol I Additional, Article 56, to the Geneva Convention, 1977.

10. President Bush obstructed justice and corrupted United Nations functions as a means of securing power to commit crimes against peace and war crimes.

President Bush caused the United Nations to completely bypass Chapter VI provisions of its Charter for the Pacific Settlement of Disputes. This was done in order to obtain Security Council resolutions authorizing the use of all necessary means, in the absolute discretion of any nation, to fulfill UN resolutions directed against Iraq and which were used to destroy Iraq. To obtain Security Council votes, the U.S. corruptly paid member nations billions of dollars, provided them arms to conduct regional wars, forgave billions in debts, withdrew opposition to a World Bank loan, agreed to diplomatic relations despite human rights violations and threatened economic and political reprisals. A nation which voted against the United States, Yemen, was immediately punished by the loss of millions of dollars in aid. The U.S. paid the UN $187 million to reduce the amount of dues it owed to the UN to avoid criticism of its coercive activities. The United Nations, created to end the scourge of war, became an instrument of war and condoned war crimes.

The conduct violates the Charter of the United Nations and the Constitution and laws of the United States.

11. President Bush usurped the Constitutional power of Congress as a means of securing power to commit crimes against peace, war crimes, and other high crimes.

President Bush intentionally usurped Congressional power, ignored its authority, and failed and refused to consult with the Congress. He deliberately misled, deceived, concealed and made false representations to the Congress to prevent its free deliberation and informed exercise of legislature power. President Bush individually ordered a naval blockade against Iraq, itself an act of war. He switched U.S. forces from a wholly defensive position and capability to an offensive capacity for aggression against Iraq without consultation with and contrary to assurances given to the Congress. He secured legislation approving enforcement of UN resolutions vesting absolute discretion in any nation, providing no guidelines and requiring no reporting to the UN, knowing he intended to destroy the armed forces and civilian economy of Iraq. Those acts were undertaken to enable him to commit crimes against peace and war crimes.

The conduct violates the Constitution and laws of the United States, all committed to engage in the other impeachable offenses set forth in this Complaint.

12. The United States waged war on the environment.

Pollution from the detonation of 88,000 tons of bombs, innumerable missiles, rockets, artillery and small arms with the combustion and fires they caused and by 110,000 air sorties at a rate of nearly two per minute for six weeks has caused enormous injury to life and the ecology. Attacks by U.S. aircraft caused much if not all of the worst oil spills in the Gulf. Aircraft and helicopters dropping napalm and fuel-air explosives on oil wells, storage tanks and refineries caused oil fires throughout Iraq and many, if not most, of the oil well fires in Iraq and Kuwait. The intentional destruction of municipal water systems, waste material treatment and sewage disposal systems constitutes a direct and continuing assault on life and health throughout Iraq.

The conduct violated the UN Charter, the Hague and Geneva Conventions, the laws of armed conflict and constitutes war crimes and crimes against humanity.

13. President Bush encouraged and aided Shiite Muslims and Kurds to rebel against the government of Iraq causing fratricidal violence, emigration, exposure, hunger and sickness and thousands of deaths. After the rebellion failed, the U.S. invaded and occupied parts of Iraq without authority in order to increase division and hostility within Iraq.

Without authority from the Congress or the UN, President Bush continued his imperious military actions after the cease fire. He encouraged and aided rebellion against Iraq, failed to protect the warring parties, encouraged migration of whole populations, placing them in jeopardy from the elements, hunger, and disease. After much suffering and many deaths, President Bush then without authority used U.S. military forces to distribute aid at and near the Turkish border, ignoring the often greater suffering among refugees in Iran. He then arbitrarily set up bantustan-like settlements for Kurds in Iraq and demanded Iraq pay for U.S. costs. When Kurds chose to return to their homes in Iraq, he moved U.S. troops further into northern Iraq against the will of the government and without authority.

The conduct violated the Charter of the United Nations, international law, the Constitution and laws of the United States, and the laws of Iraq.

14. President Bush intentionally deprived the Iraqi people of essential medicines, potable water, food, and other necessities.

A major component of the assault on Iraq was the systematic deprivation of essential human needs and services. To break the will of the people, destroy their economic capability, reduce their numbers and weaken their health, the United States:

- imposed and enforced embargoes preventing the shipment of needed medicines, water purifiers, infant milk formula, food and other supplies;
- individually, without congressional authority, ordered a U.S. naval blockade of Iraq, an act of war, to deprive the Iraqi people of needed supplies;
- froze funds of Iraq and forced other nations to do so, depriving Iraq of the ability to purchase needed medicines, food and other supplies;
- controlled information about the urgent need for such supplies to prevent sickness, death and threatened epidemic, endangering the whole society;
- prevented international organizations, governments and relief agencies from providing needed supplies and obtaining information concerning needs;
- failed to assist or meet urgent needs of huge refugee populations including Egyptians, Indians, Pakistanis, Yemenis, Sudanese, Jordanians, Palestinians, Sri Lankans, Filipinos, and interfered with efforts of others to do so;
- consistently diverted attention from health and epidemic threats within Iraq caused by the U.S. even after advertising the plight of Kurdish people on the Turkish border;

- deliberately bombed the electrical grids causing the closure of hospitals and laboratories, loss of medicine and essential fluids and blood; and
- deliberately bombed food storage, fertilizer, and seed storage facilities.

As a result of these acts, thousands of people died, many more suffered illness and permanent injury. As a single illustration, Iraq consumed infant milk formula at a rate of 2,500 tons per month during the first seven months of 1990. From November 1, 1990, to February 7, 1991, Iraq was able to import only 17 tons. Its own productive capacity was destroyed. Many Iraqis believed that President Bush intended that their infants die because he targeted their food supply. The Red Crescent Society of Iraq estimated 3,000 infant deaths as of February 7, 1991, resulting from infant milk formula and infant medication shortages.

This conduct violates the Hague and Geneva Conventions, the Universal Declaration of Human Rights and other covenants and constitutes a crime against humanity.

15. The United States continued its assault on Iraq after the cease fire, invading and occupying areas at will.

The United States has acted with dictatorial authority over Iraq and its external relations since the end of the military conflict. It has shot and killed Iraqi military personnel, destroyed aircraft and material at will, occupied vast areas of Iraq in the north and south and consistently threatened use of force against Iraq.

This conduct violates the sovereignty of a nation, exceeds authority in UN resolutions, is unauthorized by the Constitution and laws of the United States, and constitutes war crimes.

16. The United States has violated and condoned violations of human rights, civil liberties and the U.S. Bill of Rights in the United States, in Kuwait, Saudi Arabia and elsewhere to achieve its purpose of military domination.

Among the many violations committed or condoned by the U.S. government are the following:

- illegal surveillance, arrest, interrogation and harassment of Arab-American, Iraqi-American, and U.S. resident Arabs;
- illegal detention, interrogation and treatment of Iraqi prisoners of war;
- aiding and condoning Kuwaiti summary executions, assaults, torture and illegal detention of Palestinians and other residents in Kuwait after the U.S. occupation; and
- unwarranted, discriminatory, and excessive prosecution and punishment of U.S. military personnel who refused to serve in the Gulf, sought conscientious objector status or protested U.S. policies.

Persons were killed, assaulted, tortured, illegally detained and prosecuted, harassed and humiliated as a result of these policies.

The conduct violates the Charter of the United Nations, the Universal Declaration of Human Rights, the Hague and Geneva Conventions and the Constitution and laws of the United States.

17. The United States, having destroyed Iraq's economic base, demands reparations which will permanently impoverish Iraq and threaten its people with famine and epidemic.

Having destroyed lives, property and essential civilian facilities in Iraq which the U.S. concedes will require $50 billion to replace (estimated at $200 billion by Iraq), killed at least 125,000 people by bombing and many thousands more by sickness and hunger, the U.S. now seeks to control Iraq economically even as its people face famine and epidemic.[12] Damages, including casualties in Iraq, systematically inflicted by the U.S. exceed all damages, casualties and costs of all other parties to the conflict combined many times over. Reparations under these conditions are an exaction of tribute for the conqueror from a desperately needy country. The United States seeks to force Iraq to pay for damage to Kuwait largely caused by the U.S. and even to pay U.S.

costs for its violations of Iraqi sovereignty in occupying northern Iraq to further manipulate the Kurdish population there. Such reparations are a neocolonial means of expropriating Iraq's oil, natural resources, and human labor.

The conduct violates the Charter of the United Nations and the Constitution and laws of the United States.

18. President Bush systematically manipulated, controlled, directed, misinformed and restricted press and media coverage to obtain constant support in the media for his military and political goals.

The Bush Administration achieved a five-month-long commercial for militarism and individual weapons systems. The American people were seduced into the celebration of a slaughter by controlled propaganda demonizing Iraq, assuring the world no harm would come to Iraqi civilians, deliberately spreading false stories of atrocities including chemical warfare threats, deaths of incubator babies and threats to the entire region by a new Hitler.

The press received virtually all its information from or by permission of the Pentagon. Efforts were made to prevent any adverse information or opposition views from being heard. CNN's limited presence in Baghdad was described as Iraqi propaganda. Independent observers, eyewitnesses' photos, and video tapes with information about the effects of the U.S. bombing were excluded from the media. Television network ownership, advertizers, newspaper ownership, elite columnists and commentators intimidated and instructed reporters and selected interviewees. They formed a near-single voice of praise for U.S. militarism, often exceeding the Pentagon in bellicosity.

The American people and their democratic institutions were deprived of information essential to sound judgment and were regimented, despite profound concern, to support a major neocolonial intervention and war of aggression. The principal purpose of the First Amendment to the United States was to assure the press and the people the right to criticize their government with impunity. This purpose has been effectively destroyed in relation to U.S. military aggression since the press was denied access to assaults on Grenada, Libya, Panama and, now on a much greater scale, against Iraq.

This conduct violates the First Amendment to the Constitution of the United States and is part of a pattern of conduct intended to create support for conduct constituting crimes against peace and war crimes.

19. The United States has by force secured a permanent military presence in the Gulf, the control of its oil resources and geopolitical domination of the Arabian Peninsula and Gulf region.

The U.S. has committed the acts described in this complaint to create a permanent U.S. military presence in the Persian Gulf, to dominate its oil resources until depleted and to maintain geopolitical domination over the region.

The conduct violates the Charter of the United Nations, international law, and the Constitution and laws of the United States.

Ramsey Clark

May 9, 1991

Notes

1 *Covert Operations: The Persian Gulf and the New World Order* (Washington, DC: Christie Institute, 1991).

2 Rhodri Jeffreys-Jones, *The CIA and American Democracy* (New Haven: Yale University Press, 1989), p. 206.

3 Independent Commission of Inquiry on the U.S. Invasion of Panama, *The U.S. Invasion of Panama: The Truth Behind Operation Just Cause* (Boston: South End Press, 1990).

4 *Amnesty International Reports*, 1991, pp. 122-124.

5 *Congressional Record*, June 12, 1990, S8605.

6 "Saddam's Oil Plot." *London Observer*, October 21, 1990.

7 Rick Atkinson, "U.S. to Rely on Air Strikes if War Erupts," *Washington Post*, September 16, 1990: A1+. Eric Schmitt, "Ousted General Gets A Break," *New York Times*, November 7, 1991: A19.

8 *Joint WHO / UNICEF Team Report: A Visit to Iraq* (New York: United Nations, 1991). A report to the Secretary General, dated March 20, 1991 by representatives of the

U.N. Secretariat, UNICEF, UNDP, UNDRO, UNHCR, FAO and WHO. *Reprinted in Appendix B, below.*

[9] Patrick E. Tyler, "Powell Says U.S. Will Stay In Iraq," *New York Times*, March 23, 1991: A1+.

[10] Patrick J. Sloyan, "Massive Battle After Cease Fire," *New York Newsday*, May 8, 1991: A4+.

[11] "U.S. Prepares UN Draft on Claims Against Iraq," *New York Times*, November 1, 1990.

Facts substantiating the charges of U. S. War Crimes may be obtained from the International Action Center, 39 W. 14th Street #206, New York, NY 10011, http://ww.iacenter.org.

City of the First Century

Sa'di Yusuf

Mediterraneans

Basra—were it a ground, I would have gone beyond it;
but Basra is a sky.

The sky is green. Look, there are the palm trees, and the water too is green. Green shared by water and sky. And we, the little ones, are the descendants of a rare colour in the civilization of the Arabs. Was it sheer coincidence that the first two cities to become regions in the first Islamic century were Kufa and Basra? Yellow is the first, still, from verging on sand; green—the latter (still?) from verging on water and sky.

There is nothing to be lost in Basra;
it has everything that could be missed;

The wooden ship from Mombasa; the scent of apples in syntax; the
people of Al-Jahiz, ever so puzzled by Life's perpetual surprise;
the first strike of an underground union.

I say No to murder.
The fifty thousands of Basrans (so loved by Al-Hariri!) were not strewn under the American sorties. The Americans took good care of the soldiers whose only attribute of soldiering was the uniform that pronounced them targets.
I say: The fifty thousands of Basrans were not killed by the Americans except through the beast who, in one minute, had strangled thousands in a Kurdish village named Halabjah.

Full circle came the great rupture.

The Abbasid caliph's brother, Al-Muwaffaq, once led the army to Basra, to slaughter the rebellious black slaves, the Zanj, and to keep a street in the city named after him to this day. But the beast who aimed the artillery of his T72 tanks at the houses of the city, and at the chests of its children—the descendants of that rare colour in the civilisation of the Arabs—did not leave a single street that might, one day, be towered with an obelisk from which our martyrs' names, the children of Basra, would stare at us.

It's the desert then, reclaiming a city of the first Islamic
century, its crude decorum.
Yet, Basra is not a ground;
It's a sky.

Paris, March 7, 1991

The Iraqi Intifada, 1991

Kanan Makiya

from *Cruelty and Silence*

The First Spark

The spark that touched off the intifada began in the predominantly Shi'i city of Basra, the largest city of southern Iraq. It seems to have started around the time that the formal cease-fire in the Gulf war came into effect at 5:00 A.M. on February 28, 1991. A column of tanks fleeing from Kuwait rolled into Sa'ad Square, a huge rectangular open space in downtown Basra. The commander at the head of the column positioned his vehicle in front of a gigantic mural of Saddam in military uniform located next to the Ba'th Party Headquarters Building in the square. Standing on the chassis of his vehicle and addressing the portrait, he denounced the dictator in a blistering speech: "What has befallen us of defeat, shame, and humiliation, Saddam, is the result of your follies, your miscalculations, and your irresponsible actions."

A crowd assembled. The atmosphere became highly charged. The commander jumped back into his tank and swiveled the gun turret to take aim at the portrait. He blasted away with several shells. A delirious crowd cheered him, chanting, "Saddam is finished. All the army is dead." None of the other tanks or soldiers in the square intervened. Soon they were joining in the demonstration that was fast developing. "They were all shooting in the air," recalled 'Abdallah al-Badran, a twenty-four-year-old Kuwaiti who had been taken hostage and was a witness to what was going on. Guns were handed out to eager grasping hands and the crowd stormed the Ba'th Party headquarters. They burned the palatial residence of the governor of Basra and attacked police stations wherever they could find them. They looted the security offices, destroying all files. The rebellion spread like wildfire, and within hours of those fast shots in Sa'ad Square, the local residents from Basra and the returning soldiers from Kuwait had set up roadblocks and were in control of the city. It was a classic revolutionary moment.

The Aftermath

The Allied forces left four Republican Guard divisions intact during the Gulf war. These were the backbone of the force that Saddam Husain dispatched to suppress the intifada in the south. When these divisions, supported by tank and artillery units, made a three-pronged entry into the city of Najaf on Wednesday morning, March 20, 1991, the tanks had the words *"la shi'a ba'da al-yawm"* painted on them: "No more Shi'a after today."

Napalm and cluster bombs had already been dropped on residential areas, and as many as thirty-five SCUD missiles fired into the city, to soften up the resistance. Fired from far away, these inaccurate ballistic missiles struck without pattern or warning. Among many others, they killed Sayyid Basi Abu al-Tananir and everyone else in his house; Hasan Kamouna's wife and daughter; and Hilal Gashoosh's wife, two sons, and daughter-in-law. These missiles, whose proclaimed purpose was to "eat up half of Israel," according to Saddam Husain, demolished the homes of Abu Hameed al-Shukri, Salim Hashim, Sayyid Yousuf, Sayyid Salman, and Kadhum al-Naddaf, among others. The bombing, shelling, and ballistic missile attacks were designed to sow terror, with the intention of letting every Najafi know that this regime had the means and the will to demolish the entire city and kill every individual in it if necessary.

The ground assault was supported by a fleet of helicopter gunships, which began operations by encircling the residential area of Ayatollah Khoei and bombing the neighboring houses. Hundreds gathered around the house to protect him, many of whom were killed. The surrounding area was flattened. A unit of heliborne commandos then descended upon the house of the Ayatollah and kidnapped him and his companions. Walking over the bodies of the defenders littered around the house, the pontiff of Shi'ism, and all his relatives and entourage, were loaded into helicopters and transported to a specially prepared detention center in Baghdad. "They forced the Imam," said an eyewitness, "to walk without assistance, and since he cannot, he fell to the ground. Then his son helped him up and all were taken away." The next day, the ninety-two-year-old cleric, who had done more than anyone else to curb the wild men of the intifada, was put on television with Saddam Husain, whose audience, it was alleged, he had "sought" so that he could denounce the intifada. A video tape of that appearance shows an old man wearing a flowing brown wool cape and a black turban as is the custom of all *sayyids* (descendants of the Prophet). A long white beard hung from a roundish face marked by brown spots around the temples. His demeanor was gentle and critically distressed; his voice breathless and the barest of whispers. After that appearance, he was kept under house arrest in Kufa for the next seventeen months. On August 8,1992, Ayatollah Khoei (the embodiment of the history of the Shi'a from the Ottomans through the regime of the Ba'th) died in Kufa, Iraq."

The soldiers deployed in the attack on Najaf (and in southern Iraq generally) appear to have been selected from the Sunni towns of Hit, Mosul, Shirkat, Beigi, and from the Yazeedi community, a tiny sect based in northern Iraq which has a history of conflict with Shi'a Muslims. Iraqi soldiers who managed to escape from these units and reach the American post at Checkpoint 5 Alfa reported that they were offered a reward of 250 Iraqi dinars for each woman or child they killed and as much as 5,000 dinars for adult males. However, each soldier was only entitled to claim on an upper limit of one hundred dead people a day. The slogan painted on the tanks of the Republican Guard, "No more Shi'a after today," was clearly not a local initiative; it was official policy.

In the course of entering the city, troops used women and children as human shields, forcing them to walk in front of infantry patrols and tanks so that the rebels would be unable to fire without killing innocent civilians." Soldiers also forced women and children to remain in buildings which the army had turned into strongpoints. These hostages were sometimes placed on the roof of the building in full view, so the rebels would know that any attack on the building would result in their deaths. Civilians who had survived the initial artillery and aerial bombardment found themselves in even greater danger from the advancing Republican Guard and the security police who followed in their wake. A favorite army tactic was to send a loudspeaker-equipped helicopter over an area of a city to announce that the citizens would be given time to evacuate before the army attacked. Leaflets were also dropped containing threats to use chemical weapons, but advising the populace to leave by specified safe routes reserved for them. For example, in Kerbala, people were advised to leave by the Hindiyya road. Along this road queues several kilometers long of civilians desperate to escape the fighting formed. Helicopter gunships then strafed them with machine guns, creating scenes of horror that have been described by several eyewitnesses. On other occasions, the army opened fire on mobs of fleeing refugees with artillery.

Government forces paid special attention to those doctors who had kept their hospitals open during the uprising. Many stories of what happened to medical people have emerged. One doctor who managed to escape to the American lines reported that the security forces threw his wife, children, and brother out of a helicopter to punish him for treating wounded insurgents. Another surgeon reported that fifteen doctors at the Jumhouri Hospital in Basra were executed on the spot and then artillery was fired at the building, even though four thousand civilians—patients and their families—were still being held there. Um Husain told me of one doctor who was "made to look like a sieve" in full view of all the employees working at the central hospital in Basra, who had to stand around in a huge circle and watch. At Saddam Hospital in Najaf, army troops molested female doctors, murdered men with knives, and threw injured patients out of windows. Dr. Muhammad al-Khilkhali was paraded on television to set an example, and has since disappeared. Drs. Muhammad 'Ali Qraidi and Qays Hilal al-Jilawi, on the other hand, were among those executed in public by firing squads."

The families of insurgents and suspected insurgents suffered particularly hideous fates. Security forces routinely murdered relatives to punish rebels. In one case, security forces surrounding the Shrine of 'Ali recognized a fighter inside. A squad then raided the man's house and "captured" his infant son. They returned to the shrine with the boy. When the father appeared, the infant was flung at the shrine and perished on impact. On another occasion, a refugee in Iran reported that army troops surrounding the Shrine of 'Ali threw severed human limbs at the fighters inside.

Children who would not give their parents' names to soldiers were doused with gasoline and set on fire. Some were tied to moving tanks to discourage sniper fire from the rebels. Security forces also burned entire families in their houses when they would not give or did not know the location of the head of the household. One hundred and fifty people in Amara were tossed into the river with concrete blocks tied to their legs; thirty people suffered the same fate in Basra. The army made liberal use of "necklacing"—a form of punishment made famous in South Africa. In one incident, three children belonging to the Turfi family, the oldest of whom was nine, had tires soaked in gasoline placed around their necks and set alight. Some rebels, it has been alleged, were forced to drink gasoline before being shot. It appears that instead of crumpling into an undramatic lifeless heap, the victim explodes and burns like a torch for a short while. Executions of this sort had more impact on onlookers than lining people up against walls and mowing them down.

More routine atrocities included summary executions of any man caught with his face covered. Families that returned to their homes after the fighting suffered a similar fate. "The families that had fled the fighting returned with their children. They lined them up and executed them." If an army patrol was fired on from a house or neighborhood, the entire area was held accountable. In one case, a sniper firing from a hotel along Zain al-'Abideen Street killed a soldier. In reprisal, the army emptied all of the houses on the surrounding streets, gathered the residents together, and demanded that they produce the sniper. When they could not do so, the men and women were separated. The women were released after a day in uncomfortable detention. The men disappeared.

The initial military assault forces were followed by units of the security police, the Intelligence services, the Special Security, the local police force, and even the traffic police. These forces ranged through the cities, snatching young men for questioning and arresting suspected opposition leaders. House-to-house searches produced new levels of outrage. According to interviews conducted by the Organisation of Human Rights in Iraq, the forces making the sweeps had a standard modus operandi: They would search all houses in a given area, confiscating anything that looked like a weapon and arresting every able-bodied male. If the sweep found no one in a house, the soldiers looted and ransacked it. Women in the houses were often abused, raped, and forbidden to wear their veils, (as a way of impugning the family's honor). Following one such sweep, on March 15, 1991, Muhammad 'Ali al-Rumahi, a fifty-five-year-old man from Najaf, set himself on fire and burned to death after being forced to witness Republican Guard soldiers raping his three daughters.

Men and boys picked up in such sweeps had little or no chance of survival. Iraqi refugees arriving in Iran in early April reported that more than four thousand people had been executed in the previous ten days in Najaf. Indiscriminate arrests and executions were the order of the day. A survivor interviewed by Middle East Watch reports that "the army started sealing up area after area, looking for men. Everyone they found—youths, men, foreigners—they took to the sports stadiums, and from there, in large convoys, to Baghdad. These operations went on until [April 10]. . . . We don't know what has happened to them since."

Organized rebel resistance first collapsed in Basra, sometime between March 7 and March 9. Bands of rebels continued to engage in hit and run operations with government forces, but the city never passed out of government hands. Samawa held out the longest, falling on March 29, after local tribal leaders switched their allegiances back to the government. Najaf fell around March 16, 1991, and Kerbala followed suit shortly afterwards. A senior figure in the Ba'th Party told the foreign correspondent of the BBC, John Simpson, that he thought four times as many people lost their lives in the uprising as from the Allied bombing. By the middle of April 1991, some five thousand religious scholars and students from Najaf alone had been arrested. With all of their students and faculty in police custody, the religious schools shut down. Entire families disappeared into the hands of the regime. Sayyid Muhammad Bahr al-'Uloum, who first told me about the tank commander in Sa'ad Square, lost dozens of members of his extended family. They were seized in an army sweep on March 22. All are still missing, presumed dead. The Iraqi security forces detained or killed all of the religious scholars of Najaf who did not escape from the country. According to one member of the Bahr al-'Uloum family who managed to avoid death or arrest, "Every turbaned person has been killed or arrested."

Everything that set the Shi'a apart, and that gave them their identity, became for the first time in modern Iraqi history a target. In Najaf, the Imam 'Ali Mosque in the Amir district, the Baqee'a and Imam Sadiq mosques in Medina Street, and the Murad Mosque on Tusi Street have all been leveled. Government bulldozers have flattened portions of the vast cemeteries of Najaf with their monumental family tombs, some of which are centuries old, in order that they be concreted over. About fifteen hundred Najafis had fled into the extensive catacombs underneath these cemeteries, hoping to avoid napalm attacks. Many were buried alive as the tunnels collapsed in on them. One survivor made his way to Saudi Arabia and told the tale. During the intifada, the golden dome of the Shrine of 'Ali took several direct artillery hits; its main gait was destroyed; the interior was ravaged. Husain's shrine in Kerbala was much more extensively damaged. But the government's cultural offensive against holy sites, religious buildings, seminaries, and libraries continued long after the fighting in the cities was over. All the palm groves surrounding Kerbala were cut down and the city center around the two shrines leveled, in the first stage of what the penniless regime claims is a massive urban renewal program for Kerbala. Ancient treasuries that have survived centuries were looted or transported to Baghdad. The "jewels, gold, [and] manuscripts, all invaluable," that were stored in the Shrine of 'Ali in Najaf, representing "gifts, made over a thousand years by princes and kings," were gone. An enormous diamond which Ottoman Sultan Murad I gave to the shrine in 1634 is missing.

Physical destruction is at least reparable. The same cannot be said for the burning of the libraries of the religious schools and seminaries of Najaf, Kufa, and Kerbala containing ancient manuscripts, most of which have never been properly studied or catalogued by modern methods. The Dar al-Hikma Library established by the late Ayatollah Muhsin al-Hakim and the public library run by the Hakim family on Rasoul Street (containing some 60,000 books and 20,000 manuscripts) were both burnt and ransacked. So was the Dar al-'Ilm Library belonging to the late Ayatollah Khoei which, is estimated to have contained some 38,000 books and 7,500 manuscripts. Even a proper inventory of these priceless treasures may now never be made since so many of the people who were in charge of them have either been arrested or murdered. The very real danger exists that the scale and organized character of the assault launched by the regime in Baghdad has ended a thousand-year tradition of religious scholarship and learning in Najaf, with unpredictable future consequences.

By way of making a balance sheet of all of this, *al-Thawra*, the official mouthpiece of the Ba'th, ran a series of six unsigned major articles in April 1991. These mark a sea-change in Baghdad's official position on its Shi'a citizens. As was to be expected, the regime described the intifada in the south as "a dirty foreign conspiracy." The novelty came in the idea that the perpetrators were not only "foreign by virtue of their identity and nationality," but were "alien to Iraq by virtue of their mentality, conscience, and feelings." Instead of loyal Iraqis, working for the good of the Ba'th revolution and the Arab nation, which is how the Shi'a were extolled in official propaganda all through the Iraq-Iran War, they became degenerate subhumans, who observed a debased religion that had no proper moral code. This kind of language has never been used in Ba'thi publications before, and it was followed up by a stream of articles in the Iraqi press and reports of "doctoral dissertations" through the summer of 1992, all denigrating the Shi'a and their religion.

The *al-Thawra* articles went to great lengths to "prove" that Iraq's Shi'a were actually "un-Iraqi." Iranian influence over southern Iraq, it was claimed, has debased the culture and especially the religion of the Shi'a. They have lost the self-respect and close understanding of Islam that is a characteristic of the true Arab. The Shi'a are presented as a primitive and superstitious people, who worship the descendants of the Prophet—so-called *sayyids*—with a fawning adoration that disgusts the true Arab: "The adulation sometimes reaches a point where some people kiss the feet or the footmarks of the *sayyid* on the ground. . . ." Such habits, introduced by the Iranian clergy into Iraq, border on heresy and "reveal how foreigners try to belittle the Iraqis and . . . to subject them to their own will through practices which they dishonestly call religious." True Arabs "are not used to bowing down before other people."

The articles go on to attack the Marsh Arabs for their poverty, backwardness, and immorality. They are referred to as a naturally vicious, slatternly, and dirty people, descendants of Indian slaves and not true Arabs at all. Their sexual practices are disgusting and their women sluttish and immodest. "One often hears stories of perversion that would make your mouth drop," writes *al-Thawra*. Nonetheless, the unnamed author concludes, Saddam Husain treats these people "humanely, in accordance with . . . pure Arab traditions and proper Islamic principles. Whereas the *sayyid* scarcely mixes with his followers, except on big occasions, to maintain his authority and influence on an ignorant people, Saddam Husain mixes with ordinary people in the marshes without the trappings of authority, sleeps and eats with them, and shares their joy and sadness."

Arab intellectual, religious, and official opinion ignored what was going on in Iraq during March and April 1991. Not one of the intellectuals who fulminated against the West for getting itself involved over Kuwait, wrote or spoke up in defense of a people that had finally gathered the courage to rise against the regime that had napalmed, gassed, tortured, and terrorized them for twenty-three years. Distinguished Arab professors speculated across dinner tables in the West about how much better off Iraqis would be if Saddam survived. Others made the rounds with American legislators and policymakers, urging them not to intervene in the relentless mass killing of Iraqis that was under way, ostensibly because of the dire consequences to the region of doing so. Such reactions are a proof of moral bankruptcy; sadly, they are not even founded upon ignorance. Rather, they are founded upon a complete lack of empathy with the suffering of fellow human beings who happen—in this case—to be fellow Arabs. I can do no better than to close this chapter with the moving response of the Shi'i cleric Sayyid Mustafa Jamal al-Din, a poet and man of letters from Najaf, to the silence of the whole Arab-Muslim world.

> Let us suppose that the intifada was a southern Shi'i phenomenon, and not a generalized Iraqi one. And let us suppose that the Islamic allegiances of the Shi'a are the object of suspicion—as some

Sunni extremists contend. Do not these Holy Shrines and mosques belong to Islam? Are not the fourth caliph of Islam, ‘Ali ibn Abi Talib (may God's blessings be upon his face), and his sons (God's blessings be upon them), buried here? Does the bombardment of their tombs with SCUD missiles . . . not deserve one leaflet, one denunciatory statement coming out of some Arab or Islamic source—even if it is non-governmental—like the al-Azhar in Egypt for instance, or the Zaytouna Mosque in Tunis, or the Mosque of the Qaraween in Morocco, or the Islamic League in Saudi Arabia, or any other mosque, group, Islamic party, or man of religion. . . .

Is the sanctity of all these holy shrines to be defiled, only because we Shi‘a live beside them?

I am not a sectarian, and there is nothing in my literary or political history which would show that. On the contrary, I have always emphasized our own ignorance, we Muslims, of the true nobility of spirit in Islam. We let confessional sectarianism overrule the tolerance and humanity of this religion. We Arabs are ignorant of the tolerance and humanity of our own Arabism. We have let it move in the direction of chauvinism.

These are my beliefs in Islam and in Arabism and they can be summarized in the fact that I consider the greatest sickness of Muslims in the current period to be religious sectarianism and racism.

We are all Arabs because we live in one part of the world and share in the feelings of all Arabs, wherever they may be. We speak their tongue and we feel their feelings, and we are bound to one another by a common fate. Arabism is not the blood that flows in some people's veins and not in others—it is these feelings, this common fate."

The Cost of Conflict

John Pilger

from *The New Rulers of the World*

> We do not seek the destruction of Iraq. Nor do we seek to punish the Iraqi people for the decisions and policies of their leaders.
>
> *President George Bush Senior*

> We think the price is worth it . . .
>
> *US Ambassador Madeleine Albright, when asked if the deaths of half a million Iraqi children were a price worth paying for sanctions*

> They know we own their country . . . we dictate the way they live and talk. And that's what's great about America right now. It's a good thing, especially when there's a lot of oil out there we need.
>
> *Brigadier-General William Looney, US air force, director of the bombing of Iraq*

Wherever you go in Iraq's southern city of Basra, there is dust. It rolls down the long roads that are the desert's fingers. It gets in your eyes and nose and throat; it swirls in markets and school playgrounds, consuming children kicking a plastic ball; and it carries, according to Dr Jawad Al-Ali, 'the seeds of our death'. Dr Al-Ali is a cancer specialist at the city hospital and a member of Britain's Royal College of Physicians. He has a neat moustache and a kindly, furrowed face. His starched white coat, like the collar of his shirt, is frayed.

'Before the Gulf War, we had only three or four deaths in a month from cancer,' he said. 'Now it's thirty to thirty-five patients dying every month, and that's just in my department. That is twelve times the increase in the cancer mortality. Our studies indicate that 40 to 48 per cent of the population in this area will get cancer: in five years' time to begin with, then long afterwards.

That's almost half the population. Most of my own family now have cancer, and we have no history of the disease. It has spread to the medical staff of this hospital; yesterday, the son of the medical director died. We don't know the precise source of the contamination, because we are not allowed to get the equipment to conduct a proper survey, or even test the excess level of radiation in our bodies. We strongly suspect depleted uranium, which was used by the Americans and British in the Gulf War right across the southern battlefields. Whatever the cause, it is like Chernobyl here; the genetic effects are new to us. The mushrooms grow huge, and the fish in what was once a beautiful river are inedible. Even the grapes in my garden have mutated and can't be eaten.'

Along the corridor, I met Dr Ginan Ghalib Hassen, a paediatrician. At another time, she might have been described as an effervescent personality; now she, too, has a melancholy expression that does not change; it is the face of Iraq. 'This is Ali Raffa Asswadi,' she said, stopping to take the hand of a wasted boy I guessed to be about four years old. 'He is nine years,' she said. 'He has leukaemia. Now we can't treat him. Only some of the drugs are available. We get drugs for two or three weeks, and then they stop when the shipments stop. Unless you continue a course, the treatment is useless. We can't even give blood transfusions, because there are not enough blood bags . . .'

In the next bed, a child lay in his shrouded mother's arms. One side of his head was severely swollen. 'This is neuroplastoma,' said Dr Hassen. 'It is a very unusual tumour. Before 1991, we saw only one case of this tumour in two years. Now we have many cases.' Another child had his eyes fixed on me and I asked what would happen to him. She said, 'He has an abdominal mass. We have operated on him, but unless the tumour receives treatment, it will recur. We have only some drugs. We are waiting for the full course. He has renal failure now, so his future is bad. All the futures here are bad.'

Dr Hassen keeps a photo album of the children she is trying to save and has been unable to save. 'This is Taum Saleh,' she said, turning to a photograph of a boy in a blue pullover and with sparkling eyes. 'He is five-and-a-half years old. This is a case of Hodgkin's Disease. Normally, with Hodgkin's, a patient can expect to live and the cure can be 95 per cent. But if the drugs are not available, complications set in, and death follows. This boy had a beautiful nature. He died.'

I said, 'As we were walking, I noticed you stop and put your face to the wall.'

'Yes, I was emotional . . . I am a doctor; I am not supposed to cry, but I cry every day, because this is torture. These children could live; they could live and grow up; and when you see your son and daughter in front of you, dying, what happens to you?'

I said, 'What do you say to those in the West who deny the connection between depleted uranium and the deformities of these children?'

'That is not true. How much proof do they want? There is every relation between congenital malformation and depleted uranium. Before 1991, we saw nothing like this at all. If there is no connection, why have these things not happened before? Most of these children have no family history of cancer. I have studied what happened in Hiroshima. It is almost exactly the same here; we have an increased percentage of congenital malformation, an increase of malignancy, leukaemia, brain tumours: the same.'

Under the economic embargo imposed by the United Nations Security Council in 1990 and upgraded the following year, Iraq is denied equipment and expertise to decontaminate its battlefields, in contrast to how Kuwait was cleaned up after the Gulf War. The US army physicist responsible for cleaning up Kuwait was Professor Doug Rokke, whom I met in London. Today, he himself is a victim. 'I am like many people in southern Iraq,' he said. 'I have 5,000 times the recommended level of radiation in my body. The contamination was right throughout Iraq and Kuwait. With the munitions testing and preparation in Saudi Arabia, uranium contamination covers the entire region. The effect depends on whether a person inhaled it or ingested it by eating and drinking, or if they got it in an open wound. What we're seeing now, respiratory problems, kidney problems, cancers, are the direct result of the use of this highly toxic material. The controversy over whether or not it's the cause is a manufactured one; my own ill-health is testament to that.'

Professor Rokke says there are two urgent issues to be confronted by people in the West, 'those with a sense of right and wrong': first, the decision by the

United States and Britain to use a 'weapon of mass destruction', such as depleted uranium. He said, 'In the Gulf War, well over 300 tons were fired. An A-10 Warthog attack aircraft fired over 900,000 rounds. Each individual round was 300 grams of solid uranium 238. When a tank fired its shells, each round carried over 4,500 grams of solid uranium. These rounds are not coated, they're not tipped; they're solid uranium. Moreover, we have evidence to suggest that they were mixed with plutonium. What happened in the Gulf was a form of nuclear warfare.

'The second issue is the denial of medical care to American and British and other allied soldiers, and the tens of thousands of Iraqis contaminated. At international symposiums, I have watched Iraqi officials approach their counterparts from the Department of Defence and the Ministry of Defence and ask, plead, for help with decontamination. The Iraqis didn't use depleted uranium; it was not their weapon. They simply don't know how to get rid of it from their environment. I watched them put their case, describing the deaths and the horrific deformities that are showing up; and I watched them rebuffed. It was pathetic.'

The United Nations Sanctions Committee in New York, dominated by the Americans and British, has vetoed or delayed a range of vital medical equipment, chemotherapy drugs, even pain-killers. (In the jargon of denial, 'blocked' equals vetoed, and 'on hold' means delayed, or maybe blocked.) In Baghdad, I sat in a clinic as doctors received parents and their children, many of them grey-skinned and bald, some of them dying. After every second or third examination, Dr Lekaa Fasseh Ozeer, the young oncologist, wrote in English: 'No drugs available.' I asked her to jot down in my notebook a list of drugs the hospital had ordered, but had not received, or had received intermittently. She filled a page.

I had been filming in Iraq for my documentary *Paying the Price: Killing the Children of Iraq*. Back in London, I showed Dr Ozeer's list to Professor Karol Sikora who, as chief of the cancer programme of the World Health Organisation (WHO), wrote in the *British Medical Journal*: 'Requested radiotherapy equipment, chemotherapy drugs and analgesics are consistently blocked by United States and British advisers [to the Sanctions Committee]. There seems to be a rather ludicrous notion that such agents could be converted into chemical and other weapons.' He told me, 'Nearly all these drugs are available in every British hospital. They're very standard. When I came back from Iraq last year, with a group of experts I drew up a list of seventeen drugs that are deemed essential for cancer treatment. We informed the UN that there was no possibility of converting these drugs into chemical warfare agents. We heard nothing more. The saddest thing I saw in Iraq was children dying because there was no chemotherapy and no pain control. It seemed crazy they couldn't have morphine, because for everybody with cancer pain, it is the best drug. When I was there, they had a little bottle of aspirin pills to go round 200 patients in pain. They would receive a particular anti-cancer drug, but then get only little bits of drugs here and there, and so you can't have any planning. It's bizarre.'

I told him that one of the doctors had been especially upset, because the UN Sanctions Committee had banned nitrous oxide as 'weapons dual use'; yet this was used in caesarean sections to stop bleeding, and perhaps save a mother's life. 'I can see no logic to banning that,' he said. 'I am not an armaments expert, but the amounts used would be so small that, even if you collected all the drugs supply for the whole nation and pooled it, it is difficult to see how you could make any chemical warfare device out of it.'

I asked him how his criticisms were received by the World Health Organisation. 'We were specifically told not to talk about it afterwards, about the whole Iraq business. The WHO was embarrassed; it's not an organisation that likes to get involved in politics.'

Mohamed Ghani's studio in Baghdad is dominated by a huge crucifix he is sculpting for the Church of the Assumption in Baghdad. As Iraq's most famous sculptor, he is proud that the Vatican has commissioned him, a Muslim, to sculpt the Stations of the Cross in Rome, a cultural acknowledgement, he says, of his country as Mesopotamia, the 'cradle of western civilisation'. When I visited him, Mozart was playing on his venerable tape deck, which perched on a refrigerator of similar vintage and in which were two small bottles of beer. He handed me one. 'Here's to life and no more sorrow please,' he said. His latest work is a twenty-foot-high figure of a woman, her child gripping her legs, pleading for food. 'Every morning I see her,' he said, 'waiting, with others just like her, in a long line at the hospital at the end of my road.' He has produced a line of figurines that depict their waiting; all the heads are bowed before a door that is permanently closed. 'The door is the dispensary,' he said, 'but it is also the world, kept shut by those who rule the world.'

The next day, I saw the same line of women and children at the Al Mansour children's hospital. Their doctors' anguish had a terrible echo. 'Children with meningitis can survive with the precise dosage of antibiotics,' said Dr Mohamed Mahmud. 'Four milligrams can save a life, but so often we are allowed only one milligram. This is a teaching hospital, but children die because we are not allowed parts for machines that separate blood platelets.'

It was here, as we walked along the line of people waiting, that my companion Denis Halliday had an extraordinary reunion. A courtly Irishman who the previous year (1998) had resigned as the UN's Co-ordinator of Humanitarian Relief to Iraq in protest against the effects of the embargo on the civilian population, he had returned with me to Baghdad. Now he spotted a man and his daughter, and the three erupted with greetings.

'Saffa!' he said, dropping to his knees to take the hands of a nine-year-old girl.

'John, this is Saffa Majid and her father, Majid Ali. Saffa I met two years ago in this hospital, when I was the UN chief in Iraq and she was in a very poor condition with leukaemia. One cannot deal with thousands, but one can deal with two or three or four children. And I was able, with the help of the World Health Organisation, to bring in drugs, on the quiet. They were enough for two years of treatment for this little girl. And today, look at her! She looks wonderful and her father says she has only to come once a month now. So I think she's almost cured of the leukaemia. Saffa was one of four I helped. Two little girls died.'

'Why did they die?'

'They died because the medications were not available.'

'And when you set out to help these children, you were the United Nations representative here.'

'That's right. And to help them, I had to act illegally. I had to breach my own economic sanctions, so to speak, established by the Security Council, led by

Washington and London. In this hospital, we have seen the evidence today of the killing that is now the responsibility of the Security Council member states, particularly Bill Clinton and Tony Blair. They should be here with us. They should see the impact of what their decisions and their sustaining of economic sanctions mean.

'The very provisions of the Charter of the United Nations and the Declaration of Human Rights are being set aside. We are waging a war, through the United Nations, on the children and people of Iraq, and with incredible results: results that you do not expect to see in a war under the Geneva Conventions. We're targeting civilians. Worse, we're targeting children like Saffa, who of course were not born when Iraq went into Kuwait. What is this about? It's a monstrous situation, for the United Nations, for the western world, for all of us who are part of some democratic system, who are in fact responsible for the policies of our governments and the implementation of economic sanctions on Iraq.'

Denis Halliday had resigned after thirty-four years with the UN. He was then Assistant Secretary-General of the United Nations, with a long and distinguished career in development, 'attempting to help people, not harm them'. His was the first public expression of an unprecedented rebellion within the UN bureaucracy. 'I am resigning,' he wrote, 'because the policy of economic sanctions is totally bankrupt. We are in the process of destroying an entire society. It is as simple as that . . . Five thousand children are dying every month . . . I don't want to administer a programme that results in figures like these.'

Since I met Halliday, I have been struck by the principle behind his carefully chosen, uncompromising words. 'I had been instructed,' he said, 'to implement a policy that satisfies the definition of genocide: a deliberate policy that has effectively killed well over a million individuals, children and adults. We all know that the regime, Saddam Hussein, is not paying the price for economic sanctions; on the contrary, he has been strengthened by them. It is the little people who are losing their children or their parents for lack of untreated water. What is clear is that the Security Council is now out of control, for its actions here undermine its own Charter, and the Declaration of Human Rights and the Geneva Convention. History will slaughter those responsible.'

In the UN, Halliday broke a long collective silence. On February 13, 2000, Hans Von Sponeck, who had succeeded him as Humanitarian Co-ordinator in Baghdad, resigned. Like Halliday, he had been with the UN for more than thirty years. 'How long,' he asked, 'should the civilian population of Iraq be exposed to such punishment for something they have never done?' Two days later, Jutta Burghardt, head of the World Food Programme in Iraq, another UN agency, resigned, saying that she, too, could no longer tolerate what was being done to the Iraqi people.

When I met Von Sponeck in Baghdad in October 1999, the anguish behind his measured, self-effacing exterior was evident. Like Halliday's, his job had been to administer the so-called Oil for Food Programme, which since 1996 has allowed Iraq to sell a fraction of its oil for money that goes straight to an account controlled by the Security Council. Almost a third is not used on humanitarian aid, but pays the UN's 'expenses', as well as reparations demanded by Kuwait, one of the world's wealthiest nations, and compensation claims by oil companies and other multinational corporations. Iraq must then tender on the international market for food and medical supplies and other humanitarian resources. Every contract has to be approved by the UN Sanctions Committee in New York.

When sanctions were imposed, following Iraq's invasion of Kuwait in August 1990, all imports, including food, were effectively banned for eight months, even though Security Council Resolution 661 of August 6, 1990 explicitly exempted food and medicines. For a year, the UN refused to allow Iraq the means of raising funds beyond its exhausted cash reserves. As Iraq imported almost everything, the effect was immediate and devastating, compounded by the results of a bombing campaign designed to cripple the civilian infrastructure. 'US military planners,' reported the *Washington Post*, 'hoped the bombing would amplify the economic and psychological impact of international sanctions on Iraqi society . . . Because of these goals, damage to civilian structures and interests, invariably described by briefers during the war as "collateral" and unintended, was sometimes neither. The worst civilian suffering, senior officers say, has resulted not from bombs that went astray but from precision-guided weapons that hit exactly where they were aimed—at electrical plants, oil refineries and transportation networks. Among the justifications offered is that Iraqi civilians were not blameless. A senior air force officer said, "They do live there . . ." '

Reporting on the aftermath of the bombing, UN Under Secretary-General Martti Ahtisaari described the 'near apocalyptic' state of the country's basic services. 'Iraq has for some time to come been relegated to a pre-industrial age,' he wrote, 'but with all the disabilities of post-industrial dependency on an intensive use of energy and technology.' A Harvard University study team concluded that Iraq was heading for a 'public health catastrophe', with tens of thousands of deaths by the end of 1991 alone, the majority of them young children. The team of independent American professionals and academics estimated that, during the first eight months of sanctions when all shipments of food and medicines were blockaded, 47,000 children under the age of five had died. The administration of George Bush Senior appeared to concur with these assessments; and yet, wrote Dr Eric Herring of Bristol University, a sanctions specialist, 'comprehensive economic sanctions remained in place. Those policymakers who backed the sanctions cannot say that they did not know what was going to happen. Whatever the political purpose, it was a conscious and callous choice to deny an entire society the means necessary to survive.'

In 1991, the Security Council, in its Resolution 687, stated that, if Iraq renounced 'weapons of mass destruction' (nuclear, biological and chemical weapons) and ballistic missiles with a range of more than 150 kilometres, and agreed to monitoring by a UN Special Commission on Iraq (UNSCOM), the embargo would be lifted. In 1998, UNSCOM reported that, despite Iraqi obstruction in some areas, 'the disarmament phase of the Security Council's requirements is possibly near its end in the missile and chemical weapons areas.' On December 15, 1998, the International Atomic Energy Agency reported that it had eliminated Iraq's nuclear weapons programme 'efficiently and effectively'.

Scott Ritter, for five years a senior UNSCOM weapons inspector, agreed. 'By 1998, the chemical weapons infrastructure had been completely dismantled or destroyed by UNSCOM or by Iraq in compliance with our mandate,' he told me. 'The biological weapons programme was gone, all the major facilities eliminated. The nuclear weapons programme was completely eliminated. The long-range ballistic missile programme was completely eliminated. If I had to quantify Iraq's threat, I would say [it is] zero.'

While food and medicines are technically exempt, the Sanctions Committee has frequently vetoed and delayed requests for baby food, agricultural equipment, heart and cancer drugs, oxygen tents, X-ray machines. Sixteen heart and lung machines were put 'on hold' because they contained computer chips. A fleet of ambulances was held up because their equipment included vacuum flasks, which keep medical supplies cold; vacuum flasks are designated 'dual use' by the Sanctions Committee, meaning they could possibly be used in weapons manufacture. Cleaning materials, such as chlorine, are 'dual use', as is the graphite used in pencils; as are wheelbarrows, it seems, considering the frequency of their appearance on the list of 'holds'. As of October 2001, 1,010 contracts for humanitarian supplies, worth $3.85 billion, were 'on hold' by the Sanctions Committee. They included items related to food, health, water and sanitation, agriculture and education.

Most members of the Security Council want the sanctions eased considerably or lifted. The French have called them 'cruel, ineffective and dangerous'. However, American dominance of the Council is such that the US and British representatives on the Sanctions Committee alone veto and delay contracts. The British claim they hold up only 'one per cent' of humanitarian contracts. This is sophistry; by never objecting to American obstruction, they give it tacit support. Moreover, a veto or 'hold' can only be rescinded by the Council member who orders it.

So blatant is the obstruction that Kofi Annan, the UN Secretary-General virtually appointed by the Americans, complained that the delays and vetoes were 'seriously impairing the effective implementation of the [Oil for Food] programme'. He urged the approval of water, sanitation and electricity contracts 'without delay' because of 'their paramount importance to the welfare of the Iraqi people'. The Executive Director of the UN Office of the Iraq Programme,

Benon Sevan, has attacked the Council for holding up spares for Iraq's crumbling oil industry, warning that the less oil Iraq is able to pump, the less money will be available to buy food and medicine. In 1999, a senior Clinton administration official told the *Washington Post*, 'The longer we can fool around in the [Security] Council and keep things static, the better.'

In Britain, Customs and Excise have stopped parcels going to Iraqi relatives, containing children's clothes and toys. The chairman of the British Library, John Ashworth, wrote to Harry Cohen MP that, 'after consultation with the Foreign Office', it was decided that books could no longer be sent to Iraqi students. The British Library had already distinguished itself by informing a translator in Baghdad that it was not permitted to send him a copy of James Joyce's *Ulysses*. From the petty and craven to the farcical: an attempt to send documents to Iraq advising Iraqis on human rights and press freedom was blocked by the Department of Trade and Industry in London. The package, which also contained advice on family planning and Aids, was posted to Mosul University but was intercepted and returned to Article 19, the anti-censorship group.

When Denis Halliday was the senior United Nations official in Iraq, a display cabinet stood in the foyer of his office. It contained a bag of wheat, some congealed cooking oil, bars of soap and a few other household necessities. 'It was a pitiful sight,' he said, 'and it represented the monthly ration that we were allowed to spend. I added cheese to lift the protein content, but there was simply not enough money left over from the amount we were allowed to spend, which came from the revenue Iraq was allowed to make from its oil.' He describes food shipments as 'an exercise in duplicity'. A shipment that the Americans claim allows for 2,300 calories per person per day may well allow for only 2,000 calories, or fewer. 'What's missing,' he said, 'will be animal proteins, minerals and vitamins. As most Iraqis have no other source of income, food has become a medium of exchange; it gets sold for other necessities, further lowering the calorie intake. You also have to get clothes and shoes for your kids to go to school. You've then got malnourished mothers who cannot breastfeed, and they pick up bad water. What is needed is investment in water treatment and distribution, electric power production for food processing, storage and refrigeration, education and agriculture.'

His successor, Hans Von Sponeck, calculates that the Oil for Food Programme allows $100 for each person to live on for a year. This figure also has to help pay for the entire society's infrastructure and essential services, such as power and water. 'It is simply not possible to live on such an amount,' Von Sponeck told me. 'Set that pittance against the lack of clean water, the fact that electricity fails for up to twenty-two hours a day, and the majority of sick people cannot afford treatment, and the sheer trauma of trying to get from day to day, and you have a glimpse of the nightmare. And make no mistake, this is deliberate. I have not in the past wanted to use the word genocide, but now it is unavoidable.'

The cost in lives is staggering. A study by the United Nations Children's Fund, Unicef, found that between 1991 and 1998, there were 500,000 deaths above the anticipated rate among Iraqi children under five years of age. This, on average, is 5,200 preventable under-five deaths per month. Hans Von Sponeck said, 'Some 167 Iraqi children are dying every day.' Denis Halliday said, 'If you include adults, the figure is now almost certainly well over a million.'

In 1999, a humanitarian panel set up by the Security Council reported that Iraq had slipped from 'relative affluence' prior to 1991 into 'massive poverty'. The panel criticised the Oil for Food Programme as 'inadequate' to remedy a 'dire' humanitarian situation 'that cannot be overstated'. The panel's members took the remarkable step of attacking their sponsor, charging that 'the Iraqi people would not be undergoing such deprivations in the absence of the prolonged measures imposed by the Security Council'. Once again, children were found to be the main victims, with the infant mortality rate soaring from one of the lowest in the world in 1990 to the highest.

In a separate study, Richard Garfield, a renowned epidemiologist at Columbia University in New York, says that, in tripling since 1990, the death rate of children in Iraq is unique. 'There is almost no documented case,' he wrote, 'of rising mortality for children under five years in the modern world'. Extrapolating from these statistics, American researchers John Mueller and Karl Mueller conclude that 'economic sanctions have probably already taken the lives of more people in Iraq than have been killed by all weapons of mass destruction in history.'

In 1999, seventy members of the US Congress signed an unusually blunt letter to President Clinton, appealing to him to lift the embargo and end what they called 'infanticide masquerading as policy'. The Clinton administration had already given them their reply. In 1996, in an infamous interview on the American current affairs programme *60 Minutes*, Madeleine Albright, then US Ambassador to the United Nations, had been asked: 'We have heard that half a million children have died . . . is the price worth it?' Albright replied, 'I think this is a very hard choice, but the price—we think the price is worth it.'

My journey to Iraq was almost surreal. With Denis Halliday and my television colleagues Alan Lowery, Preston Clothier and Grant Roberts, I spent sixteen anxious hours on a road that is a ribbon of wreckage. Pieces of tyre drifted towards us, like giant black birds escaping the squalls of sand and dust. Beside the road lay two bodies. They were old men in suits, as if laid out for their funeral, their arms stiffly by their sides. A taxi rested upside-down. The men had been walking to the border, each with his meagre belongings, now scattered among the thornbushes. The taxi's brakes had apparently failed and it had cut them down. Local people came out of the dust and stood beside the bodies: for them, on this, the only road in and out of Iraq, it was a common sight.

The road from Amman in Jordan to Baghdad was never meant as an artery, yet it now carries most of Iraq's permissible trade and traffic to the outside world. Two narrow single lanes are dominated by oil tankers, moving in an endless convoy; cars and overladen buses and vans dart in and out in a *danse macabre*. The inevitable carnage provides a roadside tableau of burnt-out tankers, a bus crushed like a tin can, an official United Nations Mercedes on its side, its once-privileged occupants dead. Of course, brakes fail on rickety taxis everywhere, but the odds against survival here are greatly shortened. Parts for the older models are now non-existent, and drivers go through the night and day with little sleep. With the Iraqi dinar worth virtually nothing, they must go back and forth, from Baghdad to Amman, Amman to Baghdad, as frequently and as quickly as possible. And when they and their passengers are killed or maimed, they, too, become victims of the most ruthless economic embargo of modern times.

Baghdad was just visible beneath a white pall of pollution. Young arms reached up to the window of our van: a boy offering an over-ripe banana, a girl a single stem flower. Before 1990, begging was almost unknown and frowned upon. Baghdad today is an urban version of Rachel Carson's *Silent Spring*. The birds have gone as avenues of palms have died, in what was once the land of dates. The splashes of colour, on fruit stalls, are three-dimensional. A bunch of Dole bananas and a bag of apples from Beirut cost a teacher's salary for a month; only foreigners and the rich eat fruit.

The rich, the black marketeers, the regime's cronies and favoured supplicants, are not visible, except for an occasional tinted-glass late-model Mercedes navigating its way through the rustbuckets. Having been ordered to keep their heads down, the elite keep to their network of clubs and restaurants and well-stocked clinics, the presence of which make nonsense of claims in Washington and London that the sanctions are hurting the regime.

The Al Rasheed Hotel is where Saddam Hussein's people are glimpsed. Dark glasses, large dyed moustaches and spooks proliferate. You enter by way of an icon of dark Iraqi humour, crossing a large floor portrait, set in tiles, of George Bush Senior, a good likeness, and the words: 'George Bush is a war criminal'. The face is forever being polished. I met an assistant manager, who had been at the hotel since the 1980s and whose sardonic sense of western double standards was a treat. 'Ah, a journalist from Britain!' he said. 'Would you like to see where Mr Douglas Hurd stayed, and Mr David Melon [sic] and Mr Tony Newton, and all the other members of Mrs Thatcher's Government . . . These gentlemen were our friends, our *benefactors*.' He has a collection of the *Baghdad Observer* from 'the good old days'. Saddam Hussein is on the front page, where he always is. The only change in each photograph is that he is sitting on his white presidential couch with a different British government minister, who is smiling or wincing.

There is Douglas Hurd, in 1981, then a Foreign Office minister who came to sell Saddam Hussein a British Aerospace missile system and to 'celebrate' the anniversary of the coming to power of the Ba'ath (Redemption) Party, a largely CIA triumph in 1968 that extinguished all hope of a pluralistic Iraq and produced Saddam Hussein. There is Hurd twice: on the couch and on page two, bowing before the tyrant, the renowned interrogator and torturer of Qasr-al-Nihayyah, the 'palace of the end'. And there is the corpulent David Mellor, also a Foreign Office man, on the same white couch in 1988. While Mellor, or 'Mr Melon' as the assistant manager preferred, was being entertained, his host ordered the gassing of 5,000 Kurds in the town of Halabja, news of which the Foreign Office tried to suppress. And there is Tony Newton, Margaret Thatcher's Trade Secretary, who, within a month of the gassing of the Kurds, was on the same white couch offering Saddam £340 million of British taxpayers' money in export credits. And there he is again, three months later, back on the couch, celebrating the fact that Iraq was now Britain's third-largest market for machine tools, from which a range of weapons was forged. As the subsequent inquiry by Sir Richard Scott revealed, these celebrities of the *Baghdad Observer* knew they were dealing illegally with the tyrant. 'Please give Mr Melon my greetings,' said the assistant manager.

Read carefully, history will usually offer an explanation. A few miles from the Al Rasheed is a cemetery girded by iron railings, behind which lines of stone crosses are just visible through drifting skeins of dust and sand. This is the British Cemetery, where soldiers who fought the Turks near the end of the First World War are buried. 'Here have been recovered or interred,' says a plaque, 'the bodies of British officers and men who, after the fall of Kut, being prisoners in the hands of the Turks, perished . . . These are they who came out of great tribulation.' Private FR Reynolds of the Imperial Camel Corps was nineteen when he was killed on October 11, 1918. His cross has crumbled. Frederic Ivor Hesiger, Second Lieutenant Royal Field Artillery, was twenty when he was mortally wounded at the battle of Shatt-Eladhaim on April 30, 1917. Being the eldest son of the Third Baron Chelmsford, Viceroy of India, he has his own tomb, which weeds and vines have claimed. None of the inscriptions says: 'He died to secure a stupendous source of strategic power, and one of the greatest material prizes in world history'. That was how the US State Department in 1945 described the oilfields of the Middle East.

After oil was discovered in the late nineteenth century, the European powers lost no time in getting their hands on 'the greatest prize'. By 1918, they had seen off the Ottoman Turks and divided up their empire. Iraq and all the Arab lands became colonies, despite earlier promises of independence after the war. France kept Syria, Lebanon and northern Iraq; Britain seized Baghdad and Basra in the south. The long-suffering Kurds were kept in a separate region under the British; and when they rose up, Winston Churchill, the Colonial Secretary, mused: 'I do not understand this squeamishness about the use of gas. I am strongly in favour of using poisoned gas against uncivilised tribes.'

Having crowned a puppet Iraqi king, Faisal, the British set about destroying the independence movement by pulverising villages with artillery and bombing farmlands with phosphorus bombs and metal crowsfeet designed to maim livestock. Iraq, source of the world's highest-grade oil, remained a British colony in all but name until the Suez invasion in 1956.

Two years later, the Iraqi monarchy was overthrown by a nationalist, Abd al-Karim Kassem, who himself fell victim to an internecine struggle. The new regime called itself an 'Arab socialist union', and a measure of plurality included a decentralised administration and recognition of the Kurdish language and national identity. When the Iraq Petroleum Company, the foreign consortium that exploited Iraq's oil, was threatened with nationalisation in 1963, the new imperial power, the United States, engineered what the Central Intelligence Agency called its 'favourite coup'. 'We regarded it as a great victory,' said James Critchfield, then head of the CIA in the Middle East. The Secretary-General of the Ba'ath Party, Ali Saleh Sa'adi, concurred. 'We came to power on a CIA train,' he said, thereafter instigating a reign of terror that produced Saddam Hussein, who became the top man in 1979. He was America's man. 'Saddam has a great deal to thank the CIA for,' Said Aburish, his biographer, told me. 'He can thank them for bringing the Ba'ath Party to power, for helping him personally, for providing him with financial aid during the war with Iran, for protecting him against internal coups d'état. It's a continuing relationship from the early 1960s until now, and it's a love/hate relationship.'

So enduring was America's ardour, or rather its gratitude to Iraq for protecting its client Arab states from Iran's revolutionary virus, that Saddam Hussein was given everything he wanted, almost up to the day he invaded Kuwait in August 1990. When John Kelly, the US Assistant Secretary of State, visited Baghdad in 1989, he told him: 'You are a force for moderation in the region, and the United States wants to broaden her relationship with Iraq.' The 'force for moderation' had just claimed victory in a war against Iran, which resulted in more than a million casualties on both sides, dead and wounded. When human rights groups presented evidence that Saddam Hussein had used mustard gas and nerve gas against Iranian soldiers and Kurdish civilians, the State Department refused to condemn him. As Saddam Hussein was preparing his forces for the attack on his southern neighbour, a US Department of Energy official discovered that advanced nuclear reactors were being shipped to Iraq. When he alerted his superiors, he was moved to another job. 'We knew about their bomb programme,' said a former member of the Bush administration, 'but Saddam was our ally . . .'

In 1992, a Congressional inquiry found that President George Bush Senior and his top advisers had ordered a cover-up to conceal their secret support for Saddam Hussein and the illegal arms shipments being sent to him via third countries. Missile technology was shipped to South Africa and Chile and then 'on sold' to Iraq, while Commerce Department records were altered and deleted. (This mirrored the emerging scandal across the Atlantic, which saw British weapons technology being illegally shipped to Iraq, with Jordan listed on the 'end-user' certificates.) Within weeks of the Iraqi invasion of Kuwait, the CIA was still feeding copious intelligence to Baghdad. Congressman Henry Gonzalez, chairman of the House of Representatives banking committee, said, 'Bush and his advisers financed, equipped and succoured the monster they later set out to slay, and they were now burying the evidence.'

A 1994 Senate report documented the transfer to Iraq of the ingredients of biological weapons: botulism developed at a company in Maryland, licensed by the Commerce Department and approved by the State Department. Anthrax was also supplied by the Porton Down laboratories in Britain, a government establishment. A Congressional investigator said, 'It was all money, it was all greed. The US Government knew, the British Government knew. Did they care? No. It was a competition with the Germans. That's how the arms trade works.'

During the parallel Scott Inquiry in London into the arms-to-Iraq scandal, Tim Laxton, a City of London auditor, was brought in to examine the books of the British arms company Astra, which the Thatcher Government covertly and illegally used as a channel for arms to Iraq. Laxton was one of the few observers to sit through the entire inquiry. He believes that if Sir Richard Scott's brief had been open and unlimited, and Thatcher's senior aides and civil servants had been compelled to give evidence under oath, as well as numerous other vital witnesses who were not called, the outcome would have been very different from the temporary embarrassment meted out to a few ministers. 'Hundreds,' he said, 'would have faced criminal investigation, including top political figures, very senior civil servants from the Foreign Office, the Ministry of Defence, the Department of Trade . . . the top echelon of government.'

In the centre of Baghdad is a monolith that crowds the eye; it commemorates, or celebrates, the 1980–90 Iran–Iraq war, which Saddam Hussein started, urged on by the Americans who wanted him to destroy their new foe in the region, the Ayatollah Khomeini. Cast in a foundry in Basingstoke, its two huge forearms, reputedly modelled on Saddam Hussein's own, hold triumphant crossed sabres. Cars are allowed to drive over the helmets of dead Iranian soldiers embedded in the concourse. I cannot think of a sight anywhere in the world that better expresses the crime of sacrificial war and the business of making and selling armaments: America and Britain supplied both sides with weapons.

We stayed at the Hotel Palestine, a far cry from the Al Rasheed. The smell of petrol is constant; if you stay too long inside, you feel sick. With contracts for disinfectant 'on hold' in New York, petrol, more plentiful than water, has replaced it. In the lobby there is an Iraqi Airways office, which is open every day, with an employee sitting behind a desk, smiling and saying good morning to passing guests. She has no clients, because there is no Iraqi Airways, which died with sanctions. Two of the pilots are outside, waiting beside their empty taxis; others are sweeping the forecourt or selling used clothes.

In my room, the plaster crumbled every night and the water ran gravy brown. The one frayed towel was borne by the maid like an heirloom. When I asked for coffee to be brought up, the waiter hovered outside until I was finished; cups are at a premium. 'I am always sad,' he said matter-of-factly. In a month, he will have earned enough to pay for somebody to go to Amman to buy tablets for his brother's epilepsy.

A melancholia shrouds people. I felt it at Baghdad's evening auctions, where intimate possessions are sold in order to buy food and medicines. Television sets are common items up for sale. A woman with two infants watched their pushchairs go for pennies. A man who had collected doves since he was fifteen came with his last bird; the cage would go next. My film crew and I had come to pry, yet we were made welcome; or people merely deferred to our presence, as the downcast do. During three weeks in Iraq, only once was I the brunt of someone's anguish. 'Why are you killing the children?' shouted a man in the street. 'Why are you bombing us? What have we done to you?' Passers-by moved quickly to calm him; one of them placed an affectionate arm on his shoulder, another, a teacher, materialised at my side. 'We do not connect the people of Britain with the actions of the government,' he said, reassuringly. Those Muslims in Britain, terrified to leave their homes after the bombing of Afghanistan, have little of the personal security I felt in Iraq.

Through the glass doors of the offices of Unicef, the United Nations Children's Fund in Baghdad, you can read the following mission statement: 'Above all, survival, hope, development, respect, dignity, equality and justice for women and children.' Fortunately, the children in the street outside, with their pencil limbs and long thin faces, cannot read English, and perhaps cannot read at all. 'The change in such a short time is unparalleled, in my experience,' Dr Anupama

Rao Singh, Unicef's senior representative in Iraq, told me. 'In 1989, the literacy rate was more than 90 per cent; parents were fined for failing to send their children to school. The phenomenon of street children was unheard of. Iraq had reached a stage where the basic indicators we use to measure the overall wellbeing of human beings, including children, were some of the best in the world. Now it is among the bottom 20 per cent.'

Dr Singh, diminutive, grey-haired and, with her preciseness, sounding like the teacher she once was in India, has spent most of her working life with Unicef. Helping children is her vocation, but now, in charge of a humanitarian programme that can never succeed, she says, 'I am grieving.'

She took me to a typical primary school in Saddam City, where Baghdad's majority and poorest live. We approached along a flooded street, the city's drainage and water distribution system having collapsed since the Gulf War bombing. The headmaster, Ali Hassoon, guided us around the puddles of raw sewage in the playground and pointed to the high-water mark on the wall. 'In the winter it comes up to here. That's when we evacuate. We stay for as long as possible but, without desks, the children have to sit on bricks. I am worried about the buildings coming down.' As we talked, an air-raid siren sounded in the distance.

The school is on the edge of a vast industrial cemetery. The pumps in the sewage treatment plants and the reservoirs of potable water are silent, save for a few wheezing at a fraction of their capacity. Those that were not bombed have since disintegrated; spare parts from their British, French and German manufacturers are permanently 'on hold'. Before 1991, Baghdad's water was as safe as any in the developed world. Today, drawn untreated from the Tigris, it is lethal. Touching two brothers on the head, the headmaster said, 'These children are recovering from dysentery, but it will attack them again, and again, until they are too weak.' Dr Singh told me that, in 1990, an Iraqi child with dysentery, or other water-borne illness, stood a one-in-600 chance of dying; today, it is up to one in fifty.

Just before Christmas 1999, the Department of Trade and Industry in London restricted the export of vaccines meant to protect Iraqi children against diphtheria and yellow fever. Dr Kim Howells told Parliament why. His title of Parliamentary Under-Secretary of State for Competition and Consumer Affairs perfectly suited his Orwellian reply. The children's vaccines were, he said, 'capable of being used in weapons of mass destruction'.

'Much of the suffering is unseen,' said Dr Singh. 'There has been a 125 per cent increase in children seeking help for mental health problems. In a society that takes education very seriously, most homes have been denuded of the very basic stimulation materials, books and toys, because most families, in order to cope, have sold everything except the bare essentials. We have here a whole generation who have grown up with a sense of total isolation and a feeling of dependency, and the lack of hope. I often think of my own nieces and nephews, and I ask myself, "Would I accept this for my own family?" and, if I wouldn't, then it's unacceptable for the children of Iraq. This is not an empty emotion. It's a fundamental tenet of the [UN] Convention of the Rights of the Child: Article Two, the Principle of Non-Discrimination. It is simply their right not to lose out in terms of their life.'

American and British aircraft operate over Iraq in what their governments have unilaterally declared 'no fly zones'. This means that only they and their allies can fly there. The designated areas are in the north, around Mosul, to the border with Turkey, and from just south of Baghdad to the Kuwaiti border. The US and British governments insist the no fly zones are 'legal', claiming that they are part of, or supported by, the Security Council's Resolution 688.

There is a great deal of fog about this, the kind generated by the Foreign Office when its statements are challenged. There is no reference to no fly zones in Security Council resolutions, which suggests they have no basis in international law. To be sure about this, I went to Paris and asked Dr Boutros Boutros-Ghali, the Secretary-General of the UN in 1992, when the resolution was passed. 'The issue of no fly zones was not raised and therefore not debated: not a word,' he said. 'They offer no legitimacy to countries sending their aircraft to attack Iraq.'

'Does that mean they are illegal?' I asked.

'They are illegal,' he replied.

The scale of the bombing in the no fly zones is astonishing. During the eighteen months to January 14, 1999, American air force and naval aircraft flew 36,000 sorties over Iraq, including 24,000 combat missions. During 1999, American and British aircraft dropped more than 1,800 bombs and hit 450 targets. The cost to British tax-payers is more than £800 million. There is bombing almost every day: it is the longest Anglo-American aerial campaign since the Second World War; yet it is mostly ignored by the British and American media. In a rare acknowledgement, the *New York Times* reported, 'American warplanes have methodically and with virtually no public discussion been attacking Iraq . . . pilots have flown about two-thirds as many missions as Nato pilots flew over Yugoslavia in seventy-eight days of around-the-clock war there.'

The purpose of the no fly zones, according to the British and American governments, is to protect the Kurds in the north and the Shi'a in the south against Saddam Hussein's forces. The aircraft are performing a 'vital humanitarian task', says Tony Blair, that will give 'minority peoples the hope of freedom and the right to determine their own destinies'.

Blair's specious words are given the lie by a secret history. When Saddam Hussein was driven from Kuwait, in 1991, his generals were surprised to be told by the victors that they could keep their helicopter gunships. The British commander, General Sir Peter de la Billière, defended this decision with the following astonishing logic: 'The Iraqis were responsible for establishing law and order. You could not administer the country without using the helicopters.' Law and order? The same law and order that approved the gassing of 5,000 Kurds at Halabja? A clue was given in a chance remark by Prime Minister John Major. 'I don't recall,' said Major, 'asking the Kurds to mount this particular insurrection . . .'

Turkey is critical to the American 'world order'. Overseeing the oilfields of the Middle East and former Soviet Central Asia, it is a member of Nato and the recipient of billions of dollars' worth of American arms. It is where American and British fighter-bombers are based. A long-running insurrection by Turkish

Kurds, led by the Kurdish Workers' Party (PKK), is regarded by Washington as a threat to the 'stability' of Turkey's crypto-fascist regime. Following the Gulf War, the last thing the Americans wanted was tens of thousands of Iraqi Kurds arriving in Turkey as refugees and boosting the struggle of local Kurds against the regime in Ankara. Their anxieties were reflected in Security Council Resolution 688, which warned of a 'massive flow of refugees towards and across international frontiers . . . which threatens international peace and security in the region . . .'

What the refugees threatened was Turkey's capacity to continue to deny basic human rights to the Kurds within its borders. The northern no fly zone offered a solution. Since 1992, the zones have provided cover for Turkey's repeated invasions of Iraq. In 1995 and 1997, as many as 50,000 Turkish troops, backed by tanks, fighter-bombers and helicopter gunships, occupied swathes of the Kurds' 'safe haven', allegedly attacking PKK bases. In December 2000, they were back, terrorising Kurdish villages and murdering civilians. The US and Britain said nothing; the Security Council said nothing. Moreover, the British and Americans colluded in the invasions, suspending their flights to allow the Turks to get on with the killing. Virtually none of this was reported in the western media.

In March 2001, RAF pilots patrolling the northern no fly zone publicly protested for the first time about their role in the bombing of Iraq. Far from performing the 'vital humanitarian task' described by Tony Blair, they complained that they were frequently ordered to return to their Turkish base to allow the Turkish air force to bomb the Kurds in Iraq, the very people they were meant to be 'protecting'. Speaking on a non-attributable basis to Dr Eric Herring, the Iraqi sanctions specialist at Bristol University, they said that whenever the Turks wanted to bomb the Kurds in Iraq, the RAF aircraft were recalled to base and ground crews were told to switch off their radar so that the Turks' targets would not be visible. One British pilot reported seeing the devastation in Kurdish villages caused by the attacks when he resumed his patrol. 'They were very unhappy about what they had been ordered to do and what they had seen,' said Dr Herring, 'especially as there had been no official explanation.'

In October 2000, the *Washington Post* reported: 'On more than one occasion [US pilots who fly in tandem with the British] have received a radio message that "there is a TSM inbound": that is, a "Turkish Special Mission" heading into Iraq. Following standard orders, the Americans turned their planes around and flew back to Turkey. "You'd see Turkish F-14s and F-16s inbound, loaded to the gills with munitions," [pilot Mike Horn] said. "Then they'd come out half an hour later with their munitions expended." When the Americans flew back into Iraqi air space, he recalled, they would see "burning villages, lots of smoke and fire".'

During the Gulf War, President George Bush Senior called on 'the Iraqi military and the Iraqi people to take matters into their hands and force Saddam Hussein to step aside'. In March 1991, the majority Shi'a people in the south rallied to Bush's call and rose up. So successful were they, at first, that within two days Saddam Hussein's rule had collapsed across southern Iraq and the popular uprising had spread to the country's second city, Basra. A new start for the people of Iraq seemed close at hand. Then the tyrant's old paramour in Washington intervened just in time.

'The opposition,' Said Aburish told me, 'found themselves confronted with the United States helping Saddam Hussein against them. The Americans actually stopped rebels from reaching arms depots. They denied them shelter. They gave Saddam Hussein's Republican Guard safe passage through American lines in order to attack the rebels. They did everything except join the fight on his side.' In their book, *Out of the Ashes: the Resurrection of Saddam Hussein*, Andrew and Patrick Cockburn describe the anguish of one of the rebel leaders, a brigadier, who watched American helicopters circling overhead as Iraqi government helicopter crews poured kerosene on columns of fleeing refugees and set them alight with tracer fire. 'I saw with my own eyes the American planes flying over the helicopters,' he said. 'We were expecting them to help; now we could see them witnessing our demise . . . They were taking pictures and they knew exactly what was happening.' In Nasiriyah, American troops prevented the rebels from taking guns and ammunition from the army barracks. 'The Iraqis explained to the American commander who they were and why they were there,' wrote the Cockburns. 'It was not a warm reception . . . the US officer went away for ten minutes and then returned with the curious claim that he was out of touch with his headquarters. [He] curtly suggested that they try and find the French forces, eighty miles to the west.'

The rebels eventually found a French colonel, who wanted to help; but when he tried to set up a meeting with General Schwarzkopf, the American commander, he was told this was not possible. The revolt was doomed; crucial time had been lost. The first city to fall to Saddam Hussein was Basra. Tanks captured the main road and demolished the centres of resistance. 'It was a bad time,' said a doctor at the hospital. 'You could see dogs eating bodies in the streets.'

In the north, the Kurds, too, had risen up: the revolt John Major said he had 'never asked for'. Saddam Hussein's Republican Guards, who had been pointedly spared by Schwarzkopf, entered the Kurdish town of Sulaimaniya and extinguished the Kurdish resistance. Saddam Hussein had survived by a whisker; as his troops were celebrating their victory, their ammunition ran out. Five years later, when Saddam Hussein sent his tanks into another rebellious Kurdish town, Arbil, American aircraft circled the city for twenty minutes, then flew away. The CIA contingent among the Kurds managed to flee to safety, while ninety-six members of the CIA-funded Iraqi National Congress were rounded up and executed. According to Ahmed Chalabi of the INC, tacit American support for the regime was 'the most significant factor in the suppression of the uprising. They made it possible for Saddam to regroup his forces and launch a devastating counter-attack with massive firepower on the people.'

Why? What the Americans fear is that the Kurds might establish their own state, perhaps even socialist and democratic, and that the Shi'a might forge an 'Islamic alliance' with Iran. What they do not want is for them to 'take matters into their own hands'. The American television journalist Peter Jennings put it this way: 'The United States did not want Saddam Hussein to go, they just didn't want the Iraqi people to take over.' Brent Scowcroft, President Bush Senior's National Security Adviser, concurred. In 1997, he said: 'We clearly would have preferred a coup. There's no question about that.' The *New York Times* columnist Thomas Friedman, a guard dog of US foreign policy, was more to the point.

What Washington wants is 'an iron-fisted Iraqi junta', which would be 'the best of all worlds'. The clear conclusion is that they want another Saddam Hussein, rather like the one they had before 1991, who did as he was told.

'Perhaps the most repulsive thing about the whole policy,' wrote Eric Herring, 'is that US and British decision-makers have exploited popular humanitarian sentiment for the most cynical *realpolitik* reasons. They have no desire for the Shi'ite majority to take control or for the Kurds to gain independence. Their policy is to keep them strong enough to cause trouble for Saddam Hussein while ensuring that Saddam Hussein is strong enough to keep repressing them. This is a direct descendant of British imperial policy from the First World War onwards [and is about the control] of Iraqi oil . . . Divide and Rule was and is the policy.'

In 1999, the United States faced a 'genuine dilemma' in Iraq, reported the *Wall Street Journal*. 'After eight years of enforcing a no fly zone in northern [and southern] Iraq, few military targets remain. "We're down to the last outhouse," one US official protested. "There are still some things left, but not many." '

Part III

Beirut Summit Talk

Saddam Hussein

from *Saddam Hussein's address to Arab leaders,* 22nd April, 2002

In the name of God, Most Gracious, Most merciful,

Dear Arab brothers, Kings, Presidents, Emirs and officials, And through you, to our dear Arab people everywhere,

Assalamu Alaykum—Peace be upon you.

Once again, I bring to you my viewpoints and suggestions. I may be exasperating but my only excuse to you, after God, is that I am seeking what might please God and what might give us glory before our people and history. And make us gain the true respect of the nations and peoples of the world. At a time when our Palestinian brothers are being killed, our sacred places violated, our wealth being ransacked, or about to be, on a large scale, we must agree upon a plan of action with the help of God, to summon our will and faith.

I don't think that we need worry that the will of our people in all our countries is not behind us, thanks to God. This will was clearly seen throughout the current crisis by everybody, in officials, decision makers, and every single citizen.

Dear brothers,

Similar conditions have put our nation [the Arab Nation in general.-Ed.] in a difficult dilemma in past times, but our glorious nation had always proved to be equal to the challenge, and faced it in the name of God, and proved itself and gained victory over those who wanted to humiliate it, usurp its right in life in general, or its right to choose its way and aims that do not harm the principles of humanity at large, and its right to recover its rights from usurpers, so as to lead a free and decent life, after making due sacrifices by a unified and organized action that leads the nation to achieve certain aims on the basis of the good intentions and collective will of joint action. But when the nation ignores this and does not see the suitable moment for the right action, its fate will be not only humiliation but also a lot of bloodshed of its people. It will furthermore lose respect and will no longer be able to mount to higher milestones that may make it effective in life, and will not be able to protect its wealth, and values.

There is no doubt now that we are all facing, as leaders or peoples of the countries of our one Arab nation, such a choice. I think that if anyone of us deeply thinks of his surroundings, he will find himself before this choice.

I must now ask you, dear brothers: shall we choose the right aims and methods, and succeed in distributing duties among us in a spirit of collective and brotherly leadership as faithful sons of our nation? Or shall we miss the chance and leave the initiative in the hand of the enemies of our nation, who are the enemies of God and humanity, and the allies of Satan? If we do so, each and everyone of us will live in disgrace before God, himself, his nation and this generation of which we must be proud for having demonstrated the highest level of awareness, faith and readiness to make sacrifices, in a way that no one can miss or not recognize.

What I wish for you and for myself dear brothers, is that we make our choice without hesitation, get together and not separate, work and not be lazy, and prepare ourselves together for the way we choose and not to allow our enemy and his evil choices to succeed and defeat us, after subjecting us to a bitter fait-accompli that no one could accept, since we all by the grace of God, will work to please God and our nation, and to defeat evil and evil doers.

Brothers,

Our history, like the history of other nations and peoples, tells us that one of the most important weak points in which the vicious enemy finds a breach by which he can kill that nation, is the separation between the ruler and his people, or the separation or disagreement between rulers in the same nation and people, so that each acts on his own.

Hence, the greedy foreign enemies resort to enhance and create fear to trouble and frighten the ruler from his own people. They make every ruler afraid of other rulers, or they make him believe that he is their preferred ruler in his nation.

Most of you are military men, or at least have a certain knowledge and experience in this domain, this is why I say: just as armies try in the battlefield to separate the infantry from the armored forces and the frontline forces from the others in order to weaken their performance and consequently easily defeat them, in a similar manner, those who want to exploit us, resort to making the rulers afraid of their people, or making them seem weak in the eyes of their people in order to weaken both sides or anyone of them. The weakness of anyone of them would result in the weakness of both of them.

Furthermore, the enemy, tries to make anyone of us as regimes or individuals, according to our responsibilities, believe that this or that act, this collective Arab action or that, and this idea and suggestion or that, in fact serve the interests of this or that party alone, or distinguishes this or that ruler or leader at the expense of the others. The same plots and schemes are made by the enemy with the people of our countries and even at the level of the entire nation, using the same methods for the same purposes, by suggesting to this or that political party or trade union and federation when they try to organize a joint work, that this or that joint action or decision would only be in the benefit of this or that side, at the expense of this or that organization.

This discourages and weakens their common will for collective action.

We have reached such a point: our greedy enemy is preparing the psychological, political and intellectual arena to further weaken the nation and achieve his aims by division or at least by the absence of the unity of opinion, aims, stands and necessary action. The enemy is furthermore exploiting the fact that our nation consists of more than twenty countries, to say or make believe that this or that idea, opinion, suggestion, plan or goal is only meant to serve this or that Arab country at that expense of this or that country. They do this in order to enhance doubts, fears or the unoriginal tendency of those whose hearts and minds may weakly respond to the values and principles of our being one nation, or might misinterpret or not see the real motives of this or that foreigner who wants to exploit us.

Moreover, the enemy is encouraging and creating feelings of jealousy and envy among our nation of even the natural resources in some of our countries.

In order to diminish the feeling that any natural resource or wealth, or the number of the population, are, in fact, elements of strength for the entire Arab nation, and not a negative factor, that must be used in favor of the nation not against it.

In addition to that, the foreigners are encouraging some people to think that the steadfastness of any Arab country, regime or ruler, or even of any mujahid who stands against the foreigner's greed, is a stand that would lead to a weakening of the other Arab countries, rather than as something that should strengthen and encourage them to face the enemy. The enemy is even presenting weakness as an equivalent to wisdom and reason, and presenting the option of thwarting his vicious needs as an equivalent of foolishness and impatience. He is even endeavoring and hoping to transfer the conflict between the rulers on the one hand and the people on the other, to something that would prevent the rulers from undertaking their basic duties.

Dear brothers, we are the people of one nation, and this is a great honor for which we must thank God. But, at the same time, this identity represents a great responsibility, if we carry it with honor and enthusiasm; but it would become a heavy burden if we fell in contradiction of it or if we parted from it in mind and in action. We must uphold our right to belong to the Glorious Qura'an, of historical glories, of the cradle of Heavenly religion, Prophets and Messengers, and the land of the banner and the sword of justice that has honored our nation and humanity at large.

Brothers, the people, every country of our nation, have said their word about what is going on around them, and about what they want loudly and clearly. They favor a strong action in favor of our nation, its higher interests, and national security. This should not be considered a burden and a weight on us. The conditions prevailing in the world today are not the same conditions in which our people in their countries fought to free themselves of the old colonialism. Nevertheless, even in those conditions, was there any country, big or small, that did not take strength from the very name of the Arab nation, and remind its people of the fact that they belonged to this nation? Is their anyone who has not turned to the nation's potential, in part or in whole, against foreign occupation forces, for liberation, or in the wars against them?

In any case if we cannot encourage, we should not be inconvenienced by the initiative of the people doing what they believe would harm our enemy. For example, trade and professional unions and federations can do much to harm the enemy including calling for a strike of the workers of oil exporting ports or oil tankers with contracts with the country meant to be harmed, the loading and unloading workers of cargo ships of a certain country, the staff and workers of railways, ports, airports, external communication, etc.There are other such examples, as you know. In fact, trade unions and federations used to do something of that, but now they have become used to weighting their words and sentences by the balance of their ministries of foreign affairs . . .

The presence of a stronger opinion, that is expressed in a direct way in a different style and language of that of the concerned diplomats, is useful to the governments and their policies in a conflict like this.

When diplomacy fails, other means and capabilities begin their role of action, which may last.

Zionism, the American administrations, and any who has or will become their allies, have prepared themselves to confront the Arab nation, including Palestine as one nation. So it is our duty, by the rule of our doctrine (to avoid saying by the rule of the Sharia and of integrity), to prepare ourselves on this basis: we are guided by the rule of history and destiny. We are bound by duty to stand together with the guidance of God the merciful. Zionism has the upper hand over the American administrations to use them against us, and it becomes one and the same with us, against our nation, as we have repeatedly said, to facilitate the realization of the Zionists' covetous schemes in our Arab nation. Therefore, it is our duty to stand together, to mobilize our utmost forces in all fields, and not to hope for anything good for our nation and Arab security from the US. For the American administration will walk as they walk now up to their knees in Arab and Muslim blood. We must all believe that no one can defeat our nation by injustice since it is justly on its own land. Our nation would only be defeated if it abandons its distinctive attributes, and duties, and if its guides go to sleep. Our people are awake, dear brothers, so it is our patriotic, national, moral, Arab, faithful, and constitutional duty that is calling us in our capacity of rulers not to go to sleep, nor to be inadvertent or weaken. Anyone who does not follow this in his attitude with his nation, will lose himself and lose his way. Even when the people find that they have to change anyone of us if they get angry, it would be a loss had he taken the right path. And I do not think that anyone of us, including the writer of this letter, would choose this fate or accept it for himself.

The strength of the nation is a living part of its capability to defend its national security from any threats. The wealth of the nation is part of its strength and effective means. Other nations have used it throughout history, and they may have even used what is contradictory to the law they put in the UN documents, as did the US in particular with cereal contracts. You probably remember its policy against Egypt, how it cancelled the cereal contract which it had signed with Iraq in Feb. 1990, and how it used this against the ex-Soviet Union and is using it against Russia now. You may also know that the US with the support of the UK has hindered medicine contracts for the Iraqi people despite the fact that their prices had already been paid long before August 1990. They have stopped all the other means of life for the Iraqi people in order to kill them and decrease the number of the population. The US and UK do all these things although their national security is not threatened by our countries. If it is security for themselves and for the world that they want, they will get it by respecting other peoples, their land, national and Arab choices, their choice of doctrine, beliefs and values.

I am not ignoring the comments made by some of my brothers in oil producing countries; that oil is not a weapon, it is not a cannon, a tank, or a jet fighter. I say: Yes, oil is not a tank, a jet fighter or a cannon, but it can be used as a weapon, when the muzzles of the cannons, tanks and jet fighters are not working, or are not meant to be used. As for saying: we cannot, or we are not ready to use the weapon for those who have no weapons, and that oil is not a cannon, a tank or a jet fighter for those who have oil, then what would, and by what can we confront those who want to exploit us, the aggressors, and the usurpers?

On this occasion, I would like remind my brothers of some of their fathers' and grandfathers' values when they confronted any aggression. Every man would go out to face the enemy even if the battle was at its fiercest stage, or if the aggressor had launched the attack with rifles, cannons, and jet fighters. It would be disgraceful for any man not to go out to the battlefield even if he had nothing but an axe, a dagger, or club, otherwise the law (of who does not have a weapon equal to the weapon of the aggressor or the usurper, must surrender to those who have better weapons) would be applied.

If anyone was late or stayed behind, he would be called names that I do not think that anyone of us would accept for himself. He would even be forbidden to sit on the chairs of men in gatherings and meetings and no one would serve him coffee. The history of our nation is full of such examples, whether in the wars and struggles for independence or in the annals of conflicts between fighting tribes.

Now, haven't the Palestinians faced the bombs, jet fighters, cannons, missiles and rifles? What would be said of the attitude of Palestinians had they not confronted the aggressors in this way?! Haven't the Zionists used even water and food when they besieged the Palestinians, especially in heroic Jenin? Did they use water and food as a weapon in the battle against those heroes?

The history of the wars between polytheists and the Muslims under the leadership of the Prophet (Praise Be Upon Him) is full of such lessons. When the conflict begins each party tries to overcome the will of the other, or to subject it to his own will. Hence, the one who is defending his will from being subjected, and his sanctities and land from being violated and humiliated, must use his weapons in harmonized succession, each in its own field, so that he can defeat the will of his enemy, or to stop it from defeating his will and humiliating him. Therefore, oil should be used as a weapon that will come in succession in the battle, and not as an absolute alternative weapon. As for the question: what weapon do we begin with? Well, let's begin brothers . . . we did not suggest the weapon of oil until we were aware that our Arab brothers were not ready to use the other weapons, and so that no one could say that we have a weapon, the use of which does not require any bloodshed, or that we have not used the oil weapon, so let's try it, before resorting to other weapons.

At any rate, any weapon that restores our rights, and is more effective compared to another weapon, is something we wish for, and are ready to try. If you want to use the weapons of our armies to be succeeded by the oil, we are with our armies, oil and people, ready to do so, along with whomever is ready to so, although we would prefer that we all should share this honor.

Brothers,

I must also say, that I have not read or heard of anyone ever saying to their enemy that they would not use their weapons against him, despite his aggression on them. Wouldn't this encourage the enemy to speed up his aggression? Or to continue it to accomplish all their goals without paying any price?

In this case, don't the Arabs have the right to use the elements of their strength to defend their lives, sovereignty, honor, and beliefs? Neutralizing the elements of our strength leaves our weakness breaches without protection. Therefore, neutralizing our oil, which is one of the elements of our economic strength, means that we are strengthening our enemy over ourselves and enabling him to overcome us.

For these reasons, I see that:

1. Arabs should express their solidarity with their brothers' security and safety, and the oil exporters, including Iraq, immediately decrease the production of their oil for exportation by 50% and directly deprive the US and the Zionist entity from the other exported half and to threaten any country or company with the same measure if they export the oil they import from Arab countries. We should thus be strongly ringing the bells of protest and solidarity, so that those who harm and kill our people can see and hear. We will thus embarrass the American Administration before its people, and make them hear the voice of Arab with a respect that is equal to their obedient or humiliating submission to the Zionist Lobby and its evil aims. This measure should be immediately effective, once agreed upon, until further notice, and until the nation's demands in solidarity with the rights of the heroic people of Palestine are met, without any bargaining or procrastination. The Arabs

should take a collective attitude, and if anyone of them deviated, God forbid, he would be described and treated by the Arab nation as if he had abandoned his duties regarding his nation and its national security. This attitude should be publicly unveiled before the people of the concerned country. In this way, we can save the Arab nation, and provide the Palestinian people with the support by other measures funded by the increase in the prices of oil after stopping its exportation.

2. To allocate a quota of the exported oil proportional to the stand taken by the countries that express understanding of or support for Arab rights. By contrast, the quota will be decreased according to the stands of the countries, which condemn us. In this respect, special attention should be given to the members of the Security Council, especially the permanent members.

3. The Arab countries should work in solidarity with Islamic oil producing countries to take the same measures as Arabs as mentioned in paras. 1 and 2, above.

4. The Arab countries should work together, represented by oil producing countries that are members of OPEC, with the support of Muslim members, to have the OPEC adopt a resolution of full solidarity with this and the measures afore mentioned.

5. A council of a number, that will be agreed upon, of Arab ministers of Oil and Foreign Affairs, or of the minister of Oil and Foreign Affairs of oil producing countries, should be appointed to follow up the details of paras. 2,3,4. The Arab Summit should be in a position that enables it to convene urgent meetings, whenever necessary, according to a number of Presidents and Kings who will be nominated by the Summit.

6. The Arab nation should be prepared from every side to confront any reaction or aggression, in solidarity and as one nation, with the faith that the foreigner cannot force us to do anything we collectively refuse, and that if the foreigner tries anything against the weakest country among us, this country will be stronger that all the force of the foreigner, when it is in bosom of its Nation, under its banner and the protection of its sword, and the solidarity of its people.

Saying this, I pray to God to guide us together in implementing it, or in any other opinion you deem is a better one, if it is capable of stopping the wrong-doers' aggression on our nation, at the forefront of which are the people of Palestine, and to restore the usurped rights of our nation, at the forefront of which is Palestine.

* God is Great. . . . Alahuakbar. . . .
Long live our glorious nation.
God is Great. . . . Alahuakbar. . . .
Long live Palestine from the sea to the river,
God is Great. . . . Alahuakbar . . .

Let Zionism be despised along with its aggressive criminal and damned entity of occupation, and led its counterpart in evil doing; American policies and their representatives, be despised.

Rogue States

Noam Chomsky

from *Rogue States: The Rule of Force in World Affairs*

The concept of "rogue state" plays a preeminent role today in policy planning and analysis. The April 1998 Iraq crisis is only one of the most recent examples. Washington and London have declared Iraq a "rogue state," a threat to its neighbors and to the entire world, an "outlaw nation" led by a reincarnation of Hitler who must be contained by the guardians of world order, the United States and its "junior partner," to adopt the term ruefully employed by the British foreign office half a century ago.[1]

The concept merits a close look. But first, let's consider its application in the current crisis.

The Iraq Crisis

The most interesting feature of the debate over the Iraq crisis is that it never took place. True, many words flowed, and there was dispute about how to proceed. But discussion kept within rigid bounds that excluded the obvious answer: the US and UK should act in accord with their laws and treaty obligations.

The relevant legal framework is formulated in the Charter of the United Nations, a "solemn treaty" recognized as the foundation of international law and world order, and under the US Constitution, "the supreme law of the land."

The Charter states that "the Security Council shall determine the existence of any threat to the peace, breach of the peace, or act of aggression, and shall make recommendations, or decide what measures shall be taken in accordance with Articles 41 and 42," which detail the preferred "measures not involving the use of armed force" and permit the Security Council to take further action if it finds such measures inadequate. The only exception is Article 51, which permits the "right of individual or collective self-defense" against "armed attack . . . until the Security Council has taken the measures necessary to maintain international peace and security." Apart from these exceptions, member states "shall refrain in their international relations from the threat or use of force."

There are legitimate ways to react to the many threats to world peace. If Iraq's neighbors feel threatened, they can approach the Security Council to authorize appropriate measures to respond to the threat. If the US and Britain feel threatened, they can do the same. But no state has the authority to make its own determinations on these matters and to act as it chooses; the US and UK would have no such authority even if their own hands were clean—hardly the case.

Outlaw states do not accept these conditions: Saddam's Iraq, for example, or the United States. The US position was forthrightly articulated by Secretary of State Madeleine Albright, then UN ambassador, when she informed the Security Council during an earlier US confrontation with Iraq that the US will act "multilaterally when we can, and unilaterally as we must," because "we recognize this area as vital to US national interests" and therefore accept no external constraints. Albright reiterated that stand when UN Secretary-General Kofi Annan undertook his February 1998 diplomatic mission: "We wish him well," she stated, "and when he comes back we will see what he has brought and how it fits with our national interest," which will determine how we respond. When Annan announced that an agreement had been reached, Albright repeated the doctrine: "It is possible that he will come with something we don't like, in which case we will pursue our national interest." President Clinton announced that if Iraq failed the test of conformity (as determined by Washington), "everyone would understand that then the United States and hopefully all of our allies would have the unilateral right to respond at a time, place, and manner of our own choosing," in the manner of other violent and lawless states.[2]

The Security Council unanimously endorsed Annan's agreement, rejecting US/UK demands that it authorize their use of force in the event of non-compliance. The resolution warned of "severest consequences," but with no further specification. In the crucial final paragraph, the Council "decides, in accordance with its responsibilities under the Charter, to remain actively seized of the matter, in order to ensure implementation of this resolution and to ensure peace and security in the area"—the Council, no one else; in accordance with the Charter.

The facts were clear and unambiguous. Headlines read: "An Automatic Strike Isn't Endorsed" (*Wall Street Journal*), "UN Rebuffs US on Threat to Iraq If It Breaks Pact" (*New York Times*), etc. Britain's UN ambassador "privately assured his colleagues on the Council that the resolution does not grant the United States and Britain an 'automatic trigger' to launch strikes against Iraq if it impedes" UN searches for chemical weapons. "It has to be the Security Council who determines when to use armed force," the ambassador of Costa Rica declared, expressing the position of the Security Council.

Washington's reaction was different. US Ambassador Bill Richardson asserted that the agreement "did not preclude the unilateral use of force" and that the US retains its legal right to attack Baghdad at will. State Department spokesperson James Rubin dismissed the wording of the resolution as "not as relevant as the kind of private discussions that we've had": "I am not saying that we don't care about that resolution," but "we've made clear that we don't see the need to return to the Security Council if there is a violation of the agreement." The president stated that the resolution "provides authority to act" if the US is dissatisfied with Iraqi compliance; his press secretary made clear that that means military action. "US Insists It Retains Right to Punish Iraq," the *New York Times* headline read, accurately. The US has the unilateral right to use force at will. Period.

Some felt that even this stand strayed too close to our solemn obligations under international and domestic law. Senate majority leader Trent Lott denounced the administration for having "subcontracted" its foreign policy "to others"—to the UN Security Council. Senator John McCain warned that "the United States may be subordinating its power to the United Nations," an obligation only for law-abiding states. Senator John Kerry added that it would be "legitimate" for the US to invade Iraq outright if Saddam "remains obdurate and in violation of the United Nations resolutions, and in a position of threat to the world community," whether the Security Council so determines or not. Such unilateral US action would be "within the framework of international law," as Kerry conceives it. A liberal dove who reached national prominence as an opponent of the Vietnam War, Kerry explained that his current stand was consistent with his earlier views. Vietnam taught him that force should be used only if the objective is "achievable and it meets the needs of your country." Saddam's invasion of Kuwait was therefore wrong for only one reason: it was not "achievable," as matters turned out.[3]

At the liberal-dovish end of the spectrum, Annan's agreement was welcomed, but within the narrow framework that barred the central issues. In a typical reaction, the *Boston Globe* stated that had Saddam not backed down, "the United States would not only have been justified in attacking Iraq—it would have been irresponsible not to," with no further questions asked. The editors also called for "a universal consensus of opprobrium" against "weapons of mass destruction" as "the best chance the world has of keeping perverted science from inflicting hitherto unimagined harm." A sensible proposal; one can think of easy ways to start, without the threat of force, but these are not what are intended.

Political analyst William Pfaff deplored Washington's unwillingness to consult "theological or philosophical opinion" (the views of Thomas Aquinas and Renaissance theologian Francisco Suarez), as "a part of the analytical community" in the US and UK had done "during the 1950s and 1960s," but not the foundations of contemporary international and domestic law, which are clear and explicit, though irrelevant to the intellectual culture. Another liberal analyst urged the US to face the fact that if its incomparable power "is really being exercised for mankind's sake, mankind demands some say in its use," which would not be permitted by "the Constitution, the Congress, nor television's Sunday pundits"; "the other nations of the world have not assigned Washington the right to decide when, where, and how their interests should be served" (Ronald Steel).

The Constitution does happen to provide such mechanisms, namely, by declaring valid treaties "the supreme law of the land," particularly the most fundamental of them, the UN Charter. It further authorizes Congress to "define and punish . . . offenses against the law of nations," undergirded by the Charter in the contemporary era. It is, furthermore, a bit of an understatement to say that other nations "have not assigned Washington the right"; they have forcefully denied it that right, following the (at least rhetorical) lead of Washington, which largely crafted the Charter.[4]

Reference to Iraq's violation of UN resolutions was regularly taken to imply that the two warrior states have the right to use force unilaterally, taking the role of "world policemen"—an insult to the police, who in principle are supposed to enforce the law, not tear it to shreds. There was criticism of Washington's "arrogance of power" and the like—not quite the proper terms for a self-designated violent outlaw state.

One might contrive a tortured legal argument to support US/UK claims, though no one has really tried. Step One would be that Iraq has violated UN Resolution 687 of April 3, 1991, which declares a cease-fire "upon official notification by Iraq" that it accepts the provisions that are spelled out (destruction of weapons, inspection, etc.). This is probably the longest and most detailed Security Council resolution on record, but it mentions no enforcement mechanism. Step Two of the argument, then, would be that Iraq's non-compliance "reinvokes" Resolution 678.[5] That resolution authorizes member states "to use all necessary means to uphold and implement Resolution 660,"[6] which calls on Iraq to withdraw at once from Kuwait and for Iraq and Kuwait "to begin immediately intensive negotiations for the resolution of their differences," recommending the framework of the Arab League. Resolution 678 also invokes "all subsequent relevant resolutions" (listing them: 662, 664); these are "relevant" in that they refer to the occupation of Kuwait and Iraqi actions relating to it. Reinvoking 678 thus leaves matters as they were: with no authorization to use force to implement the later Resolution 687, which brings up completely different issues, authorizing nothing beyond sanctions.

There is no need to debate the matter. The US and UK could readily have settled all doubts by calling on the Security Council to authorize their "threat and use of force," as required by the Charter. Britain did take some steps in that direction, but abandoned them when it became obvious, at once, that the Security Council would not go along. Blair's initiative, quickly withdrawn, was a "mistake" because it "weakened the Anglo-American position," a *Financial Times* editorial concluded.[7] But these considerations have little relevance in a world dominated by rogue states that reject the rule of law.

Suppose that the Security Council were to authorize the use of force to punish Iraq for violating the cease-fire resolution (UN 687). That authorization would apply to *all* states: for example, to Iran, which would therefore be entitled to invade southern Iraq to sponsor a rebellion. Iran is a neighbor and the victim of US-backed Iraqi aggression and chemical warfare, and could claim, not implausibly, that its invasion would have some local support; the US and UK can make no such claim. Such Iranian actions, if imaginable, would never be tolerated, but would be far less outrageous than the plans of the self-appointed enforcers. It is hard to imagine such elementary observations entering public discussion in the US and UK.

Open Contempt

Contempt for the rule of law is deeply rooted in US practice and intellectual culture. Recall, for example, the reaction to the judgment of the World Court in 1986 condemning the US for "unlawful use of force" against Nicaragua, demanding that it desist and pay extensive reparations, and declaring all US aid to the contras, whatever its character, to be "military aid," not "humanitarian aid." The Court was denounced on all sides for having discredited itself. The terms of the judgment were not considered fit to print, and were ignored.

The Democrat-controlled Congress immediately authorized new funds to step up the unlawful use of force. Washington vetoed a Security Council resolution calling on all states to respect international law—not mentioning anyone, though the intent was clear. When the General Assembly passed a similar resolution, the US voted against it, joined only by Israel and El Salvador, effectively vetoing it; the following year, only the automatic Israeli vote could be garnered. Little of this, let alone what it signifies, received mention in the media or journals of opinion.

Secretary of State George Shultz meanwhile explained that "negotiations are a euphemism for capitulation if the shadow of power is not cast across the bargaining table."[8] He condemned those who advocate "utopian, legalistic means like outside mediation, the United Nations, and the World Court, while ignoring the power element of the equation"—sentiments not without precedent in modern history.[9]

The open contempt for Article 51 is particularly revealing. It was demonstrated with remarkable clarity immediately after the 1954 Geneva accords on a peaceful settlement for Indochina, regarded as a "disaster" by Washington, which moved at once to undermine them. The National Security Council secretly decreed that even in the case of "local Communist subversion or rebellion *not constituting armed attack,*" the US would consider the use of military force, including an attack on China if it is "determined to be the source" of the "subversion."[10] The wording, repeated verbatim annually in planning documents, was chosen so as to make explicit the US right to violate Article 51. The same document called for remilitarizing Japan, converting Thailand into "the focal point of US covert and psychological operations in Southeast Asia," undertaking "covert operations on a large and effective scale" throughout Indochina, and in general, acting forcefully to undermine the accords and the UN Charter. This critically important document was grossly falsified by the Pentagon Papers historians, and has largely disappeared from history.

The US proceeded to define "aggression" to include "political warfare, or subversion" (by someone else, that is)—what Adlai Stevenson called "internal aggression" while defending JFK's escalation to a full-scale attack against South Vietnam. When the US bombed Libyan cities in 1986, the official justification was "self-defense against future attack." *New York Times* legal specialist Anthony Lewis praised the administration for relying "on a legal argument that violence [in this case] is justified as an act of self-defense" under this creative interpretation of Article 51 of the Charter, which would have embarrassed a literate high school student. The US invasion of Panama was defended in the Security Council by Ambassador Thomas Pickering by appeal to Article 51, which, he declared, "provides for the use of armed force to defend a country, to defend our interests and our people," and entitles the US to invade Panama to prevent its "territory from being used as a base for smuggling drugs into the United States." Educated opinion nodded sagely in assent.

In June 1993, Clinton ordered a missile attack on Iraq, killing civilians and greatly cheering the president, congressional doves, and the press, who found the attack "appropriate, reasonable, and necessary." Commentators were particularly impressed by Ambassador Albright's appeal to Article 51. The bombing, she explained, was in "self-defense against armed attack"—namely, an alleged attempt to assassinate former president Bush two months earlier, an appeal that would have scarcely risen to the level of absurdity even if the US had been able to demonstrate Iraqi involvement; "administration officials, speaking anonymously," informed the press "that the judgment of Iraq's guilt was based on circumstantial evidence and analysis rather than ironclad intelligence," the *New York Times* reported, dismissing the matter. The press assured elite opinion that the circumstances "plainly fit" Article 51 (*Washington Post*). "Any president has a duty to use military force to protect the nation's interests" (New York Times, while expressing some skepticism about the case in hand). "Diplomatically, this was the proper rationale to invoke," and "Clinton's reference to the UN Charter conveyed an American desire to respect international law" (*Boston Globe*). Article 51 "permits states to respond militarily if they are threatened by a hostile power" (*Christian Science Monitor*). Article 51 entitles a state to use force "in self-defense against threats to one's nationals," British Foreign Secretary Douglas Hurd instructed Parliament, supporting Clinton's "justified and proportionate exercise of the right of self-defense." There would be a "dangerous state of paralysis" in the world, Hurd continued, if the US were required to gain Security Council approval before launching missiles against an enemy that might—or might not—have ordered a failed attempt to kill an ex-president two months earlier.[11]

The record lends considerable support to the concern widely voiced about "rogue states" that are dedicated to the rule of force, acting in the "national interest" as defined by domestic power—most ominously, rogue states that anoint themselves global judge and executioner.

Rogue States: The Narrow Construction

It is also interesting to review the issues that did enter the non-debate on the Iraq crisis. But first a word about the concept "rogue state."

The basic conception is that although the Cold War is over, the US still has the responsibility to protect the world—but from what? Plainly it cannot be from the threat of "radical nationalism"—that is, unwillingness to submit to the will of the powerful. Such ideas are fit only for internal planning documents, not the general public. From the early 1980s, it was clear that the conventional techniques for mass mobilization—the appeal to JFK's "monolithic and ruthless conspiracy," Reagan's "evil empire"—were losing their effectiveness: New enemies were needed.

At home, fear of crime—particularly drugs—was stimulated by "a variety of factors that have little or nothing to do with crime itself," the National Criminal Justice Commission concluded, including media practices and "the role of government and private industry in stoking citizen fear" "exploiting latent racial tension for political purposes" with racial bias in enforcement and sentencing that is devastating black communities, creating a "racial abyss," and putting "the nation at risk of a social catastrophe." The results have been described by criminologists as "the American Gulag" "the new American Apartheid" with African Americans now a majority of prisoners for the first time in US history, imprisoned at well over seven times the rate of whites, completely out of the range of arrest rates, which themselves target blacks far out of proportion to drug use or trafficking.[12]

Abroad, the threats were to be "international terrorism" "Hispanic narcotraffickers" and most serious of all, "rogue states." A secret 1995 study of the Strategic Command, which is responsible for the strategic nuclear arsenal, outlines the basic thinking. Released through the Freedom of Information Act, the study, *Essentials of Post-Cold War Deterrence,* "shows how the United States shifted its deterrent strategy from the defunct Soviet Union to so-called rogue states such as Iraq, Libya, Cuba, and North Korea," the Associated Press reports. The study advocates that the US exploit its nuclear arsenal to portray itself as "irrational and vindictive if its vital interests are attacked." That "should be a part of the national persona we project to all adversaries," in particular the "rogue states." "It hurts to portray ourselves as too fully rational and cool-headed," let alone committed to such silliness as international law and treaty obligations. "The fact that some elements" of the US government "may appear to be potentially 'out of control' can be beneficial to creating and reinforcing fears and doubts within the minds of an adversary's decision-makers." The report resurrects Nixon's "madman theory": our enemies should recognize that we are crazed and unpredictable, with extraordinary destructive force at our command, so they will bend to our will in fear. The concept was apparently devised in Israel in the 1950s by the governing Labor Party, whose leaders "preached in favor of acts of madness," Prime Minister Moshe Sharett records in his diary, warning that "we will go crazy" ("*nishtagea*") if crossed, a "secret weapon" aimed in part against the US, not considered sufficiently reliable at the time. In the hands of the world's sole superpower, which regards itself as an outlaw state and is subject to few constraints from elites within, that stance poses no small problem for the world.[13]

Libya was a favorite choice as "rogue state" from the earliest days of the Reagan administration. Vulnerable and defenseless, it is a perfect punching bag when needed: for example, in 1986, when the first bombing in history orchestrated for prime-time TV was used by the Great Communicator's speechwriters to muster support for Washington's terrorist forces attacking Nicaragua, on grounds that the "archterrorist" Qaddafi "has sent $400 million and an arsenal of weapons and advisors into Nicaragua to bring his war home to the United States," which was then exercising its right of self-defense against the armed attack of the Nicaraguan rogue state.

Immediately after the Berlin Wall fell, ending any resort to the Soviet threat, the Bush administration submitted its annual call to Congress for a huge Pentagon budget. It explained that "in a new era, we foresee that our military power will remain an essential underpinning of the global balance, but . . . the more likely demands for the use of our military forces may not involve the Soviet Union and may be in the Third World, where new capabilities and approaches may be required," as "when President Reagan directed American naval and air forces to return to [Libya] in 1986" to bombard civilian urban targets, guided by the goal of "contributing to an international environment of peace, freedom, and progress within which our democracy—and other free nations—can flourish." The primary threat we face is the "growing technological sophistication" of the Third World. We must therefore strengthen "the defense industrial base"—a.k.a. high-tech industry—creating incentives "to invest in new facilities and equipment as well as in research and development." And we must maintain intervention forces, particularly those targeting the Middle East, where the "threats to our interests" that have required direct military engagement "could not be laid at the Kremlin's door"—contrary to endless fabrication, now put to rest. As had occasionally been recognized in earlier years, sometimes in secret, the "threat" is now conceded officially to be indigenous to the region, the "radical nationalism" that has always been a primary concern, not only in the Middle East.[14]

At the time, the "threats to our interests" could not be laid at Iraq's door either. Saddam was then a favored friend and trading partner. His status changed only a few months later, when he misinterpreted US willingness to allow him to modify the border with Kuwait by force as authorization to take the country over—or, from the perspective of the Bush administration, to duplicate what the US had just done in Panama. At a high-level meeting immediately after Saddam's invasion of Kuwait, President Bush articulated the basic problem: "My worry about the Saudis is that they're . . . going to bug out at the last minute and accept a puppet regime in Kuwait." Chair of the Joint Chiefs Colin Powell posed the problem sharply: "[In] the next few days Iraq will withdraw," putting "his puppet in," and "everyone in the Arab world will be happy."[15]

Historical parallels are never exact, of course. When Washington partially withdrew from Panama after putting its puppet in, there was great anger throughout the hemisphere, including Panama—indeed, throughout much of the world—compelling Washington to veto two Security Council resolutions and to vote against a General Assembly resolution condemning Washington's "flagrant violation of international law and of the independence, sovereignty, and territorial integrity of states" and calling for the withdrawal of the "US armed invasion forces from Panama." Iraq's invasion of Kuwait was treated differently, in ways remote from the standard version, but readily discovered in print.

The inexpressible facts shed interesting light on the commentary of political analysts: Ronald Steel, for example, who muses on the "conundrum" faced by the US, which, "as the world's most powerful nation, faces greater constraints on its freedom to use force than does any other country"—hence Saddam's success in Kuwait as compared with Washington's inability to exert its will in Panama.[16]

It is worth recalling that debate was effectively foreclosed in 1990-91 as well. There was much discussion of whether sanctions would work, but none of whether they already had worked, perhaps shortly after Resolution 660 was passed. Fear that sanctions might have worked animated Washington's refusal to test Iraqi withdrawal offers from August 1990 to early January 1991. With the rarest of exceptions, the information system kept tight discipline on the matter. Polls a few days before the January 1991 bombing showed 2 to 1 support for a peaceful settlement based on Iraqi withdrawal along with an international conference on the Israel-Arab conflict. Few among those who expressed this position could have heard any public advocacy of it; the media had loyally followed the president's lead, dismissing "linkage" as unthinkable—in this unique case. It is unlikely that any respondents knew that their views were shared by the Iraqi democratic opposition, barred from mainstream media. Or that an Iraqi proposal in the terms they advocated had been released a week earlier by US officials, who found it reasonable, and had been flatly rejected by Washington. Or that an Iraqi withdrawal offer had been considered by the National Security Council as early as mid-August but dismissed, and effectively suppressed, apparently because it was feared that unmentioned Iraqi initiatives might "defuse the crisis," as the *New York Times* diplomatic correspondent obliquely reported administration concerns.

Since then, Iraq has displaced Iran and Libya as the leading "rogue state." Others have never entered the ranks. Perhaps the most relevant case is Indonesia, which shifted from enemy to friend when General Suharto took power in 1965, presiding over a Rwanda-style slaughter that elicited great satisfaction in the West. Since then Suharto has been "our kind of guy," as the

Clinton administration described him, while carrying out murderous aggression and endless atrocities against his own people—killing 10,000 Indonesians just in the 1980s, according to the personal testimony of "our guy," who wrote that "the corpses were left lying around as a form of shock therapy."[17] In December 1975 the UN Security Council unanimously ordered Indonesia to withdraw its invading forces from East Timor "without delay" and called upon "all States to respect the territorial integrity of East Timor as well as the inalienable right of its people to self-determination." The US responded by (secretly) increasing shipments of arms to the aggressors; Carter accelerated the arms flow once again as the attack reached near-genocidal levels in 1978. In his memoirs, UN Ambassador Daniel Patrick Moynihan takes pride in his success in rendering the UN "utterly ineffective in whatever measures it undertook," following the instructions of the State Department, which "wished things to turn out as they did, and worked to bring this about." The US also happily accepts the robbery of East Timor's oil (with participation of a US company), in violation of any reasonable interpretation of international agreements.[18]

The analogy to Iraq/Kuwait is close, though there are differences: to mention only the most obvious, US-sponsored atrocities in East Timor were vastly beyond anything attributed to Saddam Hussein in Kuwait.

There are many other examples, though some of those commonly invoked should be treated with caution, particularly concerning Israel. The civilian toll of Israel's US-backed invasion of Lebanon in 1982 exceeded Saddam's in Kuwait, and it remains in violation of a 1978 Security Council resolution ordering it to withdraw forthwith from Lebanon, along with numerous other resolutions regarding Jerusalem, the Golan Heights, and other matters; and there would be far more such resolutions if the US did not regularly veto them. But the common charge that Israel, particularly its current government, is violating UN 242 and the Oslo accords, and that the US exhibits a "double standard" by tolerating those violations, is dubious at best, based on serious misunderstanding of these agreements. From the outset, the Madrid-Oslo process was designed and implemented by US-Israeli power to impose a Bantustan-style settlement. The Arab world has chosen to delude itself about the matter, as have many others, but it is clear in the actual documents, and particularly in the US-supported projects of the Rabin-Peres governments, including those for which Netanyahu's Likud government has been denounced.[19]

It is clearly untrue to claim that "Israel is not demonstrably in violation of Security Council decrees,"[20] but the reasons often given should be examined carefully.

Returning to Iraq, it surely qualifies as a leading criminal state. Defending the US plan to attack Iraq at a televised public meeting on February 18, 1998, Secretaries Albright and Cohen repeatedly invoked the ultimate atrocity: Saddam was guilty of "using weapons of mass destruction against his neighbors as well as his own people," his most awesome crime. "It is very important for us to make clear that the United States and the civilized world cannot deal with somebody who is willing to use those weapons of mass destruction on his own people, not to speak of his neighbors," Albright emphasized in an angry response to a questioner who asked about US support for Suharto. Shortly after, Senator Lott condemned Kofi Annan for seeking to cultivate a "human relationship with a mass murderer," and denounced the administration for trusting a person who would sink so low.

Ringing words. Putting aside their evasion of the question raised, Albright and Cohen only forgot to mention—and commentators have been kind enough not to point out—that the acts that they now find so horrifying did not turn Iraq into a "rogue state." And Lott failed to note that his heroes Reagan and Bush forged unusually warm relations with the "mass murderer." There were no passionate calls for a military strike after Saddam's gassing of Kurds at Halabja in March 1988; on the contrary, the US and UK extended their strong support for the mass murderer, then also "our kind of guy." When ABC TV correspondent Charles Glass revealed the site of one of Saddam's biological warfare programs 10 months after Halabja, the State Department denied the facts, and the story died; the department "now issues briefings on the same site," Glass observes.

The two guardians of global order also expedited Saddam's other atrocities—including his use of cyanide, nerve gas, and other barbarous weapons—with intelligence, technology, and supplies, joining with many others. The Senate Banking Committee reported in 1994 that the US Commerce Department had traced shipments of "biological materials" identical to those later found and destroyed by UN inspectors, Bill Blum recalls. These shipments continued at least until November 1989. A month later, Bush authorized new loans for his friend Saddam, to achieve the "goal of increasing US exports and [to] put us in a better position to deal with Iraq regarding its human rights record," the State Department announced with a straight face, facing no criticism (or even report) in the mainstream.

Britain's record was exposed, at least in part, in an official inquiry (the Scott Inquiry). The British government has just now been compelled to concede that it continued to grant licenses to British firms to export materials usable for biological weapons after the Scott Inquiry Report was published, at least until December 1996.

In a February 28, 1998, review of Western sales of materials usable for germ warfare and other weapons of mass destruction, the *New York Times* mentions one example of US sales in the 1980s that included "deadly pathogens," with government approval—some from the army's center for germ research in Fort Detrick. Just the tip of the iceberg, however.[21]

A common current pretense is that Saddam's crimes were unknown, so we are now properly shocked at the discovery and must "make clear" that we civilized folk "cannot deal with" the perpetrator of such crimes (in Albright's words). The posture is cynical fraud. UN reports of 1986 and 1987 condemned Iraq's use of chemical weapons. US Embassy staffers in Turkey interviewed Kurdish survivors of chemical warfare attacks, and the CIA reported them to the State Department. Human rights groups reported the atrocities at Halabja and elsewhere at once. Secretary of State George Shultz conceded that the US had evidence on the matter. An investigative team sent by the Senate Foreign Relations Committee in 1988 found "overwhelming evidence of extensive use of chemical weapons against civilians," charging that Western acquiescence in Iraqi use of such weapons against Iran had emboldened Saddam to believe—correctly—that he could use them against his own people with impunity—actually against Kurds, hardly "the people" of this tribal-based thug. The chair of the committee, Claiborne Pell, introduced the Prevention of

Genocide Act of 1988, denouncing silence "while people are gassed" as "complicity," much as when "the world was silent as Hitler began a campaign that culminated in the near extermination of Europe's Jews," and warning that "we cannot be silent to genocide again." The Reagan administration strongly opposed sanctions and insisted that the matter be silenced, while extending its support for the mass murderer. In the Arab world, "the Kuwait press was amongst the most enthusiastic of the Arab media in supporting Baghdad's crusade against the Kurds," journalist Adel Darwish reports.

In January 1991, while the war drums were beating, the International Commission of Jurists observed to the UN Human Rights Commission that "after having perpetrated the most flagrant abuses on its own population without a word of reproach from the UN, Iraq must have concluded it could do whatever it pleased"; UN in this context means US and UK, primarily. That truth must be buried along with international law and other "utopian" distractions.[22]

An unkind commentator might remark that recent US/UK toleration for poison gas and chemical warfare is not too surprising. The British used chemical weapons in their 1919 intervention in North Russia against the Bolsheviks, with great success, according to the British command. As Secretary of State at the War Office in 1919, Winston Churchill was enthusiastic about the prospects of "using poisoned gas against uncivilized tribes"—Kurds and Afghans—and authorized the RAF Middle East command to use chemical weapons "against recalcitrant Arabs as [an] experiment," dismissing objections by the India office as "unreasonable" and deploring the "squeamishness about the use of gas": "We cannot in any circumstances acquiesce in the non-utilization of any weapons which are available to procure a speedy termination of the disorder which prevails on the frontier," he explained; chemical weapons are merely "the application of western science to modern warfare."[23]

The Kennedy administration pioneered the massive use of chemical weapons against civilians as it launched its attack against South Vietnam in 1961-62. There has been much rightful concern about the effects on US soldiers, but not the incomparably worse effects on civilians. Here, at least. In an Israeli mass-circulation daily, the respected journalist Amnon Kapeliouk reported on his 1988 visit to Vietnam, where he found that "thousands of Vietnamese still die from the effects of American chemical warfare," citing estimates of one-quarter of a million victims in South Vietnam and describing the "terrifying" scenes in hospitals in the South, where children were dying of cancer and hideous birth deformities. It was South Vietnam that was targeted for chemical warfare, not the North, where these consequences are not found, he reports. There is also substantial evidence of US use of biological weapons against Cuba, reported as minor news in 1977, and at worst only a small component of continuing US terror.[24]

These precedents aside, the US and UK are now engaged in a deadly form of biological warfare in Iraq. The destruction of infrastructure and banning of imports to repair it has caused disease, malnutrition, and early death on a huge scale, including more than 500,000 children, according to UNICEF investigations—an average of 5,000 children dying each month. In a bitter condemnation of the sanctions on January 20, 1998, 54 Catholic bishops quoted the archbishop of the southern region of Iraq, who reports that "epidemics rage, taking away infants and the sick by the thousands," while "those children who survive disease succumb to malnutrition." The bishops' statement, reported in full in Stanley Heller's journal *The Struggle,* received scant mention in the press. The US and Britain have taken the lead in blocking aid programs—for example, delaying approval for ambulances on the grounds that they could be used to transport troops, and barring insecticides for preventing the spread of disease and spare parts for sanitation systems. Meanwhile, Western diplomats point out, "The US had directly benefited from [the humanitarian] operation as much, if not more, than the Russians and the French," for example, by purchase of $600 million worth of Iraqi oil (second only to Russia) and sale by US companies of $200 million in humanitarian goods to Iraq. They also report that most of the oil bought by Russian companies ends up in the US.[25]

Washington's support for Saddam reached such an extreme that it was even willing to overlook an Iraqi air force attack on the USS *Stark,* killing 37 crewmen, a privilege otherwise enjoyed only by Israel (in the case of the USS *Liberty*). It was Washington's decisive support for Saddam, well after the crimes that now so shock the administration and Congress, that led to Iranian capitulation to "Baghdad and Washington," Dilip Hiro concludes in his history of the Iran-Iraq war. The two allies had "co-ordinate[d] their military operations against Teheran." The shooting down of an Iranian civilian airliner by the guided-missile cruiser USS *Vincennes* was the culmination of Washington's "diplomatic, military, and economic campaign" in support of Saddam, he writes.[26]

Saddam was also called upon to perform the usual services of a client state: for example, to train several hundred Libyans sent to Iraq by the US so they could overthrow the Qaddafi government, former Reagan White House aide Howard Teicher revealed.[27]

It was not his massive crimes that elevated Saddam to the rank of "Beast of Baghdad." Rather, it was his stepping out of line, much as in the case of the far more minor criminal Noriega, whose major crimes were also committed while he was a US client.

Exempt Rogue States

The qualifications of "rogue state" are illuminated further by Washington's reaction to the uprisings in Iraq in March 1991, immediately after the cessation of hostilities. The State Department formally reiterated its refusal to have any dealings with the Iraqi democratic opposition, and just as before the Gulf War, they were virtually denied access to the major US media. "Political meetings with them would not be appropriate for our policy at this time," State Department spokesperson Richard Boucher stated. "This time" happened to be March 14, 1991, while Saddam was decimating the southern opposition under the eyes of General Schwarzkopf, who refused even to permit rebelling military officers access to captured Iraqi arms. Had it not been for unexpected public reaction, Washington probably would not have extended even tepid support to rebelling Kurds, subjected to the same treatment shortly after.

Iraqi opposition leaders got the message. Leith Kubba, head of the London-based Iraqi Democratic Reform Movement, alleged that the US favors a military dictatorship, insisting that "changes in the regime must come from within, from people already in power." London-based banker Ahmed Chalabi, head of the Iraqi National Congress, said that "the United States, covered by the fig leaf of non-interference in Iraqi affairs, is waiting for Saddam to butcher the insurgents in the hope that he can be overthrown later by a suitable officer," an attitude rooted in the US policy of "supporting dictatorships to maintain stability."

Administration reasoning was outlined by *New York Times* chief diplomatic correspondent Thomas Friedman. While opposing a popular rebellion, Washington did hope that a military coup might remove Saddam, "and then Washington would have the best of all worlds: an iron-fisted Iraqi junta without Saddam Hussein," a return to the days when Saddam's "iron fist . . . held Iraq together, much to the satisfaction of the American allies Turkey and Saudi Arabia," not to speak of Washington. Two years later, in another useful recognition of reality, he observed that "it has always been American policy that the iron-fisted Mr. Hussein plays a useful role in holding Iraq together," maintaining "stability." There is little reason to believe that Washington has modified the preference for dictatorship over democracy deplored by the ignored Iraqi democratic opposition, though it doubtless would prefer a different "iron fist" at this point. If not, Saddam will have to do.[28]

The concept "rogue state" is highly nuanced. Thus, Cuba qualifies as a leading "rogue state" because of its alleged involvement in international terrorism, but the US does not fall into the category despite its terrorist attacks against Cuba for close to 40 years, apparently continuing through 1997, according to important investigative reporting of the *Miami Herald,* which failed to reach the national press (here; it did in Europe). Cuba was a "rogue state" when its military forces were in Angola, backing the government against South African attacks supported by the US. South Africa, in contrast, was not a rogue state then, nor during the Reagan years, when it caused more than $60 billion in damage and 1.5 million deaths in neighboring states, according to a UN commission, not to speak of some events at home—and with ample US/UK support. The same exemption applies to Indonesia and many others.

The criteria are fairly clear: a "rogue state" is not simply a criminal state, but one that defies the orders of the powerful—who are, of course, exempt.

More on "The Debate"

That Saddam is a criminal is undoubtedly true, and one should be pleased, I suppose, that the US and UK, and the mainstream doctrinal institutions have at last joined those who "prematurely" condemned US/UK support for the mass murderer. It is also true that he poses a threat to anyone within his reach. On the comparison of the threat with others, there is little unanimity outside the US and UK, after their (ambiguous) transformation from August 1990. Their 1998 plan to use force was justified in terms of Saddam's threat to the region, but there was no way to conceal the fact that the people of the region objected to their salvation, so strenuously that governments were compelled to join in opposition.

Bahrein refused to allow US/UK forces to use bases there. The president of the United Arab Emirates described US threats of military action as "bad and loathsome," and declared that Iraq does not pose a threat to its neighbors. Saudi Defense Minister Prince Sultan had already stated that "we'll not agree, and we are against striking Iraq as a people and as a nation," causing Washington to refrain from a request to use Saudi bases. After Annan's mission, long-serving Saudi Foreign Minister Prince Saud al-Faisal reaffirmed that any use of Saudi air bases "has to be a UN, not a US, issue."

An editorial in Egypt's quasi-official journal *Al-Ahram* described Washington's stand as "coercive, aggressive, unwise, and uncaring about the lives of Iraqis, who are unnecessarily subjected to sanctions and humiliation," and denounced the planned US "aggression against Iraq." Jordan's Parliament condemned "any aggression against Iraq's territory and any harm that might come to the Iraqi people"; the Jordanian army was forced to seal off the city of Maan after two days of pro-Iraq rioting. A political science professor at Kuwait University warned that "Saddam has come to represent the voice of the voiceless in the Arab world," expressing popular frustration over the "New World Order" and Washington's advocacy of Israeli interests.

Even in Kuwait, support for the US stance was at best "tepid" and "cynical over US motives," the press recognized. "Voices in the streets of the Arab world, from Cairo's teeming slums to the Arabian Peninsula's shiny capitals, have been rising in anger as the American drumbeat of war against Iraq grows louder," Boston Globe correspondent Charles Sennott reported.[29]

The Iraqi democratic opposition was granted slight exposure in the mainstream, breaking the previous pattern. In a telephone interview with the *New York Times,* Ahmed Chalabi reiterated the position that had been reported in greater detail in London weeks earlier: "Without a political plan to remove Saddam's regime, military strikes will be counterproductive," he argued, killing thousands of Iraqis, perhaps even leaving Saddam strengthened along with his weapons of mass destruction, and with "an excuse to throw out UNSCOM [the UN weapons inspectors]," who have in fact destroyed vastly more weapons and production facilities than the 1991 bombing. US/UK plans would "be worse than nothing." Interviews with opposition leaders from several groups found "near unanimity" in opposing military action that did not lay the basis for an uprising to overthrow Saddam. Speaking to a parliamentary committee, Chalabi held that it was "morally indefensible to strike Iraq without a strategy" for removing Saddam.

In London, the opposition also outlined an alternative program: (1) declare Saddam a war criminal; (2) recognize a provisional Iraqi government formed by the opposition; (3) unfreeze hundreds of millions of dollars of Iraqi assets abroad; and (4) restrict Saddam's forces by a "no-drive zone," or extend the "no-flight zone" to cover the whole country. The US should "help the Iraqi people remove Saddam from power," Chalabi told the Senate Armed Services Committee. Along with other opposition leaders, he "rejected assassination, covert US operations, or US ground troops," Reuters reported, calling instead for "a popular insurgency." Similar proposals have occasionally appeared in the US. Washington claims to have attempted support for opposition groups, but their own interpretation is different. Chalabi's view, published in England, is much as it was years earlier: "Everyone says Saddam is boxed in, but it is the Americans and British who are boxed in by their refusal to support the idea of political change."[30]

Regional opposition was regarded as a problem to be evaded, not a factor to be taken into account any more than international law. The same was true of warnings by senior UN and other international relief officials in Iraq that the planned bombing might have a "catastrophic" effect on people already suffering miserably, and might terminate the humanitarian operations that have brought at least some relief.[31] What matters is to establish that "what we say goes," as President Bush triumphantly proclaimed, announcing the New World Order as bombs and missiles were falling in 1991.

As Kofi Annan was preparing to go to Baghdad, former Iranian president Rafsanjani, "still a pivotal figure in Teheran, was given an audience by the ailing King Fahd in Saudi Arabia," British Middle East correspondent David Gardner reported, "in contrast to the treatment experienced by Madeleine Albright . . . on her recent trips to Riyadh seeking support from America's main Gulf ally." As Rafsanjani's 10-day visit ended on March 2, 1998, Foreign Minister Prince Saud described it as "one more step in the right direction towards improving relations," reiterating that "the greatest destabilizing element in the Middle East and the cause of all other problems in the region" is Israel's policy towards the Palestinians and US support for it, which might activate popular forces that Saudi Arabia greatly fears, as well as undermine its legitimacy as "guardian" of Islamic holy places, including the Dome of the Rock in East Jerusalem (now effectively annexed by US/Israeli programs as part of their intent to extend "greater Jerusalem" virtually to the Jordan Valley, to be retained by Israel). Shortly before, the Arab states had boycotted a US-sponsored economic summit in Qatar that was intended to advance the "New Middle East" project of Clinton and Peres. Instead, they attended an Islamic conference in Teheran in December, joined even by Iraq.[32]

These are tendencies of considerable import, relating to the background concerns that motivate US policy in the region: its insistence, since World War II, on controlling the world's major energy reserves. As many have observed, in the Arab world there is growing fear and resentment of the long-standing Israel-Turkey alliance that was formalized in 1996, now greatly strengthened. For some years, it had been a component of the US strategy of controlling the region with "local cops on the beat," as Nixon's defense secretary put the matter. There is apparently a growing appreciation of the Iranian advocacy of regional security arrangements to replace US domination. A related matter is the intensifying conflict over pipelines to bring Central Asian oil to the rich countries, one natural outlet being via Iran. And US energy corporations will not be happy to see foreign rivals—now including China and Russia—gain privileged access to Iraqi oil reserves, second only to Saudi Arabia's in scale, or to Iran's natural gas, oil, and other resources.

For the present, Clinton planners may well be relieved to have escaped temporarily from the "box" they had constructed, which was leaving them no option but a bombing of Iraq that could have been harmful even to the interests they represent. The respite is temporary. It offers opportunities to citizens of the warrior states to bring about changes of consciousness and commitment that could make a great difference in the not-too-distant future.

Notes

List of Abbreviations

AFP	*Agence-France Presse*
AP	Associated Press
BG	*Boston Globe*
BW	*Business Week*
CSM	*Christian Science Monitor*
GW	*Guardian Weekly*
NYT	*New York Times*
WP	*Washington Post*
WSJ	*Wall Street Journal*

This article originally appeared in *Z* magazine, April 1998.

1. Mark Curtis, *The Ambiguities of Power* (Zed, 1995), 146.
2. Jules Kagian, *Middle East International,* Oct. 21, 1994; Kagian, *FT,* Feb. 19, 1998; Steven Erlanger and Philip Shenon, *NYT,* Feb. 23, 1998; Clinton press conference, *NYT,* Feb. 24, 1998; R.W. Apple, *NYT,* Feb. 24, 1998; Aaron Zitner, *BG,* Feb. 21, 1998.

3. Colum Lynch, *BG,* March 3, 1998; Weston, Costa Rica, *BG,* March 3, 1998; *WSJ,* March 3, 1998; Barbara Crossette, *NYT,* March 3, 1998; Laura Silber and David Buchan, *FT,* March 4, 1998; Steven Lee Myers, *NYT,* March 4, 1998; R.W. Apple, *NYT,* Feb. 24, 1998 (Lott); Steven Erlanger and Philip Shenon, *NYT,* Feb. 23, 1998 (McCain, Kerry); Aaron Zitner, "A Visible Kerry Turns Tough on Crisis," *BG,* Feb. 21, 1998.
4. Editorial, *BG,* Feb. 27, 1998; William Pfaff, *BG,* Feb. 23, 1998; Ronald Steel, *NYT,* March 1, 1998.
5. Nov. 29, 1990.
6. Aug. 2, 1990.
7. Editorial, *FT,* March 2, 1998.
8. See chap. 1, p. 4, in this volume.
9. See my *Culture of Terrorism,* 67f.; and my *Necessary Illusions,* 82f., 94f., 270.
10. National Security Council 5429/2; my emphasis.
11. See my *For Reasons of State,* 100ff.; *Pirates and Emperors,* 140; UN Ambassador Thomas Pickering and Justice Dept., cited in my *Deterring Democracy,* 147; and *World Orders Old and New,* 16f.; George Kahin, *Intervention* (Knopf, 1986), 74.
12. Steven Donziger, ed., *The Real War on Crime: The Report of the National Criminal Justice Commission* (HarperCollins, 1996); Nils Christie, *Crime Control as Industry* (Routledge, 1993); Michael Tonry, *Malign Neglect: Race, Crime, and Punishment in America* (Oxford, 1995); Randall Shelden and William Brown, *Criminal Justice* (Wadsworth, forthcoming). See chap. 5.
13. "Irrationality Suggested to Intimidate US Enemies," AP, BG, March 2, 1998. See chaps. 1, 7, and 8, in this volume, for further details. On the Israeli theory, see my *Fateful Triangle,* 464ff.
14. George Bush, *National Security Strategy of the United States,* White House, March 1990; for more extensive quotations, see my *Deterring Democracy,* chap. 1.
15. On these matters and what follows, see my articles in *Z* magazine in 1990-91; *Deterring Democracy* (chaps. 4-6, afterword); *Powers and Prospects,* chap. 6; my article in Cynthia Peters, ed., *Collateral Damage: The "New World Order" at Home and Abroad* (South End, 1992). Also Dilip Hiro, *Desert Shield to Desert Storm* (Routledge, 1992); Douglas Kellner, *The Persian Gulf TV War* (Westview,

1992); Miron Rezun, *Saddam Hussein's Gulf Wars* (Praeger, 1992); and a number of useful collections. There is also a much (self)-praised "scholarly history" by Lawrence Freedman and Efraim Karsh, which contains useful information but with serious omissions and errors: *The Gulf Conflict 1990-1991: Diplomacy and War in the New World Order* (Princeton, 1992). See my *World Orders Old and New,* chap. 1, note 18; and my "World Order and Its Rules," *Journal of Law and Society* (Cardiff, Wales), Summer 1993.

16. Ronald Steel, *NYT,* March 1, 1998.
17. Cited by Charles Glass, *Prospect* (London), March 1998.
18. See chaps. 1 and 4, in this volume.
19. See my articles in *Z* magazine from the Madrid conference in 1991 through the Oslo conference in 1993, and beyond. Also *Deterring Democracy,* chap. 6 and afterword; Powers and Prospects, chap. 6; *World Orders Old and New,* chap. *3* and epilogue; and sources cited. For further update, see my "The 'Peace Process' in US Global Strategy," address at Ben-Gurion University conference, June 1997, in Haim Gordon, ed., *Looking Back at the June 1967 War* (Praeger, 1999); and my *Fateful Triangle.*
20. Serge Schmemann and Douglas Jehl, *NYT,* Feb. 27, 1998.
21. See sources cited earlier. Albright, Cohen, CNN live report, Ohio State Univ., Feb. 18, 1998; partial transcript (omitting the interchange quoted), *NYT,* Feb. 19, 1998. Trent Lott, *BG,* Feb. 26, 1998. Charles Glass, *New Statesman,* Feb. 20, 1998. Bill Blum, *Consortium,* March 2, 1990. William Broad and Judith Miller, *NYT,* Feb. 26, 1998. Scott Inquiry Report, Feb. 1996. Gerald James, *In the Public Interest* (London: Little, Brown, 1996). Alan Friedman, *Spider's Web: The Secret History of How the White House Illegally Armed Iraq* (Bantam, 1993). Mark Phythian, *Arming Iraq: How the US and Britain Secretly Built Saddam's War Machine* (Northeastern Univ. Press, 1997).
22. David Korn, ed., *Human Rights in Iraq* (Human Rights Watch, Yale, 1989); CARDRI (Committee Against Repression and for Democratic Rights in Iraq), *Saddam's Iraq* (Zed, 1986, 1989), 236f.; Dilip Hiro, *The Longest War* (Routledge, 1991), 53; Rezun, *Saddam Hussein's Gulf Wars,* 43f.; Darwish and Gregory Alexander, *Unholy Babylon* (St. Martin's, 1991), 78f.; John Gittings, "How West Propped Up Saddam's Rule," *GW,* March 10, 1991.

23. Andy Thomas, *Effects of Chemical Warfare* (Stockholm International Peace Research Institute [SIPRI], Taylor & Francis, 1985), chap. 2. See my *Turning the Tide,* 126; and *Deterring Democracy,* 181f.
24. On Vietnam, see my *Necessary Illusions,* 38f. On Cuba, see Chomsky and Edward Herman, *Political Economy of Human Rights,* vol. I, 69; and much subsequent material, including Alexander Cockburn, *Nation,* March 9, 1998.
25. *The Struggle* (New Haven), Feb. 21, 1998; Maggie O'Kane, *Guardian,* Feb. 19, 1998; Scott Peterson, *CSM,* Feb. 17, 1998; Roula Khalaf, *FT,* March 2, 1998. The impact of the bombing and sanctions was known at once; see Jean Drèze and Haris Gazdar, *Hunger and Poverty in Iraq 1991,* London School of Economics, Sept. 1991. For extensive review, see Geoff Simons, *The Scourging of Iraq* (London: Macmillan, 1996).
26. Hiro, *Longest War,* 239f.
27. AP, *NYT,* May 26, 1993.
28. *NYT,* July 7, 1991; June 28, 1993. On Kubba, Chalabi, see my article in Peters, *Collateral Damage.*
29. David Marcus, *BG, Feb. 18, 1998; Roula Khalaf, Mark Suzman, David Gardner,* FT, *Feb. 23, 1998;* FT, Feb. 9, 1998; Robin Allen, *FT,* March 3, 1998; Steven Lee Myers, *NYT,* Feb. 9, 1998; Douglas Jehl, *NYT,* Feb. 9, 1998; Charles Sennott, *BG,* Feb. 18, 1998, Feb. 19, 1998; Daniel Pearl, *WSJ,* Feb. 25, 1998.
30. David Fairhall and Ian Black, *GW,* Feb. 8, 1998; Reuters, *BG,* March 3, 1998; Douglas Jehl, *NYT,* Feb. 22, 1998; Jimmy Burns, *FT,* Feb. 15, 1998.
31. Peterson, *CSM,* Feb. 17, 1998 .
32. David Gardner, *FT,* Feb. 28, 1998; Robin Allen, *FT,* March 3, 1998.

Bomb Saddam?

Joshua Micah Marshall

Washington Monthly

Imagine for a moment that you're President George W. Bush. At some point in the next several months you will have to decide whether to overthrow Saddam Hussein—not just to threaten and saber-rattle and hope something gives, but actually to pull the trigger on what could be a very costly and risky military venture. How precisely will you make that decision? It will almost certainly come down to a choice between which of two groups of advisers you choose to believe. One side is comprised of the Joint Chiefs of Staff, most of the career military, nearly every Middle East expert at the State Department, and the vast majority of intelligence analysts and CIA operations officers who know the region. These folks generally think that the idea of attacking Saddam is questionable at best, reckless at worst. On the other side are a few dozen neoconservative think tank scholars and defense policy intellectuals. Few of them have any serious knowledge of the Arab world, the Middle East, or Islam. Fewer still have served in the armed forces. In other words, to give the go-ahead to war with Iraq, you'd have to decide that the experienced hands are all wrong, and throw in your lot with a bunch of hotheaded ideologues. Oh, and one other thing: The last few times, the ideologues have turned out to be right. To anyone who's followed foreign affairs for the last couple of decades, the names of the neoconservative hawks will be familiar—or, if you're a liberal, chilling. Their *eminence grise* is Richard Perle, who serves simultaneously as a fellow at the American Enterprise Institute and chairman of the Pentagon's Defense Policy Board, a heretofore somnolent committee of foreign policy old-timers that Perle has refashioned into a key advisory group. Of all the hawks, Deputy Secretary of Defense Paul Wolfowitz probably has the most powerful job inside the Bush administration. A dozen others hold key posts at the State Department and the White House. Most are acolytes of Perle, and also Jewish, passionately pro-Israel, and pro-Likud. And all are united by a shared idea: that America should be unafraid to use its military power early and often to advance its interests and values. It is an idea that infuriates most members of the national security establishment at the Pentagon, State, and the CIA, who believe that America's military force should be used rarely and only as a last resort, preferably in concert with allies.

The neocons have been clashing with the establishment since the 1970s. Back then, the consensus view among foreign policy elites was that the Cold War was an indefinite or perhaps even a permanent fact of world politics, to be managed with diplomacy and nuclear deterrence. The neocons argued for deliberately tipping the balance of power in America's direction. Ronald Reagan championed their ideas, and brought a number of neocons into his administration, including Perle and Wolfowitz. Reagan's huge defense buildup and harsh, even provocative, rhetoric contributed significantly to running the Soviet military-industrial complex into the ground. The president went for the Hail Mary pass—whatever the dangers—and it worked.

During the Gulf War, the hawks urged President George H.W. Bush to ignore the limits of his U.N. mandate, roll the tanks into Baghdad, and bring down Saddam Hussein's regime. Bush sided with the then-chairman of the Joint Chiefs of Staff, Colin Powell (the embodiment of the establishment, who had advised Bush against liberating Kuwait), and left Saddam in power. The neocons have been saying *I told you so* ever since.

In the 1990s, as the Balkans descended into civil war, this same establishment urged President Clinton to proceed with caution. After several years of carnage, Clinton finally broke with the experts and launched air strikes against Bosnia, then Kosovo. Many conservative Republicans criticized Clinton at the time, but the neocons, despite their loathing for the president, supported his efforts. And rightly so: American action ended the bloodshed and brought stability to a key region of Europe with practically no loss of American life.

Again and again, for more than two decades, the neocon hawks have called it right. But they've gotten a lot wrong, too. Back in the 1970s and early 1980s, they portrayed the U.S.S.R. as a menacing giant about to overwhelm us, when in fact—we now know—it was already headed for collapse, and its downfall had more to do with its own terminal rot than anything America did. They cheered on (and in some cases aided) bloody proxy wars in Central America and Africa that did little to hasten the Soviets' demise, but plenty to brutalize entire populations and tarnish America's image abroad. Neocons led the successful effort to kill Bush senior's policy, fashioned by the establishment, of conditioning U.S. aid to Israel on freezing expansion of Jewish settlements in the West Bank—a policy that seems, in the wake of recent bloodshed in the Middle East, visionary. Even on Iraq the neocons' record has been marred by errors of judgment and manifest recklessness and dishonesty. Their favored means of toppling Saddam is a CIA-created opposition leader, Ahmed Chalabi, a glib exile who hasn't lived in Iraq since he was a teenager and has no discernable support, let alone control over armed forces, inside the country. In the aftermath of September 11, neocons repeatedly tried to tie Saddam to either the World Trade Center attacks or the anthrax mailings. The evidence for such a connection was always slight to nonexistent, which they understood. But they made the argument anyway. That's how they operate.

While arguments for and against invading Iraq continue, preparations for an attack are well underway. The Pentagon is moving troops and armaments to U.S.-allied Arab emirates that ring the Persian Gulf. The State Department is getting serious about organizing and uniting the Iraqi opposition. Diplomats are discussing with allies like Turkey and Kuwait the role they would play in a U.S. attack. There is talk of a military assault on Iraq as early as this winter, though a more likely target date is 12 to 18 months from now. (With victory scheduled in time for the '04 elections? Perish the thought!) Whatever the date, some kind of war seems increasingly certain—and probably wise, for the hawks have a much better argument for attacking Iraq than many people imagine. But with their peculiar mix of strategic vision, recklessness, and intellectual dishonesty, they're the last people who should be in charge of carrying it out.

Mission Impossible?

Deciding whether or not we should topple Saddam raises a number of questions that we are in a painfully poor position to answer. How close is Saddam to having weapons of mass destruction? How long will our deterrents hold him in check? How resilient would his regime be against sustained military force? And, perhaps most important, what geopolitical collateral damage would result, even if we were successful? Anyone who claims to have the answers is either a liar or a fool.

Frank Anderson is neither. As the former chief of the Near East division of the CIA's Directorate of Operations (which runs the agency's clandestine efforts), he is a certified member of the national security establishment. When asked a question, he pauses, sorting through the many complexities, before giving an answer that is balanced, hedged, and honest. Anderson told me that Saddam could probably be deterred from using weapons of mass destruction should he acquire them. "He probably will be further along the way to having a weapon of massive destruction. [But] I think it's highly unlikely that we'll be telling the story of 'and he used it.' The bad news is that if I'm wrong, I'm wrong big time." Anderson worries about the neocons' readiness to employ cowboy tactics to bring down Saddam, a concern evidently rooted in his own experience running clandestine operations—and witnessing how often things go awry.

Richard Perle could not be more different. Dubbed the "Prince of Darkness" during the Reagan years for his hatred of the Soviets and his eagerness to confront them, he radiates a cool, effortless intelligence which is both cocky and oracular. He doesn't know many of the details about Iraq or the Middle East. But, he works you like a used car salesman, avoiding questions he'd prefer not to or cannot answer, responding to uncomfortable queries (what if Saddam's Republican Guards stay loyal to him and fight?) with best case scenarios (don't worry, they won't). When asked what would happen if America encountered an embittered civilian population after fighting a grisly battle for Baghdad, Perle replied with a question: "Suppose the Iraqis are dancing in the streets after Saddam is gone?" His arguments tend to rest on abstractions and mechanistic reasoning: *Saddam is bad. Ergo the Iraqis hate Saddam. Ergo they like us*. That might be true. But if such arguments were chairs you would hear them creaking beneath you.

Perle's case for invading Iraq, which mirrors that of other hawks, is basically an escalating series of true or false propositions that leads inexorably toward massive military confrontation: Do you believe that Saddam Hussein is an evil tyrant who would use weapons of mass destruction against us or our allies if he got them? *Check.* Do you believe he is trying to acquire nuclear or biological weapons and the means to deliver them? *Check.* If so, doesn't it stand to reason that he will eventually succeed in getting them? *Check.* Aren't we then obligated to stop him? *Check!* Sooner, rather than later? *Check!!*

The trouble is that this is a syllogism—one conspicuously short on details about Iraq, geopolitics, or anything else. And yet the logic is still pretty compelling, an impression that only grows when you talk to his critics. While they can point to an endless number of pitfalls and hurdles that the hawks either gloss over or ignore, they're less able to break apart the tight chain of reasoning that gets the hawks on their war footing.

Judith Yaphe, for one, a career CIA intelligence analyst now at the National Defense University in Washington, D.C., thinks the costs of attacking Saddam probably outweigh the benefits. But when I asked her whether Saddam was as dangerous as the hawks maintain, her reply was not so different from theirs. "I'm of the school that says this guy had better never have [weapons of mass destruction] because I don't know what he'd do. You can't ignore him," she told me. "[Costs aside] you've gotta take him out because if you don't you're going to have to continue to live with this festering wound and I don't have much confidence that it can be done short of something significant. I don't think that you just rely on a little covert action. This isn't *Mission Impossible*." In other words, Yaphe's underlying assumptions about Saddam are not so different from those of the hawks. She's just better informed and more cautious.

Boxing Saddam

Since the end of the Gulf War, U.S. policy on Iraq has been premised on two notions. First, that we would never again accept Saddam Hussein's regime as just another player in the international state system. Second, that Saddam was trying to develop weapons of mass destruction and that we could not, and would not, let him do so. In the early 1990s, we quite reasonably assumed his regime could not last long in the face of his loss of Kuwait and heavy international economic sanctions—an assumption, of course, that proved entirely wrong. In the mid-1990s, the U.S. was preoccupied with the Middle Eastern peace process and the Balkans. It's easy to second guess America's inattention to Iraq, as the hawks do. But at the time, these issues were more pressing. And as long as the UNSCOM inspectors remained in Iraq and Saddam could be sufficiently prevented from procuring weapons of mass destruction, the status quo seemed tenable. The strategy of keeping Saddam "in a box," as Clinton officials liked to put it, made sense.

But as early as 1996 and 1997, this was no longer clearly true. Saddam's regime was thriving under sanctions, even as his people suffered under them (a condition he could have alleviated, but didn't). As their condition deteriorated, so too did the U.N. Security Council's support for maintaining the U.S.-backed sanctions. We were in the box now just as much as Saddam was. And time was on his side, not ours.

In late 1998, the other shoe finally dropped: Iraq expelled UNSCOM weapons inspectors. The U.S. and Great Britain responded with a thunderous four-day bombardment of cruise missiles and air strikes-Operation Desert Fox. But when the bombing was over, the inspectors were still gone and have never returned. From that point on, U.S. policy was at war with itself. There were (and are) only two real options: to accept Saddam as a regional power (and thus to risk having his weapons and control of oil dictate terms in the Middle East and elsewhere), or take him out.

Hawk Heaven

The hawks began pressing the case for overthrowing Saddam in 1998 with a letter to the Clinton administration drafted by Perle and signed by 40 neocon luminaries. Many of the signatories became advisers to then-Gov. George W. Bush. Some won top jobs in the new administration. Hawks include, at the Pentagon, Paul Wolfowitz, Douglas Feith, William Luti, and Harold Rhode; at the Office of the Vice President, Lewis "Scooter" Libby and John Hannah; at the State Department, David Wurmser; and at the National Security Council, former Gen. Wayne Downing.

The hawks came in wanting to put regime change at or near the top of the Bush administration's foreign policy agenda. What they didn't figure on was how much of a hurdle Colin Powell, and his deputy, Richard Armitage, would present (despite Armitage's having signed Perle's '98 manifesto). In bureaucratic battles over the summer of 2001, Powell and Armitage made sure that "regime change," though nominally administration policy, lacked teeth.

All of that changed after September 11. Suddenly the prospect of Saddam slipping a dirty bomb to terrorists to blow up in, say, Milwaukee, didn't seem so far-fetched. It also became clear that our efforts to contain Saddam—sanctions that wound up hurting Iraqi civilians, U.S. troops on Saudi soil—were ideal recruitment tools for Osama bin Laden. Removing Saddam was back at the top of the administration's agenda. There was even talk, briefly, of launching an attack on Iraq prior to moving against Afghanistan. Cooler heads prevailed. But by last winter, the Bush administration had come around, with the State Department securely—if reluctantly—on board.

This presented a question that most hawks had not seriously considered. Namely, *how* exactly to bring down Saddam. The war in Afghanistan offered a compelling model. With a combination of precision assault from the air, special forces on the ground, and the aid of local insurgents ready to do some of the heavy lifting, the U.S. broke the Taliban with surprising ease. In fact, the Afghan campaign bore a striking resemblance to a plan that Iraq hawks had been pitching to Washington for several years: Arm the Iraqi opposition and let them advance on Saddam under cover of U.S. air power. This plan no longer seemed so far-fetched. It didn't require the lengthy pre-positioning of forces that the joint Chiefs demanded. And it allowed for quick action, before the anger and intensity of September 11 faded.

But the closer officials and military experts looked at the plans that the hawks put forward, the more holes they found. For while the hawks possess a real talent for crafting bold theories, the same cannot be said for their ability to execute in the real world. A striking example on the diplomatic front was their strategy, eagerly adopted by the president, of not engaging in peace efforts between Israel and the Palestinians. Such efforts, the hawks reasoned, were not worth the political capital and would only detract from bigger priorities like bringing down Saddam. The result, however, is that the U.S. was not there to keep the violence from spinning out of control. The fallout from the bloodletting has almost certainly delayed the war with Iraq that the hawks had hoped to be waging by now.

Getting to Know the General

Despite stark disagreements within the administration about the costs and benefits of toppling Saddam's regime, both sides agree on some key points about how a military campaign would unfold. Much of northern Iraq is already controlled by the Kurds, who have some 70,000 armed and trained paramilitaries and are wholly beyond Saddam's authority. Southern Iraq has a restive but unarmed Shi'a population held in check by garrisons of some of the regime's least reliable troops. Any invasion would require a substantial number of U.S. ground troops in the south. But even staunch critics believe that the United States would quickly roll up the north and the south of the country with relative ease and few casualties. Then the U.S. forces would move toward Baghdad and its environs—and that's where the agreement breaks down.

Most of Saddam's elite Republican Guard and key military installations would be in and around Baghdad and his nearby hometown of Tikrit. The hawks assume that when U.S. troops converge on Baghdad, few of these troops would choose to go down with the regime. Most would defect or simply flee.

Again, the hawks may be right. Recently, I sat down with Najib Salhi, an Iraqi general who defected in 1995 and now heads the Iraqi Free Officers Movement. Salhi has been living in the Washington area since 2001 and like many exiles in recent months he is, in effect, auditioning for the coveted role as Washington's favored exile leader. Salhi insists that Saddam's regime is far weaker than we imagine. This is not a surprising statement coming from an exile eager for United States support. But Salhi added something that did surprise me. One source of Saddam's strength, he says, is that he has convinced many in the Republican Guard and his inner circle that the U.S. doesn't really want him gone. "Don't worry about what you see on TV," Salhi described Saddam as saying. "I have a special relationship with the U.S. I am very strong with them. They want me to stay as leader of Iraq. I am like a buffer zone between the Arabian countries and Iran. I have to contain Iran. Iran is Shi'a and extremist. I have to contain them. I have been told to attack other Arab countries and keep them in their place. Just ignore what you see on TV and in the media."

One need not believe Saddam's story, or even Salhi's, to see that the United States has, over the years, given such mixed messages to potential plotters in Saddam's ranks that they might reasonably conclude that the United States really hasn't decided whether it wants him there or not. If, however, we were to act boldly to remove him, Saddam's military could well abandon him in droves before the fighting got too heavy.

But what if that didn't happen? What if Saddam's troops remained loyal? Perle didn't have an entirely satisfactory answer to this point. Instead, he insisted that without access to his ports, and the ability to sell his oil, Saddam would not be able to hunker down in Baghdad: "I think we can put him in a situation where he's got to try to assert authority over his own territory. And when he does, he's highly vulnerable, his forces are highly vulnerable."

The problem with this reasoning is that it assumes Saddam would court his own destruction on the least favorable terms. Would Saddam send his outnumbered Republican Guard out into the open to be annihilated by American airpower? Or would he hold them back in his redoubts in Baghdad, place his soldiers and heavy artillery among civilians, and dare the United States to come in and dislodge him? This sort of ugly, worst-case scenario is precisely what the professional military fears and insists on preparing for. In an attack on a metropolis like Baghdad, the U.S. could have far less of the advantages of its high-tech military and precision-guided bombs. If the Iraqi army were spread throughout the city, the toll of civilian casualties would simply be too high to destroy the Iraqi military from the air. Going in with the sort of overwhelming power that the professional military envisions is actually the only strategy that would make Perle's waiting-game scenario feasible. If the U.S. invaded and bottled up Saddam and a portion of the Republican Guard in Baghdad, war planners could then survey the rest of the country and gauge the reaction of the civilian population. If it was generally positive (or at least quiescent) we could likely hold back and wait them out. But if one of the darker scenarios began to unfold—a restive civilian population, a Kurdish declaration of independence, an Iranian mobilization to the east—then we would have to choke off resistance fast. Rather than go in with relatively few troops—as the hawks propose—and risk being drawn into a volatile and dangerous waiting game outside Baghdad, the professional military wants to go in with overwhelming force—at least 200,000 troops—to do whatever is required in Baghdad rapidly, and on our terms. Many lives would certainly still be lost; but there would be fewer Iraqi civilians and American GIs among them. Equally important, moving in with overwhelming force would make a quick American victory a near certainty, greatly increasing the odds that the Iraqi army would remove Saddam before a final assault became necessary. Part of this difference of opinion stems from the starkly different concepts of warfare held by the hawks and the military. Hawks envision a quicker, more agile, make-it-up-on-the-fly model of warfare—one which actually showed itself rather well in Afghanistan. Simply put, they don't subscribe to the Powell Doctrine. But that's not all that's in play. The hawks' first priority is not how it is done or even that it is done right—it is ensuring that the opportunity to finish off Saddam does not, once again, slip away. More than anything else, they are animated by the desire to get America into the fight and committed, even if that means doing so without the full commitment of manpower and military hardware that may eventually prove necessary or fully apprising the American people of what they may be getting into. And that is what has the uniformed services nervous: that the civilians at the Pentagon and the White House may bow to the hawks' wishes and attempt to do this on the cheap. "The fear that a lot of us have is that a really honest debate is not being conducted," says a recently retired career officer with experience working the Iraq file. "There's a sense among a number of us that the American public doesn't understand the party they're being invited to. This is going to cost big bucks. There's going to be lots of bad things going to happen. A lot of terrible things you're going to see on TV."

Hope Is Not A Plan

Another terrible thing critics worry about is that attacking Saddam might rattle Arab populations in nearby countries, to the point where regimes in Egypt, Jordan, or Saudi Arabia could fall. The hawks insist that any instability will be fleeting and easily weathered, and that a demonstration of American resolve will firm up wobbly allies. Again, we are in best-case-scenario land here. Press the point further, and the hawks do a clever bit of intellectual jujitsu, insisting that it would be a *good thing* if the repressive governments of Egypt or Saudi Arabia fell. "Mubarak is no great shakes," says Perle of the Egyptian president. "Surely we can do better than Mubarak." I put the same question to Perle's colleague from the Reagan administration and fellow hawk, Ken Adelman. Did he think wobbly or upended regimes in Egypt and Saudi Arabia were worth the price of removing Saddam? "All the better if you ask me."

These neoconservatives are not just being glib. They see toppling Saddam as the first domino to fall, with other corrupt Middle Eastern regimes following—just as the fall of the Berlin Wall was followed by the collapse of communism.

Here, as in so many other cases, the hawks have an amazing vision, but a deeply flawed grasp of how to act operationally and in the moment. It may not be in our long-term interests to ally ourselves with corrupt authoritarian governments in the Arab world. But it's quite possible that these governments, which are at least nominal allies of the U.S., will be replaced by corrupt authoritarian regimes that hate us. Moreover, the U.S. military understandably does not want Saudi Arabia disintegrating at its rear while it's in the midst of an operation in Iraq.

What the national security establishment does want is for the other Middle East regimes to be brought in as part of the anti-Saddam alliance. The hawks scorn such coalition building as a brake on our ability to act with moral clarity and decision. *We're right and we don't need anyone else's permission*, is the underlying mindset. But combining an intense diplomatic effort with military action is not about getting other countries' permission. It's about covering your flanks. One of the reasons American force worked in Kosovo in 1999 is that the U.S. had Slobodan Milosevic cornered not only militarily but diplomatically.

He had no one to turn to, to play off against us. Given the state of opinion in the Arab world today, we probably cannot expect open support from the Saudis or the Egyptians or other frontline Arab states. But we do need an understanding with them because we cannot afford to see Crown Prince Abdullah materialize in Baghdad with a "peace plan" just as we are readying our assault.

The same goes for the State Department's efforts to get weapons inspectors back into Iraq. The hawks tend to view weapons inspections as a contemptible joke, a half-measure that will bog us down with kibitzing at the U.N. and rob us of our justification for invasion. Properly done, however, inspections are not a way to avoid war but to build the ground work for it. Before a single soldier hits the ground in Iraq, the U.S. should demand a virtually air-tight inspection regime—not the half-measures the U.N. is currently negotiating with Saddam. Our European allies would oppose this strenuously, as will Russia and China. But it is well worth drawing them into that conversation, because the force and logic of our argument is quite strong. Once the concept of inspections is granted, the need to make them effective is difficult to refute. If Saddam were to accept a truly robust inspections regime—one which would allow the inspectors to roam the country more or less at will—we will have achieved our aim of neutralizing the threat of Iraqi weapons of mass destruction. But, of course, when he doesn't agree—and he won't—then we will have forced our allies to confront the reality of Iraqi intransigence head-on. Some may still oppose our imminent military action. But others might join us, and that will make us stronger.

Taking our time, deploying large numbers of troops and weaponry, working the diplomatic channels, defusing possible sources of opposition from European states and the Arab world, all will help accomplish another aim. It will telegraph our seriousness, and by so doing increase the chance that domestic forces will overthrow (or at least weaken) Saddam before our soldiers even have to begin an attack.

It's difficult to imagine that the establishment and national security bureaucracies would have brought us to our current and correct focus on Iraq. But it's even more clear that the hawks' record of breezy planning, reckless prediction, and indifferent fidelity to the truth makes them unfit to be the ones in control of how the job gets done. The hawks have a vision. But as the folks in uniform are so fond of saying, "Hope is not a plan." Getting rid of Saddam really is necessary. But it has to be done right. So, Mr. President, when the time comes for you to make a decision about Iraq, talk with Paul Wolfowitz and let him tell you what the goal should be. Escort him to the door and lock it behind you. Then sit down for a serious talk with Colin Powell.

Saddam's Nuclear Program

Khidhir Hamza

from *Bulletin of the Atomic Scientists*

In the early 1970s, Saddam Hussein, then Iraq's vice president and vice chairman of the ruling Revolutionary Council, ordered the development of a clandestine nuclear weapons program. I was one of those who initiated the program.

The plan's long-range objective was to produce nuclear weapons, but the immediate objective was to acquire nuclear technology. To achieve that goal, the manipulation of the International Atomic Energy Agency (IAEA) was key. The elaborate plan of deception that gradually evolved included the signing of nuclear cooperation treaties with friendly states and the invention of bogus projects.

Iraq had impeccable credentials for receiving nuclear assistance. It had signed the Nuclear Non-Proliferation Treaty in 1968 and ratified it in 1969. That made our nuclear-power cover stories internationally acceptable and justified our major nuclear purchases with the full backing of the IAEA. Over the years, I had many roles. I was chief of the fuel division in the 1970s, head of the theoretical division of the enrichment program in the 1980s, scientific adviser to the chairman of the Iraqi Atomic Energy Commission (IAEC) in the mid-1980s, and—for a brief period in 1987—director of weaponization. It was never smooth sailing, and after the Persian Gulf War, I grew disenchanted with the regime. In 1994 I decided to leave Iraq. Not allowed to leave legally, I had to follow a circuitous route that led through several countries. And for reasons that are still unclear, in April 1995 the Sunday Times of London published an erroneous story reporting that I had been killed by the Iraqi intelligence service after sneaking out secret documents exposing Iraq's reconstituted nuclear weapon program.

After that report appeared, I moved to the United States, where I now live. I write this now to highlight the long history of Iraq's nuclear weapon program and my past involvement in that program, and to describe how Iraq hoodwinked the IAEA during the 1970s and 1980s.

The Chicken Farm

Since the end of the Gulf War in 1991, the U.N. Special Commission (UNSCOM) and the International Atomic Energy Agency Action Team have spent tens of thousands of man-hours deciphering the secrets of Iraq's clandestine nuclear weapons program and dismantling its components.

The Action Team eventually came to a pretty thorough understanding of the program, which was far-reaching and well funded. But an important controversy remains about when the weapons program was created, and by whom.

Until 1995, Iraq denied having had any serious intention of building nuclear weapons, despite abundant evidence to the contrary uncovered by Action Team investigations. Then, after Hussein Kamel, Saddam's son-in-law and head of the Ministry of Industry and Military Industrialization, defected in August 1995, his revelations about the scope and intensity of the nuclear weapons program threatened the credibility of the government's denial.

In response to Kamel's defection, the Iraqi government produced the so-called "chicken farm documents." Several days after Kamel fled to Jordan, senior UNSCOM and Action Team officials were taken to Kamel's farm, where a half-million-page cache of documents was stashed in a shed. The documents shed light on extensive programs to develop and build weapons of mass destruction, particularly nuclear weapons.

The Iraqi government said it had not made a decision to manufacture nuclear weapons. The government said, in effect, that it had been duped—that Kamel had developed these programs without authorization and had hidden the incriminating evidence at his farm.

To complete the scenario, a new story was concocted as to how the nuclear program started. This story was even included in Iraq's so-called "Full, Final, and Complete Document" on its weapons programs, submitted in several versions in 1996 to the Action Team. In its briefest form, the new story went like this: In 1987 Gen. Hussein Kamel visited the Iraqi Atomic Energy Establishment (AEE) and asked if there were any plans to develop a nuclear device. Learning there were not, he ordered the preparation of a report outlining the requirements for developing a device.

This scenario gave the impression—reinforced by the Iraqi media—that Kamel had acted on his own, without Saddam's approval. Otherwise, why would he hide the documents on his personal property? Later, Deputy Prime Minister Tariq Aziz insinuated that Kamel had tried to restart the nuclear weapons program on his own after the Gulf War, in violation of the cease-fire agreement. Although no one bought that story (at least in private), it was one more effort to exonerate the Iraqi government from any nuclear wrongdoing before or after the Gulf War.

But the idea that a program employing thousands of scientists, engineers, technicians, and support staff, involving major facilities, and costing billions of dollars could have been carried out without Saddam Hussein's knowledge is absurd on its face—although it is the kind of diplomatic fiction that may eventually make it easier for the Security Council to lift sanctions against Iraq.

The truth is that the nuclear-weapons program started much earlier than most people realize—and on the direct orders of Saddam Hussein.

An Unasked Question

In 1971, Iraq's nuclear research program had been under way for a few years but was poorly funded. The IAEC, which was replaced in the mid-1980s by a cabinet-level agency, was then a small department within the Ministry of

Higher Education. It had made little headway. The work, considered a low priority, was almost at a standstill.

In my early 30s, I was the chairman of the physics department of the Nuclear Research Center, located at Al-Tuwaitha, 20 miles south of Baghdad. My salary was $150 a month, about a tenth of what I had made a few years earlier, teaching in the United States.

Much of our equipment had been obtained through assistance programs underwritten by the IAEA. As for our own government's contributions, we didn't even get enough money to attend scientific conferences. One day in late 1971, I was approached by the two men in charge of the IAEC, Moyesser Al-Mallah and Husham Sharif, both of whom were U.S.-educated and old and trusted members of the ruling Ba'ath party. They explained that as long as our objectives were peaceful, the government would provide little support. They said we needed to attract the attention of Saddam Hussein, a fast-rising star in the government, and that we could do so only by adopting a strategic objective—that is, we should propose a bomb program based on first acquiring a civil fuel cycle followed by a full-blown program to build nuclear weapons.

I was naive in those days. I recall thinking that proposing a bomb program was a gambit. I thought the plan, if carefully worded, would bring in money without our having to make a full commitment to producing a bomb, at least in the near future. We could fool Saddam; we would maneuver him into sending money our way, but we would escape close scrutiny. I later learned that few people were able to fool Saddam, and I came to realize that Saddam probably initiated the program in the first place.

After a review of our 50-page proposal by a group affiliated with the Revolutionary Council, Saddam accepted the plan. Iraq's president at the time was A. Al-Bakr, an army officer with little interest in the daily affairs of government. Saddam dominated planning and follow-up.

Acquiring nuclear technology within the IAEA safeguards system was the first step in establishing the infrastructure necessary to develop nuclear weapons. In 1973, we decided to acquire a 40-megawatt research reactor, a fuel-manufacturing plant, and nuclear fuel-reprocessing facilities, all under cover of acquiring the expertise needed to eventually build and operate nuclear power plants and produce and recycle nuclear fuel. Our hidden agenda was to clandestinely develop the expertise and infrastructure needed to produce weapon-grade plutonium.

As it turned out, few of Iraq's suppliers—or the IAEA itself—ever bothered to ask a simple question: Why would Iraq, with the second largest oil reserves in the world, want to generate electricity by burning uranium? For its part, Iraq was careful to avoid raising IAEA suspicions; an elaborate strategy was gradually developed to deceive and manipulate the agency.

A Seat on the Board

A two-man Iraqi delegation—Al-Mallah, who was then secretary general of the Iraqi Atomic Energy Commission, and I—attended the IAEA's annual General Conference in September 1973. Our post-conference report, sent directly to Saddam, described the IAEA and its role in implementing safeguards and providing nuclear assistance.

It was clear from the IAEA charter and many of its publications that, rhetoric aside, the IAEA served the interests of the nuclear weapon states. Under President Eisenhower's "Atoms for Peace" program, and later under the Nuclear Non-Proliferation Treaty, the IAEA was described as an organization that would facilitate the transfer of nuclear technology to nations that agreed not to use that technology to develop nuclear weapons.

In turn, the nuclear weapon states had pledged to reduce their inventories of nuclear weapons and to help transfer peaceful nuclear technology to the "have-not" states. The IAEA's role was to verify that the non-nuclear weapon states were using nuclear technology strictly for peaceful purposes.

Our examination of the IAEA's budget revealed that the agency's main role was to conduct inspections. Member contributions for the inspection program were mandatory; contributions for technical assistance programs were voluntary.

This signaled only one thing: that the IAEA's primary role was as a watchdog. As for the nuclear powers actually reducing their arsenals, few believed reductions were possible in the political climate of the 1970s. To Iraq, signing the NPT meant acceding to the wishes of the nuclear weapon states and receiving only marginal technical assistance in return. Our report on the Vienna meeting concluded that the IAEA's chief activity was spying for the nuclear weapon states.

After studying our report, Saddam issued new orders: There would be no requests for IAEA assistance that concerned personnel—that is, we would not ask for IAEA help in attending conferences or in training or in buying equipment. Meanwhile, we would sharply limit our requests for IAEA consultation; close contact might reveal sensitive information.

Our report included a summary of the IAEA's organizational structure, noting that the nuclear powers retained permanent seats on the Board of Governors, with a portion of the remaining seats open for election every year at the general conference. Saddam wanted to increase Iraq's participation in the agency, mainly to penetrate this "intelligence-gathering organization." We decided to seek a seat on the board.

When our delegation arrived in Vienna for the 1974 general conference, we learned that the Iraqi embassy was not prepared to carry out Saddam's orders. No effort had been made to win votes—in fact, Iraq's candidacy had not even been announced.

Iraq's ambassador to Austria, who was the official representative to the IAEA and automatically the head of the Iraqi delegation, was immediately sent into retirement. Other embassy staff members were transferred to less desirable locations. After that, the embassy expedited atomic energy matters.

Despite the late start, Hisham Al-Shawi, minister of higher education, was elected to the board. After the conference, however, Saddam took control, transferring the Atomic Energy Commission to the Revolutionary Council and appointing himself its chair, an appointment that was never disclosed to the IAEA.

Gaining a seat on the board was only a preliminary step. To get better access to the inner workings of the IAEA, the position of "scientific attaché" was created at the embassy in Vienna. Suroor Mahmoud Mirza, a brother of Saddam's senior bodyguard, was appointed to this position.

With his winning ways and generous budget, Mahmoud quickly became a popular figure among IAEA employees and other delegations, who remained ignorant of his underlying purpose. Mahmoud succeeded so well that he remained in Vienna for nearly 10 years. He lost his job in the late 1980s, when his brother fell out of favor with Saddam.

Mahmoud provided detailed reports on many subjects not covered in open publications—including the role of inspectors in uncovering clandestine programs, how information given to inspectors was controlled, and how limited their leverage was. He also realized the importance of having Iraqis work as inspectors to gain a more complete understanding of inspection procedures and processes. Most important of all, he alerted us to the success of satellite remote sensing in uncovering clandestine, and especially underground, activities. As a result, Iraq built no underground facilities.

New Ground Rules

Saddam's orders limiting interaction with the IAEA were not well understood at home. Although the IAEA offered little technical assistance, the agency provided long-term training opportunities for Iraqi scientists and helped to place them in other nuclear-related organizations. The IAEA was able to open doors that had previously been closed.

At home, many Iraqi scientists found the security mode instituted by the IAEC particularly repugnant. It included a vast increase in security personnel. Foreigners—including Arabs—were no longer welcome. Saddam's new deputy, Dr. Abdul-Razzaq A1-Hashimi, ordered Iraqis married to foreign wives to divorce them. In many cases these men preferred to leave the country instead. Morale deteriorated.

Saddam had to act. In late 1974, two day-long meetings were held at the Presidential Palace Conference Hall. Any encounter with Saddam was problematic. He could be charming and you could get what you wanted. Or he could be cruel and unreasonable, as many found to their regret.

In these two meetings, we met the charming Saddam. Even as he paced the conference hall in an elegant French suit, he apologized to his audience for pacing. It was doctor's orders, he explained. He needed to walk because of back problems.

When one IAEC employee complained about some problem he was having with his boss, Saddam simply laughed and ordered him to see him later so they could solve the problem. A woman who complained about being harassed by her landlord was relocated to a government housing project. Many people had money problems, which they voiced later in private meetings; some of these problems were resolved with cash on the spot. In short, the meetings convinced atomic energy personnel that they were very important to the government.

The first day of the meeting was with senior staff—about 20 people. The next day there was a general meeting with many more of the agency's employees, which numbered about 200 at the time. Saddam laid down the rules employees were to follow from then on:

All foreigners, including those representing international organizations, should be thought of as spies. Foreigners might appear friendly and helpful, but they were really trying to gain your confidence in an effort to discover what you were doing. Contacts with foreigners were to be limited, and each contact had to be reported in detail.

Each member of the IAEC had to be security-conscious. A scientist or engineer who was not security-conscious was useless, dangerous, and not wanted.

Scientists and engineers should not divulge what they knew to outsiders; in fact, they should try to appear less knowledgeable than they were.

These were the directions of the most powerful man in the country, and they were phenomenally effective. Unauthorized contacts with foreigners became the equivalent of treason. An Office of Policy and International Relations was created within the IAEC, and all foreign contacts, including technical assistance and inspections, had to go through this office.

But within the new ground rules, Iraq could receive more IAEA technical assistance. For instance, the Soviet-provided research reactor was upgraded from two to five megawatts/thermal, and there were consultations about the possible future purchase of a power reactor. If the IAEA did not have to be involved, it was excluded.

Easily Manipulated

Abdul-Wahid Al-Saji, a mild mannered physicist, became the first Iraqi to serve as an IAEA inspector. He was replaced in the late 1980s by Abdul-Wahab Al-Hani.

Ironically, the understanding that gradually emerged from a closer relationship to the IAEA was how weak and easily manipulated the agency was. With little leverage on member states, inspectors were in a difficult position. If an inspector wrote about a suspicious activity in the state he visited, and if it leaked out (which was often the case), the inspector could be denied future access to that state. Further, according to Al-Saji and Mahmoud, if an inspector gained a reputation as antagonistic or aggressive, few states would allow him to inspect their facilities.

Overall, the IAEA proved extremely useful to the Iraqi weapons program in obtaining nuclear technology. The agency accepted Iraq's importation of highly enriched uranium fuel for its research reactor, without evaluating the possibility that Iraq might divert it to military use. Much later, in 1987, I was instructed by Hussein Kamel, then my boss, to keep open the option of diverting the safeguarded fuel in case the clandestine enrichment programs failed. After Kamel's defection, Iraq revealed to the Action Team that it had initiated a crash program after the invasion of Kuwait in August 1990. (This program, aimed at making an atomic bomb from the safeguarded highly enriched uranium, failed.)

The IAEA accepted and promoted power reactor programs in both Iraq and Iran—two oil-rich countries with high military expenditures, centuries-old antagonisms, and many possibilities for conflict. Under cover of safeguarded civil nuclear programs, Iraq managed to purchase the basic components of plutonium production, with full training included, despite the risk that the technology could be replicated or misused. Iraq took full advantage of the IAEA's recommendation in the mid-1980s to start a plasma physics program for "peaceful" fusion research. We thought that buying a plasma focus device, which operates in the nanosecond range, and which requires ultrafast electronic components, would provide an excellent cover for buying and learning about fast-electronics technology, which could be used to trigger atomic bombs. We even considered the plasma focus device as a possible neutron initiator for a bomb, but abandoned that approach when we discovered how unreliable the system was for producing neutrons. In any case, IAEA personnel brokered the purchase of the system together with the necessary training.

To be fair, the IAEA personnel had no expertise in making nuclear weapons. They simply viewed plasma focus research as a cheaper and more readily available alternative to building a tokomak, a fusion-research device that was far too expensive for most countries.

Invisible Buildings

Iraq built a number of new buildings at Al-Tuwaitha that were dedicated to developing ways to produce bomb-grade uranium. These new buildings-constructed in the early and mid-1980s—housed the research and development phases of both the electromagnetic isotopic separation (EMIS) and gaseous diffusion enrichment programs. The diffusion program, which lasted from 1982 to at least mid-1987, occupied three large buildings. Several other buildings housed the EMIS research and development program.

Many researchers and administrators in the enrichment program objected to putting the covert enrichment program at Al-Tuwaitha, a declared site that was regularly inspected by the IAEA. The Israeli bombing of the French-built Osirak reactor in June 1981 and the subsequent media discussions about the Iraqi nuclear program also showed that Tuwaitha was under close scrutiny.

The Israelis had already complained in 1981 about the huge conglomeration of buildings at Al-Tuwaitha, as revealed in a 1982 book describing the bombing, Two Minutes Over Baghdad. To add more buildings and work on the early stages of a nuclear weapons program in an area where IAEA inspectors had access struck most of us as the ultimate folly. But the program's top administrators knew better. They had come to understand how poorly the IAEA system worked.

In any event, the head of the research and development division, Jaafar D. Jaafar, wanted the projects located at Tuwaitha for the sake of convenience, and the chair of the Atomic Energy Commission, Humam Al-Ghafoor, simply did not want the bother and logistical problems of managing several sites. (When Hussein Kamel was put in charge of the clandestine nuclear program in 1987, he ordered additional buildings to be located outside Tuwaitha.)

Tuwaitha had 100-foot-high berms, and IAEA inspectors were carefully escorted along pre-designated paths that did not expose the new buildings. Questions by inquisitive inspectors were answered carefully to avoid revealing new information. Iraqi authorities spent considerable time before each inspection rehearsing answers to possible questions and planning the routes of the inspections. The IAEA never learned about many of the buildings at Tuwaitha until after the Persian Gulf War, when for the first time it received aerial photos of the site.

Some of the EMIS developmental activities were housed inside the same buildings that were inspected by the IAEA. Important research on ion sources—the heart of the EMIS program, because intense ionized uranium beams are essential for producing highly enriched uranium—was conducted in the fuel-manufacturing building, which had been supplied by an Italian firm and was under IAEA safeguards. Under the old IAEA inspection rules, however, the IAEA could inspect only certain rooms. The ion research activities took place in rooms where inspectors were not allowed. To avoid risk of discovery, workers were told to stay out of the building or remain behind locked doors during an inspection.

Asleep at the Switch

By any estimate, Al-Tuwaitha must have housed thousands of technical people. Yet for two decades, only a handful of scientific articles were published by those working at this huge complex. We worried about how this would look to the IAEA or to foreign intelligence organizations. But to our relief, no one ever raised questions about the lack of publications by Al-Tuwaitha's scientists.

The research center was carrying out Saddam's original orders, and it permitted only a few publications. Jaafar, for example, had 32 publications listed on his resume when he returned to Iraq in 1974, most of which he wrote during a four-year period in the early 1970s when he worked at Cern, the European accelerator center in Switzerland. From the time he returned to Iraq in 1974 through the Gulf War in 1991, he published only two or three additional articles.

Despite the size of the Iraqi program, it had only a dozen or so scientists and engineers who were in a position to plan and implement nuclear projects. Without these key people, the nuclear program could not have existed. Before the Gulf War, the IAEA had no idea who they were or what they did, nor did Western intelligence agencies seem to have much interest. More than 400 Iraqis were trained in France and Italy during the late 1970s, yet none of them reported being approached about what they were doing. Nearly all the current leaders of the program were drawn from those trainees.

Most surprising to the Iraqi scientists after the Gulf War was how little was known about them, especially among UNSCOM and IAEA Action Team personnel who were supposed to uncover the nuclear program. Iraqi scientists found it unbelievable that IAEA member states did not share critical intelligence about Iraq before the Gulf War. Iraq's scientific attaché at IAEA headquarters in Vienna regularly sent back all published IAEA reports concerning Iraq's nuclear activities, including video clips. In 1989, an article in Der Spiegel detailed the participation of German nationals in Iraq's centrifuge program. Still the IAEA voiced no concern about a possible secret enrichment program.

The only explanation my colleagues and I could imagine was that the major powers did not think the IAEA could be trusted with intelligence information because of its reputation for leaks. But more important, the agency's safeguards division showed little willingness to follow up on leads, even if it obtained provocative information. This situation has improved markedly since the embarrassment of uncovering Iraq's clandestine program. The new safeguards system that has gown out of the "93+2 program," set up in 1993 to overcome past failings, is capable of detecting future Iraqs. But if the old IAEA safeguards culture prevails, the new system will not be a match for a determined and untiring Saddam or other proliferators.

The Road to the United States

Working for Saddam proved to be nerve-wracking and thankless. Terror tactics were his favored means of control. Since Saddam became president in 1979, the country has lived in a constant state of war. As the system turned more cynical, it became unbearable. Everyone was treated as a possible defector.

Since 1981 Iraq has prevented workers in the nuclear program from traveling outside the country with their families. Scientists and engineers were conscripted into the program without their consent. The program had many disgruntled employees and many personnel problems. One worker defected in 1991. Two of the program's leaders, Jaafar and Dr. Hussein Al-Sharistani, were thrown in jail in late 1979 and early 1980 with no official reason given. My colleagues and I believed the reason was that they did not cooperate adequately with the bomb program. Jaafar was released after 20 months, but only after he agreed to take charge of the clandestine uranium enrichment program. Except for an escorted trip to the Soviet Union, he was never permitted to leave the country.

The Gulf War was the last straw. Living conditions and security deteriorated to a degree that made life in Iraq a living hell. Many of the country's intelligentsia and professional class left by any means they could. Many of those lucky enough to be outside the country during the war, including several ambassadors, simply did not return. One of them was the ex-chairman of the IAEC, Dr. Al-Shawi, Iraq's ambassador to Britain and later to Canada. In a press conference in 1993 he and another ambassador asked for the overthrow of Saddam's regime. It was in 1994, after the brutal and bizarre murder of a chief procurement officer near my farm, that I decided to leave.

The problem with trying to learn the truth about the Iraqi nuclear weapons program is the complete secrecy and the security measures that surround it. The movements of insiders, including members of their families, are restricted, and breaking the rules can be a death sentence. Muayad Naji, a centrifuge program worker, left Iraq without authorization in 1992. He was shot down by Iraqi intelligence agents on a street in Amman, Jordan, in front of his wife and children. People who knew him reported that all he wanted was to go to Libya for a teaching job.

Some are luckier or do better planning. An electrical engineer who defected after the war in 1991 was instrumental in uncovering important EMIS sites. He was careful to smuggle his family out with him. When the fact that I had left the country was publicly reported in the April 2, 1995 edition of the Sunday *Times* of London, the Iraqi government was not worried because my family remained in Iraq. The government even covered for me by saying that I was on a business trip.

When my family managed to slip out of the country, however—and after the defection of Kamel four months later—the situation changed. Kamel's name and mine are the only names that appear in Iraq's "Full, Final, and Complete Declaration," where we are accused of having essentially created the weaponization program on our own.

After two disastrous wars and the large-scale massacre of Kurds and Shiites, the criminal nature of the Iraqi regime is internationally recognized. (Kamel described one massacre—in which 4,600 were killed because of a rumor—in a September 21, 1995 interview broadcast on CNN.) What is not recognized by the world community, though, is the determination with which the regime of Saddam Hussein intends to pursue programs to produce weapons of mass destruction, including nuclear weapons, once sanctions are lifted. The nuclear weapons group is still in place; the expertise is still there; and Saddam Hussein and his colleagues are well practiced in the arts of deception.

The Politics of Weapons Inspection

Patrick and Andrew Cockburn

from *Out of the Ashes: The Resurrection of Saddam Hussein*

In her four years as U.S. ambassador to the United Nations, Madeleine Albright had staked a claim to be regarded as Saddam Hussein's most unremitting foe. Her answer to the question posed in a 1996 TV interview regarding the cost of sanctions in Iraqi childrens' lives—"We think the price is worth it"—which became famous in the Arab world, only underscored her hawkish credentials at home on the issue and did nothing to impede her eventual elevation as secretary of state.

Soon after Mrs. Albright's arrival in Washington, word spread that she would be making a major policy address on the subject of Iraq at Georgetown

University. Expectations ran high, on all sides. Before the speech, a prominent businessman of Iraqi extraction, known to be in close touch with Nizar Hamdoon, Saddam's UN envoy, was circulating word among the Iraqi exile community in Washington that the speech would contain dramatic new initiatives.

On the appointed day, March 26, 1997, Mrs. Albright strode onto the dais and announced that "We do not agree with the nations who argue that if Iraq complies with its obligations concerning weapons of mass destruction, sanctions should be lifted." Sanctions, she made clear, would remain. Almost six years had passed since Robert M. Gates, President Bush's deputy National Security adviser, had declared that sanctions would remain as long as Saddam Hussein ruled Iraq, and that in the meantime "Iraqis will pay the price." Nothing, it seemed, had changed.

There could have been no clearer message to Saddam that he had little to gain in further cooperation with the UN inspectors. Even had he been of a mind to yield the secrets of the weapons he had so tenaciously concealed since 1991, Albright had told the world that he would gain nothing by doing so.

Yet while stating that Saddam's putative arsenal of mass-destruction weapons was unconnected to the maintenance of sanctions, the United States still emphasized the importance of the weapons inspectors' mission, the execution of which, paradoxically, depended on Iraqi cooperation and assistance. It was up to the Iraqis to escort inspectors to sites where weapons or documents might be hidden. The Iraqis had repeatedly demonstrated their power to exclude the inspectors from any site if they so wished. The extensive program of remote cameras and other sensors monitoring former weapons-related factories and laboratories could be removed with a simple phone call from Baghdad. In that event, the only remaining sanction for the United States and its allies would be military action—a renewed bombing offensive. But the threat of force was a diminishing asset because, as the failure to secure support for bombing Saddam in retaliation for the Arbil operation had vividly demonstrated, every potential military confrontation highlighted declining support for the United States both in the Middle East and around the world. By 1997, recalls a senior Unscom official, Security Council resolutions condemning Iraq had "all the impact of traffic tickets." Thus, a crisis over Iraqi cooperation with Unscom carried significant risks for the United States. Saddam, as he well recognized, could choose the timing of those crises. As 1997 went on, he had plenty of opportunity to do so. The inspectors were testing the limits of the Iraqi leader's patience.

Ever since the inspectors first arrived, Saddam had been forced to give up much. His initial expectation that his Unscom problem would last only a few months and that the inspectors could easily be fooled or bribed had soon been proved false, as we have seen. Thereafter, the Iraqis had waged a fighting retreat. Up until the summer of 1995, they had successfully concealed their most modern chemical capabilities—the VX nerve agent—as well as their homegrown missile program and almost the entire biological effort. Then, in August 1995, the defection of Hussein Kamel had brought disaster. Unscom officials now knew that they had been successfully fooled by their Iraqi opponents. The inspectors set to work to uncover the full truth.

In April 1997, Rolf Ekeus reported to the Security Council that after six years of work, "Not much is unknown about Iraq's retained proscribed weapons capabilities. However, what is still not accounted for cannot be neglected." Even a few long-range missiles, he wrote, would be a source of deep concern if those missiles were fitted with the most deadly of chemical nerve agents, VX. "A single missile warhead filled with the biological warfare agent anthrax could spread many millions of lethal doses in an attack on any city" in the Middle East.

Ironically, the publicity about Saddam's secret arsenal, attendant on Ekeus's investigations, helped him project a chill of fear over his neighbors. The primary effectiveness of these weapons was psychological. In 1991, the Kurds had fled in panic when Saddam's troops dropped flour on them from helicopters. "I lie awake at night worrying about those terrible biological weapons," a tremulous King Fahd of Saudi Arabia once told a visiting Kuwait diplomat. To divest Saddam of the psychological advantage he derived from his tiny but famous arsenal, Unscom would have to find or account for every single missile, all the VX, and every pound of anthrax, as well as the machines and materials used to make them. That was most certainly an impossible undertaking, but even in making the attempt, the inspectors would have to penetrate and defeat the system of concealment created on Saddam's orders in the early summer of 1991.

As with so much else, the existence of this system had come to light thanks to Hussein Kamel. The sudden appearance of the huge cache of "chicken farm" documents together with the fact, soon deduced by the Unscom sleuths, that certain categories of files that would naturally belong in such a collection of records were absent led them to the inescapable conclusion that the missing documents must still exist under the protective guard of a concealment apparatus dedicated to frustrating Unscom. Hussein Kamel's cousin and fellow defector, Major Izz al-Din al-Majid of the Special Republican Guard, who had actually had missile parts buried in his own garden in Baghdad, provided confirmation and wealth of detail in interviews with Unscom officials.

As we have seen, concealment was in the hands of especially trusted members of elite security organizations: the Mukhabarat, the Special Republican Guards, and the Special Security Service. Once upon a time, this arrangement had operated under the supervision of Hussein Kamel, but after his departure, control had passed to the capable and hardworking Qusay, operating in conjunction with the immensely powerful Abed Hamid Mahmoud, Saddam's private secretary. Not everyone, of course, in the twenty-thousand-man Special Republican Guards, and the Special Security Organization, which comprised a total of two thousand people, was involved in the exercise. Those directly concerned numbered no more than a hundred, selected on the basis of absolutely unquestioned loyalty and, usually, a direct family relationship with the leader.

At the end of 1995, Ekeus commissioned Nikita Smidovich, the mustachioed Russian expert who so maddened senior Iraqi officials, to begin leading an inspection team targeted specifically on the "mechanism" for concealing missile parts, tools, and most important, documents. Since the weapons were being guarded by the same security organizations that protected Saddam Hussein himself, that meant Smidovich and his team would inevitably be getting very close to the central nervous system of the regime itself. In March and June

1996, Smidovich had tried to get into what became known as "sensitive sites" occupied by these security organizations and had been blocked, or at least delayed, by the guards. Ekeus managed to hammer out a compromise in June 1996 with Tariq Aziz under which the teams would be allowed into such places. But the following month, the team was blocked again at a Special Republican Guard camp, although they saw long, round objects looking for all the world like Scud missiles being hurriedly driven away. The Iraqis had a ready explanation: The admittedly suspicious "Scud-like objects" being removed from the site were, they claimed, concrete pillars that coincidentally resembled missiles.

As the Unscom teams continued their hunt, they found that time and again they were just too late. Despite stringent efforts to make their descent on a suspected site a total surprise, the Iraqis appeared to have been forewarned in the nick of time and the team would arrive to see trucks speeding away in the opposite direction. Either Iraqi intelligence had managed to find some way of listening in on the last-minute planning sessions at Unscom's Baghdad headquarters in the Canal Hotel or there was a mole inside the organization. Hussein Kamel had unmasked Ekeus's translator as an Iraqi agent, but that individual had never had access to information as sensitive as this.

The Unscom offices in the Canal had been modernized in 1994 and were equipped with the best in countersurveillance technology that American and British intelligence could provide, making it unlikely that the Iraqis had succeeded in planting a bug. There was, however, a Russian scientist assigned to the teams who always seemed suspiciously inquisitive about upcoming "no-notice" inspections. Therefore, in strictest secrecy, a few of the senior members of the special commission staff planned and executed a sting operation. With only the suspect present, they discussed a purported upcoming surprise inspection at a specific location. Sure enough, discreet observation at the nominated site revealed the guards fully prepared for an Unscom visit. The Russian, who appeared to have been operating under the auspices of his country's foreign intelligence service, the SVR, was sent home amid conditions of deepest secrecy. The penetration of Unscom, using corruptible foreign intelligence agencies that Saddam had discussed years before with Wafiq al-Samarrai, had been brought to fruition, at least for a while.

If Iraqi intelligence had scored a coup against Unscom, the inspection agency had itself turned into a formidable intelligence organization. Things had come a long way since Rolf Ekeus had been forced to give a personal guarantee for the cash advance from the UN secretary general's special fund that had launched the organization.

"We became extremely successful at penetrating the concealment mechanism," says one former Unscom official. "We had gotten into [i.e., developed the ability to intercept] their communications. So we were only missing them by minutes. The Iraqis may have thought that the first time it might have been just luck, but the second, third, and fourth time it was obviously something more.

"This wasn't about biological weapons hidden in Saddam's palaces, as the press was suggesting. This was about the trucks moving around that moved the things we were after. When we went into places like the Special Republican Guard installations, we checked the drivers' logs to see who had been driving what truck and where. Our people knew almost by heart the names of the various people, drivers and so on, who were involved."

The units involved in the concealment effort did not operate in isolation. As Rolf Ekeus, the man the Iraqi leader once referred to as the "miserable spy," said after he left Unscom in July 1997: "It is the Special Republican Guards we are interested in, the concealment force. But they are also the protection force for Saddam. He can build new palaces, he can rebuild the weapons program, but he cannot replace the Special Guards, because they are the key loyal force. He does not have a replacement."

When the inspectors did manage to penetrate the compounds of this and other equally important units in pursuit of trucking records and other information germane to their enquiries, they inevitably saw evidence of other tasks assigned to these loyal servants of Saddam: lists of people to be arrested, logs of drivers who had transported prisoners to the grim confines of Abu Ghraib prison, duty rosters for standing guard at the palace. An inspector once opened a door in one of these complexes only to find a roomful of people sitting at desks wearing headphones. They were the telephone eavesdroppers. The inspector excused himself and closed the door.

Sometimes the interaction between Unscom officials and the Iraqi high command bordered on the surreal. Charles Duelfer, the Unscom second-in-command, recalls one occasion when he and Roger Hill, who succeeded Nikita Smidovich as chief of the concealment team, were making an exploratory survey of a presidential site. They had a map but were finding it difficult to figure out the perimeters of the site. Suddenly a large black Mercedes purred to a halt beside them. A rear window slid down, to reveal Abed Hamid Mahmoud, the much-feared presidential secretary. Extending a genial greeting to the inspectors, Saddam's right-hand man asked if he could help. This was not as surprising as it may seem. Despite TV images of Unscom personnel engaged in grim, snarling face-offs with Saddam's minions, the two sides spent so much time in each other's company that they had inevitably become, if not friends, at least amiably civil with each other. Duelfer had even managed to strike up an amicable relationship with the previously shadowy Mahmoud, so he explained their problems with the map. "Let me see if I can help," said the Iraqi. Removing a large cigar from his mouth, he peered at the map and supplied helpful directions. Then, in response to a rapid command, one of his bodyguards opened the trunk of the limousine and reached inside. Duelfer wondered what the Iraqi leadership kept in the trunks in their cars—Kalashnikovs? rocket launchers?—and craned his neck to see. The bodyguard emerged with a tray of chilled Pepsis. After finishing their sodas, the Americans thanked their high-powered guide and he drove off.

Minutes later, another large Mercedes purred to a halt at the same spot. This one was white. The window slid down to reveal General Amer Rashid, minister for oil and the official responsible for negotiating with (and frustrating) Unscom. He too inquired as to what the two inspectors were doing. They explained that Abed Mahmoud had been most helpful in interpreting the map. "Nonsense," snorted Rashid. "Abed can't read a map. He probably had it upside down. Let me look." Duelfer explained that they were still puzzled by the precise placement of a particular boundary line. "Let's go see," said Rashid.

The line in question turned out to run along a thirteen-foot-high wall with a deep, square pit just in front. The Americans and Rashid surveyed it to check that they were in the correct place, all three stepping carefully around the pit. No one brought up the fact that the wall was heavily pitted with bullet holes, most of them grouped at chest height. Clearly, this was where the firing squads did their work, the pit providing temporary storage for dead bodies between shifts.

Any reference to the wall's gruesome function would have been an intelligence question," i.e., raising a matter that lay outside Unscom's mandate and expressly barred from discussion. So, with the surveying completed, the two inspectors thanked Rashid and went on their way.

Rolf Ekeus finally left the organization he had created at the end of 1997. Richard Butler, the Australian diplomat who replaced Ekeus as special commissioner, promoted Scott Ritter to run the concealment inspections. The former marine was determined on an aggressive approach. He later described the Iraqi system of shifting the weapons and related materials from site to site, one jump ahead of the inspectors, as a "shell game." He declared that Unscom, rather than going after the shells (weapons, documents, etc.), should pursue "the man moving the shells." Not all the inspectors agreed with this single-minded tactic. "Ritter was obsessed with this notion that he was finally going to find the document that exposed 'the architecture of concealment,' " says one official in close touch with the inspection effort. "But other people wanted to find out what the Iraqis were actually doing, and that meant looking for the weapons themselves."

By the summer of 1997, the main effort of these others was concentrated on tracking the elusive remnants of the Iraqi biological and VX nerve gas programs effort as well as the possibility that Saddam might still have missiles and warheads with which to deliver these potent agents. Central to their concerns was the lack of evidence to support Baghdad's claim that it had destroyed the 25 missile warheads and as many as 150 bombs it had filled with anthrax and botulinum toxin before the Gulf War. In addition, after sifting through the sites where Iraq insisted all its forbidden missiles had been secretly held in 1991 and 1992, Unscom announced that two remained unaccounted for.

Other bones of contention included seventeen tons of the "growth media" necessary for reproducing the toxins, nine hundred pounds of anthrax, and the possible existence of sprayers suitable for the technically highly difficult task of distributing the anthrax in fine enough particles to be absorbed in victims' lungs, as well as the true documentary history of the entire project. When Iraq submitted a sixth "Full, Final, and Complete Declaration" on the biological program in September 1997, Special Commissioner Richard Butler described it as "not even remotely credible."

The pressure from Unscom was matched by an increasingly defiant attitude from Iraq. In June 1997, an Iraqi "minder" accompanying inspectors in one of the Unscom helicopters seized the controls of the machine in order to prevent them from taking pictures of vehicles leaving a suspect site, causing a near crash. In the same week, another team was blocked from entering a site on instructions, said the Iraqi officials at the gate, "from the highest authority."

Following yet another censorious Security Council resolution demanding that Iraq cooperate with the inspectors, Saddam, sitting in council with the uniformed notables of the Revolutionary Command Council, issued a stern statement: "We would like to summarize and clarify our position as follows: Iraq has complied with and implemented all relevant resolutions. . . . There is absolutely nothing else. We demand with unequivocal clarity that the Security Council fulfill its commitments toward Iraq. . . . The practical expression of this is to respect Iraq's sovereignty and to fully and totally lift the blockade imposed on Iraq."

With hindsight, it is clear that the Iraqi leader had resolved to go on the offensive. All he needed was an excuse. That was to come soon enough.

In September, the obstruction of the inspectors grew more blatant. There was another helicopter incident on the thirteenth. On the seventeenth, a team hunting for details of VX production was kept outside the gate of the Iraqi Chemical Corps headquarters for hours while files were openly trucked away and other documents burned on the roof of the building. A week later, inspectors making a routine visit to a food-testing laboratory encountered several men carrying briefcases and trying to escape through a back door. Diane Seaman, an American microbiologist who was leading the team, seized one of the briefcases and opened it. Inside were kits for testing three deadly organisms as well as a logbook indicating that the lab had been conducting tests in secret for eight months under the supervision of the Special Security Organization.

By the end of October, the crisis was reaching a head. Insisting that Unscom had become no more than an espionage agency operating on behalf of the United States to prolong sanctions, Tariq Aziz announced on October 29 that no more Americans would be allowed into Iraq to work on the inspection teams. Four days later, he announced that the U-2 high-altitude photo-reconnaissance plane lent by the United States to Unscom was operating as a spy plane for the Americans. (Aziz was presumably unaware that by this time Scott Ritter was routinely—with the approval of his superiors—sharing U-2 photo intelligence with the Israelis.) These threatening statements were followed by news that the Iraqis were sabotaging the work of the Unscom longterm monitoring effort, in which erstwhile weapons sites were surveyed by remote cameras to ensure that forbidden work had not resumed. A few days later, the remaining American inspectors were expelled from Iraq.

As a U.S. military riposte to this defiance appeared to be increasingly inevitable, the familiar features of an Iraqi crisis reappeared. Once again, Saddam's picture adorned the covers of news magazines. *Time* declared somberly that this was "the gravest international crisis of [Bill Clinton's] presidency." On television and in print, biological warfare experts solemnly described the massacres that could be perpetrated with only a minute fraction of the Iraqi leader's presumed stockpile of anthrax. Eminent columnists began sounding like Tikritis, calling glibly for a "head shot" against Saddam, while the nightly network news displayed stirring scenes of the U.S. military gearing up for action. The atmosphere summoned up memories of the Gulf War, when White House correspondents asked President Bush in all seriousness why he was not making greater efforts to kill the president of Iraq.

The reality, however, was very different from those heady days. Most important, the coalition built by George Bush had almost completely disappeared. This time the Saudis made it clear that they did not even want to be asked to let their territory be used by U.S. warplanes in bombing Iraq. The

United States did not dare ask the Security Council for the authorization to launch an attack for fear that Russia or France, both increasingly sympathetic to Iraq's position, would cast a veto. As it was, Washington was "stunned" by the indifference of the Security Council to Saddam's expulsion of the American inspectors. The most severe sanction the council was willing to pass was a ban on international travel by Iraqi weapons scientists, the last people Saddam was likely to allow to leave the country.

The Clinton administration insisted that it had every right to bomb Iraq under existing resolutions, and prepared targeting plans. But here again, President Clinton and his advisers were faced with problems. The targets attacked in the first days of the Gulf War had been easy to choose—power plants, the presumed centers of Iraqi nuclear and other mass-destruction weapons production, Saddam Hussein himself. Subsequent inquiries had revealed that while the power-plant bombings had done permanent damage to Iraq's civilian infrastructure, they had not brought down the regime or even hindered its military capabilities to any great extent. The most important weapons plants—al-Atheer for nuclear, al-Hakam for biological production—had not even been targeted, let alone destroyed. Saddam and all other important officials had simply stayed away from obvious targets and had escaped unscathed. The rationale advanced by the White House for attacking this time was that if Saddam was preventing Unscom from rooting out his weapons capabilities, the job would have to be done with high explosives. But no one knew where these weapons and systems were actually hidden at any particular time. Some of the suspected production facilities were "dual use," with legitimate civilian applications in, among other places, hospitals. The United States could hardly bomb them.

As Clinton and his advisers mulled over these awkward choices, Saddam chose to back off, at least for the moment. Having tested the strength of the U.S. alliance, he chose to accept mediation from an old friend, Russian foreign minister Yevgeny Primakov. Primakov pledged to press for the lifting of sanctions. In return, the Iraqi leader agreed that American inspectors could return to Baghdad. The Clinton administration greeted the news with relief. By November 20, the immediate crisis was over.

From Saddam's point of view, the confrontation had yielded eminently satisfactory results. The United States had declared that Unscom's right to inspect was an issue on which it was prepared to go to war, and had then found itself, except for the British, entirely bereft of useful allies. Unscom, from being a threat to the Iraqi leader, had turned into an advantage. He now had the initiative because he could provoke a confrontation any time he chose, simply by refusing to cooperate. In pursuing this strategy, Saddam had an unlikely ally (albeit one with a different agenda), Scott Ritter, who returned to Baghdad on November 21 as determined as ever to search for Saddam's secrets, regardless of the consequences—which as likely as not would be renewed Iraqi obstruction that in turn would necessitate a forceful U.S. response.

The realization that the power to provoke crises appeared to rest in the hands of President Saddam Hussein and Major Scott Ritter had by this time dawned on the Clinton administration. An aggressive effort by Ritter, just when they had drawn back from military action in the hope of garnering more international support, was not at all what was required. According to Ritter, Special Commissioner Richard Butler now came under heavy pressure to rein in the energetic inspector, pressure to which he yielded. State Department and Unscom officials indignantly deny that Butler was following instructions from outside. "It wasn't just Madeleine Albright who didn't want Scott Ritter starting a crisis whenever he felt like it," says one State Department official indignantly. "Richard Butler didn't want him doing that either." For whatever reason, for the time being Butler canceled Ritter's planned inspections.

Meanwhile, both the United States and Iraq were readying themselves for a fresh confrontation. The Clinton administration had concluded that Saddam had gotten the better of the United States in the November crisis and the Pentagon was dusting of its target lists. The casus belli would be the principle of access for Unscom to the eight sprawling complexes comprising Saddam's somewhat gaudy palaces, security forces offices, and barracks, as well as other government facilities generically referred to as "presidential sites." When Iraq announced it was denying access to these areas, the United States rose to the bait and embraced the sites as the defining issue.

Saddam was quite ready for a second round. In November, the government had admitted the foreign press en masse, a move that yielded ample dividends in the form of sympathetic descriptions of the plight of the Iraqi people after seven years of sanctions. Now Baghdad began to fill up once again with journalists and TV crews from around the world. By mid-February, the number had reached eight hundred. Their all-too-accurate depiction of hospitals without medicines, schools without books, and mothers without food for their children had a searing impact on international public opinion. Pope John Paul II eloquently expressed the feelings of many when he declared, in an address to the Vatican diplomatic corps in January 1998:

"As we prepare for a new round of bombings, we cry out in anguish over seven years of United Nations sanctions against the Iraqi people, which can only be understood as biological warfare against a civilian population. During the Gulf War, U.S.-led coalition forces deliberately targeted Iraq's infrastructure, destroying its ability to provide food, water and sanitation to its civilian population and unleashing disease and starvation on an unimaginable scale. United Nations reports claim that over 1 million civilians have died as a direct result of the sanctions. UNICEF reports that 4,500 children are dying each month. As people of faith, we are ashamed that the actions of the UN, whose mission is to foster peace, can be so deliberately directed toward the sustained slaughter of innocent civilians."

Nevertheless, U.S. officials pressed on doggedly to make the case and gain the necessary support for bombing. Defense Secretary William Cohen sought to rouse European officials by stating that "a poison that kills" (actually ricin, the most toxic substance known) can be extracted from "six or seven castor beans," also the source of castor oil. In Iraq, Cohen noted darkly, "they are growing hundreds of acres of castor beans," leaving his audience wondering if bean fields were being added to the target list. A stream of high-ranking American officials touring the capitals of the Gulf states failed in many cases to extract even the mildest endorsements for an American attack. The most telling rejection came from Bahrain, the tiny island-state lying off the coast of Saudi Arabia, long a staunch American ally and the staging area for Unscom since its inception.

President Clinton had personally spoken with the emir to ensure his support. Even so, the Bahraini information minister issued a statement declaring that the United States could not attack Iraq from his country.

The Arab leaders had not come to love Saddam in the seven years since the Gulf War. Their chilly attitude toward the American pleadings was derived from the fact that no U.S. strike was likely to get rid of the Iraqi leader and also the growing public outrage among their subjects over the suffering of ordinary Iraqis. In 1990 and 1991, the public in the Gulf and the rest of the Arab world had been comparatively deprived of access to information. (The Saudi government withheld news of the invasion of Kuwait from its citizens for forty-eight hours.) They could listen to the BBC or Radio Monte Carlo for news that their rulers preferred to keep out of the local (tightly controlled) media, but such an audience was, in most cases, limited. In the 1990s, however, the region had been swept by a communications revolution. Arab-language satellite, TV channels brought comparatively uncensored news into the homes of anyone with a dish. The uncontrollable Internet served the same function. The public, thus informed, was resolutely against support for the United States and its perceived agent, Richard Butler, in raining more bombs on Iraqi children already decimated by sanctions. Even the most absolute of monarchs had to pay attention.

The effect of changing patterns in communications was further brought home to the administration when Madeleine Albright, William Cohen, and National Security Adviser Sandy Berger attempted to market their policy at a "town hall meeting" at Ohio State University. The event was a fiasco. Amid continuous heckling, angry citizens challenged America's "moral right" to bomb Iraq. The proceedings, humiliating for Albright, Cohen, and Berger, were televised internationally by CNN. Iraqi TV ran them in full.

By coupling the issue of a putative secret Iraqi missile force armed with biological weapons with the issue of the presidential sites, Washington had given a hostage to fortune. "All we ever believed was in these places," says Unscom deputy chief Charlie Duelfer, "was documents." Any weapons were almost certainly hidden elsewhere. But the impression took hold among press, public, and politicians that Saddam was concealing the deadly missiles in the recesses of his infamous palaces, immune from the attentions of the inspectors. In an ill-advised remark to the *New York Times,* Richard Butler suggested that such missiles could be fired "at Tel Aviv," thereby igniting panic in the Israeli capital, where long lines quickly formed to pick up gas masks and the government rushed in 6 million doses of anthrax vaccine from the United States. But the United States itself did not really appear to take the threat of an Iraqi biological or chemical missile strike very seriously. In Kuwait, which would presumably have been high on Saddam's list of possible targets, U.S. citizens were advised by their embassies that there was no cause for alarm and certainly no need to equip themselves with gas masks.

In the months between the invasion of Kuwait and the outbreak of the Gulf War, the Bush White House had been haunted by the fear of a "diplomatic solution" that would allow Saddam to extricate himself from Kuwait without undue loss of face. In those days, the United States, aided by the Iraqi leader's intransigence, had ruthlessly quashed any initiatives aimed at such a solution. But by February 1998, the world had changed. The French, who in any case had been busily negotiating business relationships with Iraq, had argued that there was little point in an inconclusive military action that would not get rid of Saddam. Now they suggested that UN secretary general Kofi Annan travel personally to Iraq to seek a way out of the crisis over the presidential sites.

Annan thought this an excellent idea. Washington did not. "You can't go," UN ambassador Bill Richardson told Annan. "It will box us in." But even the British thought the secretary general should be allowed to go to Baghdad. Clinton agreed with reluctance.

The secretary general's trip was a breakthrough for Saddam. For the first time since the war, a world statesman was coming to visit, addressing him respectfully and seeking a favor. The Iraqi leader speedily agreed to a compromise under which Unscom could inspect the presidential sites, but only when accompanied by a newly formed team of diplomats who would monitor the activities of the obstreperious inspectors. Thus, rather than asserting the principle of free and unfettered access to any site that Unscom needed, the agreement created a new and cumbersome procedure for this special category of site.

None of this mattered to Annan. After he had smoked one of Saddam's cigars, the secretary general described his host as "calm" and "very well informed and . . . in full control of the facts."

Since the crushing of the 1991 uprisings, Saddam had rarely been seen in public. Now, in the fullness of his triumph, he embarked on a program of public appearances. On March 17, for example, he visited al-Dhour, a small town in the Sunni heartland. This locality held a special significance in the Saddam Hussein story because it was here, in 1959, that he had swum the Tigris following his abortive attempt to assassinate President Qassim. He took phone calls from local citizens and accepted the "greetings of the masses, who received him with shouts of praise and dancing," according to Iraqi TV. Afterward the crowd slaughtered sheep in celebration while the leader waved from the back of an open car, firing his rifle in the air again and again.

The fact that Annan's visit had endowed Saddam with a legitimacy he had not enjoyed in years was not lost on the Republican Party leadership in Washington. Denouncing the administration's weak acquiescence to Annan's "appeasement," the Republicans in Congress looked for a means to discommode both Clinton and Saddam simultaneously and found it in none other than Ahmad Chalabi.

Ever since the CIA had withdrawn funding from the Iraqi National Congress at the beginning of 1997, the opposition group had fallen on hard times. Chalabi claimed to be supporting the opposition group out of his own pocket, to the tune of no less than $5 million a month, but the INC London headquarters had taken on a semi-deserted look. The once-bustling INC center at Salahudin in Kurdistan had been abandoned since the massacre and headlong flight of September 1996. As an active opposition movement within Iraq, the INC was defunct. Nevertheless, to powerful senators like Trent Lott and Jesse Helms and their advisers, including the formidable cold-war veteran Richard Perle, the articulate Chalabi was a godsend.

Speaking as an "elected representative" of the Iraqi people (a claim based on a vote by the three hundred delegates at the inaugural INC meeting in

Salahudin back in October 1992), Chalabi told a Senate committee that the INC was "confronting Saddam on the ground" and had the support of "thousands of Iraqis." After leveling some abuse at the CIA and paying tribute to the "warrior" Scott Ritter, he proposed that the United States should deploy its forces to establish "military exclusion zones" in northern and southern Iraq. The northern zone he had in mind was far larger than the area controlled by the Kurds, including the major cities of Mosul and Kirkuk and Iraq's northern oil fields. The southern area included Basra and the southern oil fields. The INC would take over the administration of these areas, assisted by the United States, and would eventually establish itself as the provisional government of Iraq. The whole undertaking would be financed either from Iraqi assets frozen in U.S. banks since 1991 or by the sale of oil from the southern zone.

This ambitious scheme went down well with the Senate majority party. A Democrat who had the bad taste to bring up the issue of the embezzlement charges against Chalabi in Jordan following the collapse of the Petra Bank in 1989 was roundly abused by the former banker's supporters, along with a suggestion that even the mention of this event "had the earmarks of a plant from the White House or the CIA." In the following months, support for the Iraqi opposition and Chalabi in particular blossomed in Congress, which voted $5 million to establish a "Radio Free Iraq" along the lines of the Radio Free Europe that had been beamed into Eastern Europe during the cold war. Another $5 million was voted for the "Iraqi democratic opposition," with the proviso "that a significant portion of the support for the democratic opposition should go to the Iraqi National Congress, a group that has demonstrated the capacity to effectively challenge the Saddam Hussein regime with representation from Sunni, Shia, and Kurdish elements of Iraq."

Thus, while many of its former leading Iraqi members—including the Kurdish leaders Barzani and Talabani—considered Chalabi's organization extinct, the INC, as a weapon in the Republicans' armory, was going from strength to strength on Capitol Hill. For the first time since the debate that preceded the Gulf War, Iraq had become a partisan issue in U.S. politics.

This being the case, the administration had to fight back. Officials briefed journalists on the all too evident weakness of the opposition, including the INC. Others leaked word that the CIA was hard at work on a whole new covert scheme of "sabotage and subversion" to undermine Saddam. Kurdish and Shiite agents would be enlisted to destroy "key Iraqi pillars of economic and political power, like utility plants or broadcast stations." Whoever was responsible for this "plan" had evidently forgotten Abu Amneh, the mercenary bomber and self-proclaimed veteran of the last CIA covert action against Saddam. Nor did the mooted scheme indicate much knowledge of contemporary conditions inside Iraq, where the utility plants were failing without the need of any outside intervention by the CIA. By the summer of 1998, the hottest in fifty years in Iraq, even the power plants in Baghdad were regularly out of action for twelve hours and more a day.

On a more practical level, the administration made efforts to reach out to Saddam's enemy to the east, Iran. For years, the "dual containment" policy, by which the Iranians were accorded equal status as pariahs with the Iraqis, had precluded any effective collaboration between Tehran and Washington. But by 1998, the cold war between Washington and Tehran showed signs of winding down, aided by appeals for better relations from the liberal cleric Mohammed Khatami, elected president of Iran in May 1997. Accordingly, Mohammed Baqir al-Hakim, the leader of the Iranian-backed Supreme Council for the Islamic Revolution in Iraq, began to receive earnest appeals to visit Washington. Hakim rejected these overtures, presumably with the encouragement of the powers that be in Tehran. The Iranian authorities were not about to help solve Washington's Iraq problem without receiving something tangible in return, such as U.S. blessing for shipment of Central Asian oil across Iranian territory.

At the same time, the State Department moved to rebuild old alliances. Before August 1996, northern Iraq had been a "military exclusion zone" denied to Iraqi forces. Ruminating on various possible means of challenging Saddam, the State Department now took steps to restore the status quo in Kurdistan. Accordingly, in early September 1998, Massoud Barzani and Jalal Talabani were invited to Washington for a peace meeting, lodging at the Key Bridge Marriott Hotel. In return for a firm guarantee of American military protection against Saddam, the two leaders agreed to swallow their mutual enmity once again and unite in a reformed Kurdish government, with elections to follow. Barzani agreed to share the money from the border-crossing tolls and Talabani agreed that Arbil should be jointly controlled by the two groups. As Barzani and his delegation came and went through the Marriott lobby during the negotiations, they were surveyed with vocal enmity by Jahwar al-Sourchi who, by coincidence, had booked himself into the same hotel while in Washington on a business trip. As he muttered imprecations against his tribal enemies, the blood feuds of the distant mountains of Kurdistan seemed suddenly very near.

Chalabi greeted the initial news of the Kurdish agreement with exultation. "Things are really moving," he said the day after the agreement was announced. But these high hopes were dashed when the Kurdish leaders flatly refused to have anything to do with him. Even an imperious summons from the office of Senator Jesse Helms for the pair to come to a joint meeting with the Chalabi could not sway them. The discussion with Helms's messenger became acrimonious, with ugly words such as "embezzler" being tossed about. It did not appear that the INC would be returning to Salahudin anytime soon. To add to Chalabi's vexation, the CIA leaked word that the agency's inspector general was investigating the agency's prior handling of both the INC and the Accord operations, including the use of funds. This did not sway Chalabi's partisans in Congress, however, who by October had passed the "Iraq Liberation Act," authorizing $97 million for the arming and training of the Iraqi opposition. Precisly where this training was to take place and who would be trained was not specified.

Meanwhile, reviewing the recent crises over Unscom, U.S. officials concluded that the confrontations with Saddam had been a disaster. In late April, President Clinton secretly decreed that, for the time being, there would be no more attempts at military action to force the Iraqis to allow access to presidential sites or anywhere else to the Unscom inspectors. Even when tests on a missile warhead excavated from one of the sites where Iraq had secretly destroyed weapons in 1991 indicated that it had once contained VX, thus giving the lie to Iraqi denials that it had ever succeeded in "weaponizing" the lethal chemical, the adminstration showed little appetite for an immediate face-off.

In Baghdad, Saddam was stepping up the level of his rhetoric by demanding a speedy conclusion of the Unscom mission and threatening grave but unspecified retaliation if sanctions were not lifted. Unscom was still going about its work, seeking elusive documents and other evidence of Iraqi perfidy. On August 5, however, the Iraqi government announced that it was ending all cooperation with the inspectors, thus ending their searches. The White House, true to the April decision to swear off military confrontations over the issue, had little reaction.

By now, Washington knew for certain that Saddam had been deliberately seeking a provocation. An electronic intelligence interception of a conversation between Tariq Aziz and Russian foreign minister Primakov revealed Aziz angrily complaining that "the Americans are not reacting" to the action against the inspectors. If the fact that the recent intrusive searches had been to the advantage of Saddam was now clear to high-level officials such as Madeleine Albright, the point was irrelevant to Scott Ritter. On August 27, he resigned, citing the interference with his work by high-level officials in Washington and London and complaining that "the illusion of arms control is more dangerous than no arms control at all." With this and subsequent denunciations of the administration's weakness in the face of Saddam's defiance, the articulate ex-marine swiftly became as much a hero as Ahmad Chalabi to the Republicans, anxious as they were to malign Clinton administration policy on Iraq.

Ritter lost no time in asserting the magnitude and imminence of the threat from Saddam's hidden arsenal, declaring that Saddam had at least three nuclear weapons ready for use as soon as he laid his hands on the necessary fissile material (uranium 235 or plutonium). This was too much for many of his former colleagues on the inspection teams. Gary Dillon, leader of the "action team" deployed by the International Atomic Energy Agency (the IAEA) to work on the specifically nuclear aspects of Iraq's weapons programs, asked Ritter how he had learned of these three nuclear devices. "From a northern European intelligence source," replied Ritter. The response from the nuclear experts was laughter.

"For political reasons, the United States pushes the IAEA to find little discrepancies in Iraq's nuclear accounting so that the file can be kept open," explains one official closely involved in the operation, "but short of lobotomizing or killing all the Iraqi nuclear scientists, the Iraqi nuclear program is finished. We have closed down all their nuclear facilities and activities."

Having achieved fame as the Unscom martyr, Ritter now inflicted another wound on the organization. In an interview with the Israeli newspaper *Haaretz*, he spoke in glowing terms of his close and fruitful relationship with Israeli intelligence, as well as detailing such hitherto closely held Unscom secrets as the organization's ability to monitor Iraqi communications. On the same day his *Haaretz* interview appeared, the *Washington Post* reported that Ritter, with his superiors' approval, had been in the habit of bringing film taken by Unscom's U-2 spy plane to Israel for processing and analysis. Only a few months before, the United States had been seeking to rally Arab support in asserting Unscom's right to inspect at will. Given this admission of collusion with Israel, however well intentioned, the prospect of any Arab support for Unscom was clearly fading away.

As they maneuvered, both sides were using Unscom as a tool. On November 1, Saddam upped the ante by suspending all cooperation with Unscom's long-term monitoring program, meaning that the inspectors could no longer check to ensure that sites already visited were not being used for work on weapons. Events now followed a familiar pattern. The United States and Great Britain announced that they were ready to bomb Iraq. Statements of defiance poured forth from Baghdad. At the very last minute, with U.S. warplanes actually in the air on their way to attack Iraq, the Iraqi government offered to resume "full cooperation" with Unscom. The bombers returned to their bases, but only for a brief period.

The Clinton Administration and Saddam Hussein, it appeared, were both intent on fomenting the much postponed bombing attack. Richard Butler's inspectors returned to Baghdad and went about their searches. Most of these passed off without incident, but the Iraqis on some occasions provided just enough non-cooperation to justify Butler's subsequent report that Saddam had once again failed to live up to his commitments. Reliable reports at the time suggested that Butler had composed his report in close consultation with Washington. Indeed the vociferous Scott Ritter went on record with the claim that the inspections had been a "set-up," designed to "generate a conflict that would justify a bombing." Saddam for his part, in insisting that Butler stick to the letter of the agreement negotiated by Rolf Ekeus in June 1996 and send no more than four inspectors to sensitive sites such as Baath Party headquarters, appears to have been no less eager to have the bombs fall.

In Washington, of course, everything was overshadowed by the ongoing impeachment proceedings against President Clinton. When he duly ordered the long heralded bombing strike on December 16, his Republican opponents reacted with angry suspicion, claiming with some justice that the attack had been timed to serve as a distraction from the president's problems at home. However, apart from the postponement of the House of Representatives' debate on impeachment by one day, the attack on Iraq was of little political benefit to the commander in chief.

The bombing elicited furious protests from France, Russia, China, and Egypt, while angry crowds demonstrated in the Arab world on behalf of the Iraqi people. Palestinians set fire to the American flags they had been given to wave in honor of President Clinton's visit to Gaza only a few days before. Nor was the attack effective in humbling Saddam or eliminating his alleged arsenal of weapons of mass destruction. Ninety seven targets overall were attacked, of which only nine were reported by the Pentagon as fully destroyed. Of eleven chemical and biological weapons production facilities targeted, none were destroyed. The Special Republican Guards and other bastions of the regime associated with weapons concealment were similarly slated for destruction, but even assuming they had not evacuated their peacetime barracks and offices as they did in January 1991, the results in terms of facilities destroyed appear to have been meager.

The Pentagon expressed surprise at the lack of antiaircraft fire, but Iraq's most effective defenses were the massed ranks of television news cameras from around the world on the roof of the international press center in Baghdad. Under such scrutiny, the United States could not risk high-profile "collateral damage" such as the attack on the Amariya shelter that had incinerated four hundred women and children eight years before. In Baghdad itself, people greeted the renewed offensive with weary resignation. "Iraqis," as one of them remarked, "fear that a game is being played over which they have no interest. They feel they are always the victims, whether it is sanctions or bombs." The streets emptied as the air-raid sirens wailed at nightfall, but wedding parties continued at the al-Rashid hotel and the Iraqi dinar in contrast to previous crises, retained its value against the dollar. "Operation Desert Fox," repeatedly threatened and postponed for more than a year, had turned out to be only a shabby and diminished echo of the storm unleashed on Iraq in the distant days of January 1991.

Dr. Hussain al-Shahristani, the man who had defied Saddam's orders to build a nuclear weapon so many years before, was living in Tehran. His dedicated work on behalf of Iraqi refugees endowed him with considerable moral authority among the Iraqi Shia and a wide range of contacts inside Iraq, especially in the south. Two days into the bombing he wrote one of the present authors an urgent message. "A number of people have contacted us from inside Iraq," he wrote, "and asked if the Americans are really going to continue this [bombing] campaign to weaken Saddam to a point where people can rise up and free themselves from the regime. The memory of betrayal during the last intifada is vivid in people's minds, and they do not want to repeat that tragic experience." The Iranian government had made its own attitude clear by closing its border with Iraq in order to prevent any assistance to a potential uprising.

Following seventy hours of bombing, President Clinton gave al-Shahristani and his people their answer. He declared victory—"I am confident we have achieved our mission"—and called off the attacks. Saddam Hussein also pronounced himself the winner. "God rewarded you," the Iraqi leader told his subjects in a TV address that was broadcast across the Arab world, "and delighted your hearts with the crown of victory." Iraqi spokesmen insisted that there would be no further cooperation with Unscom, while in Washington, President Clinton promised to "sustain what have been among the most intensive sanctions in UN history." It was an ominous prospect.

Amid the furor over Scott Ritter's resignation in the summer of 1998, another resignation passed with little attention. Denis Halliday, the Irish Quaker who had been sent to Baghdad to supervise the oil-for-food arrangement under which revenues from exports of Iraqi oil were entrusted to the custody of the United Nations to buy food and other humanitarian supplies, was leaving Baghdad in disgust. As he left, he directed a bitter blast at the policy that caused "four thousand to five thousand children to die unnecessarily every month due to the impact of sanctions because of the breakdown of water and sanitation, inadequate diet, and the bad internal health situation."

In her March 1997 speech at Georgetown announcing the indefinite continuation of sanctions, Secretary of State Albright had described the oil-for-food deal just then coming into effect as being "designed to ease the suffering of civilians throughout Iraq." As it so happened, the month after she spoke, UNICEF conducted a survey of some fifteen thousand children under five across Iraq. The results showed little difference between the cities and the countryside. Just under a quarter of the children were underweight for their age. Slightly more than a quarter were chronically malnourished. Almost one in ten was acutely malnourished. In March 1998, after the oil-for-food program had been in effect for twelve months and indeed had been vastly increased in value, UNICEF did another similar survey. The percentage of underweight children had gone down by a statistically insignificant margin. Those with chronic malnutrition had declined by eight tenths of a percentage point, while the acutely malnourished infants and toddlers had actually increased by a tiny fraction. Commenting on these chilling statistics, the authors of the report noted in bold type that "it would appear that the 'oil-for-food' program has not yet made a measurable difference to the young children of Iraq."

For Halliday, the hungry and dying children in a land where overeating had been the major prewar pediatric problem were only the most obvious effect of the United Nations blockade. Sanctions, he said, were biting into the fabric of society in less visible but almost equally devastating ways. They had, for example, increased the number of divorces (up to 3 million Iraqi professionals had emigrated, leaving their womenfolk behind to head the household) and reduced the number of marriages because young people could not afford to marry. Crime had increased. An entire generation of young people had grown up in isolation from the outside world. He compared them, ominously, to the orphans of the Afghan war who had spawned the cruel and fanatical Taliban movement. These young Iraqis were intolerant of what they considered to be their leaders' excessive moderation. 'What should be of concern is the possibility of more fundamentalist Islamic thinking developing," concluded Halliday. "It is not well understood as a possible spin-off of the sanctions regime. We are pushing people to take extreme positions."

Following the suppression of the great insurgencies of 1991, Saddam Hussein had announced his intention of sitting back and waiting to take advantage of his enemies' mistakes. In the ensuing years, those mistakes had been plentiful. Saddam himself had survived unscathed. But the biggest mistake of all was to make the Iraqi people pay the price of besieging Saddam. One day, the bill will come due.

Notes

p. 430 "price is worth it": CBS News, *60 Minutes*, 5/12/96.

p. 432 "Not much is unknown": Report by the Secretary General, 4/11/97, S/1997/301.

p. 432 King Fahd: Interview with a Western diplomatic source; Washington, D.C.; 10/10/97.

p. 433 First concealment inspection:Unscom Report,10/11/96, S/1996/848.

p. 434 Concrete pillars: Ibid.

p. 434 Russian spy: Interview with former Unscom official; Washington, D.C.; November 1997.

p. 435 "miserable spy": Saddam Hussein, speech, 7/17/97, reported FBIS, 7/22/97.

p. 435 "It is the Special Republican Guards": Interview with Rolf Ekeus; Washington, D.C.; 6/16/98.

p. 437 Shell game: *Haaretz*, 9/29/98.

p. 438 Helicopter, highest authority: Unscom Report,10/6/97, S/1997/774.

p. 438 Saddam's statement from RCC: Iraq TV News, 6/22/97.

p. 439 Ritter gives U-2 photos to Israel: *Washington Post*, 9/29/98.

p. 439 "gravest crisis of [Bill Clinton's] presidency': *Time* magazine, 11/24/97.

p. 439 "head shot": *New York Times* columnist Thomas Friedman, quoted in *Time* magazine, op. cit.

p. 440 "stunned": *Washington Post*, 3/1/98.

p. 441 Ritter pulled back: *Washington Post*, 8/27/98.

p. 442 Castor beans: Jim Hoagland, *Washington Post*, 2/11/98.

p. 442 Bahrain: FBIS, 2/21/98.

p. 443 Town hall meeting: 2/18/98. Text released by Department of State, 2/20/98.

p. 444 "You can't go": *Washington Post*, 3/1/98.

p. 445 Annan statement: *Washington Post,* 2/24/98.

p. 445 Saddam on tour: Iraqi TV, 3/17/98, as reprinted in the online newsletter *Iraq News*.

p. 445 "appeasement": Senator Trent Lott, *Washington Post,* 2/26/98. Senator John D. Ashcroft (Republican from Missouri) summed up the prevailing mood of his party when he declared that "U.S. foreign policy ought not to be subjected to Kofi Annan or written at the United Nations. And as long as I have a voice, America will not sacrifice another ounce of her sovereignty to the architects and acolytes of a one-world government" *(Washington Post,* 3/4/98).

p. 446 Chalabi testimony: Senate Foreign Relations Committee, Subcommittee Hearings on the Middle East, 3/2/98.

p. 446 Embezzlement question a plant: Jim Hoagland, "From Pariah to Iraq's Hope," *Washington Post,* 3/5/98.

p. 446 Congress votes money: H.R. 3579 Sec. 2005, 4/30/98, *Iraq News,* 5/1/98.

p. 446 Kurdish leaders considered INC defunct: Interview with Jalal Talabani, London, 6/6/98. Interview with Hoshyar Zibari, Washington, 3/16/98.

p. 447 Sabotage plan: *New York Times,* 2/26/98.

p. 449 Three nuclear weapons: Senate Foreign Relations and Armed Services Committees Hearings, 9/3/98.

p. 450 *Haaretz,* 9/29/98.

p. 451 Scott Ritter: Interview with Ritter in the *New York Post,* 12/17/98.

p. 452 Message from al-Shahristani: E-mail from Dr. al-Shahristani to Andrew Cockburn, 12/18/98.

p. 453 UNICEF: Nutritional status survey at primary health centers during polio national immunization days (PNID) in Iraq, March 14-16, 1998. Made available to authors by UNICEF office in Baghdad. The actual figures were: April 1997: Underweight—24.7 percent; chronically malnourished—27.5 percent; acutely malnourished—9.0 percent. March 1998: Underweight—22.8 percent; chronically malnourished—26.7 percent; acutely malnourished—9.1 percent.

p. 453 Half of all Iraqi children still malnourished: *Washington Post,* I, 12/13/98.

The Hostage Nation

Hans Von Sponeck and Denis Halliday

The Guardian

Thursday November 29, 2001

A major shift is occurring in US policy on Iraq. It is obvious that Washington wants to end 11 years of a self-serving policy of containment of the Iraqi regime and change to a policy of replacing, by force, Saddam Hussein and his government.

The current policy of economic sanctions has destroyed society in Iraq and caused the death of thousands, young and old. There is evidence of that daily in reports from reputable international organizations such as Caritas, Unicef, and Save the Children. A change to a policy of replacement by force will increase that suffering.

The creators of the policy must no longer assume that they can satisfy voters by expressing contempt for those who oppose them. The problem is not the inability of the public to understand the bigger picture, as former US secretary of state Madeleine Albright likes to suggest. It is the opposite. The bigger picture, the hidden agenda, is well understood by ordinary people. We should not forget Henry Kissinger's brutally frank admission that "oil is much too important a commodity to be left in the hands of the Arabs".

How much longer can democratically elected governments hope to get away with justifying policies that punish the Iraqi people for something they did not do, through economic sanctions that target them in the hope that those who survive will overthrow the regime? Is international law only applicable to the losers? Does the UN security council only serve the powerful?

The UK and the US, as permanent members of the council, are fully aware that the UN embargo operates in breach of the UN covenants on human rights, the Geneva and Hague conventions and other international laws. It is neither anti-UK nor anti-US to point out that Washington and London, more than anywhere else, have in the past decade helped to write the Iraq chapter in the history of avoidable tragedies.

The UK and the US have deliberately pursued a policy of punishment since the Gulf war victory in 1991. The two governments have consistently opposed allowing the UN security council to carry out its mandated responsibilities to assess the impact of sanctions policies on civilians. We know about this first hand, because the governments repeatedly tried to prevent us from briefing the security council about it. The pitiful annual limits, of less than $170 per person, for humanitarian supplies, set by them during the first three years of the oil-for-food programme are unarguable evidence of such a policy.

We have seen the effects on the ground and cannot comprehend how the US ambassador, James Cunningham, could look into the eyes of his colleagues a year ago and say: "We (the US government) are satisfied that the oil-for-food programme is meeting the needs of the Iraqi people." Besides the provision of food and medicine, the real issue today is that Iraqi oil revenues must be invested in the reconstruction of civilian infrastructure destroyed in the Gulf war.

Despite the severe inadequacy of the permitted oil revenue to meet the minimum needs of the Iraqi people, 30 cents (now 25) of each dollar that Iraqi oil earned from 1996 to 2000 were diverted by the UN security council, at the behest of the UK and US governments, to compensate outsiders for losses allegedly incurred because of Iraq's invasion of Kuwait. If this money had been made available to Iraqis, it could have saved many lives.

The uncomfortable truth is that the west is holding the Iraqi people hostage, in order to secure Saddam Hussein's compliance to ever-shifting demands.

The UN secretary-general, who would like to be a mediator, has repeatedly been prevented from taking this role by the US and the UK governments.

The imprecision of UN resolutions on Iraq—"constructive ambiguity" as the US and UK define it—is seen by those governments as a useful tool when dealing with this kind of conflict. The US and UK dismiss criticism by pointing out that the Iraqi people are being punished by Baghdad. If this is true, why do we punish them further?

The most recent report of the UN secretary-general, in October 2001, says that the US and UK governments' blocking of $4 billion of humanitarian supplies is by far the greatest constraint on the implementation of the oil-for-food programme. The report says that, in contrast, the Iraqi government's distribution of humanitarian supplies is fully satisfactory (as it was when we headed this programme). The death of some 5-6,000 children a month is mostly due to contaminated water, lack of medicines and malnutrition. The US and UK governments' delayed clearance of equipment and materials is responsible for this tragedy, not Baghdad.

The expectation of a US attack on Iraq does not create conditions in the UN security council suited to discussions on the future of economic sanctions. This year's UK-sponsored proposal for "smart sanctions" will not be retabled. Too many people realize that what looked superficially like an improvement for civilians is really an attempt to maintain the bridgeheads of the existing sanctions policy: no foreign investments and no rights for the Iraqis to manage their own oil revenues.

The proposal suggested sealing Iraq's borders, strangling the Iraqi people. In the present political climate, a technical extension of the current terms is considered the most expedient step by Washington. That this condemns more Iraqis to death and destitution is shrugged off as unavoidable.

What we describe is not conjecture. These are undeniable facts known to us as two former insiders. We are outraged that the Iraqi people continue to be made to pay the price for the lucrative arms trade and power politics. We are reminded of Martin Luther King's words: "A time has come when silence is betrayal. That time is now."

We want to encourage people everywhere to protest against unscrupulous policies and against the appalling disinformation put out about Iraq by those who know better, but are willing to sacrifice people's lives with false and malicious arguments.

The US Defense Department, and Richard Butler, former head of the UN arms inspection team in Baghdad, would prefer Iraq to have been behind the anthrax scare. But they had to recognize that it had its origin within the US.

British and US intelligence agencies know well that Iraq is qualitatively disarmed, and they have not forgotten that the outgoing secretary of defense, William Cohen, told incoming President George Bush in January: "Iraq no longer poses a military threat to its neighbours." The same message has come from former UN arms inspectors. But to admit this would be to nail the entire UN policy, as it has been developed and maintained by the US and UK governments.

We are horrified by the prospects of a new US-led war against Iraq. The implications of "finishing unfinished business" in Iraq are too serious for the global community to ignore. We hope that the warnings of leaders in the Middle East and all of us who care about human rights are not ignored by the US government. What is now most urgently needed is an attack on injustice, not on the Iraqi people.

Attack on Clinton Administration Policy

Cynthia McKinney

Middle East Research and Information Project

Few members of Congress are critical of US policy toward Iraq; fewer still are those willing to go public in their criticism of that policy. Not representative Cynthia McKinney. She is one of four members of congress who decided to send their senior aides on a fact-finding tour to Iraq in September '99 in spite of repeated attempts by the State Department to scuttle that tour. In an interview with the Middle East Research and Information Project (MERIP), McKinney, a Democrat from Georgia, questions the nine-year US-led sanctions against Iraq, arguing that the reason behind the sanctions is not even to "find an alternative" to the Iraqi leader or to "arouse a democratic fervor" in that country. The real reason, she says, is "to continue the status quo and, in the process, test a few weapons," in order to market them to other countries. Representative McKinney from Georgia's 4th District, and the ranking member on the Subcommittee on International Operations and Human Rights, believes that the sanctions are killing babies and other innocent Iraqis and, therefore, should be lifted immediately. She also calls US attempts to topple foreign leaders "reckless and irresponsible." Following is the full interview:

Q: You have adopted a stand regarding Iraqi sanctions that goes against that of the majority of your colleagues in both houses. Assuming that they have the same information you do about the sanctions' consequences in Iraq, what made you move to your present position?
A: Well, unfortunately, it's not the information you have, but what you do with it that matters. The fact is that the US is very isolated in the international community when it comes to Iraq and is at odds with France, Russia, China (permanent members of the UN Security Council) and the Arab League. The outcry from the international community has been uniform. When you have the United Nations High Commissioner for Human Rights, Mary Robinson, saying that the policies supported by her institution have become a tool for the violation of human rights, that is mighty powerful. The United Nations Children's Fund (UNICEF), the World Health Organization, the Pope, former Oil-for-Food Coordinator Denis Halliday and former weapons inspector Scott Ritter have all decried the effects of sanctions on the people of Iraq and have called for an end to the embargo. The most recent statement by the highest-ranking United Nations representative in Iraq, Hans Van Sponeck, calling for the immediate lifting of sanctions tells me that the US is increasingly isolated and, as I suspected a long time ago, wrong on this issue.
Q: Considering the domestic political and social atmosphere of hostility toward Iraq, and the inability, or unwillingness of this government to distinguish

between the innocent people and the regime there, what did it take for you to agree to dispatch your aide to investigate the situation there?
A: I wanted to find the truth. I was not satisfied with our government policy . . . and I wanted to explore ways in which we could perhaps facilitate change in the effects of the policy, if not in the overall policy itself. Peter Hickey, my aide who traveled to Iraq, has painted a vivid picture for me: desperately malnourished babies, dying of treatable diseases formerly eradicated from Iraq as their under nourished mothers fan them in hot, dim hospital wards. Barefoot children, walking in the raw sewage surrounding their barracks-like housing complexes without railings on upper-floor balconies. Medicine in short supply. Families living on meager government rations, and clean water almost non-existent.
Q: Objective sources that you quote report that a million Iraqi's have died and 4,500 children under the age of 5 are dying every month from the sanctions? How do you read the US government's insistence that sanctions should stay?
A: The overall outcome of the Administration's commitment to sanctions has been to decimate the very people that they expect to rise up and overthrow Saddam Hussein. By taking food out of the mouths of babies, they have hurt, in a very real and substantial way, the United States' ability to have a positive image before the Iraqi people and a positive and lasting impact on development inside the country. We have grossly overplayed our hand in Iraq. We are quite exposed in that we don't have a clear policy toward Iraq, or the policy we do have is one that allows for the continuation of Saddam Hussein's leadership. This betrays a deeper truth than one would like to admit: the United States, for whatever reason, has not been able to find an alternative to Saddam. In fact, the policy does not aim to find an alternative to Hussein or to arouse a democratic fervor in the people, but rather to continue the status quo and, in the process, test a few weapons to see how well they work, so they can be marketed to other countries. Unfortunately, innocent women and children are being killed along the way.
Q: We understand that the State Department tried very strenuously to convince the staffers and others not to go to Iraq. They still went. How do you feel charting an independent course—on a foreign policy issue—different from that of the State Department and the administration as a whole?

A: Congress has a right and a responsibility to oversee foreign policy. As the Ranking Member of the Subcommittee on International Operations and Human Rights, I was carrying out my responsibility. If it were left up to the State Department, no Member of Congress, nor any staffer, would go anywhere other than London or Paris.

Q: Where does your constituency in Georgia stand on this issue, and have you received any feedback from them?

A: I have received several calls and letters from my constituents who supported my staff member taking the trip to Iraq. Many of them expressed their displeasure with the sanctions because innocent men, women, and children are being killed as a result. And they hoped that by seeing first hand the devastation, Congress and the Administration would see that the sanctions are not an effective tool in trying to get rid of Saddam Hussein.

Q: What was your colleagues' reaction, if any, to you consenting to the visit in Iraq?

A: I was pleased to have my staff joined by the staff from the offices of four other Members of Congress: Sam Gejdenson (D-CT), Bernie Sanders (I-VT), Earl Hilliard (D-AL), and Danny Davis (D-IL). We have been asked by other Member offices to put together a briefing of the findings of our staff delegation to Iraq.

Q: Were you or your aide asked by the White House or State Department for a briefing about the situation in Iraq? If not, why?

A: No. The State Department and the White House are well aware of the situation in Iraq, but they choose to ignore it and continue to support the economic sanctions. When asked about Iraqi children starving and dying as a result of the UN sanctions, US Secretary of State Madeleine Albright said, "It's a hard decision, but we think the price . . . is worth it." Whatever the merits of the accusations about Iraq, there is no way to justify the wholesale killing of hundreds of thousands of innocent human beings.

Q: Does the fact that you are an African-American have anything to do with your stand on this issue?

A: No. I believe in human rights for all people, regardless of their race, color, gender, or religious beliefs. It is a fundamental right.

Q: In your article, you restate the Administration's open secret position that the sanctions are there to "topple the regime" of Saddam Hussein and not necessarily to get rid of Iraq's weapons of mass destruction. Is it legitimate for the US or other governments to use innocent people and children as weapons to topple a regime they cannot influence?

A: Of course it's not legitimate to use innocent people and children as weapons to topple a regime. Yet that seems to be what we are doing. The result of the Administration's sanctions-at-any-cost policy has been to decimate the very people that they expect to rise up and overthrow Saddam Hussein. It's very hard to get people to think about revolting when their primary concern is feeding their families or saving their dying children. It's also reckless and irresponsible to talk of toppling leaders of other countries. Democracy is not something that can be manufactured at Foggy Bottom or at the Pentagon. The way to produce change is through incentives—for both the people and regime. We must show the Iraqi people that there is light at the end of the tunnel. We need to distinguish between the Iraqi regime and the innocent people of Iraq. This can be done by lifting sanctions on the people and maintaining or even tightening military sanctions on the regime.

Q: Do you believe that it is going to be possible to prevent an Arab country from acquiring nuclear weapons as long as Israel has them? What should be done in this situation?

A: As you know, I feel strongly about the dangerous proliferation of nuclear weapons all over the world. But the United States must recognize its role in promoting regional arms build-ups. We've already turned the Middle East into the most arms-bloated region in the world. I think it's very telling, that in its zeal to implement every aspect of UN resolutions against Iraq, there is one article that the U.S. overlooks and, consequently, nobody knows about: The very same resolution that calls for the elimination of Iraq's weapons of mass destruction, UN Resolution 687, also calls for "the establishment of a nuclear-weapons-free zone" throughout the Middle East. Any approach to arms control should be done in a regional context.

Inside Saddam's Terror Regime

David Rose

Vanity Fair

The most senior officer ever to defect from Iraq's Mukhabarat intelligence service, brigadier general Abu Zeinab al-Qurairy was forced into exile in the summer of 2000 when he crossed Saddam Hussein's son Uday. After a three-day interview in Beirut, DAVID ROSE has the exclusive on al-Qurairy's brutal history of rape, torture, and mass murder, his training of a previously unknown elite force called al-Qare'a—including an untraceable 30-commando unit that left Iraq a year ago and his strong belief that Iraq was involved in the September 11 attacks.

April 28, 2000, was a very special day in Iraq. The president, Saddam Hussein, had turned 63. Along the 106 miles of highway from the capital, Baghdad, to Saddam's official birthplace in the town of Tikrit, government officials had erected a line of marquees, from which they dispensed free rice and lamb from steaming cauldrons. In Tikrit itself, top presidential aide Izzat Ibrahim cut an enormous, flower-shaped cake to the tune of "Happy Birthday to you." He ended the ceremony with a prayer: "We ask God . . . to prolong his [Saddam's] life, and make this an occasion of victory to us and to our nation against our enemies and the enemies of humanity." Later that evening, Saddam's elder son, Uday, gave his father the perfect birthday gift. It had been a long time in the making. Uday had ordered his closest aide and confidant, Abu Zeinab al-Qurairy—a brigadier general in Iraq's feared intelligence service, the Mukhabarat—to put together a team of 30 specially trained fighters. In al-Qurairy's seasoned judgment, the men were the finest members of the secret unit he administered—the 1,200-strong commando force known as al-Qare'a, "the Strikers," Iraq's elite of elites, trained to a level far beyond ordinary special forces in sabotage, urban warfare, hijacking, and murder.

Al-Qurairy had given the 30 men new identities, complete with genuine United Arab Emirates passports supplied by a corrupt U.A.E. minister in the pay of the Mukhabarat: a means of travelling anywhere, without creating the least suspicion they had originally come from Iraq. He had overseen their final training project—an exercise, using limpet mines and diving gear, to blow up a specially constructed mock-up of a U.S. Navy Fifth Fleet destroyer, moored in central Iraq's Habbaniya Lake. Like all al-Qare'a exercises, it had been conducted using real explosives and live ammunition. Uday had the fake ship's destruction videotaped, and that birthday evening he played the recording to his father.

Al-Qurairy never found out what happened to his 30 fighters. Less than three months after Saddam's birthday, his glittering, 20-year career as a Mukhabarat officer was at an end, and he was fighting for his life. Somehow, he managed to escape, and today he is trying to find a safe haven. At the end of November 2001, in a sparse hotel room in Muslim West Beirut in Lebanon, Henry Porter, Vanity Fair's London editor, and I interviewed him, over three intense days. The most senior Mukhabarat officer who has ever left Iraq, he gave a complete picture of his career, including his personal involvement in mass murder, torture, abduction, and rape. He supplied details of Iraq's terrorist training for Islamic fundamentalists, and described al-Qare'a—its very existence previously unknown to the Western public—for the first time.

As for the 30 fighters, al-Qurairy says all he knew about their future missions was that they would shortly be going abroad, for a long but unknown period. Abu Omer, the unit's former cook, whom we also met in Lebanon, described the first stage of their journey. In January 2001 they boarded the ferryboat which plies daily from the Iraqi port of Umm Qasr to one of the emirates, Dubai. There, untraceable as Iraqis, they vanished. They could, says al-Qurairy, be anywhere.

Like many defectors, al-Qurairy, who is 41, crossed from Iraq to its northern neighbour, Turkey. There, stuck in a Spartan refugee camp, his life going nowhere, in August 2001 he did what would once have been unthinkable: he made contact with Iraq's democratic opposition, the Iraqi National Congress, which brought him to us in Beirut. The photograph on his Turkish temporary residence permit depicts him, as he was when he served the Mukhabarat: a stocky, gnome-like figure, bald, with a Saddam-style mustache. The man we met had disguised himself with a red Palestinian headscarf and a carved goatee. His manner was cheerful; his small brown eyes seemed kind. The only sign he might have been under stress was his prodigious consumption of alcohol and tobacco. On the second night, he drank a fifth of Johnnie Walker Black Label scotch. There were no ashtrays in the hotel room, forcing him to extinguish his cigarettes in a glass of water. By the end of the first morning's interview, the water was stained the color of strong tea. It is not uncommon for intelligence officers to cultivate an air of inscrutable stillness. Al-Qurairy seemed to have taken this to extremes. He'd left a wife and four children in Baghdad. Surely he must miss them, I asked. He shrugged. "Not really. They're just little kids."

It is not until al-Qurairy begins to talk of the terrorist training camp he used to run at Salman Pak, a 45-minute drive south from Baghdad, that he speaks with real feeling—unconcealed pride. "It's got a long-established history and we're proud to be associated with it," he says, "because it's trained the elite—the people who've carried out operations abroad, who are on the Interpol wanted lists. By the time a trainee leaves our school he can protect any V.I.P. or assassinate any V.I.P. In 1979, when Saddam Hussein executed half his Cabinet, they had the honor of executing them at the camp." Alone of all Iraq's myriad security installations, Salman Pak remains directly answerable to Saddam. "When he writes to the camp," says al-Qurairy happily, "he calls it 'the school of the liars.' "

On a satellite photo, he picks out Salman Pak's main features. In the southern part of the camp, at a bend in the Tigris River, is the barracks used for non-Iraqi Arabs, Islamic fundamentalists who first came to Salman Pak in 1995 to be trained in classes of 24 by al-Qurairy's closest friend, Brigadier General Jassim Rashid al-Dulaimi. He is a man who practices what he preaches: he is wanted by Lebanese authorities for the 1994 murder of an opposition leader in Beirut. As recently as the summer of 2000, al-Qurairy saw the Arab students being taught to hijack aircraft on Salman Pak's own passenger jet, an Old Russian Tupolev. They all took a special course, he says—"how to gain control of the cockpit and passengers without using firearms." Professional pride meant the Iraqis ensured the Islamists reached a high standard: "When we train non-Iraqis, we're not training them to preach in a mosque. We don't expect them to preach in a mosque, but to carry out offensive duties." But al-Dulaimi and his fellow instructors, all members of Saddam's secular Baath Party, regarded their Islamist students with contempt. "When Jassim and I go for a drink after work, Jassim says they are sons of bitches. They have all this work to do, but they spend half their time praying."

Al-Qurairy was responsible for running the north part of Salman Pak, and for al-Qare'a. He served as the unit's staff general and supervised its formation, at Uday's behest, from the best and most politically reliable fighters from an earlier and larger special-forces group—the Fedayeen Saddam, 'Saddam's Martyrs." (He remained in charge of the Fedayeen as well.) From the time of its conception in 1995, al-Qurairy says, al-Qare'a was seen as a super-elite, as a force inured to violent death.

Faced with the aftermath of defeat in the Gulf War, Saddam believed that "to defend the country, sometimes you have to go on the attack." That could mean several things, including assassination, hijacking, and suicide missions. "Trainees who fail are used as targets in live ammunition exercises," al-Qurairy explains. "So they die. . . . The training is purely offensive and not only offensive but suicidal. They are made to sign a document when they join that specifically says that orders will ask individual members to commit suicide on missions." The suicide-attacker principle was not original. Al-Qurairy says, "They got that idea from the Islamists."

In one training procedure, regularly repeated, students had to land three helicopters on the roof of a speeding train on Salman Pak's own railroad, and then hijack it. With sudden animation, al-Qurairy gets up from his chair and performs a series of jumps and pirouettes, demonstrating the difficulty of the necessary maneuvers. "Fifty took part; 38 passed," he says. "Twelve failed. They were used as 'passengers' in subsequent exercises."

Part of the role envisaged for al-Qare'a is to crush future internal rebellion. But the unit's primary ethos remains aggression against enemies abroad. "That's the very nature of our training," al-Qurairy says. "We have to go outside Iraq—why would we train to blow up a building in Baghdad?" In July

2000, al-Qare'a moved en masse from Salman Pak to a camp near Basra on the Kuwait border, with orders to begin a campaign of sabotage and murder inside Kuwait. On that occasion, the plan was aborted.

In Arabic, says Nabeel Musawi, the Iraqi National Congress member who acted as our translator, there is a saying: "Evil comes back to the evildoer." If any individual could be said to prove this maxim's veracity, it is al-Qurairy. He, it swiftly became apparent, was no reluctant, press-ganged recruit to what the Iraqi writer Kanan Makiya calls Saddam's "republic of fear." He embraced its beliefs and inhuman practices with unrestrained enthusiasm. Even in exile, he still refers to Saddam by his respectful title, "Haji." He proudly relates how, when Uday was lying in the hospital after the 1996 shooting that left him crippled, he had the honor of bending over his hospital bed and kissing him.

Al-Qurairy was born to a wealthy, prominent family north of Baghdad. His parents were Baath Party members, and he joined at the age of 10. By 18, he was the party's youngest full-time organizer. In al-Qurairy's opinion, Michel Aflaq, the party's founder, "was a greater prophet than Muhammad himself." The Baath Party's official ideology—in fact a vague mishmash of socialism and nationalism—was "written to serve humanity." Cursed by poor high-school grades, al-Qurairy missed university, and in 1980, a year after Saddam became president, he began to train for the Mukhabarat.

In London, I met another of Iraq's Mukhabarat defectors, who like al-Qurairy, spent six months at the Mukhabarat's "April 7th" camp at Diyala, northeast of Baghdad. "The fatal-casualty rate was 5 percent," this defector says. "In my course, we lost three men." The graduation ceremony was peculiarly brutal. The new graduates were put in a yard with 200 or 300 dogs. "We had to show what we can do" the defector continues.

"So we catch them with our bare hands and kill them with our teeth, by biting the arteries in their necks. Then we had to jump off a bridge into filthy, sewage-laden water, holding another dog. You mustn't let the dog go. If the dog lives, you are out of the Mukhabarat."

Al-Qurairy recalls the same experience. But as far as he is concerned, "to

Mukhabarat people that was just a joke. Mukhabarat training was much more serious than that."

In 1990, by now a captain, al-Qurairy joined with the Iraqi forces that invaded Kuwait, and helped administer the seven-month occupation. It was a time for frolics. One day a young Palestinian woman made the mistake of visiting the Mukhabarat office, to complain that her estranged husband was failing to pay child support. In a conversation with Iraqi National Congress officers, al-Qurairy said the woman was beautiful—and that he, along with others in the Mukhabarat, raped her and let her go. Then al-Qurairy told the husband of what they had done, reminding him to pay up.

Saddam's defeat in Kuwait in March 1991 was followed by rebellion, by Kurds in the North of Iraq and by Shiite Muslims in the South. (Saddam and the Baathists come from the other principal Muslim sect, the Sunni.) George H. Bush had made a televised call to the Iraqi people to "force Saddam Hussein, the dictator, to step aside." For the Baath regime and its servants, it was the moment of deepest peril. Fourteen provinces were lost, and in most of them all Mukhabarat agents and officers were killed. "Once the people woke up," says al-Qurairy, "they were out to get revenge."

He turns to us with a smile. "We have you to thank for letting us save the day." The U.S. had already halted the allied advance, failing to take the road to Baghdad when it lay almost undefended, and allowing Saddam's best troops, the Republican Guard, to escape the military debacle unscathed. To the regime's barely suppressed amazement, America said it had no objection to Iraq's flying its helicopter gun ships. Iraq's Mukhabarat, says al-Qurairy, interpreted this announcement as a "green light" for repression. Far from planning to protect the rebels from the air, thus ensuring Saddam's downfall, it seemed America intended Saddam to survive. If Saddam's orders were 'Lash out, take the land back, even if it's bare land,' " al-Qurairy says. The Mukhabarat were to do whatever it took to regain the lost territory, however great the human cost. In the first phase of the repression, the Mukhabarat and the army asked no questions at all. In some Shiite cities, says al-Qurairy, all the young men were rounded up and killed.

At Razaza, on the shores of Milh Lake in central Iraq, thousands of people from the Shiite city of Kerbala, including women and children, gathered in the open air. Although the air force and Republican Guard were storming their city, they thought they would be safe there. "The orders came: 'Use helicopters, gun them all down.' Then they immediately called for bulldozers to dig mass graves. The bulldozer drivers radioed back, 'Quite a lot are still alive.' The order came in response: 'Don't waste bullets. Bury them!' " While these and other massacres unfolded, U.S. fighters and reconnaissance planes watched uselessly from the skies high above.

After the first month, al-Qurairy says, the operation became marginally more discriminating. He was transferred to a camp at Radwaniya, north of Baghdad. Alleged rebels were brought to the camp each morning, subjected to cursory interrogation, then dispatched. "They brought them in buses, and they left in lorries, dripping with blood. Every lorry we and the special-security agency possessed was being used for dead bodies, taking them to mass graves. We kept each grave open for days; when it was full, we'd dig another one. . . . When you see the bullets being fired all the time, and the lorries coming out, drenched in blood, and blood drenching the ground because there was nowhere for it to go—the effect stays with you forever. . . . It took me days during that period before I could sleep. Some of my friends in the Mukhabarat simply lost their minds. They could not cope with the level of murders we were committing."

One recalls the historian Daniel Jonah Goldhagen's account of the massacres of Jews perpetrated by the German Police Battalions in Poland in 1942. Like the Mukhabarat, the Police Battalions killed their victims with shots to the head. Goldhagen quotes one killer's recollection: "The executioners were gruesomely soiled with blood, brain matter, and bone splinters. It stuck to their clothes." It can have been no different at Radwaniya. On one morning, al-Qurairy says, he checked his list of prisoners' names. He was up to No. 4,300. That was the number of killings that had taken place that morning. In all, he says, at least 100,000 were killed there in a few weeks. The Iraqi National Congress estimates that 330,000 Iraqis were murdered in the spring of 1991. Al-Qurairy believes the true figure may well be higher.

Al-Qurairy claims he is still haunted by the memory of these terrible events.

Yet as he describes them, he seems devoid of emotion, and matter-of-fact. Does he believe in God? I ask. For the first and only time, he pauses, apparently unable to provide an answer. "This is a hard question. I'm not a strong believer. We mention God by instinct, not because we think about it. I had to think!" The Iran-Iraq war of 1980-88 "hardened our attitudes towards death." Yet the killings of 1991 were on such a scale, "even our own people can't come to terms with what they did," he says.

If I ever went back to Iraq," al-Qurairy says, "they would put me on a machine and cut me to pieces." There are taxis with Baghdad license tags for hire on Beirut's streets, some almost certainly driven by members of the Mukhabarat; from Beirut to Baghdad by road takes less than nine hours. The Iraqi National Congress had arranged our meetings with al-Qurairy with care. Until the previous evening, he had been staying in a safe house in another Middle Eastern state. He was brought to Lebanon by a member of that country's intelligence service, who had the experience and the paperwork to travel the region freely. He was introduced to us by Nabeel Musawi, our translator and effectively al-Qurairy's case officer.

Based in an office in London protected by bulletproof glass, the Iraqi National Congress is an underground intelligence network that hopes to topple Saddam. Led by Ahmed Chalabi, a genial, wealthy intellectual with a mathematics Ph.D. from the University of Chicago, it has built its own network, its effectiveness enhanced by technology. In London, Ahmad Allawi, the Iraqi National Congress's director of operations, exchanges dozens of highly encrypted E-mails each day with agents in Iraq who have been given digital cameras, small titanium laptops, and satellite phones. The Iraqi National Congress has handled many other defectors from within the regime—Khidhir Harnza, for example, who ran Saddam's nuclear-weapons program, and Wafiq Samaraii, his head of military intelligence. Before arranging our interviews with al-Qurairy, Musawi and his colleagues had debriefed him thoroughly, checking every aspect of his story with sources inside Iraq and with other defectors. There was no doubt he was what he claimed. Before we met him, he had spent three days in Ankara, Turkey, with agents from the FB.I and C.I.A. A senior

C.I.A. analyst told me that, as far as the agency was concerned, al-Qurairy was telling the truth.

On our first night in Lebanon, we all dined together in a traditional Lebanese restaurant next to a Roman bridge. Shouting over the noise of the cabaret, Musawi laughed at al-Qurairy's jokes, slapped his back good-humoredly, and played the convivial host. It was left to his fellow opposition activist, Zaab Sethna, to tell us later how much effort this bonhomie required. Musawi's father and two cousins disappeared in 1981, taken as prisoners by the Mukhabarat. His quest to uncover their fate cost him years and thousands of dollars in bribes. It was not until 1995 that he learned they had been murdered shortly after their abduction and were buried in an unmarked grave.

Toward the end of our stay in Beirut, Musawi and Sethna left abruptly on another assignment—a meeting in Bangkok with a new Iraqi defector. This man, a building contractor, claimed to have been working to construct new facilities that Saddam would use to restore his biological- and chemical-weapons arsenals and to develop a nuclear bomb. Before their departure, the two activists showed us "contracts the defector had sent them. The documents suggested he had been building radiation-proof underground laboratories. That same day, President Bush ordered Saddam to admit U.N. weapons inspectors or "face consequences."

In 1995, when Saddam's son Uday took control of the Fedayeen, the unit that was to spawn al-Qare'a, al-Qurairy found himself cast as his principal henchman. In addition to his duties at Salman Pak, he had a new office in the Iraqi Olympic Committee's downtown-Baghdad building that Uday had made his headquarters. What happened there had little to do with the noble ideals of athletics. Beneath the building's ground floor, its cells slotted into the spaces between the piles of its foundation, is a dungeon that has housed as many as 520 detainees. "We were under strict orders to deny its existence, al-Qurairy says. "For a long time, even Saddam didn't know about it." Worst were the sensory-deprivation cells—almost sealed, painted red, with red lightbulbs and only a tiny slot for the passage of food. Prisoners would be kept there for up to three months before being removed for release, a determinate prison sentence, or execution.

Many of the Olympic committee's victims had committed no transgression, even by the warped standards of Saddam's Iraq. They were businessmen or children of wealthy families whom Uday saw as ripe targets for extortion. In one case, al-Qurairy says, a businessman had arranged to import a shipment of steel for construction, and had deposited his payment with a bank in Baghdad to transfer to his foreign supplier. Uday arranged for the paperwork to disappear, "and then they brought him to us." Uday had stolen the money, and after interrogation the businessman was given a stark choice: pay for the steel again or die. On other occasions, people were simply ransomed, for as much as $100,000.

Sometimes the reasons for arrest were more personal. Al-Qurairy named a famous Iraqi concert pianist, who was seized from his own wedding and brought to the committee. When al-Qurairy arrived at work the next day, he was baffled: "I looked at his record. There was nothing obvious to do with politics or business." The man was a yoga practitioner, al-Qurairy says, "so I decided to take advantage of his presence and asked him to teach me some yoga." A few days later, the pianist was transferred to the prison at the Presidential Palace. Finally, after the victim had been imprisoned for 40 days, al-Qurairy asked Uday why he was there. Uday replied, speaking of the pianist's bride, "I fucked her two years ago!" Eventually, the pianist was released.

Other committee victims had been arrested for political offences, drug dealing, prostitution, theft, or minor corruption. Whatever the reason, at night they would be taken, blindfolded, to the building's third floor and interrogated. "Usually they're ready to confess, but they're tortured anyway. It's just part of the process: they have to go through torture and a confession." The luckier ones would merely go through "light beatings, just kickings and punchings." Those who showed signs of resistance would be handed over to the "real professionals": hard-core sadists whose names were well known—men al-Qurairy named as Ghalib Jawad, Samir Adrian al-Obeidi, and, the most infamous of all, Kadum Sharqia. I ask al-Qurairy what methods Sharqia used, and he shrugs. "To him, torture is like an exercise. Once they're out of our control, it's none of our business."

Al-Qurairy says he personally supervised at least 1,000 arrests on the committee's behalf, a small fraction of the total. Many of his victims were women: "Mainly pharmacists who were overcharging, and nurses. I followed one nurse's case very closely, because I really fancied her—she'd been arrested for trying to restore a girl's virginity. I liked her a lot."

Were the prisoners raped? "Once they get in there, they're open to all. Most of them are more than happy to be had if it means the end of their ordeal. Those who resist, they take them anyway. Most of the women hope it will reduce their sentence or get them discharged, so they submit to it. To them, we're one step below God. If they're nurses or university students, it's great."

Many of the committee's prisoners are later executed. Al-Qurairy doesn't know exactly how many: "It's like the flow of oil. It never stops. Thousands come through the gates of the Olympic committee. We don't know what happens to them. There's no judicial process. They just disappear." The committee, he stresses, is only one of many portals to Iraq's apparatus of detention, torture, and extrajudicial killing. Since the Gulf War, Iraq's gulag has expanded substantially. "My estimate is that thousands die each year. And this continues.

As we were interviewing al-Qurairy in Beirut, becoming lost in the horror he so baldly described, it became apparent that the defeat of the Afghan Taliban was only a matter of time. America and its partners in the anti-terrorist coalition were conducting a furious debate over whether to extend military action to Iraq. The Pentagon appeared to be the main source of hawks. The Europeans, including Britain's prime minister, Tony Blair, were urging caution, claiming that a strike against Saddam was unjustified and might easily destabilize the Middle East. One argument was being repeated often: that there was no conclusive evidence of an Iraqi role in terrorism in general, nor in the September 11 atrocities specifically.

As yet, there isn't a case that would stand up in a court of law. We know Mohammed Atta, the hijackers' leader, who flew the first airplane into the World Trade Center, twice met a notorious Mukhabarat special-operations expert in Prague in the months before the attacks; and it is believed that his former roommate in Hamburg, Marwan al-Shehhi (who flew the second

W.T.C. plane), and an Hamburg associate, Ziad Jarrah (the hijacker who piloted Flight 93 before it crashed into the ground in Pennsylvania), both met Mukhabarat men in the U.A.E. That amounts to strong evidence of a connection with the 19 hijackers. Al-Qurairy says: "When I saw the World Trade Center attack on television I turned to a friend and said, 'That's ours.' "

Yet there are other issues besides responsibility for September 11-such as justice for the people of Iraq. By granting Saddam his "green light" in 1991, the West appeared to condone a further decade of killing. Now, perhaps, it has a chance to put that right.

In the roughest way possible, justice started to catch up with al-Qurairy. Nabeel Musawi's Arabic proverb was coming true. In February of 2000, Saddam gathered his top 400 officials, including al-Qurairy, and warned he was launching a major drive against a corruption, backed by a military committee. Offenders could expect only one penalty: death. It placed al-Qurairy in a very difficult position. Uday had been running a vast, multimillion-dollar scam against his father's government, involving illegal transfers of dozens of government buildings. Al-Qurairy had signed many of these contracts, and now he feared they would come to light. So he wrote a report denouncing Uday to Saddam's personal secretary, hoping—as Saddam had promised his loyal disciples—it would remain confidential.

On July 24, 2000, he returned to Baghdad from a mission to inspect the al-Qare'a camp on the Kuwaiti border. A driver was waiting at the station, saying Uday wanted a meeting. Ushered into Uday's office at the Olympic committee, al-Qurairy spent an hour reporting on his inspection of the al-Qare'a camp, then, he says, Uday changed. "He said, 'You sonofabitch, you think you care more about government money than we do?' I was so shocked, I immediately stood up. I said, 'Sir, there is a military committee investigating, this means execution.' He produced an electric cattle prod from nowhere, and he jabbed me with it between my legs. I lost consciousness. When I woke up, I was in a red cell in the Olympic-committee prison."

Al-Qurairy was moved to an isolation cell at the Presidential Palace. After 40 days he was released. But first, he had to see Uday again. There was a gold scimitar on his wan, a gift from one of the U.A.E. sheikhs. Uday said, "If I see your face or hear your voice again, I'll cut your head off.", As al-Qurairy was well aware, temporary release, followed by re-arrest and execution, was a common tactic. Abandoning his family and everything he owned, he fled by taxi.

As we say our good-byes to al-Qurairy, I wonder what will become of him. His admitted crimes make political asylum in the West an unlikely possibility. It seems the C.I.A. has no further use for him. He speaks of returning to Turkey and trying again to become a refugee, using a "clean" false identity. Perhaps America will topple Saddam through bombing or supporting a coup d'etat, he muses. In that case, there might be a role for him in a reconstructed, yet still Baathist, Iraq: "The truth is, I was born a Baathist. If you're born Christian, you don't question your mom and dad taking you to church. . . . Till September 2000, the thought of ever leaving Iraq, of leaving my position or the party, never entered my mind."

Al-Qurairy believes that Saddam and his family's hold on power, though hard, has become brittle. "Nobody does my job for the love of Saddam. . . . There is a lot of anger inside many people. If there is a U.S. strike on Baghdad, and it's clear the regime is being targeted, for example by bombing the Presidential Palace, no one will stand and fight—not al-Qare'a, not the special forces. They will turn against the regime, because they remember when."

I look into those warm, brown eyes a final time. I realize that his eventual destiny will make little difference. Whatever happens to al-Qurairy, they are the eyes of a man who is already dead.

Inside Saddam's World

Johanna McGeary

Time

The mad hatter might feel at home in the Wonderland of Iraq. The day is already growing hot as lines of ramshackle buses and black-windowed Mercedes jam the normally empty highway to Tikrit, the rural hometown of Saddam Hussein. It's April 28, Saddam's 65th birthday. Crowds of military men with fat moustaches, sheiks in flowing robes and farmers in shabby pants spill onto the expansive parade ground Saddam has built for special occasions like this. High-ranking guests fill up chairs in a large pseudohistorical reviewing stand where Mussolini would have felt at home.

As the guest of honor arrives, groups of schoolgirls, including a unit clad in the black face masks of suicide-bomber trainees, perform dances dedicated to Saddam's "pulse of life." Then an interminable line of marchers files through, maybe 10,000 strong, singing "Happy year to you, President Saddam Hussein, who brought victory to us." As a group of fist-waving farmers tramps past, one of its members, Abdullah, offers, "We volunteered to come to show how much we love our President."

Trouble is, the man standing high above on that imposing podium is not Saddam Hussein. It's Ali Hassan al-Majid, the Saddam intimate foreigners have dubbed "Chemical Ali" for his role overseeing the 1988 poison-gas attacks that killed thousands of Iraqi Kurds. Al-Majid raises his right arm with palm open in the gesture Saddam uses, smilingly acknowledging the crowd's chants as if he were the ruler. "We sacrifice our blood, our souls for you, Saddam," the mob trills.

Saddam is nowhere in sight for his Tikrit party or any of the other parades and cake cuttings orchestrated across Iraq during the six-day birthday celebration. He is, more than ever, an invisible ruler, his authority wielded from the shadows, where he hides from potential assassins. The Potemkin parties were intended to deliver a message to any Iraqi citizen feeling restive, to any foreign government contemplating his overthrow. The all-powerful puppet master can make his whole nation sing his praises as a blunt reminder: I am still here. It won't be easy to get rid of me.

The Bush Administration hopes the hollowness of that birthday scene is a symbol of the true state of the archenemy's regime: brittle and rotting from within, held together only by force and bribery. The White House has concluded that Saddam poses a clear and present danger that must be eliminated. "He is a dangerous man possessing the world's most dangerous weapons," President Bush has said. "It is incumbent upon freedom-loving nations to hold him accountable, which is precisely what the United States of America will do."

Beyond Bush's advisers, objective monitors too are convinced that Saddam possesses hidden chemical and biological weapons and is working feverishly to build a still elusive nuclear bomb. He's a serial aggressor. Sept. 11 probably opened Saddam's eyes to powerful and unorthodox methods of attack. Terrorists want weapons of mass destruction, and he has them. "The lesson of 9/11 for us," says a senior State Department official, "is you can't wait around."

As Bush repeatedly telegraphs his intention to finish Saddam, the Iraqi leader is not exactly sitting on his hands. "He's not so naive as to ignore the seriousness of this threat," says Wamidh Nadhmi, a Baghdad political scientist in contact with the regime. "He knows it would be very difficult for Bush to retreat from his declared intent." There are signs Saddam is bracing for attack: beefing up his personal security, bucking up the ruling Baath Party and repositioning his military while playing at diplomatic delay with the U.N. He knows the issue for him is existential.

Both Washington and Baghdad foresee confrontation ahead. Here's what it looks like from inside Iraq.

Saddam's Mind

The West has been trying to understand Saddam's psyche for years. A few intimate details have long been observed. Saddam never sleeps in his grand palaces but moves each night to a secret house or tent. He smokes Cohiba cigars supplied by Fidel Castro. He dyes his graying hair black. He walks with a slight limp, allegedly from back trouble, but he looks remarkably fit when seen, usually sitting or standing, on TV. Invariably he now appears wearing immaculately tailored suits in place of the green army fatigues he once favored. Iraqis say he has not worn his uniform publicly since 1998, when, according to local legend, U.N. Secretary-General Kofi Annan told him his image would vastly improve if he donned a statesman's suit instead.

Saddam has limited knowledge of the West and surrounds himself with yes-men who tell him only what he wants to hear. But he shows an eager appetite for certain kinds of information. He constantly monitors CNN and BBC news programs, likes American thriller movies and admires Stalin and Machiavelli. He writes romance novels, supposedly without assistance: just last week a play based on a novel widely believed to have been written by Saddam, Zabibah and the King, opened at Baghdad's elegant new theater. It tells of a lonely monarch in love with a virtuous commoner who is raped on Jan. 17—the day in 1991 that the U.S. attacked Iraq to expel it from Kuwait, which Saddam had invaded the previous August—and killed by a jealous husband egged on by foreign infidels. The king decides he must follow the martyred Zabibah's advice: only strict measures keep the people in line.

In all things about Saddam, contradictions abound. He is known to surround himself with paranoiac security. Yet when Saddam invited Mohammed Sobhi, an Egyptian actor performing in Baghdad last year, to one of his palaces, security seemed almost nonchalant. Sobhi and his troupe were ushered inside with nary a frisk. Saddam chatted easily, about Iraqi poetry, about the Palestinian problem. He allowed each guest to pose for a picture with him. The notorious dictator struck his Egyptian visitors as steady, smiling, relaxed, cheerful, sensitive, amiable, hospitable. He sounded confident that he had weathered a storm. "Saddam said every Iraqi feels inside him that he is a winner, with his pride intact," recalls Sobhi. "Saddam said, 'We did not lose anything. We refuse to be humiliated in front of the Americans.' "

In the weeks before the Gulf War, the CIA presented George Bush Sr. with a psychological profile of Saddam that hasn't altered in its essentials since. Analysts concluded that Saddam was a stable personality and a rational, calculating decision maker. They had no evidence he suffered from mental illness. He was not exactly reckless but was comfortable wielding absolute power, using naked force and taking risks. He was wary and opportunistic and relied only on himself to make decisions. And his sense of mission could taint his judgment.

Saddam's Iraq

For Saddam, the Gulf War was not a defeat but a victory: though he was evicted from Kuwait, he remained in power. In the decade since, he has endured strict economic sanctions and has evaded U.N. inspections designed to eliminate his weapons of mass destruction. Today Iraq has emerged significantly from its isolation.

Saddam's "Republic of Fear"—as Iraqi exile Kanan Makiya dubbed Iraq in the title of his 1989 book—looks remarkably tame these days. You can fly into Baghdad's Saddam International Airport on one of the embargo-busting planes from Jordan or Syria or Lebanon that make regular runs—even if you are greeted by blood-red down with america slogans daubed along the gangway in English. All the capital's buildings, bridges and roads damaged in the 1991 war and in follow-up American attacks in 1998 have been rebuilt. Fancy shops selling the goods of globalization line the posh streets of the al-Mansur neighborhood, and even the poor man's market in the Washash neighborhood peddles plentiful fruit and cheap Chinese TVs.

As goods of all kinds flood in, incomes are rising to pay for them. In 1998 Yusef, a Baghdad resident, drove a broken-down taxi and lived in a house that was bare after he sold the furniture to support his five children. Today Yusef is a partner in a fleet of GMC vans that carry people and merchandise to Amman, Damascus and Beirut. "Life is so much better," he says. "We have some money, we have a good house, my children are healthy."

The supply of medicine from abroad, bought with money the U.N. allows Iraq to earn from limited exports of oil, has improved substantially over the past year. Electricity now runs 24 hours a day, at least in Baghdad. There is plenty of money too for Saddam's fantastic construction projects: giant mosques, more palaces and enough statues of him, goes the joke, to have one for each of Iraq's 24 million people. These grandiose projects are widely resented as a waste of money better spent on desperately needed housing. But the new mosques, at least, address a surging religious faith among dispirited Iraqis seeking escape from the bitter realities of daily life.

For years, Saddam ruthlessly milked the suffering of the Iraqi people to erode the global determination on maintaining the U.N. sanctions. Now he has shifted gears to meet a different objective: to keep those same long-suffering Iraqis from rebelling against him. So the taps have opened: more of the money from his legal oil sales and illicit oil smuggling, once reserved for the purpose of bribing regime loyalists, is now being spread around to the populace.

Saddam has always had to buy his friends. "The only ones who love Saddam," says an Iraqi businessman, 32, whom we'll call Ahmed, "are his family. Everyone else, even his closest circle, must be paid to love him." Saddam rules with an exquisite combination of terror and reward. "He will make you a millionaire or kill you," says Francis Brooke, an American adviser to the Iraqi National Congress (I.N.C.), the London-based, U.S.-funded, main Iraqi-opposition group. "Both are effective levers." Sometimes the two are applied almost simultaneously, as when an individual tortured in prison is welcomed home with a new Mercedes.

In his book Saddam's Bombmaker, the defector Khidhir Hamza, who ran Saddam's atom-bomb program until he fled in 1994, writes frankly of the seductive power of Saddam's largesse. His way of maintaining power has always involved carrots and sticks. Club memberships, chauffeured cars, lavish houses, foreign travel and Johnnie Walker scotch are the means by which Saddam keeps the allegiance of those he needs to protect him and advance his interests. Torture, imprisonment and execution are the lot of those who fail or offend.

The tales of Saddam's brutish violence are legion. Abu Harith (not his real name) spent his life in Saddam's inner circle. He still looks the part: he has the characteristic paunch, the moustache, the Rolex, the confident walk of a senior officer. He spent a year in the foreign directorate of the Defense Ministry, then transferred into Jihaz al-Amin al-Khas, or Special Security Organization (SSO), the elite intelligence outfit responsible for Saddam's personal security, the construction and hiding of weapons of mass destruction and other sensitive tasks. In the 1990s, Abu Harith ran a front company in Jordan purchasing computers, chemical-analysis equipment and special paper for forging passports; then he moved on to Dubai to oversee a lucrative oil-smuggling enterprise.

Abu Harith can't feel his fingertips or his right leg anymore. His joints ache, and his fingers are puffy. These, he says, are the aftereffects of being poisoned by the guards of Saddam's son Uday in 1998. One day that October, he was out walking with a young female cousin when Uday, cruising in his car, spotted her and ordered his guards to snatch her for his evening's entertainment, as is his notorious practice. Abu Harith fended them off. That night Uday's thugs grabbed him at his house and sped him to Uday's farm, where he says he was tied to a palm tree for two days and repeatedly beaten. Uday branded him with a hot iron on his back and shoulder. Then one of the guards injected Abu Harith's arm with something that hurt; he still has a lump there. He was driven back to Baghdad and dumped near his home. When he fled to the Kurdish-controlled north, his suspicions were confirmed: he had been given thallium, a heavy metal used in rat poison that kills slowly through internal bleeding. Kurdish officials got him to Turkey, where he received medical attention.

Colonel Hamadi (not his real name) was commander of a tank unit in Iraq's Third Army before he was arrested for links—which he denies—to an opposition party. He was held for 10 months. Saddam's military intelligence, he says, tortured him several times a week. "Sometimes they hung me from a ceiling fan to make me confess to something that was not true," says the colonel. When he was released last spring, he fled to northern Iraq, where the country's Kurdish minority functions almost autonomously from Baghdad under the protection of the U.S.-British no-fly patrols. But Hamadi left his family behind. His father was recently arrested. "If you are against them," says the colonel, "every one of your relatives is in danger."

Inside Iraq, Saddam's constituents can express despair about such oppression only quietly. An entire population has developed a sixth sense about keeping genuine feelings buried deep. "I can never say what I think," Layla, 38, a former office worker, says from the privacy of her home. With those they trust, Iraqis do grumble about Saddam and his excesses, about the way his ruling circle assesses 7% "for the family" on every business deal. But 30 years of Saddam have instilled in Iraqis a reflexive habit of survival. They seem too tired, too disillusioned, too frightened of one another to plot serious conspiracies. And they have total disdain for the opposition exiles scheming abroad.

If Saddam's hold on power is as tenuous as some officials in Washington claim, that is not visible in Baghdad. The government has lost control over the Kurdish north but has tightened it somewhat in the Shi'ite-dominated south and still firmly grips the Sunni center. The country has been weakened, the army especially, but Saddam remains the strongest of the weak. His control over the intelligence and security services appears unshakable. Officers' families are hostages, and the regime is very good at creating a community of guilt, in which everyone has committed crimes from corruption to execution and fears judgment by a more democratic successor government.

Especially since the Sept. 11 attacks, for which he feared immediate American retaliation, Saddam has taken measures to tighten his protection. The inner circle of guardians, known as al-Himaya, is made up exclusively of close relatives. Says a senior U.S. official: "They're the ones standing with weapons in the background of photos you see of Saddam." The next circle is the Murafiqoun, also related by blood or from unimpeachable families, who are in charge of broader personal and family security and crowd control for Saddam. The outermost circle is the elite SSO, run by son Qusay.

For years Saddam's elder son, the wild, thuggish Uday, was considered the heir apparent. But Uday's penchant for excess was too much even for Saddam after the son, in a fit of pique, murdered a beloved bodyguard of Saddam's in 1988; Uday was jailed for several months. He has largely recovered from a 1996 assassination attempt that has left him barely able to walk. Though he is still a feared man, he has clearly been eclipsed by Qusay, 36. Qusay, say observers in Baghdad and Washington, is a force to be reckoned with. Sober, hardworking and deferential to his father, he is considered as cruel and ruthless as Saddam, though lacking his father's charisma. He never appears in public, but his accumulating strength is evident. He has been "elected" to a leading position in the Baath Party.

Qusay's SSO is increasingly the crucial force, in charge of both internal security and internal intelligence. Members of the SSO are recognized even by the military as having near absolute power; soldiers call these civilian watchdogs "the Masters." Says Falah al-Nakib, a senior member of the Iraqi National Movement, a rival of the I.N.C.: "Every corps commander has one of them in his office watching what he's doing every minute."

Saddam appears to be preparing for war. I.N.C. officials and Kurdish intelligence sources say that for the past two months, government agencies have been conducting preparatory exercises, sending top officials to designated safe locations, for example, and protecting official archives. The sources claim that the commanders of the army have been reshuffled and that various military units have been moved around the country. The I.N.C. says its sources report that military factories are being dismantled so that key components can be hidden from bombing.

But ex-Colonel Hamadi says the army he left behind last year was in sorry shape, demoralized, underpaid and ill equipped. Of the 33 tanks in his sector, he says, 15 were out of commission. In a land of oil wells, there was even a shortage of tank lubricant. Washington officials say sanctions have worked well to undermine Saddam's 424,000-man army. Only the 100,000 or so Republican Guards are still considered serious fighters. So a cataclysmic collapse of the army under pressure from U.S. attack is possible. But experts inside and outside Iraq count 15,000 to 25,000 Saddam loyalists in Qusay's SSO and the Special Republican Guard, the elite of the elite, who would put up a tougher fight.

Saddam's Intentions

Saddam has always been obsessed with building. The Pharaonic size of his enterprises—vast palaces, gigantic mosques, even the idea of an atom bomb—reflect his self-image as history's hero. He never forgets he was born in Tikrit, home nine centuries ago to the great Saladin, the Islamic victor in the Crusades. Saddam's latest Baghdad palace features columns topped with huge replicas of his own head bearing Saladin's helmet. He shaped the minarets on the grand new Mother of All Battles mosque to resemble the Scud missiles he fired at Israel during the Gulf War. These things give concrete expression—literally—to his central ambition: to be remembered and revered as the leader who restored Iraq and the Arab world generally to their rightful glory. He considers himself, says Charles Duelfer, the former deputy executive chairman of the U.N. weapons-inspection team in Iraq, "the incarnation of the destiny of the Arab people."

Like his hero Stalin, Saddam sees weapons of mass destruction as the great equalizers that give him the global position he craves. A nuke plus a long-range missile make you a world power. Deadly spores and poisonous gases make you a feared one. These are the crown jewels of his regime. He sacrificed the well-being of the Iraqi people and billions of dollars in oil revenues to keep the unconventional weapons he had before the Gulf War and to engage in an open-ended process of acquiring new ones. During the cat-and-mouse game of U.N. inspections that ended in 1998, he seemed determined to hold on to some of everything, as if to keep all options open. The weapons clearly are critical to his ambitions. But no one, perhaps not even Saddam, seems to know what he will do with them.

He appears to have not so much a strategy as a concept of grandeur. He is never satisfied with what he has. He operates by opportunity more than by plan and takes devastating risks if the gambles might expand his power. He believes in the ruthless use of force. When he thought Iran was weak, he invaded. When he thought he could get away with taking Kuwait, he invaded. Such conventional warfare is probably not available to him anymore. But intimidation is just as good, maybe better. Weapons of mass destruction could help him coerce the oil-rich Gulf and other Arab states to act in his favor.

Of course, blatantly using such weapons against his greatest enemies, the U.S. and Israel, would expose him to a nuclear reprisal that would almost surely end his rule. But if he could punish either country and survive, he might do it. He has not contracted out his aggressions up to now. But he might risk supplying terrorists with his deadliest weapons if he saw a way it might redound to his power.

Meanwhile, Saddam is working hard to undercut international support for a U.S. attack on him by deploying his diplomatic weapons. He has found a rich issue to exploit in the Palestinian crisis and has made it a constant theme. His offer of $25,000 to the family of every suicide bomber and every Palestinian family made homeless by the Israeli assault last month on a refugee camp in the West Bank city of Jenin has won wide admiration at home and in the larger Arab world. He is showing muscle in the oil market with his 30-day moratorium on Iraqi oil sales to protest Israel's aggression. He has burnished his reputation as the one Arab leader who says no to Washington and stands up against Israel.

At the same time, he has conducted an astute, quiet campaign to integrate Iraq's economy with those of neighboring countries and to convince Europe that the sanctions are wrong and pointless. He made a rapprochement with Kuwait and Saudi Arabia at the Arab summit in March that he hopes will quiet any regional enthusiasm to join an anti-Saddam coalition. He is playing a fresh chess match with the U.N. on weapons inspections. If he can get more favorable terms, he'll probably let them resume. That would undercut European eagerness for a war on Iraq.

While others would find the situation desperate, Saddam has always managed to make his way through. If the U.S. indeed attacks, his paramount strategy will be to weather the assault, hoping that it will prove inadequate and the world will turn against the Americans before they succeed in taking him down. Until that day comes, if it comes, Saddam will rule on from the shadows that protect him from a lifetime's worth of enemies. For him, as long as he's alive, every birthday that passes is another glorious victory.

Saddam and the US

Christopher Hitchens

The Mirror

The discovery by an American president that nuclear weapons can be useful is not as new as some shocked people appear to believe. General MacArthur had eventually to be fired because he thought them too potentially useful in the Korean war.

Presidents Eisenhower, Kennedy and Nixon were prepared to use them against Cuba or Vietnam or the Arab states. Even the latest rather candid nuclear "doctrine" can be traced directly to an authorisation made by President Clinton in 1996. The message is always the same. Take us seriously: we are in principle prepared to destroy you utterly.

The problem with such a "stand tall" policy is that it always has to be based upon a bluff. The warheads are essentially unusable. A superpower looks sillier and less super, each time it rattles this particular sabre. The old problems resurface, just as stubborn as they were before.

During the Gulf War, Saddam Hussein was emphatically told by Washington that if he unleashed any chemical or biological weapons, his country would be turned into glowing ashes. But he ended the war as the undisputed leader of Iraq, while American doctors continued to puzzle over the symptoms of malady shown by their soldiers, a malady still known neutrally under the name "Gulf War Syndrome". As the Bush administration sends Vice-President Cheney around the world to recruit support for another and presumably more conclusive assault upon Iraq, there is a little-noticed controversy taking place back home in Washington DC.

Last month, Dr Ahmed Chalaby, leader of the Iraqi opposition, was in town. And nobody in the government would agree to meet him. Indeed, it became plain from making a few inquiries that there was a formal ban on any contact between him and any member of the administration. If we are to liberate the Iraqi people from the vile despotism of Saddam Hussein, how is this to be done by treating one of that country's leading dissidents as a pariah?

Dr Chalaby's umbrella resistance organisation, the Iraqi National Congress, is the main recipient of the funds allotted by Congress under the terms of the Iraq Liberation Act, which was passed during the Clinton years but never really pursued.

It is said by various Bush bureaucrats that there are some accounting questions about how exactly the money was spent. But this innuendo, even if founded in truth, cannot possibly be the real reason for official frigidity. Since when has the CIA been choosy about accountancy? Since when are Kurdish rebels and other fighters supposed to submit immaculate expense accounts? (If only the administration were as high-minded about its former friends at Enron and Arthur Andersen . . .). No, behind all this is a dirty political secret, which may, if ignored, lead to a calamity in Mesopotamia.

The awful, undiscussed truth is this. In many ways, the United States quite likes the Saddam regime. It was its best friend and chief financier and supplier during the 80s and the presidency of Bush senior. Indeed, on that endlessly recalled occasion when Saddam "used chemical weapons on his own people", the Pentagon solemnly and falsely reported that the deadly stuff had come from the Iranian side. (By the way, to refer to the Kurds as Saddam's "own people" is also rather to beg the question. They are not Arabs and many of them wish they were not even Iraqis.) If Washington were designing a system for Iraq, it would choose a Sunni Muslim military dictatorship, with a strong central government in Baghdad, held in place by a ruthless but secular political party.

That is exactly what it now has—except that this ideal regime is headed by a megalomaniac. So the suspicion must be that the United States really wants, in Dr Chalaby's words, "Saddamism without Saddam".

A rising by the Shi'a majority in the south (Dr Chalaby is a Shi'a) might lead to an Iraq that was more friendly to Iran—which is also a member of the so-called "Axis of Evil". A rising by the long-suffering Kurds in the North would greatly inconvenience the American client state in Turkey, which eyes restiveness among its own Kurds with great apprehension.

To realise this is to understand why Washington has been denouncing Saddam Hussein as "Hitler" for more than a decade without ever summoning the nerve to depose him. The difference now is supposed to be made by his frantic efforts to build or to acquire the Weapons of Mass Destruction that deserve their capital letters. Nor is this a frivolous point: credible defectors have told of serious work on thermo-nuclear bombs—"dirty" ones if you like, as if there could be "clean" ones—and the development of a range of hideous plague devices as well.

In its current mood, the Bush administration is not prepared to wait and find out whether such an arsenal will be used or not. It has decided to err on the side of active mistrust and to smash the Iraqi military capacity before it becomes any more sophisticated. But here another enormous difficulty presents itself.

Saddam Hussein has been very quiet of late but if his country were invaded he would very probably unleash at least some horror weapons in the direction of Israel. (These would run the risk of killing the Palestinians as well, as few people ever bother to point out but it could well be that a desperate dictator would not mind this "collateral damage".) In other words, an attack upon Iraq might precipitate the very contingency that it is designed to forestall.

I have asked several people in the "national security" world how they reply to this—and they say that the invasion will be so overwhelming that no Iraqi commander will find it worth his while to obey orders from the doomed leader. Not a completely convincing response. After all, what would the United States do if that "scenario" didn't work out? Nuke Iraq? Tell the Israelis they were free to nuke Iraq? Goodbye then to the oilfields and—depending on how the prevailing wind was blowing—goodbye to much else besides.

In the recent tussles with Milosevic and the Taliban, the declared objectives were to halt further self-evident aggression and to emancipate populations held hostage by fanatical regimes. In both cases, local allies were more than willing to welcome intervention as a liberation. These favourable conditions do not appear to apply so far in the Iraqi case and, what is worse, the Bush administration does not appear to feel that it owes anybody, including the hostage people, an explanation.

US Strategic Options for Iraq

Michael Isherwood

The Washington Quarterly

When George W. Bush was elected president, he assumed more than the office that his father occupied a decade earlier; he also inherited his father's foreign policy nemesis, Iraq's Saddam Hussein. Saddam has steadfastly been high on the list of the Bush administrations foreign policy priorities. The key questions are, how high of a priority is Iraq? Where does it fit in the counterterrorism campaign? Clearly, however, the United States must change its policy toward Iraq.

In place of the oil-for-food regime and no-fly-zone enforcement, the Bush administration should foster cooperative security alliances with conservative Persian Gulf nations. This traditional approach to containing a hostile nation is all the more compelling when viewed in light of the new global campaign against terrorism. The United States lacks the means, that is, resources and political capital, to confront Iraq more forcibly and battle terrorism worldwide simultaneously.

The rationale for a new policy approach toward Iraq is evident after examining three options for U.S. Iraq policy—a patient approach, a moderate approach, and a bold strategy. The costs, benefits, and risks associated with each option are set forth, and the defining question is posed for Bush and his national security team: what is the end state of this administration's Iraq policy? Do the president and his team envision a region less threatened by Iraq? Or do they look at Iraq "through a glass, darkly" and seek a reflection of U.S. society and values? The options presented focus primarily on U.S. policy toward Iraq. Regardless of the policy it pursues, the Bush administration must integrate its Iraq policy within a broader U.S. strategy toward the Middle East, a strategy that includes Iran and Israel and the Palestinian territories.

U.S. Iraq policy will succeed if it does the following:

- *Articulates the nature of U.S. interests with respect to Iraq.* Are these interests vital, important, humanitarian, or a combination? To what extent is the administration willing to endanger U.S. military personnel?
- *Matches its resources with its objectives.* The Clinton administration set an alluring goal—a law-abiding Iraq with a democratically supported regime[1]—but failed to commit the resources to match the ambition.
- *Expends enough political capital to gain both domestic and international support for its policy.*
- *Rebuilds consensus between the United States and its allies in the Middle East.* Countries such as Syria and Turkey abandoned the 1991 Persian Gulf War coalition because of their immediate national interests: their benefit from black market activities that circumvent Iraqi sanctions. The failure to back up the rhetoric with action has fractured the coalition in the past, as in 1996 when the United States ignored Saddam's move against Irbil that crushed PUK (Patriotic Union of Kurdistan) forces in that city. The U.S. response of launching 44 cruise missiles against primarily air-defense targets appeared disproportionate and weak compared to Saddam's crushing blow with tanks against PUK forces and Kurds.[2] Inconsistent actions reinforce allies' skepticism and undermine U.S. prestige in the region. No U.S. objective is achievable without the support of Iraq's neighbors as well as U.S. allies in Europe and Asia. The United States must gain its allies' support by elucidating the similarities between U.S. interests and their own. Reinvigorated relations with allies will support any new U.S. policy toward Iraq; without stronger alliances, any new policy is doomed to fail.

A more patient approach to U.S.-Iraqi relations is necessary. Foreign policy, like war and wrestling, is a two-sided contest. Every coercive action provokes resistance. The greater the sacrifice the United States expects of Saddam, the more the United States should anticipate resistance by Saddam, requiring an increasing level of U.S. resources and will. Given Iraq's current capabilities, the survival of the United States is not at stake; Saddam's survival is. If the Bush administration seeks a new regime in Baghdad, it should not expect Saddam to leave quietly.

Toward a New Strategy

After 11 years, no one should have any illusions that a silver bullet exists to solve the problem of Iraq and Saddam. Simple solutions will not create conditions that meet all U.S. interests immediately. The legacy of the past decade reinforces the belief that the United States risks further erosion of its prestige unless it alters its Iraq policy.

Option I : The Strategy of Patience: Emphasizing U.S. Strengths

The objectives of option 1 are that the United States:

- *Seek a united Iraq.* Iraq maintaining its territorial integrity is in the United States' interest. The disintegration of Iraq threatens regional stability and access by industrialized nations to oil resources.
- *Seek a non-nuclear Iraq that possesses limited conventional forces.* The United States should reinvigorate political and diplomatic efforts to deny Iraq access to weapons of mass destruction (WMD) and to restrict Iraq's ability to rearm its conventional forces.
- *Reinforce a long-term, formal security relationship with conservative Gulf nations.* The core U.S. interest is regional stability. An enduring, viable, and positive relationship with regional allies—not a negative relationship with Iraq—reinforces this interest.
- *Foster an alternative, tolerant, and democratic Iraqi government that respects the rights of its citizens.* The United States should train a cadre of alternative government leaders who would respect the rights of Iraqi citizens.

If it were to choose a patient approach, the United States would seek to reinforce cooperative relations with Gulf Cooperation Council (GCC) nations and secure long-term influence in the region. It would accept an increase in immediate risk in order to reduce the near-term diplomatic, military, and financial costs. Six critical pillars would support this policy.

Course of Action

Pillar One: *The United States would support the cessation of economic sanctions.* Many U.S. allies endorse this critical first step to any revitalized U.S. policy for two reasons. First, ending economic sanctions will help key regional allies. Turkey, for example, estimates that it has lost $35 billion in trade during the past decade.[4] At the same time, Turkey could benefit from a windfall of $30–50 billion in construction contracts for rebuilding Iraqi dams, roads, and refineries.[5] Second, ending economic sanctions will deny Saddam the lucrative black market that he uses to support his patronage network. Iraq recently repaired the pipeline between the Kirkuk oilfields and the Syrian port of Baniyas, allowing Syria to funnel $2 million per day to Saddam in illegal revenues by purchasing, transferring, and reselling Iraqi oil.[6] Average Iraqis, however, do not benefit from these proceeds. By lifting economic sanctions, the Bush administration would demonstrate its concern for the welfare of the Iraqi people and deny Saddam the ability to blame the United States for their suffering. Without sanctions, Saddam will have to improve the quality of life for all Iraqis.[7] This pillar would be a vital part of sustaining a constructive, long-term U.S. relationship with its regional allies.

Pillar Two: *The United States would curtail, and ultimately halt, no-fly-zone enforcement.* Reducing and eventually phasing out the daily no-fly-zone flights in Operation Northern Watch (ONW) and Operation Southern Watch (OSW) would offer a means to reduce the burden on scarce U.S. military resources and gain a key bargaining chip with the international community. The United States could transition from a daily to a periodic presence, returning the ONW and OSW missions to their original purpose—denying Saddam the use of his fixed-wing aircraft to terrorize the Kurdish and Shi'a populations—while still perhaps providing the Iraqi Kurds the margin of security they need. To implement the random enforcement, the United States could stay out of Iraqi air space for 3–6 weeks at a time and then, using U.S. naval aircraft from a carrier battle group or an air force air expeditionary force that deploys for 30–45 days to the region, return for a 2–3 week interval of patrolling. During lulls, U.S. Air Force long-range bombers—B-2, B-1, and B-52 aircraft—and carrier-based fighters could provide an immediate response, should Saddam violate the no-drive sanction or use his fixed-wing aircraft against Iraqi citizens, rapidly restoring the full no-fly zones. Reducing and halting daily operations in the no-fly zones would not negate the legal justification for the flights or the U.S. ability to protect Iraqi citizens—only the timing would be changed.

Pillar Three: *The United States would gain renewed access for United Nations (UN) weapons inspectors.* The September 2001 terrorist attacks and subsequent anthrax deaths have created the optimum international conditions for all countries to demand that Saddam allow an unobstructed return of international inspectors to confirm his compliance with UN Security Council directives. The world community has no tolerance for state sponsors of terrorism and would support a return of UN inspectors. Although many suspect Iraq's complicity in the anthrax mailings, no conclusive link to Saddam's laboratories is apparent,[8] but Saddam should be eager to avoid being the next target in the U.S. global war on terrorism. Accepting (or at least appearing to accept) the return of international weapons inspectors would allow Saddam to deflect possible U.S. military action. Saddam's refusal to accept the return of inspectors provides the most logical path to increased hostilities and the actions in option 3 (below). This pillar, combined with the first two, could help the United States build international support.

Pillar Four: *The United States would expand the Missile Technology Control Regime (MTCR) to deny Iraq WMD technology and obtain a weapons embargo on conventional armaments.* This pillar is the second part of the "smart-sanctions" regime proposed by the United States and the United Kingdom (UK) in the spring of 2001. It would rely on tougher external monitoring of exports bound for Iraq to ensure that they do not include materials that would enhance Iraq's WMD and military rearmament programs.[9] Pillar four goes beyond the existing smart-sanctions measure, however, by recommending that the United States expand the voluntary MTCR to include China, India, and Pakistan. Currently, the MTCR is an association of 29 nations, some of which might supply Saddam with advanced weapons technology.[10] An expanded MTCR would prove more palatable to U.S. allies in the Gulf because it would focus on those nations outside the region that sell WMD and conventional weapons to Saddam.

To augment the expanded MTCR initiatives and smart sanctions, the United States should seek a more effective enforcement mechanism, such as one that imposes severe financial penalties against those companies that violate the Iraqi arms embargo under the MTCR banner. The host government of any offending company would impose penalties worth hundreds of millions or billions of dollars. In addition to the physical inspection of exports bound for Iraq, fines would provide a disincentive for firms that want to supply Iraq with weapons-related products. Currently, the UN Special Commission on Iraq (UNSCOM) has a list of countries and companies that have supplied Iraq with military equipment, but the UN prohibits the release of those names.[11] This restriction should be removed.

Gaining allied and regional support will require the United States to offer economic assistance. Syria, Jordan, and Turkey rely on trade and cheap oil from Saddam to sustain their economies.[12] The July 2001 UK-U.S. effort to revamp Iraq's oil-for-food program failed in part because Saddam used his economic clout more effectively. He has used his buying power to punish nations that do not support his agenda. For example, since the late 1990s, he has curtailed imports from France because of its training of UN inspectors.[13] To counter Saddam's economic pressure, the United States must be ready to provide significant economic aid. Smart sanctions and expanded MTCR efforts will only succeed with the support of Iraq's immediate and future trading partners. The Bush administration should expect that support to have a price tag.

Pillar Five: *The United States and its allies would forge a formal security alliance.* The United States would pursue a formal security alliance with the GCC and other regional allies, such as Jordan, to offset any increased risk associated with a reduced U.S. presence in the no-fly zones. This alliance would pre-position military hardware, such as brigade sets and munitions storage, and modernize commend-and-control networks. The alliance could extend beyond the GCC nations to include European Union countries such as France and Great Britain as well as Pacific nations such as Japan and Singapore. Periodic military exercises and deployments to the region would underscore the commitment of these nations to peace in the region. A formal security alliance answers the most pressing interests of the United States and its allies: ensuring that Iraq—under any leadership—does not threaten regional stability and the world's economic system.

Pillar Six: *The United States would sponsor a civic-development program for Iraq.* The United States could nurture a cadre of future Iraqi government and municipal leaders who would create a tolerant, effective, and democratic society. The United States could offer to sponsor several hundred Iraqis to travel to the United States and other Western or Islamic nations to gain theoretical and hands-on experience in how a modern civil society provides for its citizenry, administers municipal governments, and manages key industries and public utilities. This program would offer a year of advanced university study followed by 1–2 years of on-the-job experience in areas including judicial systems, law enforcement, hospital administration, electrical and agricultural industry development, modern financial institutions, and media operations. Turkey could offer the experience it gained building on its Kemalist tradition and offer a valuable perspective for the Iraqi Kurds. Following their training, these Iraqis could return to work with the Iraqi Kurds in the north or form a government in exile. This initiative could be repeated during the course of a decade or more. With 42 percent of Iraqis under the age of 14, the United States must offer an atypical experience to Iraq's future leaders if the United States envisions a different Iraq.[14] This initiative seeks to capture the youth of Iraq, and its success must be measured over a generation.

Risk Assessment

To adopt option 1, the United States would have to believe that a long-term relationship with key allies and the citizens of Iraq better serve its interests. This approach provides for stability by defending key allies while seeking to reverse the increasingly negative view of the United States in the region. It stresses diplomatic initiatives while reserving the military instrument for a primarily deterrent role. The United States would also benefit from a reduced military budget and a reduced operations tempo associated with curtailing ONW and OSW. Considering that the United States intends to conduct a global war on terrorism, reducing military requirements elsewhere is prudent. The risks, however, cannot be ignored. The United States and its allies could bear a significant cost if Saddam evades MTCR efforts. In addition, should Saddam rebuild his conventional forces, he could invade Kuwait and move south to seize the oil fields of Saudi Arabia, exacting a high price for Saudi support of U.S. policy in the 1990s. Finally, reduced ONW operations might cause Kurds in northern Iraq to flee into Turkey, as they did in the spring of 1991, prompting an internal crisis in Turkey, one of the strongest allies of the United States in the region. Still, option 1 incurs the lowest diplomatic and economic costs in the short term. If unsuccessful, it incurs significant risk in the long run.

Option 2: Strategy of Moderation: Creating a Climate for Change

This option's objectives are to:

- *seek a united Iraq* (see option 1);
- *seek a nonnuclear Iraq that possesses limited conventional forces* (see option 1);
- *foster a tolerant and democratic Iraqi government that respects the rights of its citizens* (see option 1); and
- *actively undermine Saddam.*

If the United States chooses option 2, it would actively seek to undermine Saddam's power structure. The United States would expand its strategic use of military, economic, and diplomatic tools to create an alternative Iraqi society, as well as weaken Saddam's domestic political power base.

Course of Action

To reach these expanded objectives, the Bush administration would add the two pillars that follow to the six pillars discussed in option 1. Creating a climate for change requires a more assertive approach.

Pillar Seven: *The United States would support safe havens in northern and southern Iraq governed by a viable alternative government to Saddam's regime.* Currently, the UN facilitates safe havens in northern Iraq. This initiative would extend the protected enclaves concept into southern Iraq. If the UN mandated such safe havens, they would reinforce the safe havens' humanitarian objective to protect Iraqi citizens from Saddam's brutality. Strong evidence supports the efficacy of such enclaves. Where the UN supervises food and medicine distribution in northern Iraq, for example, infant mortality rates are lower than they were in 1990 and less than twice that elsewhere in Iraq. The distinctive difference is the presence of an effective administering body.[15]

The boundaries of the proposed enclaves would approximate the boundaries of the no-fly zones without a firm "red line" south of the 32nd parallel and north of the 36th parallel that the United States would have to defend. Instead, the safe havens would gradually expand as the UN expanded humanitarian aid and as graduates of the civic-development program returned to provide social services such as schools, hospitals, law enforcement, and a judicial system.

To support the enclaves' economic viability, the United States could provide financial and economic development funds. To encourage trade, the United States and its allies could offer other countries special free-trade status with the enclaves. These economic initiatives in the enclaves would reinvigorate key segments such as agriculture, electrical production, manufacturing, and water purification. The aid would be critical to ensuring that Iraq becomes a viable state with an economy able to provide for its people's basic needs: jobs, income, goods, and services. The development of safe havens reinforced with economic aid would create an alternative in Iraq to Saddam's brutality.

Pillar Eight: *The United States would arm the opposition to Saddam and support the opposition with airpower.* The enclaves must be able to defend themselves if they are to survive. The Bush administration would provide military aid to opposition members in the enclaves, enabling them to defend themselves. Lethal aid would extend beyond rifles, grenades, and mortars to include light mobile vehicles and antitank weaponry. Such equipment is defensive in nature, providing the opposition forces with mobility and fire-power but not the survivability needed for offensive operations. As such, it would not encourage the opposition to launch a campaign on Baghdad or threaten a neighboring state. Because the allies originally established the no-fly zones to prevent Saddam from using his military forces to kill Iraqis who oppose him, coalition aircraft could provide additional firepower in support of the opposition by fully enforcing the intent of the no-fly zones and no-drive mandates of the UN Security Council resolutions.

OSW and ONW are tools to provide immediate firepower to the opposition and undermine Saddam's regime when he violates UN Security Council mandates. As such, the military objectives of these forces must be expanded. Broader air operations would seek to protect Iraqi civilians in the safe havens, destroy any Iraqi WMD infrastructure, and target Saddam's command-and-control structures in order to degrade his ability to govern and to command his military forces. A liberalized air effort would also hit critical elements of Saddam's power structure: the Republican Guard headquarters, leadership, and command and control; security services' headquarters and forces; prisons; the Ba'th Party network; and even financial institutions. These air strikes would methodically strip away Saddam's support system by physically removing it or intimidating those who support him. Saddam's supporters would realize that association with him incurs a personal cost. Making use of Pillar Eight would reinforce U.S. objectives by physically denying Saddam the ability to threaten Iraqi citizens or neighbors and by undermining his political power base within Iraq.

Risk Assessment

This option requires an expanded U.S. military, political, and financial commitment to the region. The costs are significant. Economic and military aid must be matched with considerable funding for the safe havens. In addition, the U.S. Department of Defense would require additional funds to provide the necessary air support to assist the opposition forces. The size of U.S. forces deployed would have to increase significantly over the number currently deployed for ONW and OSW, required for homeland defense, and engaged in the global counterterrorism campaign.

This option also entails increased risks. Saddam may interpret the safe havens as a violation of Iraqi sovereignty and move to prevent their establishment. Countering such a move will challenge U.S. prestige and require significant military forces to defend the enclaves, endangering U.S. military personnel.

A second risk is that the opposition may not coalesce into a viable, coherent national government. The PUK, the Kurdistan Democratic Party (KDP), and the Supreme Council for Islamic Revolution in Iraq (SCIRI) could have divergent expectations and might not share a common view of a regime tolerant of their values. This realization, however, underscores the importance of the civic-development initiative. Iraq is not the first nation to deal with the coexistence of multiple ethnic and religious groups. A hopeful sign is SCIRI's recent statement that it is more willing to cooperate with an opposition coalition, the Iraqi National Congress (INC).[16] The United States must show the opposition groups how their interests are linked in a unified, post-Saddam Iraqi government.

With or without the civic nation building, post-Saddam Iraq might disintegrate into two or three separate states. Saddam's son, Uday, could forge an allegiance with Ali Hassan al-Majid, Saddam's cousin, and Barzan Ibrahim al-Tikriti, Saddam's half brother, to force out Saddam's other son, Qusay. The ensuing chaos could cause the Kurds to attempt to secede, providing Syria, Turkey, or Iran with an excuse to intervene. These risks are not insignificant. Finally, if this option fails, the United States will lose its prestige and influence in the Gulf region in the long run.

Option 3: Strategy of Boldness: Compelling Change

This option's objectives propose that the United States:

- *seek a united Iraq* (see option 1);
- *seek a nonnuclear Iraq that possesses limited conventional forces* (see option 1);
- *remove Saddam from power forcibly with a robust military campaign.*

Course of Action

Although the first two objectives of this third option are consistent with earlier objectives, the third objective marks an unabashed departure. The end state of this option is clear: to eliminate Saddam's regime. As such, only two of the previously discussed pillars, Pillar Six (nation building) and Pillar Eight (arming the opposition), are immediately applicable to this option. Three additional critical pillars would support this policy.

Pillar Nine: *The United States must conduct a successful public relations campaign to demonstrate Saddam's threat to international peace.* This effort must involve more than senior U.S. government leaders summarily stating that Saddam threatens peace. It requires more than the United States declaring that Saddam has failed to comply with the UN Security Council resolutions or the Safwan cease-fire of 1991 (which demanded that Iraq demonstrate that it had ceased all WMD programs and account for all Kuwaiti citizens missing following the 1990 invasion). The U.S. effort must link Saddam directly and unequivocally to the September terrorist attacks, to the anthrax events, or to similar pending hostile action against the world community. A successful public relations campaign must create conditions such that regional and world leaders expect, support, and even demand military action. An effective military campaign will require access to GCC nations for staging and basing operations. Islamic governments will require convincing and unambiguous proof of Saddam's complicity or his threat to peace. Islamic communities and Arab public opinion view the U.S. campaign in Afghanistan against the Taliban and Al Qaeda in a purely West-versus-Islam context. Without an effective public relations campaign, military actions against Iraq will only reinforce that view and fortify Osama bin Laden's intent to isolate the Middle East from the West.

Pillar Ten: *The United States would employ decisive special operations and land, air, and maritime power to remove Saddam and secure Iraqi WMD sites.* The U.S. military forces required for this pillar are significant although the outcome is not in doubt. If the requisite political and diplomatic efforts enable the United States to base its forces in the region, U.S. forces will need months to prepare for military operations that will revive Operation Desert Storm where it concluded in March 1991. This option offers the most assured and direct means to remove Saddam from power.

Pillar Eleven: *The United States would support UN sponsorship of a transitional, pluralistic Iraqi government.* U.S. policymakers must think beyond merely removing Saddam and recognize that peace will come to the region only with an Iraqi government that respects the international rule of law and the rights of all its citizens. In the 1920s, Kemal Ataturk led Turkey in its transition from an autocratic regime to a foundation for democracy. The challenge for the United States and Iraq is finding a similar mechanism or leader to gain similar effects. Shaping this new regime will be an immense challenge.

Risk Assessment

This bold approach demands the greatest immediate costs in terms of political, economic, and military resources. Weaning key regional allies from their addiction to Saddam's cheap oil will require financial resources. UN Security Council members such as Russia and France must envision potential economic benefits from a different regime in Baghdad and be willing to defer more immediate benefits to this new relationship. In addition, this option will be costly in terms of a lost opportunity as U.S. military resources are diverted from the global campaign against terrorism.

The military costs of this campaign will be significant. The size and shape of Iraq's military forces dictate that U.S. forces look more like those employed in 1991 than those employed against Afghanistan in 2001. One view estimates that a minimum of 200,000 troops is required to defeat Iraq.[17] Even the economical approach attributed to retired General Wayne Downing—to use Iraqi opposition groups, special operations forces, and over-whelming U.S.

airpower, as the United States did in Afghanistan—requires a significant U.S. footprint for staging air forces.[18] As such, the United States would require international support for basing and overnight rights to execute the military campaign. Turkey, Saudi Arabia, and other GCC nations would have to allow offensive operations from their territory against Iraq. In the past, these nations have been circumspect to provide such approval for enforcing the no-fly zones; the United States should not lightly assume these nations would extend approval to unseat an Arab leader in Baghdad.

The risks associated with this option must not be minimized. Without an effective alternative government and cadre of leadership, the United States risks allowing Iraq to disintegrate into chaos as competing Kurdish, Shi'a, and Sunni factions contend for power. Such turmoil may invite Iran or Turkey, claiming their vital interests are threatened, to take action and reshape the political borders. This option also places in danger significant numbers of U.S. personnel—during both the buildup of forces and the invasion of Iraq. The Bush administration would have to explain the action to U.S. citizens by articulating the nature of the U.S. interest at stake that is worth risking U.S. lives.

The influence campaign could backfire on the United States. Instead of being convinced of the moral good and value of an increased U.S. presence in the region, Arab public opinion could reject the arguments and compel Arab governments to invite the United States to leave. Alternatively, a revolt of fundamentalist Muslims against conservative political regimes could cause the United States to lose its unprecedented access to the Gulf region. Being summarily kicked out of the region would represent a catastrophic failure of U.S. foreign policy. Finally, just as the U.S. presence in the Gulf region and the U.S. attack on Iraq gave rise to bin Laden, attacking Saddam again would serve as a rallying point for those fundamentalist Islamic groups attracted to bin Laden's cause. A renewed assault against Iraq could bring fresh momentum to Islamic terrorist groups and new attacks against U.S. citizens.

Nonetheless, the benefits of this option are appealing. If successful, this option would provide a near-term solution to the enduring problem of Saddam. It would allow the United States to shape the region in its own image, to demonstrate global leadership, to establish that hostile and aggressive behavior will not be tolerated, and to signal its determination to other hostile nations or state sponsors of terrorism.

The Way Ahead: Balancing Political Capital, Risks, and Benefits

After a decade, U.S. policy toward Iraq has not realized its full objective of a more stable and peaceful region. Saddam flaunts the UN disarmament mandate and continues his bellicose rhetoric toward his neighbors. His regime jeopardizes the industrialized world's access to oil, threatens to use force to redraw national borders, and intimidates other nations with WMD. His determination to develop WMD remains a salient concern for the United States and its allies. Saddam remains a threat.

Anything seems easy, it is often said, to someone who does not have to do it. The options presented here "easily" connect the objectives with the ways and means to reach the desired end state. Carrying out an option in the current domestic and international environments is far more difficult.

Option 3 is attractive because it positions the United States to shape the region. The costs and risks associated with option 3, however, may be beyond the political capital that Bush is willing or able to expend. Suggesting that the UN Security Council back up its resolutions with authorizations to use force if necessary to enforce them is logical, but the UN is unlikely to approve the military measures required to strip Saddam of WMD and remove him from power. Many in the international community would wonder whether the United States was pursuing a common interest, holding a grudge, or boosting its ego by removing Saddam. Although some polls suggest that the U.S. public would like to solve the Saddam problem once and for all, the lack of an immediate connection between Saddam and terrorism means that removing him from power would be done at the expense of striking against a concrete terrorist threat—the threat that is directly responsible for those killed in the attacks on September 11.

Option 2 may appear as a middle-of-the-road solution, but the United States would find it as daunting to execute as option 3. The UN is unlikely to authorize safe havens and arm the opposition unless an overwhelming international outcry results from a highly publicized humanitarian catastrophe or threat. Events in Afghanistan demonstrated that the United States needs allies and some form of international support to act; the U.S. need for basing and overflight rights impedes unilateral action. A concurrent, extensive public relations campaign would also be needed to set the conditions and gain international support for option 2. Middle Eastern nations have not sought this type of solution because they do not see it in their interests. The United States would need to expend significant political and economic resources—at least as much as the reported $1 billion in aid to Pakistan enabling U.S. operations in Afghanistan—to persuade nations of the region to accept U.S. objectives.

Proponents of options 2 and 3 should remember that, for those in the Middle East, the path to Baghdad runs through the Palestinian territories. Regional allies place a higher priority on resolving the Israeli-Palestinian problem and will expect U.S. leadership to solve this situation before the United States receives their support to deal with Saddam.

Option 1 provides the best match of resources to objectives for the Bush administration. It satisfies the U.S. core interest: regional stability. It allows the United States to pursue stability in a manner that fosters and reinforces its long-term access, influence, and prestige in the region. Option 1 moves diplomatic and economic tools to the forefront of U.S. efforts to prevent Saddam from obtaining WMD capability. It employs the military tool in its traditional peacetime role: to deter aggression through cooperative peace-time alliances. Option 1 also enables the United States to conserve scarce military, financial, and diplomatic resources for the higher-priority task of neutralizing the global terrorist threat to U.S. interests and U.S. citizens. Should Saddam (or his successor) ultimately pursue aggressive behavior, the United States would have solid and positive relations with key nations in the region, such as Turkey and Saudi Arabia, to meet that challenge.

The United States must weigh the ultimate domestic and international costs associated with any approach it takes. Washington must also appreciate that Saddam will resolutely oppose U.S. initiatives and that any approach will require time to reach its objectives. Whatever strategy the United States pursues, rebuilding allied consensus vis-à-vis Iraq is a fundamental challenge in the months ahead. Options described here are crafted so that U.S. tools and means correspond with the specific objectives the United States seeks. In formulating strategies and choosing options to deal with Saddam and Iraq, it is important to recognize that some things are easier said than done.

Notes

[1] *Iraq Liberation Act of 1998*, Public Law 338, 105th Cong., 2d sess. (October 31, 1998).

[2] Michael Eisenstadt, "The U.S. Strikes on Iraq: What Was Accomplished? What Is Next?" *Policy Watch* no. 215 (Washington, D.C.: Washington Institute for Near East Policy, September 4, 1996), www.washingtoninstitute.org/watch/Policy watch/policywatchl996/215.htm (accessed January 15, 2001).

[3] Ofra Bengio, "How Does Saddam Hold On?" *Foreign Affairs* 79, no. 4 (July/August 2000): 101–102.

[4] John W. Anderson, "Ankara Supports Lifting UN Sanctions against Iraq," *Washington Post*, January 26, 2001, p. A7.

[5] Terry Boyd, "Future Cloudy for Operation Northern Watch," *European Stars and Stripes*, January 19, 2001, p. 2.

[6] "Syria Has Opened a Pipeline for Iraqi Oil, Observers Say," *Los Angeles Times*, January 23, 2001, p. l.

"Iraq Country Profile 2000," *Economist Intelligence Unit*, http://db.eiu.com/report_dl.asp?mode=pdf&valname=CPAIQB (accessed January 6, 2001) (hereinafter "Iraq Country Profile 2000").

[8] Rick Weiss, "Germ Tests Point Away from Iraq," *Washington Post*, October 30, 2001, p. A9.

[9] Charles Recknagel, "Iraq: U.S., Britain Step Up Talk of 'Smart' Sanctions," Radio Free Europe/Radio Liberty, March 2, 2001, www.rferl.org/nca/features/2001/03/02032001114030.asp (accessed May 25, 2001).

[10] U.S. Arms Control and Disarmament Agency, "The Missile Technology Control Regime," dated September 15, 1997, www.fas.org/nuke/control/mtcr/docs/mtcr96.htm (accessed May 25, 2001). The following countries are part of the Missile Technology Control Regime: Argentina, Australia, Austria, Belgium, Brazil, Canada, Denmark, Finland,

France, Germany, Greece, Hungary, Iceland, Ireland, Italy, Japan, Luxembourg, Netherlands, New Zealand, Norway, Portugal, Russian Federation, South Africa, Spain, Sweden, Switzerland, Turkey, United Kingdom, and the United States.

[11] Phyllis Bennis and Stephen Zunes, "Four Days in December: Answers to Some of the Unanswered Questions behind the U.S.-British Bombing of Iraq," *Foreign Policy in Focus*, www.foreignpolicy-infocus.org/media/opeds/oped_iraqqa.html (accessed January 6, 2001).

[12] Colum Lynch, "Iraq Uses Its Buying Power for Political Leverage," *Washington Post*, July 3, 2001, p. A1.

[13] Ibid.

[14] "Syria Country Profile 2000," *Economist Intelligence Unit*, http://db.ciu.com/report_dl.asp?mode=pdf&valname=CPAIQB (accessed January 17, 2001).

[15] "Iraq Country Profile 2000."

[16] "Iraqi Group to Accept U.S. Help," *Washington Post*, April 8, 2001, sec. A, p. 18.

[17] Philip Gordon and Michael O'Hanlon, "A Tougher Target," *Washington Post*, December 26, 2001, p. A31.

[18] Michael Dobbs, "Old Strategy on Iraq Sparks New Debate," *Washington Post*, December 27, 2001, p. A1.

Saddam Hussein's Would-be Successors

Heidi Kingstone

The Jerusalem Report

In Mid-March Iraq.net, a two-year old website owned by a prominent member of the Iraqi opposition in London, ran a poll asking who could head a transitional government in Baghdad, should President Bush make good on his declaration that he intends to get rid of Saddam Hussein. The U.S.-funded opposition Radio Free Iraq gave the poll good coverage, and commentators good-humoredly dubbed it the first democratic election in Iraqi history.

About 2,500 respondents—mostly exiled Iraqis—chose from a list of 14 names. The results indicate the dilemma faced by the Americans, who say they are determined to "change the regime" in Baghdad but are much less clear on who, or what, they want to see replace Saddam Hussein. The most popular answer was "none of the above." The top "candidate" of the 14 named, with 19 percent of the votes, was Najib Salhi, a former Iraqi army brigadier general who defected in 1995. Salhi heads the Free Officers Movement based in Fairfax, Virginia. The group supports regime change in Iraq, but not by military coup.

Because the Salhi clan is found throughout Iraq and spans the country's Sunni and Shi'ite Muslim populations, he's a plausible consensus candidate. (About 65 percent of Iraqis are Shi'ites though the country's current leadership is Sunni.)

Second, with about 15 percent, came Sharif Ali, a cousin of Faisal II, the Iraqi king who was assassinated in the original Free Officers revolution of 1958. Ali, 45, left Baghdad at the age of 3, grew up in Beirut and now lives in London. A banker, he heads a movement for a constitutional monarchy for Iraq based on the British model, and favors democratic elections.

Ali's party, the Constitutional Monarchy Movement, is a member of the Iraqi National Congress (INC), the pro-democracy umbrella movement that represents all the main segments of the Iraqi opposition in exile. Ali finished ahead of INC founder Ahmed Chalabi, long tagged as the Pentagon's favorite for the successor role, who scored only 12-13 percent in the poll. The London-based INC, which has U.S. funding but is riven with rivalries, advocates new leadership but so far has not put forward names of those it considers candidates to succeed Saddam.

Unsurprisingly for a poll taken in the Iraqi diaspora, two candidates related to Saddam—his son Qusai and his half-brother Barazan Tikriti—garnered less than 3 per cent between them.

In addition to being inconclusive, the results were tainted by the fact that the poll was called off a few days ahead of schedule. Critics say that was because Chalabi was not winning. The website's managers deny that, saying they pulled the poll because they suspected someone was falsely inflating the figures of front-runner Salhi.

If anything, the poll serves as an ironic microcosm of Iraqi politics, reflecting just how murky the future after Saddam looks.

President Bush, worried about Iraq's weapons of mass destruction, has now clearly stated that Saddam needs to go. But the administration is being much more coy about how or when that goal will be achieved, and observers can't make out whether Washington will follow through or not. David Mack, vice president of the Middle East Institute, a Washington think tank, echoes a common sentiment: "America is getting serious about getting rid of Saddam Hussein, but they have not yet figured out how to do it."

Washington appears to be mulling several options, ranging from diplomatic pressure through covert activity to a full military invasion. And, Iraq watchers say, Washington officials are on the lookout for potential new leaders. "It's one of the strands in the administration's bow," says a former U.S. government official.

Some traditional Washington lines about who or what could replace Saddam seem to be getting blurred. State Department skeptics who once ruled out any dealings with what they saw as the non-credible INC, favoring a military coup scenario instead, now seem open to other options. And Pentagon hawks who once looked upon anyone who didn't back Ahmed Chalabi as an agent of Saddam now recognize that the INC head might not be the ideal or only vehicle for change after all.

Despite the uncertainty of U.S. intentions, scores of Saddam opponents, rivals and potential heirs, many of whom live in exile, are gearing up to seize the moment. Mack, a retired U.S. diplomat with considerable experience in dealing with Iraq, reckons about 40 people are in the running.

Among these, the most recognizable is Chalabi. A Shi'ite from Baghdad, Chalabi left Iraq in 1958, at the age of 13. His father had been the head of the Senate under the monarchy. A former banker and former professor of mathematics at the American University of Beirut, Chalabi now operates out of London and Washington. Supported and funded by the Pentagon and Congress, he founded the INC in 1992, is the organization's representative in Washington and sits on its six-seat leadership council. One criticism leveled at Chalabi is that he has little support in present-day Iraq.

Another would-be contender in the eyes of the think-tank world is Ayatollah Baqir Al-Hakim, a Shi'ite from a clerical family in the southern city of Najaf. Hakim heads the Shi'ite Supreme Council for the Islamic Revolution in Iraq, an armed opposition group based in Iran, as is Hakim. SCIRI claims to stand for democracy, not theocracy. But its critics say that should the organization ever come to power, Iraq would effectively become an Iranian province. Obviously, Hakim would not be the Americans' idea of a desirable successor.

Also being tossed around Washington is the name of Fawzi al-Chamari, one of a clutch of generals now in the United States who might take part in any future action. "For some reason Washington is fixated on the notion that only a military leader can force Iraqis to live in one cohesive state," says Ibrahim Marashi of the Middle East Centre at Oxford University. He notes that Najib Salhi has been dubbed in some circles as a "Hamid Karzai of Iraq," a reference to the interim Afghani leader—a comparison that greatly annoys the INC.

Then there's Gen. Nizar al-Khazraji, a former Iraqi army chief of staff who now lives in Denmark under virtual house arrest. Danish police are investigating his possible role in the Anfal campaign of the 1980s, when the Iraqi army used chemical weapons against Kurdish villages in the north, killing thousands. Khazraji has denied any part in the attacks. A former national hero of the Iran-Iraq war, Khazraji has pro-Saudi leanings. His name has been put forward by Iraqi opposition splinter groups known to have close links with the CIA.

Other mooted contestants include Dr. Ayad Allawi (head of the Iraqi National Accord, a Ba'athist party based in south London that was originally organized by British intelligence, and that is dedicated to staging a coup in Baghdad) and Adnan al-Pachachi (a former foreign minister who left Iraq before Saddam came to power in 1979.)

To complicate matters, the INC may no longer be the only opposition umbrella in town. Emerging as an alternative is the "Gang of Four," a coalition including the INA, the Patriotic Union of Kurdistan (PUK), the Kurdistan Democratic Party (KDP) and SCIRI. Though technically members of the INC, the four groups have recently distanced themselves from Chalabi and the INC core.

While the leaders of the KDP and the PUK, Masoud Barazani and Jalal Talabani, already represent powerful rival forces on the ground in the Kurdish "safe haven" of northern Iraq, the fact that they are Kurds takes them out of the running for the top job in Baghdad. But both would certainly be involved in any future central government.

There is a natural empathy between Iraq's Shi'ites and Kurds. Both see themselves as the oppressed victims of Saddam's brutality, though that doesn't mean they work closely together. The Kurds are not in a hurry for political change, due to a lucrative sanction-busting and oil trade thriving in the autonomous Kurdish zone of northern Iraq. But any potential leader will have to be able to reach out to the country's Shiites, Sunnis and Kurds.

The INC is certainly the most all-embracing Iraqi opposition organization, but it lacks credibility as a real force capable of effecting change inside the country.

"It is unrealistic to think that a political umbrella group, the INC, which is not on the ground in Iraq the way the Northern Alliance was in Afghanistan, could actually engage in operations as opposed to merely providing a sort of form for political consensus," believes David Mack.

And while many would-be Iraqi leaders are putting themselves forward, the outcome will depend at least in part on who will be effective when the moment for change comes. Says Patrick Clawson, deputy director of the Washington Institute for Near East Policy: "There is going to be a moment of opportunity. Hamid Karzai is where he is today in part because he was effective when he first got in."

The would-be contestants have one thing in common: none has any real power base inside Iraq. So a crucial factor will be who the army and the internal security agencies support.

"If you have a truly military government," says Clawson, "you are likely to get a succession of coups. If you want to have a semi-stable Iraq that doesn't dissolve in some kind of general chaos you need a broader based government than just the Iraqi army. That should include some people in the Shi'ite community, probably named by the ayatollah there, and you would include some prominent Kurds."

The U.S. administration is not looking to create a government in exile or leaders in waiting, according to a former U.S. official. Rather, it is trying to get the lay of the land to figure out what options are available to it and asking if there are other people in the Iraqi Diaspora who could create the foundation for a new Iraq.

Ken Pollack, a former CIA military analyst and now deputy director of national security studies at the Council on Foreign Relations in Washington, says: "If the States did invade Iraq, it would be nice to have a small contingent of Iraqi forces alongside us; kind of like the Free French in WWII. No one would expect a whole lot of them during the fighting but the symbolism would be important. It could have some impact on Iraqis inside Iraq, seeing free Iraqis as part of a liberation rather than us just coming to conquer them."

One problem the U.S. faces in working with the opposition is that key opponents of Saddam's regime are Shi'ites or Kurds. The Sunnis now in control of Baghdad see U.S.-led efforts as undermining their position. Bringing in more Sunnis would convey the message that this is not a Shi'ite or Kurdish plot, but an exercise by all Iraqis to liberate Iraq.

But the American government needs more experience and knowledge, experts say, about the Iraqi opposition's organizational, propaganda and military abilities.

"The first step is to ask those questions," says Pollack. The next is to test the candidates. "Give them resources and tasks, then see if they can use those resources to accomplish those tasks. This is what experienced foreign service and intelligence professionals in the State Department and the CIA will be looking to do."

Does Iraq Have A Future?

Kanan Makiya

from a public talk at Brandeis University

The title of my talk is suggestive of a situation which is bleak and full of dark portent for the future, not only Iraq's future I might add but that of the whole Middle East. The plight that Iraqis find themselves in today shares something very important with the Middle East Peace Process. Both are intimately bound up with the outcome of the 1991 Gulf war.

The Peace Process, as we have all come to know the process begun in Oslo, has its beginnings in the scale and magnitude of the military defeat of Iraq in that war. Iraq's plight today on the other hand has its roots not in that defeat but in the politically unfinished nature of the war—the fact that five years after its end George Bush, Margaret Thatcher and all kinds of leaders of the Allied coalition forces that waged that war have come and gone while Saddam is still in power. But this parting of the ways of Iraq and the rest of the Arab world, which began with Iraq's occupation, annexation and looting of Kuwait in August 1990, cannot go on forever. At some point the affairs of a country which has been in effect been left to rot, are going to boomerang back with great consequence to everyone in the region. Iraq is simply too big, too rich and too advanced a country for that not to be the case.

If I were giving this talk one or two years ago, I might not have given it such a bleak title in spite of the fact that what I have just said would still apply. However, it is a fact of life that too many factors all working in the same negative direction have been conspiring to undermine even my usual optimism.

There are two kinds of catastrophic outcomes to consider in relation to the future of Iraq. One is that a transition from the regime of Saddam Husain does not come about. The other is that when it does it will do so with the force of a giant, unpredictable and powerful whirlpool which sucks everything into its raging vortex beginning with the people of Iraq.

Consider this little story, which took place in Salahaldin, northern Iraq, in the so-called "safe-haven" area of northern Iraq at a time when it was supposedly being protected by the Allied forces. Think of the story as a kind of dress rehearsal for what could happen in Iraq in the not-too distant future.

In the summer of 1995 a bomb went off in what was thought to be the safest city in the Kurdish enclave killing 26 members of the Iraqi Arab and Kurdish opposition coalition against Saddam Husain known as the INC. I knew three of those who died. They had escorted, guided and generally helped me gather information for the book, *Cruelty and Silence*. Moreover they were critical members of the INC's operations in northern Iraq, acting as links to various well-placed individuals working inside the Ba'thist state apparatus. In one fell swoop, measured by the seconds and minutes it took for them to die, a crippling blow was dealt to the project to topple the regime of Saddam Husain by opponents interested in democracy and in working with the West from the safe-haven area created by the Allied coalition after the Gulf war.

Who set off the bomb that killed these crucial 26 members of the INC? How did they know that they would all be gathered in one place on that day at that hour? How was a bomb smuggled into such carefully guarded premises? The answer to all these questions is like the truth behind the story of Rashomon—and this is why the incident is so depressing to anyone familiar with the deadly logic of civil wars.

In the affairs of northern Iraq, which once held so much promise following the Kurdish elections of 1992, it is impossible today to know anything for certain. The

INC had failed to stop the internecine fighting that broke out among the Kurds in May 1994 and which I accidentally got caught up in being in northern Iraq at the time.

I ended up spending a whole month shuttling around acting as a mediator between the warring Kurdish parties. But those talks failed, and they were followed by other talks with INC mediation, and other breakdown and so on until finally with US and Turkish government representation, a last ditch INC effort broke down last October.

The Iranians were in the meantime positioning themselves to take over. Large numbers of their security personnel, recruited from among the 3/4 of a million or so in Iran, have been infiltrated inside northern Iraq. To complicate matters even more the Turkish government is waging its own private war against the PKK inside Iraqi territory. I will spare you the agaonizing details but almost anyone could have planted the bomb with the most likely candidates being the regimes in Baghdad and Tehran both of whom think of the INC as the eyes and ears of the West inside their own backyard. The bottom line situation today is that Turks, Kurds, Iranians, Saddam's agents and God-knows who else—other than the West itself—battle and conspire and negotiate and make claims over a country whose future is crucial to the peace and stability of the whole region, and they are doing all of this in a safe-haven area protected by the Allied coalition as a legacy of the 1991 Gulf war.

So what affect does this have on "The Problem of Justice in the Transition to a Post-Saddam Iraq?" The underlying assumption of the title after all is that there will remain such a thing as "Iraq" which will therefore face a transition problem sometime in the future. How reasonable is such an assumption in the light of such developments? "Does Iraq even have a Future," given the way things are going.

This is the real existential question facing Iraqis today and it is the only reasonable context within which to look at the whole thorny problem of justice in a post-Saddam Iraq. The point I am trying to make is that there is no way of separating the question of politics from that of justice in the case of Iraq without having a completely academic discussion that is not going to be of very great value to anyone. It is certainly not why we are here. Do 'politics' and 'justice' belong together? Or, put differently, is it not the case in Iraq as it may very well be in Bosnia, that the one can only take place at the expense of the other?

I am reminded in this context of a discussion that took place over NPR with General Trainor who was told by one listener that since the brief of the NATO mission to Bosnia did not include the apprehension of war criminals it was bound to fail in the long run. The General answered by observing that the mission was not about justice; it was about peace. I understand the sense in which the General is right, but I guess there is something in me that refuses to want to let these two things go their separate ways. And certainly the case I want to put before you today is that whatever may be the case elsewhere in the world, in Iraq the central problem of politics—which is a problem of the nature of the Iraqi state—this problem is the prerequisite to any experience or hope of justice in the country as a whole in the forseeable future. Let me illustrate the issues involved by way of a familiar metaphor.

You all know the story of the Tower of Babel, the foundations of which still exist, less than seventy miles from where I grew up. In Genesis, we are told that, Noah's progeny who built the city after the flood, forgot their side of the covenant made with the Lord and abandoned his worship. The symbol of this presumptuousness and arrogance on their part took the form of the building of a tower, a house for false gods. The shape that justice took in their case—their punishment in other words—was the breakup of the power that derived from agglomeration, from being one people, from having one policy. The Lord paid a visit to the city to see the tower that the people had built. "So they are all a single people with a single language" he said! "This is only the start of their undertakings! Now nothing they plan to do will be beyond them."

Babylon's Tower symbolized everything that had gone wrong with the city. Yet it held the people together. And that is why the form of the punishment that was brought to bear on this people which had so grievously sinned, was to bring down this arrogant edifice, scattering the people who had built it all over the face of the earth, and confusing their language, so that they would never again understand one another.(1) That, you might say, is a very apt image illustrating the complete inextricability of the question of justice from that of politics.

Many Iraqis fear that when the Ba'thist tower that Saddam Husain has built comes tumbling down, as it surely will in our lifetime, "Things [will] fall apart; and the center [will not] hold;" unloosing, to continue paraphrasing Yeats, a "blood-dimmed tide" upon everything that they hold familiar. Such fears for the future keep Saddam Husain in power. Ironically the UN-imposed sanctions on Iraq, as manipulated by Saddam Husain's propaganda machine, helps to stoke them up thus undoing the effect of the sanctions in weakening the Ba'thist state in the first place. It is a vicious circle in which Iraqis have been caught for the last four years since the Gulf war.

The experience of Iraq shows, it seems to me, that we still have a lot to learn about sanctions as a means of bringing about change in an incalcitrant or outlaw regime. They do not work in the way one expects, and they can have completely unpredictable and undesirable social and even moral consequences even when they are imposed on the most odious of regimes. I am not, with these observations, arguing for or against sanctions. I do think, however, that both opponents and supporters of the sanctions often seem to lose sight of why they were imposed in the first place. In this talk I want to return and stick with these fundamentals of the dilemma of Iraq. Let us review the current conjuncture.

Four years after the Gulf war and Saddam Husain is not only still in power, but he even seems to be increasingly successful in driving apart the allies who so successfully drove him out of Kuwait. Most governments, including most members of the Security Council, believe that the time is coming when the ban on Iraqi oil sales should be lifted, at least in part. This, whether we like it or not, has got to mean the international rehabilitation of the regime of Saddam Husain, its re-entry from the cold into the community of world states.

America, with an ever decreasing number of allies, wants to keep the pressure of the sanctions on. The rationale for doing this is increasingly a purely formal one, namely that Iraq is still not in compliance with UN Resolutions on a whole range of issues. The unspoken and increasingly tenuous subtext of the American argument is that sanctions will eventually do away with the odious regime in Iraq. With what should it be replaced? On this no one is willing to make a statement because the policy is not officially about the outlaw nature of a fellow member of the United Nations. To think even in this way is tantamount to extending the application of the idea of human rights in politics to societies not identified with the Western tradition. That would set up too complicated a precedent, and it amounts to a reversal of trends that have been working themselves out at least since decolonization and the end of World War Two.

We live in a world of multiple cultures, and born out of the struggle for the emancipation of peoples has come the idea of the relativism of all values, and the right of all peoples of different traditions to live by the laws of their own cultures. Therefore the West, the International community, the United States, whatever apellation you choose, cannot tell other peoples how they ought to be ruled. It can only pretend to be talking about what Saddam needs to do next to be in compliance with this and that UN Resolution. And thus the sanctions policy has drifted into aimlessness, turning into an end in itself, justified by external and increasingly not very honorable considerations.

The unsaid theoretical premise behind the policy is that sanctions will do indirectly what the Untited States is no longer able or willing to say directly: turn Iraqis against their dictator. And that the whole problem will in this way resolve itself. The great irony of course is that the Gulf war did that. And at the time, the world balked, and turned its back on those Iraqis who rose up against their regime in the single most unusual and promising reversals of the traditional pattern of Middle East politics. Instead of rallying around their regime when the nation came under attack in January 1991, and in spite of enduring one of the most ferocious and comprehensive bombing campaigns since the fire-bombing of Dresden, the population which had had all those bombs rained on its head rose up against the local dictator and reached out for help to the very so-called imperialist armies that had been bombing them.

Nothing like this has ever happened before in the politics of the modern Middle East. Far more Iraqis have ended up dying from the subsequent crushing of that rebellion, and from the effect of the sanctions, than ever died during the Gulf war itself. Is it any wonder then that most Iraqis today are going back to that old bogey-horse of Arab politics: blaming the West or someone else for one's agony. Iraqis think that the United States has a policy, and that that policy is to keep Saddam Husain in power and punish them. Whether or not one agrees that that is in fact US policy—and I for one do not agree—can you blame them? What many Iraqis don't understand—or rather find very hard to understand—is that in fact the situation is even worse than they think.

The United States which, for whatever reason, right or wrong, sent 450,000 men to fight the Iraqi dictator in 1991, today has no coherent policy towards Iraq. It is unwilling to plan beyond the need to contain him. The West, whose armies created and still safeguard the safe-haven area in the north of Iraq, today sits by and watches while that whole situation blows up in its faces. But the United States has not conspired to bring about this unbelievable mess as virtually all Iraqis think; it does not manipulate things from the sidelines. At best you might say it is watching over the unfolding of things, unable to decide what if anything it wants to happen, and whether or not it even has the right to want it in the first place.

The West is conspicuous by its reluctance or absence with regards to any question that has to do with the future of Iraq. Why that is the case, given the enormous fact of the Gulf war, is, I suspect a very complicated question, one that has more to do with post World War Two multicultural politics and the abandonment of international humanism, and the whole idea of a universal value system which came with the Enlightenment. That is a whole big, other subject which I certainly don't want to get into now. The main point I would, however like to reiterate, is that contrary to what most Iraqis and virtually the whole of the so-called Third World thinks, the United States is conspicuous by its unwillingness and possibly even I have come to think in recent months, structural inability to formulate what it wants to happen in the post-Saddam era in Iraq.

By way of furthering the discussion, let me ask the following question: "Why not let the whole house of cards come tumbling down?" Why shouldn't the state that the Ba'th have built get broken up into smaller, or as its proponents would put it, 'more organic and natural' units. Don't the Kurds deserve a state after all the horrors that have been inflicted upon them by this and previous Arab nationalist regimes in Iraq? Is that not what they really want anyway? And what about the Shi'ites and the Sunnites of Iraq? Doesn't history teach us that these two branches of Islam can never live in peace with one another? If so, if this is how the people of

Iraq are—riven by ancient prejudices, fears and hatreds—then let a hundred flowers bloom, as Mao used to put it. Iraq was always too artificial a framework for a proper state; it never made sense as a project. So let the baby go the way of the bath water. Let the whole deck come tumbling down and then we shall then see what the cards really have in store for the people of Iraq.

It is almost impossible to speculate about this scenario for the future in Iraq without passing it through the prism of post-1989 events in Europe, namely through the experience of the collapse of the Soviet Union and Yugoslavia. Was it not the toppling of the Soviet Tower of Babel that was behind the release of all kinds of ethnic and sectarian tensions in that unfortunate country? The wounded and humiliated little nationalisms of the Serbs and the Croats and the Bosnians, and the Armenians and the Turkomans, lashed back like twigs—as Isaiah Berlin put it I believe just before he died—bent down by the oppressive weight which had been crushing them. They lashed back with the fury of one who is reacting to a hurt, to an insult. They emerged from under the oppressive weight of the Tower enraged and wounded. Is there not an inevitability about such a reaction? Especially in a country like Iraq where the legacy of blood is all still so close to the surface. After all the Anfal campaign which resulted in the extermination of possibly as many as 100,000 Kurds was a mere six years ago. The repression of the intifada, the attack on Shi'i holy cities, the draining of the marshes, all of this has happened since the Gulf war.

More fundamental, I would argue, than even all of this loss of life—speaking politically of course, and not merely in human terms—is the fact that the underlying premise of the polity that the Ba'th have built in Iraq since 1968 has been complicity, the involvement of larger and larger numbers of people—in large part unwillingly—in the criminal behavior of the state. The Ba'th, over a period of 25 years, have woven together a state built upon circles upon circles of complicity and it is upon these that they have legitimized themselves. Almost any scenario of a post-Ba'thist future in a wounded country like this is going to be a balancing act, like walking a tightrope balancing the legitimate grievances of all those who have suffered on one side and the knowledge that if everyone is held accountable who is in fact guilty for this legacy, then that too will tear the country asunder. It is going to be a country in which justice is both the first thing that everybody wants, and the last or most difficult thing that anyone can deliver.

Tens of thousands of Iraqis were either willing or unwilling participants in what was done to other Iraqis during the 1980s and 1990s. Very large numbers of people informed on one another or stood by while their neighbours were humiliated, imprisoned, abused, deported, tortured, made to "disappear" and killed in countless horrible ways. Virtually every adult male has had to serve long terms in an army that has consistently brutalized both its own soldiery and ordinary Iraqi citizens. The multi-layered, highly secretive security organizations regularly employed hundreds of thousands of people to watch over, police, and abuse individuals in a variety of ways.

You could only do this in an oil-rich country where the level of the state's disposable income bore no relation at all to the size of the country, or the level of its real wealth-producing economic activity. According to a calculation I made in Republic of Fear for 1980, one-fifth of the economically active urban labour force (677,000 people) were institutionally charged with one form or another of violence (whether "policing", "defending" or "controlling" the society at large). If this was the picture on the eve of the Iraq-Iran war (before the decision to go to war had been made) one can imagine the extraordinary state of affairs that has developed after twelve more years of this kind of dictatorship and two gruelling wars.

Defenders of the 'let it all come tumbling down' scenario therefore have a Biblical notion of where justice lies. They conclude that there is no way out but to let Saddam's Tower fall. That this should be American policy, for instance. The ensuing turmoil will certainly be very painful and destructive. That is just the way things are and have to be for something better to emerge in the end. But the city I was born and brought up in is not a Biblical metaphor; it is a real place, with people made of flesh and blood and filled with the same kinds of phobias and hopes as any of you in this room. And when I think of the collapse of the existing edifice of the state system in Iraq—deformed and horrible as it certainly is—I am to be perfectly frank with you filled with dread and horror at what is likely to follow. Which brings me to a second scenario for the future of Iraq linked to a completely different and most un-Biblical notion of justice which I would like to now sketch out. In fact there is no need for me to reformulate it since a recent issue of *The Economist* has already done the job.

"The world still has a strong interest in Mr. Hussein's good behaviour" opens an important editorial published on the eve of the last debate in the Security Council on renewal of sanctions. "On the face of it, the decision to lift or maintain the oil ban should turn on a judgement about whether Mr Hussein has complied with the post-war conditions placed by the UN upon Iraq." Realizing, however, that this was going to get endlessly bogged down in the minutaie of the weapons inspection reports versus French and Russian commercial interests in Iraq, *The Economist* proposed a compromise that everyone might accept—not a lifting of the ban but its suspension. This provides what *The Economist* calls a way "to relax some of the pressure on Iraq without losing the ability to restore it in full." [*The Economist,* April 8, 1995]. In other words the future that is envisaged here is one of soldiering on with the same nasty state suitably weakened and therefore no longer a regional threat.

This is what virtually every state in the region thinks is best, including Israel incidentally. It is what Saddam Husain himself wants, and the underlying rationale for it is summed up in phrases like regional stability in the case of Iran, preservation of the existing state system in the case of the Arab countries, commercial interests in the case of Turkey, containing the Islamic threat from Iran in the case of Israel and so on.

The kindest thing that one can say about this scenario is that it is cynical. More importantly, however, it is very short-sighted and foolish in that it fails to understand what has happened inside Iraq since and because of the Gulf war. I liken the country to a rotting fruit on a tree which remains still firmly attached to its branch because the degree to which the fruit has rotted does not correspond to the weakness or strength of the stem attaching it to the branch.

Consider, by way of illustration, how forms of punishment have been changing over the last year or so in Iraq. Law number 109, was promulgated six weeks before President Saddam Husain began redeploying his troops to make the world think that he was about to do the unthinkable—invade Kuwait a second time. It reads as follows: "According to Section 1, Article 42 of the Iraqi Constitution, the

Revolutionary Command Council has decreed that. . . . the foreheads of those individuals who repeat the crime for which their hand was cut off will be branded with a mark in the shape of an "X." Each intersecting line will be one centimeter in length and one millimeter in width."[2] The crimes "for which their hand was cut off" are theft and army desertion. Branding is restricted to repeat offenders. The law specifies that the operation must take place at the same hospital where the right hand was amputated at the wrist.

As of the end of last year up to two thousand brandings may have been performed on soldiers foreheads, according to two military personnel recently escaped to Kuwait. The Kurdish opposition radio in northern Iraq has declared that eight hundred branded soldiers were captured by Kurdish forces near villages along the border of the safe-haven zone in northern Iraq.[3] Car thieves are being singled out for prosecution on the basis of the new laws. Iraqi newspapers reported that 36,000 cars were stolen last year. The law, however, is unambiguous and formulated in general terms: stealing anything worth more than 5,000 dinars—worth roughly twelve dollars—by anyone who is not a minor, is today punishable in Iraq first by amputation and second by branding.

Something went wrong in the case of thirty-seven year-old 'All Ubaid Abed 'Ali because he had his hand amputated and his forehead branded with an "X" for stealing a television set and 250 Iraqi dinars (worth roughly 50 cents). 'Ali was shown on Iraqi television on September 9, 1994, still under anaesthetic, with his bandaged arm and closeups of his branded forehead.[4] Amputation was introduced before branding. The earlier law (number 59, dated June 4, 1994) stated that a second offence of stealing was punishable by severance of the left foot from the ankle. No mention of branding.

Rumours circulating in Baghdad have it that Saddam Husain discerned a problem with this law when he realized that disabled veterans of the two Gulf wars, who could very well have lost a limb or two, were not differentiable from common thieves. The honour of the country was at stake. Cruelty has shape and form to it; how it progresses can be very revealing of what is going on in a country. In Saddam Husain's Iraq, in the period from the show trials of 1969 to the debacle of the 1991 Gulf war, the politics of bodily disfigurement moved from the public stage to the private confines of secret torturing centers. The stronger the state got, the more secret became its torturing practices.

One always knew that one lived in a torturing state, but its omniscience and omnipotence lay in the total environement of secrecy which surrounded the whole operation. Everything was secret including the arrest, the charges, the interrogation, the extraction of the evidence, the trial, the judgement, and the execution of the sentence. If there was a corpse, bearing in its markings that last record of the whole affair, even it was returned to the family in a sealed box.

This is what has changed and probably irreversibly or for a whole historical period. The fact is the absolutism of the system is disintegrating, more soldiers than ever before are deserting, law and order is breaking down in Baghdad, and even army Generals like the former head of military intelligence, Wafiq al-Samarraie, are defecting to the main opposition force operating out of the north—the INC.

So what is one to do? After all, you can't shoot or torture everybody. You make examples of some people, the relatively few that you can catch, hoping to reinstill the environment of fear that once controlled everyone but no longer does. The number of ways in which the state can legally publicly disfigure the bodies of its subjects has mushroomed, and this is a sign of weakness not strength. Depending on the crime, the foreheads of offenders get branded with a mark in the shape of one horizontal three to five centimetre line, or in the shape of two parallel horizontal lines of the same dimensions, or in the shape of a circle or an "X" as spelled out in law number 109. Army deserters, draft dodgers, and those who shelter them, get special treatment: the outer part of one ear is cut off for the first offence; a repeat offence results in the second ear being cut off and so on (unconfirmed reports from inside Iraq claim that the word, jaban, coward, is also being branded on the forehead, and two parallel horizontal lines three to five centimetres in length for I know not what crime). Upon his third attempt an army deserter is shot. This seems to be an improvement on the situation before the passage of these new laws when the penalty for desertion was a firing squad, instantly. In fact it is a confirmation of how deep is the rot today inside Iraq.

Consider also the reaction to these measures inside Iraq. For they too are signs of how far the rot has proceeded in a country with the highest literacy levels and what used to be the most highly developed infrastructure and services systems of anywhere in the Middle East barring Israel. Two men whose ears had been cut off in accordance with the laws I have just mentioned immolated themselves in central Baghdad in the summer of 1994. Following the murder of a doctor in the southern city of Nassirriyya by an amputee, and the storming of the headquarters of the Ba'th party in the city of 'Amara by a crowd which cut off the ears of the Ba'thi officials it got its hands on, several hundred doctors protested at having to carry out the new punishments.[5] Upon being threatened with having their own ears cut off, the doctors called off their strike. Law number 117 was then promptly issued clearly directed at the whole medical profession. It threatened anyone who assisted in the cosmetic improvement of the appearance of an officially disfigured bodily part with immediate amputation. The law's wording ends with this strange acknowledgement of the public outrage: "The effects" of the punishment of amputation of the hand or ear and branding, "will be eliminated [by the state] if those so punished go on to perform heroic and patriotic acts."[6]

If I have gone on for too long describing these grisly punishments, it is in order to drive home the following point. The Gulf war, the uprising against the regime, the savagery of its suppression, and the continuation of a regime of sanctions for nearly four years, and everything else that has happened since, represent the crossing of a kind of the Rubicon as far as the Ba'thist experience in Iraq goes. I don't see any turning back. Things may get worse; in fact they are more likely to get worse than they are to get better. The one thing they won't do is go back to anything like what they were before the Gulf war. To count in such an environment on the regimes "good behavior" as *The Economist* put it, makes no sense at all. It is to live in the past. Even if the sanctions were to be removed tomorrow, I personally would not be willing to conclude that the regime automatically becomes less likely to be overthrown than it is today.

I would like to end by underlining something that the two previous scenarios share in common: a disregard of the central importance of the character of the state. In the case of the first scenario, the state is simply not there and that is not perceived to be a major catastrophe. In the name of cultural incompatabilities or deeprooted ethnic and religious hatreds, or the relativity of all values, the idea of a fabricated artifice of institutions which acts as an arbiter and guarrantees a monopoly of the means and instruments of violence for some purpose or another, this idea is losing ground as something that it is positively desirable to fight for and argue over. Identity politics is where everything is at. In the case of the second scenario, the autocratic, absolutist character of the state is simply taken for granted. Tradition and continuity is what is good and it is all that ever works anywhere, the argument goes. It is assumed in other words that Iraqis cannot be ruled any other way than via the likes of Mr. Saddam Husain. In both cases the character or quality or nature of the state is not the issue.

What is lacking is a third scenario, one that is distinguished from the other two in that on the contrary the character of the state, that great big artificial dispenser of justice and regulator of human relations, is the key to everything. But the fact is such a scenario, in the concrete circumstances of Iraq today, can only be brought about with outside help, preferably in the shape of a concerted international effort spearheaded by a new and more energetic UN armed with a new sense of its own mission in the world, and the kind of institutions to back up such a mission including in particular an army independent of the will of individual member states.

The mandate of such an international effort would have to be the establishment of a transitional government in Iraq under UN auspices. The key legacy of the outgoing regime which will have to be dealt with right away will be the fact that during a quarter of a century or so of rule, all notion of procedure in the country has been effectively destroyed and needs to be rebuilt. Many years of administrative decrees, of edicts by the Revolutionary Command Council or Saddam Husain, have done away with justice as a tradition in Iraq. In fact justice has lost its personnel, its lawyers and independent judges, its reliance on custom, precedent and procedure. To avoid a slide into anarchy during the transition, a top priority of such an international effort therefore has to be an all-encompasing reform of the Iraqi legal system. A system of justice will have to be introduced that is both forgiving and holds some people accountable for the legacy of the Saddam Husain regime.

I headed a team of Iraqis which produced some detailed proposals along these lines which was published as a policy paper of the INC and submitted to the UN some two years ago. The title of the report that came out is Crimes Against Humanity and the Transition to Democracy in Iraq. The central idea of the document is that because of the extraordinary circumstances that prevailed in a country like Iraq for so many years, the collective interest of all Iraqis cannot possibly translate into the prosecution of everyone who is in fact guilty. Yet some people have to be held accountable for what happened. The document is essentially an attempt to work out the criteria and spell out the names even of those who should be held accountable.

How these two considerations are to be combined has to become foundational in a new Iraqi state if a new blood bath is to be avoided. Legitimate fears of present and former civil servants of the present regime have to be addressed, and a system of justice introduced that walks a tightrope between punishment and forgiveness.

I should emphasize that I do not make these suggestions under any illusion that they are likely to be picked up. Quite the contrary. A whole paradigmatic shift in Western thinking is required, one which clearly has implications that go far beyond Iraq. Moreover there are prerequisites for all of this to happen, interim stages needed before we get to UN mandates to reshape entire state systems. None of this is going to transpire, certainly not in the next few months or years that a country like Iraq still has left to it, years in which we all stand staring into an abyss knowing we are about to fall in and yet being unable to do much of anything about it.

The 1990-91 Gulf war was a dress rehearsal for all sorts of new developments in the international arena. Sometimes someone has to pay the price in order for others to see the way forward. On that unhappy note I will end citing these lines written by the First World War poet Siegfried Sassoon (1886-1967), who looked into all the carnage of his own times, and wrote: "Babylon the merciless, now a name of doom, Built towers in Time, as we today, for whom Auguries of self-annihilation loom."[7]

Prerequisites for a Third Scenario. To suggest a contemporary Iraqi political program for change, one which has at least the chance of working in a less destructive and more honorable way than either of the two previous scenarios, would mean the following: (a) Elevating the outlaw character of the existing Iraqi state to the top of the international agenda whenever the issue of Iraq is brought up. (b) Openly and publicly seek the ouster of Saddam Husain personally and the inner clique around him, utilizing whatever means might help including promises of removal of sanctions and other inducements that would convince Iraqis that the UU or the US had no interest whatsoever in this regime's continuation. (c) In order to do this, work through the Iraqi opposition based in northern Iraq. (d) Don't leave the Kurds to the tender mercies of the Iranians and the Turks. Enter actively in the resolution of their internal disputes, and with a view to convincing them that Kurdish self-interest in the long run passes through the restructuring of power in Baghdad. (e) Actively participate in efforts already underway among Iraqi opposition groups and individuals to draft a new inspiring constitutional framework for the post-Saddam state. Seek to use the full weight of Western authority to publicize the ideas of a newly restructured state to the maximum. (f) Insist upon the implementation of UN Resolutions 688 and 986. These, among other things, involve UN repsonsibility for the placing of human rights monitors throughout the country.

Notes

[1] Genesis, 11, v.29.

[2] The law was published in the official daily newspaper, Al-Thawra, August 26, 1994.

[3] See report in Al-Hayat, September 8, 1994. [check]

[4] See Amnesty International, Urgent Action notification dated October 6, 1994. (AI index: MDE 14/12/94

[5] Reported in The Times, 13 September, 1994.

[6] Published in Al-'Iraq, 6 September, 1994.

[7] Siegfried Sassoon, 'Babylon,' reprinted in Chapters Into Verse, vol I: Genesis to Malachi, edited by Robert Atwin & Laurence Wieder (Oxford University Press, 1993), p.391-92.

Will the Next Mid East War Go Nuclear?

Mark Gaffney

Middle East Policy Journal

Does Iraq Have the Bomb?

There is some evidence that Saddam Hussein revived his nuclear weapons program following the 1998 ouster of U.N. weapons inspectors.[1] Unfortunately, in October 2001 the key question, does Iraq have the bomb, remains unanswerable. Earlier this year two alarming but so far unconfirmed reports appeared in the London press, the first in January in the London Telegraph. The story quoted an unnamed source, allegedly a defector from Iraqi's nuclear bomb program, who asserted that Iraq possesses two "fully operational" weapons.[2]

A more substantial report appeared in February in the London Times. The story alleged that Saddam Hussein clandestinely acquired as much as 50 kilograms of highly enriched uranium in 1988 and tested an underground nuclear device on September 19, 1989.[3] Three different sources were cited in the article. All claimed to be former Iraqi scientists. Allegedly the test went undetected because the device was small, on the order of 10 kilotons, and because it was positioned in an evacuated cavern beneath Lake Rezzaza, southwest of Baghdad. The cavern supposedly muffled the blast. The same technique, known as "decoupling," was developed by the United States and may have been used by Israel to conceal one or more nuclear tests in the Negev desert in 1966.[4] The sources quoted in the *Times* said that Iraq obtained the fissile uranium from South Africa, which pursued the uranium-enrichment path to the bomb at its Valindaba plant between 1978 and early 1990. The plant was closed in 1990 following President F.W. de Klerk's historic 1989 decision to dismantle South Africa's bomb program. According to the *Times,* the alleged diversion was substantiated by a former South African intelligence officer, who stated that the material reached Baghdad by way of Brazil. One of the Iraqi sources also insisted that Saddam Hussein currently has nine nuclear weapons stored in a repository in the Hemrin Mountains north of Baghdad.[5] I reiterate that these reports remain unconfirmed. Indeed, the story in the *Times* was disputed by Terry Wallace, a geophysicist at the University of Arizona, who undertook a seismological analysis.[6] When Wallace compared the available seismic signals from Iraq with data from U.S. decoupling experiments, he found that the seismic data from Iraq was not consistent with a nuclear test. Weak seismic waves were present, but "from an event so tiny that it is difficult to determine its location accurately."[7] Wallace explained the difference between man-made waves and those generated by earthquakes: "In U.S. decoupling experiments the seismic signals always showed very large primary-to-secondary amplitude ratios at high frequencies, a powerful tool for discriminating between explosions and earthquakes. The phases in this case all clearly had both [primary and secondary] wave energy and significant high-frequency [secondary] energy, which would indicate a natural earthquake source."[8]

Wallace could not rule out a fizzled test. But he noted that a cavern under a lake is a poor choice for a secret nuclear test site, because the overpressures from such a blast would almost certainly collapse the lake bed, causing a sudden drop in the water level: an obvious signature of a test. Wallace believes the story was a hoax.[9] And this appears to be the view of most western intelligence experts. When I discussed the *Times* report with Frank Barnaby, the former nuclear-weapons designer suggested that the 1989 event might have been a radiological bomb.[10] Such weapons require less fissile uranium, and never achieve a sustained chain reaction; hence no nuclear explosion. They do release large amounts of deadly radiation. Such a bomb might be attractive to a state with a shortfall of fissile material.

But even if the *Times* report is false, the possibility remains that Iraq may soon acquire, or has already acquired, enriched uranium or plutonium. The danger of a diversion is very real. The existence of a nuclear black market has been known since the 1980s. And the problem became much more serious after the end of the Cold War. In the years following the breakup of the former Soviet Union, there have been hundreds of reported cases of attempted smuggling of fissile materials from former communist states. In one year alone, 1994, the number of cases doubled.[11]

Moreover, as with drug smuggling, it is safe to assume that for every known case, numerous others go unreported. As early as 1994, Sam Nunn, then chairman of the U.S. Senate Armed Services Committee, called the smuggling of nuclear materials "the primary security challenge not only for the United States, but the world."[12]

The matter is especially urgent in the case of Iraq, which faces few other remaining barriers to the bomb. Scott Ritter, a former U.N. Special Commission (UNSCOM) weapons inspector in Iraq, warned in 1998 that Iraq has the components for three "implosion-type devices, minus the fissile material."[13] Numerous other experts have expressed similar views." Should Iraq succeed in acquiring sufficient plutonium or enriched uranium, the government of Saddam Hussein could probably produce a nuclear weapon within months, perhaps weeks. It is in this context that the recent reports in the London press, as well as the likelihood of intensified U.S. military action against Iraq, must be evaluated.

Why Did Iraq Not Use Chemical Weapons During the Gulf War?

At the onset of the Gulf War, Western intelligence experts were convinced that Iraq was still years away from a usable nuclear weapon. The same experts believed that Iraq already had deployed chemical and possibly biological weapons. No one doubted that Saddam Hussein would use them.[14] The prewar assessment about chemical weapons was later confirmed. Massive stockpiles of Iraqi chemical munitions survived the U.S. bombing campaign.[15] But Iraq never used its chemical weapons. A declassified Defense Intelligence Agency (DIA) document reported that analysis of Scud impact points uncovered no traces of chemical-warfare agents or their decomposition products.[16] The Central Intelligence Agency (CIA) agreed and also found no evidence of the use of biological weapons.[17]

Israeli officials reported similar findings. None of the Scud attacks on Israel involved weapons of mass destruction. All the Scuds had been armed with conventional ordnance.[18] The matter of why Iraq refrained from using the chemical and biological weapons in its arsenal is one of the intriguing questions to emerge from the war.

Some analysts speculated that the Iraqis had not yet mastered the fuse technology needed to detonate chemical warheads. Apparently, the successful delivery of a chemical agent is not a simple matter. For a chemical warhead to function properly, it must dispense the liquid agent in an aerosol form in the moments prior to impact. This is accomplished by means of a specially designed fuse located in the nose of the warhead. These proximity fuses must withstand the missile's high terminal speed, nearly one mile per second, and the substantial heat build-up, shock and vibration of descent. The fuse charge must also breach the warhead casing without destroying the small load of toxic liquid. If any part of the fuse fails to work properly, dispersal of the chemical agent will not occur within the critical time period, and the toxic liquid will be destroyed or absorbed on impact.[19] A very different sort of explanation was given by Husayn Kamil, Saddam Hussein's brother-in-law and former chief of Iraqi nuclear-biological-chemical weapons development. Kamil stated in August 1995, after defecting to the West, that Iraqi officials were deterred from using chemical weapons by fears that the United States would respond with tactical nukes.[20] An interesting twist on this question of deterrence was recently given in congressional testimony by Charles Duelfer, a former UNSCOM official. In his remarks before the House International Relations Committee on October 4, 2001 (less than a month after the terrorist attack on the World Trade Center), Mr. Duelfer stated that in his many discussions with Iraqi citizens during his UNSCOM tour of duty in Baghdad, he found that all Iraqis, from high government officials to the man on the street, were convinced that Iraq's chemical weapons had deterred the coalition forces from advancing on Baghdad.[21] And—who knows—those taxi drivers in Baghdad may well be correct. Deterrence probably worked both ways. By holding chemical weapons in reserve, Saddam Hussein survived to fight another day. This would certainly explain Saddam's determination to acquire weapons of mass destruction, at any price.

The Scud Missile

Although the Iraqi Scud missile has the capability to deliver chemical, biological and nuclear warheads, the conventionally armed Scuds fired at Israel and coalition forces during the Gulf War caused few casualties. Aside from its dubious value as a terror weapon, the conventionally armed Scud proved ineffective from a military standpoint. So unimpressed was the U.S. field commander General Norman Schwarzkopf that he contemptuously told the press that a coalition soldier had "a greater chance of being struck by lightning in south Georgia than of being hit by a Scud in Riyadh."[22]

The Scud's lackluster performance was due, in part, to Iraqi modifications to the Scud design, which were intended to increase the range of the missile. These alterations did succeed in extending the Scud's range quite substantially, in fact, but also caused flight-instability problems. Unlike more modern ballistic missiles, the Scud warhead does not detach from the body of the missile after the boost phase (the period when the rocket motor fires and accelerates the missile). The missile body reenters the atmosphere still attached to the warhead. The modifications made the missiles unstable and often caused them to disintegrate before impact. Such break-ups seriously degraded accuracy and overall performance.[23]

But the Scud's poor showing during the Gulf War should be no cause for complacency. Iraq has an abundance of scientists and skilled technicians to work on these kinds of problems and has had a decade in which to do so. We know, for example, that during the 1990s, Iraq sought and probably acquired advanced gyroscopes and guidance systems from cash-starved Russia.[24] It is therefore reasonable to suppose that in a future war, Iraqi missiles will not simply fall into the desert or break up in flight. We should expect Scud performance to improve significantly.

"The Great Scud Hunt"

It is interesting that the so-called "Master Attack Plan" developed by coalition forces prior to the Gulf War ignored Iraq's mobile Scud-missile launchers because they were deemed strategically insignificant and too difficult to attack.[25] Consistent with his low opinion of the Scud, General Schwarzkopf believed that he had more important things to worry about.

The flaw in this strategy became glaringly evident in the first days of the war, when Baghdad began lobbing Scuds at Israel from the western desert. Overnight, the mobile Scuds became a source of grave concern. Washington feared that a chemical-weapons attack on Tel Aviv would trigger a massive Israeli retaliation that would shatter the solidarity of the anti-Iraq coalition. No doubt, though he stopped short of using chemical weapons, this was precisely—and predictably—Saddam Hussein's intention.

On orders from Washington, the coalition immediately changed gears and mounted an ad hoc campaign to seek out and destroy the Iraqi mobile Scud launchers in western Iraq. It had no great success in doing so. The campaign developed into a cat-and-mouse affair that appears to have been won decisively by the Iraqis. During the 43 days of the war, coalition aircraft flew approximately 1,500 sorties against the mobile launchers yet were unable to confirm a single kill.[26] Coalition air crews did report the destruction of about 80 mobile launchers. Another score or so were claimed by special-operations forces, but not one of the claimed kills was actually confirmed. An official post-war survey concluded that "... most, if not all, of the objects involved now appear to have been decoys or vehicles such as tanker trucks with infrared and radar signatures that are impossible to distinguish from mobile launchers. Few mobile Scud launchers were actually destroyed."[27] This sober assessment was cited in a later report with the added words, "Luckily, the Iraqi Scuds were inaccurate and carried only conventional ordnance."[28]

The primary reason for the ineffectiveness of the air campaign was the lack of a "real time" intelligence-response capability. Time and again the position of a Scud launcher would be reported by a coalition spotter either from the ground or the air. And time and again the launcher would escape into the desert before strike aircraft could arrive on the scene. During the course of the war, U.S.-led forces never did succeed in overcoming the mobility of the Iraqi Scud launchers. Scud attacks continued throughout the war.

This outcome helps to explain the imposition after the war of the no-fly zones. Despite the rhetoric about protecting the Kurds in the north and the

Shiites in the south—and events proved this to be just rhetoric—it appears the zones were imposed to "box" Saddam into central Iraq, thus preventing him from posing a threat to Kuwait, Saudi Arabia and Israel. The zones enabled the coalition air forces to better monitor the desert launching areas where the mobile Scuds had proved so elusive.

After the war, it appeared that Iraq still retained a substantial missile inventory. In 1992, the CIA estimated the residual force at "perhaps hundreds" of missiles.[29] The early estimates were scaled down, however, as U.N. weapons inspectors proceeded to deconstruct Saddam Hussein's war machine. UNSCOM supervised the destruction of 48 Scuds plus additional components and found evidence that Iraq had unilaterally destroyed another 83 missiles.[30] Ultimately, UNSCOM was able to account for nearly all of Iraq's original inventory of 819 Soviet-made Scuds. However, in 1995, U.N. inspectors learned that before the Gulf War, Iraq had launched its own program to manufacture missiles based on the Scud design. And the following year UNSCOM concluded that Iraq had indigenously produced as many as 80 Scuds, none of which have yet been accounted for.[31]

Guns Over Butter

Iraq's pattern of military spending in the 1980s made it dependent on a wide spectrum of technological imports. The country's economy was in crisis even before the Gulf War because of the high military cost of the conflict with Iran. The war in the Gulf and the subsequent sanctions hastened the collapse of the Iraqi economy and turned the fiscal crisis into a humanitarian catastrophe.[32]

At the cost of incalculable suffering to the Iraqi people, U.N.-imposed sanctions did prevent Iraq from recovering its military readiness, which in the view of analyst Anthony Cordesman is today at only a fraction of the level of 1990.[33] Nevertheless, by pursuing an aggressive policy of "guns over butter," again at great cost to his own people, Saddam Hussein was able to revive key military programs, especially those associated with ballistic missiles and weapons of mass destruction. Such a policy is perfectly understandable, given the above-noted view inside Iraq that Iraqi chemical weapons prevented the occupation of Baghdad by coalition forces in 1991.

Massive air strikes by the United States and United Kingdom during Operation Desert Fox in December 1998 were aimed, in part, at destroying Iraqi missile-production facilities. The attack prompted Saddam Hussein to order U.N. inspectors out of the country. Later the CIA reported that Iraq had begun the reconstruction of these same facilities.[34] In 2001, it is safe to assume that in the absence of U.N. inspections Saddam Hussein has continued to rebuild his missile force. With regard to weapons of mass destruction, UNSCOM reported to the Security Council in 1997 that Iraq still had not provided a clear picture of the country's biological weapons program. Indeed, it was not until the defection of Husayn Kamel to the West in 1995 that Iraq even admitted that such a program existed. With regard to chemical weapons, the same report included a laundry list of concerns about Iraqi refusals to account for inventories or permit verification by inspectors.[35] Today few experts doubt that Iraq has both kinds of weapons.[36]

Pondering the Imponderable

In 2001, the same concerns about the mobile Scuds that prompted sober reflection in the first days of the 1991 war need to be revisited, especially by those eager to rid the world of Saddam Hussein. The Gulf War was an exercise in restraint, in the sense that neither side used weapons of mass destruction. Next time things may be very different.

The Scud missile may be primitive by U.S. standards, but it is nonetheless capable of delivering biological, chemical and nuclear warheads. If the United States moves militarily to topple Saddam Hussein, does anyone believe that the Iraqi leader will hesitate to use all of the weapons at his disposal? Even if Iraq does not have nuclear weapons, a "successful" war from the standpoint of the United States would still necessitate 100-percent detection, identification, pursuit and kill rates of the same Iraqi hardware that proved so elusive in Desert Storm. Anything less would have consequences that few care to contemplate. To be sure, since 1991, the U.S. military has greatly improved its ability to counter mobile missile launchers. The question is whether "better" will be good enough.

A surprise attack by the United States would not be easy to achieve. More likely, U.S. intentions would become known days and perhaps weeks ahead of time. Tensions during this period would reach an impossible level. Wired to a hair-trigger, the entire region would wait, breathless, for the first shot to be fired.

Nor is it likely that Saddam would wait to be attacked; since he who strikes first is always at an advantage. Israel too would be tempted for the same reason to break ranks and preemptively hit Iraqi positions in the western desert. Washington might find it impossible to restrain Ariel Sharon, who would angrily cite the failure of coalition forces to halt the Scud attacks during the 1991 Gulf War. Hizballah forces in Lebanon would launch Katusha rockets at northern Israel, and Syria might well be drawn in with its massive arsenal of chemical weapons. Should missiles fall on Tel Aviv, Israel would probably respond with the nuclear weapons that officially do not exist.

The United States would prevail in such a war. Saddam Hussein would be defeated—but at what cost? The use of nukes against one or more Arab states would be the end of the nuclear nonproliferation regime. The United States would be confronted with its own duplicitous policies vis-à-vis Israel and very likely would lose its remaining influence in the Middle East. The world would face a terrible conundrum: how to find its way, our way—back to a common humanity. The alternatives will be neither pleasant nor easy. But almost anything is better than the scenario just described. When a man (or a nation) arrives at the edge of a precipice, the only sane move is to stop, take a deep breath, turn around, and find another way forward.

Notes

[1] Kelly Motz, "Terrorism: Iraq Watch," The Wisconsin Project on Nuclear Arms Control, posted at http://www.iragwatch.org/updates/update.asp?id=po 1200109211811.

[2] Kelly Motz, "What has Iraq been doing since inspectors left? What is on its shopping list?," posted at http://www.iragwatch.org/updates/update.asp?id=wpn207231601.

[3] Jessica Berry, "Saddam Has Made Two Atomic Bombs, Says Iraqi Defector," London Telegraph, January 28, 2001.

Gwynne Roberts, "Saddam Has Tested Nuclear Weapon," *London Sunday Times,* February 25, 2001. 1 Taysir N. Nashif, Nuclear Warfare in the Middle East: Dimensions and Responsibilities, (Princeton: Kingston Press, 1977), pp. 24-25.

[4] Gwynne Roberts, op. cit.

[5] Terry Wallace, "Did Iraq Conduct a Nuclear Weapon Test?," Trust and Varify, March-April 2001, posted at http://www.vertic.org/tnv/maraprOI/irag.html.

[6] Ibid.

[7] Ibid.

[8] Ibid.

[9] Telephone conversation, October 21, 2001.

[10] Craig Whitney, "Smuggling of Radioactive Material Said to Double in a Year," *The New York Times,* February 18, 1995.

[11] Statement on ABC's Primetime Live, 10:00 p.m., August 19, 1994.

[12] "Iraq's Breakout Potential," Carnegie Endowment for International Peace, Vol 1. No. 12, September 22, 1998, http://ceip.org/programs/npp/briefl2.htm.

[13] For example, David Albright, president of the Institute for Science and International Security (ISIS), stated in 1998 that " . . . if Iraq were to obtain weapons-grade uranium or plutonium from abroad, they may be able to turn this into a nuclear weapon fairly quickly—within a year." "Special Policy Forum Report, Iraq's Nuclear Weapons Program: Past, Present, and Future Challenges," No. 301, February 18, 1998, posted at http://www.washingtoninstitute.org/watch/Policywatch/policy watchl998/301 htm; also see the testimony of Paul Leventhal, president of the Nuclear Control Institute, before the Subcommittee on Near Eastern and South Asian Affairs, Senate Foreign Relations Committee, Wednesday, March 22, 2000, posted at http://www.nci.org/index.htm; also see Gary Milhollin, director, The Wisconsin Project on Nuclear Arms Control, "Saddam's Nuclear Shopping Spree," The New Yorker, The Talk of the Town, December 13, 1999, p. 44.

[14] Defense Intelligence Agency, "Chemical and Biological Warfare in the Kuwait Theater of Operations; Iraq's Capability and Posturing," undated; Central

Intelligence Agency, "Report on Iraqi Chemical/Nuclear Warhead Systems," 1991; Defense Intelligence Agency, "Scud Chemical Agent Coverage Patterns," August 1990.

[15] Thomas A. Keaney and Eliot A. Cohen, eds., Gulf War Air Power Survey: Summary Report, (Washington, DC: USGPO, 1993), pp. 80-82.

[16] Defense Intelligence Agency message, subject: "IIR 6 284 0008 94/Detection of Chemical Agents By Czechoslovak Unit during Desert Storm, Part III," 141325Z, October 1993.

[17] Central Intelligence Agency, "CIA Report on Intelligence Related to Gulf War Illnesses," August 2, 1996.

[18] Special Assistant for Gulf War Illnesses, "Middle East Trip Provides Useful Information Exchange," January 27, 1998.

[19] "No Chem Scuds?" *Armed Forces Journal International,* March 1991, p. 23.

[20] Central Intelligence Agency, "Review of NESA Files," February 21, 1996; Central Intelligence Agency, "Why WMD were Withheld," March 1991.

[21] U.S. Policy Towards Iraq, Hearing of the House International Relations Committee, Subcommittee on the Middle East and South Asia, Rep. Benjamin A. Gilman (NY), chairman, October 4, 2001.

[22] Counterforce Ops, The Centre for Defence and International Security Studies (CDISS), Department of Politics and International Relations, Lancaster University, U.K., posted at http://www.cdiss.org/scudnt2.htm.

[23] Dale A. Vesser, acting special assistant for Gulf War Illnesses, Medical Readiness and Military Deployments, Department of Defense, "Iraq's Scud Ballistic Missiles," 2000236-0000003 Ver 1.1, posted at http://www.gulflink.osd.mil/scud-info-ii/index.htm.

[24] Vladimir Orlov and William C. Potter, "The Mystery of the Sunken Gyros," *Bulletin of the Atomic Scientists,* November/December 1998, Vol. 54, No. 6.

[25] Counterforce Ops, CDISS, posted at http://www.cdiss.org/scudnt2.htm.

[26] Thomas A. Keaney and Eliot A. Cohen, op. cit., pp. 78-79.

[27] Ibid., p.83.

[28] McNair Paper Number 41, Institute for National Strategic Studies, Radical Responses to Radical Regimes: Evaluating Preemptive Counter-Proliferation,

May 1995: Lessons of the Gulf War. posted at http://www.fas.org/spp/starwars/program/docs/41 war.html.

[29] David C. Isby, "The Residual Iraqi 'Scud' Force," *Jane's Intelligence Review,* Vol. 7, No. 3, p. 115.

[30] United Nations Special Commission, "UNSCOM's Comprehensive Review," Annex A, Status of the Material Balances in the Missile Area, and cover letter, January 25, 1999, web site: www.un.org (as of March 10, 2000).

[31] "John Pike, "UNSCOM and Iraqi Missiles," Federation of American Scientists, November 2, 1998, posted at http://www.fas.org/nuke/guide/iraq/missile/unscom.htm.

[32] Anthony H. Cordesman, "The Military Balance in the Gulf," Center for Strategic and International Studies, July, 2001.

[33] Ibid.

[34] CIA report, August, 2000, cited in Cordesman, July, 2001.

[35] "What is at Stake in the UNSCOM Crisis in Iraq: Summary of the Iraqi Threat," Report of the Secretary General on the Activities of the Special Commission, S/1997/774, October 6, 1997.

[36] Anthony H. Cordesman, "Weapons of Mass Destruction in the Middle East," Center for Strategic and International Studies, June 2001. Consider also the recent Congressional testimony of Gary Milhollin, director of the Wisconsin Project on Nuclear Arms Control: "In biological weaponry, the experts that I have spoken to, who seem to be the foremost ones, believe that Saddam Hussein is now essentially self-sufficient that Iraq has the strains, the equipment, and the know-how necessary to make biological weapons—that it is pretty much independent now of imports. We know that Iraq did not account for all the biological agent that it made before the Gulf War, and we know that it produced anthrax. I think a reasonable assumption is that that capability still exists and is an active threat." Statement before the House International Relations Committee, Subcommittee on the Middle East and South Asia, October 4, 2001.

Iraq Today

Howard Schneider

The Washington Post

BAGHDAD, Iraq—It was a breezy Monday night, and the mood in Horreya Square was festive as a crowd that included college students, old men and shy young girls gathered outside the Faqma ice cream shop to indulge.

In the Iraq of the mid-1990s, such a scene would have been impossible. People were penniless and the government strictly rationed milk and sugar to ensure that the country's embargoed food supplies covered necessities.

But those days are past. Step by step, economic and social life is rebounding and the country is breaking out of limits imposed on it by the United States and other Western powers after the Persian Gulf War a decade ago.

Iraq is now sufficiently flush to independently launch an oil embargo, as it did last month, suspending exports of crude as a protest against Israeli occupation of Palestinian cities in the West Bank. That won Iraq admiration in many Arab countries, as have its payments of $25,000 that U.S. officials said have been made to the families of each Palestinian suicide bomber.

Many Iraqis and foreign diplomats here said the country's resurgence will make the U.S. goal of unseating President Saddam Hussein all the more difficult to achieve. And, in the meantime, the growing prosperity is allowing Hussein's political apparatus to proclaim that Iraq was the ultimate victor in the Persian Gulf conflict.

"Many people predicted that Iraq would collapse in 1991, but we have reconstructed our country," Oil Minister Amir Mohammad Rasheed said recently at a news conference in Baghdad. "We know it is difficult for those without thousands of years of history to understand, but oil is not the only resource of the Iraqi people."

Oil, however, is what's driving the rebound. Iraq is allowed to sell as much petroleum as it wants under U.N. sanctions to buy food, medicine and other necessities. But money is also entering the country illegally through oil smuggling and a complicated surcharge scheme that a Wall Street journal analysis recently estimated provides around $2.5 billion annually outside the control of sanctions.

While U.S. officials contend that much of the money is being spent to refit the Iraqi military, develop long-range missiles and possibly assemble nuclear, biological or chemical weapons, clearly some of it is improving the lives of Iraqi citizens.

Per capita income now stands at around $2,500 annually—double that of Egypt, according to the CIA World Factbook. Iraq's gross domestic product grew about 15 percent in the year 2000.

"Little by little, things are getting better. You can find everything," said Sinan Abdul Hamid, 20, an engineering student whose chief complaint about life is that the lasers used in his classes are out of date.

Entrepreneurs are bringing shiploads of computers, televisions, stereos, appliances and other goods from Dubai to stock the the shelves of Baghdad's shops. Wealthy Iraqis can arrange long-distance special deliveries of their favorite foods from grocery stores in Amman, Jordan, 12 hours by car and a few bribes away from the Iraqi capital.

Farmers are buying new trucks; new double-decker buses are moving about the capital. A few privately owned luxury cars are breaking the previous monotony of wobbly taxis and private cars with shattered windshields.

Even such areas as an impoverished corner of Saddam City south of Baghdad are feeling gains. There, vegetable seller Rabbia Jassim at first pointed to his 6-year-old son's dilapidated sneakers and said that for the poorest in Iraq, many basics remain out of reach. But later he conceded there was some improvement: His family can now afford an occasional chicken.

As part of the upturn, Iraq has again become a major force in the regional economy. Much of its $13 billion in annual imports come from Turkey, Egypt, Saudi Arabia, Syria and Jordan, Iraqi officials said, helping bolster economies in the region. They added that Turkey's sales to Iraq doubled in the past year, to nearly $1 billion, while Egypt, starved for hard currency, now gets $2 billion a year from goods its sells to Iraq.

Iraqis are traveling abroad more easily, too, on the expanding network of flights available since Saddam International Airport reopened a year ago. Royal

Jordanian Airlines offers four flights a week between Amman and Baghdad, and service is also available to the Syrian capital, Damascus, and to Moscow.

Iraqi diplomats circle the globe pressing their nation's case, while business leaders from the Arab world, Russia and Europe fill Iraq's version of a five-star hotel, the Al Rasheed.

The future of Iraq and Hussein has been a chief preoccupation of the region, as well as of world powers, for more than a decade now. While there is agreement that Iraq's isolation as a nation should end, there is disagreement over whether that should happen while Hussein is still in power.

To Washington, he remains a global menace, intent on developing weapons of mass destruction and likely to use them against Israel, Arab neighbors or even the United States. At a recent U.N. Security Council briefing, U.S. officials presented evidence of new long-range missile sites, and foreign diplomats in Baghdad cite suspicions that Iraqi officials have stepped up efforts to acquire material for a nuclear device.

President Bush has called Iraq part of an "axis of evil" that includes its neighbor Iran and North Korea. U.S. officials have not made a case linking Iraq with al Qaeda or any terrorist attack against U.S. interests. But they insist that Iraq is developing weapons of mass destruction and say action against the country, perhaps armed action, is needed.

"The combination of a dangerous regime with such destructive weapons is not acceptable," said Patrick Clawson, research director at the Washington Institute for Near East Policy.

Among Iraq's Arab neighbors, the view is less apocalyptic. Hussein is viewed as a brutal leader, but many say he became more cautious after seeing his army expelled from Kuwait in 1991. An international coalition might well retaliate against any aggressive act tied to Baghdad, spelling an end to the Baath Party that controls the country.

One diplomat here, whose government has counseled the United States to avoid military action in the absence of clear provocation, said the risks of toppling Hussein might be as great as the risks of leaving him in power.

In society here, the diplomat said, "there is a big hate for the U.S. Every malaise is attributed to them and not the regime. The complexity of the problem is that once Pandora's box is open, are we in a more difficult position than now?"

A U.S. attack could lead to a fracturing of the country among the quasi-autonomous Kurdish region in the north, the Iranian-influenced Shiite populations in the south, and the Sunni Muslims who dominate the central region, the diplomat said.

Some Iraqis who privately dislike the regime are also uneasy about the prospect of an attack. They would rather wait for the 65-year-old Hussein's natural demise than risk a war or revolution. "Borders are closed, brains are closed," said one businessman, who asked not to be identified. "But it has been 20 years. What is three or four more? This is what is in the heart of Iraqis."

Advisers in the president's office, meanwhile, say the government's public bravado—defiant, anti-American and ready for a fight—isn't the whole story. "What are we going to say if [Bush] says we are the axis of evil? We fought Iran for eight years. How can you just throw us in one bottle?" one Iraqi official said. "We have learned lessons, and we will make use of those lessons. We will try to avoid our people suffering again."

Despite the talk of war, the United States hasn't much changed the military pressure that it has exerted against Iraq since the end of the Gulf War. Every day a panoply of U.S. planes, including high-flying U-2 reconnaissance jets and RC-135 eavesdropping aircraft, course the skies of northern Saudi Arabia and southern Turkey, monitoring the Iraqi military. Warplanes stage periodic strikes against antiaircraft positions.

But some diplomats in Baghdad and analysts in Washington say that Bush's war threats may already be paying off with the rise of what amounts, by Iraqi standards, to a group of pragmatists on the Baath Party's ruling Revolutionary Command Council.

The diplomats said they believe Foreign Minister Naji Sabri has developed an influential voice in alliance with Hussein's younger son and possible successor, Qusay. Sabri is said to have pushed for recent efforts to mend fences with Kuwait and Saudi Arabia. At a recent Arab League summit in Beirut, Iraq went further than ever, promising to respect Kuwait's sovereignty.

Iraq has also reopened talks with the United Nations on the possible return of U.N. weapons inspection teams, who were withdrawn from the country in 1998 hours before the United States and Britain launched airstrikes on Baghdad. The talks now involve Iraqi scientists and generals. Before Sept. 11, Iraq maintained that inspectors would never return.

Hussein remains the ultimate arbiter, however, holding on to power despite a record of domestic mismanagement, political executions and atrocities against his people.

Increasingly elaborate statues of Hussein continue to sprout throughout the capital, as do state-financed mosques. The Mother of All Battles Mosque opened recently. Still in progress is Saddam Mammoth Mosque, intended to be the largest in the world. Along one boulevard stands what people call The Big "La," (" No" in Arabic), a granite symbol of the country's defiance.

Hussein is lionized in party tracts as the rightful heir of history's great Muslim leaders, such as the 12th-century warrior Saladin, who fought the Christian Crusaders. The revisionism has turned the invasion of Kuwait into a "Zionist trap" that ended with U.S. troops encircled and begging for a cease-fire.

It is unclear how many people accept that account, doled out incessantly by Iraqi newspapers and television. But the hardships of the last decade have been real, and many ordinary Iraqis appear to view the recent easing as a triumph over the United States.

In their offices in the capital, Iraqi officials tried to build on those feelings. They said that what is really behind Bush's talk of war is Hussein's refusal to follow the recent path of Egypt, Saudi Arabia, Jordan and other Arab states and submit to what they perceive as U.S. dominance.

Bush "wants Iraqi oil. Saddam Hussein won't let him. He wants to put a stooge government in. Saddam Hussein won't let him," said Abdelrazak Hashimi, a semi-official government spokesman. "Nobody has the right to go into another country and change the system of government. . . . Nobody can just scratch Iraq off their calendar."

Contributors

Michel Aflaq was a Greek Orthodox Syrian, educated at the Sorbonne, who, together with the Sunni Muslim political reformer Salah ad-Din al-Bitar, formed the Arab Baath (or Renaissance) Party in 1940. He lived in Iraq, with minimal political influence, from 1974 until his death in 1989.

Said K. Aburish is a Palestinian-born journalist and author, who, in the 1970s and 1980s worked as a consultant in Iraq on construction and armament issues. His other books include *The Rise, Corruption and Coming Fall of the House of Saud, A Brutal Friendship: The West and the Arab Elite,* and *Arafat: From Defender to Dictator.*

Sheikh Isa bin Salman al-Khalifa was the **Amir of Bahrain** from independence in 1971 until his death in 1999, when the Amirate passed to his son Sheikh Hamad bin Isa al-Khalifa.

Amatzia Baram teaches in the Department of Middle East History and is the Director of the Jewish-Arab Center and Gustav Von Heinemann Middle East Institute at the University of Haifa. He is one of Israel's pre-eminent specialists on Iraq.

Ofra Bengio is a Senior Research Fellow at the Moshe Dayan Center for Middle Eastern and African Studies, and Senior Lecturer at Tel Aviv University, specialising in the history and political discourse of the modern Middle East.

George Black is the Research and Editorial Director for Human Rights Watch. He is also the author of three books *Iraq's Crime of Genocide, Black Hands of Beijing: Lives of Defiance in the Chinese Democracy Movement 1976-1992,* with Robin Munro, and *The Good Neighbor: How the United States Wrote the History of Central America and the Caribbean.*

Noam Chomsky is Institute Professor in the department of linguistics and philosophy at the Massachusetts Institute of Technology, and one of America's leading Left-wing intellectuals.

Ramsey Clark is a former US Attorney General.

Patrick and Andrew Cockburn are pre-eminent journalists. Patrick has been covering the Middle East for over twenty years, and Andrew is best known for his reportage on American policy-making. They are brothers.

Anthony H. Cordesman holds the Burke Chair in Strategy at CSIS, the Center for Strategic and International Studies, an independent think-tank in Washington. He is national security analyst for ABC News, and the author of a great number of books on the Middle East. He has held numerous posts in government, most recently as national security advisor to Senator John McCain.

John Esposito is the Founding Director of the Center for Muslim-Christian Understanding, and Professor of Religion and International Affairs and of Islamic Studies at Georgetown University. He is one of the foremost scholars of Islam in the United States, and is Editor-in-Chief of *The Oxford Encyclopedia of the Modern Islamic World* and *The Oxford History of Islam.*

Dr. Robert Fisk is one of the UK's leading foreign correspondents. He has been covering the Middle East for over thirty years, and is Middle East Correspondent for *The Independent.* His book on the Lebanese Civil War, *Pity the Nation,* is an international bestseller.

Mark Gaffney is a journalist, writer, and researcher specialising in the proliferation of nuclear weapons in the Middle East.

Khidhir Hamza is an American-trained nuclear physicist, who headed Iraq's

Nuclear Weapons Programme before defecting to the West in 1994. He is the author of *Saddam's Bombmaker,* an autobiography.

Jad al-Haqq, Sheikh al-Azhar was Grand Mufti of Egypt, before becoming Sheikh al-Azhar—head of Al-Azhar, the oldest, most important and most prestigious Islamic University in the world. Al-Azhar is in Cairo, and he held the post until his death in 1996.

Christopher Hitchens is a British journalist and author living in Washington, D.C. He is a longtime contributor to *The Nation* magazine and Washington editor at *Harper's.*

Michael Isherwood is a Lt. Colonel in the US Air Force.

Efraim Karsh is Professor and Head of the Mediterranean Studies Programme at King's College, University of London, where **Lawrence Freedman** has been Professor of War Studies since 1982.

Heidi Kingstone is a Canadian journalist based in London.

Kanan Makiya was born in Baghdad, where he trained and practiced as an architect. He now teaches at Brandeis University and runs the Iraq Research and Documentation Project at Harvard. He is the author *Republic of Fear, The Monument* and *Cruelty and Silence,* all highly controversial accounts of life in Iraq under Saddam Hussein. His latest book, *The Rock,* is a novel set in 7th century Jerusalem.

Joshua Micah Marshall is a writer living in Washington, D.C.

Fuad Matar is a Lebanese journalist and political commentator, whose biography *Saddam Hussein* was authorized by the president himself.

Johanna McGeary is a senior foreign correspondent at *Time.*

Cynthia McKinney is Congresswoman for Georgia at the US House of Representatives.

Middle East Watch is an offshoot of Human Rights Watch, the largest human rights non-governmental organization in the United States. It is based in New York but has offices in Brussels, London, Moscow, Hong Kong, Los Angeles, and Washington. The organization publishes reports annually, of which *Institutions of Repression* was one.

John Pilger is an Australian journalist and filmmaker, based in London. His work has twice won Britain's "Journalist of the Year" award, its highest prize for journalism, and has won the "United Nations Association Media Prize." He is known for his reporting on Cambodia, Iraq, and East Timor.

David Rose is a journalist at *Vanity Fair.*

Edward Said, a Christian Palestinian, brought up in Egypt and the US, is University Professor of English and Comparative Literature at Columbia University in New York, and one of the most prominent intellectuals in the United States today.

Howard Schneider is a foreign correspondent for the *Washington Post.*

Stephen Shalom teaches political science at William Paterson University in New Jersey. He writes regularly for *Z Magazine*. He is on the editorial board of *New Politics,* and is active with the Montclair Civil Rights Coalition.

Avi Shlaim is Professor at the Middle East Centre, St. Antony's College, Oxford University, and one of the pre-eminent historians of the modern Middle East. He was one of the first Israeli historians to challenge the traditional history of the creation of the State of Israel.

Charles Tripp is senior lecturer in the department of political studies at the School of Oriental and African Studies, University of London, and the author of *A History of Iraq*.

Hans Von Sponek and Denis Halliday are former UN Humanitarian Aid Coordinators to Iraq.

Sa'di Yusuf is a native poet of Basra, living in Basra at the time of the bombings his poem refers to.

Permissions

I would like to thank the following publishers, journals, and magazines for permission to reprint the articles and book chapters contained in this volume.

Excerpts from "An Interview with Saddam Hussein" by Fuad Matar. Originally published in *Saddam Hussein: The Man, the Cause, the Future*, Third World Centre for Research and Publishing, 1982.

Excerpts from "Ba'ath Founder's Thought" by Michel Aflak. Originally published in pamphlet form by the Arab Ba'th Socialist Party, London.

Excerpt from *Saddam Hussein: The Politics of Revenge* by Said K. Aburish. Copyright © 2000 by Said K. Aburish. Reprinted with permission of Bloomsbury Publishing plc.

Excerpt from *Saddam's Word: Political Discourse in Iraq* by Ofra Bengio. Copyright © 1998 by Oxford University Press, Inc. Used by permission of Oxford University Press, Inc.

"In Praise of Saddam Hussein" by Amir of Bahrain, translated from *al-Khalij al-'Arabi*. Published by the University of Basra, 1981.

Excerpt from *War and Peace in the Middle East* by Avi Shlaim. Copyright © 1994 by Avi Shlaim. Used by permission of Viking Penguin, a division of Penguin Putnam, Inc.

"The Iran-Iraq War and the Iraqi State" by Charles Tripp from *Iraq: Power and Society* Ed. Derek Hopwood, et al. © 1993 by Charles Tripp. Reprinted with permission of Garnet Publishing.

Excerpt from *Iraq and the War of Sanctions: Conventional Threats and Weapons of Mass Destruction* by Anthony Cordesman. Reprinted courtesy Praeger Publishers and the author.

"The United States and the Iran-Iraq War" by Stephen R. Shalom. Copyright © 1990 by Stephen R. Shalom. Reprinted with kind permission of the author.

Permissions

Excerpts from *War Crimes: A Report on United States War Crimes Against Iraq* by Ramsey Clark et al. Copyright © 1992 by Ramsey Clark. Reprinted with the permission of the International Action Center.

"City of the First Century" by Sa'di Yusuf. Copyright © 1991 by Sa'di Yusuf. Appeared in *Mediterraneans,* vol. 2-3, Didsbury Press, 1991.

Excerpts from *Cruelty and Silence* by Kanan Makiya. Copyright © 1994 by Kanan Makiya. Reprinted with kind permission of the author.

Excerpts from *The New Rulers of the World* by John Pilger. Copyright © 2002 by John Pilger. Reprinted with permission of Verso.

"Rogue States" from *Rogue States: The Rule of Force in World Affairs* by Noam Chomsky. Copyright © 2000 by Noam Chomsky. Reprinted with kind permission of the author.

"Bomb Saddam?" by Joshua Micah Marshall. Copyright © 2002 by The Washington Monthly Company, 773 15th St NW, Suite 1000, Washington DC 20005. (202) 393-5155. Web site: www.washingtonmonthly.com.

"Inside Saddam's Secret Nuclear Program" by Khidhir Hamza. Copyright © 1998 by Bulletin of Atomic Sciences. Reprinted with permission. *The Bulletin of the Atomic Scientists* is published by the Educational Foundation for Nuclear Science, 6042 South Kimbark, Chicago, IL, 60637. A one-year subscription is $28.

Excerpt from *Out of the Ashes: the resurrection of Saddam Hussein* by Andrew Cockburn and Patrick Cockburn. Copyright © 2000 by Andrew Cockburn and Patrick Cockburn. Reprinted with permission of Verso.

"The Hostage Nation" by Hans Von Sponeck and Denis Halliday. Copyright © 2001 by Hans Von Sponeck and Denis Halliday. Reprinted with permission of *The Guardian,* London.

"The Situation in Iraq: Democracy Cannot Be Manufactured at Foggy Bottom or the Pentagon" by Cynthia McKinney. Copyright © 1999 by the Middle East Research and

Information Project. Reprinted with permission of the Middle East Research and Information Project.

"Inside Saddam's Terror Regime" by David Rose. Copyright © 2002 by David Rose. Reprinted with kind permission of the author.

"Inside Saddam's World" by Johanna McGeary. Copyright © 2002 by Time, Inc. Reprinted with permission.

"The Awful Truth Is America Quite Likes the Saddam Regime" by Christopher Hitchens. Copyright © 2002 by Christopher Hitchens. Reprinted with kind permission of the author.

"U.S. Strategic Options for Iraq: Easier Said than Done" by Michael W. Isherwood. Copyright © 2002 by the Center for Strategic and International Studies (CSIC) and the Massachusetts Institute of Technology. Originally appeared in *The Washington Quarterly*, 25:2 (Spring 2002), pp 145-159.

"Saddam Hussein's Would-be Successors" by Heidi Kingstone. Copyright © 2002 by Heidi Kingstone. Reprinted with permission of *The Jerusalem Report*.

"Does Iraq Have a Future?" by Kanan Makiya. Copyright © 1996 by Kanan Makiya. Reprinted with kind permission of the author.

"Will the Next Mid East War Go Nuclear?" by Mark Gaffney. Copyright © 2001 by Mark Gaffney. Reprinted with permission of Blackwell Publishing.

"Iraq Shows Signs of Economic Life" by Howard Schneider. Copyright © 2002 by *The Washington Post*. Reprinted with permission.